(continued on back endpapers)

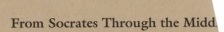

Living Issues
in Philosophy

NINTH EDITION ◆ ■■■ ◆ ◆ ■■■ ◆

Living Issues
in Philosophy

HAROLD H. TITUS

MARILYN S. SMITH

RICHARD T. NOLAN

New York   Oxford
OXFORD UNIVERSITY PRESS

Oxford University Press

Oxford   New York
Auckland   Bangkok   Buenos Aires   Cape Town
Chennai   Dar es Salaam   Delhi   Hong Kong   Istanbul   Karachi
Kolkata   Kuala Lumpur   Madrid   Melbourne   Mexico City   Mumbai   Nairobi
São Paulo   Shanghai   Singapore   Taipei   Tokyo   Toronto

Copyright © 1995 by Oxford University Press, Inc.

Published by Oxford University Press, Inc.
198 Madison Avenue, New York, New York 10016
http://www.oup-usa.org

ISBN: 0-19-515509-2

Cover Photo: Erich Lessing/Art Resource. Roman mosaic from Pompeii.
A Conversation between Philosophers. Museo Archeologico Nazionale,
Naples. Details are used on the Part Opening pages.

Printing number: 9 8 7 6 5 4

Printed in the United States of America
on acid-free paper

PART THREE   *Knowledge and Science*   167

PART FIVE   Religion: East and West   357

There are many approaches to teaching an introduction to philosophy class. As the title of our book indicates, we believe students learn best through analysis of philosophical issues. When Professor Harold Titus first introduced this text, he emphasized the importance of an issues-oriented approach. Clearly he was on the right track. A great number of students have been introduced to philosophy through this text; by the time the seventh edition of *Living Issues in Philosophy* appeared, the book had sold well over a million copies.

Professor Harold H. Titus, the original author of *Living Issues in Philosophy*, died in 1984. He was widely known for his successful textbooks in philosophy, especially for his ability to communicate basic philosophical issues and for his lucid style. He was a person for whom philosophy meant continually confronting the issues common to his culture and presenting them in a fashion that would be understandable to a philosophical novice. As his fellow authors, we have already discovered how much his wisdom guided us in our thinking and writing.

The New Edition. The ninth edition continues the traditions of previous editions and updates the content. We want to assure readers and old friends that certain fundamental characteristics have been retained. The ninth edition continues to make accessible to students a wide range of living philosophical issues. Both the introduction and the concluding reflection emphasize the importance of dealing with issues closely related to everyday life. Once the relevance of these questions has been grasped, students can move on to more specialized courses such as ethics, history of philosophy, logic, and others.

Insofar as possible, the material is presented in nontechnical language. When necessary for the purpose of introducing philosophical viewpoints, the text does use terms such as *fundamentalism* and *dualism*. These terms, however, are only labels for different philosophical positions; more important than the labels are the philosophies they represent.

Level of Presentation. A concerted effort has been made to gear the level of presentation to the student who has had no previous philosophical experience. The prose is more direct, and unfamiliar terms are clearly defined upon first appearance and in the end-of-chapter glossaries.

Treatment of Important Topics. Many sections have been revised or expanded. Examples of updated material include the following:

- Chapter 1, "The Task of Philosophy," is arranged differently, with philosophy of education included as an elaboration on the uses of philosophy.

- Metaphysics, which encompasses many issues related to Chapters 2 through 5, introduces the second chapter.

- Functionalism and eliminative materialism are new to Chapter 4, "The Mind."

- "What Is a Value?" is discussed at the beginning of Chapter 6, "The Meaning of Values."

- Kohlberg's levels of moral development; classical moral philosophy; natural law ethics; contemporary principles; and distinctions among moral certainties, moral relativism, and moral pluralism are new to Chapter 7, "Ethics and Morality."

- Chapter 8 provides an orientation to several issues of individual and societal living, including new clarifications of human rights, civil rights, and civil liberties; philosophical issues in sexual ethics are included for the first time.

- The chapters on knowledge have been consolidated from three to two.

- Space–time relativity has been clarified in Chapter 11, "Science and Philosophy," and a new section, Darwinism and Genetics, added.

- In Chapter 17, "The Nature of Religion," new sections include discussions of the nature of faith and the sacred, cults and sects, and meanings of *jihad* in Islam.

- Paley's argument for the existence of God is new to Chapter 18, "Belief in God."

- Chapter 19, "Asian Thought," has been updated significantly with current scholarship.

Special Features. The ninth edition includes updated material on individual philosophers. Special pedagogical features have also been included to benefit students.

- Excerpts from more than sixty philosophers' writings, accompanied by photos and biographies. These give students a "taste" of primary source material.

- End-of-chapter glossaries, as well as a comprehensive glossary at the end of the book. Important terms appear in boldface upon first appearance in the text.

- Chapter review and suggested study questions and projects at the end of every chapter.

An introductory text should, of course, be adaptable to instructors' needs. Thus, we have divided the text into five parts to permit instructors to omit an entire part or only certain chapters. The order of presentation of topics may also be changed if one prefers to begin with, for example, The Realm of Values or Philosophical Perspectives.

Acknowledgments. We would like to acknowledge those who assisted in our effort, who lent advice and encouragement along the way. To Wadsworth Publishing Company we are pleased to continue this joint effort and especially thank Tammy Goldfeld, our editor, and Kristina Pappas, editorial assistant to Ms. Goldfeld. Many advisors have stood in the background: We thank John E. Smith, Clark Professor of Philosophy *Emeritus*, Yale University, for his ready expertise whenever called upon; Robert C. Pingpank for his continuing supportive comments and help with the proofreading; Joseph F. Wassong IV for bibliographical assistance; and several colleagues for their suggestions, especially David Blitz (Associate Professor of Philosophy, Central Connecticut State University), Frank G. Kirkpatrick (Professor of Religion, Trinity College, Hartford), Stephen R. Morris (Assistant Professor of Philosophy, Central Connecticut State University), Jerome A. Shaffer (Chair and Professor of Philosophy, University of Connecticut), and John G. Troyer (Associate Professor of Philosophy, University of Connecticut).

The authors acknowledge with appreciation the 1984 Indonesian translation and publication of *Living Issues in Philosophy* as *Persoalan-persoalan Filsafat* by P. T. Bulan Bintang Publishing Co. of Jakarta. Indonesia has been added to our international readers in Guam, Canada, England, the Netherlands, Jamaica, West Africa, and New Guinea.

We discovered in Merrill Peterson both a production coordinator and a colleague.

Harold H. Titus (1896–1984) earned a B.A. degree from Acadia University, B.D. and M.Th. degrees at Colgate-Rochester Divinity School, and a Ph.D. from the University of Chicago. The founding author of *Living Issues in Philosophy* and the five editions of *Ethics for Today*, he also wrote *What Is a Mature Morality?*—an alternate Book-of-the-Month-Club selection. At the time of his death Dr. Titus was professor of philosophy *emeritus* at Denison University, where he had taught for over thirty-five years.

Marilyn S. Smith earned a B.A. degree from Barnard College and an M.A. degree from Union Theological Seminary and Columbia University. She is chair of the humanities department and associate professor of philosophy in Hillyer College of the University of Hartford. Prof. Smith coauthored the sixth through the ninth editions of *Living Issues in Philosophy* and the third edition of *The Range of Philosophy*; she appeared as a panelist in the "Do unto Others" program of the nationally televised series *Ethics in America*. Prof. Smith is married to John E. Smith, Clark Professor of Philosophy *Emeritus*, Yale University.

Richard T. Nolan earned a B.A. degree from Trinity College (CT), M.Div. from the Hartford Seminary, an M.A. degree from Yale University, and a Ph.D. from New York University. Editor of *The Diaconate Now* and coauthor of *Living Issues in Ethics*, he has coauthored the seventh through the ninth editions of *Living Issues in Philosophy*. Prof. Nolan taught philosophy in Connecticut's community college and university systems for more than two decades. He is president of The Litchfield Institute, Inc., Ft. Lauderdale, Florida.

What Is Philosophy?

The Task of Philosophy

CHAPTER OBJECTIVES

In this chapter we will address the following questions:

◆ What Does "Philosophy" Mean?

◆ Why Do We Need Philosophy?

◆ What Are the Traditional Branches of Philosophy?

◆ Is There a Basic Method of Philosophical Thinking?

◆ How May Philosophy Be Used?

◆ Is Philosophy of Education Useful?

◆ What Is Happening in Philosophy Today?

*Reflection—thinking things over—. . .
[is] the beginning of philosophy.*[1]

The Meanings of Philosophy

◆ ◆ ◆ ◆ ◆ ◆ ◆ ◆ ◆ ◆

Each of us has a philosophy, even though we may not be aware of it. We all have some ideas concerning physical objects, our fellow persons, the meaning of life, death, God, right and wrong, beauty and ugliness, and the like. Of course, these ideas are acquired in a variety of ways, and they may be vague and confused. We are continuously engaged, especially during the early years of our lives, in acquiring views and attitudes from our family, from friends, and from various other individuals and groups. These attitudes also may be greatly influenced by movies, television, music lyrics, and books. They may result from some reflection on our part, or they more likely may result from a conventional or emotional bias. This broad, popular, man-in-the-street (*common-sense*) view of philosophy is not adequate for our purposes. It does not describe the work and task of the philosopher. We need to define philosophy more specifically; the broad view is vague, confused, and superficial.

The word philosophy is derived from the Greek words *philia* (love) and *sophia* (wisdom) and means "the love of wisdom." A definition of philosophy can be offered from a number of perspectives. Here we present five, although some philosophers may wish to exclude one or more of them. Each approach must be kept in mind for a clear understanding of the many meanings of *philosophy* and what particular philosophers may say about the nature and function of philosophy.

1. *Philosophy is a set of views or beliefs about life and the universe, which are often held uncritically.* We refer to this meaning as the informal sense of philosophy or "having" a philosophy. Usually when a person says "my philosophy is," he or she is referring to an informal personal attitude to whatever topic is being discussed.

2. *Philosophy is a process of reflecting on and criticizing our most deeply held conceptions and beliefs.* This is the formal sense of "doing" philosophy. These two senses of philosophy—"having" and "doing"—cannot be treated entirely independent of each other, for if we did not *have* a philosophy in the formal, personal sense, then we could not *do* a philosophy in the critical, reflective sense.

Having a philosophy, however, is not sufficient for doing philosophy. A genuine philosophical attitude is searching and critical; it is open-minded and tolerant—willing to look at all sides of an issue without prejudice. To philosophize is not merely to read and know philosophy; there are skills of argumentation to be mastered, techniques of analysis to be employed, and a body of material to be appropriated such that we become able to think philosophically.

Philosophers are reflective and critical. They take a second look at the material presented by common sense. They attempt to think through a variety of life's problems and to face all the facts involved impartially. The accumulation of knowledge does not by itself lead to understanding, because it does not necessarily teach the mind to make a *critical evaluation* of facts that entail consistent and coherent judgment.

Critical evaluations often differ. Philosophers, theologians, scientists, and others disagree, first because they view things from different points of view and with different assumptions. Their personal experiences, cultural backgrounds, and training may vary widely. This is especially true of people living at different times and in different places. A second reason philosophers disagree is that they live in a changing universe. People change, society changes, and nature changes. Some people are responsive and sensitive to change; others cling to tradition and the status quo, to systems that were formulated some time ago and that were declared to be authoritative and final. A third reason philosophers disagree is that they deal with an area of human experience in which the evidence is not complete. The evidence we do have may be interpreted in various ways by different people. Despite these disagreements, however, philosophers continue to probe, examine, and evaluate the material with the hope of presenting consistent principles by which we can live.

3. *Philosophy is a rational attempt to look at the world as a whole.* Philosophy seeks to combine the conclusions of the various sciences and human experience into some kind of consistent world view. Philosophers wish to see life, not with the specialized slant of the scientist or the businessperson or the artist, but with the overall view of someone cognizant of life as a totality. In speaking of "speculative philosophy," which he distinguishes from "critical philosophy," C. D. Broad says, "Its object is to take over the results of the various sciences, to add to them the results of the religious and ethical experiences of mankind, and then to reflect upon the whole. The hope is that, by this means, we may be able to reach some general conclusions as to the nature of the universe, and as to our position and prospects in it."[2]

Although there are difficulties and dangers in setting forth any world view, there also are dangers in confining attention to fragments of human experience. Philosophy's task is to give a view of the whole, a life and a world view, and to integrate the knowledge of the sciences with that of other disciplines to achieve a consistent whole. Philosophy, according to this view, attempts to bring the results of human inquiry—religious, historical, and scientific—into some meaningful interpretation that provides knowledge and insight for our lives.

4. *Philosophy is the logical analysis of language and the clarification of the meaning of words and concepts.* Certainly this is one function of philosophy. In fact, nearly all philosophers have used methods of analysis and have sought to clarify the meaning of terms and the use of language. Some philosophers see this as the main task of philosophy, and a few claim this is the only legitimate function of philosophy. Such persons consider philosophy a specialized field serving the sciences and aiding in the clarification of language rather than a broad field reflecting on all of life's experiences. This outlook has gained considerable support during the twentieth century. It would limit what we call *knowledge* to statements about *observable facts* and their interrelations—that is, to the business

of the various sciences. Not all linguistic analysts, however, define *knowledge* so narrowly. Although they do reject and try to "clean up" many nonscientific assertions, many of them think that we can have knowledge of ethical principles and the like, although this knowledge is also experientially derived. Those who take the narrower view neglect, when they do not deny, all generalized world views and life views, as well as traditional moral philosophy and theology. From this more narrow point of view, the aim of philosophy is to expose confusion and nonsense and to clarify the meaning and use of terms in science and everyday affairs.

5. *Philosophy is a group of perennial problems that interest people and for which philosophers always have sought answers.* Philosophy presses its inquiry into the deepest problems of human existence. Some of the philosophical questions raised in the past have been answered in a manner satisfactory to the majority of philosophers. Many questions, however, have been answered only tentatively, and many problems remain unsolved.

What are philosophical questions? The question "Did John Doe make a false statement on his income tax return?" is merely a question of fact. But the questions "What is truth?" and "What is the distinction between right and wrong?" have philosophical importance.

Most of us stop at times—sometimes because of startling events, often out of simple curiosity—and think seriously about fundamental life issues: What is life and why am I here? Why is there anything at all? What is the place of life in this great universe? Is the universe friendly or unfriendly? Do things operate by chance or through sheer mechanism, or is there some plan or purpose or intelligence at the heart of things? Is my life controlled by outside forces, or do I have a determining or even a partial degree of control? Why do people struggle and strive for their rights, for justice, for better things in the future? What do concepts like "right" and "justice" mean, and what are the marks of a good society? Often men and women have been asked to sacrifice their lives, if need be, for certain values and ideals. What are the genuine values of life and how can they be attained? Is there really a fundamental distinction between right and wrong, or is it just a matter of one's own opinions?

What is beauty? Should religion count in a person's life? Is it intellectually valid to believe in God? Is there a possibility of a "life after death?" Is there any way we can get an answer to these and many related questions? Where does knowledge come from, and can we have any assurances that anything is true?

These questions are all philosophical. The attempt to seek answers or solutions to them has given rise to theories and systems of thought, such as *idealism, realism, pragmatism, analytic philosophy, existentialism, phenomenology,* and *process philosophy. Philosophy* also means the various theories or systems of thought developed by the great philosophers—Socrates, Plato, Aristotle, Augustine, Aquinas, Descartes, Spinoza, Locke, Berkeley, Kant, Hegel, Nietzsche, Royce, James, Dewey, Whitehead, and others. Without these people and their thoughts philosophy would not have the rich content it has today. Even though we may be unconscious of the fact, we are constantly influenced by ideas that have come down to us in the traditions of society.

Why We Need Philosophy

♦ ♦ ♦ ♦ ♦ ♦ ♦ ♦ ♦ ♦

We are living in a period that resembles the late stages of the Graeco-Roman civilization, the Renaissance, the Reformation, and the Industrial Revolution, when basic shifts took place in human thinking, values, and practices. Changes are occurring that reach to the foundations of human life and society. We now have immense power over nature, including outer space; we have made giant strides in the areas of science, technology, agriculture, medicine, and the social sciences. In this century, especially in the last few decades, we have seen great advances in society—men and women live longer, travel faster, have more comforts and labor-saving devices, and produce more goods in fewer hours than ever before. The extension of the role of the computer and the age of automation undoubtedly will eliminate more drudgery and further increase production and reduce working hours. Controlling new sources of energy from the atom, the sun, the tides, and the winds is likely to change our lives beyond even our wildest imaginations.

Yet despite our amazing advances, many thoughtful people are disturbed and anxious. They are concerned that our physical power, scientific knowledge, and wealth stand in sharp contrast with the failure of governments and individuals to come to grips with the pressing intellectual and moral problems of life. Knowledge seems divorced from values; it is possible to have great power without insight.

Perhaps the most striking example is to be found in the onset of a nuclear age, which we have created through an application of scientific and technological power. We are unable, however, to solve the question of arms control. Nuclear weapons cannot be realistically used in the actual fighting of a war; using even one is likely to lead to an earthly cataclysm. Despite the appalling dangers of nuclear war, some people argue that we need to manufacture nuclear weapons as a means of deterring nuclear aggression by a potential enemy; that is, a nuclear war cannot be planned with the aim of winning it. Once again, we are in a paradoxical situation: we are unable to offer a solution to a problem that stems from our own ingenuity.

The twentieth century has been characterized by a war of ideas as well as of people, materials, and conflicting national interests. Irreconcilable philosophies compete for allegiance. Earlier in the century, the difference between life in the democratic and in the fascist countries was not a difference in technology, or in science, or even in general education; it lay in basic ideas, ideals, and loyalties. In a similar way, communism challenged many of our beliefs and ideals.

Editorials, articles, books, films, and television commentators unite in appealing for a redirection of our society. They believe that we are adrift without moral and intellectual leadership. No doubt our period is characterized by personal and social instability. We are at a loss to form genuine communities that would lend satisfaction and hope to their members; we find commitment to selfishness and competition rather than to self-interest and cooperation. Our civilization often has been diagnosed; the diagnosticians are eloquent in their descriptions of the diseases, but it is a rare individual who proposes a cure; the most the critics can agree on is that it is time for a change.

Changes in customs and in history usually begin with people who are convinced of the worth of some ideal or who are captured by some vision of a different way of life. Following the Middle Ages, many people began to conceive of a way of life motivated by a belief that life on this earth is worthwhile in itself. In the broadest sense, this belief made possible the Renaissance, the Reformation, and our modern world with its factories, mass production, money and banks, rapid transportation, and, more recently, atomic power and exploration of outer space. All these are calculated to make this world better and to give us more control over it. But unless we develop some fairly consistent and comprehensive view of human nature, the nature of the total order within which we live, and some reasonable scale of values based on an order beyond mere human desires, such things are not likely to provide an enduring basis for our world. Philosophy, in conjunction with other disciplines, plays a central role in guiding us toward new desires and aspirations.

In his book *The Illusion of Technique*,[3] William Barrett proposes that today, more than any other time in history, it is necessary to place the idea of scientific technique in a new relation to life. As we have noted, ours is a society more and more dominated by technique. Barrett is convinced that modern philosophy must respond to technique and technology, or humanity will permanently lose purpose, direction, and freedom.

. . . anyone who would argue for freedom today has to concern himself with the nature of technique—its scope and its limits— . . . The question of technique is, in itself, an important one for philosophy—and more important particularly for modern philosophy, which has so often let matters of technique blind its vision. More significantly still, the question bears upon the uncertainties of a whole technological civilization, which even as it wields its great technical powers is unsure of their limits or possible consequences.[4]

Traditional Branches of Philosophy

♦ ♦ ♦ ♦ ♦ ♦ ♦ ♦ ♦ ♦

Historically, philosophical concerns have been treated under these broad categories: logic, metaphysics, epistemology, and value theory. We have organized our text around the basic *issues* of philosophy; therefore we will merely glance at the definitions of the traditional branches, trusting that the chapters that follow will further develop these definitions.

In addition to the broad categories mentioned, philosophy also deals with the systematic body of principles and assumptions underlying a particular field of experience. For example, there are philosophies of science, education, art, music, history, law, mathematics, and religion. Any subject pursued far enough reveals within itself philosophical problems.

LOGIC

Philosophy endeavors to understand the nature of correct thinking and to discover what is valid reasoning. One thread running throughout the history of philosophy is its appeal to reason, to argumentation, to logic.

We all use arguments in everyday life to support our opinions and to refute the opinions of others with whom we disagree. But how do we distinguish between valid and invalid arguments? Basically, an argument is simply the reasons (called the **premises**) for or against a position (called the **conclusion**). An **inference** is a conclusion derived either from general premises (deduction) or from factual evidence (induction). **Deduction** and **induction** are both processes of reasoning that we need to understand if we are to avoid serious fallacies in our thinking. They are terms used to describe methods by which we move from evidence to conclusions based on the evidence. Deduction is the process by which we draw a conclusion from one or more premises. If our inference is correct and the conclusion does follow, we say that the deduction is valid. For example, if we say, "All men are mortal" and "Socrates is a man," we may conclude that "Socrates is mortal." Here the premises are all the evidence that is relevant to the soundness of the conclusion. Induction, on the other hand, is **empirical**, in that it deals with matters of fact. It attempts to draw conclusions concerning all the members of a class after examining only some of them or concerning an unexamined member of a class. The aim is to make statements or propositions that are true. For example, after examining some crows, or even a large number of them, is it valid for us to conclude that all crows are black? May we conclude that the next crow we see will be black?

Argumentation and **dialectic** are indispensable tools of the philosopher. The arguments must have a sound and reasonable basis. The task of devising tests to determine which arguments are valid and which are not belongs to that branch of philosophy known as *logic*. **Logic** is the systematic study of the rules for the correct use of these supporting reasons, rules we can use to distinguish good arguments from bad ones. Most of the great philosophers from Aristotle to the present have been convinced that logic permeates all other branches of philosophy. The ability to test arguments for logical consistency, understand the logical consequences of certain assumptions, and distinguish the kind of evidence a philosopher is using are essential for "doing" philosophy.

METAPHYSICS

Some of the philosophical outlooks that we will consider in Part Four will take us into that branch of philosophy traditionally known as **metaphysics.** For Aristotle (See biography and excerpt, pp. 8–9), the term *metaphysics* meant "first philosophy," discussion of the most universal principles; later the term came to mean "comprehensive thinking about the nature of things."

Metaphysics undoubtedly is the branch of philosophy that the modern student finds most difficult to grasp. Metaphysics attempts to offer a comprehensive view of all that exists. It is concerned with such problems as the relation of mind to matter, the nature of change, the meaning of "freedom," the existence of God, and the belief in personal immortality.

Today philosophers disagree about whether a world view or a metaphysics is possible. Some contemporary philosophers, with their emphasis on sense perception and objective scientific knowledge, are skeptical about the possibility of metaphysical knowledge and the meaningfulness of metaphysical questions. There are, however, many philosophers, ancient and modern, who believe that problems of value and religion—metaphysical problems—are closely related to one's conception of the fundamental nature of the universe. Many of these philosophers believe there is in humanity something that transcends the empirical order of nature.

EPISTEMOLOGY

In general, **epistemology** is the branch of philosophy that studies the sources, nature, and validity of knowledge. What is the human mind capable of knowing? From what sources do we gain our knowledge? Do we have any genuine knowledge on which we can depend, or must we be satisfied with opinions and guesses? Are we limited to knowing the bare facts of sense

Aristotle

Aristotle (384–322 B.C.E.) was a philosopher, scientist, and educator. He is widely considered to be one of the most influential thinkers in Western civilization. He was born in Stagira in Northern Greece and at age eighteen years entered Plato's Academy, where he remained for nearly two decades until the death of Plato. For a time he traveled, and for four years he was the tutor of the prince Alexander, who later became "The Great." About 334 B.C.E., Aristotle returned to Athens and founded his own school, the Lyceum. He summarized and developed the knowledge of his day and enriched it by his own investigations and critical thinking.

Aristotle was interested in medicine and zoology among many other things, and set up laboratories and museums. At one time his royal patrons are said to have placed at his disposal one-thousand men throughout Greece and Asia who collected and reported details concerning the life conditions and habits of living things. He also collected constitutions and documents concerning the political arrangements of many states.

His writings show an interest in all areas of knowledge including science (nature), society and the state, literature and the arts, and the life of man. His logic (*Organon*) developed deductive, or syllogistic, logic; his ethics (*Nicomachean Ethics*) was the first systematic treatise in the field and is still read.

experience, or are we able to go beyond what the senses reveal?

The technical term for the theory of knowledge is *epistemology,* which comes from the Greek word *episteme,* meaning "knowledge." There are three central questions in this field: (1) What are the *sources* of knowledge? Where does genuine knowledge come from or how do we know? This is the question of origins. (2) What is the *nature* of knowledge? Is there a real world outside the mind, and if so can we know it? This is the question of appearance versus reality. (3) Is our knowledge *valid*? How do we distinguish truth from error? This is the question of the tests of truth, of verification.[5]

Traditionally, most of those who have offered answers to these questions can be placed in one of two schools of thought—**rationalism** or **empiricism.** The rationalists hold that human reason alone can discover the basic principles of the universe. The empiricists claim that all knowledge is ultimately derived from *sense experience* and, thus, that our knowledge is limited to what can be experienced. It should be clear that there is a necessary relation between metaphysics and epistemology. Our conception of reality depends on our understanding of what can be known. Conversely, our theory of knowledge depends on our understanding of ourselves in relation to the whole of reality.

Excerpt from Aristotle:

Nicomachean Ethics,
Book I (1094)

Every art and every inquiry, and similarly every action and pursuit, is thought to aim at some good; and for this reason the good has rightly been declared to be that at which all things aim. But a certain difference is found among ends; some are activities, others are products apart from the activities which produce them. Where there are ends apart from the actions, it is the nature of the products to be better than the activities. Now, as there are many actions, arts, and sciences, their ends also are many; the end of the medical art is health, that of shipbuilding a vessel, that of strategy victory, that of economics wealth. But where such arts fall under a single capacity—as bridle-making and the other arts concerned with the equipment of horses fall under the art of riding, and this and every military action under strategy, in the same way other arts fall under yet others—in all of these the ends of the master arts are to be preferred to all the subordinate ends; for it is the sake of the former that the latter are pursued. It makes no difference whether the activities themselves are the ends of the actions, or something else apart from the activities, as in the case of the sciences just mentioned.

R. McKeon, ed., *The Basic Works of Aristotle* (New York: Random House, 1941).

VALUE THEORY

Value theory is the branch of philosophy that studies values. It can be subdivided into ethics, aesthetics, and social and political philosophy.

In broad terms ethics concerns itself with the question of morality. What is right and what is wrong in human relations? Within morality and ethics there are three major areas: *descriptive* ethics, *normative* ethics, and *metaethics*. Descriptive ethics seeks to identify moral experience in a descriptive way. We seek to identify, within the range of human conduct, the motives, desires, and intentions as well as overt acts themselves. We consider the conduct of individuals,

or *personal morality;* the conduct of groups, or *social morality;* and the culture patterns of national and racial groups. Descriptive ethics is in part an attempt to distinguish what *is* from what *ought to be.*

A second level of inquiry is *normative ethics* (what ought to be). Here philosophers try to work out acceptable judgments regarding what ought to be in choice and value. "We ought to keep our promises" and "you ought to be honorable" are examples of normative judgments—of the *moral ought,* the subject matter of ethics. From the time of the early Greeks, philosophers have formulated principles of explanation to examine *why* people act the way they do, and what the principles are by which people ought to live; statements of these principles are called *ethical theories*.[6]

Third, there is the area of *critical* or *metaethics*. Here interest is centered on the analysis and meaning of the terms and language used in ethical discourse and the kind of reasoning used to justify ethical statements. Metaethics does not propound any moral principle or goal (except by implication), but rather consists entirely of philosophical analysis. What is the meaning of "good?" and Can ethical judgments be justified? are typical problems for metaethics.

Philip Wheelwright has written a clear and precise definition of ethics: "Ethics may be defined as that branch of philosophy which is the systematic study of reflective choice, of the standards of right and wrong by which it is to be guided, and of the goods toward which it may ultimately be directed."[7]

Broadly speaking, **aesthetics** concerns the theory of art and beauty. Questions of art and beauty are considered to be part of the realm of values because many philosophical problems in aesthetics involve critical judgments. There are wide differences of opinion as to what objects call forth the aesthetic response, and what beauty really is. Our concepts of beauty may differ not because of the nature of beauty itself, but because of varying degrees of preparation in discerning beauty. Therefore, if we cannot perceive beauty in objects that others find beautiful, it may be wise to withhold judgment until we are capable ourselves of making a competent analysis of the aesthetic experience.

Social and political philosophy investigates value judgments concerning society, the state, and the individual's relation to these institutions. The following questions reflect the concerns of social and political philosophy: Why should individuals live in society? What social ideals of liberty, rights, justice, equality and responsibility are desirable? Why should anyone obey any government? Why should some individuals or groups have political power over others? What criteria are to be used in determining who should have political power? What criteria are to be used in determining the scope of political power, and what rights or freedoms should be immune from political or legal control? To what positive goals should political power be directed, and what are the criteria for determining this? Conflicting answers and applications of these philosophical questions permeate human history; the values and moral convictions of human beings are reflected in our daily social and political life.

Philosophical Methodology— Socratic Dialectic

◆ ◆ ◆ ◆ ◆ ◆ ◆ ◆ ◆ ◆ ◆

Because philosophy begins with wondering, questioning, and reflecting about our fundamental assumptions, we need to consider *how* it proceeds to answer questions. Philosophical problems cannot be resolved by appealing exclusively to the facts: how then does philosophy solve the problems it raises? What method does philosophy employ?

We have defined philosophy as a process of reflecting on and criticizing our most deeply held beliefs. To achieve that end, we believe that the basic method of philosophical inquiry is *dialectical*.

Philosophy proceeds through the **dialectic of argument**. The term *dialectic* refers to a process of thinking that originated with the philosopher Socrates. In Plato's dialogues, Socrates (See biography and excerpt from Plato's writings, pp. 12 and 13) is the main character—the protagonist. Socrates employs the method of dialectic; he engages in argumentation, in a relentless analysis of any and every subject. Socrates was convinced that the surest way to attain reliable knowledge was through the practice of disciplined conversation, with the investigator acting as an intellectual midwife; we call the method he used *dialectic*. This is a deceptively simple technique. It always begins with a discussion of the most commonly accepted aspects of any problem. The dialectical process is a dialogue between opposing positions. Socrates, and many later philosophers,[8] believed that through the process of this dialogue, in which each participant in the conversation was forced to clarify her or his ideas, the final outcome of the conversation would be a clear statement of what was meant. What is important is that the dialectic is *the development of thought through an interplay of ideas.*

Dialectical thinking, and consequently dialectic as a method, attempts to develop a sustained pattern of argument in which the implications of different positions are drawn out and interact with each other. As the argument unfolds, we find that neither position represents a complete understanding of the truth; new considerations and alternatives emerge. At each stage of the dialectic we gain a deeper insight into the original problem, and by so doing perhaps come closer to the truth.

When entering a course of study, a student is generally prepared to memorize facts, learn formulas, or master a set of material; philosophy demands something quite different. By using the dialectical method, we come closer to the truth but often, in fact frequently, the original philosophical problem remains unsolved. There are always more questions to be asked, more arguments to be challenged. The student of philosophy, however, must not despair. With this method we can arrive at tentative answers; some answers will appear to be more philosophically satisfactory than others, some we will abandon altogether.

In Socratic fashion, philosophy proceeds by attempting to correct incomplete or inaccurate notions, by "coaxing" the truth out of the situation. Socrates is famous for his belief that the unexamined life is not worth living. Similarly, philosophy proceeds with the conviction that the unexamined idea is not worth having. Dialectic necessarily involves critical reflection.

The Uses of Philosophy

♦ ♦ ♦ ♦ ♦ ♦ ♦ ♦ ♦ ♦ ♦

Before registering for an introductory philosophy course, students frequently ask: "Why study philosophy?" "What use is philosophy?" "Is philosophy of any value to me personally, and will it help my career?"

PHILOSOPHY AS INESCAPABLE

Everybody has some notion of reality. Whether fully examined or not, ideas about the origin, destiny, and fabric of existence—including views about God and human nature—have a place in each person's mind. Everyone also has some notion of knowledge. Ideas about the authentic sources of knowledge, about subjective beliefs in contrast to objective truths, and about methods that prove a conclusion true or false form a part of everyday life. We all have some notion of values, including right or wrong. Most of us try to think correctly and to reason in a valid fashion so that others will heed us when we set forth our ideas. Far from being merely a classroom exercise, issues of metaphysics, epistemology, values, and logic are part of everyday living.

THE STUDY OF PHILOSOPHY

Shallowness, incompleteness, poor reasoning, and assertions with flimsy foundations prevent a truly enlightened citizenry. Persuasive orators can sway minds and hearts and thereby wage wars, gain political control, establish cults, and otherwise seduce an unsuspecting public. Unaware of the complexities of an issue, unfamiliar with a comprehensive view of a topic, unable to distinguish between valid and invalid reasoning, ready to yield to authoritarian approaches, individuals and entire communities have been asked to sacrifice their lives for certain values and ideals. However, people who have studied philosophy are more likely to pursue an issue in depth and to examine it comprehensively with sound reasoning. Having the courage to question the conventional and traditional is useful for individuals in achieving intellectual autonomy and in helping communities to make informed choices.

Failure to obtain a specific answer to a philosophical question or an acceptable solution to a problematic issue frequently leads to frustration.

Socrates

Socrates (469–399 B.C.E.) was a Greek philosopher of Athens. Famous for his view of philosophy as a pursuit necessary to all intelligent humans, Socrates lived by his principles even though they ultimately cost him his life. Socrates was widely known for his intellectual power and use of the dialectical method. According to Plato's report of Socrates' speech in the *Apology*, the oracle at Delphi pronounced that there was no one wiser than Socrates in all of Greece. However, Socrates never himself claimed to be wise; he always professed ignorance. Thus, he became convinced that his calling was to search for wisdom about right conduct by which he might guide the intellectual and moral development of the Athenians. Neglecting his own affairs, he spent his time discussing virtue, justice, and piety wherever his fellow citizens congregated. In 399 B.C.E., Socrates was brought to trial for corrupting youth and for religious heresies. The trial and death of Socrates are described in the *Apology*, the *Crito*, and the *Phaedo* of Plato with great dramatic power.

Nonetheless, exploration of the possible, reasonable solutions clarifies the options open to thoughtful persons. The usefulness of choosing from reasoned, researched alternatives rather than from bigoted, impulsive, and unclear claims is apparent in all dimensions of our lives. Ideally, the study of philosophy nurtures our capacity for making ~~informed~~ choices.

wise

SPECIFIC PERSONAL USES

Examining our everyday language often leads to philosophical questions. "I want to do the *right* thing" is an expression regularly used by all of us; ethical reflection can illuminate an individual's sense of *right*. "Wait and see what happens" may imply philosophical fatalism: Is fatalism a reason-

How to make your way in the world without becoming an evil person.

Excerpt from Plato:

Meno, 71B–72A (c. 390 B.C.E.)

Socrates: . . . Meno, be generous and tell me what you say that virtue is; for I shall be truly delighted to find that I have been mistaken, and that you and Gorgias do really have this knowledge, although I have just been saying that I have never found anybody who had.

Meno: There will be no difficulty, Socrates, in answering your question. Let us first take the virtue of a man—he should know how to administer the state, and in the administration of it to benefit his friends and harm his enemies; and he must also be careful not to suffer harm himself. . . . Every age, every condition of life, young or old, male or female, bond or free, has a different virtue: there are virtues numberless, and no lack of definitions of them; for virtue is relative to the actions and ages of each of us in all that we do. And the same may be said of vice, Socrates.

Socrates: How fortunate I am, Meno! When I ask you for one virtue you present me with a swarm of them, which are in your keeping. Suppose that I carry on the figure of the swarm, and ask of you, What is the nature of the bee? and you answer that there are many kinds of bees, and I reply: But do bees differ as bees because there are many and different kinds of them; or are they not rather to be distinguished by some other quality, as for example, beauty, size, or shape? How would you answer me?

Meno: I should answer that bees do not differ from one another, as bees.

Socrates: And if I went on to say: That is what I desire to know, Meno; tell me what is the quality in which they do not differ, but are all alike. . . . *what makes a bee a bee?*

Plato, *Five Dialogues,* trans. G. Grube. (Indianapolis, Ind.: Hackett, 1981).

able view?[9] "I believe in God": How is such belief supported? What kind of God? "That painting is beautiful": What is beauty? "I'm a Gemini": Are there solid premises for the predictions of astrology?

"Developing a philosophy of life" was an objective considered essential or at least important by about 45 percent of American college freshmen in 1993.[10] More important were, in ascending order, helping others who are in difficulty, becoming an authority in one's field, raising a family, and being very well-off financially. We wonder whether the responses were based on a clear understanding of the nature of values and the possible meanings of "developing a philosophy of life." Were the surveyed students aware of the meanings, branches, and tools of philosophy? Had they any notion of the benefits of choosing adequate views of reality and maintaining a coherent, consistent world view? We propose that a mature person's philosophic beliefs are well established; such a man or woman is well integrated, and sustains a harmony between thought and action that is indispensable to his or her well-being.

As the ancient philosophers long ago discerned, philosophy is a quest for wisdom. We all are aware that a person can have a great deal of knowledge and still be a learned fool. In our age of confusion and uncertainty, we need a sense of direction. Wisdom is what provides us with that sense: it is an affair of values. As Abraham Kaplan has written regarding wisdom:

> Whatever else wisdom may be, it is in some sense an *understanding* of life. It is not a purely cerebral attainment; wisdom is as much a matter of what we do and feel as it is of how we think. But thought is central to it. . . . Wisdom is a matter of *seeing* things—but as they are, not subjectively.[11]

Wisdom is intelligent conduct of human affairs. We experience intellectual discomfort when confronted with fragmentary and confused views of the world. Without some unity of outlook, the self is divided. Among other benefits, study of philosophy gives our lives an inner integration, helps us to decide what to approve and what to disapprove, and provides a sense of the meaning of human existence.

SPECIFIC VOCATIONAL USES

In recent years, professionals and businesses have begun to pay attention to the ethical dimensions of their practices. In business ethics, many of the following issues are discussed: What is the goal of a corporation? What are the ethics of "whistle-blowing"? What is fair in competition? How can we resolve conflicts of profit making with the good of the environment? Ought we to demand truth telling in advertising? How should we view job discrimination, affirmative-action hir-

ing practices, respective rights of employers and employees, social responsibilities of business, responsibilities of business to the consumer, the role of government in business, and so on?

For those in the health-care professions, the thorny ethical issues regarding reproductive technologies, allowing or helping chronically and terminally ill patients to die with dignity, suicide, patients' rights, genetic engineering, and public health care are in the forefront of investigations.

Each occupation is in the process of identifying the ethical issues it confronts in practice. The usefulness of identifying and understanding the options—a task undertaken by philosophers—is evident. "Applied philosophy" today is not only a useful part of our lives, it is necessary to our daily existence.

Values and Education

◆ ◆ ◆ ◆ ◆ ◆ ◆ ◆ ◆ ◆ ◆

Elaborating on our discussion of personal and vocational uses of philosophy, we shall now explore briefly a pertinent philosophical area, the philosophy of education. Philosophical thinking about education (indeed, about the courses for which this textbook is intended) is linked to our values and to our convictions about the role of the liberal arts in various curricula.

Do you go to a *good* college? Is your philosophy course a *good* one? Is your instructor a *good* teacher? Such common questions ask for an evaluation of an institution, a course, and a professional. A rating based on some scale or standard of values is sought; to answer these questions, an individual must have some idea of what he or she values in a college, course, or instructor.

Some students believe that for a college to qualify as "good" it must be internationally prestigious; apparently they value privately funded and well-known institutions. By this standard, neither public nor local colleges can be rated as "good."

A philosophy course may be rated "good" if the instructor demands little work and gives high grades, if the reading assignments are short and entertaining, and if the emphasis is immediate relevance and obvious utility. A demanding course with long-range as well as some immediate benefits, dedicated to traditional knowledge, may be judged a "bad" course.

A teacher may be valued highly because of personal qualities, such as speaking ability, warmth, and participation in extracurricular student activities. Professional standards such as thoroughness, up-to-date subject knowledge, and reasonable academic expectations for students may be ignored or entirely overlooked when those students rate an instructor.

RELEVANCE OF PHILOSOPHY TO EDUCATION

If we are to give thoughtful answers to evaluative questions about education, we must acknowledge their dependence on philosophy. Educational value judgments, like all value judgments, are debatable: Do they express subjective feelings or objective knowledge? On what bases are particular educational values justified?

Other relevant philosophical considerations are: (1) *What is meant by education?* Is it the learning of skills for a job? Is it the memorization of data? Is it, as Alfred Whitehead said, a collection of "inert ideas—ideas that are merely received into the mind without being utilised, tested, or thrown into fresh combinations?"[12] Is it a process of continuous reinterpretation of one's individual and social life? (2) *What is human nature?* Which image reflects accurately the creature to be educated? How do human beings learn? What is the mind?[13] (3) *What is knowledge?* What are the sources and nature of knowledge? What methods can we use to distinguish valid from invalid knowledge?[14]

Different philosophical outlooks and religious traditions present contrasting explanations of value, human nature, knowledge, and education.[15] For example, the pragmatism of John Dewey offers a particular interpretation of reality (including human nature), knowledge, and values with definitive consequences for an approach to education. A Hindu's understanding of these issues would be quite different.

PHILOSOPHY OF EDUCATION

The application of general philosophical positions to educational problems is called *philosophy of education*. One model of this field focuses on three issues: (1) basic objectives and specific goals of education; (2) methods of teaching and learning; and (3) curricula. To establish a college requires a philosophy of education, and the answers to a number of basic questions: What are the basic objectives and specific goals of the school? What methods of teaching and learning are consistent with these basic objectives? What will constitute the curriculum? Various founders of colleges and universities have different answers to these questions. Throughout the world, institutions of higher education have different purposes, teaching and learning methods, and curricula.

If a college or university system lacks a coherent educational philosophy, the result can be a series of conflicting objectives and aims, random teaching and learning methods, and unstable, trendy curricula. Similarly, if a local public school board appoints or elects members with conflicting philosophies, an incoherent patchwork of aims, methods, and curricula may result.

A DILEMMA: LIBERAL ARTS OR VOCATIONAL TRAINING?

Many students today, perhaps the majority, believe that the basic objective of all education, especially at the college or university level, is to provide vocational training; that is, to prepare students for a job or career. They believe that the need for occupational skills should be the basis of a curriculum; methods of teaching and learning should include whatever means are available to communicate clear-cut vocational information; a diploma or college degree should be an entry ticket to a good job. One student, studying philosophy because it was required in a vocational program, exclaimed in anguish during a provocative class session, "You're messing up my mind! I didn't come here to think; I came for an education." One wonders whether such a student has connected a view of education with reflected comprehension of human nature, knowledge, and values. Are students to be trained only in order to get a job? Should worthwhile knowledge be defined only as that which can be used to earn a living? Is occupational competence the only valuable purpose of education?

Many believe that if vocational training is the sole content of education, the graduate enters the marketplace unprepared. One reason is vocational training can become obsolete very quickly. New technologies, new products, new management styles, and new industries appear so rapidly that skills learned today are inadequate only a few years later. Training of men and women solely with occupational information often ignores their need for a better understanding of themselves and the world. An education that has the humanities at its core provides the student with permanent knowledge, the ability to think critically, and exposure to powerful minds, inquiring intellects, and events of human significance. Whether vocational training takes place alongside such "freeing arts" (the literal meaning of "liberal arts"), at separate institutions, or in the marketplace depends on the educational philosophies of individual institutions. Over a decade ago a national magazine asserted that, in addition to good technical training, new leaders need to be educated in the humanities.[16] They need to have the kind of understanding of the human psyche—of the struggle against regressive and irrational forces—that comes from reading great writers such as Sophocles, Plato, Shakespeare, and Ibsen who make us see how difficult it is for human beings to deal with each other.

Some people think that many of our leaders display a lack of understanding about human nature, that they appropriate simple-minded psychological theories of what motivates people and tend to believe that everyone is motivated by the desire for money or to "keep up with the Joneses." They seem to lack the qualities gained from exposure to the liberal arts and social sciences, qualities that are essential in an effective leader.

A commission funded by the Rockefeller Foundation credits the humanities with enabling men and women to make critical judgments about ethics and social policy, to understand diverse cultures, and to interpret current events in light of the past. The thirty-two-member group described the humanities as integral to elementary and secondary education. They recommended that subjects such as languages, history, philosophy, and English, which nurture critical thinking, be taught early in the student's academic career.[17] Consistent with the commission's recommendations is the Institute for the Advancement of Philosophy for Children. Founded in 1974, the Institute has been responsible for the development of curriculum materials and teaching methods that improve thinking and problem-solving skills. For similar reasons, the American Philosophical Association has active committees concerned with the teaching of philosophy at all levels.

EVALUATING EDUCATION

Any evaluation of a school, a course, or a teacher depends on the general philosophy of the evaluators, including their position on values, philosophy of education, and commitment to the humanities. Clearly, many educational philosophies are possible, and evaluators disagree, whether they are members of an accrediting team or students chatting in a cafeteria. The evaluation of a college, course, or professor as "good" is a philosophical judgment that reflects a wide range of other philosophical convictions. If people have no understanding of logic, ethics, and metaphysics, their evaluations of philosophies of education are of questionable worth because a philosophy of education needs to be grounded in an articulated philosophy.

The educational philosophy of a university dedicated to research may differ legitimately from the aims, methods, and curriculum of a small teaching college. Both may have value if their respective philosophies are well implemented. A course or a teacher may be judged "good" if consistent with the philosophy of their institution. Frequently, poor evaluations expressed informally reflect primarily other criteria that are, at best, of secondary significance. To avoid a course in physics because of its difficulty, to degrade the University of Leipzig because it is not well known by the average American student, or to rate Nietzsche poorly as a teacher because he was not entertaining is to render an unreasonable and superficial judgment. Sound evaluations require thoughtfulness and philosophical awareness.

There are a multitude of problems facing American education today. Within a democratic society, how can we harmonize the different traditions out of which American higher education springs? Where can moral and financial support be found that will permit American scholarship to maintain its freedom and standards? How can a substantial relationship be established between an increasingly technologically oriented culture and the institutions and ideals of the humanities? As we have tried to indicate, these questions have no easy answers, but we agree with Professor Charles Frankel when he writes:

> In the final analysis, however, these are the problems of teachers and scholars whose mission is the same as that of scholars anywhere. That mission is to keep the tradition of disinterested learning alive; to add to the knowledge possessed by the race; to keep some solid, just, and circumspect record of the past; and to use what knowledge, skill, and critical intelligence exists for the improvement of the human estate. This is the function of universities wherever they are permitted to attend to their own proper business.[18]

Philosophy Today

◆ ◆ ◆ ◆ ◆ ◆ ◆ ◆ ◆ ◆

For most of its history, philosophy has been concerned with the problems of everyday, human situations; in recent decades, however, many philosophers in the Western world turned their attention almost exclusively to questions about the nature and role of philosophy or to a discussion of the terms and language through which thoughts are expressed. A knowledge of terms and the structure and uses of language is important, but we need not substitute the study of instruments—logic, semantics, and linguistic analysis—for the study of the basic problems—the perennial problems of philosophy.

Recently, however, a growing number of philosophers have broadened the scope of their interests. They are working with hospitals, business and industry to help solve the problems of health care delivery and corporate communities. Philosophers are professionals like doctors, lawyers, and tennis players: philosophers get paid for being specialists in the area of ideas.

Many people today have become dissatisfied with narrow analytic conceptions of philosophy; in the 1980s, philosophy began to be concerned with nontraditional fields, such as brain research, cognitive science, and artificial intelligence; and with new issues, such as animal rights, defining life and death, establishing the nature and role of technology in modern thought, and experimentation with human subjects; and with raising philosophical questions in relation to outer space, gender issues, literature, sports, violence, social norms, and the environment. Moreover, as is apparent from newsletters of the American Philosophical Association, many philosophers are giving attention to other topics such as "The Black Experience," "Feminism and Philosophy," "Computer Use In Philosophy," and "Philosophy and Law." Applied philosophy has captured the interest of many philosophers who do not regard linguistic analysis as the sole job of philosophy. In this book, we view philosophy as a process of reflecting upon and criticizing our most deeply held beliefs. We hope to show that the activity of philosophy belongs to all thinking persons.

Reflections

◆ ◆ ◆ ◆ ◆ ◆ ◆ ◆ ◆ ◆

The usefulness of philosophy is well attested to in this excerpt:

Far from being an academic luxury, philosophy should play a central part in any well balanced college or university curricula. The study of philosophy contributes distinctively and substantially to the development of students' critical thinking. It enhances their ability to deal rationally with normative issues. It extends their understanding of interdisciplinary questions. It strengthens their grasp of our intellectual history and of our culture in relation to others. It increases their capacity to articulate and assess world views. And it improves their skills in writing and speaking. . . .

Philosophical reflection can be brought to bear on any subject matter whatsoever; every discipline raises questions which philosophical investigation can help clarify; and every domain of human existence confronts us with problems on which philosophical reflection can shed light. The study of philosophy can help students in all the ways this suggests, and the philosophical techniques they assimilate can help them both in their other academic work and in their general problem solving over the years.[19]

◆ ◆

Glossary Terms

AESTHETICS   The branch of philosophy concerned with art and the nature of the work of art.

CONCLUSION   A proposition inferred from the premises of an argument.

DEDUCTION   An inference in which the conclusion follows necessarily from one or more premises. When the conclusion does so follow, the deduction is said to be valid.

DIALECTIC   As most frequently used by philosophers, the critical analysis of conceptions in order to determine their meaning, implications, and presuppositions. Also, a method of reasoning used by Socrates, Hegel, and others in which opposites are reconciled.

EMPIRICISM (EMPIRICAL)   The view that knowledge comes from experience or through the senses, in opposition to *rationalism*.

EPISTEMOLOGY   Theory of knowledge; the branch of philosophy which studies the sources, nature, and validity of knowledge.

ETHICS   The study of moral conduct. The term may also be applied to the system or the code followed (such as "Buddhist ethics.")

INDUCTION   Reasoning that attempts to reach a conclusion concerning all the members of a class after inspection of only some of them. Inductive knowledge is empirical. The conclusion of an inductive argument, unlike that of a deductive one, is not logically necessary.

INFERENCE   A conclusion derived either from general premises (deduction) or from factual evidence (induction). Not to be confused with *implication;* one proposition is said to *imply* another when their relation is such that if the first is true the second *must* also be true.

LOGIC   The branch of philosophy that deals with the nature and problems of clear and accurate thinking and argument.

METAPHYSICS   A critical study of the nature of reality. Metaphysics is often divided into ontology and cosmology.

PREMISE   A proposition supporting or helping to support a conclusion.

RATIONALISM   The view that the mind has the power to know some truths that are logically prior to experience and yet not analytic.

Chapter Review

THE MEANINGS OF PHILOSOPHY

1. Every individual has a philosophy, even though he or she may not be aware of it.

2. The word *philosophy* is derived from the Greek words *philia* (love) and *sophia* (wisdom) and means "the love of wisdom."

3. One must consider each approach to philosophy to have a clear understanding of the many meanings of *philosophy* and what particular philosophers say about the nature and function of philosophy.

WHY WE NEED PHILOSOPHY

1. Humanity has acquired a great new power in science and technology; numerous techniques for gaining greater security and comfort have been developed. At the same time, people feel insecure and anxious because they are uncertain about the meaning of life and of which direction they should take in life.

2. Philosophy, in conjunction with other disciplines, plays a central role in guiding us toward new desires and aspirations.

TRADITIONAL BRANCHES OF PHILOSOPHY

1. The text is organized around basic issues of philosophy. The traditional branches of philosophy are logic, metaphysics, epistemology, and value theory.

2. Logic is the systematic study of the rules for the correct use of supporting reasons, rules we can use to distinguish valid arguments from specious ones.

3. Metaphysics traditionally has been concerned with the ultimate nature of things.

4. Epistemology is in general the branch of philosophy that studies the sources, nature, and validity of knowledge.

5. Value theory is concerned with the nature of values; it can be subdivided into ethics, aesthetics, and social and political philosophy.

6. Ethics is concerned with questions of morality. Within morality and ethics there are three major areas: descriptive ethics, normative ethics, and metaethics.

7. Aesthetics focuses on the theory of art and beauty.

8. Social and political philosophy investigates value judgments concerning the individual in society.

PHILOSOPHICAL METHODOLOGY— SOCRATIC DIALECTIC

1. The basic method of philosophical inquiry is *dialectical*. The dialectic is the development of thought through an interplay of ideas. Dialectical thinking attempts to develop a sustained pattern of argument in which the implications of different positions are drawn out and contrasted with each other.

THE USES OF PHILOSOPHY

1. Philosophy is inescapable; issues of metaphysics, epistemology, values, and logic are part of everyday living.

2. The study of philosophy nurtures the capacity for making informed choices.

3. Specific personal and vocational uses add to the benefits of philosophical studies.

VALUES AND EDUCATION

1. Philosophy of education is explored briefly as an elaboration of the discussion of personal and vocational uses of philosophy.

2. To evaluate a college, course, or instructor, we must determine what we value in these areas.

3. Evaluative issues in education depend on several philosophical attitudes.

4. The application of general philosophical positions to educational problems is called philosophy of education.

5. A current educational dilemma is whether the basic objective of all education is to provide vocational training or "permanent education" of the liberal arts.

PHILOSOPHY TODAY

1. Philosophy has in recent decades been concerned almost exclusively with questions about the nature and role of philosophy or a discussion of the terms and language through which thoughts are expressed.

2. Recently a growing number of some philosophers have broadened the scope of their interests. Applied philosophy, concerned with areas such as brain research, cognitive science, artificial intelligence, definitions of life and death, the nature and role of technology in modern thought, gender issues, animal rights, value or moral problems in medicine and business, and so on, has captured the interest of many philosophers.

REFLECTIONS

1. The usefulness of philosophy is well attested to by its several theoretical and practical applications to human living.

◆ ◆

Study Questions and Projects

1. Is there justification for saying that our age is facing unprecedented problems? Are these problems any different, except in degree and intensity, from the problems of past ages? Which contemporary conditions or trends do you consider encouraging, and which discouraging?

2. Does each person need a philosophy? Can one really choose whether he or she is to have a philosophy of life?

3. What justification can you give for saying that some of the great issues of our time are philosophical problems? In what sense are some of these issues also timeless?

4. Organize some of your present beliefs and convictions regarding life and the world into a statement of no more than 2000 words. Keep a copy of this statement of personal philosophy and compare it with a similar statement that you write toward the end of the course.

5. Has your secondary and college education developed in you any set of convictions or values regarding your personal life, social relationships, and the world in general? Should education be concerned with such questions or only with descriptive knowledge in specialized areas?

6. Indicate the extent and areas of your agreement or disagreement with the following statements:

(a) "There is no more direct way of elevating our life than by elevating our ideas."
—Ernest Dimnet

(b) "Make it thy business to know thyself, which is the most difficult lesson in the world."—Cervantes

(c) "Money buys everything except love, personality, freedom, immortality, silence, and peace."—Carl Sandburg

(d) "The great sickness of our age is aimlessness, boredom, and lack of meaning and purpose in living."—Dr. Dana L. Farnsworth

7. Philosophical journals are an important storehouse of current thinking in the field. Familiarize yourself with as many of them as you can and see how many of them are in your library. Fairly complete lists may be found in *The Encyclopedia of Philosophy* and in the *Directory of American Philosophers*. The following is a partial list: *Ethics; The Humanist; International Philosophical Quarterly; The Journal of Aesthetics and Art Criticism; The Journal of Philosophy; The Journal of the History of Ideas; The Journal of the History of Philosophy; The Journal of Symbolic Logic; The Monist; The Philosophical Forum; The Philosophical Review; Philosophical Studies in Education; Philosophy and Phenomenological Re-*

search; *Philosophy East and West; Review of Metaphysics; Free Inquiry; Public Affairs Quarterly; The Thomist.*

8. State the difference between "first-order questions" and "second-order questions" and give some examples. See Mortimer J. Adler, *The Conditions of Philosophy*, pp. 42–48.

9. Do you think teachers of philosophy should be committed and speak out, or neutral and silent, on the great pressing, but controversial, issues of the day?

10. What is meant by the statement that "civilization is basically a set of ideas and ideals?"

11. What is the meaning of the word *philosophy,* and in what ways do philosophers understand the nature and function of philosophy?

12. Write an article for a junior high school newspaper entitled "Philosophy: Its Meaning, Method, and Branches."

13. Evaluate your school according to its philosophy of education as published in its current catalogue. (Offices of admissions and the registrar usually have catalogues available.)

14. Respond to the student in an introductory philosophy class who complained angrily, "I didn't come here to think; I came here for an education."

15. In a carefully organized, thoughtful essay comment on the following statement: "Many groups in the United States provide definitive answers to questions of reality, truth, and values for their members. Their firm convictions have eliminated the need to reflect philosophically."

◆ ◆

Suggested Readings

Adler, M. J. *The Conditions of Philosophy*. New York: Dell, 1967.

A clear statement of the nature of philosophy and what is needed to restore it to a place of eminence in the contemporary world.

Barrow, R., and Woods, R. *An Introduction to Philosophy of Education*. 3rd ed. New York: Routledge, 1989.

An excellent introduction for students with no previous background in philosophy.

Barth, E. M. *Women Philosophers: A Bibliography of Books through 1990*. Bowling Green, Ohio: Philosophy Documentation Center, 1992.

More than 2,800 philosophical works written by women are listed.

Brumbaugh, R. S., and Lawrence, N. M. *Philosophers on Education: Six Essays on the Foundations of Western Thought*. Lanham, Md.: University Press of America, 1986.

First published in 1963, this book studies educational theories developed by Plato, Aristotle, Rousseau, Kant, Dewey, and Whitehead.

Copleston, F. C. *History of Philosophy*. 9 vols. New York: Image/Doubleday, 1976.

An excellent, comprehensive history of Western philosophy.

Edwards, P. (ed.). *The Encyclopedia of Philosophy*. 8 vols. New York: Macmillan/Free Press, 1967.

A mine of information on the subjects related to the field of philosophy. Many articles written from the point of view of analytic philosophy.

Ewing, A. C. *The Fundamental Questions of Philosophy*. London: Routledge and Kegan Paul, 1951.

Professor Ewing seeks to deal with all the main issues of philosophy insofar as they can be stated and discussed profitably and simply. Among other questions, he treats the place of reason in knowledge and life, the relation of body and mind, the problem of evil, and the existence of God.

Hocking, W. E. *Types of Philosophy*. New York: Scribner's, 1939.

Hocking's classic introduction to the problems of philosophy is still a good book for those "who are not devoting their lives to the study of philosophy."

Hoy, R. C., and Oaklander, L. N. (eds.). *Metaphysics: Classic and Contemporary Readings*. Belmont, Calif.: Wadsworth, 1991.

An anthology that delves into five topics—time, identity, mind, freedom, and reality.

Jones, W. T. A. *A History of Western Philosophy*. 2nd ed. New York: Harcourt Brace and World, 1969–1975.

A five-volume history of western philosophy that, in addition to being an excellent history, reveals a great deal about the philosophical enterprise and the role that philosophy plays in the general culture.

Kim, J., and Sosa, E. (eds.). *A Companion to Metaphysics*. Cambridge, Mass.: Blackwell, 1993.

An alphabetically arranged survey of metaphysics with more than 200 articles by distinguished scholars.

Knight, George R. *Issues and Alternatives in Educational Philosophy,* 2nd ed. Berrien Springs, Mich.: Andrews University Press, 1989.

Knight presents a succinct and clearly written survey of the major philosophies and philosophic issues relevant to education.

Lipman, M., Sharp, A. M., and Oscanyan, F. S. *Philosophy In The Classroom*. 2nd ed. Philadelphia: Temple University Press, 1980.

The authors argue for the integration of thinking skills into every aspect of the curriculum.

Ozmon, Howard A., and Samuel M. Craver. *Philosophical Foundations of Education,* 4th ed. Columbus, Ohio: Merrill, 1990.

In their widely used text, Ozmon and Craver present a well-done introduction to the most important schools of educational philosophy.

Parkinson, G. H. R. (ed.). *The Handbook of Western Philosophy*. New York: Macmillan, 1988.

Although some articles are quite technical, the topics are of current interest and are grouped within six parts: Meaning and Truth; Theory of Knowledge; Metaphysics; Philosophy of Mind; Moral Philosophy; and Society, Art and Religion.

Pelikan, J. *The Idea of the University—A Reexamination*. New Haven, Conn.: Yale University Press, 1992.

The author provides an analysis of what a university is and ought to be; he explains why universities are indispensable to a modern society.

Post, J. F. *Metaphysics: A Contemporary Introduction*. New York: Paragon, 1991.

Topics include defining metaphysics, why there is anything at all, whether time and the universe have a beginning, conflicting ideas about God, and so forth.

Schoedinger, A. B. (ed.). *Introduction to Metaphysics: The Fundamental Questions*. Buffalo, N.Y.: Prometheus, 1991.

An introductory anthology of historical and contemporary readings concerning the problem of universals, causation, personal identity, free will and agency, and artificial intelligence.

Taylor, R. *Metaphysics*. 4th ed. Englewood Cliffs, N.J.: Prentice-Hall, 1992.

In the "Foundations of Philosophy Series," this text explores the need for metaphysics, persons and bodies, the mind as a function of body, freedom and determinism, fate, space and time, the relativity of time and space, temporal passage, causation, God, polarity, and metaphysics and meaning.

Thomson, G. *An Introduction to Modern Philosophy*. Belmont, Calif.: Wadsworth, 1993.

An introduction to the claims and arguments of Descartes, Spinoza, Leibniz, Locke, Berkeley, Hume, and Kant.

Notes

1. G. W. F. Hegel, *Encyclopedia of the Philosophical Sciences,* trans. W. Wallace (Oxford: Clarendon Press, 1975), sec. 7.

2. C. D. Broad, *Scientific Thought* (New York: Harcourt, Brace, 1923), p. 20.

3. W. Barrett, *The Illusion of Technique* (Garden City, N.Y.: Doubleday, Anchor, 1978).

4. Barrett, *The Illusion of Technique,* p. xv.

5. These questions are considered in Chapters 9 and 10. Note especially the discussion of "common sense" on pp. 169–170.

6. Ethical theories are more fully discussed in Chapter 7.

7. P. Wheelwright, *A Critical Introduction to Ethics,* 3rd ed. (New York: Odyssey Press, 1959), p. 4.

8. Philosophers as different as Plato, Aristotle, Hegel, Kierkegaard, Nietzsche, Marx, and Heidegger have stressed the importance of dialectic.

9. See pp. 87–89 for a detailed explanation of philosophical fatalism.

10. As reported in *The Chronicle of Higher Education* (January 26, 1994), p. A31.

11. A. Kaplan, *In Pursuit of Wisdom* (Beverly Hills, Calif.: Glencoe Press, 1977), p. 16.

12. A. N. Whitehead, *The Aims of Education* (New York: Macmillan, 1929), p. 1.

13. See Part I, The Nature of Human Nature, for a discussion of several aspects of this issue.

14. See Part III, Knowledge and Science.

15. See Parts IV, Philosophical Perspectives, and V, Religion: East and West.

16. M. Maccoby, "Who Will Lead 'This New Breed' of Americans?" *U.S. News and World Report* (March 15, 1982): 81.

17. See Commission on Humanities, *The Humanities in American Life: A Report* (Berkeley: California University Press, 1980). This book is the commission's full report.

18. C. Frankel, ed., *Issues in University Education* (New York: Harper, 1959), pp. 174–75.

19. *The Role of Philosophy Programs in Higher Education* (Newark: American Philosophical Association, University of Delaware, 1980), p. 13.

The Nature of Human Nature

Human Nature: What Is It?

CHAPTER OBJECTIVES

In this chapter we will address the following questions:

♦ What Does Metaphysics Have to Do with Human Nature?

♦ Is There a Human Nature?

♦ How Do Humans Differ from the Rest of Nature?

♦ What Are Some Representative Images of Human Nature?

It is a characteristic of man that the more he becomes involved in complexity, the more he longs for simplicity; the simpler his life becomes, the more he longs for complexity; the busier he becomes, the stronger is his desire for leisure; the more leisure he has, the more boredom he feels; the more his concerns, the more he feels the allure of unconcern; the more his unconcern, the more he suffers from vacuousness; the more tumultuous his life, the more he seeks quietude; the more placid his life, the lonelier he becomes and the more he quests for liveliness.[1]

Metaphysics and Human Nature

♦ ♦ ♦ ♦ ♦ ♦ ♦ ♦ ♦

Metaphysics (see Chapter 1, p. 7) encompasses many issues related to the nature of human beings, including the topics explored in this chapter and Chapters 3, "The Self," 4, "The Mind," and 5, "The Freedom To Choose." We shall begin our inquiry with the basic question, "Is there a human nature?"

Is There a Human Nature?

♦ ♦ ♦ ♦ ♦ ♦ ♦ ♦ ♦

What is it about being human that makes people different from stones or trees or rats? What do we mean when we say that all persons are brothers and sisters in some sense? People are obviously different from each other in so many ways; yet we speak of "human nature" as if all individuals also have some quality in common. Is there such a thing as human nature? Where does it come from, and what is it like?

Almost all of the important issues in philosophy, psychology, and religion, and everyday living involve the question of what it means to be human. Most thinkers of Greek antiquity, the Middle Ages, and up to the period of the **Enlightenment** in the eighteenth century assumed that there is something called "human nature," something that philosophically speaking constitutes the "essence of humans." They believed that there was a fixed human nature, an unchanging essence. There were various ideas about what this essence was like, but there was agreement that such an essence existed, that there was something that makes a human being different from anything else, something by virtue of which humans are humans.

Advances in the biological and social sciences in the twentieth century, however, have led us to raise new and different questions about humans' essential nature. For example, the study of so-called primitive peoples has shown such a diversity of customs and values that some anthropologists view a newborn child as a blank sheet of paper on which each culture fills in the text. Environmental factors are such a powerful influence in the development of personality that some anthropologists question the idea that there is a human essence that is common to all individuals no matter what cultural environment they are in. According to their view, people become what they are because their culture shapes them.

How does the concept of evolution affect views on the nature of being human? **Evolution,**[2] in the biological sense, holds that all life develops from lower, simpler forms to higher and more complex forms. *Homo sapiens* is seen by the evolutionist as a development from one-celled animals; because human beings are subject to evolutionary change, what is "human" now must be different from what will be "human" fifty thousand years from now. If this is indeed the case, what is unique or special to humans? What constitutes "human" nature in a continually evolving process?

Another factor has contributed to the modern tendency to deny the phenomenon of a fixed human nature, of an essence of being human:

> The concept of human nature, has been abused so often, has been used as a shield behind which the worst injustices are committed, that when we hear it mentioned we are inclined to seriously doubt its moral value, and even its sense. In the name of human nature Plato, Aristotle, and most of the thinkers up to the eighteenth century defended slavery; in its name, nationalism and racism were born; in the name of a supposedly superior Aryan nature, the Nazis exterminated more than six million human beings; in the name of a certain abstract nature, the white man feels superior to the Negro, the powerful to the helpless, the strong to the weak. "Human nature," in our days, too often has been made to serve the purposes of state and society.[3]

Is it necessary to come to the conclusion that there is no human nature? Such an assumption seems to imply as many dangers as those belonging to the concept of a fixed human nature. If there were no essence common to all of humanity, how could there be values that are universally applicable to all persons; or, for that matter, how could there be the disciplines called the social sciences—anthropology, psychology, or sociology—which claim "human nature" as their subject matter.

Perhaps it would be helpful to distinguish—as many contemporary philosophers do—between the concept of human nature with an essence shared by all persons and that of certain characteristics that are common to all people. Humans are described, for example, as those animals that can produce, as tool makers, as social animals, or as symbol-making animals. None of these attributes, in themselves, completely define or limit the nature of humans. They simply describe their common characteristics.

The question of human nature also has an immediate, personal, existential dimension. As one well-known theologian has pointed out, we are our own most vexing problem; we are problems to ourselves.[4] Should humans insist that they are simply children of nature, no more than animals, who respond only to their animal instincts and appetites? Or should we insist on our unique and distinctive place in nature; after all, it is the human mind that interprets and discovers meaning in the process of life and history. *Homo sapiens* is a part of nature and partakes of nature's ways; we also appear to transcend or rise above nature and to exercise considerable control over it.

How Humans Differ from the Rest of Nature

♦ ♦ ♦ ♦ ♦ ♦ ♦ ♦ ♦ ♦ ♦

Recent decades have seen rapid development not only in the biological and behavioral sciences but also in computer technology and what is sometimes referred to as "thinking machines." If humans do not differ radically from the higher mammals, and if some computer-type machines can solve problems too complicated for the human mind, then are humans in any sense unique? If there is a difference, is it merely a matter of difference of degree or do humans differ in kind? Is there evidence to show that human behavior does include abilities not found in other living things or in machines of any degree of complexity? Let us

in this chapter look at some of the objective evidence and at some widely accepted views of humans and our distinctive nature. In the following chapter, we shall consider human beings as persons, as we move beyond strictly objective and measurable traits.

We have already noted that most scientists view humans as a part of the physical order of nature and as one of more than a million species of animals. How do humans differ in our overt behavior and what can be readily inferred from this behavior?

1. *There are certain physical characteristics that set humans apart from other higher animals.* (1) Our *erect posture.* Upright posture frees the arms and hands for exploration and manipulation. Whereas most other animals can only scratch, smell, taste, and bite, we can handle objects. The human sense of sight achieves greater prominence and use, and the sense of smell tends to recede. (2) Our *free fingers and prehensile thumb,* and the *rotation capacity of the arm.* The free flexible fingers and prehensile thumb enable us to oppose the thumb to the other four fingers in grasping objects. The well-developed collarbone, which permits the rotation of the arm, gives greater freedom and flexibility to the arm than that present in the forelimbs of many animals. For example, the forelimb of the dog is stiff and limited in range compared with the arm of a human. Because of this flexibility, we are manipulators, tool makers, and inventors. (3) Our *larger brain and head and more highly organized and intricate nervous system.* Not only is the human average skull capacity about three times that of the largest anthropoid ape, but in humans the greatest development is in the cerebrum, the seat of the higher mental processes. This permits more varied and subtle behavior.[5]

2. *As we move beyond these physical traits and relationships, we come to certain social, cultural, and intellectual traits and forms of behavior possessed exclusively by human beings, at least in any marked degree.* Humans employ a propositional language, make complex sentences, and vary the order of the sentence elements; thus, syntax (the arrangement of words in grammatical construc-

tions), which is not demonstrably evident in animal communication, occurs exclusively in the language of humans, who also are capable of carrying on conversations. Articulate speech, oral and written language, and the use of symbols are the principal vehicles of culture. They keep alive and continuously feed memory and imagination. Language in its various forms is the instrument of both personal and social communication and is basic to human society. According to some social psychologists, the invention of writing enabled us to pass from barbarism to civilization.

3. *As far as we can discover, only humans invent repeatedly, make complex tools, and build machines.* They light fires, build intricate shelters, wear clothes and ornaments. They have learned to fly, to journey under the sea, to travel to interstellar space, to construct a shuttle between earth and manufactured satellites, and to project their images and voices around the world.

4. *Humans are social and political creatures who enact laws, establish rules of conduct, and are learning to cooperate in large units.* Cooperation among individuals and groups is essential for the development of the institutions of agriculture, industry, education, science, government, and religion. In this development, specialization and integration, or organization, have gone hand in hand. Human progress appears to depend on the ability of people to cooperate in larger and larger groups. Social cooperation is one condition for a good life in an interdependent society.

5. *Only humans are conscious of history and have a cumulative cultural tradition.* They look into the past and make plans for the future. They participate in the making of history by their decisions, whether these are responsible and intelligent or irresponsible and impulsive. People can influence and make history; today they can even annihilate the future.

6. *Humans have aesthetic appreciation.* They decorate themselves and their artifacts for the enjoyment it brings, often without any utilitarian purpose. People can not only appreciate beauty—they can create it. In art, the human spirit exhibits the range and depth of its appreciation and imagination.

7. *Human beings have a sense of right and wrong and of values.* That is, they are ethical creatures with a moral conscience. In light of "what is," they can ask "What ought to be?" Our conscience, our sense of "ought," our eternal restlessness are our hope. Moral progress usually comes through the insights of a quickened or haunted conscience or through creative individuals.

8. *Humans are religious beings in that they worship and engage in ritualistic or ceremonial practices.* That people worship, pray, repent, and ask forgiveness is a worldwide phenomenon. Even though some become agnostic or atheistic, they tend to replace a personal god with an impersonal one—the state, race, some process in nature, or devotion to the search for truth or some other ideal.

As we look back over this list of observable human characteristics, especially the fact that we alone have a propositional language and possess the power of syntactical speech, we are impressed that human beings alone have the power of conceptual thought. Although other species may well share with humans some higher mental abilities, human analytical capabilities appear to remain vastly superior to anything demonstrated elsewhere in the animal kingdom. Animals, apparently, are limited to the "perceptually apprehended present situation," and do not have this conceptual power. They do not develop art, philosophy, science, or a religious outlook.

However, if other creatures are more than "living robots," if to some extent they experience mental activity and feelings, human beings will have to reassess the treatment of other animals. For example, do they have moral rights? To what extent are they mere resources for humanity?

Images of Human Nature

♦ ♦ ♦ ♦ ♦ ♦ ♦ ♦ ♦ ♦

There are many different interpretations of human nature, but they can be grouped into five fairly distinct viewpoints: (1) The classical or rational view of Western philosophers, held up to and through the period of the Enlightenment.

This view has been inherited largely from the world of Greece and Rome. (2) The religious view expressed in the Hebraic traditions. Judaism, Christianity, and Islam hold variations on a basic theme; this stance has permeated the history of Western civilizations. (3) In the Asian world, we have singled out the Hindu and Buddhist heritages as representatives of the Eastern religious view. (4) The opposing images of humans in relation to society offered by the philosophers Hobbes and Rousseau. (5) The scientific view, which can be divided into two parts: the biological understanding of humans, which is largely the product of the natural sciences, and the behavioristic view, which is largely attributable to certain thinkers in the social sciences. There are various subdivisions, modifications, and transformations, but these are the general images produced by civilizations throughout history.

THE RATIONAL VIEW OF HUMAN NATURE

According to the classical rationalistic view of human nature, inherited mainly from Greece and Rome and revived in a slightly different form during the Renaissance, what most distinguishes human beings is the fact that they are rational beings. For Plato, reason is the highest part of the soul, and the function of reason is to guide conduct. Reason is independent and immortal in its essential nature. Only reason is able to penetrate to the nature of things. For Aristotle, also, reason is the highest faculty of the soul. It is our prize possession, which sets us apart from subhuman nature. The Stoics believed in a cosmic reason, or *logos,* which pervades all things. The Stoic sage is the ideal person who suppresses emotions and governs the world through self-control. Reason must check the testimony of the senses because the "assent of reason" is central in human knowledge.

According to this classical interpretation, a human is to be understood primarily from the viewpoint of the nature and the uniqueness of his or her rational powers. Mind is the unifying principle and, as such, is distinguished from the body. Reason is the pride and glory of all human persons. For Socrates, Plato, and their followers, the intelligent human is the virtuous human. To know what is right is to do it. Vice is the result of ignorance. The goal of human effort and the meaning of progress are the harmonious development of all of human functions and capabilities through the supremacy and the perfection of reason in human beings and their society.

Although the classical view of human nature is optimistic, especially in its confidence in human reason and its view that the intelligent person is virtuous, there is an undertone of melancholy in Graeco-Roman civilization. Many Greek thinkers were impressed by the brevity and mortality of humans. They did not believe that large numbers of people (or what they frequently referred to as "the Many") could be among the wise. History had little meaning, because it was viewed as a series of cycles or endless recurrences.

The Renaissance view of human nature retained a firm, optimistic confidence in human reason. It differed from the classical view in that people's uniqueness was understood in terms both of their rational independence and their relationship to God. Their religious faith, however, was not based on authoritative pronouncements, but on free inquiry and on making their own choices. With the purpose of understanding and justifying their capacity for initiative in the world, Renaissance people sought harmony between philosophy and theology. Although a Christian orientation set the perspective, they shared with their classical predecessors the focus on practical applications of truths to human life in society.

RELIGIOUS VIEWS OF HUMAN NATURE: JUDAISM, CHRISTIANITY, AND ISLAM

Engrained in the sacred literature of Judaism, Christianity, and Islam is the major motif that the individual is in a special relationship to the Creator. Human uniqueness lies not chiefly in our reason or in our relation to nature. Instead, each person is a worthwhile, unique individual created by God.

In Judaism and Christianity, we have the capacity to act under our own initiative; we have the freedom to move within the limits of time and space. We can alter the paths of history, but not God's ultimate sovereignty or the final outcome of the historical process. In Judaism and Christianity alike, God appears and intervenes in history; the Bible is the product of divine revelation such that the Creator is "he who was in the beginning, is now, and will be in all the future" (Revelations I:4). Human beings are regarded by these religions as made "in the image of God"; that is, the Creator has endowed us with the unique attributes of a free agent capable of love, characteristics analogous to God's own self-expression. However, because we have the freedom to make choices, we can choose to disobey and rebel against the Creator; a choice of false gods is one cause of an individual's separation from the true God.

In Islam, humans also are the primary, intentional creation of God. It is more difficult to derive a doctrine of human freedom from the Qur'an[6] than it is from the Bible. With an uncompromising emphasis on the omnipotence of God, Muslims have included a strong sense of predestination in their image of humans: God directs all events. In contrast, other themes in the Qur'an point to individual responsibility for actions, the very act of submission to Allah's will presupposing a measure of freedom. It is perhaps most fair to say that there is a problem of reconciling human free will with God's omnipotence in Islam.

For these three religions, the criterion for the exercise of human freedom is loving submission to the will of God. Each understands the nature of that love and breaches of the relationship (sin) in a variety of ways in their holy writings and traditions. Participation in the community of faith, as each defines that community, is an essential nurturing of persons individually and corporately in their basic goodness as "children of God." It is this participation that empowers them with love. An implication of this religious image of humans is, therefore, that personal fulfillment requires an individual and a communal loyalty or affection for God, neighbor, and self.

THE ASIAN RELIGIOUS VIEW OF HUMAN NATURE

The religions of Asia have many varying views of humans and their essence. The Hindu religion, or Hinduism, is distinctive for its complexity, and it is difficult to delineate one particular view of humans in Hindu thought. Nevertheless, the great theme of nearly all schools of Hindu thinking is that humans must recover eternal life, which is indestructible and imperishable. We must pierce through all the misleading confusions and appearances of this life to see our true, real self in the context of the eternal life. We must begin with true knowledge about ourselves. We must cut through the web of delusion as experienced by our senses, so that we can know the eternal and permanent life that is beyond the phenomena of existence. Hinduism clearly delineates between the world of the senses—the visible world—which is changing, ephemeral, and temporary, and the unchanging world, which is permanent, reliable, and eternal. It is our task to be delivered from the wheel of existence in which we find ourselves.

No aspect of Buddhist thought is more puzzling to the Western mind than the Buddhist view of human nature. Buddhist teaching begins with a diagnosis of the human situation and finds a remedy for that situation in "The Four Noble Truths."[7] Both the diagnosis and the remedy are set in a world view very different from that of the West. Buddhism sees present human existence in terms of the reappearance of *karmic* (see *karma* in glossary) attributes in continuous sequential lives. Turn where we will, nothing in present existence is permanent. In Buddhist thought, existence involves *dukkha*, or "suffering." We suffer because we are attached to things which change. The main problem for the Western mind is that Buddhism also insists that we cannot prove one way or another that there is a "self" to experience either the suffering or the bliss. Human beings are no exception to the rule that "all is change." There can be no fixed human nature. The Buddhist doctrine asserts that rather than a self or soul, there is instead a coming together of "streams," of bodily sensations, feelings, perceptions, conceptions, and consciousness. Thus, to be proud (that is, to have self-regard), we must be vain and deluded, for not only are the attachments the self makes impermanent but also anything that can be called "the self" also is impermanent, subject to change and decay.

Unlike the Western traditions, Hinduism and Buddhism view human freedom such that we can conform to the flow of rebirth in one life after another and thereby find eventual freedom in a self-aware existence; or we may choose to be out of step with this flow and consequently retard our freedom from selfhood. However, in Hinduism *all* souls will eventually find ultimate destiny in **moksa**, or release, while in Buddhism all sentient beings can be assured of the eventual experience of *nirvana*. More of this will be explained in the chapter on Asian thought; at this point we should understand that human freedom in Western religious thought is crucial to an individual's and a people's destiny. In Hinduism and Buddhism, on the other hand, the same destiny is the identical future for the entire universe.

In the philosophic schools of Hinduism and Buddhism, sin is the ignorant clinging to the world that inhibits the process of migration and liberation from the universe. We find a sense of "sin" different from the understandings in the Hebraic traditions. In Asia, human nature finds its fulfillment in flowing toward freedom; in the West, a communal fellowship with a loving Creator is the goal that we may choose or reject.

HUMAN NATURE AND SOCIETY: HOBBES AND ROUSSEAU

With the advent of the Renaissance, philosophers became aware that an important philosophical consideration had remained untapped in the earlier classical and religious images of human nature. What they began to ask was not merely how humans differ from other animals, but what pos-

sibilities we possess for becoming more human. How could people live together in peace and harmony? Would it be possible for a person to create a new form of life, one that would be more worth living? Or is there something so corrupt in human nature that we are doomed to repeat the errors of the past and present?

These questions led naturally to a concern for the relation between human nature and society. Is there an unchanging human nature that determines social forms—that makes suffering and war inevitable? Or would it be possible to alter the social form in a fashion that would lead to change and progress?

Two different pictures of the relation between human nature and society developed. First, in the seventeenth century, Thomas Hobbes (1588–1679) published *Leviathan* (1651), essentially an analysis of political authority. (See biography and excerpt, pp. 34–35.) The title for his work came from the Old Testament, where the Leviathan was a magnificent crocodile who ruled the animal kingdom and could never be overthrown. Hobbes, who had witnessed rebellion and civil war in England, was convinced that peace and order required a Leviathanlike state that would be able to resist attack and that had absolute authority over its subjects.

In *Leviathan*, Hobbes based his political position on an analysis of human nature. He argued that human beings were naturally competitive, aggressive, greedy, antisocial, and "brutish." If left to themselves, they would be continuously at war with one another. Hobbes attacked the idealistic political philosophies of Plato and Aristotle for being unrealistic and for assuming wrongly that people were naturally capable of virtue and wisdom. He appealed to human passions, particularly the passion for self-preservation. Reason suggests that human beings make an agreement with the state in the form of a **social contract** that, for Hobbes, was mainly an agreement of equally selfish and self-seeking persons not to commit mass murder and thereby destroy the human race.

Other pictures of a social contract were developed in the seventeenth and eighteenth centuries; most notable was that of John Locke (1632–1704), which greatly influenced the formulation of the American Constitution. A social contract, however, is most frequently thought of in connection with the French philosopher Jean Jacques Rousseau (1712–1778). (See biography and excerpt, pp. 36–37.) Rousseau, contrary to Hobbes, had an extremely optimistic view of human nature. He believed that people were "naturally good" and it was only the corruptions of society that made them selfish and destructive. Rousseau does not, therefore, take the social contract to be simply a doctrine of protection among mutually brutish individuals. Rather, the function of the state is to allow people to regain the "natural goodness" that they once had in the absence of any state at all. Rousseau's aim is to develop a conception of the state that would allow us to live as morally as possible.

Our basic concern here is not so much with the theory of the state that Hobbes and Rousseau proposed, but with the clear opposition of their views in respect to the moral nature of humans. For Hobbes, humans in the "state of nature" desire only to outdo their fellow humans; they mainly seek gain and glory, always at the expense of another. For Rousseau, on the other hand, a "natural" person is "naturally" good, and contemporary society has corrupted us. We are alienated from our original nature and prevented from being our real selves; instead, we are filled with inner contradictions and seek after objects outside of ourselves. We neglect the true lessons of nature to pursue the illusions of opinions.

Rousseau further believed it was competition and our lust for private property that was responsible for this corruption; as a result we must reexamine our social institutions. In his famous book, *The Social Contract* (1762), he asserts that humans must regain their freedom within society; to be a citizen is to want and to do what is good for the society as well as oneself. Rousseau has properly been regarded as the father of the most liberal and revolutionary theories of our time; he believed that the institution of any genuine political society must be the result of a social pact, or free association of intelligent human beings who deliberately choose to form the type of society to which they will owe allegiance. For Rousseau, a citizen chooses the type of society on the basis of the general will, which is a force superior to the action of any particular will. In accepting the authority of the general will, which is not an external authority but a part of our own moral law—which is directed toward the general good—we achieve true freedom by obeying a law that we prescribe for ourselves. In this fashion, the individual gains another kind of goodness: the genuine virtue of a person who is not an isolated being but part of a great whole.

SCIENTIFIC VIEWS OF HUMANS

One strict scientific interpretation of humanity asserts that we and all our activities are determined by the laws of physics and chemistry. In this view, we are merely a more complex or "higher" form of life, and may be explained by the same laws that govern all other matter. We are part of the physical order of nature; like other objects, we have size, weight, shape, and color. We occupy space and time; the laws of physics, such as the law of gravitation, apply to us as well as to other physical objects.

This scientific view of humanity does not consider the realm of science to extend beyond the objective "facts" disclosed by the various natural sciences. Since the nineteenth century, however, the scientific method has been applied in many of the human studies, resulting in the disciplines we know as the social sciences: sociology, political science, anthropology, and psychology. In contemporary behavioral science, human psychology has become the study of human behavior. According to **behaviorism,** we can be manipulated, formed, and developed in much the same manner as any other animal.

> The cry of the behaviorist is: "Give me the baby and my world to bring it up in and I'll make it crawl and walk; I'll make it climb and use its hands in constructing buildings of stone or wood; I'll make it a thief, a gunman, or a dope fiend. The possibility of shaping in any direction is almost endless."[8]

Thomas Hobbes

Thomas Hobbes (1588–1679) was born prematurely when his mother became fearful because of the threat of invasion of England by the Spanish Armada. He attended Oxford University, then became a tutor to a prominent family that gave him access to books, foreign travel, and prominent people. His royal sympathies at a time when England was torn by civil strife led him to flee to France, where he became acquainted with the philosophy of Descartes and other French thinkers. Deeply impressed by the precision of science, he sought to work out a philosophy on a mathematical basis.

Hobbes rejected the scholastic tradition in philosophy, and tried to apply the new mechanical conceptions of the physical world to his thinking about humans and mental life. His chief philosophical work, *Leviathan* (1651), gave expression to his view of the relationship between nature, the individual, and society. Hobbes describes humans as they appeared in what he called the *state of nature,* which is the condition of humans prior to the creation of a state or civil society. Life in the state of nature is brutish and short, a state of perpetual strife and war. Because people wanted preservation and peace, they transferred their will to the will of the state in a social contract that justifies absolute sovereign power.

A direct forerunner of behaviorism during the nineteenth century was the field of animal psychology, which developed from the Darwinian revolution in biology. Animal psychologists undertook extensive research on rats, cats, chickens, and chimpanzees as substitutes for the human subject, always claiming a close identity in their methods with those of the natural sciences. As a result of these studies, the behaviorist was led to conclude that the task of a psychologist is to investigate human *behavior* rather than the human mind and its consciousness.

John B. Watson, who founded the behaviorist school of psychology, held that the scientific investigation of human nature must be limited to the objectively observable. "Now what can we observe? We can observe behavior—what the organism says and does."[9] The far-reaching implication of this limitation is that the scope of observation does not include what the human organism *means* or *intends* by speech and action; all subjective terms such as *sensation, perception, drive,* and *purpose* are dropped. For Watson, a person was simply "an assembled organic machine ready to run."[10]

Many contemporary behaviorists, including B. F. Skinner, have been fascinated by the possibility that people, and thus society, could be controlled from birth. Skinner reduced the "science" of human behavior to a study of human responses to the effects of the environment. The position of the majority of the behavioral scientists is that all individuals are "by nature" identical—empty organisms furnished with the same

Excerpt from Hobbes:

Leviathan, Ch. XIII (1651)

So that in the nature of man, we find three principal causes of quarrel. First, competition; second, diffidence; thirdly, glory.

The first maketh men invade for gain; the second, for safety; and the third, for reputation. The first use violence to make themselves masters of other men's persons, wives, children, and cattle; the second, to defend them; the third, for trifles, as a word, a smile, a different opinion, and any other sign of undervalue, either direct in their persons, or by reflection in their kindred, their friends, their nation, their profession, or their name.

Hereby it is manifest that during the time men live without a common power to keep them all in awe, they are in that condition which is called war; and such a war, as is of every man against every man. For WAR, consisteth not in battle only, or in the act of fighting, but in a tract of time wherein the will to contend by battle is sufficiently known and therefore the notion of *time,* is to be considered in the nature of war as it is in the nature of weather. For as the nature of foul weather lieth not in a shower or two of rain but in an inclination thereto of many days together; so the nature of war consisteth not in actual fighting, but in the known disposition thereto, during all the time there is no assurance to the contrary. All other time is PEACE.

E. Burtt, ed., *The English Philosophers from Bacon to Mill* (New York: Modern Library, 1939).

neural and mechanical equipment, waiting to be formed accidentally or purposefully by the forces around them. Skinner sought to demonstrate through the simplifications of the laboratory and of biology that changes in human behavior can be broken down to two basic processes: *Pavlovian conditioning* and *operant modification* through the use of the controls of positive and negative reinforcement.[11] Operant modification occurs when the experimenter selects from the organism's network of responses a particular response to trigger positive reinforcement or to remove a negative stimulus. In his well-known book, *Science and Human Behavior,* and in his utopian novel, *Walden Two,* Skinner indicated that this kind of behavior control operates, and has operated, in our everyday lives through the constraints of government, the law, religion, economics, and education.

It's a little late to be proving that a behavioral technology is well advanced. . . . Many of its techniques and methods are really as old as the hills. Look at their frightful misuse in the hands of the Nazis! And what about the techniques of the psychological clinic? What about education? Or religion? Or practical politics? Or advertising and salesmanship? Bring them all together and you have a sort of rule-of-thumb technology of vast power.[12]

Strict behaviorists deny that humans have an essential nature. They see a person as a robot or a machine; all individuals come equipped with the same potential for manipulation by the world around them.

Jean Jacques Rousseau

Jean Jacques Rousseau (1712–1778) was a Swiss-born French philosopher of the Age of Reason. A forerunner of Romanticism whose thinking and writing influenced the development of the French Revolution, he was born in Geneva. His mother died soon after his birth, and he was brought up by his father who gave him no regular schooling during his first ten years. He was later apprenticed to an engraver who punished him and left him with a strong resentment against injustice. In 1728, he ran away from Geneva and began an adventurous life in France and Italy. On his way to visit Diderot, who was then in prison, he saw a notice indicating that the Academy of Dijon was offering a prize for an essay on the question of whether the revival of the sciences and the arts had helped to corrupt or to purify morals. This subject fascinated him, because he thought modern society was rotten to the core. His essay won first prize and he became famous.

In addition to his prize-winning essay, "Discourse on the Sciences and the Arts," his writings include: *The New Héloise*, which is sentimental fiction; *Emile*, a work on education that has had influence in the field of education; *The Social Contract*, a discourse on inequality; and *Confessions,* the principal authority for the first fifty-three years of Rousseau's life. At times during his life, Rousseau was the victim of severe emotional distress, and in his later years he suffered from delusions of persecution.

Heavy criticism has been leveled at this approach; Hannah Arendt (1906–1975) (see biography and excerpt, pp. 38–39) for example, was contemptuous of what she called the "all-comprehensive pretension of the social sciences which as 'behavioral sciences' aim to reduce man as a whole, in all his activities, to the level of a conditioned and behaving animal."[13]

Reflections

Modern, Western culture is a synthesis of ideals and ways of living that have come primarily from the early Greek culture, the Jewish and Christian beliefs, and the scientific progress of recent centuries. The sciences study humans as physical objects, as complicated animals, as stimulus-response mechanisms, and as social beings. These sciences have furnished us with a mass of facts or descriptive material regarding human life and relationships. They give us valuable and expert information about segments of human life. For example, knowledge of our metabolism, our allergic sensitivity, the Mendelian laws of inheritance, our defense mechanisms, and our intelligence quotients is important. There is a great quantity of technical knowledge we could not gain by other methods. We need more, rather than fewer, such facts to live well.

The scientific view of humans is one that can be accepted as far as it goes, and no limitations to the humane study of its proper subject matter should be placed in its way. Where it is deficient

Excerpt from Rousseau:
The Social Contract (1762)

Man is born free, and yet we see him everywhere in chains. Those who believe themselves the masters of others cease not to be even greater slaves than the people they govern. How this happens I am ignorant; but, if I am asked what renders it justifiable, I believe it may be in my power to resolve the question.

If I were only to consider force, and the effects of it, I should say, When a people is constrained to obey, and does obey, it does well; but as soon as it can throw off its yoke, and does throw it off, it does better: for a people may certainly use, for the recovery of their liberty, the same right that was employed to deprive them of it: it was either justifiably recovered, or unjustifiably torn from them. But the social order is a sacred right which serves for the basis of all others. Yet this right comes not from nature; it is therefore founded on conventions. The question is, what those conventions are.

J. J. Rousseau, *The Social Contract,* ed. C. Frankel (New York: Hafner, 1947).

it is usually not because it is false, but because it is incomplete. There is the danger that we may reduce the rich qualities of human personality to the functioning of the biological organism, and then attempt to interpret the organism totally according to physical and chemical action and reaction. The sciences, with their emphasis on objectivity, are likely to neglect what is distinctively human about us.

To limit the investigation of human experience to one or even a few of its segments is unphilosophical, because philosophy seeks completeness and a comprehensive answer to questions. Freud's interpretation of humans according to "libido" or sex striving, Spengler's interpretation of humans as "beasts of prey," or Marx's interpretation of humans according to economic processes—these are not totally false but extremely lopsided views.

Is it necessary, then, to come to the conclusion that there is no human nature? Such an assumption seems to invite as many dangers as those inherent in the concept of a fixed nature. If there were no essence common to all people, it is unlikely that there ever would be a unity of all people. Neither could there be a science of psychology or anthropology, which has humans as its subject matter.

The Greek view of human nature as rational is sound insofar as it goes, yet it is not complete either. Reason gives us dignity and is the logical basis of our demand for freedom. Though no human is completely and consistently rational, we are potentially rational beings. We may learn

Hannah Arendt

Hannah Arendt (1906–1975), a teacher, writer, and philosopher, was born in Hanover, Germany, and educated at the Universities of Marburg, Freiburg, and Heidelberg. Fleeing the Nazis, she left her homeland in 1933 for France. In 1941, she arrived in the United States and worked for Jewish relief agencies until 1952. Thereafter, Arendt devoted most of her time to university teaching and writing at the University of Chicago, Princeton, and the New School for Social Research in New York.

She became known as a philosopher who viewed the human condition pessimistically and thus generated much controversy. The *Origins of Totalitarianism* (1951) is a study of the decline of the political systems of nineteenth-century Europe and the expansionist, antisemitic tendencies that arose in its wake. It helped establish her reputation as a political scientist.

Arendt wrote several other books, including *The Human Condition* (1958), *Eichmann in Jerusalem* (1963), *On Revolution* (1963), *On Violence* (1970), *Crises of the Republic* (1972), and *The Life of the Mind* (1977). Her less-than-optimistic views on human nature were no doubt due in large measure to her exposure to the roots of Nazism in the late 1920s and early 1930s.

from the Greeks in respecting reason and cultivating it in human society.

The religious emphasis on humans as creatures whose lives have meaning in a meaningful universe—on the worth and dignity of each person, and on love and social-mindedness in human relations—is another contribution. This is not to deny, of course, that many earlier theological conceptions of humans need to be revised or discarded. But this outlook is crucial, because it does not reduce personality to uncontrolled

"natural" impulses or conceive of it as perfect. As we noted before, we live at the point where "nature" and "spirit" meet. We have great possibilities for both evil and good.

Under the influence of the biological sciences, modern humans are likely to explain the tension in our lives as a conflict between our animal characteristics and our higher aspirations, which accompany the development of our higher powers. We are children of nature, in continuous interaction with our environ-

Excerpt from Arendt:

The Human Condition (1958)

In 1957, an earth-born object made by man was launched into the universe, where for some weeks it circled the earth according to the same laws of gravitation that swing and keep in motion the celestial bodies—the sun, the moon, and the stars. To be sure, the man-made satellite was no moon or star, no heavenly body which could follow its circling path for a time span that to us mortals, bound by earthly time, lasts from eternity to eternity. Yet, for a time it managed to stay in the skies; it dwelt and moved in the proximity of the heavenly bodies as though it had been admitted tentatively to their sublime company.

This event, second in importance to no other, not even to the splitting of the atom, would have been greeted with unmitigated joy if it had not been for the uncomfortable military and political circumstances attending it. But, curiously enough, this joy was not triumphal; it was not pride or awe at the tremendousness of human power and mastery which filled the hearts of men, who now, when they looked up from the earth toward the skies, could behold there a thing of their own making. The immediate reaction, expressed on the spur of the moment, was relief about the first "step toward escape from man's imprisonment to the earth." And this strange statement, far from being the accidental slip of some American reporter, unwittingly echoed the extraordinary line which, more than twenty years ago, had been carved on the funeral obelisk for one of Russia's great scientists: "mankind will not remain bound to the earth forever."

H. Arendt, *The Human Condition* (Chicago: University of Chicago Press, 1958).

ment, animals living a precarious existence on a small planet. But we are also self-conscious beings who stand outside nature. We are nature's rebels, who refuse to accept conditions as we find them.

We see, then, that there are many images of human nature. Most important, however, is our belief that persons are not things and not means for ends outside of themselves. If this is the case, the understanding of human nature has never been more difficult than in our contem-

porary society. Stimulated by our increasing technical capacity, we have concentrated all our energies on the production and consumption of things. In this process, we continually experience ourselves as things, manipulating machines and being manipulated by them. There is a clear, present danger that people may forget they are persons. For these reasons, it is most important today to reassess continually the traditions of thought about the nature of being human.

Glossary Terms

BEHAVIORISM   A theory of psychology which asserts that the proper subject matter of human psychology is the observed behavior of the human being.

ENLIGHTENMENT   A philosophical period of the seventeenth and eighteenth centuries, characterized by belief in the power of human reason.

EVOLUTION   The theory of evolution is an interpretation of how the development of living forms has taken place.

KARMA   In Hinduism, the cosmic law of sowing and reaping, of cause and effect in human life. The law determines the form that will be taken in each new

existence. Action is seen as bringing upon oneself inevitable results, good or bad.

MOKSA OR MOKSHA   In Hinduism, liberation or release from the bondage of the physical world. (See Chapter 19.)

SOCIAL CONTRACT   The voluntary agreement among individuals by which, according to any of various theories, as of Hobbes, Locke, or Rousseau, organized society is brought into being and secures mutual protection and welfare for its members.

Chapter Review

METAPHYSICS AND HUMAN NATURE

1. Metaphysics encompasses many issues related to the nature of human beings, including the topics of Chapters 2, 3, 4, and 5.

IS THERE A HUMAN NATURE?

1. What is it about being human that makes people different from stones or trees or rats? Throughout history several philosophical interpretations of human nature have emerged.

2. Comprehensive investigations attempt to define the essence of being human and the characteristics common to all people.

3. Some contemporary philosophers deny the phenomenon of a fixed human nature, of an essence of being human.

HOW HUMANS DIFFER
FROM THE REST OF NATURE

1. Humans have certain observable physical characteristics.

2. People also possess certain exclusive social, cultural, and intellectual traits and forms.

IMAGES OF HUMAN NATURE

1. The classical view stresses human reason.

2. The religious view of Judaism, Christianity, and Islam focuses on a special relationship between human beings and their Creator. Each person is a unique individual, a free agent capable of making choices.

3. The Asian view, as held by Hindu and Buddhist philosophers generally, is that humans need to search for a "true" self, which can be found in only an eternal and permanent life.

4. Contrasting positions on the individual's relationship to society are found in Hobbes and Rousseau. Hobbes emphasizes our natural hostility and conceit, which necessitate a social contract enforced by a sovereign power. Rousseau argues for a social contract based on laws resulting from the general agreement of the governed.

5. Scientific views regard human beings as part of the natural order; human nature can be explained by the same laws that govern all other matter.

REFLECTIONS

1. Modern, Western Culture is a synthesis of ideas and ways of living that have come primarily from the early Greek culture, Jewish and Christian beliefs, and the scientific progress of recent centuries.

2. The scientific view of humans is one that can be accepted as far as it goes, and no limitations to the humane study of its proper subject matter should be placed in its way.

3. Whatever image of human nature is being studied or proposed, it is most important to always regard persons as neither things nor means for ends outside of themselves.

◆ ◆

Study Questions and Projects

1. In discussing the nature of human beings, J. A. V. Butler, in *Science and Human Life* (New York: Basic Books, 1957), p. 152, protests against certain "grotesque simplifications." He says, "Because they contain mechanical contrivances, living things were regarded as machines; because they were made of chemical substances, life was a chemical phenomenon; because the nervous tissue conducts electrical currents, the brain is likened to a telephone exchange." Can the dynamic and creative inner worlds of humans be subsumed under scientific headings? Discuss.

2. Some scientists think that life may exist in other parts of the universe. See what you can find on this topic in your library and marshal the evidence for and against the view that life as we know it exists beyond the area of our earth. What would be the implications of the discovery that life exists elsewhere in the universe? Would it affect your view of human nature?

3. Comment on the following statements:
   (a) "Life can be understood only by living."
   (b) "The scientist, the thinker, is being forgotten . . . Even in science the machine is being worshipped, while the inventor—the scientist who thought it out—is set aside."
   (c) "We must deal with persons as they are with a view to what they may become."
   (d) "There is no wealth but life . . . no consummation of life except in the perpetual growth and renewal of the person."

4. B. F. Skinner wrote a utopian novel, *Walden Two,* which describes a society governed by the principles of behaviorism. One of the main characters explains this society's approach to questions about human nature:

   I wish I could convince you of the simplicity and adequacy of the experimental point of view. . . . What is the "original nature of man?" . . . That's certainly an experimental question—for a science of behavior to answer. And what are the techniques, the engineering practices, which will shape the behavior of members of a group, so that they will function smoothly for the benefit of all? That's also an experimental question, Mr. Castle—to be answered by a behavioral technology. . . . Experimentation with life—could anything be more fascinating?[14]

   Describe some experiments of your own devising that would measure human nature as it has been discussed in this chapter. What, if any, qualities of human nature cannot be measured experimentally?

5. Do you agree that each one of the interpretations of human nature (the classical or rational, etc.) has contributed important insights? Explain your answer and indicate to what degree you agree with the evaluations of these interpretations given in this chapter.

6. Discuss the influence of the theory of evolution on views of human nature and indicate why there have been sharp differences of opinion on this question. (Refer also to Chapter 11.)

7. Describe the various characteristics of human beings listed in this chapter, and indicate whether you would add others, or omit some of those listed, or both.

8. Discuss the relation between the theory of evolution and the account of creation in the first two chapters of Genesis. Read those two chapters and list the events as they are related verse by verse. Is there any evidence for two accounts, as many Biblical scholars claim? Note carefully Genesis 1:1–2:4a and Genesis 2:4b–3. Why are different words for God used in these two sections? Is the order of creation the same in the two accounts? (See also Chapter 11.)

9. Compare the Jewish-Christian-Muslim religious view of human nature with the Asian religious view.

10. Does Hobbes or Rousseau describe you and your relationship to society? Does either reflect well individuals other than yourself and their relationship to society? How would you account for any differences in your view of yourself and your view of others?

Suggested Readings

Abel, D. *Theories of Human Nature: Classic and Contemporary Readings*. New York: McGraw-Hill, 1992.

An historically organized collection of readings at an introductory level.

Cassirer, E. *An Essay On Man*. New Haven, Conn.: Yale University Press, 1944.

Subtitled *An Introduction to a Philosophy of Human Culture*, Cassirer's book has become a classic study of human nature. Particularly memorable is his discussion of the symbol as a clue to human nature.

Cranston, M. *Jean-Jacques: The Early Life and Work of Jean-Jacques Rousseau, 1712–1754*. Chicago: Chicago, 1982.

The first volume of a study that corrects many of the misunderstandings concerning Rousseau.

Cranston, M. *The Noble Savage: Jean-Jacques Rousseau, 1754–1762*. Chicago: University of Chicago Press, 1991.

The continuation of the first volume.

Dodds, E. R. *The Greeks and The Irrational*. Berkeley: University of California Press, 1951.

Indispensable to an understanding of the complex cultural context of Greek rationalism.

Lovejoy, A. *The Great Chain of Being*. Cambridge: Mass.: Harvard University Press, 1936.

Meticulously traces the idea that the universe is a rationally ordered whole, from its Greek origins to the nineteenth century.

Niebuhr, R. *The Nature and Destiny of Man*. 2 vols. New York: Scribner's, 1943.

Niebuhr's Gifford lectures, which afford us a Christian interpretation of both the nature and the destiny of humanity.

Scheler, M. *Man's Place in Nature*. Trans. Hans Meyerhoff. New York: Noonday, 1962.

A phenomenological treatment of human nature by one of the founders of "philosophical anthropology."

Sherrington, Sir C. *Man on His Nature*. New York: New American Library, Mentor Books, 1951.

A renowned psychologist tells the story in this famous work of the human effort to perceive our true nature by means of the revelations of sixteenth-through twentieth-century science.

Stevenson, L. *Seven Theories of Human Nature*. 2nd ed. New York: Oxford University Press, 1987.

An introductory exploration of human nature in Christianity, Freud, Lorenz, Marx, Sartre, Skinner, and Plato.

Trigg, R. *Ideas of Human Nature: An Historical Introduction*. London: Blackwell, 1988.

Examines ten of the most influential Western thinkers in their historical context and explores their relevance to contemporary controversies.

Wilson, E. O. *The Diversity of Life*. Cambridge, Mass.: Harvard University Press, 1992.

A tour through evolutionary time that describes the creation of the living world's biological wealth and the threat that humans now pose to the diversity of nature; a central theme notes that humankind must rediscover its evolutionary origins and be true to them.

◆ ◆

Notes

1. Shin'Ichi Hisamatsu, "Zen: Its Meaning for Modern Civilization," in *The Eastern Buddhist* (new series), Vol. I, No. 1 (Kyoto, Japan: The Eastern Buddhist Society, Sept. 1965), p. 39.

2. See Chapter 11 for an extended exploration of evolution.

3. E. Fromm, and R. Xirau, eds., *The Nature of Man* (New York: Macmillan, 1968), p. 4.

4. R. Niebuhr, *The Nature and Destiny of Man*, Vol. I (New York: Scribner and Sons, 1943), p. 1.

5 A recent edition of *National Geographic* (Vol. 181, No. 3, March 1992, p. 18) describes *Homo sapiens* as follows:

> The bipedal primate, the human, habitually walks upright. Skeletal adaptations to this mode of locomotion and posture include legs that are longer and stronger than the arms and muscular buttocks and thighs that permit sprinting and long-distance walking. A curve in the lower spine places the center of gravity in the pelvis. Both a shock absorber and a pliable platform, the human foot is uniquely adapted for bipedal walking. The hand's muscular thumb is opposable and rotates to touch any finger, increasing dexterity. The human brain is two to three times the volume of any great ape's and more complex, conferring an enhanced ability to reason and develop spoken language. In common with other primates, protracted infancy and adolescence in humans are devoted to learning survival skills and social behavior. Over the species' world-wide range, male weight averages 150 pounds; females tend to be about 20 percent smaller.

6. Often written as "Koran." Contemporary Islamic scholars prefer Qur'an.

7. See Chapter 19. Note the explanation of Buddhist terms in The Buddhist Quest for Enlightenment, pp. 412–416.

8. J. B. Watson, *The Ways of Behaviorism* (New York: Harper, 1928), pp. 35–36.

9. J. B. Watson, *Behaviorism* (Chicago: University of Chicago Press, 1958), p. 6.

10. J. Watson, *Behaviorism,* p. 269.

11. E. S. Bordin, "Two Views of Human Nature," *New York University Education Quarterly* 12 (1981): 29.

12. B. F. Skinner, *Walden Two* (New York: Macmillan, 1948), p. 240.

13. H. Arendt, *The Human Condition* (Chicago: University of Chicago Press, 1958), p. 45.

14. (New York: Macmillan, 1948), p. 145. See also Don Williams' review of *Walden Two*, "The Social Scientist as Philosopher and King," *The Philosophical Review* 58 (1949): 345–59, and comments in *Psychology Today* (August 1971).

The Self

CHAPTER OBJECTIVES

In this chapter we will address the following questions:

◆ Is There a "Self"?

◆ Are There Philosophies That Deny the Existence of the Self?

◆ What Is Consciousness?

Who was she? *She turned the question over in her mind, and found that she had not the dimmest notion of who she was; except that watching the people and horses passing, she grasped that she was a human being and not a horse. And at that the question altered itself and took this form: "Am I a man or a woman?" . . . her fingertips brushed against her body. She realized more clearly than before that her body existed, and that it was her own— that it was in fact, herself.*[1]

The Nature of the Self

♦ ♦ ♦ ♦ ♦ ♦ ♦ ♦ ♦ ♦ ♦ ♦

Who am I? Who are you? We continually refer to ourselves: *I* think, *I* ought to, *I* wish. What are we saying when we tell someone, "I am not myself today"? What is the self that is conscious of itself? Is the self immediately present to consciousness? If not, how do we come to have a consciousness of self? Have we always had something we call a "self"? If not, how did the self come into being? What is the status of the self in those disciplines that take human nature as their primary subject? These questions have profound philosophical implications and have been pursued relentlessly throughout the history of philosophy. People can have just as much trouble identifying themselves as they can identifying someone else. We have explored the question of whether there is a human nature—whether humans have a common essence. We will now explore the nature of the self.

The self has defied adequate description. Terms like *being, self,* and *God* are difficult to define; trying to explain what they mean in a few explicit words seems to distort their nature and limit their implications. We are thus left with partial definitions. Although we cannot define *self* completely, it is nevertheless an important concept. Although some philosophers have asserted that the notion of a self is meaningless, others would say that the self is *the* important factor in human life. We cannot eliminate awareness, self-consciousness, and mind from our interpretations of human affairs without denying much that is central in human experience. In fact, human history itself is an account of self-conscious, intelligent beings—that is, selves—moving through time, observing, thinking, and carrying out a multitude of purposes.

THE SELF AS THE CENTER OF PERSONAL IDENTITY

The term *self* refers to the subject, to that which persists through the changing experiences of a person's existence. The self is the perceiving, conceiving, thinking, feeling, willing, dreaming, and deciding **entity.** If the self is a substance—and many modern philosophers and psychologists reject this view—then it is a substance of a special or unique kind. A substance, it is well to remember, does not have to be material; it may be nonmaterial. Even if we claim that the self is not a substance, we can still think of it as the center of personal identity.

There is evidence of an inner element of some sort, call it what you will—self, ego, agent, mind, knower, soul, spirit, or person. Phrases such as "immediate experience" and "content of consciousness" imply an agent of some kind that has the experience: there is something that supplies unity. We say "I" or "me" in connection with experiences that happened ten years ago, five years ago, yesterday, and now. I am a unity, a subject of experience, who cannot be reduced to one part of me or to any of the particular, changing elements of my experience. If the terms *mind* and *self* are not to be identified as the same thing, then the self, or person, is the part that has those experiences we call "mental."

The reality most *immediately* known to us is our own self or ego; we know it more directly and intimately than we do the external world. The objective world that can be experienced, measured, and manipulated always is viewed from the vantage point of a self or knower. The self includes that quality of uniqueness and duration through change that enables a person to say "I" or "me." **Self-consciousness** is the awareness by the self of itself. We are not only conscious of ourselves as "I"—we are also conscious of the fact that it is ourselves who are conscious.

The conviction that there is something unique about each self is expressed in many philosophical, theological, and legal systems. In philosophy, the identity of a person usually has been taken to pose a problem distinct from the question of the identity of a physical object, an organism, or, for that matter, an animal. The attempt to define the characteristic that makes a self, or person, unique leads to the conclusion that to be a person—to have a self—one must have the capacity to be aware of one's self as a distinct entity existing over time. Do animals have this capacity? That is, are any nonhuman animals persons? The most common view of philosophers on this subject is best expressed by the contemporary English philosopher Stuart Hampshire:

> The difference here between a human being and an animal lies in the possibility of the human being expressing his intention and putting into words his intention to do so-and-so. . . . The difference is not merely that an animal in fact has no means of communicating its intention. . . . It is a stronger difference, which is more correctly expressed as the senselessness of attributing intentions to an animal which has not the means to reflect upon, and announce to itself or to others, its own future behavior. . . . It would be senseless to attribute to an animal a memory that distinguished the order of events in the past, and it would be senseless to attribute to it an expectation of an order of events in the future. It does not have the concepts of order, or any concepts at all.[2]

THE SELF AS THE PART THAT TRANSCENDS

All experience implies the existence of a self or subject independent of and not completely submerged in the processes and events surrounding it. Through its integrating or synthesizing power, the self transcends the process in which it is involved. People experience the world as "a world of objects open to observation." They experience themselves as "an inner awareness of being alive." The person who denies selfhood as something apart from objective and observable behavior will insist that his or her ideas are true. But doesn't this denial of self really establish its reality? If there are such things as truth and falsity, then thinking is not merely a succession of sensations that follow one another apart from a center of personal identity that gives them unity. Truth and falsity, recognition, and knowledge presuppose a self or a thinker. How can one compare things apart from a comparer who stands outside the things compared? The conti-

nuity of thought that enables people to carry on a lengthy argument or to write a book implies a continuing self or knowing subject.

Rollo May, a psychologist, says that "the self is the organizing function within the individual. It is prior to, not the object of, our sciences; it is presupposed in the fact that one can be a scientist."[3] The self that knows and decides is inaccessible if we attempt to use only the objective methods of the sciences. Karl Heim says, "The odd thing about the ego, which takes the world of nature as the object of its perception and volition, is that although it is nearest and most familiar to us, and although each of us is immediately aware of it, yet it is downright impossible for us to describe it objectively, as we can describe a crystal or a flower or a house."[4]

The relation of the self to the time process is one of the deepest problems of human life. Humans are limited beings with a dated existence; yet we transcend, or rise above, the time sequence in the sense that we perceive and experience the self in the ever-present "now," the subjective point between the past and the future. We have the ability to deal with the past, which may be kept alive through memory. We also have foresight—the ability to project, predict with varying degrees of probability, plan for, and to some extent shape the future. My self, however, is inexorably bound to *my* present, although in memory I can move into the past, and in imagination I can roam into the future. I am inseparably attached to my present, which is different in quality from the series of points in the sequence; it thus becomes the *time center,* so that the past and the future are viewed from the standpoint of my *now.*

THE SELF AS PRIVATE

In addition to its unity (or continuity), and **transcendence,** there is a private character about the self that is not characteristic of the body. We have an immediate knowledge of the self that is personal and by its very nature cannot be described completely in objective terms. I speak of *my* body, *my* environment, *my* experiences. I can give an eye, a kidney, or some of my blood to another person; I cannot substitute the content of another's consciousness for my own. We never completely know what another person is thinking. I can never actually enter into the world of another; I cannot feel another's pain, although by various forms of communication I can come to sympathize, understand, and even express empathy.

Furthermore, the privacy of the self means no self can have direct experience of another self. The presence of the self cannot be verified objectively, as we can verify the presence of a rock or a tree; we discover no "self" among our sense perceptions, because the self is not an object. The private nature of the self makes it an entity that defies objective investigation. Thus it is that many scientifically oriented philosophers claim that either there is no self or they can deal with it only as it manifests itself objectively in behavior.

What is the self and where is it found? Let us summarize: The self is to be found neither on the inorganic nor the merely organic level. The self is found where there is personal awareness, reflective thinking, ethical and aesthetical judgment, appreciation, and the like. Just as poetry is more than grammar and music more than rhythm, so a person is more than a body in space, and this *more* is what philosophers have called the self.

THE SELF AS SUBJECT: MARTIN BUBER

In his book, *I and Thou,* Martin Buber (1878–1965) (see biography and excerpt, pp. 48–49), a Jewish scholar, sets forth his views of the self and the relationship between persons and persons, and persons and things, which he calls a **dialogic** approach.[5] According to Buber, knowledge is of two fundamentally different kinds. There are, as a result of this, two different attitudes toward experience, two approaches to the self, and two types of relation to the environment that are not interchangeable.

First, I may know another self by mutual acquaintance. Here the fundamental relation is one of *subject* to *subject,* of self to self, which in the first instance is that of the child with her or his mother. Out of this consciousness, at first indistinct, there emerges the distinction between *I* and *Thou,* between one self and another. I know another person as a thou (the I–Thou relationship). I recognize another person (another I) in her own right, and I invite response. This is a relationship of reciprocity, in which real communion is possible. This I–Thou type of relationship, or person-to-person relationship, involves a genuine meeting or encounter, so that each discloses something of the depth of his or her being to the other. Buber says that "all real life is meeting."

Second, I know a thing as an *it,* as an object outside. This object is one of many objects occupying a position in space and time, capable of being measured, and subject to causal laws. This I–It relationship is one of person to thing, or subject to object. The purpose of I–It knowledge and relationship usually is to gain control over that which is known. The knower is detached, and the relationship is essentially one of manipulation. This kind of knowledge is illustrated by science and technology, in which the self exercises control but stands detached from the experiment. Because of this detachment and concentration on the object, there is a strong tendency to deny the self.

These two attitudes, the I–Thou and the I–It, are essential to our nature. "The primary word I–Thou can only be spoken with the whole being. The primary word I–It can never be spoken with the whole being. . . . If I face a human being as my Thou, and say the primary word I–Thou to him, he is not a thing among things, and does not consist of things." I can meet a person as a self, or I can objectify that person and make her or him an It to serve my purposes. Persons can be treated as things to be conditioned, manipulated, and brainwashed. "Without It man cannot live. But he who lives with It alone is not a man. . . . If a man lets It have the mastery, the continually growing world of It overruns him and robs him of the reality of his own I."[6]

Martin Buber

Martin Buber (1878–1965), Jewish theologian and philosopher, was one of the most creative scholars of the middle decades of the twentieth century. He was born in Vienna, brought up by his paternal grandparents in the Ukraine, and studied at the Universities of Vienna, Berlin, Leipzig, and Zurich. After completing his dissertation on mysticism, he received his doctoral degree from the University of Vienna. He was influenced by the existentialism of Kierkegaard, Nietzsche, Dostoevsky, and others. While estranged from orthodox Judaism, he believed that Zionism must be built on a Jewish and cultural renaissance. He supported Hasidic piety with its emphasis on the divine in everyday life. His books *I and Thou* (1923) and *Between Man and Man* (1947) are widely read.

In 1923, Buber was appointed to the chair of Jewish Religious Thought at the University of Frankfurt. When forced to leave Germany because of his opposition to Nazism, he went to Palestine, where he became Professor of Social Philosophy at the Hebrew University.

We are born as individuals who are different from one another. We become genuine selves only as we respond to and enter into intimate relations with others. "Through the Thou a man becomes an I." The self is social and interpersonal, and real being is between person and person. The I–Thou relationship is characterized by mutuality, directness, and intensity. Only in such a relation is genuine communion or dialogue possible, be it spoken or silent. It may be a glance or look that is spontaneous and unaffected and that involves mutuality of understanding and concern.

Buber protests against "thingification" and "objectification"—the tendency to depersonalize—because this often leads us to deny the self and certainly hinders its expression. True community emerges out of the I–Thou. Only as persons are able to say *Thou* to one another will they be able to live in mutual relations. What is good is the interpenetration of spirit with life; what is evil is the separation of spirit from life. An "organic community" is based on cooperation and the recognition of persons as persons, of selves as subjects.

The realm of the interhuman goes far beyond that of sympathy. Such a simple happening can be part of it as, for instance, when two strangers exchange glances in a crowded streetcar, at once to sink back again into the convenient state of wishing to know nothing about each other. But also every casual encounter between opponents belongs to this realm, when it affects the opponent's attitude—that is, when something, however imperceptible, happens between the two, no matter whether it is marked at the time by any feeling or not. The only thing that matters is that for each of the two men the other happens as the particular other, that each becomes aware of the other and is thus related to him in such a way that he does not regard and use him as his object, but as his partner in a living event, even if it is no more than a boxing match. It is well known that some existentialists assert that the basic factor between men is that one is an object for the other. But so far as this is actually the case, the special reality of the interhuman, the fact of the contact, has been largely eliminated. As a crude example, take two men who are observing one another. The essential thing is not that the one makes the other his object, but the fact that he is not fully able to do so and the reason for his failure. We have in common with all existing beings that we can be made objects of observation. But it is my privilege as man that by the hidden activity of my being I can establish an impassable barrier to objectification. Only in partnership can my being be perceived as an existing whole.

M. Buber, *The Knowledge of Man,* ed. M. Friedman (New York: Harper and Row, 1965).

Denials of the Existence of a Self

◆ ◆ ◆ ◆ ◆ ◆ ◆ ◆ ◆ ◆

If the concept of self is so important, why have many philosophers denied the existence of a self? We can answer this best by attempting to understand the historical setting for some of the denials.

BUDDHISM

In Asia, some five hundred years before the common era, Siddhartha Gautama, the Buddha, founded the Buddhist tradition. He was called the *Enlightened One* when he turned from fruitless asceticism to engage in resolute meditation, which gave him special philosophical and religious insight. He taught a number of followers the doctrine of the Middle Way with the promise that if they followed this Way, they themselves would attain a similar enlightenment. As we have seen in our discussion of human nature (pp. 31–32), Buddhism asserts that nothing in present existence can be proved to be permanent; instead of any "soul" or "self," the Buddhist postulates five transient streams (*skandhas*) which come together to make up being. The five streams are bodily sensation, feeling, perception, mental conception, and consciousness. The negative thrust of this view can be emphasized by the popular illustration of the chariot. What is a chariot, it is asked, except a combination of wheels, axles, chariot body, yoke, reins, and the like, that is, name and form (*namarupo*)? To what can we point as constituting the chariot other than the pieces out of which it is made? To what can we point other than streams of sensation, feeling, and various stages of consciousness as constituting the soul?

Thus we find scholars of Buddhism stating, "The aim of all Buddhist endeavor is the extinction of self, the dying out of separate individuality."[7] In fact, in Mahayana Buddhism it is the supreme task of a **Bodhisattva** (a person who is destined to win full enlightenment—to become a Buddha) to be rid of personal identity. Indeed, what separates humanity in general from Buddhahood is the belief that we are separate individuals who are preoccupied with the self. We must attain insight into the interdependence of all aspects of the self (*an-atta*) before we can realize enlightenment.

DAVID HUME

The *an-atta* doctrine seems, and has been thought by many, to have great similarities with David Hume's denial of a self (see biography and excerpt, pp. 52–53). Let us look carefully at what Hume rejected and compare his denial with that of the Buddhist.

Since the seventeenth century in the West, when philosophers became concerned with questions of knowledge, there have been a number of explicit denials of the existence of a self. For example, John Locke (1632–1704) thought of the mind beginning as a passive blank tablet, with action initiated from the external world through the senses. David Hume carried the denials further. He was unable to discover any permanent self. He rejected the notion

of a permanent self-identical substance in favor of a succession of impermanent states and events. Hume wrote: "for my part, when I enter most intimately into what I call *myself,* I always stumble on some particular perception or other, of heat or cold, light or shade, love or hatred, pain or pleasure. I never can catch *myself* at any time without a perception, and never can observe any thing but the perceptions."[8] These perceptions, of course, always are fleeting or temporary. The sole content of the mind is impressions and ideas, which are both forms of perception. Hume stressed that our self is "nothing but a bundle or collection of different perceptions" united by certain relations. He further stated that only a stream of successive ideas exist; there is no permanent self within, nor is any subject of experience needed to hold the ideas together. The mind is a mere stage for its contents.

In Buddhism the "not-self teaching is not in *itself* a denial of the existence of a permanent self; it is primarily a practical teaching aimed at the overcoming of attachment. It urges that all phenomena that we *do* identify with as 'self,' should be carefully observed and examined to see that they cannot be taken as such. In doing this, a person finally comes to see *everything,* all *dhammas,* as not-self, thereby destroying all attachment and attaining *Nibbāna.* In this process, it is not necessary to give any philosophical 'denial' of self; the idea simply withers away, as it is seen that no actual instance of such a thing can be found anywhere. Buddhism sees no need to postulate a permanent self, and accounts for the functioning of personality, in life and from life to life, in terms of a stream of changing, conditioned processes."[9] The parallels, then, between Buddhism and David Hume are significant.

BEHAVIORISM

Some contemporary social scientists have followed Hume's lead in denying the self. For example, B. F. Skinner, a behavioral psychologist, asserted that "a concept of self is not essential in an analysis of behavior," that "mental or psychic events . . . lack the dimension of science," and that "the free inner man who is held responsible for the behavior of the external biological organism is only a prescientific substitute for the kinds of causes which are discovered in the course of a scientific analysis. All these alternatives lie *outside* the individual." Skinner proposed an alternative to the concept of the self: "the self is simply a device for representing *a functionally unified system of responses.*"[10] Responses are, by necessity, observable. Complete discussion of our "inner self" is not ordinarily limited to observable behavior; Professor Skinner thought that because motives, ideas, and feelings are not objectively observable events, they can have no part in determining behavior or in explaining it: science can take no account of them.

Professor Brand Blanshard (see biography and excerpt, pp. 54–55) challenged Skinner's contention that mental behavior is no more than bodily behavior. Blanshard defended the idea that consciousness is distinct from observable behavior. Through a simple example, Blanshard showed why he thinks the Skinnerian denial of consciousness is absurd:

> Consider the behaviorist who has a headache and takes aspirin. What he means by his "headache" is . . . the grimaces or claspings of the head that an observer might behold. Since these *are* the headache, it must be these he finds objectionable. But it is absurd to say a set of motions . . . is objectionable . . . except as they are associated with the conscious pain. Suppose again, that he identifies the pain with the grimaces and outward movements then all he would have to do to banish the pain would be to stop these movements and behave in a normal fashion. But he knows perfectly well that this is not enough; that is why he falls back on aspirin. In short, his action implies a disbelief in his own theory.[11]

In contrast to Blanshard, a philosopher, some psychologists say that they do not wish to retain concepts and terms like *self, mind,* and *self-consciousness* because they do not wish to

"drag in spooks." In their desire to be completely objective and empirical, these psychologists—and philosophers who share their view—omit all reference to a self, or claim that they can deal with it only as it manifests itself objectively in behavior. They talk about stimuli, responses, and "behavioral biographies" but not about a self. Methods devised for studying inorganic nature, animals, and machines are applied to the study of humanity:

> We may expose a pigeon to a black, a white, and a red disc, of which it can get food by pecking the white one, and observe how many mispecks it makes before learning to peck at the white disc only. Here we are studying the connection between observable stimuli and observable responses . . . that is the way we should study human behavior.[12]

Many modern philosophers, however, believe that such animal studies cannot be applied to humans. Suppose you present those discs to a man. He may do any one of a hundred things because he has the power—which a pigeon does not—of thinking about it. He can consider, deliberate, and plan in a manner that cannot be foreseen. Scientific methods and postulates have clearly demonstrated their usefulness in the realm of objective phenomena.

LIMITATIONS OF METHODS SCIENTIFIC

As the behavioral sciences succeed in their aim to become more like the natural sciences, they eliminate questions of meaning, value, and the self. It is precisely these questions that have been considered essential in philosophical thought for thousands of years. The current denials of the self and mind, which hold that these concepts are no more than verbal shorthand to refer to physical and psychological processes, seem to be in part a result of the desire of some scientists to extend the objective methods of science to include all reality. If this desire can be fulfilled, all questions can be answered neatly; the world and humanity can be reduced to a series of logical,

David Hume

David Hume (1711–1776), a Scottish philosopher and a man of letters, lived at a time when thinkers were engaged in discussions about the nature of morals and religion. He entered into these discussions and had major influence in the development of two movements. The first was skepticism. He was distrustful of philosophical speculation and, among other things, said that the principle of causality was without foundation. He was also an agnostic who asserted that the existence of God could be neither proven nor disproven. The second movement was empiricism, the view that all knowledge comes from sense experience. Although a world may exist beyond or outside our consciousness, this cannot be rationally asserted.

After two unsuccessful applications for positions in philosophy at Edinburgh and Glasgow, and apart from occasional diplomatic missions, Hume spent most of his life writing. His works in history include *History of England* (4 vols.), and *The Natural History of Religion*. His best known philosophical works are *A Treatise of Human Nature, An Inquiry Concerning Human Understanding*, and *Inquiry Concerning the Principles of Morals*. Later Kant said that it was Hume who wakened him from his "dogmatic slumbers."

easily manipulated constructs. Is this denial of a self the result of an interpretation of humans as merely a product of their environment? We also do not want to deal with "spooks," but there are elements of human experience that we should not ignore just because one method works only for certain kinds of investigation. Some things that cannot be explained in the language of the behaviorist school of psychology may still be the most significant part of our lives.

Departing from narrow scientific methods of behaviorism, contemporary cognitive psychology and neuropsychology both emphasize inner events, processes, and states that affect behavior; few would deny these factors today. With more comprehensive scientific research that includes consideration of inner events, processes, and states, the sciences can contribute to ongoing in-terpretations of the self. Nonetheless, we cannot expect scientific methods alone to provide complete and final explanations. Human life can never be reduced to even the best of current scientific explorations.

Consciousness

The term **consciousness** occurs in philosophy, psychology, and common speech, but has a variety of different meanings. For example, a common use of "consciousness" refers to the awareness of one's surroundings: "The patient is regaining consciousness." Philosophers have often focused on one aspect of consciousness, namely, self-consciousness. It is our intention to examine a few of the philosophical meanings briefly.

Excerpt from Hume:

A Treatise of Human Nature
(1739)

Unluckily all these positive assertions *(about the self)* are contrary to that very experience which is pleaded for them; nor have we any idea of *self,* after the manner it is here explained. For from what impression could this idea be derived? This question it is impossible to answer without a manifest contradiction and absurdity; and yet it is a question which must necessarily be answered, if we would have the idea of self pass for clear and intelligible. It must be some one impression that gives rise to every real idea. But self or person is not any one impression, but that to which our several impressions and ideas are supposed to have a reference. If any impression gives rise to the idea of self, that impression must continue invariably the same, through the whole course of our lives; since self is supposed to exist after that manner. But there is no impression constant and invariable. Pain and pleasure, grief and joy, passions and sensations succeed each other, and never exist at the same time. It cannot therefore be from any of these impressions, or from any other, that the idea of self is derived; and consequently there is no such idea.

D. Hume, *A Treatise on Human Nature,* ed. J. H. Green (London: Longmans, Green, 1874).

In *An Essay Concerning Human Understanding,* John Locke (1632–1704) defined consciousness as "the perception of what passes in a man's own mind."[13] Consciousness or reflection is a person's observing or noticing the "internal operations" of his or her own mind. It is by means of consciousness that a person acquires the ideas of the various mental states, such as perceiving, thinking, doubting, reasoning, knowing, and willing and learns of his or her own mental states at any given time. Locke's use of *consciousness* as described here was widely adapted by philosophical thinking and common sense until the late nineteenth century. At that time, the word **introspection** began to be used: "To introspect is to attend to the workings of one's own mind."[14]

Just as some philosophers have denied the existence of a self (see pp. 49–51), many have denied the possibility of introspection. One reason given is that introspection implies the absurdity that people could divide themselves in two, one part reasoning and the other observing the first reasoning. Another objection has been raised concerning the physical organ of introspection. Traditionally, introspection has been seen as analogous to perception: a nondiscursive act by which the mind contemplates its own acts. Just as we can distinguish between seeing an object and making judgments about it—"the tree is huge"—so we can distinguish between introspecting a mental state and making judgments about that state. Perceiving, however, as we shall see (pp. 191–197), involves use of the sensory organs—the eyes, ears, and so on. What is the organ of introspection? There is no physical organ

Brand Blanshard

Brand Blanshard (1892–1988) was born in Fredericksburg, Ohio. His father was a Congregational minister; both his parents were Canadians who later became American citizens. Brand and his twin brother Paul were raised mostly by a paternal grandmother who lived in modest circumstances.

Blanshard's schooling began in Grand Rapids, and in 1910 he moved to Ann Arbor to attend the University of Michigan. There he studied Greek and, in his sophomore year, began to study philosophy, inspired mainly by the hope of certainty in religion. His lifelong interest in public speaking and philosophical style also began at this time. In 1913, Blanshard won a Rhodes Scholarship to Oxford, England. His experience there at Merton College and his exposure to the idealism of F. H. Bradley had an immense impact on his future life. He served in the British Army YMCA during World War I and returned to America in 1917 positive of his commitment to philosophy.

He attended Columbia University to work with John Dewey, William P. Montague, and others. He received an M.A. from Columbia in 1917 and, after marrying, returned to Oxford, abandoned his earlier religious focus, and worked on Dewey's theory of judgment. After receiving his doctorate from Harvard in one year (1920–1921), he taught for a short time at his alma mater, the University of Michigan. In 1925 he began a twenty-year career as professor at Swarthmore College, where his wife was Dean of the College. In 1944 he began the last active phase of his teaching career at Yale University. He retired in 1961 as Professor Emeritus of Philosophy.

Among his published works are *The Nature of Thought* (1939), which contains the most comprehensive statement of his philosophical position; *Reason and Goodness* (1961), which contains his ethical theories, and *Reason and Analysis* (1962), which is a restatement of his epistemological and metaphysical theories, together with a detailed examination of the views of the logical positivists and other analytic philosophers. Blanshard was a past president of the American Philosophical Association and a Fellow of the British Academy; undoubtedly, he is one of America's most important philosophers.

These requirements he (the behaviorist) believes to be imposed upon him by science, and in the interest of science, as he conceives it, he is quite ready to part company with common sense. But in other places he clings to common sense in a manner that places him in clear conflict with science. When Professor Skinner talks about stimuli he does not ordinarily mean the impact of microwaves on nerve ends; he means observable things or changes such as coloured discs or the sounds of a voice or the impact of a hard object. Since these are observable, they are assumed to be physical. But would a physicist of sophistication take them to be physical, just as presented? Would he accept the colour of a disc as something spread out in physical space over the surface of the disc? Would he take the sounds that are heard, as distinct from waves in the air, to be physical existents? Having explained to us that a football consists of millions of microparticles in motion, would he add that this aggregate is *hard?* Most philosophers since Locke have held that the "secondary qualities" belong in consciousness, not in the physical world, and reflective physicists have thought likewise. There is no doubt that we experience them, and they must, therefore, have lodgement in some recognized realm of being. But Professor Skinner has no room for them in any realm of being. If he puts them in physical space, as he seems inclined to do, he loses the much-coveted support of natural science. He cannot put them in consciousness, for there is no consciousness to put them in. Nor would he identify them, as Watson tried to do, with nervous changes in the body; to hunt for a sound in the nervous system he would consider absurd. In our conscious experience of nature these qualities are almost everywhere, but in the world of the behaviorist they are without a home.

J. Smith, ed., *Contemporary American Philosophy* (London: Allen and Unwin, 1970).

to do the job so, traditionally, it must be the mind or one of its parts. It would seem that the mind is a nonphysical entity capable of having sensorylike experiences. This involves a specific view of the mind–body relationship and is rejected by both behaviorists and **materialists,** those philosophers who reject nonphysical entities.[15] In response to the critics of both introspection and consciousness as conceived by Locke, two questions need to be asked. How can we have any awareness of the existence of mental states if we do not have consciousness or introspection? It would appear that consciousness is the only evidence we have of the existence of mental states. How do we explain the simple, everyday phenomenon of thinking about our experiences at the time they are occurring. For example, while looking at a painting I may wonder whether I am enjoying this experience or whether I would prefer some other experience. It appears, once again, that in an attempt to apply a purely scientific approach, certain philosophers have lost sight of the "I" who is having the experiences, of the self-conscious, self-aware aspect of human existence.

Reflections

♦ ♦ ♦ ♦ ♦ ♦ ♦ ♦ ♦ ♦

Some of us are convinced that there is a uniqueness and definite reality to the human self. A private sense of one-*self* is so persuasive that to deny the reality of a self seems inconsistent with ordinary experience. Interpretations that understand human beings as physiochemical objects, physiological mechanisms, or un-self-conscious creatures appear to be at best partial representations of the united "I within." An adequate description of human nature must account for human self-awareness, our sense of individual continuity, the human faculty and processes of abstract thought, our capacities for ethical discrimination and aesthetic appreciation, and the human sense of consciously establishing purposes followed by deliberate action. The dismissal of these "I" experiences as illusory is not in accord with experience. Nonetheless, intellectually competing positions, such as those found in Hume, Buddhism, and certain scientists, are found worldwide. As our explorations of human nature continue, we shall encounter added diversity among interpretations of the human mind and "free will."

♦ ♦

Glossary Terms

BODHISATTVA   A term used in Buddhism for a person aspiring to enlightenment, one who is a Buddha-to-be; a Buddhist wise and holy individual.

CONSCIOUSNESS   Awareness of one's own existence.

DIALOGIC   Pertaining to or participating in dialogue.

ENTITY   Whatever has real existence or being; thing.

INTROSPECTION   A person's awareness of his or her own thoughts and feelings; a psychological method of study that is in contrast to the study of objective behavior, though the two methods may be used together.

MATERIALISM (MATERIALISTS)   In its extreme form, the view that nothing is real except matter. Mind and consciousness are merely manifestations of such matter and are reducible to the physical elements.

SELF-CONSCIOUSNESS   To be aware of one's existence, sensations, thoughts, and the like is to be conscious; to be self-conscious is to be fully aware of the contents and activity of one's own mind or self. When self-conscious, individuals regard themselves as subjects.

TRANSCENDENT (TRANSCENDENCE)   That which is beyond what is given in experience. In theology the term means that God is outside of or beyond nature.

Chapter Review

THE NATURE OF THE SELF

1. The terms *self* and *selfhood* refer to the subject or to that part of us which persists through the changing experiences of our existence.

2. The self is the center of personal identity. Self-consciousness is the awareness by the self of the self.

3. Through its integrating or synthesizing power, the self transcends the process in which it is involved. We are aware of our awareness.

4. The self is private and personal. No person can experience directly another person's consciousness.

5. Martin Buber proposes a dialogic approach to the self. Two types of relationships with the environment are given: "I-Thou" and "I-It."

DENIALS OF THE EXISTENCE OF A SELF

1. Buddhism, founded by Siddhartha Gautama, asserts that nothing in present existence is permanent. Instead of any "soul" or "self," there are five streams that constitute being: bodily sensation, feeling, perception, mental conception, and consciousness.

2. The aim of all Buddhist endeavor is the extinction of the self.

3. David Hume denies the existence of any personal self. He stresses that the self is nothing but a collection of different perceptions. Only a stream of successive impressions exists; there is no permanent self within.

4. B. F. Skinner, a behavioral psychologist, asserted that a concept of self is not necessary in an analysis of behavior. Skinner believed that motives, ideas, and feelings are insignificant because they are not objectively observable events.

5. Scientific methods alone can never provide complete explanations of human beings.

CONSCIOUSNESS

1. The term *consciousness* occurs in philosophy, psychology, and common speech and has a variety of different meanings.

2. Introspection and consciousness as conceived by Locke are two interpretations.

REFLECTIONS

1. Some of us are convinced that there is a uniqueness and definite reality to the human self.

2. Intellectually competing positions, such as those found in Hume, Buddhism, and the work of certain scientists, are found worldwide.

3. As our explorations of human nature continue, we shall encounter added diversity among interpretations of the human mind and "free will."

Study Questions and Projects

1. In the text's discussion, certain distinctive qualities of selfhood were presented. Can you accept these qualities as distinctive? Do you wish to add others or to omit some of those listed or both? Explain your position.

2. In his book *Reality* (New York: Macmillan, 1926), p. 36, B. H. Streeter says that what a person really knows of the "inner quality of life" depends primarily on the following three things: "first, the depth and the range of his own personal experience; secondly, how far he has the imaginative sympathy to penetrate into the inner experience of others; thirdly, the extent to which he has reflected on the material so presented." Give reasons for agreeing or disagreeing with Streeter.

3. Is there any truth in or justification for the statement that the self and the mind are evidenced not in physiological and psychological measurements, but in the greater literature, and in the art, religion, and outstanding human achievements?

4. Report on the view of the self in Indian thought. See Troy Organ, *The Self in Indian Philosophy* (The Hague: Mouton, 1964).

5. Much of a person's sense of self is related to that person's biological sex and to the sex-roles assigned by society. To what extent do you feel that you define yourself in terms of your sex? What limitations do you see in this kind of personal definition?

6. Discuss the meaning of the terms *person, self,* and *mind*. What is the reason for making a distinction between self and mind?

7. What is meant by the statement that the question of the meaning of the self or person is not just one problem among others but in many ways *the* basic issue in human life?

8. Describe some of the attempts to deny the self as something distinctive in human beings. Are these denials based mainly on methodological or on other considerations? Discuss.

9. What is the evidence for saying that the self is not completely submerged in the nonpersonal processes of nature?

10. Explain the characteristics of a person as a self. Indicate whether you can accept the distinctive qualities of selfhood, and if you would add others, or wish to omit some of those listed, or both.

11. State in your own words Martin Buber's "dialogic approach" and his view of the self.

◆ ◆

Suggested Readings

Buber, M. *I and Thou*. New York: Scribner's, 1958.

The most important statement of Buber's existential view of the self; he presents a religious and poetic exposition of the distinction between the "I-It" and "I-Thou."

Hofstadter, D. R., and Dennett, D. C. *The Mind's I: Fantasies and Reflections on Self and Soul*. New York: Bantam, 1981.

Examines the nature of the self and self-consciousness, including the mind, from verbalizing chimpanzees to the mazelike fiction of Borges, to scientific speculations about machines with souls.

Johnstone, H. W., Jr. *The Problem of the Self*. University Park: Pennsylvania State University Press, 1970

A study of the self in which distinctions are made between persons and computers and persons and selves; the uniqueness of humans is stressed.

Kolak, D. (ed.). *Self and Identity*. New York: Macmillan, 1991.

A contemporary anthology on core issues about the self, identity, and nature of the mind.

Lewis, H. D. *The Elusive Self*. Louisville, Ky.: Westminster/John Knox, 1982.

This volume deals with the nature of self and experience. It is an investigation into the question of personal identity, defending a dualism that distinguishes between mental experience, "inner being," and bodily things, and exploring the relationship of that distinction to a constant self, or soul.

Macmurray, J. *The Self as Agent*. London: Faber and Faber, 1957

In these 1953 Gifford Lectures the author holds the views that the self is a person and personal existence is constituted by the relations of persons to one another.

Morris, B. *Western Conceptions of the Individual*. New York: St. Martin's, 1992.

An interdisciplinary study of the human subject in Western traditions.

Noonan, H. W. *Personal Identity*. New York: Routledge, 1991.

A detailed introduction to the main historical theories and the current debates; designed to be useful to undergraduates.

Organ, T. W. *Philosophy and the Self: East and West*. Cranbury, N.J.: Susquehanna University Press/Associated University Presses, 1987.

A general overview presenting varying positions on the theory of self, self-realization, and humankind as knower and self-knower.

Parfit, D. *Reasons and Persons*. New York: Oxford University Press, 1984.

The author offers several arguments challenging some of our deepest beliefs about rationality, morality, and personal identity.

Shoemaker, S. *Self-Knowledge and Self-Identity*. Ithaca, N.Y.: Cornell University Press, 1963.

The author is concerned with the problems of personal identity that arise from philosophical views of the nature of self-knowledge.

Sypher, W. *Loss of Self in Modern Literature*. New York: Random House, Vintage Books, 1964.

The author interprets contemporary literature and art in the light of modern science and mathematics; he draws parallels between the ideas of modern scientists and the work of contemporary artists. He traces the tendency toward the loss of self from the post-romantic view to the present.

White, S. L. *The Unity of the Self*. Cambridge, Mass.: MIT Press, 1991.

An examination of the forms of psychological integration that give rise to self-knowable and self-conscious individuals who are responsible, concerned for the future, and capable of moral commitment; an advanced study.

◆ ◆

Notes

1. G. Orwell, *A Clergyman's Daughter* (New York: Avon Books, n.d.), p. 69.

2. S. Hampshire, *Thought and Action* (London: Chatto and Windus, 1960), pp. 98–99. Others who have similar views are: N. Malcolm, "Thoughtless Brutes," *Proceedings and Addresses of the American Philosophical Association*, Vol. 42, 1972–73 (Clinton, N.Y.: The American Philosophical Association), pp. 5–20, and D. Davidson, "Thought and Talk," in S. Guttenplan, ed., *Mind and Language* (Oxford: Clarendon Press, 1975).

3. R. May, *Man's Search for Himself* (New York: Norton, 1953), p. 91.

4. K. Heim, *Christian Faith and Natural Science* (New York: Harper, 1957), p. 36. [Torchbook Edition.]

5. See *The Writings of Martin Buber*, selected, edited, and introduced by Will Herberg (New York: Meridian Books, 1956), p. 11.

6. M. Buber, *I and Thou*, trans. R. G. Smith (Edinburgh: T. and T. Clark, 1937), pp. 3, 8, 34, 46.

7. E. Conze, *Thirty Years of Buddhist Studies* (Oxford: Cassirer, 1967), p. 75.

8. D. Hume, *A Treatise on Human Nature*, Vol. I, ed. T. H. Green (London: Longmans, Green, 1874), p. 534.

9. B. P. Harvey, *An Introduction to Buddhism* (New York: Cambridge University Press, 1990), pp. 52–53.

10. B. F. Skinner, *Science and Human Behavior* (New York: Free Press, 1965), pp. 30–31, 285, 447–48.

11. B. Blanshard, "The Limits of Naturalism," in J. E. Smith, ed., *Contemporary American Philosophy*, (London: Allen and Unwin, 1970), p. 34.

12. Blanshard, "The Limits of Naturalism," p. 30. Professor Blanshard presents a typical experiment using Skinner's method for studying the connection between stimulus and response.

13. John Locke, *An Essay Concerning Human Understanding*, 2 Vols. (London: J. M. Dent and Sons Ltd., New York: E. P. Dutton and Co., Inc., 1961.) Everyman's Library. Vol. One, p. 87).

14. G. F. Stout, *A Manual of Psychology* (New York: University Correspondence College Press, 1899), p. 14.

15. See Chapter 4 for further discussion of the traditional dualism between mind and body.

The Mind

CHAPTER OBJECTIVES

In this chapter we will address the following questions:

◆ What Is The "Mind"?

◆ Are There Difficulties in Studying the Mind?

◆ What Are Some Representative Theories of the Mind?

◆ How Is the Mind Related to the Body?

◆ Is Parapsychology Convincing?

Many definitions of mind and thinking have been given. I know of but one that goes to the heart of the matter:—response to the doubtful as such. No inanimate thing reacts to things as problematic.[1]

The Nature of the Mind

What is the mind? Is the mind different from the self? Is the distinction between mind and body valid? Is there a genuine question whether "mind rules matter" or is it more accurate to talk about matter over mind, whereby "matter" means newly discovered brain chemicals? Plato was the first philosopher to make a sharp distinction between the mind and the body. Plato believed that the mind could exist both before and after its residence in the body and that mind ruled the body during that residence. For philosophers today, interpretation and understanding of the relation between the human mind and the human body is one of the most important issues philosophy has to consider—and one of the most complex and baffling.

Since ancient times, some philosophers have tended to make a sharp division between events, substances, processes, or relations they have called material, or **physical,** and those they have called **mental,** or **psychical.** The former realm comprises the entire range of inorganic and organic matter, including animal and human bodies. The things so classified are located in space and time and are public in that they are capable of being perceived by any observer. The latter realm comprises thinking, images, sensations, desires, emotions, and the like. These events or processes are distinctively private in that they cannot be experienced by an observer, although another person can be informed of them and gain sympathetic understanding.

Before proceeding further, let us clarify a number of terms that are widely used and frequently confused: *soul, self, mind, consciousness,* and *self-consciousness.* Different writers often use these terms with different meanings, and this makes clarification more difficult. Plato used the term *psyche,* often interpreted as *soul,* to distinguish a nonmaterial entity, or substance, from humans' animal nature. The soul came to be conceived of as immortal and separable from the body at death. Philosophers now tend to avoid the term *soul* and to use others such as *self, mind, knower, ego,* or *agent.* Since the time of the early

Greeks, many thinkers have used *self* and *mind* as synonymous or have equated the "self as subject" with mind, and the "self as object" with the body. This use can be questioned, however, as the human self consists, to use the traditional terms, of the **cognitive** element—the thinking, reasoning, knowing side; the **affective** element—the feeling, emotional side; and the **conative** element—the desiring, striving, and willing side. From this point of view, mind is identified with the cognitive aspect of the self and of human life.

Mind and *consciousness* are not synonymous, although they are sometimes thought of in that way. We may or may not be conscious of our mental processes. When we arrive at a solution to some problem, we have gone through a *mental process,* but not necessarily one of which we are conscious. When we introspect these processes—that is, examine them or simply become aware of their existence—we are conscious of them. This distinction allows us to speak, for example, of animals having *mental processes* whether they are conscious of them or not. Consciousness is an awareness of a relation between the perceiving individual, the subject or knower, and some object of attention. When we are aware that it is we who are conscious, we speak of *self-consciousness.* We do not seem to be able to explain immediate conscious and self-conscious experiences satisfactorily without some notion like that of the self. We must, it appears, hold to a personal unity or identity that persists through the various experiences of life and makes those separate experiences "mine."[2]

Recent studies of mental processes and of artificial intelligence in computers has enhanced our appreciation of the complexity of the human mind and its unique self-consciousness while raising additional questions concerning "mind," "consciousness," and "self."

We have stated that we may or may not be conscious of our mental processes. If we are not, we are faced with the concept of the **unconscious** mind. In order to clarify the meaning of *unconscious,* we must concentrate on the work of Freud. We shall then discover that we are dealing not with an entity that is untestable but with a theory that is not scientifically verifiable but that nevertheless might have a sound empirical basis. Just as Pasteur showed that not only do germs exist but also there are germs that manufacture poisons, it would have been pointless for Freud simply to have proven only the existence of the unconscious; the real importance of the theory of the unconscious concerns sources, activities, and consequences.

Freud (see biography and excerpt, pp. 64–65) conceived of the unconscious as "the hidden seat" of what were then considered some of man's worst urges—sexuality, aggressiveness, and the impulse toward self-destruction. He thought that the unconscious exerted a powerful influence: it provoked phobias and hysterical paralysis and appeared disguised in dreams and unexpected turns of phrase. Contemporary explorations raise continuing profound questions about the nature of consciousness itself.

Difficulties of Studying the Mind

◆ ◆ ◆ ◆ ◆ ◆ ◆ ◆ ◆ ◆ ◆

EMPHASIS ON THE PHYSICAL WORLD

Study of the mind has involved confusion and delay for several reasons. The study of mind, and of human nature in general, traditionally received much less attention—and certainly less financial support—than did the study of the world around us. In our own age, we have been concerned mainly with the exploitation of physical nature, the construction of machines, and journeys into outer space. We have studied things and animals more than people and social relationships. When humanity has been studied, the focus usually has been on those aspects of life that belong as well to the world of things and animals. The social studies are comparatively recent, dating from the late nineteenth and early twentieth centuries. Scientific method was applied first to mathematics and astronomy, then to physics and chemistry, later to physiology and biology. In recent decades, the scientific character of sociology and psychology has been emphasized.

In earlier interpretations that were made before the concept of evolution was taken seriously, mind was seen as something quite apart from nature. The "mind" attempted to contact and know "ultimate reality." The "spectator view" of knowledge was taken for granted. The problem was to bridge the gap between the mind and the world. Now the mind is likely to be viewed as a growing instrument or function, not just an observer outside the process. More stress is being placed on research and experimentation, on the processes of the mind and how they manipulate information, and on the electrical and chemical signals produced by individual neurons of the brain.

CONFLICTING SCHOOLS OF PSYCHOLOGY

Psychology has produced conflicting schools of thought. Psychology is the special science to which we would normally look for the descriptive material on the basis of which to formulate interpretations of mind; but there is no single psychology, only psychologies. There is no agreement about what method should be used or, indeed, what subject matter should be studied. In studying mind, a number of methods may be used. The study of objective behavior; the genetic approach, involving development of the child or of the race; the study of animal behavior; abnormal behavior; physiological mechanisms and processes; introspection; cognitive science; "extrasensory perception"—each of these is used by one group or another.

The various psychologies emphasize different aspects of the human mind or behavior. The early development of psychoanalysis by Sigmund Freud, Alfred Adler, Carl G. Jung, and others took place within the medical profession. Freudian psychology, although inward-looking, dealt more with problems of human personality than with thinking as such. According to Freud, the life energy of a person, or the structure of the personality, is divided into three parts: the *id*—the deep subconscious realm of instinct, impulse, and passion; the *ego*—the element of individual consciousness that is capable of deliberation and that at times exercises some control over the impulses of the id; and the *superego*—an internalization of the demands of society that has been called *conscience*. Subservient to three masters—the id, the superego, and a harsh external world of nature—the ego is forced to recognize its weakness, and it easily develops a sense of guilt and anxiety. Psychoanalysis has stressed conflicts and fixations within and between these personality areas, and various mechanisms for coping with these problems—for example, escape or defense.

Behaviorism, developed by John B. Watson and expanded by B. F. Skinner, emerged as a result of studies of animal psychology, the methods of which were then applied to study human behavior. The behaviorist approach is to observe the relationships between external stimuli and observable responses. As mentioned in Chapters 2 and 3, behaviorists, specifically Skinner, say that to explain human behavior in terms of what goes on in the mind is as out-of-date and unscientific as is the belief that spirits dwell in material objects.

Gestalt psychology (developed by Max Wertheimer, Kurt Koffka, and Wolfgang Köhler), a reaction against the analytical and atomistic methods of the older psychologies, stresses the view that the whole is more than the sum of its parts; wholes often have qualities not present in their parts. The Gestaltists, whose researches have been mainly in the area of the psychology of perception, believe that the notion of organization or pattern is fundamental to an understanding of the observations in that realm, and have extended their views to include certain aspects of personality. For these psychologists, behavior is said to be determined, not by discrete and isolated stimulus-response events, but by an integrated personality perceiving a total situation.

Cognitive psychology is a relatively new area that covers a spectrum ranging from cognitive science to cognitive therapy.[3] Cognitive psychology, which has its roots in the Gestalt school, provides an alternative to psychoanalytically based psychology and to behaviorism. Beginning with the study of perception, memory, and thinking, cognitive psychology provides a coherent explanation of the gulf between what we perceive and what we conclude, and how this information is processed, stored, and retrieved.[4] Men and women are conceived of as seekers after information; the cognitive psychologist tries to understand how knowledge is possible: how we obtain information, order it, and use it; what we perceive and how we conceive of our perceptions. Cognitive theory is rapidly displacing behaviorism as the guiding viewpoint of psychology. In contrast to the behaviorist, students of cognitive theory hold that the human mind is highly complex, that we cannot understand human behavior without knowing what goes on in the mind and, most important, that the mind can be investigated scientifically.[5] We will discuss this new field of inquiry further when we examine theories of the mind.

HOW CAN MIND BE EXAMINED OBJECTIVELY?

Another problem in studying the mind is that it is difficult to be objective when examining what is basically a subjective entity. Science, with its ideal of objectivity, tends to ignore the unique and nonrepeatable and to deal with the external world, consciously excluding the subjective element from its investigations. There is definitely a question whether the mind can be studied as an objectively viewed entity. Can the same mind be subject and object at the same time? Can one mind be subject and another mind object? If there is an area of human existence that is private and not publicly observable, and if science is confined to knowledge that is objectively verifiable, then scientists cannot study the mind and self. Part of this difficulty can be overcome by attributing a broader task to science. For most people, scientific investigation relies on empirical methods, and uses whatever means are available to gather information about the problem under investigation. Science therefore need not necessarily be limited to looking for causal relationships; such a narrow conception excludes the

Sigmund Freud

Sigmund Freud (1856–1939) was born in Moravia. He lived most of his life in Vienna, receiving his medical degree from the university in 1881. His medical career began with studies on the use of hypnosis in the treatment of hysteria; these studies (1885–1886) marked the beginnings of psychoanalysis with the discovery that the symptoms of hysterical patients—directly traceable to psychic trauma in early life—represented undischarged emotional energy. The therapy consisted of having the patient recall under hypnosis the forgotten scenes. Freud's ideas were poorly received by the medical profession. He then rejected hypnosis and devised a technique called *free association,* which would allow the repressed material in the unconscious to emerge to conscious recognition. His writings on these subjects include *The Interpretation of Dreams* (1900) and *The Psychopathology of Everyday Life* (1904). In 1910, The International Psychoanalytical Association was formed with C. G. Jung as president, but the association of Freud, Jung, and the Austrian Alfred Adler was short-lived. Both Jung and Adler formed their own schools in protest against Freud's emphasis on infantile sexuality and the Oedipus complex. Nonetheless, the basic structure of analysis is still Freudian and he is regarded as the founder of psychoanalysis. Because of the Nazi occupation of Austria in 1938, Freud fled to England, where he died. His later, more philosophical writings include *Totem and Taboo* (1913), *Civilization and Its Discontents* (1929), and *Moses and Monotheism* (1939).

possibility of "scientific" study of the mind and self. Interpreters of the world try to interpret themselves or other selves, their own minds or other minds, and they find it difficult to investigate subjective qualities when confined to objective bias. They cannot always be sure what they have studied, how they should interpret the results, the accuracy of their observations and results, or what bearing, if any, these results have on a theory of mind.

There is no need to characterize what we call *conscious:* it is the same as the consciousness of philosophers and of everyday opinion. Everything else that is mental is in our view *unconscious.* We are soon led to make an important division in this unconscious. Some processes become conscious easily; they may then cease to be conscious, but can become conscious once more without any trouble: as people say they can be reproduced or remembered. This reminds us that consciousness is in general a very highly fugitive condition. What is conscious is conscious only for a moment. . . . Everything unconscious that can easily exchange the unconscious condition for the conscious one, is therefore better described as "capable of entering consciousness," or as *preconscious.* Experience has taught us that there are hardly any mental processes, even of the most complicated kind, which cannot on occasion remain preconscious, although as a rule they press forward, as we say, into consciousness. There are other mental processes or mental material which have no such easy access to consciousness, but which must be inferred, discovered, and translated into conscious form in the manner that has been described. It is for such material that we reserve the name of the unconscious proper. Thus we have attributed three qualities to mental processes: they are either conscious, preconscious, or unconscious. The division between the three classes is neither absolute nor permanent. What is preconscious becomes conscious, as we have seen, without any activity on our part; what is unconscious can, as a result of our efforts, be made conscious, though in the process we may have an impression that we are overcoming what are often very strong resistances. . . . A lowering of resistances of this sort, with a consequent pressing forward of unconscious material, takes place regularly in the state of sleep and thus brings about a necessary precondition for the formation of dreams.

S. Freud, *An Outline of Psychoanalysis* (New York: Norton, 1949).

ORIGIN OF MIND

Finally, there is no agreement about when or how mind originated in the long process of evolution and when and how it emerges in the development of the human from fertilized ovum to adult person. The answer depends largely on our definition of *mind* and on our world view, or interpretation of the universe. If, on the one hand, we define *mind* as "adaptive behavior," the account may well begin with the ameba or some early form of life. There is a gradual increase in delicacy and complexity of reactions as we deal with more complex organisms, but there is no clear evolutionary or classifiable break that we can point to as the "beginning of mind." On the other hand, if *mind* were interpreted as "abstract thought," then an account of mind would have to be confined to humans, and not all of them at that.

Theories of the Mind

♦ ♦ ♦ ♦ ♦ ♦ ♦ ♦ ♦ ♦

Numerous theories of mind have been developed through the years. These theories can be classified according to the following simple system used by philosophers concerned with studying the mind: (1) mind as a nonmaterial substance, (2) mind as a principle of organization, (3) mind as the sum total of experiences, (4) mind as a form of behavior, and (5) mind as a series of thought processes.

MIND AS SUBSTANCE: PLATO AND DESCARTES

The mind can be interpreted as a nonmaterial entity that is indivisible and immortal. The term **substance** generally is used in philosophy to refer to some underlying reality, in which qualities reside. For example, wax is a substance that has specific qualities: it is dull yellow (unless bleached or purified), plastic (when warm), adhesive, impressible, and so on. What is left when you turn away from the qualities? The answer is substance, or that which has the qualities. Again, take mind, which has such qualities as the ability to perceive, think, remember, and imagine. What is left when you remove these qualities? The answer again is substance, but this time it is said to be nonmaterial substance.

The source and chief representative of this view of mind in ancient times was Plato. His major interest was human nature, especially the mind of human beings.

Plato divided human nature into three parts. There is, first, the rational part, the locus of which is in the brain. Our rational element is a divine essence, or substance, not to be confused with the body in which it is imprisoned. There is, second, the feeling or sensory part, with its locus in the breast. There is, third, the desiring elements, or the appetites, the locus of which is in the abdomen. Our desiring element has no principle of order of its own. It needs to be brought under the control of reason. Mind and body are intimately related but, according to Plato, there is a clear-cut distinction between them. The indivisible soul originated in the supersensible **world of eternal Forms** or **Ideas,** beyond this fleeting, changing world of sense experience. The soul is marred considerably by contact with matter; it will eventually leave the body and return to its eternal abode.

Plato's interpretation of soul, mind, or reason strongly influenced the thinking of Plotinus and Augustine and, through them, the Christian church. A view derived from Plato was widely held during the Middle Ages. In this form, or as restated by Descartes, it permeates much modern thinking.

The seventeenth century was a transitional age. The new scientific approach to reality developed by Nikolaus Copernicus (1473–1543), Galilei Galileo (1564–1642), Johann Kepler (1630–1671), and Sir Isaac Newton (1642–1727) appeared to be in conflict with the traditional religious world view. The scientific view held that the earth was not the center of the universe, that the movements of the physical universe could be understood by the principles of mechanics, and that the human body was itself subject to the same principles. At this point, philosophy—especially Cartesian (of Descartes) philosophy—became intensely self-reflective, rooting itself in self-consciousness.

Through most of the Middle Ages, philosophy had been dominated by religious assumptions. Now the scientific explanation of the world was replacing one based on belief in a personal God and religious tradition. Descartes (see biography and excerpt, pp. 68–69) believed that it was better to take nothing for granted—neither the presuppositions of religion nor the presuppositions of science. He therefore declared that he would not accept anything as true unless it was demonstrated to be beyond doubt; he decided to question everything and begin anew, to adopt a program of systematic doubt:

> I suppose, accordingly that all the things which I see are false (fictitious); I believe that none of those objects which my fallacious memory represents ever existed; I suppose that I possess no senses; I believe that body, figure, extension, motion, and place are merely fictions of my mind. What is there, then, that can be esteemed true? Perhaps this only, that there is absolutely nothing certain.[6]

From this position of methodological skepticism, Descartes emerges with the clear-cut conviction that the self is what exists. His famous saying is "*cogito ergo sum*"—"I think; therefore I am." Descartes found the existence of at least one mind—his own—to be beyond doubt. "This alone is inseparable from me. I am—I exist: this is certain; but how often? As often as I think; for perhaps it would even happen, if I should wholly cease to think, that I should at the same time altogether cease to be."[7] In asking how he came to exist, he inferred the existence of God, which guaranteed the truth of clear and distinct ideas, of other minds, of an external world of matter. The external world impressed itself on him through his sense organs, and he could not believe that he was being deceived by God.

For Descartes, there were two substances: mind and matter. He made a sharp distinction between them. Mind is immaterial; it is conscious, and it is characterized by thinking. Because it is substance, it cannot be destroyed except by God. Matter is characterized by extension. The human body is a part of the world of matter and is subject to its laws.

Descartes' explanation of the mind as a separate substance was the beginning of a long development in modern philosophical and scientific thinking, sometimes referred to as the "bifurcation of nature." The Cartesian dualism of mind and body (or matter) enabled us to interpret the external world in mechanical and quantitative terms and to put all other aspects of existence in the realm of mind. Theories distinguishing mind from matter have been proposed in all periods of history.

MIND AS THE PRINCIPLE OF ORGANIZATION: ARISTOTLE AND KANT

Aristotle, Plato's famous pupil, although basically subscribing to many features of the theory of mind as substance, moved in a new direction. For Plato, ideas were eternal forms whose real existence was in another realm; the ideas we have in this world are merely copies, of varying degrees of accuracy, of these eternal ideas. For Aristotle, the eternal forms exist *in* things or *in* the world. They are the shaping, organizing, dynamic principles that give order and direction to matter. From this point of view, soul (*psyche*) is the life principle, the sum of the processes of life, the active principle of organization of these processes. Mind, or reason, is the highest capacity or function of the human *psyche*. In this attempt to integrate mind and body, Aristotle moved away from Plato's position and closer to the view of the mind as process and function.

Immanuel Kant, in the late eighteenth century, criticized the traditional view of mind as substance, a view that assumes the individual can make her or his "self" and "mind" direct objects of knowledge. For Kant, the mind was active; it formed into a system of knowledge all the materials presented by the various senses. Time and space were the forms of our sensible experience that, by means of judgment, were brought into unified and organized experience. Mind was not a separate mental substance; it was the organization and unity of personal human experience.

According to Kant, our knowledge is based on our experiences as organized and understood by the mind. There is unity wherever there is knowledge, and knowledge entails a knower. Where there is memory, there must be something to do the remembering. The organization of experience is made possible by reason and

René Descartes

René Descartes (1596–1650), a French philosopher, mathematician, and scientist, was educated at a Jesuit college, but also was acquainted with most of the scientific knowledge of his day. He emphasized the use of reason as the major tool of philosophical inquiry. The growing conflict between the spirit of the Middle Ages and that of the Renaissance appears in his philosophy. Often called the "father of modern philosophy," Descartes excelled in mathematics, and his philosophical method borrowed considerably from the form of proof used in geometry.

In his most famous work, *Meditations on First Philosophy*, Descartes declared that he would not accept anything as true unless it was demonstrated to be beyond doubt or, in the manner of geometry, could be derived from principles that were beyond doubt. Thus, Descartes began his reflections with what may be called a methodological doubt; that is, a philosophical doubt of everything that can possibly be doubted, regardless of whether these things really were doubted in the course of living.

In 1628, Descartes retired to Holland where he remained for twenty years. He wrote the *Discourse on Method* (1637) addressed to an educated public outside the universities. In 1649, after much hesitation, Descartes yielded to the requests of Queen Christina of Sweden that he instruct her in philosophy. The next year, as a result of the Swedish climate and the rigorous schedule imposed by the queen, he caught pneumonia and died. In addition to the *Discourse* and the *Meditations*, he published his *Principles of Philosophy* (1647) and the *Passions of The Soul* (1649).

understanding acting as a principle of organization. There is unity that transcends or is responsible for the continuity among the separate experiences. This unity we call the *self*. The self is sometimes spoken of as the locus of the forms of knowing. Sometimes, too, the self and the mind are treated as if they were identical. To understand Kant, however, we must realize that the self is a moral as well as a knowing subject.[8]

MIND AS THE SUM TOTAL OF EXPERIENCES: HUME

David Hume, in the eighteenth century, was a severe critic of the traditional view of the mind as a separate substance. Even before Kant's time, Hume attacked the dualism of Plato and Descartes. Hume did not maintain, however, as did Kant, that there was a personal unity or self.

Meditations from Philosophical Writings, "Concerning the Nature of the Human Mind, and How it is More Easily Known than the Body" (1641)

I am supposing, then, that all the things I see are false; that of all the happenings my memory has ever suggested to me, none has ever so existed; that I have no senses; that body, shape, extension, movement and location are but mental fictions. What is there, then, which can be esteemed true? Perhaps this only, that nothing whatsoever is certain.

But how do I know that there is something different from all things I have thus far enumerated and in regard to which there is not the least occasion for doubt? Is there not some God, or other being by whatever name we call Him, who puts these thoughts into my mind? Yet why suppose such a being? May it not be that I am myself capable of being their author? Am I not myself at least a something? But already I have denied that I have a body and senses. This indeed raises awkward questions. But what is it that thereupon follows? Am I so dependent on the body and senses that without them I cannot exist? Having persuaded myself that outside me there is nothing, that there is no heaven, no Earth, that there are no minds, no bodies, am I thereby committed to the view that I also do not exist? By no means. If I am persuading myself of something, in so doing I assuredly do exist. But what if, unknown to me, there be some deceiver, very powerful and very cunning, who is constantly employing his ingenuity in deceiving me? Again, as before, without doubt, if he is deceiving me, I exist. Let him deceive me as much as he will, he can never cause me to be nothing so long as I shall be thinking that I am something. And thus, having reflected well, and carefully examined all things, we have finally to conclude that this declaration, *Ego Sum, ego existo,* is necessarily true every time I propound it or mentally apprehend it.

R. Descartes, *Meditations from Philosophical Writings,* trans. J. Veitch (La Salle, Ill.: Open Court, 1941).

Hume carried empiricism to its logical conclusion and attacked both the idea of substance and the rationalism of his time. All knowledge comes through experience, he held, and the sole content of the human mind is impressions and ideas. Impressions are our simple and elemental experiences; they are lively and vivid. Ideas are only copies of impressions. When we introspect, we find only these fleeting experiences and ideas, which are constantly changing. There is no evidence of any substance or of any permanent self.

What, then, is the mind? For Hume the mind and the faculties and properties of the mental life were nothing but an association of ideas and experiences. *Mind* was only a name for the sum total of the experiences, ideas, and desires that occupy one's attention and life. It was a bundle of experiences, or a collection of sensations.

Hume's general attitude was one of skepticism; he was a thoroughgoing empiricist. He hesitated to accept anything beyond the common day-by-day experiences. The critic of Hume will point out that he continuously used such terms as "I" and "myself," which imply some fairly constant personal center of unity. Although the self finds it difficult to be both subject and object at the same time, the critic insists that we affirm the existence of a continuing self in the very act of denial. Hume denied the more traditional concepts of a self.

MIND AS A FORM OF BEHAVIOR

Psychological Behaviorism. Some psychologists believe that mind is one form of behavior.[9] For them, certain kinds of behavior lead us to postulate the existence of a mind; why not, they ask, simply study behavior and rid ourselves of abstract and unobservable entities like "mind?" A few deny that terms like *mind* and *consciousness* have any real content or value; they prefer to speak of mental events or the neuromuscular activity of an organism. (See the section Behaviorism in the previous chapter.)

Instrumentalism. A group of philosophers concerned with questions about the mind also regard mind as a form of behavior—intelligent, mental conduct rather than physiological expressions. They are of two types: the instrumentalist, such as John Dewey, and the logical behaviorist, as represented by Gilbert Ryle. Their similarity lies in their rejection of all dualisms and in their stress on intelligent behavior.

John Dewey is the chief representative of the **instrumentalist** position. We consider his overall view in Chapter 14; we shall state his views only briefly at this point. For Dewey, *mind* is not a noun; it is an adjective descriptive of certain kinds of behavior. Mind consists of what he calls "operative meanings." Mind and thinking become functional aspects of the interaction of natural events. We are not part body and part mind. Dewey rejects all dualisms and the view of mind as "knower"; he basically regards mind as the problem-solving activity, as our response to the doubtful, the uncertain. Dewey regards thinking as the transition from the problematic to the secure. When I am faced with a problem, I locate the nature of the trouble and form an idea of how it may be dealt with—this is mental action. "Many definitions of mind and thinking have been given. I know of but one that goes to the heart of the matter:—response to the doubtful as such. No inanimate thing reacts to things *as* problematic."[10]

Logical Behaviorism. Gilbert Ryle, in *Concept of Mind,* is as vehement as Dewey in his attack on mind–body dualism and insists that mind is not something separate and distinct from body and matter. Mind is a way a person behaves. "When we describe people as exercising qualities of mind . . . we are referring to overt acts and utterances themselves."[11] Mind is not another world either parallel to or beyond the ordinary world. Ryle attempts to get rid of what he calls the traditional "dogma of the ghost in the machine," and to rectify the "category mistake" or the "philosopher's myth." This myth occurs when we put the facts of mental life in a category or class to which these facts do not properly belong. Ryle uses the example of a foreign visitor on a university campus. Suppose that the visitor, after being shown the college halls, library, dormitories, playing fields, administration offices, and the activities associated with them, asks to see the university. The university, she will be told, is just the organization of the buildings and activities she has seen. To consider the university as an entity beyond what she has seen would be a mistake. In the same way, to talk about the "mind" as a world behind or beyond the activity of the organization of ideas is a mistake.

MIND AS A SERIES OF THOUGHT PROCESSES

As mentioned earlier, *cognitive science* is an interdisciplinary field that includes cognitive psychology, computer science, linguistics, psychobiology, anthropology, and philosophy.[12]

Cognitive scientists hold that we cannot understand human behavior without knowing what goes on in the mind,[13] and that the mind can be investigated scientifically. They are devising new techniques (mostly drawn from the example of the computer) to find out how the mind works. Cognitive scientists assert that, although the mind's processes cannot be observed directly, they can be explored by means of circumstantial evidence. The nature of the machinery of the mind is deduced from what happens to the information fed into it. We "process" incoming information step by step, and what those steps are can be inferred from the different amounts of time it takes us to do slightly different tasks.

> Several researchers have been confronting physicists, physicians and engineers with the kind of situations they deal with in their professional capacities. The subject is asked to say out loud everything he or she is thinking while solving the problems. Then the protocol (the transcript of these utterances) is analyzed, step by step, to show how the subject generated various hypotheses, made tentative forays in this or that direction, backed away from unpromising avenues or blind alleys of thought and so on. . . . The subject's total set of operating procedures can then be written out in the form of a computer program and actually run on a machine. If the machine deals with the problem much as the human being did, the researcher's overall analysis is confirmed.[14]

Cognitive science is thus concerned with a system of processes for manipulating information; it is this concept that now unifies and guides this new field.

The Mind–Body Relationship

♦ ♦ ♦ ♦ ♦ ♦ ♦ ♦ ♦ ♦ ♦

The mind–body problem is a persistent one; people have struggled with it for centuries. Since Descartes, it has been an issue of first importance, especially because of the growing influence of science, and the scientist's desire to describe the world in quantitative and mathematical terms. It also has been important because of the trend of thought, started by Descartes, that made a clear-cut distinction between mind and matter. Descartes' dualism leads to deep difficulties. How, according to the view that minds and bodies are distinct substances, is it possible for a mind to cause a change in the body or vice versa? Consider an action such as moving a hand, or writing, or walking. How could something so rarefied as a mind produce the physical movements involved in such actions? And how could something that happens to a body—for example, bumping into a table—produce something mental—for example, a feeling of pain? Furthermore, how could such interactions be consistent with the conservation of matter and energy, a fundamental principle of modern physics?

Interpretations of and solutions to the mind–body problem are many and varied. The solutions range from a complete denial of mind and a thoroughgoing materialism to the assertion that mind is the only fundamental reality and that what we have called *matter* is an illusion or a byproduct of mind or consciousness. Some explanations, however, have avoided these extremes.

In this section, we discuss a few of the answers to the mind–body problem found in the literature. We make no attempt to give all shades of opinion or to mention all those who have supported the various theories.

INTERACTIONISM

Let us begin with what might be called the common-sense view, which has been widely accepted; since the time of Descartes, it has been prominent in philosophical discussions. In considering the view of "mind as substance," we have seen that Descartes made a clear-cut separation between mind and matter. Mind is a nonmaterial or spiritual substance that thinks; matter is a substance the chief characteristic of which is extension. This presentation of Descartes is a classic expression of the common-sense view. We do not have to accept Descartes' philosophy or his formulation of the position to accept interactionism.

According to interactionism, in addition to a physical causal sequence and a psychical causal sequence, the mind may cause bodily changes, and bodily changes may produce mental effects. The following diagram illustrates these connections.

The white circles represent the mental, or mind; the solid black circles indicate the physical, or body. The arrows indicate the direction of cause and effect. At point A the alarm buzzes; at point B my brain is affected; at C I wake up; at D I decide to get up; at E I get out of bed; and at F I turn off the alarm; at G the alarm stops buzzing.

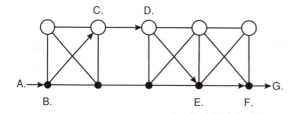

Many people have been impressed by what they believe to be a causal relationship or interaction between mental and bodily processes. Our physical condition affects our disposition; bodily changes register themselves in our mental outlook. Diseases of the brain affect our mental life and thinking. A blow on the head or chloroform fumes may cause us to lose consciousness. The mental effects of drugs, alcohol, and caffeine are universally recognized. If our digestion or bodily secretions are disturbed, we may become depressed. We usually cannot think clearly unless our bodily processes are functioning smoothly. Furthermore, as the brain and the nervous system develop, the powers of the mind increase.

Mental experiences affect bodily processes too. An idea strikes us, and we become animated and proceed to strenuous activity. Worry may cause ill health. Fear leads to quickened heart rates and other bodily reactions. Anger or even ordinary mental effort may produce a rise in blood pressure. Mental states may lead to organic as well as functional disease, and resistance to disease is affected by mental outlook. Teeth are said to decay more quickly when a person is under

emotional strain. Hypnotism has been used as anesthesia, to cure alcoholism, and to control other processes and actions. A blister was raised on a hypnotized patient when the experimenter told him he was being burned, although the metal that touched his skin was cold, not hot.[15]

Despite the array of evidence and its widespread support, the theory of interactionism has been criticized severely. People question how two substances or entities so different could possibly interact. A causal relation between a change in the brain or nervous system and a muscular movement can be understood. A causal relation between an idea and a physical motion is difficult to comprehend. The two areas seem independent and self-sufficient.

PARALLELISM

The attempt to meet objections to interactionism led to *parallelism*. According to this interpretation of the mind–body relation, there is no interaction or causal connection between the two. Mental and physical processes are equally real, but they are not causally related; they merely accompany each other in time. (Again, the white circles represent the mental, or mind; the solid black circles indicate the physical, or body.)

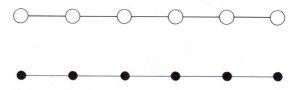

The law of causation holds in the mental realm: one mental event can cause another mental event. The law of causation also holds good in the physical realm. The illustration has been used of two railway trains running side by side on a double track. Although the trains are parallel and appear to be moving together, they are operating on different systems and are not causally connected.

The classic example of this point of view is the position of the philosopher Leibniz (1646–1716) (see biography and excerpt, pp. 74–75). He believed there was a preestablished harmony in God's mind and creativity. Two clocks run together and keep perfect time because they have been made with such skill that they always operate in harmony. Leibniz believed that the universe had been made with such skill that mind and matter always operated in harmony. The course of the universe was determined by the way its elements were endowed.

Parallelism never has had the widespread support given to interactionism and some other theories. It seems to cut the universe in two and to deny rather than solve the problem. Sudden experiences or interruptions are exceedingly difficult to explain on the basis of parallelism. How is it, when the doorbell rings, that we get the idea that someone is at the door? When we are in the midst of a train of thought, we are annoyed if unwelcome interruptions occur. Most of us believe that reflective thinking saves time and energy and that thinking makes a real difference in the world of affairs. Thus, some of us have been forced, in seeking an explanation of this apparent relationship, to adopt the doctrine of the identity of mind and body.

THE IDENTITY THEORY

The Double-Aspect Theory.
According to the double-aspect interpretation of the identity theory, neither mind nor body is a completely separate and independent entity. Both mind and matter are expressions of some underlying reality that appears as "mind" when we experience it from the inside—or subjectively—and as "body," or matter, when we view it from the outside—or objectively. Mind and body are thus in a sense identical; they are two different aspects of the same thing. As people, we know our inner life intimately; we speak of it as "mental." The rest of the world we know only at second hand, through its impression on our sense organs; we speak of this part of our world as "physical."

Spinoza regarded the mind and body as two aspects of one reality. For Spinoza, a pantheist, that one reality was God. The two series, the physical and the psychical, only seem to be causally connected with each other since each is causally connected with the one reality.

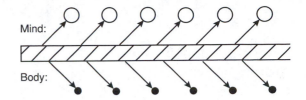

Mind:

Body:

Contemporary Identity Theory.
A view of the mind–body problem that has been widely discussed in recent philosophical writings is the identity thesis. The view, as the name suggests, is that mental states are literally identical with brain states. Specifically, as formulated by J. J. C. Smart,[16] the identity thesis claims that future scientific inquiry will show that all experiences are identical with processes taking place in the brain. At first sight, it may seem strange that so obvious a suggestion as this identification has not, until recently, been much discussed by philosophers. The reason is that, since Descartes, philosophers have tended to define the mental in terms that are incompatible with their definitions of the physical; thus, it seems that saying mental *is* physical is paradoxical, if not contradictory—and perhaps logically it is. The justification given for the identity theory is that we now know that the brain, although it is a physical organ, bears some intimate relation to the mind. The English language includes a number of expressions indicative of this relation: we speak of "racking one's brains," "picking another's brains," and so on. In recent years, the conviction has grown that a view that *identified* the mind and the brain would assert a philosophical monism, thus avoiding the mind–body dualism.

There are many alternative forms of contemporary identity theory, but they all stem from a basic conviction: recent research on the biological correlates of human thought and emotion—especially in the neurochemistry of the brain—indicates a clear connection between brain research, psychiatry, and mind–body theory. Some researchers assume that thoughts and feelings will one day be traced to chemical events or that the mind is a particular type of electrical field that arises from the operation of the brain.

Gottfried Wilhelm Leibniz

Leibniz (1646–1716) was a German scholar whose father was a professor at the University of Leipzig. He developed rapidly, knew considerable Latin at age eight, and was considered to be a classicist at age twelve. He was admitted to the University of Leipzig when he was fifteen, and received his Ph.D. five years later. He possessed one of the world's greatest intellects, and had considerable knowledge in philosophy, mathematics, science, history, and theology. He shares with Sir Isaac Newton the credit for developing differential calculus. He developed a calculating machine that was an improvement of the one invented by Blaise Pascal. He demonstrated this machine before the Royal Academy of the Sciences in Paris and the Royal Society of London, and was elected to membership in the latter. He was sent on important diplomatic missions, and was thus able to meet many leading scholars. Whereas Spinoza had achieved unity in a monism, Leibniz believed that individuality must be stressed. His philosophy, called monadology, asserts that every person or thing is a separate entity, or *Monad*, whose existence is established by God; thus there is continuity with no real break in nature. Nothing is dead, because everything is in some degree of activity. With Leibniz we pass from the idea of passive matter to the concept of force or energy. His most important writings include *The New System* (1695), *Theodicy* (1710), and *Monadology* (1720).

This particular aspect of the identity theory simply argues that neurotransmitters found in the brain regulate everything we do; the task of the pharmacologist is to synthesize drugs that mimic the brain's chemicals and thus direct the brain's processes that constitute the mind, thereby directing the body as well.

Supporters of this view claim that it clearly avoids the unhappy split between mind and body. There is one integrated spatiotemporal world, without any breaks in continuity. Thus, this theory, unlike parallelism, asserts that mental states can be causally effective: itches do cause us to scratch, decisions result in appropriate ac-

Excerpt from Leibniz:

Theory of Knowledge and Metaphysics, "What is an Idea?" (c. 1686)

By the term *Idea* we mean, first of all *something which is in our mind;* traces of brain-impressions, therefore, are not ideas, for I take it to be certain that the mind is something else than the brain or some ethereal substance in the brain.

But there are many things in our mind, for example, opinions, perceptions, emotions, etc., which we know well enough are not simply ideas though they would not be produced without ideas. What I mean by an idea is *not a certain act of thinking, but a power or faculty* such that we have an idea of a thing even if we are not actually thinking about it but know that we can think it when the occasion arises.

However, there is a certain difficulty here for we have the power of thinking about remote things of which we may not have any ideas, in so far as we have the power of recalling things; *an idea, therefore, requires a certain power or faculty of thinking things near at hand.*

But even this will not suffice, for whoever has a method to follow in order to understand a thing, does not yet have an idea of it. For example, if I should go through all the sections of a cone in order, I am bound to come across a pair of hyperbolas although until I do so I may not yet have an idea of them. Therefore there must be something in me *which not only leads to the thing but also expresses it. . . .*

Thus the idea of things which exists in us is exclusively due to the fact that God, the author of both things and the mind, has endowed our mind with this power to infer from its own internal operations the truths which correspond perfectly to those of external things. Whence, although the idea of a circle is not exactly like the circle, we may yet infer from the idea truths which experience would undoubtedly confirm concerning the true circle.

G. Leibniz, *Discourse on Metaphysics and Monadology,* trans. G. R. Montgomery. (La Salle, Ill.: Open Court, 1937).

tion, and the like, since itches and decisions are brain states that can produce behavior.

Those who criticize the identity theory argue that the case has not yet been made convincingly; the logical objections to declaring that mental *is* physical have not been answered adequately. Identity theorists reply that we simply redefine these terms to allow for identity. Why not *physical* is *mental?* There is, as yet, insufficient empirical justification to assert that mental states are identical with brain processes. The very intelligibility of the position is in dispute; of course, any final acceptance must await further scientific research, including psychical research.

FUNCTIONALISM AND ELIMINATIVE MATERIALISM

The theory that mental activity consists of certain functions of the brain—which might well be duplicated in non-brain material such as computers—is termed *functionalism*. This theory accounts for mental characteristics (e.g., perceptions, memories, beliefs, thinking, desires, wants, feelings, willing, and emotions) as interacting parts of a complex system of internal causes of bodily responses and behavior. Each part is understood in terms of its function within the system of inner causes. The brain is regarded as a marvelous piece of machinery or hardware, and there is no reason to rule out the possibility of a future computer duplicating the functions of the human brain. Today a human chess player and a computer chess player can be in the same functional state, about to make the same move for the same strategic purpose.

Functionalism proposes system explanations of all psychological states, events, and processes; psychological processes are defined in terms of a system of causes and effects. For example, a belief is regarded as an inner state caused by perceptions, which can cause other beliefs, through thinking, which in turn interacts with wants and desires to cause deliberate action. In sum, consciousness is the variety of internal functions interacting with an environment.

Though consistent with materialism, functionalism is not necessarily a form of materialism. The inner system could be physical (such as nerve cells that constitute our brains) or nonmaterial qualities of spirit or a soul. However, some functionalists suggest that the material brain performs the internal functional relationships.

Eliminative materialism differs from functionalism in its conclusion that mental concepts (e.g., desires, pains, fears, intelligence, and so on) are part of "folk psychology"—our common-sense psychological categories—and will eventually be replaced by the concepts of a mature neuroscience.

COGNITIVE THEORY

Cognitive scientists also reject the dualist mind–body view that mind or spirit exist apart from body or material things. Most cognitive scientists do not believe in incorporeal substance on the grounds that there are no scientific tests that would prove the dualist position true or false. What they do assert, based on their understanding of contemporary identity theory, computer theory, and information theory, is that the thought processes that make up the mind are organizations of billions of neural events that process physical stimuli in highly complex operations to, in the end, produce physical responses. The nature of these complex operations is currently being studied by teams of psychologists, linguists, artificial-intelligence researchers, and logicians.

Parapsychology

Popular literature reflects a growing interest in the unusual aspects of the mind. Throughout history people have made claims concerning phenomena beyond (para) the range of known sensory processes and conventional psychology.

Founded in London in 1882, The Society for Psychical Research has included among its presidents philosophers William James and C. D. Broad; other executive officers have been university psychologists, physicists, and other responsible academicians. The terms *parapsychology, psychical research,* and *paranormal* have no precise definitions, and their investigators differ on matters of content, method, and interpretation.

Two focal points of parapsychology concern the powers of the mind and perceptions of unusual events.

POWERS OF THE MIND

Psychokinesis refers to a particular application of "mind over matter." Some persons claim they can influence the objective environment by using only their minds; they use no muscles or glands, for example, in moving an object across a table. *Extrasensory perception* (ESP) is the acquisition of knowledge without aid of the senses. It is claimed that various data are known by *telepathy* (communication between minds by some means other than sensory perception), *clairvoyance* (the power of seeing objects or actions beyond the range of natural vision), and *precognition* (knowledge of future events through extrasensory means).

PERCEPTIONS OF UNUSUAL EVENTS

For centuries, rational and reliable people have reported apparent interruptions of the natural order: apparitions, demonic possession, healings and other "miracles;" responses of plants to human communication; colored auras around persons; levitations; disappearances of persons, ships, and airplanes in particular geographical areas; and premonitions. Assuming that *something* is encountered in at least a small number of these cases, the problem becomes one of human perception and interpretation, attributed in large degree to a function of the mind.

In 1977, a Committee for the Scientific Investigation of Claims of the Paranormal was established by reputable philosophers and other scholars. This group is committed to the use of reason and evidence in evaluating claims to extrasensory knowledge, and it is aggressive in its scrutiny of all phases of parapsychology. The claims of parapsychology should not be denied a hearing; the same rigor, however, ought to apply here as in other scientific inquiry. At present, accounts of knowledge gained without sense experience require further investigation and assessment; the validity of parapsychological claims remains an open question.

Reflections

♦ ♦ ♦ ♦ ♦ ♦ ♦ ♦ ♦ ♦ ♦

Obviously, there are many psychological methods of study and explanations of mind. The various psychological interpretations use methods, terms, and symbols that differ greatly. They almost use different languages when they set forth their explanations.

Even though a few people assert that the subject matter of psychology is so complex and elusive as to make impossible any strictly scientific treatment, some progress is being made. There are some converging lines of evidence and some generally accepted conclusions. For example, most psychologists recognize that the traditional structural approach is inadequate; that function and human activity are especially important; and that the traditional notion of a person as a purely "rational animal" needs to be modified to the extent that we recognize the importance of impulse, emotion, habit, and custom in the explanation of behavior. The extreme empiricism of Hume and the behaviorists are likewise inadequate. However, each psychological school is organized around some main emphasis and therefore tends to impose its order or system on that aspect of the complex individual that attracts its attention.

Each of the psychological interpretations has given us some valuable knowledge about mind and its powers and functions. Behaviorism has made a significant contribution through its concept of conditioning. Psychoanalysis has given us information about mental conflicts and repressions. Gestalt psychology has called our attention to the qualities of wholes and to the dangers involved in dealing with parts separately. Cognitive science is exploring the workings of the human mind. As total explanations however, these interpretations are inadequate. A combination of methods and a receptive attitude toward knowledge gained from any source might be considered reasonable. Just as the psychologists differ about methods of study and interpretations of the mind, so philosophers differ about the theory of the mind and the mind–body relationship.

We do not have the space to compare and contrast all the different interpretations of mind. We would like to point out, however, that the question of the truth or falsity of the various interpretations of mind is *not* a purely academic issue. The acceptance or rejection of particular views has widespread implications for the interpretation of other questions and for our lives. For example, consider briefly two views of mind: those set forth by Plato and Freud. The two have some points in common as well as sharply contrasting assertions. Both men divided the psychic life of the individual into three parts, but the division and emphasis are different. For Plato, the function of reason was to master life and rule the passions. For Freud, the *id*, which represents our passionate nature, was largely beyond the control of reason. The ego, which represents our conscious and reflective life, was weak, easily frightened, and cowed by the passions and the pressures and dangers of the external world. Plato's picture of people is perhaps too optimistic and that stresses too strongly the power of the intellectual elements in human life. On the other hand, Freud probably underestimated these elements. Freud's long study of neurotic people gave him, in the opinion of many, a somewhat distorted view of the human mind. Because ideas have consequences for our lives and society, it is important for us to discover whether Plato's or Freud's views of mind are applicable. If we think that Freud's view is valid, we may expect less of people's self-discipline and self-control than if we accept Plato's interpretation.

Glossary Terms

AFFECTIVE   Relating to emotion or feeling.

COGNITION (COGNITIVE)   The attainment of knowledge of something; the mental process by which we become aware of objects of perception; thought.

CONATION (CONATIVE)   The part of mental life having to do with striving, including desiring and willing.

INSTRUMENTALIST (INSTRUMENTALISM)   (1) Another term for the pragmatism of John Dewey and others. (2) Instrumentalism stresses experience and interprets thinking, ideas, and beliefs as means for the adjustment of an organism to its environment.

MENTAL   Of or pertaining to the mind.

PHYSICAL   Of or pertaining to empirical realities, including the human body.

PSYCHICAL   Of or pertaining to the human soul or mind.

SUBSTANCE   That which exists in and of itself; that in which attributes, properties, and qualities reside.

UNCONSCIOUS   Without awareness, sensation, or cognition.

WORLD OF ETERNAL FORMS OR IDEAS   Plato's supersensible world which contains the universal definitions of ideas, known as forms.

Chapter Review

THE NATURE OF THE MIND

1. Throughout time, people have made distinctions between the material or physical world and the mental or psychical world. The former may be perceived by any observer; the latter remains a private experience.

2. The concepts of soul, self, mind, consciousness, and self-consciousness are often confused.

DIFFICULTIES OF STUDYING THE MIND

1. The study of the mind has received much less attention in the past than the study of the natural world. Things and animals have been studied more than people and social relationships.

2. In studying the mind, many conflicting schools of psychology have emerged.

3. Objectivity becomes difficult when studying the mind. We cannot isolate the mind. Our methods of study, our interpretations, and the consequences of our findings are often ambiguous.

4. There is no agreement as to when or how mind originated in the long process of evolution. The answer depends on our definition of mind and our interpretation of the universe.

THEORIES OF THE MIND

1. Plato and Descartes interpreted mind as a nonmaterial substance that is indivisible and immortal.

2. Aristotle and Kant saw mind as the principle of organization.

3. David Hume saw mind as the sum total of experiences. As a skeptic and an empiricist, Hume refused to accept any knowledge that is not a direct result of experience. Self is understood only in terms of perceptions. The act of perceiving constitutes a knowing self.

4. Others consider mind as a form of behavior or as a series of thought processes (cognitive science).

THE MIND–BODY RELATIONSHIP

1. The relationship between mind and body has been questioned throughout the centuries. Interpretations are many and varied. Most views propose that mind and body are essentially different.

2. Interactionism, often called the common-sense view, has been widely accepted. Presented by Descartes, this view interprets mind and matter as distinct, different forms of substance.

3. Parallelism asserts that there is no interaction between the mind and the body. Mind and body processes are equally real but are not causally related.

4. The identity theory in the form of the double-aspect theory asserts that the mind and body are two different aspects of the same thing. Reality experienced from the outside is called the body and reality experienced from the inside is called the mind.

5. Functionalism is the theory that mental activity consists of certain functions of the brain, that mental characteristics are interacting parts of a complex system of internal causes of bodily responses and behavior.

PARAPSYCHOLOGY

1. Parapsychology and psychical research focus on phenomena beyond the range of known sensory processes and conventional psychology. Two focal points of parapsychology are the powers of the mind and perceptions of unusual events.

REFLECTIONS

1. There are many psychological methods of study and explanations of mind, each of which has contributed valuable knowledge about mind and its powers and functions.

2. Any single interpretation of mind is inadequate.

3. The question of the truth or falsity of the various interpretations of mind is not a purely academic issue. The acceptance or rejection of particular views has widespread implications for the interpretation of other questions and other areas of our lives.

4. When analyzing mind, we must recognize life itself. Our theories must remain synthetic and adaptable to new information.

◆ ◆

Study Questions and Projects

1. Read "Is The Mind An Illusion?" in *Newsweek* (April 20, 1992; pp. 71f.) and "Biology of the Mind" in *U.S. News and World Report* (December 14, 1992; pp. 66*ff*.). In an essay discuss why major news magazines are interested in the mind and how the information in the articles is related to specific interpretations explored in this chapter.

2. Read the book *Animal Minds* (University of Chicago Press, 1992) by D. R. Griffin. In an essay discuss the author's justifications for his claim that animals are conscious. Do you agree with his position? Justify your response. (Check the review of the book by H. Cronin in the *New York Times Book Review,* November 1, 1992, p. 14. Do you agree with the reviewer?) Also, read the cover story "Can Animals Think" in *Time* magazine (March 22, 1993; pp. 54ff.). Does the *Time* presentation agree with or differ from Griffin's proposals?

3. Computers have been called "thinking machines." Do machines really "think" or do they do only what they are programmed to do by a thinking person? Read a few of the many books and articles on this topic.

4. Comment on the following statements:
   (a) "I think, therefore I am."
   (b) "Mental events are only brain events; thinking is subvocal speech."
   (c) "One never really knows other minds."
   (d) "Men are tormented by the opinions they have of things, rather than by the things themselves."
   (e) "Knowledge has altered the world. We must rely on knowledge to accommodate ourselves to new surroundings."
   (f) "When a person depends for his happiness upon the interests and activities of his own mind, he has become to a considerable extent independent of his material surroundings.

5. One of the crucial issues facing this generation is whether humanity is going to neglect and weaken its latent powers of reflection and control and permit impulses and passions to have free sway, or whether blind and unconscious animal passions are to be brought under control by the powers of human rationality and insights. Which seems more beneficial to you as a way of life for individuals and societies: a life ruled by passion or a life ruled by reason? Why?

6. According to a concept called *self-fulfilling prophecy,* a person is influenced by what he or she believes to be true so that it sometimes becomes true as a result of this belief. If you think that someone else does not like you, for example, you may behave in a hostile and defensive manner toward that person and that person,

in turn, may come to dislike you. What does the concept of self-fulfilling prophecy suggest to you about the relationships between the mind and behavior?

7. In the past, individuals have made a distinction between material and mental processes, or between the physical and the psychical. Why have these distinctions been made, and do you think the mind–body problem is still a live issue?

8. Explain the various methods of studying and interpreting mind as set forth by the different schools of psychology. Is any one method sufficient, or do you think it advantageous to use many different approaches to study the mind? Discuss.

9. What problems do we encounter when we attempt to be strictly objective in our experiments with and studies of the mind or mental phenomena?

10. State the general theories of the nature of the mind.

11. Distinguish between "mind as substance" and "mind as personal unity or principle of organization." How do the views of Plato, Aristotle, and Descartes relate to this distinction?

12. State the interpretations of mind given by Hume and by the behaviorists. How adequate are these interpretations?

13. Explain the important theories of the mind–body relationship. Be ready to present the case for and against any one of these interpretations and to indicate which side of the argument seems most convincing.

14. Are all the interpretations of the mind–body problem mutually exclusive, or would it be possible to hold, say, the theory of interactionism and that of emergent evolution at the same time?

15. Select an area of parapsychology and discuss some related philosophical issues and problems. (See "ESP Phenomena, Philosophical Implications of" in *The Encyclopedia of Philosophy* and the periodical *The Humanist,* Vol. 37, No. 3 (May/June 1977), and such recent books as J. Nickell and J. Fischer, *Mysterious Realms;* C. Hansel, *The Search for Psychic Power;* J. Randi, *Flim-Flam!;* and T. Hines, *Pseudoscience and the Paranormal.*

Suggested Readings

Churchland, P. *Matter and Consciousness: A Contemporary Introduction to the Philosophy of Mind.* Rev. ed. Cambridge, Mass.: MIT Press, 1988.

The author presents the advantages and disadvantages of such difficult issues as behaviorism, reductive materialism, functionalism, and eliminative materialism. Developments in neuroscience, cognitive science, and artificial intelligence and their relevance to philosophical issues are explored.

Dennett, D. C. *Consciousness Explained.* Boston: Little, Brown, 1991.

A good-humored, imaginative, and wide-ranging discourse in which the author attempts to explain the conscious mind; he contends that human consciousness is the product of what humankind tells itself. For each position stated, a compelling or counter-argument is given.

Fetzer, J. *Philosophy and Cognitive Science.* New York: Paragon, 1990.

An introduction that includes computer science, artificial intelligence, and linguistic/cognitive psychology.

Hofstadter, D. R. *Gödel, Escher, Bach: An Eternal Golden Braid.* New York: Vintage Books, 1980.

Hofstadter, Pulitzer prize–winning author, tries to stimulate not only the most sophisticated thought processes but also the most basic. He develops a theory of the mind that contains elements of artificial intelligence, neuroscience, and philosophy.

Hook, Sidney (ed.). *Dimensions of Mind: A Symposium.* New York: Collier Books, 1961.

These papers of the New York Institute of Philosophy represent many points of view on the mind–body problem, the brain and the machine, and concept formation.

Hunt, M. *The Universe Within: A New Science Explores the Mind.* New York: Simon and Schuster, 1982.

In a successful presentation of a cognitive science, the author criticizes psychologists who believe little human thinking; Hunt's view is that human beings are radically different from all other forms of life and from computers and that it is human thinking that makes us unique.

Mayer, R. E. *The Promise of Cognitive Psychology.* Lanham, Md.: University Press of America, 1990.

An introduction to cognitive psychology that provides the reader with a definition, a history, the tools, and the models of cognitive psychology.

McGinn, C. *The Problem of Consciousness: Essays Towards A Resolution.* London: Blackwell, 1991.

The author proposes that consciousness exists and cannot be explained away by the physical sciences.

Priest, S. *Theories of the Mind.* Boston: Houghton Mifflin, 1991.

An investigation into the ideas of seventeen leading philosophers on the nature of the mind and its relation to the body.

Rosenthal, D. (ed.). *The Nature of Mind.* New York: Oxford University Press, 1991.

A framework for understanding mental functioning from contributors that include Fodor, Dennett, Nagel, Putnam, Davidson, Searle, Ryle, Strawson, Burge, Chisholm, Rorty, and Sellars.

Ryle, G. *The Concept of Mind.* Chicago: University of Chicago Press, 1949.

Ryle's classic challenge to the Cartesian "myth" of the separation of mind and matter.

Shaffer, J. *Philosophy of Mind.* Englewood Cliffs, N.J.: Prentice-Hall, 1968.

A classic summary of the problems in the publisher's *Foundations of Philosophy* series.

Smythies, J. R. (ed.). *Brain and Mind: Modern Concepts of the Nature of Mind.* New York: Humanities Press, 1965.

Nine scholars representing different viewpoints discuss the mind–body problem and the nature of mind.

Notes

1. John Dewey, *The Quest for Certainty* (London: Allen and Unwin, 1930), p. 214.

2. See Chapter 3 for a discussion of the self and self-consciousness.

3. See p. 70 for further comments on cognitive science.

4. The authors are indebted to Professors Maxine Morphis and Christopher Riesbeck for guiding our discussions of cognitive science.

5. M. Hunt, *The Universe Within: A New Science Explores the Human Mind* (New York: Simon and Schuster, 1982), p. 52.

6. R. Descartes, "Meditation II," in *Descartes' Meditations and Selections from the Principles of Philosophy,* trans. John Veitch (La Salle, Ill.: Open Court, 1941), pp. 29–30.

7. Descartes, "Meditation II," p. 33.

8. A discussion of Kant's view of morality can be found in Chapter 7.

9. Psychological behaviorism has been discussed in Chapters 2 and 3. It will be further alluded to in the discussion of freedom in Chapter 5.

10. J. Dewey, *The Quest For Certainty* (London: Allen and Unwin, 1930), p. 214.

11. G. Ryle, *The Concept of Mind*, p. 25. See a discussion of this book in *The Journal of Philosophy* 48 (1951): 257.

12. See p. 63.

13. *Mind* as used by cognitive scientists is generally understood as the computational or information processing function.

14. Hunt, *The Universe Within*, pp. 253–56.

15. See A. Huxley, *Ends and Means* (New York: Harper, 1937), p. 299.

16. J. J. C. Smart, "Sensations and Brain Processes," *The Philosophical Review* 48 (1959): 141.

The Freedom to Choose

CHAPTER OBJECTIVES

In this chapter we will address the following questions:

◆ In Philosophy What Does "Freedom" Mean?

◆ Are There Views That Deny Freedom?

◆ What Does Indeterminism Propose?

◆ Does Self-Determination Advocate Freedom?

Man is not fully conditioned and determined; he determines himself whether to give in to conditions or stand up to them. In other words, man is ultimately self-determining . . . every human being has the freedom to change at any instant.[1]

The Philosophical Meaning of Freedom

♦ ♦ ♦ ♦ ♦ ♦ ♦ ♦ ♦ ♦

Few words have been used in so many different senses as *freedom*. Freedom may mean physical freedom—being able to move from one place to another; it may mean psychological freedom—open expression of the spontaneous character of human nature; or it may mean civil freedom—the right to act within the framework of the law, or as Montesquieu put it, "to do whatever the law permits." Everyday English speech is filled with expressions about freedom: "freedom of the press," "freedom of speech," "academic freedom." Most of these expressions have ambiguous popular definitions.

To the philosopher, however, freedom has meant not so much political, economic, or physical freedom, but rather the capacity to choose freely. Every day we make decisions. We decide what to order at a restaurant, what to wear, which TV show to watch. Some decisions have more long-term consequences: deciding on a career, on whether to marry, or whether to fight for one's country. In each case, nonetheless, it *appears* to us that we have chosen freely.

Are we free in the sense that we have some power to choose among alternatives and initiate action? Or, in fact, is our every act caused? Probably no issue in philosophy is more alive today or has as large an influence on other questions. For example, if all events in the world, including our actions, are rigidly determined by forces beyond our control, then what is the point of someone making future plans in an attempt to guide the course of human events? And what of moral responsibility? If a person could not have acted differently, how is it possible to hold him or her responsible for the action?

Philosophically, this age-old conflict has been known as the free will versus **determinism** controversy. The term *will* in modern thought refers to a person's ability to choose whether to perform acts of all sorts. The central problem is knowing whether and to what extent we are free to make choices.

In our intimate, personal relationships with other men and women we assume that we are free to decide many issues. Many such contacts are permeated with ideas of purpose and freedom. We take for granted spontaneity—the quality of acting without premeditation and without effort—and feel that it is the essence of life. We meet to decide certain questions, and we persuade others to accept our plans.

The world of the sciences holds quite different assumptions. There it is assumed that everything is determined (caused) by the laws of nature, and that the realm of nature—including humans—is an unbroken chain of cause and effect (determinism), governed by the laws of matter and motion (**mechanism**). The universe as a whole and all its parts participate in and are governed by an orderly causal sequence. Effects follow causes with often predictable regularity. The causal sequence is thought to hold not only in the physical sciences but in the biological, social, and psychological sciences as well. All these sciences have made considerable progress operating on the basis of a strict determinism.

Here, then, is a seeming paradox: in our personal relations we take freedom for granted, whereas in the sciences we assume that necessity and determinism rule.

The Denial of Freedom

♦ ♦ ♦ ♦ ♦ ♦ ♦ ♦ ♦ ♦

Today the denial of freedom appears as a result of the **postulate** of determinism as accepted by the natural sciences.[2] We will first consider "hard" determinism and then other forms of the rejection of freedom of choice, such as **predestination** and **fatalism**.

HARD DETERMINISM AS A SCIENTIFIC DOCTRINE

Determinism is the theory that everything in the universe, including people, is entirely governed by causal laws. It asserts that whatever happens at some specific moment is the outcome of something that happened at a previous moment; that is, that the present is always "determined" by the past. The laws of causality, which govern nature, also govern the actions of humans. Wherever nature has been studied, orderly causal sequences have been found. From the orbit of the stars to the fall of the snowflake, natural laws reign. Sciences such as physics, chemistry, biology, psychology, and sociology have shown that we also are ruled by cause and effect. Our organs, complexes, unconscious drives, conditioning, and conventions all influence our lives; a whole range of hereditary and environmental pressures are present and are powerful determining factors.

The case for determinism can be impressive. Here is an example offered by a hard determinist:

> Let us suppose that a doctor after carefully examining a patient, announces that unfortunately he cannot offer any assistance since the patient suffers from a mysterious ailment—one, in fact, which has no cause. The patient would in these circumstances undoubtedly be justified in angrily turning to somebody else for help. If the doctor had merely said that he had never come across this kind of illness before and that he knew of no cause for it or that the cause had not yet been discovered, we would not necessarily consider his statement absurd. We are ready to admit that there are illnesses whose causes are unknown. We are not ready to admit that there are illnesses without a cause.[3]

Imagine the consternation that would arise if a doctor signed a death certificate that asserted there was no cause of death!

Determinism has the appearance of being more "scientific" than **indeterminism,** the theory that personal choices in some cases are independent of antecedent events. The temptation is to apply the law of causality not only to physical phenomena but also to the phenomena treated in the social sciences. After noting that Western thought has emphasized the importance and dignity of the individual, Skinner (see biography and excerpt, pp. 86–87) goes on to say:

The use of such concepts as individual freedom, initiative, and responsibility has, therefore, been well reinforced. When we turn to what science has to offer, however, we do not find very comforting support for the traditional Western point of view. The hypothesis that man is not free is essential to the application of scientific method to the study of human behavior. The free inner man who is held responsible for the behavior of the external biological organism is only a prescientific substitute for the kinds of causes which are discovered in the course of a scientific analysis. All these alternatives lie *outside* the individual.[4]

In a somewhat similar vein, philosopher John Hospers tells us that our conscious lives, including our choices and decisions and the "entire train of deliberations leading up to them," are merely the expression of unconscious urges and desires. After relating cases of people who have gone astray, he says of children who have turned out all right that it is "through no virtue of their own. . . . The machine turned them out with a minimum of damage. . . . We do not blame people for the color of their eyes, but we have not attained the same attitude toward their socially significant activities."[5] If people's desires, as well as the acts resulting from them, are rigidly determined, then they are not responsible for their actions; they are merely playthings of forces beyond their control.

PREDESTINATION

Predestination in its most thoroughgoing form is the doctrine that God has decreed every event that is to take place, or at least that each person's destiny is fixed by divine decree. If God is omnipotent and omniscient—that is, all-powerful and all-knowing—then things must be determined by Him. This means that events in nature and human conduct, including human will, are determined by the sovereign will of God. The view is thus theological in its outlook and emphasis. The doctrine ranges from an extreme form, in which every event and each individual's

B. F. Skinner

Burrhus Frederic Skinner (1904–1990), a native of Susquehanna, Pennsylvania, was educated at Hamilton College and at Harvard, where he received a Ph.D. degree in 1931. He held academic appointments at the University of Minnesota, Indiana University, and—for most of his career—Harvard.

Skinner followed in the behavioral footsteps of John Watson by introducing the theory of operant conditioning. He contends that a system of rewards and punishments governs an individual's behavior. In a classic experiment, Skinner deprived a laboratory rat of food for a specific time; the rat was placed in a "Skinner Box," which is bare except for a protruding bar with a food dish underneath. The rat's behavior, he assumed, is governed by the hunger drive. Alone in the box, the rat pressed the bar accidentally, thereby establishing the preconditional operant level of bar pressing. Then food was allowed to fall into the dish whenever the bar was pressed; discovering this process, the rat pressed the bar repeatedly. The behavior was stopped eventually when the rat received no food when it pressed the bar. Skinner believed that human beings also learn by such conditioning.

B. F. Skinner wrote extensively, his books include *The Behavior of Organisms* (1938), *Science and Human Behavior* (1953), and his more popularly known *Walden Two* (1948) and *Beyond Freedom and Dignity* (1971).

destiny are fixed, to interpretations that call for some initiative or choice on the part of the individual. Some contemporary theologians use the term *predestination* to mean that "God is seeking us even before we are aware of Him," or that "a person's decision is a response to the initiative of God."

The doctrine of predestination is found in Judaic, Christian, and Muslim religious thought.[6] Although Judaism and Christianity have placed emphasis mainly on our responsibility to God, there is a development of the notion of predestination from passages in the writings of Paul through Augustine to John Calvin. In his later writings, Augustine (see biography and excerpt, pp. 88–89) elaborated the doctrine

and gave it a prominent place in his thinking. In Calvinism, the doctrine of predestination achieves its most complete expression in Christian thought. In extreme Calvinism, as expressed, for example, by the early Puritans, salvation is not dependent on anything that a person can do. Jonathan Edwards, an eighteenth-century American philosopher and theologian (see biography and excerpt, pp. 90–91), writes: "There is an absolute and universal dependence of the redeemed on God. The nature and contrivance of our redemption is such, that the redeemed are in every thing directly, immediately, and entirely dependent on God: They are dependent on him for all, and are dependent on him every way."[7]

Almost all living things act to free themselves from harmful contacts. A kind of freedom is achieved by the relatively simple forms of behavior called reflexes. A person sneezes and frees his respiratory passages from irritating substances. He vomits and frees his stomach from indigestible or poisonous food. He pulls back his hand and frees it from a sharp or hot object. More elaborate forms of behavior have similar effects. When confined, people struggle "in rage" and break free. When in danger they flee from or attack its source. Behavior of this kind presumably evolved because of its survival value; it is as much a part of what we call the human genetic endowment as breathing, sweating, or digesting food. And through conditioning similar behavior may be acquired with respect to novel objects which could have played no role in evolution. These are no doubt minor instances of the struggle to be free, but they are significant. We do not attribute them to any love of freedom; they are simply forms of behavior which have proved useful in reducing various threats to the individual and hence to the species in the course of evolution.

B. Skinner, *Beyond Freedom and Dignity* (New York: Knopf, 1971).

FATALISM

Fatalism is the belief that some (perhaps all) events are irrevocably fixed; thus, human effort cannot alter them. It is the doctrine that the happenings in the world of nature and the events in people's lives are predetermined at the beginning of time, so no human will has a part in shaping the course of things. A person's lot is determined independently of her or his choices and actions; the future is always beyond individual control.

Fatalism holds to the notion of the inevitable appearance of an event at a specific time. Such convictions are expressed in common usage: "When your number is up, it's up," "What will be, will be," "If there is a bullet with my name on it, I'll get it. If there isn't, I'll come through unscratched, so why worry?"

Fatalism logically may set forth a definite theory of causation, but it is in fact more likely to consider the question of causes of an inscrutable mystery.

A fatalist—if there is any such—thinks he cannot do anything about the future. He thinks it is not up to him what is going to happen next year, tomorrow, or the very next moment. He thinks that even his own behavior is not in the least within his power, any more than the motions of the heavenly bodies, the events of remote history, or the political developments in China. It would, accordingly, be pointless for him to

Saint Augustine

Saint Augustine (Aurelius Augustinus, 354–430 C.E.) was born in Tagaste, North Africa. Son of a pagan father and a devout Christian mother, he had embraced Manichaeism (a dualistic belief system that views human nature quite negatively) before his conversion to Christianity. While a teacher of rhetoric, he came into contact with Ambrose, the Christian Bishop of Milan, who encouraged Augustine's conversion to Christianity in 386. He then resigned his professorship, partly on account of illness, and remained with friends to await baptism the next year. To further his project of founding a monastery, Augustine went to Hippo (in Algeria) where he was ordained to the priesthood and became a very active bishop four years later.

The fullest expression of his spiritual journey is found in his *Confessions,* written about 400. His great work *On The Trinity* borrowed concepts from Neo-Platonism and became one of the primary models for Christian thinking in Western civilization. He began his greatest treatise, *City of God,* in 412, and did not finish it until about 426. These and other works have made Augustine one of the strongest influences in subsequent Western thought.

deliberate about what he is going to do, for a man deliberates only about such things as he believes are within his power to do and to forego, or to affect by his doings and foregoings.[8]

In Greek and Roman thought, the concept of Fate is prominent. It is a determining power sometimes identified with the will of Zeus (Greek), or Jupiter (Roman), or often thought of as superior to the gods, as well as to mortals. Fate is omnipresent in the Greek plays, especially the tragedies. The Stoics identified Fate with the course of Nature and with Providence. The Romans were influenced by the Greek beliefs regarding Fate, and they reproduced much of the spirit of Greek mythology. In place of Fate, the Romans sometimes used the similar concept of Fortune.

The view that as individuals or in groups we are incapable of changing the course of events seems to have its origin in the fact of human helplessness in the presence of certain inescapable evils, especially death. Fatalism is in part an emotional reaction growing out of recognition that we live in a universe the nature of which far exceeds our power to understand and control. As a theoretical position, fatalism is not subject to refutation. What it does, however, is to blur important and useful distinctions. It classifies all *[handwritten margin note:] Why would God allow His creation to sin and bring evil into the world?*

But though I said and firmly held that the Lord God was incorruptible and unalterable and in no way changeable, the true God who made not only our souls but our bodies also, and not only our souls and bodies but all things whatsoever, as yet I did not see, clear and unravelled, what was the cause of Evil. Whatever that cause might be, I saw that no explanation would do which would force me to believe the immutable God mutable; for if I did that I should have been the very thing I was trying to find (namely a cause of evil). From now it was with no anxiety that I sought it, for I was sure that what the Manichees said was not true. With all my heart I rejected them, because I saw that while they inquired as to the source of evil, they were full of evil themselves, in that they preferred rather to hold that Your substance suffered evil than that their own substance committed it.

So I set myself to examine an idea I heard—namely that our free-will is the cause of our doing evil, and Your just judgment the cause of our suffering evil. I could not clearly discern this. I endeavoured to draw the eye of my mind from the pit, but I was again plunged into it; and as often as I tried, so often was I plunged back. But it raised me a little towards Your light that I now was as much aware that I had a will as that I had a life. And when I willed to do or not do anything, I was quite certain that it was myself and no other who willed, and I came to see that the cause of my sin lay there.

Augustine, *Confessions,* trans. E. Pusey (New York: Modern Library, 1949).

events as the same—even those as apparently different as the man in prison who cannot go to the movies and the man who decides not to go to the movies. In modern Western civilization, with its concepts of democracy, progress, and human control, fatalism has never been a popular view.

Indeterminism

Many people are repelled by a doctrine of hard determinism; they believe that determinism is not compatible with freedom and moral responsibility. This position is justified by pointing out that nothing can be more certain than what is given in immediate experience. If, for example, I see a flash of red, or feel happy, this is far more certain than a complicated theory about causality. My experience of freedom is thus a datum of immediate experience and has intuitive certainty.

Other philosophers reject determinism on the grounds that they believe the world to be "open" rather than "closed." They point to novelty, spontaneity, and genuine creativity; a rigid determinism allows none of these. We shall consider the American philosopher William James (1842–1910) as the outstanding representative of this position.

Jonathan Edwards

Jonathan Edwards (1703–1758), Congregational minister, theologian, and philosopher born in East Windsor, Connecticut, grew up in an atmosphere of Puritan piety and learning. He graduated from Yale College, and for a time was an ordained pastor serving with his grandfather at Northampton, Massachusetts. When his grandfather died (1729), he remained as minister until he was dismissed in 1750 because he wanted to exclude from the Lord's Supper those who had not had an intense religious experience. He then served as a missionary to a Native American settlement in Stockbridge, where Edwards attacked the notion of a self-determining will in his famous work: *Freedom of the Will*. He defended the revivals, called the "Great Awakening," of his day. He had an ability to combine insights from Locke's philosophy, Newtonian science, and Calvinistic theology: a combination heretofore unseen. Edwards has been called one of the greatest theologians in American history. In 1758, he became President of the College of New Jersey (later Princeton), but he died as a result of volunteering for a smallpox vaccination shortly after his appointment.

Edwards' books include *Religious Affections* (1746), in which he distinguishes genuine from false piety, and *Original Sin* (1758), a discussion of the fact and nature of original sin.

William James was a forceful exponent of the theory of freedom of the will, or "indeterminism," as he called it. Determinism, according to James, is the view that past factors decree what the future will be. Consequently, the future has no ambiguous or indeterminate possibilities hidden within it. James says that indeterminism, on the other hand, is the view that the parts of the universe have a considerable amount of "loose play"—that is, not all things are causally connected and there is a genuine pluralism in the nature of things. There are genuine alternative possibilities existing in the future. For example, there may be many possible routes for you to choose from to reach home, even though you actually *take* only one route.

The possibilities exceed the actualities in many situations. James says that "our first act of freedom, if we are free, ought in all inward propriety to be to affirm that we are free."[9] Although freedom is a postulate—that is, an unproved rule or basic assumption from which to reason—so also are causality and uniformity. James is not afraid of the term *chance*. If we accept the real existence of chance, novelty, and spontaneity, our world is just as consistent as is the world of the strict determinist. For example, before the action we often cannot predict which

Excerpt from Edwards:

Freedom of the Will, "Concerning the Nature of the Will" (1754)

It may possibly be thought, that there is no great need of going about to define or describe the "will"; this word being generally well understood as any other words we can use to explain it: and so perhaps it would be, had not philosophers, metaphysicians and polemic divines brought the matter into obscurity by the things they have said of it. But since it is so, I think it may be of some use, and will tend to the greater clearness in the following discourse, to say a few things concerning it.

And therefore I observe, that the will (without any metaphysical refining) is plainly, that by which the mind chooses anything. The faculty of the will is that faculty or power or principle of mind by which it is capable of choosing: an act of the will is the same as an act of choosing or choice.

If any think 'tis a more perfect definition of the will, to say, that it is that by which the soul either chooses or refuses; I am content with it: though I think that 'tis enough to say, it's that by which the soul chooses: for in every act of will whatsoever, the mind chooses one thing rather than another; it chooses something rather than the contrary, or rather than the want or nonexistence of that thing. . . . So that whatever names we call the act of the will by—choosing, refusing, determining, directing, commanding, forbidding, inclining or being averse, a being pleased or displeased with—all may be reduced to this of choosing. For the soul to act voluntarily, is evermore to act electively.

J. Edwards, *Freedom of the Will,* ed. P. Ramsey (New Haven: Yale University Press, 1957).

---

of two possible items an individual will buy. The indeterminists do not assert that *any imaginable* action is possible for *any* person; they claim merely that, among two or more mutually exclusive choices, more than one is possible; only one becomes actual—that is, occurs. Freedom is limited to the field of voluntary action and conscious selection.

In his essay "The Dilemma of Determinism," James shows how judgments of regret and tragedies such as murders present a dilemma for the determinist. If the murder has been fully determined by the rest of the universe, a judgment of regret seems inappropriate or foolish.

Calling a thing bad means, if it means anything at all, that the thing ought not to be, that something else ought to be in its stead. Determinism, in denying that anything else can be in its stead, virtually defines the universe as a place in which what ought to be is impossible—in other words, as an organism whose constitution is afflicted with an incurable taint, an irremediable flaw.[10]

The only escape for the determinist, according to James, is in the direction of a subjectivism that assumes that a certain amount of evil is good, because it may further some higher good. Such a view is gained only at the price of suppressing our judgments of blame and remorse.

Insofar as determinists attempt to think things through, without denying evident facts of experience, they tend toward pessimism, which may in turn lead to the pathetic hope that everything really is good. This type of optimism results in an ethical indifference that is likely to bring trouble in its wake.

> The only consistent way of representing a pluralism and a world whose parts may affect one another through their conduct being either good or bad is the indeterministic way. What interest, zest, or excitement can there be in achieving the right way, unless we are enabled to feel that the wrong way is also a possible and a natural way— nay, more, a menacing and an imminent way? and what sense can there be in condemning ourselves for taking the wrong way, unless we need have done nothing of the sort, unless the right way was open to us as well? I cannot understand the willingness to act, no matter how we feel, without the belief that acts are really good or bad. I cannot understand the belief than an act is bad, without regret at its happening. I cannot understand regret without the admission of real, genuine possibilities in the world.[11,12]

Self-determination

♦ ♦ ♦ ♦ ♦ ♦ ♦ ♦ ♦ ♦ ♦

In dealing with the problem of freedom versus necessity, many people have been led to make extreme claims and draw unreasonable conclusions from portions of the evidence. Some, impressed by the evidence for determinism, have claimed that freedom in the sense of personal choice is an illusion. They have agreed with the player in As You Like It that "All the world's a stage, And all the men and women merely players." Others have been impressed by the evidence for freedom of choice and have declared that the doctrine of determinism is false. There is a third possible position—that both those who deny all freedom and power of alternative choice and those who deny determinism are taking false and extreme stands. The supporters of this third position say that it is not an "either–or" issue; we need not accept freedom alone or determinism alone. They see determinism and freedom as a "both–and" issue.

Self-determination links determinism and freedom and stresses the causal effectiveness of human participation in events. We are not only creatures of our environment; we are also at times critics and creators of it. This position does not defend indeterminism, which holds that some decisions may be independent of any antecedent causative factors. (Indeterminism is the extreme position on the side of freedom.) On the other hand, it denies the opposite extreme of hard determinism, which rejects freedom and, as a logical concomitant, moral responsibility. Self-determination holds that the self acts as the causal agent, is the center of creativity, and has a degree of freedom of choice.

How is it possible to accept both determinism and freedom? Let us look at determinism a little more closely, and then see why it is also possible to accept a degree of freedom. Determinism is a necessary scientific assumption. The scientist, to work, must follow the directive "Behave as though every event has a cause." The idea of a dependable order of nature is the guiding principle of scientific thinking; on the basis of this assumption the sciences have made outstanding progress. Even the actions of human beings, it is claimed, arise out of a given set of conditions and have little meaning apart from those conditions. Case studies of the behavior of delinquents, as well as the life histories of other people, indicate that conduct may be determined by specific causative factors. Determinism is said to be a presupposition of all intelligent explanations.

Although determinism in some form is a necessary scientific assumption, there are many different kinds of determined events or causal relationships. In the physical realm there are causal sequences of the collision type, where there is direct contact: for example, when one billiard ball strikes another and *causes* it to move. There are also gravitational, electromagnetic, and chemical causative factors. In the organic realm, vital processes contribute to (cause) the maintenance of the organism as a whole. In the realm of human behavior, there are geographical, biological, psychological, social, and cultural determinants.

There is clear evidence that certain determining factors influence our behavior. For example, various aspects of human biology rhythmically rise to a peak, fall to a valley, and return to a peak at periodic intervals. Circadian (daily) rhythms occur, for example, in our sleep-wake cycle, temperature, heart rate, and the release of various hormones. Moreover, an alteration in the timing of these rhythms can lead to a disruption of the body's physical *and* psychological performance. In addition, recent discoveries have revealed surprising links between the chemistry of behavior and that of other body functions in humans and animals. Chemical compounds of a group called *peptides* have been found to perform key roles in signaling within the brain and in the control of such perceptions as thirst, pain, emotion, and perhaps even memory. In one study, a chemical extracted from the urine of mental patients immediately caused rats to fight so violently that scientists found four of them dead in one cage and the sole survivor licking his wounds. In another experiment, a substance extracted from patients who have the illness called anorexia nervosa (loss of appetite and aversion to food), produced a reluctance to eat that lasted for weeks in laboratory animals. In everyday discussion, we often refer to the effect of the weather on our moods and behavior. Scientific investigation has confirmed what heretofore was thought to be merely speculation: day-to-day atmospheric changes can affect the way we feel and behave.

Other factors that researchers believe determine our behavior are genetic characteristics of brain structure and function; differences in behavior at the time of birth, for example, are to a large extent determined genetically. The main problem for the behavior geneticist is to decide the extent to which a behavioral characteristic is environmentally versus genetically determined. There appears, however, to be no question that there are some determining factors, be they chemical, genetic, meteorological, or biological.

Although determinism has been a scientific postulate, present trends in the sciences appear to be against the acceptance of any completely mechanistic or physical determinism. To what extent the principle of uncertainty or indeterminacy, as set forth by Heisenberg, has played a part we cannot say, but this and other recent developments in science undoubtedly have had some influence. There are scientists who recognize determinism and causality but insist that modern science does not banish freedom from the universe and certainly from human affairs. Speaking about "opinion in physics with regard to the question of determinism as it is presented by quantum mechanics," Percy W. Bridgman says that "seldom in the history of physics . . . has there been such a radical difference of fundamental outlook between the acknowledged leaders."[13]

Reflections

It seems that humans, as self-conscious beings, have the ability to undertake personal initiative and response, that they are capable of creativity, and that within limits they are able to reshape themselves, to influence the behavior of their fellows, and to redirect the processes of the outer world. What is the evidence for a degree of freedom of choice?

1. *The immediate consciousness of freedom.* Practically all human beings have a direct and distinct consciousness of freedom. They believe they are able to choose among alternative courses of action. After they have acted, they usually believe that they could have chosen other than they did. This experiential fact must be recognized. If we actually have some freedom, then it is easy to understand how this consciousness of freedom arises; if we are not free in any sense, then it is difficult to understand.

To claim that we think we are free merely because we are ignorant of the causes of our action is not adequate refutation of this point. In many situations we know just why we are acting, but still we believe we are free. If the organism or the self is a center of activity, it may choose that stimulus to which it desires to respond from among a number of stimuli. The increase of self-consciousness, knowledge, and intelligence—that is, of stimuli—does not make us less free. On the contrary, we have more alternatives before us, and we have a greater sense of personal choice.

To claim that we are not free because we always act on the basis of the strongest motive is likewise an inadequate refutation of the argument for freedom. This apparent refutation is circular in that whatever motive wins is called the strongest and is so called merely because it wins.[14] We may also say that it wins and is the strongest because it is chosen by the self. We admit at once that choice or selection does involve determination by motives; free choices are not undetermined, but they are within our control.

2. *The sense of personal responsibility.* The sense of personal responsibility that expresses itself most clearly in our feeling of obligation, or the sense of "ought," is quite meaningless if the power of choice is denied. After some actions we say, "I could not have done otherwise"; but after other actions we say, "I ought to have done the other thing" or "I ought to have chosen differently." Sometimes we have a keen feeling of guilt and remorse.

We experience a sense of obligation and we need to explain it; its existence cannot be denied. If freedom is a reality and the person has some power of alternative choice, the sense of "ought" is meaningful and important.

3. *Moral judgments on human conduct and character.* We not only hold ourselves personally responsible for our own choices but hold others responsible for their actions. Praise and blame, approval and disapproval, rewards and punishments, and the norms and standards we set up in society assume human freedom. They assume that the chain of causal sequences is not fixed solely by outside determinants and that new ones can sometimes be added at will.

The majority of judgments of conduct and character assume that people are free moral agents. Children are held responsible only in proportion to their age, experience, and degree of maturity. Why do we speak of an "age of accountability" if all actions of both children and adults are equally determined or if the adult has no more power of selection than the child? In the courts, we could not hold people responsible or guilty unless we believe that they could have done otherwise, that they are free moral agents. In some cases, much of the court's effort is directed to discovering the degree of guilt—that is, the degree to which the defendent intended the consequences of his or her action.

In a discussion of "Free Will and the Laws of Nature," Werkmeister says:

> It is generally conceded that our ethical notions are meaningful and significant only if they pertain to free agents. In a world in which there is no freedom, *loyalty,* for example, is a meaningless word; for what sense is there in saying that a person is loyal—or truthful or honest or just—if factors and forces beyond his control determine his every word and deed, and if he cannot help doing what he does? Do we call a particle of dust loyal because gravitation and adhesion keep it securely in its place? . . . One need only ask these questions in order to see the absurdity of the very idea of moral significance in a world in which no freedom exists. Even truth and falsity lose their meaning in such a world.[15]

4. *The fact of deliberation.* Reflective thinking is another fact of human experience that indicates that persons are not mere playthings of external forces. Sometimes an individual stops to deliberate before acting. As a result of this deliberation, a person may select a course of action that he or she would not have selected without deliberation. In reflective thinking, human beings can place before themselves a number of possible courses of action. They may consider the consequences of first this and then that action, and weigh all the possibilities carefully. Reflective thinking has been called "trial and error by ideas." A person may carry out a number of courses of action in imagination and then select one of them as the actual course. In this way ideas, ideals, and goals may determine conduct. Conduct may be guided by the anticipation of future consequences, as well as by the pressure of past or present events.

Why should an individual stop and deliberate if the choice is not influenced by the deliberation? Why do we say so frequently to ourselves and to others, "Why don't you stop and think?" When hit by the racket, a tennis ball does not stop to deliberate. It goes at once, and it goes in a direction that is determined by mechanical forces. Sometimes when we are stimulated we do not act at once; we stop to think. Our action may be influenced by what we consider to be our interests. We may decide on a course of action that runs counter to one that appeals strongly to our emotions. We may even resolve to modify some well-established habit. Thought and deliberation are meaningless if we are not free to choose among alternatives.

It is human beings—thinking, self-conscious beings—who have formulated the laws of nature. We are accustomed to speaking of heredity and environment as determining our actions, and certainly no person can doubt the importance of these factors. However, it should be pointed out that we do not know exactly which the hereditary and which the environmental determinants are in rats and guinea pigs, and evaluating the roles of these determinants is even more difficult in the case of individual human beings. Furthermore, when we become aware that some hereditary or environmental factor is influencing us, it ceases to be the same determinant. We may accept it and yield to its influence, we may modify it, or we may reject or counteract it. In any case, our consciousness of it has some effect. If we accept our humanity and self-consciousness, we have considerable freedom. When we talk about nonhuman species, the terms *heredity* and *environment* seem sufficient.

Supporters of the notion of *freedom* in its philosophical sense do not deny the evidence presented by the various sciences in support of causal relationships; nor do they claim that humanity is completely free—that is, not subject to causal determinants, be they internal (such as genetic bases of behavior, mental disorders, or biological rhythms) or external (such as the many environmental determinants to which we respond). They claim merely that the self at times is a causal agent, as well as an entity acted on by causes, and that an individual has considerable power to choose among alternatives. If the things we have said about humans and their powers and capabilities are correct, then people are real causes. In other words, everything is caused, and I (the self) cause some things. If the self is a determining agent, then a degree of freedom and some kind of determinism may be combined. Self-conscious beings, at least at times, are capable of initiating events that lead to goals that are self-chosen. Human freedom is neither freedom from causes nor freedom from laws; it is the ability to act on the basis of self-chosen ends, which are themselves influenced by experiences, thoughts, motives, desires, and needs. Freedom is the power to direct mechanisms so that they contribute to fulfillment of our purposes. Without reliable cause-and-effect relationships, our human purposes would be frustrated at every turn.

> Despite the controversy, despite the overgeneralizations, we remain conditioned—as is every other known organism. Yet the distinguishing feature of human nature is not our conditioning but our ability to transcend its limits, as does no other known species. Rarely, in any single person's life, but often enough to create our civilization, our society, our languages, art and ideas, we go beyond the "contingencies of reinforcement" to develop an unheralded mastery over the body, create an image never seen, even understand a complete vision of life.[16]

If contemporary human sciences tell us anything, it is that we possess abilities far greater than is dreamt of in the view of the determinists.

Self-consciousness, as we have seen, is one of the distinctive human traits. Whereas animals are conscious, only human beings are self-conscious. Consciousness is awareness of the environment; self-consciousness includes the additional awareness of the contents and activity of one's own mind or self. Self-consciousness makes reflective thinking and the sense of right and wrong possible. It enables us to consider ourselves as subjects and as objects of action. It is a prerequisite for freedom of choice.

Glossary Terms

DETERMINISM   The view that human choice is entirely controlled by previous conditions or governed by causal laws. The realm of nature, including human beings, is an unbroken chain of cause and effect. (Sometimes called "hard determinism.")

FATALISM   The belief that events are irrevocably fixed so that human effort cannot alter them, though sometimes things appear otherwise. "What will be, will be."

INDETERMINISM   The belief that personal choices in some cases are independent of antecedent events. William James, for example, held that there are genuine possibilities existing in the future, and that the universe has a considerable amount of novelty, chance, and spontaneity.

MECHANISM   The view that everything is to be explained by mechanical principles or by the laws that govern matter and motion.

POSTULATES   A postulate is a fundamental assumption used as a basis for developing a system of proofs, but not subject itself to proof within the system. Though some logicians use *axioms* and *postulates* as synonymous, for others an axiom is a self-evident truth, whereas a postulate is a presupposition or premise of a train of reasoning and not necessarily self-evident. In this latter sense, all axioms are postulates, but not all postulates are axioms. A postulate is a basic statement "taken for granted" from which other statements may be deduced.

PREDESTINATION   The doctrine that all events in the life of humans have been decreed or determined from the beginning of time by the sovereign will of God.

SELF-DETERMINATION   Position that links determinism and freedom and stresses the causal effectiveness of human participation in events.

Chapter Review

THE PHILOSOPHICAL MEANING OF FREEDOM

1. *Philosophical freedom* refers to the capacity to choose freely. The possibility and extent of human freedom is a living issue in philosophy, often referred to as the "free will versus determinism" controversy.

THE DENIAL OF FREEDOM

1. Hard determinism asserts that everything in the universe is entirely governed by causal laws. Humans are no exception.

2. Predestination asserts that each person's destiny is determined by divine decree. Events in human conduct and nature are determined by the will of God.

3. Fatalism asserts that events in nature and in our lives are fixed at the beginning of time.

INDETERMINISM

1. William James proposed a theory of free will or indeterminism that stressed that there are genuine possibilities in the future. Not all things are causally connected. He recognized the existence of chance and spontaneity.

SELF-DETERMINATION

1. Self-determination is the middle road between determinism and freedom. We are affected not only by our environment; we create change within that environment.

2. Determinism is a necessary scientific assumption; a dependable order of nature is essential for scientific thinking. However, there are differences among scientists as to kinds of determinism. The tendency today is to reject mechanical determinism.

REFLECTIONS

1. Self-determination proposes specific evidence to support a degree of human freedom of choice.

2. Self-determination proposes that the self is at times a causal agent; thereby a degree of freedom and determinism may be combined.

● ●

Study Questions and Projects

1. When unjustly sentenced to death, Socrates had ample opportunity to escape, and his friends urged him to do so. Reflecting on the entire situation, he decided to stay in prison and drink the poisonous hemlock, because he considered it more just and honorable to obey the laws of the city than to break them. Was Socrates free or casually determined or both when he held to an ideal even though it meant death?

2. Evaluate the following statements and indicate your areas of agreement and disagreement with them:
   (a) "If everything is determined, let's relax; we do not need to exert ourselves."
   (b) "A philosophy that denies all human freedom cannot be lived."
   (c) "From early times some individuals have refused to accept the world in which they live as it is."
   (d) "Since people do not ultimately shape their own characters, it follows that they are not morally responsible."
   (e) "The impulse to frame ideas or values and to strive for their realization is one of human nature's peculiar endowments."
   (f) "The most permanent thing in creation is the demand of the human soul for freedom, the thirst after fullness of life and opportunity. These demands are written into nature itself."

3. Explain as clearly as you can the "dilemma of freedom and necessity," or the problem that centers around freedom of choice. Why is this question important?

4. What is meant by thoroughgoing or "hard" determinism and what are its implications? Name some people who have held this position.

5. Distinguish among *predestination*, *fatalism*, and *scientific determinism*.

6. State the evidence or the case for indeterminism as William James sees it.

7. What are the more extreme positions on the question of freedom versus determinism? What is meant by the view that this question is not an "either-or" issue?

8. What is the evidence for the position that there is some freedom of choice? State this evidence as fully and clearly as possible and in your own words.

9. Explain what is meant by self-determination? What part do heredity, environment, self-consciousness, and knowledge play in a consideration of the problem of freedom?

10. What are the broad implications for human life of the denial of freedom of choice, and the implications of the acceptance of the position that there is some freedom?

● ●

Suggested Readings

Anglin, W. S. *Free Will and the Christian Faith*. New York: Oxford University Press, 1991.

   The author proposes that free will and traditional Christian convictions about God's omnipotence and omniscience are compatible.

Dennett, D. *Elbow Room: Varieties of Free Will Worth Wanting*. Cambridge, Mass.: MIT Press, 1985.

   An attempt to dissolve the traditional problem of free will and determinism by defending a version of soft determinism.

Dobzhansky, T. G. *The Biological Basis of Human Freedom*. New York: Columbia University Press, 1960.

Five lectures dealing with some philosophical implications of modern biology. The ability of humans to choose between alternatives is presented as a characteristic product of human evolution.

Fischer, J. M. (ed.). *God, Foreknowledge, and Freedom*. Stanford, Calif.: Stanford University Press, 1989.

A collection of essays dealing with the relationship between divine foreknowledge and human freedom. The central study is Nelson Pike's "Divine Omniscience and Voluntary Action."

Hook, Sidney (ed.). *Determinism and Freedom in the Age of Modern Science*. New York: Collier Books, New York University Institute of Philosophy, 1961.

Philosophers and scientists discuss determinism and freedom in their respective fields and in law and ethics. Excellent as a reference.

James, W. "The Dilemma of Determinism," in *The Will to Believe and Other Essays in Popular Philosophy*. New York: Longmans, Green, 1912.

James, one of the founders of American pragmatism, states in this classic essay the case for indeterminism, or for freedom of choice.

O'Connor, D. J. *Free Will*. Garden City, N.Y.: Anchor Books, 1971.

A short volume in a series, *Problems in Philosophy,* which is an introductory examination of a selection of arguments for and against the view that some human actions are freely chosen. The series includes short volumes directed to the main problems critical to basic philosophical thinking.

Thornton, M. *Do We Have Free Will?* New York: St. Martin's, 1990.

The author asserts that the question to be asked is, "Do we have autonomy?" To answer the question the author takes an historical overview of religious and scientific attempts to understand human nature.

Trusted, J. *Free Will and Responsibility*. New York: Oxford University Press, 1984.

A clear, basic introduction to the subject.

Watson, Gary (ed.). *Free Will*. New York: Oxford University Press, 1982.

The eleven essays in this volume illuminate a number of issues, moral and metaphysical, relevant to the discussion of free will. Among the contributors are A. J. Ayer, Roderick M. Chisholm, Peter Strawson, and Norman Malcolm.

Weiss, P. *Man's Freedom*. Carbondale, Il.: Southern Illinois University Press, 1967.

The author explores the issue of determinism and free-will.

White, M. *The Question Of Free Will: A Holistic View*. Princeton, N.J.: Princeton University Press, 1993.

A defense of the position that we may believe in free will without denying or accepting determinism.

Williams, C. *Free Will and Determinism*. Indianapolis, In.: Hackett, 1980.

An imaginary dialogue between a proponent of free will and a determinist and self-determinist.

♦ ♦

Notes

1. V. E. Frankl, *Man's Search For Meaning* (New York: Washington Square Press, 1963), pp. 206–207.

2. Consult the end-of-chapter glossary for the difference between "postulates" and "axioms."

3. P. Edwards, and A. Pap, eds., *A Modern Introduction to Philosophy,* 3rd ed. (New York: Free Press, 1972), p. 2.

4. B. F. Skinner, *Science and Human Behavior* (New York: Macmillan, 1953), pp. 447–48.

5. J. Hospers, "Meaning and Free Will," *Philosophy and Phenomenological Research* 10 (1950): 326.

6. One element of Protestant Christianity rejected the doctrine of predestination, called *Arminianism* after Jacobus Arminius (1560–1609). Although declared heretical by orthodox Calvinism, Arminianism had broad implications for seventeenth-century humanism.

7. J. Edwards, "God Glorified in Man's Dependence," in W. Muelder and L. Sears, eds. *The Development of American Philosophy* (Boston: Houghton Mifflin, 1940), p. 17.

8. R. Taylor, "Fatalism," *The Philosophical Review* 71 (1962): 56.

9. W. James, *The Will to Believe and Other Essays in Popular Philosophy* (New York: Longmans, Green, 1912), p. 146.

10. W. James, *The Will to Believe and Other Essays in Popular Philosophy,* pp. 161–62.

11. W. James, *The Will to Believe and Other Essays in Popular Philosophy,* p. 175.

12. See the section Jean-Paul Sartre in Chapter 16 (pp. 335–338) for a discussion of Sartre's belief in human freedom.

13. In Hook, *Determinism and Freedom,* p. 57.

14. See W. H. Werkmeister, *A Philosophy of Science* (Lincoln: University of Nebraska Press, 1965), Chapter 12.

15. W. H. Werkmeister, *A Philosophy of Science,* p. 436.

16. R. Ornstein, "Reconsiderations of *Science and Human Behavior* by B. F. Skinner," *Human Nature* 6 (1978): 96.

The Realm of Values

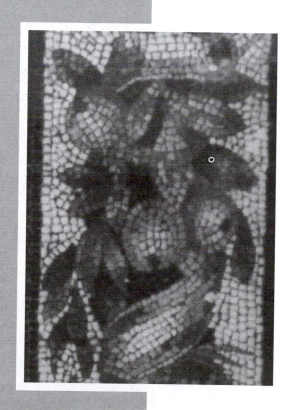

The Meaning of Values

Moral judgments, whatever else they are, are a species of judgments of value. They characterize acts and traits of character as having worth, positive or negative. Judgments of value are not confined to matters which are explicitly moral in significance. Our estimates of poems, pictures, landscapes, from the standpoint of their esthetic quality, are value-judgments. Business men are rated with respect to their economic standing of giving credit, etc. We do not content ourselves with a purely external statement about the weather as it is measured scientifically by the thermometer or barometer. We term it fine or nasty: epithets of value.[1]

Value Judgments

We all make value judgments at one time or another: "I like chocolate ice cream." "What a great film!" "There is too much poverty in the world." Valuing occurs for most people almost constantly, and whenever anything—whether a physical object, a way of acting or a person—is preferred or chosen, a value has been expressed. From the simple cry of a baby that needs attention to the shopper making selections at the supermarket to the diplomat deciding issues of national or foreign policy, we are all involved in behavior in which values are at stake. Some choices are trivial, such as whether we say "coffee" or "tea" when asked which we prefer; others may affect our entire lives, such as when we choose a trade or profession, select a marriage partner, or join a political party or religious congregation.

WHAT IS A VALUE?

Several overlapping interpretations of "value" are in use, including these four: (1) a value may be a guiding *principle,* such as honesty; (2) a value may be a *quality,* such as persistence; (3) a value may be a *goal,* such as happiness; or (4) a value may be the artistic or monetary *worth* of something. Values are found in morality, the arts, religion, economics, politics, laws, customs, and even in some areas of science (see page 222). Whenever standards are set, criteria established, preferences expressed, or assessments of worth made, one or more values are stated.

VALUES INESCAPABLE

Life forces us to make choices, to rate things as better or worse, and to formulate some scale or standard of values. We praise and blame, call actions right or wrong, and declare the scene before us beautiful or ugly. Each person has some sense of values, and no society has been found that is devoid of some value system. If we do not make our own choices, time, our friends, or other external forces will decide for us, which is in a sense our decision too. Therefore, the question is not so much whether we have standards, convictions, loyalties, and ideals around which our lives are organized as whether these are consistent or inconsistent, life-promoting or life-destroying.

Various professionals (for example, some counselors) claim to be "value free" with their clients; that is, they resist imposing their own values on their clientele. Moreover, they are not truly free of values; instead, they attempt to value their client's standards.

Since the time of the early Greeks, philosophers have written about the theoretical side of the problem of values.[2] Today, the study of what humanity values, and what *should* be valued, has taken on new interest and importance. Studies of the general theory of value, including the origin, nature, classification, and place in the world of values are appearing regularly in the popular press and scholarly publications.

Ethics, the study of values in human conduct, and **aesthetics,** the study of values in art, are two major fields concerned with values.

In a relatively static society, values are embedded in habits and traditions. They may be accepted and followed by all the members of a society such that its members are hardly conscious of them. In a rapidly changing society, such as the one in which we live, values may be topics of controversy. The contemporary crisis in values is deep-seated, seen by many as an aspect of a more pervasive crisis of authority.[3] The seat of authority has become elusive and its basis questionable, so that its pronouncements are no longer believed. We may attribute such distrust to recent historical events, but the question is more than one of not trusting spokespersons of authority; it is a matter of no longer being able to believe anything at all.

Facts and Values

A crucial philosophical distinction is made between a factual judgment and a value judgment. Judgments about such things as the distance between New York and San Francisco, the make of some particular automobile, or the age of a friend are factual.

Factual judgments are *descriptive* statements of empirical qualities or relations. Judgments about such things as whether a particular picture is beautiful, one ought to visit a sick relative, or your friend's behavior is right are *evaluative*. Value judgments appraise the worth of objects, acts, feelings, and so on. There is little agreement among philosophers as to how the term *value* is to be defined. In general, we can say that value judgments are judgments of *appraisal*.

VALUES AS FACT-DEPENDENT

Although we can ordinarily distinguish between judgments of fact and judgments of value, we cannot separate them completely. There is an interaction between facts and values. For example, if I am a student, the answer to the question of whether I should play football (or some other sport) or spend more of my time on my studies depends in part on the facts regarding my health, intellectual ability, and standing in course work. If I am weighing the merits of two people as prospective life partners, I should seek out and consider many facts, and make certain that logic and analysis, as well as immediate feelings, play an important part in my decision. The observable characteristics of things enter into our appraisals of value. If facts or conditions change, our evaluations often change too; that is, value judgments are generally fact-dependent.

VALUES AS KNOWLEDGE OR FEELINGS

One of the main issues in the area of values is whether value judgments express knowledge or feelings. When I say that the Mona Lisa is beautiful, that kindness is good, and that murder is wrong, am I making assertions about things that are true or false or am I merely expressing preferences, making entreaties, or issuing commands? Value judgments may be thought of merely as expressions of our feelings and desires—that is, as subjective. For example, a value has been called an emotion or "sentiment of approval or disapproval," the satisfaction of a human want or desire. In recent decades, the claim that values are subjective often has been made to depend on a theory about what sorts of expressions can be said to be "meaningful." The most extreme position, that of *positivism*, restricted the scope of meaning to those statements involving reference to data verified by sense experience. Statements referring to matters of fact, according to this view, are the only meaningful expressions there are. The conclusion of this position is that value judgments either mean nothing at all or must be taken as no more than the *expression* of someone's feelings, as when a person responds to a painful blow by exclaiming "ouch!"

Other philosophers think of a value as the quality of objects or situations that have worth—that is, as an objective quality of things, such as "that quality of things that evokes an appreciative response." Still others interpret value judgments as some combination of both the subjective and the objective.

VALUES AND DESIRES

Does a thing have to be desired to have value? Although something with value is something desirable and is usually desired by people, its value is not equivalent to the fact that it happens to be desired by someone. I may desire to kill someone, set fire to homes, to steal a watch—things that are not usually considered to be in themselves desirable. Being desired is thus only part of the meaning of *valuable*. Not all things that are desired are valuable. Likewise, some things that are not desired by many people are undoubtedly valuable. Some examples include healthy, nutritional diets, probing psychotherapy, and painful surgical and dental procedures.

How Values Are Justified

♦ ♦ ♦ ♦ ♦ ♦ ♦ ♦ ♦ ♦

A basic issue in value theory has to do with the ground of values and their place in the scheme of things. What is the relationship of values to the mind that does the evaluating? Are values only in the mind, in the sense that they pertain only to the imagination, the thinking, the interests, and the desires of the person? Or are they outside the mind, in the sense that they belong to (are qualities of) things, just as temperature, size, and shape do? Or does the truth lie between the two extreme positions, so that values are both subjective and objective and also depend in part on the circumstance or context in which they are found?

During the past two thousand years, Western philosophy, which had its beginning in Greece, and the Judaeo-Christian tradition, which had its source in Palestine, furnished Westerners with a world view, a life view, and a scale of values by which to live. This outlook on life came to be embraced by most thinkers in Western Europe and was carried to those parts of the world, including the Americas, where Western civilization came to prevail. According to this outlook, there are certain fundamental, persistent values. The defense of these values may be stated in a number of ways.

First, there is the view that certain values are absolute and eternal. They are given to us by God, or they are grounded in the nature of the universe. They transcend, it is claimed, the everyday world of things disclosed to us by the senses and examined by science. That is, beyond the "passing show" or phenomenal world in which we live, there is a more permanent order of reality, which gives the basis and justification for such disciplines as metaphysics, theology, ethics, aesthetics, and logic. Because there is a moral order, we have a solid basis for calling some things "right" and others "wrong," some things "good" and others "evil;" because an aesthetic order is part of the nature of things, we can call some things "beautiful" and others "ugly;" because there is such a thing as truth, some judgments are true and others false. These things are such, it is claimed, regardless of what people think or believe or say about them.

VALUES AS GROUNDED IN HUMAN NATURE

A second way of defending values is stated in more experiential, functional, and dynamic terms. It appeals to many who do not accept absolute and authoritative systems. We are, it is claimed, growing persons in a changing, dynamic, or creative universe. From this point of view, the ground of values is found in human nature, and the basic value is the worth of persons. Just as in science the quest is for knowledge and the discovery of truth, in ethics the quest is for the development of people or the good life. The quest for the truth and the quest for the good are always continuing; circumstances change and knowledge is accumulating at a rapid rate.

VALUES AS SUBJECTIVE

Those who believe that values are subjective think that value statements express sentiments or emotions of liking or disliking, and nothing more. Eating, drinking, playing, listening to music, observing a gorgeous sunset—all are valuable in that they evoke pleasurable feelings, or furnish us with experiences that we enjoy.

George Santayana (see biography and excerpt, pp. 106–107) tells us that "there is no value apart from some appreciation of it."[4] Emotions as well as consciousness are necessary for the existence as well as the apprehension of good in any form. Dewitt H. Parker says that values belong wholly to the inner world, to the world of mind. The satisfaction of desire is the real value; the thing that serves is only an instrument. A value is always an experience, never a thing or object. Things may be *valuable,* but they are not values. We project value into the external world, attributing it to the things that serve desire.[5]

Those who present arguments for the subjective interpretation of values are likely to stress that values—judgments of goodness and beauty—have varied from individual to individual, from group to group, and from one age to another. If values were wholly objective, would judgments vary? Values are in some sense subjective; they depend on a relationship between an observer and that which is evaluated.[6] One might say, on this view, values are human inventions.

VALUES AS OBJECTIVE

Those who consider values objective believe that the latter are strictly out there in our world to be

George Santayana

George Santayana (1863–1952), philosopher, poet and novelist, was born in Madrid of a Spanish father and an American mother. His undergraduate studies and doctorate were completed at Harvard, where he also taught until 1912. A small inheritance allowed him to retire, live in England and Paris, and finally settle in Rome. During World War II, he found shelter in a Roman convent of English nuns, where he lived until his death.

The Sense of Beauty, written in 1896, was his first important philosophical work. His aesthetic theory was developed further in *Reason In Art* (1905), which is Volume IV of *The Life of Reason.*

In his earlier work, he defined beauty as "pleasure objectified" and distinguished among the materials of a work of art, its form, and its expressiveness. In *Reason In Art,* Santayana explored the place of art, as one good among many, within the life of reason; the most important justification of art is that it adds significantly to human enjoyment, and thereby to human happiness.

Santayana's major writings also include *Scepticism and Animal Faith* (1923), *Realms of Being* (4 volumes; 1927–1940), and *Dominations and Powers* (1949).

discovered. The value fact—some quality, or some assemblage of qualities—calls forth our judgment. Something independent of the observer appeals to his or her "moral sense" or "aesthetic faculty." People take an interest in those things and experiences that appear to them to possess value; it is not their interest that creates the value.

We must make a clear distinction—according to objectivism—between the act of judging and the thing or situation about which the judgment is made. People differ in their judgments about temperature, yet we do not say that temperature is subjective. In this case we can check their judgments with a thermometer and declare them correct or incorrect. In ethics and aesthetics, there are no thermometers, but there are cri-

teria on the basis of which correct judgments are made. To say that a value is present in an object is to declare that the object is in some sense *good.* What is felt to have value need not on reflection be *judged* to have value. Judgment can correct our immediate feelings of value. If I judge a landscape to be beautiful, it is not my judging that is beautiful but the colors and shapes before me. There is a quality present that is independent of my judgment. Values seem to reside in objects just as truly as do color, smell, temperature, size, and shape.

Such widely varying systems as the philosophies of Plato and Aristotle, medieval realism, neo-Thomism, and various types of modern realism and idealism agree that values are in some sense objective. For Plato, the world of concepts, universals, and values is the real and permanent world. There is a hierarchy of values—leading up to the Good or the supreme value—that determines the organization of the world. For Aristotle, the relation of a thing to its end or value is an essential part of its nature. The objectivity of value is central also in medieval thought. Roman Catholic philosophy, as a whole, holds that truth, goodness, and beauty exist in their own right and that God is the ultimate ground of values.

The supporters of the view that values are objective point out that beauty and goodness are valued by all and that, among cultured people and critics in general, there is a large measure of agreement as to aesthetic value judgments. The objectivist claims that agreements concerning fundamental values reflect the physical, psycho-logical, and social conditions and needs of people everywhere. If values were subjective, they would reflect a person's own desires, interests, or wishes exclusively. Yet whether the values sought are social, moral, or aesthetic, our choices are definitely limited.

DECONSTRUCTION

A contemporary school of thought called **deconstruction** neither accepts nor rejects problems relating to values, choosing instead to reduce the issues to investigations of language. The individuals who belong to this school are called deconstructionists. Instead of examining values in terms of fact-value distinctions, subjective-objective stances, deconstructionists focus on language and the continuous reassessment of words. They maintain that values have nothing to do with either the object or the subject or the situation; as a result, the deconstructionists have often been accused of being nihilists. Values are nothing more than the products of our ability to exercise our linguistic skills: the only reason values exist is because value statements are grammatically possible.[7] Words are difficult, even impossible to define. For these thinkers, questions of value are frequently underplayed. Nonetheless, many literary critics, philosophers, and creative thinkers have been taking a second look at their crafts in order to understand the meaning of their disciplines.

Values and the Aesthetic Experience

♦ ♦ ♦ ♦ ♦ ♦ ♦ ♦ ♦ ♦ ♦

THE NATURE OF THE AESTHETIC EXPERIENCE

The word *aesthetic* comes from the Greek verb meaning "to sense or perceive"; it has the same root as the words *theory* and *theater*. *Aesthetic experience* pertains to the perceptual level of human experience as related to beauty. For reasons of clarity, let us distinguish a **sensation**, a **percept**, and a **concept**. As a result of a stimulus we receive a *sensation* through one of our sense organs, which produces a state of consciousness. We may see, hear, touch, smell, or taste something. Such sensations may be unorganized or vague and convey little or nothing in the way of ideas. But when these sensory impulses are organized into units or wholes so that we recognize objects, such as stones, trees, books, or people, we speak of *percepts* or *perception*. I have a sensation of redness; I perceive an apple. When we move from particular things to general ideas, class terms, or universals, we enter the realm of concepts. When I see a particular man, John Doe, I have a percept. When I talk about humanity, I am talking not about any particular person but about what is common to people in general, or the *concept* "human being." Philosophers and scientists generally deal with conceptual problems.

Aesthetic experience that is the result of perceptual experience is most frequently visual or auditory, but it is not limited to these areas. It may be related to our sense of touch, taste, or smell. Aesthetic experience includes any pleasurable absorption in these perceptual experiences insofar as it arises from a disinterested contemplation of phenomena, whether natural or manmade. The aesthetic "emotion" may be aroused by artistic productions, in which the artist has attempted to evoke an aesthetic response, or it may be aroused by many different kinds of objects or experiences that occur, sometimes quite unexpectedly, in everyday living. Perception and conception are closely related; we often are led to see what we expect or want to see; we recognize an object because it answers our conception of it. The ways of identifying a work of art that we will discuss depend heavily on the conceptions of the artist and experts on art and perhaps not heavily enough on the viewer's perceptions of the work itself.

AESTHETIC VALUE

There are wide differences of opinion about what objects call forth the aesthetic response, and what a work of art really is.[8] Not everything deliberately made by humans is a work of art. An ordinary pencil, for instance, is not a work of art. How do works of art differ from other manmade articles?

Three of the most widely accepted criteria for determining whether something is a work of art are: (1) that the object or event is intended to be a work of art by its maker; (2) that the object or event is made by an artist; and (3) that important or recognized "experts" consider it to be art. Let us take two examples from the world of sculpture.

Our first photograph is of a sculpture by Marcel Duchamp called *Bottle Rack*. At first glance, this object does not fulfill the first criterion for a work of art, as a bottle rack is simply an industrial tool. Duchamp exercised no special "artistic skills" in the execution of this sculpture. As its name makes clear, it is an industrial object,

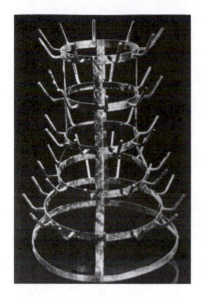

DUCHAMP, Marcel. Photograph of *Bottlerack* (original lost) from Box in a Valise. (1935–1941). Leather valise containing miniature replicas, photographs, and color reproductions of works by Duchamp, 16″ × 15″ × 4″. Collection, The Museum of Modern Art, New York. James Thrall Soby Fund.

PICASSO, Pablo. *Baboon and Young.* 1951. Bronze (cast 1955), after found objects, 21″ high, base 13¼ × 6⅞″. Collection, The Museum of Modern Art, New York. Mrs. Simon Guggenheim Fund. Right: Detail.

made to serve a practical function. Duchamp's "artistry" has entered, not into its making, but into its recognition and selection. He has isolated it from its familiar practical context and posed it, forcing us to contemplate it. By treating it like a work of art, he has transformed it into one.

Similarly, our second example, a sculpture by Pablo Picasso entitled *Baboon and Young,* involved only one single act—an act of the imagination. Picasso had the artistic genius to see how he could fashion a toy automobile into a baboon's head such that an art object was derived from this chance resemblance. Part of the fascination of the artistic creation lies in the fact that the old parts are unaltered; it is the combination of the parts that changes them altogether.[9]

As these examples illustrate, we often cannot tell whether contemporary pieces are works of art, or have aesthetic value. Two elements are needed. First, we need clues given to us from the context. If we find Duchamp's *Bottlerack* standing in a garden surrounded by other sculptures, we are more likely to have an aesthetic response and thereby discover its aesthetic value. Second, if we cannot perceive aesthetic value in objects that others find valuable, it may be wise for us to withhold judgment until we are ourselves capable of making a competent analysis of the aesthetic experience. William James has made this point: "Men have no eyes but for those aspects of things which they have already been taught to discern . . . in poetry and the arts someone has to come and tell us what aspects we may single out, and what effects we may single out, and what effects we may admire, before our aesthetic nature can 'dilate' to its full extent."[10]

Objects and events do have qualities that can be perceived without the help of artists or experts, although these specialists can be helpful. To consider the artistic qualities of objects or events, we need to develop an approach that is flexible and depends on a willingness to perceive artistic form as well as content and subject matter.[11]

The Selection of Values

◆ ◆ ◆ ◆ ◆ ◆ ◆ ◆ ◆ ◆

How are we to select the values by which we live? There is widespread agreement about the existence of certain groups of values: religious, moral, aesthetic, social, scientific, economic, political, and the like. There is not nearly the same measure of agreement concerning their number, nature, relationship to each other, rank in a scale, and the principles to be used in selecting them.

Our value decisions have been influenced by a wide range of traditional values that have come down to us from the past and are embedded in our language, customs, and institutions. The thinkers of ancient Greece discussed many values: goodness, truth, beauty, happiness, and so forth. Aristotle in his *Ethics* presented many virtues for consideration. In the West, many values have a biblical background. The Ten Commandments; the teachings of the Hebrew Prophets, and the Sermon on the Mount and other teachings of Jesus have been especially influential. For Muslims, the Qur'an contains all the traditional values. From time to time new values have been added: the rule of law, the principle of consent, and the concepts of liberty, security, education, health, and social welfare are examples.

We shall make no attempt to set forth a rigid classification of values as higher or lower. There are, however, certain principles that are generally accepted in philosophical discussions.

1. **Intrinsic values** are to be preferred to those that are **extrinsic**. Something is intrinsically valuable (good in itself) when it is valued for its own sake and not for its capacity to yield something else. Something is extrinsically valuable (good for something) when it is an instrument for attaining other things. Most of the things we see and use in our everyday activities, from books and typewriters to buildings and institutions, have extrinsic value.

Intrinsic and extrinsic values are not necessarily mutually exclusive. The same things may be valued for themselves and for what they may bring, or a thing may be valued now intrinsically and later extrinsically. For example, knowledge may be valued as a good in itself and also as a means to other things that have value, such as economic success or power. A great work of art may be valued for itself, or it may be viewed as a means for making profit or achieving distinction. We can say in general that the good of a surgical operation is extrinsic: it points to the greater health that is to come. The enjoyment of a glass of wine is an intrinsic good, a good "in itself": the wine is not enjoyed as an instrument to something beyond enjoyment. Those things that are sought as good in themselves are the *ends* we seek in life. The other things are the *means* we use to attain these ends.

2. *Values that are productive and relatively permanent are to be preferred to those that are less productive and less permanent.* Some objects that are valued, such as wealth, tend to be used up in the activities of life, whereas others, such as friendship, tend to increase as they are used. To share the values of the mind and spirit with other people does not lessen their value for us. Physical and economic values, although necessary for life, are not permanently satisfying ends in themselves. Many people think that human experience shows that the social, intellectual, aesthetic, and religious values tend to give more permanent satisfaction than do the material values. The productive and permanent values tend also to be the intrinsic values.

3. *We ought to select our values on the basis of self-chosen ends or ideals.* The values we seek ought to be *our* values, and these values ought to be consistent with each other and with the demands life makes on us.

Reflections

♦ ♦ ♦ ♦ ♦ ♦ ♦ ♦ ♦ ♦ ♦

Human beings have been concerned about values from the beginning of philosophical thought, even though value theory (axiology) as such was not formulated until the end of the nineteenth century. Only since then have justice, goodness, beauty, and other particular values been studied as values. When we consider the question of "value free" disciplines, the study of isolated values acquires new meaning. Both ethics and aesthetics have profited immensely from the study of value as such.

The discovery of a new area of study cannot be underrated. If philosophy tends by its very nature to give an explanation of the totality of what exists, anything unearthed that broadens our vision will be a true philosophic discovery.[12] When a new area is discovered, two contrary movements are generally produced. There is the basic question: What can values be reduced to? First, we can attempt to reduce values to experiences (*subjective value*). On this view, value is equivalent to that which pleases us; it is identified with what is desired; moreover, it is the object of our interest. Pleasure, desire, and interest are experiences; value for these philosophers is reduced to personal experiences, or the emotional expression of those experiences. Those who contend that value is merely subjective identify it with some kind of feeling, satisfaction, or other psychological state. For example, Hume denied that beauty is an objective quality:

> Euclid has fully explained all the qualities of the circle; but has not in any proposition said a word of its beauty. The reason is evident. The beauty is not a quality of the circle. . . . It is only the effect which the figure produces upon the mind. . . . Till . . . a spectator appears, there is nothing but a figure of such particular dimensions and proportions: from his sentiments alone arise its elegance and beauty.[13]

In opposition, the objective view states that things are not valuable because we desire them, but rather that we desire them because they are valuable. This question of subjective and objective value is raised in Plato's *Euthyphro* when Socrates asks whether piety is pious because it is loved by the gods, or whether the gods love piety because it is pious. Value is objective if its existence and nature is *independent* of a subject; conversely, it is subjective if its existence and its validity are *dependent* on the feelings or attitudes of the subject.

There is an alternative to the approach of the subjectivist, such as Hume, who puts exclusive emphasis on the subjective component in the value situation, and of the objectivist, who must logically conclude that values exist independently of any individual consciousness. That alternative is to maintain that subjective and objective values interlock. Value is always related to desire—this is the *subjective pole*—the fact, however, that something is desired, does *not settle* the question of its value, but raises the problem: Is what was desired, desirable? And the resolution here is in terms of a critical appraisal, involving a consideration of means and ends—the objective pole—aimed at answering the question. Is the object of desire *satisfactory*? For John Dewey, the answer to this question is not a matter of subjective preference. Thus both subjective and objective factors are brought together.

In this interpretation of value, the relation between subject and object is one of interdependence—a change in either one brings about a change in the other and the character of the parts is more or less determined by the character of the whole. As Melvin Rader points out, a good example is a melody. To appreciate a melody, we must be aware of a pattern of tones. We hear each tone, and determine its value not as a detached sound, but as an integral part of that pattern. The beauty of the melody springs from the combination of sounds (objective) and mood (subjective). Value emerges when there is a synthesis of objective and subjective factors.

Glossary Terms

AESTHETICS   The branch of philosophy concerned with art and the nature of the work of art.

AXIOLOGY   The branch of philosophy that deals with values.

CONCEPT   A general idea, as distinct from a percept. I may have a concept of "man" or "humanity," but I have a percept when I see a particular man, John Doe. We have percepts of particular, experienced objects; we have concepts of universals, classes, and unexperienced objects.

DECONSTRUCTION   A philosophical and critical movement, starting in the 1960s that questions all traditional assumptions about the ability of language to represent reality.

ETHICS   The study of moral conduct. The term may also be applied to the system or code followed (such as "Buddhist ethics.")

EXTRINSIC VALUE   A value or good that leads to another good; valued for something other than itself

(such as a common pencil whose chief value is what it *does*, not what it *is*.)

INTRINSIC VALUE   A value or good that is good in itself.

NIHILISM (NIHILISTIC)   (1) An extreme form of skepticism; the denial of an objective basis for truth and meaning. (2) The doctrine that nothing exists; therefore, nothing can be known or have value. (3) The term is often used to refer to social doctrine that conditions are so evil that the present order ought to be swept aside or destroyed to make room for something better.

PERCEPTS OR PERCEPTION   The organization of sensory impulses into units or wholes; apprehending by means of the senses; that which is immediately given in perception.

SENSATION   A state of consciousness, an awareness, a mental condition resulting from stimulation of a sense organ.

Chapter Review

VALUE JUDGMENTS

1. Life forces us to make choices, to rate things as better or worse, and to formulate some scale or standard of values. Every society has some type of value system.

2. What is a value? A value may be a guiding principle, such as honesty; a quality, such as persistence; a goal, such as happiness; or the artistic or monetary worth of something.

3. Two major fields concerned with values are ethics, the study of values in human conduct, and aesthetics, the study of values in art.

FACTS AND VALUES

1. Factual judgments are descriptive statements, whereas value judgments appraise the worth of objects, acts, feelings, and so on.

2. Facts or conditions may change, and therefore our evaluations are subject to change; value judgments are generally fact-dependent.

3. A main area of controversy concerning value judgments is whether they express knowledge or feelings.

4. Value judgments may be thought of as expressions and therefore as subjective; they may be viewed as qualities of objects or situations and therefore as objective, or they may be considered as a combination of both the subjective and the objective.

5. Being desirable is only part of the meaning of "valuable." Not all things that are desired are valuable; some things that are not desired are valuable.

HOW VALUES ARE JUSTIFIED

1. Western philosophy has certain fundamental, persistent values.

2. Values may be viewed as subjective or objective.

3. Deconstructionism focuses on language and the continuous reassessment of words; values are nothing more than the products of our ability to exercise our linguistic skills.

VALUES AND THE AESTHETIC EXPERIENCE

1. Aesthetic experience pertains to the perceptual level of human experience of beauty. This experience frequently is visual or auditory but is not limited to these senses.

2. There are many different opinions concerning aesthetic value. Works of art can be recognized by means of contextual clues.

THE SELECTION OF VALUES

1. Value decisions are influenced by traditional values from the past that are embedded in our language, customs, and institutions.

2. Although there is widespread agreement about the existence of certain groups of values, there is little agreement concerning, among other things, the principles to be used in selecting them. Certain principles are generally accepted in philosophical discussions.

REFLECTIONS

1. There are certain principles that are generally used to select values. These principles are related to intrinsic values, permanence, and self-chosen ideals.

2. The quality of value may be found in a synthesis of objective and subjective factors.

◆ ◆

Study Questions and Projects

1. Read "Whose Values?"—the cover story of *Newsweek* for June 8, 1992. Discuss the related essays (pp. 19–27) with reference to the following sections of Chapter 6: Facts and Values, How Values Are Justified, and The Selection of Values. Have the *Newsweek* essays' issues been resolved, or do they remain problematic?

2. Explain whether you agree or disagree that we have been living half a life, in the sense that we live by the values "more is better," "winning is everything," and "everyone for himself or herself."

3. Discuss one or more of the following claims: "Values are a matter of opinion," "Values can be discovered within nature itself," "Values have been revealed by God."

4. Read the article "Family" in *The Anchor Bible Dictionary* (Vol. 2, pp. 761–69). What are "family values" in the *Bible*?

5. Why are the philosophical problems of value important in daily life?

6. What distinguishes factual judgments from value judgments?

7. On what bases do you select your own values?

8. What are "traditional American values?" Have they been consistent? Support your claims with historical references.

9. Should public funds support the arts? Should limitations be placed on the subject matter of publicly funded art? Are there differences between publicly funded art and publicly funded religion?

10. Read a critic's appraisal of a work of art. Write an essay that explores the criteria, implied or stated, used by the critic. Would your own criteria be the same as the critic's? Why or why not?

11. Comment on the following view of William Muehl, as presented in "The View from Philistia," from *Reflection* (Vol. 75, No. 1, November 1977), an alumni periodical from Yale Divinity School:

In recent years . . . I have been increasingly troubled about the veneration accorded artists by the more highly educated segments of our society. People who are inclined to lay about them irreverent critical glee in matters political, economic, and religious tend to go all hushed and mushy in the presence of anything that claims to be a "work of art." . . . To suggest that works of art can be corrupt . . . is to make a statement . . . which our age finds unacceptable.

12. Read "Art and the Morality of the Artist" by Anne Bernays in the January 20, 1993, edition of *The Chronicle of Higher Education* (Vol. 39, No. 20; p. B1*f*). What are the author's main points, and on what bases do you agree or disagree with her?

13. Are clothing fashions an art form? By what criteria do you judge the annual trends in men and women's fashions as covered by televised news programs (such as CNN) or newspaper advertisements?

14. Is it possible for an atheist to have worthwhile values?

15. What values are stated or implied in the U.S. Constitution?

◆ ◆

Suggested Readings

Almond, B., and Wilson, B. (eds.). *Values: A Symposium*. Atlantic Highlands, N.J.: Humanities Press, 1988.

A collection of essays exploring the ways in which values are transmitted in a variety of fields.

Berleant, A. *Art and Engagement*. Philadelphia: Temple University Press, 1991.

The author utilizes phenomenology and pragmatism to develop a theory of aesthetic perception based on the idea of engagement. Extensive knowledge of various modern and postmodern art movements enables the author to contend persuasively that a constitutive and participatory model of perception is essential to aesthetic experience.

Cothey, A. L. *The Nature of Art*. New York: Routledge, 1990.

An attempt to develop a theory of art midway between those who deny the existence of beauty and those who accept the actuality of beauty but doubt the human capacity to create it.

Davies, S. *Definitions of Art*. Ithaca, N.Y.: Cornell University Press, 1991.

The author describes and analyzes the definition of art as it has been discussed in Anglo-American philosophy during the past thirty years; he also introduces his own perspective on ways we should reorient our thinking.

Derrida, J. *Of Grammatology*. Trans. G. C. Spivak. Baltimore: Johns Hopkins University Press, 1976.

Although difficult reading, this resource is of immense importance to understanding deconstruction. Moreover, the author's reinterpretations of phenomenology, of psychoanalysis, and of structuralism have heavily influenced contemporary criticism and aesthetics alike.

Dewey, J. *Art As Experience*. New York: Capricorn Books, 1959.

Based on Dewey's lectures on aesthetics, this study considers the formal structures and characteristic effects of most of the arts: architecture, sculpting, painting, music, and literature.

Dickie, G., et al. (eds.). *Aesthetics: A Critical Anthology*. 2nd ed. New York: St. Martin's, 1989.

A text that combines historical studies, works of scholarship, and contemporary criticism in an effort to present a comprehensive account of aesthetics; included are works by Kant, Tolstoy, and Nietzsche.

Eaton, M. M. *Basic Issues in Aesthetics*. Belmont, Calif.: Wadsworth, 1988.

Part of the Wadsworth Basic Issues in Philosophy series, this small volume is of particular interest because of its concluding section on aesthetic value.

Fisher, J. A. *Reflecting on Art*. Mountain View, Calif.: Mayfield, 1993.

Written specifically for undergraduates, this text introduces readers to the philosophy of art with a blend of traditional theory, compelling readings, high-quality reproductions, and extensive coverage of the social questions concerning art.

Fried, C. *An Anatomy of Values: Problems of Personal and Social Choice*. Cambridge, Mass.: Harvard University Press, 1970.

Influenced by Kant and Rawls, the author develops a scheme of human values that stresses impartiality, equality, justice, and the rational ideal of the person.

Gaus, G. *Value and Justification: The Foundations of Liberal Theory*. New York: Cambridge University Press, 1990.

The author explores the nature of valuing and the morality that can be justified in a society that deeply disagrees on what is truly valuable.

Grice, P. *The Conception of Value*. New York: Oxford University Press, 1991.

The author explores and defends a modern view of value.

Hartmann, N. *Ethics*. 2nd ed. 3 vols. London: Allen and Unwin, 1950.

First published in Germany in 1926, the three volumes *Moral Phenomena, Moral Values,* and *Moral Freedom* exhibit the subject matter of ethics in a new light.

Lewis, H. *A Question of Values*. San Francisco, Calif.: Harper, 1991.

A primer defining personal ethics and values based on perceptions of truth. The author isolates six characteristic systems grounded in authority, deductive logic, science, sense experience, intuition, and emotion, contending that most individuals are influenced by a combination of these systems.

Margolis, J. (ed.). *Philosophy Looks at the Arts*. 3rd ed. Philadelphia: Temple University Press, 1987.

An anthology containing a broad sample of the principal strands of thought across the range of contemporary aesthetics.

Martin, F. D., and Jacobus, L. A. *The Humanities Through the Arts*. 3rd ed. New York: McGraw-Hill, 1983.

This book provides an excellent introduction to questions of value in the humanities and the arts. The authors discuss what constitutes a work of art in many fields: painting, sculpture, architecture, literature, music, dance, and film.

Murphey, M. G., and Berg, I. (eds.). *Values and Value Theory in Twentieth-century America*. Philadelphia: Temple University Press, 1988.

A collection honoring the breadth and unity of Elizabeth Flower's philosophical work; humanistic pragmatism is the underlying theme.

Nerlich, G. *Values and Valuing: Speculations on the Ethical Life of Persons*. New York: Oxford University Press, 1990.

The author argues that human beings are naturally endowed with personhood and its qualities, which require self-appraisal, which in turn requires an evolution of desires into values.

Novitz, D. *The Boundaries of Art*. Philadelphia: Temple University Press, 1992.

Novitz asserts that society underestimates the role of art in daily life; he explores how this viewpoint has developed, how it is to be remedied, and the extent to which art contributes to humanity's daily endeavors.

Quintas, A. L. *The Knowledge of Values: A Methodological Introduction*. Washington, D.C.: University Press of America, 1989.

The author proposes that the interplay between persons and their environment must form the core of value study; values are born of personal encounters emerging from acts of participation, which are both personal and communal.

Stocker, M. *Plural and Conflicting Values*. New York: Oxford University Press, 1990.

Stocker explores attitudes toward choices between lower pleasures and higher values. Hedonistic utilitarianism is discussed with a recurrent theme of moral judgment before, during, and after intentional actions.

Notes

1. J. Dewey, *Theory of the Moral Life* (New York: Holt, Rinehart & Winston, 1960), p. 122.

2. The branch of philosophy that deals with the nature of values is known as **axiology.**

3. A. Kaplan, *In Pursuit of Wisdom* (Beverly Hills, Calif.: Glencoe Press, 1977), p. 309; also see D. Cupitt, *Crisis of Moral Authority* (Philadelphia: Westminster, 1972).

4. G. Santayana, *The Sense of Beauty* (New York: Scribner's, 1899), pp. 18–19.

5. D. H. Parker, *Human Values* (New York: Harper and Brothers, 1931), pp. 20–21. See also a later volume by Parker, published posthumously, *The Philosophy of Value,* with a preface by William K. Frankena (Ann Arbor: University of Michigan Press, 1957), pp. 14, 20.

6. See the discussion of ethical relativism in Chapter 7.

7. For further examination of this position, see Jacques Derrida, *Of Grammatology* (Baltimore and London: Johns Hopkins University Press, 1976).

8. For a more complete and exacting study of the nature of a work of art, consult I. A. Reid, *A Study in Aesthetics* Chapter 7 (New York: Macmillan, 1954), pp. 156–201.

9. See R. Goldwater, *What Is Modern Sculpture?* (New York: The Museum of Modern Art, 1969).

10. W. James, *Principles of Psychology* (2 vols. bound as one), Part I (New York: Dover Publications, 1950), p. 443.

11. For a complete investigation into the characteristics of artistic form, content, and subject matter, see F. D. Martin, and L. A. Jacobs, *The Humanities Through the Arts* (New York: McGraw-Hill, 1975), pp. 21–26.

12. R. Frondizi, *What is Value?* (La Salle, Ill.: Open Court, 1971).

13. D. Hume, *An Enquiry Concerning the Principles of Morals* (London: Oxford University Press, 1902), pp. 291–92.

♦ ♦ ♦ ♦ ♦ ♦ ♦ ♦ ♦ ♦

Ethics and Morality

CHAPTER OBJECTIVES

In this chapter we will address the following questions:

♦ Are There Levels of Moral Development?

♦ What Is Involved in Moral Situations and Assessments?

♦ What Are Some Representative Ethical Norms?

♦ How May Ethical Standards Be Approached?

♦ Are There Useful Ethical Principles?

♦ Are There Differences Among Moral Certainties, Moral Relativism, and Moral Pluralism?

"Throughout most of the nineteenth century, the most important course in the college curriculum was moral philosophy, taught usually by the college president and required of all senior students. The moral philosophy course was regarded as the capstone of the curriculum. It aimed to pull together, to integrate, and to give meaning and purpose to the student's entire college experience and course of study. In so doing it even more importantly sought to equip the graduating seniors with the ethical sensitivity and insight needed in order to put their newly acquired knowledge to use in ways that would benefit not only themselves and their own personal achievement, but the larger society as well."[1]

Moral Judgments

The question of morality—what is right and what is wrong in human relations—may be the central issue of our time. Other questions that often are thought to outrank this one in importance—such as how we should relate to modern technology, or how nations should act in the interest of maintaining peace and of the future of the civilized world—also are moral questions. Classes in ethics are taught not only in the undergraduate curriculum but also in the professional schools. Doctors, lawyers, and school and public administrators attend seminars about morality. Our techniques and skills have developed faster than our comprehension of our goals and values; perhaps the renewed interest in these ends will help to provide us with much-needed answers to the crises and anxiety that are part of our lives.

Individuals are continually judging their own conduct and that of their fellows. They approve of some acts and call them "right" or "good." They condemn other acts and call them "wrong" or "evil." Moral judgments always have to do with the actions of human beings and, in particular, with voluntary actions—those actions freely chosen. *Involuntary actions*—those over which people have no control—are rarely open to moral judgment, as a person usually is not held responsible for an action that she or he did not initiate.

LEVELS OF MORAL DEVELOPMENT

A significant interpretation of three levels of moral development was presented several years ago.[2] According to this model, people at the preconventional level make moral decisions based on avoiding punishment by authorities or on satisfying their own needs; morally right behavior is defined in terms of what brings satisfaction to oneself. An example of this level is the choice to behave in a particular way primarily to avoid punishment; another is generous or kind acts toward others primarily for the resulting good feelings within oneself. Individuals at the conventional level choose their moral options according to customary societal norms, in order to obtain the approval of others, or to preserve social harmony; right action is defined as loyalty to others and respect for law and order. At the postconventional level of moral development, one relies on internalized personal principles of responsibility or on principles believed to be universally valid; right action is defined in terms of general principles chosen independently. The literary portraits we have of Socrates, Jesus, and Gandhi suggest their highly principled morality at the third level. Understood in Kohlberg's way, we may expect to discover people who make their moral judgments ranging from reliance upon external authorities to carefully selected, internalized principles. In fact, a given individual might make social-moral decisions at the preconventional level, establish business-moral conclusions at the conventional level, and develop political-moral resolutions at the postconventional level.

The Moral Situation

A moral situation involves moral agents—human beings who act, are empowered to make choices, and consciously make decisions. As moral agents, demands are made on us and place us under obligations: we have both duties and rights. We are faced with moral alternatives, and we can better weigh those alternatives when we have an understanding of the ingredients of the moral situation.

RIGHTS AND DUTIES

"We generally understand 'human right' to mean a kind of universal moral right that belongs equally to all human beings simply by virtue of the fact that they *are* human beings."[3] Human rights are *universal* rights and should be contrasted with *legal* or *civil* rights.[4] For example, it might be argued that parents have a moral right to their grown children's care should they become old or infirm or for some reason unable to care for themselves. Most people would, as a result of this view, hold that children of such parents have a moral *duty* to aid their parents. Rights and duties are reciprocal: I have a right to my life and therefore have a duty *not* to take away your life. The same holds for my property. As regards *legal* rights, under the U.S. Constitution I have the right to free speech. I also have the duty to exercise that right such that other citizens may also exercise free speech, even when their expressions oppose my most cherished convictions. Rights and duties go hand in hand and are frequently the subject of debate in moral situations.

VIRTUES AND VICES

In society, certain approved traits, such as unselfishness, honesty, courage, and self-control, are almost universally encouraged; these qualities are called virtues. Other characteristics, such as treachery, murder, theft, and cheating are regarded as undesirable; these failings are called vices. The virtues and vices of one's own society is another fact of life at a particular time in history.

AGREEMENTS AND LAWS

One way for a group of people to protect their rights and lead an orderly social life is through agreements, including understandings, principles, and laws. All human societies have well-established rules of procedure. Some agreements are embedded in the customs of the group and are taken for granted; others are formally recognized, such as codes of law; still others may be subjects for discussion (e.g., whether to take one's pet on a family trip).

CHANGES IN MORALS

Morals evolve, as do social life and institutions. Moral standards may be the customs of primitive humans or the carefully reasoned theories of modern life. A society's moral practices and standards are influenced by its stage of social development, its general level of intelligence, and the knowledge (including new information from the social and biological sciences) available to its citizens. That moral insights and codes change, however slowly, is another ingredient in the moral situation.

ASSESSING MORALITY

Finding the right course of action, choosing the right alternative, is not always simple. When conflicts of interest arise, the solution may require the greatest intelligence and goodwill, and even then we may doubt whether we have acted rightly. In judging conduct we have to consider **motives, means,** and **consequences.**

Motives. Motives, as Jesus, Kant, and others have pointed out, are basic for a determination of morality. A good motive is a prerequisite to conduct that we approve without qualification. If a good motive is present when an act, through some unforeseen factor, leads to harmful effects, we tend to disapprove less severely and to say, "Anyway, he meant well."

Kant, for example, defined the good as the "good will." "Nothing can possibly be conceived in the world, or even out of it, which can be called good, without qualification, except a good will."[5] For Kant, a rational being strives to do what he or she *ought* to do and this is to be distinguished from an act that a person does from either inclination or self-interest. In other words, a person must act out of **duty** to the moral law—that is, do what one ought to do. The truly moral act, for Kant, not only agrees with the moral law, but is done for the sake of the moral law—not only *as* duty requires but *because* duty requires. In Kantian thinking the seat of moral worth is the individual's will, and the good will acts out of a sense of duty.

Means. Just as there may be many motives for desiring something, there may be many means for achieving it. The term *means* can be defined as an agency, instrument, or method used to attain an end. Though we expect people to use the best available means to carry out their purposes, we condemn them if their choice of means impresses us as unjust, cruel, or immoral. On rare occasions we may approve of an act when means are used that under other conditions would be condemned. However, there is a danger in proposing that any means may be used, provided the end is good, or that "the end justifies the means." Once chosen, the means become part of the general effect of an act.

Consequences.   Consequences are the effects or results of a moral decision based on a value. We expect the consequences of an act that we call "right" to be good. Ordinarily, when people ask, "What is right?" they are thinking about the consequences of the action. This depends on what ethical principle is in operation. Kant agrees to the good motive, utilitarians to the result. In general, society judges conduct "right" if it proceeds from a good motive, through the use of the best available means, to consequences that are good. If these conditions are not fulfilled, we condemn the action or approve it with reservations. We rarely approve an action when the results are evil or wrong.

Ethics: The Study of Morality

CLARIFICATION OF TERMS AND CATEGORIES

♦ ♦ ♦ ♦ ♦ ♦ ♦ ♦ ♦ ♦

The terms *morals* and *ethics* are closely related in their original meanings. The former comes from the Latin *moralis,* and the latter from the Greek *ethos.* Both mean "the custom or way of life." Modern usage of *morality* refers to conduct itself and *ethics* (or moral philosophy) to the study of moral conduct. We speak of "a moral act" and "an ethical code."

The word *right* comes from the Latin *rectus,* meaning "straight" or "in line." It implies conformity to some standard. The term *good* applies to that which has desirable qualities, satisfies some need, or has value for human beings.

In **descriptive ethics,** we consider the actual conduct of individuals—or personal morality—and of groups—or social morality. This purely descriptive examination is distinguished from

normative ethics, which is concerned with the principles by which we *ought* to live. From the time of the early Greeks, principles of explanation have been formulated and ethical theories have been set forth. Plato expressed the importance of these principles more than two thousand years ago: "For you do see, Callicles, that our conversation is on the subject which should engage the most serious attention of anyone who has a particle of intelligence: in what way should one live one's life."[6] The highest values by which moral judgments are made are often referred to as *norms, principles, ideals,* or *standards.* For example, happiness is chosen by some philosophers as the highest value by which we should judge morality; happiness may also be regarded as a norm, a principle, an ideal, or a standard. As one considers this norm, one might develop additional principles consistent with happiness, such as pleasure.

Norms regarded as absolute are unchanging moral certainties; in this view there are absolute moral truths to which we must adhere in all situations.

There is also the area of critical ethics, or **metaethics.** Here interest is centered on the analysis and meaning of the terms and language used in ethical discourse and the kind of reasoning used to justify ethical statements. This area has received considerable emphasis in recent years, and involves highly technical issues. We shall be more concerned with normative ethics, as we seek to establish criteria by which individuals can judge whether an action should be regarded as right or wrong.

A Variety of Ethical Standards— Normative Ethics

♦ ♦ ♦ ♦ ♦ ♦ ♦ ♦ ♦ ♦ ♦

Awareness of the moral situation leads us to the issue of ethical standards. Ethical standards are principles by which we judge whether a moral action is right or wrong; examples are statute law, religious authority, public opinion, or conscience. These standards often conflict; we need to have a hierarchy of values to help us make satisfactory moral decisions.

Since the time of the early Greeks and Hebrews, humanity has been reflecting on the principles and problems of right and wrong. Ethical thought has been expressed in many forms. Some that have been influential and that have persisted include the writings about pleasure such as those of Epicurus; the philosophy of Kant, the ablest representative of principles of duty and obligation; John Stuart Mill, the outstanding proponent of utilitarianism; and Plato, the supreme humanist. Other standards have stressed civil law, self-realization, or religious ideals.

PLEASURE OR HAPPINESS AS THE ETHICAL STANDARD

Teleological ethical theories are those that judge conduct as right or wrong in relationship to some end or goal considered good. The doctrine that pleasure or happiness is the greatest good in life has been known by three labels: **hedonism,** *Epicureanism,* and *utilitarianism.* The first of these is derived from the Greek word for "pleasure"; **Epicureanism** is named for Epicurus (see biography and excerpt, pp. 122–123) an early Greek exponent of the pleasure theory; since the time of Jeremy Bentham (see biography and excerpt, pp. 124–125) and John Stuart Mill in the nineteenth century, the term **utilitarianism** has been used.

According to John Stuart Mill (1806–1873), utilitarianism "accepts as the foundation of morals, Utility, or the Greatest Happiness Principle, which holds that actions are right in proportion as they tend to promote happiness, wrong as they tend to produce the reverse of happiness."[7] Mill's brief but brilliant treatise *Utilitarianism* should be read by all students of moral philosophy. Mill accepted the general position of Jeremy Bentham (1748–1832), who used the phrase "the greatest happiness of the greatest number." Bentham asserted that nature has placed humans under the guidance of two masters, pleasure and pain. Humans are "pleasure-seeking, pain-avoiding" creatures. Bentham stated his theory in quantitative terms and hoped to establish utilitarian ethics on a strictly scientific basis. In answering the criticisms directed against Bentham's position, Mill modified the position and added some new elements.

The most important change that Mill made in utilitarianism was to add a qualitative standard. Human beings with refined faculties are not satisfied with the pleasures of the body; they seek the higher pleasures of the mind. The pleasure of the intellect, of feelings and imagination, and of the moral sentiments have a higher value than the pleasures of sensation. Although Mill had referred to these higher pleasures originally to answer the critics of utilitarianism, his concern over higher pleasures led him to criticize the very foundation of Bentham's doctrine of utility: he said that "it would be absurd that . . . the estimation of pleasures should be supposed to depend on quantity alone." Once an individual has lived on a higher level, he or she can never wish to sink into a lower level of existence. This is because of the human sense of dignity. "It is better to be a human being dissatisfied than a pig satisfied; better to be Socrates dissatisfied than a fool satisfied."

Mill vigorously defended utilitarianism against the charge that it encourages selfishness. He maintained that the good of all, or the greatest happiness of the greatest number, must be the standard of what is right in conduct. Because we live in an unjust society, some have to sacrifice themselves for the happiness of others. Such sacrifice is not an end in itself; it is a means to the greater happiness of a larger number of people. Although all people may not actually seek happiness, they ought to do so. To promote not individual pleasure but the greatest total happiness is the essence of Mill's position.

THE MORAL LAW AS THE ABSOLUTE

One of the great systems of ethics was formulated by Immanuel Kant (1724–1804) (see biography and excerpt, pp. 126–127). To

Epicurus

Epicurus (371–270 B.C.E.), a Greek philosopher, founded the school of thought called *Epicureanism*. Before opening his school in Athens, he studied with followers of Plato and Democritus. The school, later called *The Garden,* accepted women and slaves. This policy, combined with Epicurus' teachings concerning pleasure, led to public criticism of the school as a place of the sexual excesses practiced among many hedonists of the day.

Actually, life in the school was fairly austere. Epicurus taught that pleasure and happiness (and the avoidance of pain) are the natural purpose of life; people should forget their fear of gods and punishment after death and live for pleasure. However, pleasures of the mind are superior to sensual pleasures; physical enjoyments are not even possible without mental pleasures. If pleasures of the mind are truly wise, then physical pleasures will be prudent as well.

Epicurus viewed all areas of life within the context of this world. His many writings encompassed a broad system of thought. Of these, however, only three letters and several fragments have survived.

Excerpt from Epicurus:

Principal Doctrines (c. 310 B.C.E.)

I. The blessed and immortal nature knows no trouble itself nor causes trouble to any other, so that it is never constrained by anger or favour. For all such things exist only in the weak.

II. Death is nothing to us: for that which is dissolved is without sensation; and that which lacks sensation is nothing to us.

III. The limit of quantity in pleasures is the removal of all that is painful. Wherever pleasure is present, as long as it is there, there is neither pain of body nor of mind, nor of both at once.

IV. Pain does not last continuously in the flesh, but the acutest pain is there for a very short time, and even that which just exceeds the pleasure in the flesh does not continue for many days at once. But chronic illnesses permit a predominance of pleasure over pain in the flesh.

V. It is not possible to live pleasantly without living prudently and honourably and justly, not again to live a life of prudence, honour, and justice without living pleasantly. And the man who does not possess the pleasant life, is not living prudently and honourably and justly, and the man who does not possess the virtuous life, cannot possibly live pleasantly.

VI. To secure protection from men anything is a natural good, by which you may be able to attain this end.

VII. Some men wish to become famous and conspicuous, thinking that they would thus win for themselves safety from other men. Wherefore if the life of such men is safe, they have obtained the good which nature craves; but if it is not safe, they do not possess that for which they strove at first by instinct of nature.

VIII. No pleasure is a bad thing in itself: but the means which produce some pleasures bring with them disturbances many times greater than the pleasures.

IX. If every pleasure could be intensified so that it lasted and influenced the whole organism or the most essential parts of our nature, pleasures would never differ from one another.

W. Oates, ed., *The Stoic and Epicurean Philosophers* (New York: Random House, 1940).

Jeremy Bentham

Jeremy Bentham (1748–1832) was born in London, studied at Oxford University, then entered Lincoln's Inn to study law. Although law was his major concern throughout his life, he never practiced law, but set himself the task of reforming both civil and criminal law, which he considered harsh, antiquated, obscure, and expensive. Bentham wrote many thousands of pages, including pamphlets on a variety of subjects. The major work published during his lifetime was *Introduction to the Principles of Morals and Legislation* (1789). Bentham is a widely recognized leader of the English Utilitarians and a proponent of the view that we should judge ideas, actions, and institutions on the basis of their utility or usefulness, or their ability to produce happiness. Other writings include *Manual of Political Economy* (1793) and *Panopticon* (1791).

appreciate Kant fully, we need to read his ethical writings, especially *The Fundamental Principles of the Metaphysics of Morals* and *Critique of Practical Reason.* Kant's moral philosophy is sometimes called **formalism,** because he was looking for moral principles that are inherently right or wrong apart from any particular circumstances. These moral principles, or laws, according to Kant, are recognized immediately or directly as true and binding. This approach, in contrast with the **teleological** theories (sometimes referred to as "consequentialist" because of their emphasis on ends or results), is one representative of normative ethical theories called **deontological.** *Deon* is the Greek word for "duty." Both the Judeo-Christian ethic and that of Kant primarily emphasize duty and obligation.

Kant inherited the Christian reverence for divine law and the worth of the individual self. He also was profoundly influenced by the Greek and the eighteenth-century respect for reason. According to Kant, moral philosophy is properly concerned not with what is, but with what ought to be. Each of us possesses a sense of duty, the "I ought," or the moral law, which is logically prior to experience and which springs from our innermost nature. The moral law brings us into contact with the order of the universe itself, because the laws of nature and the laws of reason are essentially one.

Next to the moral law, or the sense of duty, Kant emphasized the good motive, or the good will, as central. "Nothing can possibly be conceived in the world, or even out of it, which can be called good without qualification, except a Good Will." Intelligence and courage are usually

Excerpt from Bentham:

The Principles of Morals and Legislation (1789)

The principle of utility is the foundation of the present work: it will be proper therefore at the outset to give an explicit and determinate account of what is meant by it. By the principle of utility is meant that principle which approves or disapproves of every action whatsoever; according to the tendency which it appears to have to augment or diminish the happiness of the party whose interest is in question: or, what is the same thing in other words, to promote or oppose that happiness. I say of every action whatsoever; and therefore not only of every action of a private individual, but of every measure of government.

By utility is meant that property in any object, whereby it tends to produce benefit, advantage, pleasure, good, or happiness . . . or to prevent the happening of mischief, pain, evil, or unhappiness to the party whose interest is considered: if that party be the community in general, then the happiness of the community: if a particular individual, then the happiness of that individual.

J. Bentham, *On Government and an Introduction to the Principles of Morals and Legislation*, ed. W. Harrison (Oxford: Basil Blackwell, 1948).

good, but they may be used to promote evil. Happiness may be gained in ignoble ways: we may contribute to charity because we want publicity or lack the courage to refuse requests. The good will is the dutiful will, which acts solely out of respect for the principle of duty. If an individual acts from a good motive, the act is good regardless of the consequences. Kant did not say that consequences are not to be considered or that they are unimportant; he did say that the moral quality of the act is not determined by the consequences.

If the will or the motive is governed by reason and not by mere desire, it is absolute and unconditional—that is, obeying it is one's duty, admitting of no exceptions. This call to duty that comes from within is the moral law, or, to use Kant's phrase, "the categorical imperative."

He gives us three criteria, or formulations, of the moral law.

The Principle of Universality. "Act in conformity with that maxim, and that maxim only, which you can at the same time will to be a universal law." Actions should spring not from desires or inclinations but only from principles that can be universalized. Kant uses the example of the man who, after a series of misfortunes, contemplates suicide. When he attempts to universalize such behavior, he realizes at once that it cannot be approved. If everyone were to commit suicide, it would lead to the elimination of humanity. Kant universalized the general type of conduct and not the particular act under particular circumstances. The latter interpretation might lead to extreme laxness; the former leads

Immanuel Kant

Immanuel Kant (1724–1804) was a little man, physically frail, whose life was an undeviating routine of meals, daily walks, lectures, hours of reflection, and writing. He seldom ventured beyond the city of his birth, Königsberg, and never went outside the province, East Prussia, Germany. Yet in his thinking, he was a giant. His thoughts and writings brought a far-reaching revolution in modern philosophy. He was influenced by the pietism of his mother, but he lived in an age of skepticism and read the works of skeptics like Voltaire and Hume; consequently his problem became: What can we know? What is the nature and what are the limits of human knowledge? Kant spent most of his life investigating the knowing process and studying the relation among the logical processes of thought, the external world, and the reality of things. Since his time, philosophers have had to consider and reckon with his arguments.

Although Kant's minor writings are many and encompass a variety of topics, his major works are his three critiques: *Critique of Pure Reason* (1781), which discusses reason and the knowing process, on which he worked for fifteen years and which startled the philosophic world; *Critique of Practical Reason* (1788), which sets forth his moral philosophy; and *Critique of Judgment* (1790), which supplements the earlier critiques and depicts nature as purposive in its laws.

to a rigorism that admits few if any exceptions to moral principles.

The Principle of Humanity as an End, Never as Merely a Means.

"Act so as to use humanity, whether in your own person or in the person of another, always as an end, never as merely a means." This principle has received more widespread approval than any other part of Kant's moral philosophy. People, as rational beings, are ends in themselves and should never be used merely as means to other ends. We may use physical things as means, but when we use people simply as means, as in slavery, prostitution, or commercial exploitation, we degrade them and violate their innermost beings as people.

The Principle of Autonomy.

The moral laws that we obey are not imposed on us from the outside. They are the laws that we impose on ourselves. The sense of duty and the reason that we obey come from within; they are expressions of our higher selves.

SELF-REALIZATION AS THE IDEAL

The theory of self-realization considers as right that which tends to promote the development of all the normal capacities of humans as thinking, feeling, and acting individuals. Many able philosophers in both ancient and modern times have subscribed to this theory. It has frequently been referred to as *humanism* and has two es-

Since my purpose here is directed to moral philosophy, I narrow the proposed question to this: Is it not of the utmost necessity to construct a pure moral philosophy which is completely freed from everything which may be only empirical and thus belong to anthropology? That there must be such a philosophy is self-evident from the common idea of duty and moral laws. Everyone must admit that a law, if it is to hold morally, i.e., as a ground of obligation, must imply absolutely necessity; he must admit that the command, "Thou shalt not lie," does not apply to men only, as if other rational beings had no need to observe it. The same is true for all other moral laws properly so called. He must concede that the ground of obligation here must be sought in the nature of man or in the circumstances in which he is place, but sought a priori solely in the concepts of pure reason, and that every other precept which rests on principles of mere experience, even a precept which is in certain respects universal, so far as it leans in the least on empirical grounds, may be called a practical rule but never a moral law.

I. Kant, *Fundamental Principles of the Metaphysic of Morals,* trans. T. Abbott (Indianapolis: Bobbs-Merrill, 1949).

---

sential characteristics. First, it does justice to the entire nature of humanity. Enjoyment of pleasure, on which the hedonists build their theories is only one part of our nature. A sense of justice is equally our concern. Second, the ethics of humanism finds its center in humanity and does not reduce people to a fragment of some larger whole—whether nature, society, or God.

Platonic Humanism. In his great work, *The Republic,* and in other writings, Plato says that there are three active principles within humans. There is, first, the rational part; this is the mind, or intellect, the proper function of which is to rule other parts of the soul. Reason alone comprehends the true nature of things. There is, second, the "spirited" part; this includes the emotions and is the seat of the heroic virtues. There are, third, the appetites, or the desiring part. There is no order within the human soul except as the appetites and emotions are controlled by reason. Each part or function has its proper place and role in life, and when the three parts operate in harmony, each carrying out its own function, there is order and peace.

Aristotle and Self-Realization. Aristotle, in his *Nicomachean Ethics,* wrote the first systematic treatise on ethics. Reason, well-being, and moderation are central concepts. Just as the excellence of the sculptor lies in the skill with which she or he applies his art, so the excellence of humans lies in the fulfillment of their function as human beings. The function peculiar to humans is their life of reason. They should live a life that fully actualizes their rational capacities, and by principles that best express what it means to be a human being.

According to Aristotle, human action should aim at its proper end. Everywhere people aim at pleasure, wealth, and glory. But none of these ends, although they have value, can occupy the place of the chief good for which we should aim. To be an ultimate end, an act must be self-sufficient and final—"that which is always desirable itself and never for the sake of something else"—and it must be attainable. Aristotle seemed certain that all people would agree that happiness is the only end that meets all the requirements for the ultimate end of action. Indeed, we choose pleasure, wealth, and glory only because we think that "through their instrumentality we shall be happy." Happiness, it turns out, is another name for the good for human beings; like the good, happiness is the fulfillment of our distinctive function as human beings—our self-realization. The highest good is *eudaemonia,* or well-being. The good life avoids the extremes of both excessive repression and excessive indulgence. The good life involves the harmonious development of the normal functions of the organism. The theory of self-realization has emphasized the development of all the functions of the person as the greatest good. Nothing short of the harmonious development of all sides of human nature can be accepted as a satisfactory standard.

Classical Moral Philosophy. Plato and Aristotle's use of reason to discover moral truths is representative of *classical moral philosophy.* Ethical absolutes, like the certainties of their notions of geometry, may be determined rationally; after self-evident moral norms are established by means of disciplined reflection, other moral principles can be deduced logically. (John Locke, a seventeenth-century philosopher, argued that all rational persons would agree on those self-evident moral absolutes.)

NATURAL LAW ETHICS

The medieval period (thirteenth century C.E.) revived interest in Aristotle by showing the compatibility of Aristotelian thought with Christian dogma. At the center of medieval ethics was the concept of natural law. This ethic stemmed from Aristotle's view of nature as *teleological*—as having a purpose and end. According to these thinkers, there is an inherent tendency in the nature of man expressed in moral conscience and informed reason; by conforming to this nature, man fulfills the commands of God as revealed in the Scriptures. *Natural law is the divine law as discovered by reason;* the teachings of the Church and the Bible, therefore, are a standard of ethical judgment. Today, belief in natural law ethics is the basis for the Roman Catholic Church's position on abortion and birth control as well as homosexuality.

RELIGIOUS ETHICAL IDEALS: JEWISH AND CHRISTIAN NORMATIVE VIEWS

There are two broad types of religious ethics, and these two approaches are found in Judaism, Christianity, and other religions. The first view is that ethical duties neither have nor need a justification or reason beyond the fact that they are God's will. This keeps ethics strictly theological and requires that it be expressed in theological concepts. The more conservative form of this approach is a biblical literalism in which religion is viewed as a final body of truth that has been completely revealed. All we need to do is to discover this truth through reading the sacred writings, and obey its laws. God does not require certain things because they are right; they are right because God requires them. The task of ethics is to ascertain what God expects us to do.

According to the second type of religious ethics, we are inspired by our view of humanity and of God and our love of God to discover the good and to live so as to achieve it. Loyalty to Christ or to God means leading the best possible life in the situation in which we find ourselves. The religious or ethical spirit is best expressed as a supreme concern for people. We discover through experience and growing knowledge the tasks that we need to do; then we view these tasks as part of our duty to God. Religion is thus a strong motivating force, emphasizing both purity of motive and the continuous quest for a more abundant life for all.

Judaism. The ethical ideals of Judaism are based on the Hebrew Bible (Law, Prophets, and Writings) and the belief in **ethical monotheism,** or the doctrine of the "One only and Holy God" who has disclosed his righteous will for all to follow. Religion and morality are bound together; Judaism is a way of life that has to do with the individual, the home and family, and the welfare of the group as a whole. To do God's will, one must "do justly, love mercy, and walk humbly with God." Truth, justice, faithfulness, and loving kindness are stressed. Depending on the branch of Judaism, the emphasis varies from strict obedience to the revealed Law among the more orthodox to an emphasis on the changing experiences and needs of people as they seek fulfillment in today's world.

Christianity. Christian ethics regards ethics and religion as inseparable. To live the good life is to obey God. Central to all Christian ethics have been the teachings of Jesus as found in the New Testament. Jesus swept aside many old requirements that did not appear to have a vital relation to persons or to human need and welfare. Jesus brought together certain central convictions of morality and religion in a simple and direct fashion and exemplified them in his own life. Inheriting a rich legacy of morality from Judaism, he gave it a different emphasis. He took the rather exclusive nationalistic morality of his day and made it into a universal morality that embraced all humankind.

Central to the ethical teachings of Jesus is his emphasis on the value of the self, or person. Individuals are treated as ends in themselves. Humans, who are seen in relation to God, are of greater value than anything else. When asked a question regarding the observance of the Sab-

bath, the most sacred of institutions at that time, Jesus replied, "The Sabbath was made for man, not man for the Sabbath." Only people are ends in themselves; all other things are means.

For Jesus morality was inner and positive, a matter of the "heart" or a disposition of the feeling and will. Goodness resided not simply in obedience to The Law, but in one's heart. Love was the supreme virtue. When asked about the great commandments, Jesus said, "Thou shalt love the Lord thy God with all thy heart, and with all thy soul, and with all thy mind, and with all thy strength; this is the first commandment. And the second is like, namely this, Thou shalt love thy neighbor as thyself. There is none other commandment greater than these." Love of God and love of other humans is required. Each of us is under an obligation to promote the interests of the other people with whom we come in contact. Mutual love, unselfishness, humility, equal regard, and generosity of spirit received a new emphasis in human relations. As a general rule, Christian ethics has included belief in God's grace (gift) as necessary for human beings to behave morally; people are unable by their unassisted efforts to be good.

Throughout history, some Christians have thought that Christian ethics is a repository of absolute truth revealed by God. For an increasingly large number of Christians, however, the Christian life is a loving concern for the welfare of persons under the inspiration of devotion to the ideals of Jesus. We are thus encouraged to discover the tasks that need to be done and then to view these tasks as part of our duty to God and to our fellows.

Approaches to Ethical Standards

There are three quite different approaches to the problems of morality. The first, called absolutism, is to hold to some belief or line of conduct and to appeal to some absolute authority for its support. The second is to claim that morality is entirely relative and that there are no fixed moral standards; the ethical relativists regard morality as a matter of personal or group opinion, preference, or custom. The third approach is situation ethics: a norm is applied to situations, each somewhat unique and perhaps calling for varying applications of the norm; the situational approach is often confused with relativism, which acknowledges no norm.

AUTHORITY

Reliance on authority has been widespread in human history. The authoritarian was almost entirely in control in the past, and even today most people behave as though right conduct means conduct in obedience to some established authority. For some people, it is a matter of habit and inertia; they are glad to let others do the thinking or deciding for them, because they do not want to assume the responsibility. Others want the assurance of certainty that comes when they invest some established authority with final wisdom and infallibility.

Many authorities have been chosen. They include custom and tradition, moral codes, creedal statements, churches and other institutions, sacred literature or some portion of it, natural law, commands of the state or of "divinely ordained" rulers, statute law, or the word of some individual.

Much of our knowledge is gained through the testimony of others, or from authority, and authority that is open to free and honest examination is a legitimate source of knowledge under certain circumstances. Authority accepted without regard for the extent to which it harmonizes with one's experience and reason, however, is a dangerous thing and is regarded by some philosophers as fallacious. Today, we live under rapidly changing conditions, and we face problems about which the ancient authorities were silent. They did not tell us whether it is right to prosecute homosexuality as criminal behavior, to impeach a president of the United States, to grant amnesty to those who refuse to fight in what they regard as an unjust war, or to withhold life-support from a severely impaired infant. Authoritarian ethics are likely to delay progress in a changing society. They also are likely to be destructive of a sound moral perspective; acts are condemned because they violate the code rather than because they are injurious to human welfare. Whatever tends to discredit the authority tends to discredit all its pronouncements, leaving no system at all.

Many people in our society accept custom or public opinion as the basis of right and wrong. Although many customs are beneficial insofar as they represent a sort of collective wisdom, custom may not be a good gauge of morality. To accept custom and tradition as the standard is to submerge the individual's morality to that of society. In the past, progress has come mainly through some individual's challenging the customary actions of the group.

Divine law in one of its forms is not as certain a standard as it may appear to be at first. Even if we decide that it is right to do the "will of God," there is no set of rules that can be identified as "God's will." The codes and commands attributed to God are diverse, and they have changed with the development of society. Many modern religious leaders say that God inspires us to discover the good and to live in pursuit of it. They do not think of religious ethics as an authoritarian and fixed system.

The role of authority has been weakening in modern society, partly because of the influences of the Renaissance, the Reformation, modern science, the democratic spirit (which stresses the worth of people and their right to think and judge for themselves), historical studies, and rapid changes in our life and work.

RELATIVISM

The position that rejects ethical absolutism and the appeal to any external authority is **ethical relativism**—the view that there are no fixed moral values. Some people, having rejected the older authorities, have discovered no new ones that they believe have any objective validity. Many people also have been influenced by the findings of anthropologists, sociologists, and psychologists concerning the great diversity of moral practices and codes found among the cultures of the world.[8] Human views of what is right and wrong vary over time and from place to place. Morals, ethical relativists assert, come from the *mores,* the folkways that have grown up and are considered the right ways.

The ethical relativists claim that there are no standards accepted by all people everywhere and that custom can make anything appear right. They do not merely say that what some people *think* is right in one place or at one time is *thought* to be wrong by some other people in another time or at another place; they claim that what *is* right at one time or place *is* wrong at another time or place (or even at the same time and place, if judgments differ) because there are no objective or universal standards.

Subjectivism. Ethical relativism holds that all ethical norms and pronouncements originate in the human intellect or emotions and are therefore subjective. There is nothing about moral standards that is objective or independent of human experiences; there are no moral absolutes. Moral principles are not divinely revealed, built into nature, or rationally self-evident. Value statements, including moral values and their diverse elaborations, express only sentiments or feelings.[9]

APPEAL TO THE SITUATION

In the 1960s, especially in the United States and Great Britain, philosophers have been interested in **situation ethics.** It has appeared in various forms and has often been confused with relativism; proponents see it as a middle ground between two extreme approaches: absolution and relativism.

On the one hand, absolutism in its legalistic application consists of final codes, prefabricated rules, and regulations that permit few if any exceptions. These absolutes are derived philosophically through reason (Kant); through divine revelation in the form of natural laws; or through consensus, tradition, and laws enacted by human beings.

On the other hand, schools of relativism stress freedom from all norms other than what is the practiced morality of a given time. This view is concerned not with the rightness or wrongness of what is chosen, but with what actually has been chosen and is practiced in a given culture.

In theory, situation ethics has an absolute norm or standard; this approach calls for the selection or acknowledgment of an absolute, but a nonlegalistic, flexible application of the standard to each individual situation. This norm could be love, personal power, or any other principle around which one could build an interpretation of morality. Guidelines that assist in the application of the selected norm may or may not be included in a given interpretation. For example, a certain dictator views personal power as his moral absolute; if he takes a situational approach, he reflects on every situation in which he finds himself and involves himself such as to acquire personal power. He may or may not have useful guides in mind as he enters new situations.

The uproar that occurred in religious circles in the 1960s was the result of a view interpreting Jesus as a situationist. Many Christians understood the Old and New Testaments as containing clear-cut moral laws. Some scholars now claim that Christian ethics is situational, not authoritarian in the legalistic sense. Advocates of this position respect the ethical maxims and the wisdom that have come down from the past. As Joseph Fletcher proposed in his controversial book *Situation Ethics:*

> The situationist enters into every decision-making situation fully armed with the ethical maxims of his community and its heritage, and he treats them with respect as illuminators of his problems. Just the same he is prepared in any situation to compromise them or set them aside *in the situation* if love seems better served by doing so.[10]

For these Christians, the only absolute is love (*agapé*); only love is universally good. "Anything and everything is right or wrong, according to the situation," says Fletcher, because the good is the most loving, concerned act.[11] Love can rightly be directed only toward a person and not toward some abstract good.

The supporters of situation ethics claim that many cases or decisions are unique and must be considered on their merits. This approach allows freedom in a changing society. Ethical judgments are meaningless apart from the benefiting or the injuring of persons. The critics, on the other hand, say the view that circumstances alter cases is as old as Aristotle. In its modern form, perhaps situationism places too great an emphasis on the motive and attitude of the one who makes the decision and carries out the action, and not enough on the fact that we always act within a community that is affected by our acts. Love can be blind and uninformed; it may be prudent to add some principles or guidelines based on knowledge and reason.

Contemporary Principles

◆ ◆ ◆ ◆ ◆ ◆ ◆ ◆ ◆ ◆ ◆

A DILEMMA

If the question of morality is the central issue of our time, we may appear to have a dilemma! On the one hand, we might agree on such matters as the levels of moral development, ingredients of the moral situation, and the many basic terms and categories of ethics. On the other hand, philosophers and other reflective people have never agreed on a method for *doing* normative ethics. Varying methods employing reason, inferences from nature, divine revelation, and/or intuition have led to contrasting moral standards both ancient and modern. Where does this variety leave us as we attempt to make sound moral choices individually and as a society?

PRINCIPLES IN USE TODAY

Hospital ethics committees—often composed of nurses, physicians, clergy, ethicists, lawyers, and others—would never be able to offer advice or make decisions if consensus on the many issues we have been studying were required. Instead, several principles have been widely adopted, be-cause they seem to offer practical guidance for discussion of specific cases. These principles are justified on the grounds that their opposites are repugnant to the cross section of people wrestling with moral dilemmas. For some persons on a committee, these principles are of divine origin; for others, they are reasonable; and, for others, they are built into human nature or the very fabric of reality. For some individuals, these norms are absolutes; for others, they function as highly valued guidelines. In all instances, the meanings of the principles must be interpreted and applied, and sharp differences frequently remain.

Respect For Persons. There is, however, one clear area of agreement: human beings should be treated as subjects, not objects; human life is of significant value. This principle is essentially the same as Kant's *Principle of Humanity as an End, Never as Merely a Means* (see page 126). A primary value of this norm is that it excludes its opposite—treating individuals as objects, as things, whether in medical research, business activities, or social relationships. However, this standard's application to specific situations of health care, employment, or human relationships is subject to debate and may result in more than one reasoned conclusion. For example, when an employer must fire 10 percent of her employees for legitimate financial reasons, how does *respect for persons* apply to issues of age, seniority, gender, competence, severance pay and benefits, possibilities for future recall, personal and vocational counseling, and so forth? Although different policies will result from the application of this principle, at least employees will be treated as human beings instead of mere numbers or objects. The final choice of policies will be made according to the decision-making process in place, such as a negotiated compromise, a management committee, the "boss," or the courts.

May this principle ever be set aside? If a maniac is about to lower an ax on your head, are you morally obliged to respect this person? One might affirm the principle and call for martyrdom of the intended victim. Others might claim that such attackers have waived their rights to personhood and may be killed in self-defense. No doubt other reasoned options are possible; in this situation, the intended victim is the decision maker, who will be accountable morally and legally afterward.

The following principles are equally difficult to apply; our discussion of them will be brief.

Autonomy. Human beings deserve personal liberty in order to make informed judgments and decisions about their lives; individual informed consent is valued. Women and men should be self-determining within the context of their own societies. (Note Kant's principle of autonomy; see page 126.)

As with the principle of humanity as an end, the ideal of autonomy rejects its opposite—absolute external control. However, the degrees of autonomy in actual situations are subject to debate; to what extent should autonomy be offered to prisoners, the mentally ill, children, the military, property owners, and employees? Resolution will occur, according to available decision-making procedures in each case.

Beneficence. Do good; promote goodness! This standard rejects knowingly doing evil.

Nonmaleficence. Do no harm; prevent harm. This principle rejects knowingly doing harm.

Justice. Human beings ought to be provided with what is fair and what is deserved; goodness should be distributed among people in fair and equitable ways. Does this mean distribution according to need? according to merit? or equally without regard for need, ability, or merit? Calculated injustice is ruled out, but arguable interpretations of justice remain.

Honesty. Telling the truth is the norm; it is essential to promote and maintain respect for persons and for autonomy. However, there is a question as to whether a "moral lie" may ever be justified.

Other Principles. In addition to the principles heretofore discussed, others are helpful; they may be viewed as deriving from those we have mentioned or as having equal status. *Informed consent* is the understanding of and consent to a procedure an individual is about to undergo. *Confidentiality* is the restriction of information based on the right to privacy. *Double effect* means that the intended good result requires a secondary harmful or bad effect. *Paternalism* involves the interference with an individual's liberty of action.

WHEN PRINCIPLES COLLIDE

In certain situations, honesty may conflict with confidentiality; for example, a supervisor might not be able to reveal pending dismissals to workers in her department. Autonomy might be in opposition to paternalism, as when adult children face the problem of nursing home placement unwanted by their parents. Beneficence collides with nonmaleficence when individuals defend themselves from unjust agressors. Solutions to such conflicting norms are shaped according to the principle(s) valued most highly by the decision maker(s) in the actual situation.

Reflections

◆ ◆ ◆ ◆ ◆ ◆ ◆ ◆ ◆ ◆

MORAL CERTAINTIES

"I just want to do the right thing," is a familiar statement made by morally concerned women and men. The moral codes of some absolutists are persuasive to people seeking clear-cut ethical certainties. When their absolutes and implications are perceived as divinely revealed, unmistakably located in nature, or discovered by infallible reason, one can live "by the book" with moral clarity.

MORAL RELATIVISM

Other people also wanting to do the right thing propose that the global community will continue to develop contrasting and conflicting moral norms and practices. This observation will lead some individuals to the conclusion that no universal norms are appropriate and the practice of the moment is the only actual norm.

MORAL PLURALISM

Others will formulate and/or choose principles believed universally applicable, principles such as those explored in the previous section of this chapter. Where these ideals originate is less pivotal than our agreement to apply them with utmost care and reasonableness. Hospital, business, political, and educational committees attempting to come to grips with current moral dilemmas are already functioning quite well with these principles. Only those individuals con-vinced that their positions are the only viable ones are difficult to deal with, but they deserve to be heard, too.

"Moral pluralism" refers to the existence of thoughtful, contrasting interpretations of moral matters. The use of moral principles, such as those discussed in this chapter, does not lead to one clear and certain conclusion. For example, a committee might adopt these principles and yet conclude differently about the morality of capital punishment. Schools of thought exist in virtually all areas of human inquiry, including the range of moral issues. Nonetheless, the principles outlined above provide a reasoned framework for moral discourse, a distinct alternative to relativism.

◆ ◆

Glossary Terms

CONSEQUENCES   The effects or results of something occurring earlier.

DEONTOLOGICAL   Refers to theories which hold that right and wrong is determined by true and binding, formal rules of conduct, independently of any consideration of consequences.

DESCRIPTIVE ETHICS   The study of the ingredients of a moral situation, of the actual conduct of individuals, groups, and peoples.

DUTY   Doing what one ought to do.

EPICUREANISM   The doctrine that pleasure (as understood by Epicurus) or freedom from pain is the highest good in life.

ETHICAL MONOTHEISM   The belief in one God who has revealed moral standards all must follow.

ETHICAL RELATIVISM   The view that there are no fixed, universal moral values; also called moral relativism.

ETHICAL STANDARDS   Principles or norms by which moral actions are judged right or wrong.

FORMALISM   Adherence to prescribed forms. In ethics, *formalism* means that certain types of acts follow fixed moral principles, apart from consideration of any particular situation or probable consequences.

HEDONISM   The doctrine that the chief good in life is pleasure.

MEANS   An agency, instrument, or method used to attain an end.

METAETHICS   The study of the meaning of terms and language used in ethical discourse and the kind of reasoning used to justify ethical statements. Differs from *normative* ethics, which is the study of the principles underlying the moral forms of human conduct.

MORAL AGENT   The individual who is participating in a moral situation.

MORAL OUGHT   Used to express duty or moral obligation.

MOTIVE   Whatever it is that prompts a person to act in a certain way or that determines volition (willing).

NORMATIVE ETHICS   The area of ethics that is concerned with principles by which we *ought* to live.

SITUATION ETHICS   According to Joseph Fletcher, the doctrine contending that truly moral actions produce the greatest amount of love possible in each situation; love is the only moral absolute. A version of teleological ethics.

TELEOLOGICAL ETHICS   The theory that the consequences of a moral act determine its rightness or wrongness.

UTILITARIANISM   An ethical theory that claims that utility, in the sense that whatever increases pleasure and decreases pain, should be the aim of acts and the criterion by which we judge them.

VICES   Immoral or evil habits or practices.

VIRTUES   Particular moral excellences; righteousness, goodness.

VOLUNTARY   Done, made, or brought about by one's own accord or by free choice.

◆ ◆

Chapter Review

MORAL JUDGMENTS

1. The question of morality may be the central issue of our time; there is a renewed interest in rethinking goals and values in contemporary society.

2. Kohlberg's levels of moral development are the preconventional, conventional, and postconventional.

THE MORAL SITUATION

1. The moral situation involves moral agents with both rights and duties.

2. Other ingredients in the moral situation are virtues and vices, agreements and laws, and change.

3. In assessing morality we have to consider motives, means, and consequences.

ETHICS: THE STUDY OF MORALITY

1. "Morality" generally refers to conduct itself, whereas "ethics" refers to the study of moral conduct.

2. Ethics includes descriptive ethics, normative ethics, and metaethics.

A VARIETY OF ETHICAL STANDARDS— NORMATIVE ETHICS

1. Ethical standards are principles by which we judge whether a moral action is right or wrong; they include statute law, religious authority, public opinion, and conscience.

2. Teleological ethical theories are those that judge conduct as right or wrong in relationship to some end or goal considered good.

3. Hedonism, epicureanism, and utilitarianism consider pleasure or happiness to be the highest goal. John Stuart Mill denies the criticism that utilitarianism encourages selfishness; he maintains the greatest happiness of the greatest number is the standard of right conduct.

4. Kant proposes a moral philosophy in which principles are either right or wrong, regardless of the situation. This position is sometimes called formalism.

5. Self-realization, often referred to as humanism, promotes the development of humans to the highest possible degree. Platonic humanism and Aristotle's view of self-realization are historically significant.

6. Classical moral philosophy proposed that moral absolutes can be determined rationally.

7. Natural law ethics is based on natural law, which can be discovered by reason.

8. Religious ethical ideals, as found in Judaism and Christianity, include two major views: (1) the will of God is sufficient justification to obey traditional maxims, and (2) the love of God inspires people to do the best to live as caring individuals.

APPROACHES TO ETHICAL STANDARDS

1. Authoritarianism has been a dominant ethical standard. Revered authorities include custom, tradition, churches or other institutions, sacred literature, and statements made by rulers or other individuals.

2. Relativism and subjectivism reject authoritarianism.

3. Situation ethics has been called the middle ground between authoritarianism and relativism. A standard is chosen and then applied to each individual situation.

CONTEMPORARY PRINCIPLES

1. Ethical principles in use today include respect for persons, autonomy, beneficence, nonmalefi- cence, justice, honesty, informed consent, confidentiality, and double effect.

2. When principles collide, the most highly valued principle(s) may lead to solutions for specific situations.

REFLECTIONS

1. Some people appeal to their moral certainties, others to the practice of the moment. Still others formulate or choose moral principles; moral pluralism is inevitable. Nonetheless, we have principles on which we can choose to rely.

◆ ◆

Study Questions and Projects

1. In 1943 the founding author of this textbook, the late Dr. Harold H. Titus (1896–1984), wrote in his book *What Is a Mature Morality?* (New York: Macmillan, 1943, p. 1):

   Many thoughtful persons in our time are speaking of the 'decay' or 'decline' or the 'crisis' of Western Civilization, or of the 'end of an era.' The older moorings and authorities seem to be disintegrating and people find it difficult to build new and stable foundations. Many of the standards and ideals that once were thought to be absolute and eternal are being questioned or disregarded. Many persons do not seem to know where to turn for guidance and direction. We are suffering not so much because of a lack of technology, of science, or even of general education, but because we have lost a sense of the meaning and goals of living.

   Are Professor Titus' words relevant today? Would a reflective person in every generation offer similar comments? What, if anything, is unique about the moral situation today?

2. State in your own words what you consider the basis of the distinction between right and wrong. Are you able to affirm that there is "an independent order of things" which is unaf- fected by human wishes and beliefs and which should play a part in our moral judgments?

3. What is the relation between morality and religion? Does morality depend on religion for support, or does it stand on its own feet in that it is autonomous?

4. If one compares the outlook today with that of some centuries ago, how is one to explain the changed views of most members of society on such questions as hanging for theft, capital punishment, the status of women, slavery, homosexuality as a criminal offense, labor conditions, usury and interest, war, and the like?

5. Discuss the following comment: "Ethics is just a matter of opinion."

6. Evaluate authoritarianism in ethics. When is it advisable to accept the authority of others, and when is it inadvisable or dangerous?

7. What is ethical relativism? What reasons are advanced for it? Evaluate this position critically, indicating its strengths and weaknesses.

8. What are the central points in the following positions: (a) formalism, or Kant's appeal to the

moral law; (b) pleasure as the guide to morality; and (c) the development of persons or self-realization as the moral standard?

9. Discuss situation ethics indicating points of strength and of weakness.

10. In an essay respond to one or more proposals made by philosopher Sissela Bok in her book *Lying: Moral Choice in Public and Private Life* (New York, Pantheon Books, 1978).

11. Select a moral issue in medicine, and write a paper that includes the basic philosophical issues, moral options, and your own conclusions on the issue. (*The Encyclopedia of Bioethics* and "The Hastings Center Report," a bimonthly periodical, are two excellent resources for such topics.)

12. In what sense is one's personal health (nutrition, exercise, chemical intake, balanced diet, leisure, emotions, etc.) an individual and a community moral issue?

◆ ◆

Suggested Readings

Bailey, C. *The Greek Atomists and Epicurus.* New York: Russell and Russell, 1964.

A classic exposition of Epicurus and of the philosophical atomism that preceded him. Epicureanism is almost universally misunderstood; Bailey's book is a good remedy.

Beauchamp, T. L. *Philosophical Ethics.* 2nd ed. New York: McGraw-Hill 1991.

An introductory ethics text in which the author moves freely from case studies and issues in private, professional, and public ethics to various more traditional concerns in ethical theory. Included are works by Mill, Hume, Kant, Sartre, and MacIntyre, among others.

Becker, L. C. (ed.). *A History of Western Ethics.* New York: Garland, 1992.

A collection of original articles by well-known scholars which provide a useful summary of the history of ethics in Western philosophy, ranging from the presocratic Greeks to twentieth-century Americans.

Bok, S. *Lying: Moral Choice in Public and Private Life.* New York: Pantheon, 1978.

Sissela Bok looks at lying and deception in public and private life—in government, medicine, law, academia, journalism, and in the family and between friends. She explores the consequences of lying through concrete situations: white lies, lies to the dying, lies of parents to children, and more.

Frankena, W. *Ethics.* 2nd ed. Englewood Cliffs, N.J.: 1988.

A careful presentation of the main types of ethical theory in modern philosophy.

Gert, B. *Morality: A New Justification of the Moral Rules.* New York: Oxford University Press, 1988.

The author presents a coherent, comprehensive account where he asserts that morality is a public system that applies to all rational persons. Issues of good versus evil, virtue and vice, and morality as impartial rationality are discussed.

Holmes, R. L. *Basic Moral Philosophy.* Belmont, Calif.: Wadsworth, 1993.

An introduction to the main issues and concepts of Western moral philosophy. A clear, systematic approach to ethical theories enables the author to discuss the historical roots and contemporary theories of morality.

Kant, I. *Fundamental Principles of the Metaphysic of Morals.* Trans. L. W. Beck. New York: Bobbs-Merrill, The Library of Liberal Arts, 1959.

One of the most influential ethical treatises ever written.

Kekes, J. *Moral Tradition and Individuality.* Princeton, N.J.: Princeton University Press, 1991.

The author develops the view that a good life depends on maintaining a balance between one's moral tradition and individuality. Moral tradition provides the forms of good lives and the permissible ways of trying to achieve them. Self-knowledge and self-control, he asserts, enable us to realize our aspirations.

Louden, R. B. *Morality and Moral Theory*. New York: Oxford University Press, 1992.

Using insights from both Kant and Aristotle, the author focuses his attention on the importance of moral theory and of morality in general. He asserts that morality serves as a unifying force for structuring and assessing the fabric of our lives.

MacIntyre, A. *After Virtue: A Study in Moral Theory*. 2nd ed. Notre Dame, Ind.: University of Notre Dame Press, 1984.

MacIntyre reveals his dissatisfaction with the conception of "moral philosophy" as an independent area of inquiry. His conclusion that we must reject the modern *ethos*—particularly liberal individualism—to develop a morally defensible standpoint from which to judge and to act.

Mackie, J. L. *Ethics: Inventing Right and Wrong*. New York: Viking Penguin, 1977.

The author uses a systematic approach to discuss the content and status of ethics, considering such issues as moral skepticism, obligation and reason, and consequentialism.

Nolan, R. T., and Kirkpatrick, F. G. *Living Issues in Ethics*. Belmont, Calif.: Wadsworth, 1982. [5th printing 1991].

A companion to *Living Issues in Philosophy,* this text is organized into four parts: The Search for a Moral Philosophy; Personal Identity and Fulfillment; Health and Sexuality; and Social Ethics. Ethical theory is presented in the first part's four chapters.

Rachels, J. *The Elements of Moral Philosophy*. New York: McGraw-Hill, 1992.

An introduction to moral philosophy for those who know nothing about the subject.

Rogerson, K. (ed.). *Introduction to Ethical Theory*. Fort Worth, Tex.: Holt, Rinehart and Winston, 1991.

An introductory anthology focusing on normative ethical theories. The central theme is that ethical theories are more careful, consistent, and coherent versions of familiar ethical ideas. The author hopes to encourage the reader to regard philosophical ethics as a part of everyday experience.

Wagner, M. (ed.). *An Historical Introduction to Moral Philosophy*. Englewood Cliffs, N.J.: Prentice-Hall, 1991.

A collection of essays that approaches moral philosophy as a living tradition best understood by studying the great ideas and thinkers from every major period of Western thought.

Williams, B. *Ethics and the Limits of Philosophy*. Cambridge, Mass.: Harvard University Press, 1985.

A text which offers criticism of current philosophical issues while raising the question of how philosophy could help humankind recreate ethical life. The author introduces a picture of ethical thought with a set of ideas that apply to the current state of ethics while provoking thoughts about how it might be.

Notes

1. Douglas Sloan, quoted in D. Amy, "Teaching the Moral Analysis of Policy Issues," *News for Teachers of Political Science* (Winter 1983):1*ff.*

2. A brief presentation of these levels may be found in Lawrence Kohlberg, "The Claim To Moral Adequacy of a Highest State of Moral Judgment," *The Journal of Philosophy* 70 (1973): 630–46.

3. Morton E. Winston, *The Philosophy of Human Rights* (Belmont, Calif., Wadsworth, 1989), p. 7.

4. See Chapter 8.

5. I. Kant, *Fundamental Principles of the Metaphysics of Morals,* trans. L. W. Beck (New York: Bobbs-Merrill, 1959), p. 9.

6. Plato, *Gorgias* (New York: Liberal Arts Press, 1952), p. 73.

7. J. S. Mill, *Utilitarianism,* ed. Oskar Piest (Indianapolis, Ind.: Bobbs-Merrill, 1957), p. 10.

8. See, for example: W. G. Sumner's *Folkways* (New York: Dover, 1959), E. A. Westermarck's *Ethical Relativity* (New York: Harcourt, Brace and Company, 1932), and J. G. Frazer's *The Golden Bough* (New York: St. Martin's Press, 1966).

9. See discussion of subjective value, in Chapter 6, p. 105.

10. J. Fletcher, *Situation Ethics: The New Morality* (Philadelphia: Westminster, 1966), p. 26.

11. Fletcher, *Situation Ethics,* p. 124. See also H. Cox, ed., *The Situation Ethics Debate* (Philadelphia: Westminster, 1968).

Individual and Social Morality

CHAPTER OBJECTIVES

In this chapter we will address the following questions:

♦ How Do "Human Rights," "Civil Rights," and "Civil Liberties" Differ?

♦ May Civil Disobedience Ever Be Justified?

♦ Are There Limits on Liberty?

♦ Should Morals Be Enforced by the State?

♦ What Are the Basic Philosophical Issues in Medical Ethics, Sexual Ethics, and Business Ethics?

What is freedom and why is it prized? Is desire for freedom inherent in human nature or is it a product of special circumstances? Is it wanted as an end or a means of getting other things? . . . Does freedom in itself and in the things it brings with it seem as important as security of livelihood; as food, shelter, clothing, or even having a good time? Did man ever care as much for it as we in this country have been taught to believe? Is there any truth in the old notion that the driving force in political history has been the effort of the common man to achieve freedom?[1]

A Contemporary Challenge

♦ ♦ ♦ ♦ ♦ ♦ ♦ ♦ ♦ ♦ ♦

As we prepare to enter a new millennium, several issues of individual and societal living remain problematic, all requiring philosophical considerations. Many moral problems continue to form a lively national and global agenda. In this chapter we shall explore some of the philosophical elements in the areas of civil liberties, medical ethics, sexual ethics, and business ethics. These topics are among the many moral issues challenging us to continue to ask, "What is right and what is wrong in today's society?"

Civil Liberties

♦ ♦ ♦ ♦ ♦ ♦ ♦ ♦ ♦ ♦ ♦

Humanity's age-old struggle for freedom continues unabated. There is an especially strong Anglo-Saxon tradition of civil liberties, based on English common law and practice and on American constitutional law and practice. Humans seek to safeguard and maintain freedom while preserving order and security. Order is necessary for the maintenance and enlargement of freedom, but sometimes appears to be in conflict with it. The problem is to maintain a balance that will protect the rights of the individual and of the community; freedom can be jeopardized if government has too little or too much power.

Some of the great historical struggles have grown out of the democratic spirit, the attempt to secure freedom under law and order and to eliminate the artificial restrictions on its development and expression. People have fought to curb arbitrary and irresponsible power and to broaden political and economic liberty. For example, people have dedicated their lives to the elimination of slavery, serfdom, and peonage from most parts of the world, the growth of representative assemblies, the broadening of political and religious freedom, the emancipation of women and minority racial groups, and the like. After centuries of struggle and debate, free societies have worked out certain principles and safeguards and have sought to guarantee some of them in formal legal enactments.

"HUMAN RIGHTS," "CIVIL RIGHTS," AND "CIVIL LIBERTIES"

As mentioned in the previous chapter (see p. 118), **human rights** may be understood as universal moral rights belonging equally and absolutely to all human beings. Among the human rights accepted in the United States are the rights to life, liberty, equality, and the pursuit of happiness. However, the very characterization of universal human rights may be debated by raising questions such as, How do we know that universal rights exist? Are they provided by God, by irrefutable human reason, and/or by nature? If they truly exist, who interprets them? By way of contrast, are human rights relative to various cultures and historical periods; that is, are they the prevailing opinion of a given time and place?

"**Civil rights**" and "**civil liberties**," cornerstones of a free society, are used broadly and sometimes interchangeably; they have no fixed and uniform definitions. Both categories overlap and refer to whatever a person is legally entitled to have or to do or to receive from others; both include freedom of speech and religion, the right of citizens to participate in the political process, and the right to equal treatment under the law. Civil rights and civil liberties refer to freedoms guaranteed citizens even though these freedoms may not always be available in practice.

Civil rights are frequently specified as rights belonging to people by virtue of their citizenship. Legally protected and enforced, civil rights include many freedoms and entitlements for individuals, regardless of race, religion, gender, or other similar characteristics. Examples of civil rights are the rights to privacy, to own property, to education, and to work, and equal rights for women, for the handicapped, for the elderly, and for sexual minorities. Various civil rights movements may be viewed as attempts to put into practice the ideal of equality under the law for all citizens.

Civil rights often encompass "civil liberties" that are intended to protect individuals from intrusions of government. Examples of civil liberties are freedom of thought, of speech, of the press, of religion, of assembly, the right of dissent, and freedom from unreasonable search and arbitrary arrest. Civil liberties limit the power of the state to restrain or dictate the actions of individuals.

Some people claim there should be complete freedom, with no limitations other than that of preventing harm to others. Others claim there should be additional limitations.

The advocates of complete freedom believe that opinions on matters of public concern should be expressed freely. No one should be restrained for expressing a point of view. This appears to be the position that the First Amendment to the United States Constitution seeks to protect: "Congress shall make no law respecting an establishment of religion, or prohibiting the free exercise thereof; or abridging the freedom of speech, or of the press; or the right of the people peaceably to assemble, and to petition the government for a redress of grievances."

Thomas Jefferson in his day and the American Civil Liberties Union in ours supported this position. Jefferson said, "It is time enough for the rightful purposes of civil government for its officers to interfere when principles break out into overt acts against peace and good order."

JOHN STUART MILL

In the nineteenth century, John Stuart Mill (see biography and excerpt, pp. 144–145), an Englishman, stated the classic defense of individual liberty and freedom of expression in his treatise *On Liberty:*

> The object of this Essay is to assert one very simple principle . . . that the only purpose for which power can be rightfully exercised over any member of a civilised community, against his will, is to prevent harm to others. His own good, either physical or moral, is not a sufficient warrant. He cannot rightfully be compelled to do or forbear because it will be better for him to

do so, because it will make him happier, because in the opinion of others, to do so would be wise, or even right.[2]

Mill's position is that the only purpose for which power can be rightfully exercised over the individual against his or her will is to prevent that person from doing harm to others.

LIMITED OR UNLIMITED CIVIL LIBERTIES

Civil liberties are among our most important rights. For a considerable portion of the population, especially for minority groups and women, they exist in only a very limited form. Some people advocate few limitations. For example, restrictions on freedom of speech might include laws against slander, libel, indecency in public places, and immediate incitement to riot. Others say there should be no restrictions on the presentation of opinion on social, political, economic, scientific, or religious issues. Society or the state should proceed cautiously—if it proceeds at all—in restricting the expression of opinions. They suggest we distinguish between "preserving the peace" and "preserving the status quo." Lack of criticism, or agitation, or tampering with things as they are can mean no progress.

In the second half of the twentieth century both gains and losses for civil liberties have been recorded. Recent decades show a moderate improvement over the early 1950s. The Supreme Court of the United States has handed down some notable decisions: the Civil Rights Act of 1957 established a Civil Rights Commission and the government took steps to revise its security program. The Civil Rights Commission has moved away from granting indiscriminate civil liberties. Various individuals and groups, however, protest what they consider to be some dangerous trends. Space does not permit us to give details of the numerous cases involving the denial of liberties in education, art, religion, the banning of books and speakers.

Justice William O. Douglas noted in 1958 that the time had come for us "to become the champions of the virtues that have given the West great civilizations." These virtues include the ideas of "justice, liberty, and equality." The rights of the people, the civil liberties, "distinguish us from all totalitarian regimes." Justice Douglas contended that there is "no free speech in the full meaning of the term unless there is freedom to challenge the very postulates on which the existing regime rests. . . . Condemnation of public servants for their beliefs or expressions has the inevitable result of substituting pallid orthodoxy for the independence of thought, ingenuity, and boldness of decision which effective public service demands."[3]

Civil Disobedience

♦ ♦ ♦ ♦ ♦ ♦ ♦ ♦ ♦ ♦

How should we proceed when we are dissatisfied with and wish to change some law, institution, or public policy? One way is through the constitutional right to express dissent and opposition through the normal channels of speech, press, and assembly, which may include participation in demonstrations, parades, and picketing, and through the ballot box. In addition, protest and opposition may take the form of **civil disobedience** or the open refusal to obey a law that we believe to be wrong or unconstitutional. Civil disobedience differs from ordinary modes of dissent, because opposition is expressed through the deliberate but nonviolent refusal to obey some law or laws. In an especially fine essay devoted to the topic of civil disobedience, Hannah Arendt writes:

> Civil disobedience arises when a significant number of citizens have become convinced either that the normal channels of change no longer function, and grievances will not be heard or acted upon, or that, on the contrary, the government is about to change and has embarked upon and persists in modes of action whose legality and constitutionality are open to grave doubt. Instances are numerous: seven years of an undeclared war in Vietnam; the growing influence of secret agencies on public

affairs; open or thinly veiled threats to liberties guaranteed under the First Amendment; attempts to deprive the Senate of its constitutional powers, followed by the President's invasion of Cambodia in open disregard for the Constitution, which explicitly requires congressional approval for the beginning of a war. . . . In other words, civil disobedience can be turned to necessary and desirable change or to necessary and desirable preservation or restoration of the *status quo*—the preservation of rights guaranteed under the First Amendment, or the restoration of the proper balance of power in the government.[4]

Civil disobedience has become a fairly widespread tactical weapon used by minority groups who believe they have been discriminated against. They seek more direct methods of change than the electoral process. Sit-ins, freedom marches, and demonstrations are means of expressing opposition to laws.

Justifications of Civil Disobedience. Is civil disobedience ever justified? Is it ever right to disobey the law? When individuals are faced with customs and laws they believe to be injurious, compliance with which rests on legal sanction or is embedded in some venerable institution, what are they to do? Should they obey or disobey? What are people to do when their consciences and the demands of society are in conflict? These are serious and complex questions. In discussing them, we assume that we live in a democratic society in which the rule of law and the principle of consent (majority rule) are accepted. Keep in mind that no human being and no societies are perfect. Mistakes are common, and we are not always ruled by reason and compassion. Democracy, even at its best, is an ideal. Respect for law is one of the foundations of an orderly society; there are a number of courses open to an individual in such a society.

First, when we do not agree with some law we may, although we do not believe the judgment of the majority to be wise, accept the decision because we believe in the rule of law, and wish to be good citizens and maintain respect for

John Stuart Mill

John Stuart Mill (1806–1873), a distinguished philosopher and economist, was born in London and educated by his eminent father, James Mill. He never attended school, although for a time he read law with John Austin. His father gave him a most remarkable education; at the age of fourteen he had read most of the major Greek and Latin classics and had read widely in history, logic, and mathematics. When he was fifteen years old, Mill read a treatise by Jeremy Bentham that captivated him, crystallized his thinking, and fixed his goal in life—to be a social reformer. He became one of the most influential spokesmen for the liberal view of humanity and society. From 1823 to 1858, he was employed at the East India Company, where he worked his way up to a post of great administrative responsibility. His *System of Logic* (1843), *Principles of Political Economy* (1848), *Utilitarianism* (1863), and *On Liberty* (1859) make him one of the most influential philosophers in the English-speaking world in the nineteenth century.

the law. Probably few persons agree with all laws in any city, state, or nation, but many people follow this course.

Second, we can obey the law while protesting it and working to have it changed. We may talk to others, make public addresses, write letters to the newspaper and to Congress, and try to influence public opinion. This course is desirable when the injustice of the law is not great and impairment of respect for law and government might work more evil than would obedience to a law considered unfair.

Third, when the law requires us to do something we consider clearly immoral or extremely unjust, we may choose to protest, make known our objection to the law, and disobey the law

Excerpt from J. S. Mill:
On Liberty (1859)

What, then is the rightful limit to the sovereignty of the individual over himself? Where does the authority of society begin? How much of human life should be assigned to individuality, and how much to society?

Each will receive its proper share if each has that which more particularly concerns it. To individuality should belong the part of life in which it is chiefly the individual that is interested; to society, the part which chiefly interests society.

Though society is not founded on a contract, and though no good purpose is answered by inventing a contract in order to deduce social obligations from it, everyone who receives the protection of society owes a return for the benefit, and the fact of living in society renders it indispensable that each should be bound to observe a certain line of conduct towards the rest. This conduct consists, first, in not injuring the interests of one another, or rather certain interests which, either by express legal provision or by tacit understanding, ought to be considered as rights; and secondly, in each person's bearing his share of the labours and sacrifices incurred for defending the society or its members from injury or molestation. These conditions society is justified in enforcing at all costs to those who endeavor to withhold fulfilment. . . . As soon as any part of a person's conduct affects prejudicially the interests of others, society has jurisdiction over it, and the question whether the general welfare will or will not be promoted by interfering with it becomes open to discussion. But there is no room for entertaining any such question when a person's conduct affects the interests of no persons besides himself, or needs not affect them unless they like. In all such cases, there should be perfect freedom, legal and social, to do the action and stand the consequences.

J. S. Mill, *On Liberty* (London: J. M. Dent, 1910).

openly. We make clear why we are breaking the law and accept any penalty that results. This nonviolent refusal to obey some law was used effectively by the early Christians and by people like Mahatma Gandhi, Henry Thoreau, and Martin Luther King, Jr.

In his "Letter from Birmingham Jail" on April 16, 1963, Martin Luther King, Jr. (see biography and excerpt, pp. 146–147) wrote, "One who breaks an unjust law that conscience tells him is unjust, and who willingly accepts the penalty of imprisonment in order to arouse the conscience of the community over its injustice, is in reality expressing the highest respect for the law."[5] This is the stand of those who practice civil disobedience—nonviolent resistance to what

Martin Luther King, Jr.

Martin Luther King, Jr. (1929–1968) was born in Atlanta, Georgia. His father and maternal grandfather were Baptist ministers. He graduated from Morehouse College, Crozer Theological Seminary, and received his Ph.D. from Boston University in 1955. As a Christian minister and American civil rights leader, he worked for racial justice, equality for blacks, and full civil rights for all persons to be obtained through peaceful means. For his efforts and leadership in these areas, he received the Nobel Peace Prize (1964). He led peaceful demonstrations in cities such as Birmingham and Washington.

King wrote five books: *Stride Toward Freedom* (1958), *Strength to Love* (1963), *Why We Can't Wait* (1964), *Where Do We Go from Here?* (1967) and *The Trumpet of Conscience* (1968). His "Letter from Birmingham Jail" has been widely quoted. In all these writings and in his addresses, he rejected separatism and violence, but stressed nonviolent resistance to discrimination and other forms of injustice. He helped establish the Southern Christian Leadership Conference, and he won the support of millions of persons both black and white. In the summer of 1963, a coalition of black leaders, joined by nationwide organizations of both blacks and whites, organized a march on Washington, D.C. More than 200,000 people from all over the country participated in the march, and millions more watched on television as Dr. King addressed the throng in front of the Lincoln memorial. "I have a dream!" he intoned again and again, and the dream was the American Dream of freedom, justice, equality, and brotherhood among God's children. At the height of his career, at age 39, he was assassinated.

Excerpt from Martin Luther King, Jr.:

Acceptance Speech for Winning the Nobel Peace Prize (1964)

Your Majesty, your Royal Highness, Mr. President, Excellencies, ladies and gentlemen:

I accept the Nobel Prize for Peace at a moment when twenty-two million Negroes of the United States of America are engaged in a creative battle to end the long night of racial injustice. I accept this award in behalf of a civil rights movement which is moving with determination and a majestic scorn for risk and danger to establish a reign of freedom and a rule of justice. I am mindful that only yesterday in Birmingham, Alabama, our children, crying out for brotherhood, were answered with fire hoses, snarling dogs, and even death. I am mindful that only yesterday in Philadelphia, Mississippi, young people seeking to secure the right to vote were brutalized and murdered. And only yesterday more than forty houses of worship in the State of Mississippi alone were bombed or burned because they offered a sanctuary to those who would not accept segregation. I am mindful that debilitating and grinding poverty afflicts my people and chains them to the lowest rung of the economic ladder.

Therefore, I must ask why this prize is awarded to a movement which is beleaguered and committed to unrelenting struggle; to a movement which has not won the very peace and brotherhood which is the essence of the Nobel Prize.

After contemplation, I conclude that this award which I receive on behalf of that movement is a profound recognition that nonviolence is the answer to the crucial political and moral question of our time—the need for man to overcome oppression and violence without resorting to violence and oppression. Civilization and violence are antithetical concepts. Negroes of the United States, following the people of India, have demonstrated that nonviolence is not sterile passivity, but a powerful moral force which makes for social transformation. Sooner or later, all the people in the world will have to discover a way to live together in peace, and thereby transform this pending cosmic elegy into a creative psalm of brotherhood. If this is to be achieved, man must evolve for all human conflict a method which rejects revenge, aggression and retaliation. The foundation of such a method is love.

Nobel Lecture by The Reverend Dr. Martin Luther King, Jr., Recipient of the 1964 Nobel Peace Prize, Oslo Norway, December 11, 1964 (New York: Harper and Row, 1964).

they consider evil. On occasions it has led to severe penalties—death in the case of Socrates and many early Christians—but judges in modern democracies are sometimes lenient when they know the protest is genuine and based on conscience or religious scruples. Some societies make special provisions for conscientious objectors to military service. Refusal to obey a law frequently brings the unjust law vividly to the attention of the general public and may mold public sentiment by appealing to the conscience and sense of fair play of the majority of citizens, who through ignorance, indifference, or fear have become insensitive to the injustices involved.

In some cases of civil disobedience in the 1950s and 1960s (sit-ins at lunch counters by blacks, freedom marches, and the like), those who resisted broke a state or local law that they believed was in clear conflict with a federal law, the decision of a federal court, or even the Constitution. That is, they broke the local law or ordinance in the belief that it would be declared invalid by the higher courts. In some situations, this has been the only way to test the validity or constitutionality of a law.

Can resistance to law and the state reasonably go beyond these? The fourth course is the illegal resort to force or violence. In the 1960s and early 1970s, some groups went far beyond nonviolent civil disobedience and resorted to extreme methods to gain their ends.

Of all the means that people may use to gain civil liberties, the only one that we believe can justify calling them "revolutionaries" is violence. A generally accepted characteristic of civil disobedience is nonviolence, and it follows that "civil disobedience is not revolution. . . . The civil disobedient accepts, while the revolutionary rejects, the frame of established authority and the general legitimacy of the system of laws."[6] Civil disobedients share with revolutionaries the wish "to change the world," and the changes they wish to accomplish can be drastic—as were those pursued by Gandhi (see biography and excerpt, pp. 150–151), who is regarded as an excellent example of a nonviolent protestor. Did Gandhi accept the frame of established authority—at the time, British rule of India? Did he respect the general legitimacy of the system of laws in the colony? There is a very fine line, often, between the revolutionary and the civil disobedient.

The choice of violence as a tactic for social change raises serious problems of justification. Under what circumstances does violence become creative, and under what circumstances should violence be the tool of a broad commitment to revolution? Answers to these questions depend to some extent on how bad the existing order is; it also depends on whether we believe it is possible to create an order that is substantially better. Can we conceive of an alternative system that avoids imbalances of power, unjust laws, and inequitable distributions of burdens and benefits? Tactics used on occasions by those living under tyranny often are unnecessary in societies in which there is some degree of freedom. "In a world of great injustice, we need social change. Social change requires action. Action may result, either by design or by accident, in violence. This fact must be faced. And violence is an evil, along with injustice."[7] Is it possible to develop an ethics that might suggest appropriate limits for violence while not condemning as always evil the use of violence?

One recognition of the validity of rebellion or revolution was expressed in British and American political philosophy and used by the early colonists. John Locke (see biography and excerpt, pp. 152–153), who set forth the classical liberal theory of representative government that influenced the United States Declaration of Independence and the Bill of Rights in the Constitution, laid the foundation. In *Two Treatises of Government* (1690) he made clear that popular consent is the basis of government and the function of the state is to protect human rights. There is a "law behind the law," a higher law than the formally enacted law, and some rights of the individual are inalienable. The state does not create these rights but has a duty to recognize and defend them. When rulers become tyrannical, abuse their mandate, and rule unjustly, citizens have the right to resist and rebel.

Read the strong words of the Declaration of Independence: "that whenever any form of government becomes destructive of these ends, it is the right of the people to alter or abolish it, and to institute new government." Societies that recognize the right of revolution seldom experience revolutions, whereas those that deny such rights seem to experience violent upheavals with some frequency.

The Limits of Liberty

♦ ♦ ♦ ♦ ♦ ♦ ♦ ♦ ♦ ♦

The legal safeguards set up to assure fairness in the administration of justice include rules of procedure to prevent arbitrary arrest. In the United States, people cannot be arrested on mere suspicion, but only for "probable cause." When a person is arrested without a warrant, he or she is taken without unnecessary delay before a judge for arraignment. He or she must be permitted to secure counsel. A writ of *habeas corpus* by a judge requires the person to be presented and cause shown why he or she should be detained rather than set free. To keep prisoners incommunicado or prevent them from obtaining counsel is unlawful, as are "third degree" tactics or brutal and inhumane treatment, forced confessions, and unreasonable search and seizure. These are just a few of a long list of safeguards that are intended to prevent abuses and help obtain justice.

Order, one necessary element for the preservation of liberty, requires the enforcement of law by some governmental authority. The enforcement of law entails the use of power, which sometimes takes the form of physical restraint or the use of force against those who violate the law. The people who exercise the authority and administer the laws are fallible; they occasionally show excessive zeal and go to extremes. When a crime is committed, the public may become emotionally aroused and demand immediate and drastic action. Law enforcement officers often are under pressure from the underworld and special interest groups, and they may be tempted by bribery. Furthermore, some people think that

the promotion of worthy ends, such as the protection of society and the reduction of crime, justifies the use of any means, even the bypassing of procedural regulations. For this reason, law enforcement officials must be subject to scrutiny and judicial supervision. Some people, although they want effective law enforcement, think that it is better that some guilty persons escape than that innocent individuals be deprived of their freedom and wrongly punished.

The Enforcement of Morals

♦ ♦ ♦ ♦ ♦ ♦ ♦ ♦ ♦ ♦

It has long been taken for granted that law is the servant of morals; that the law was designed, among other things, to protect the moral tone of society. This theory has been rejected by a variety of thoughtful persons. In 1957, the Wolfenden Committee recommended that England's law on homosexuality be liberalized so that homosexual activity between consenting adults in private would no longer be considered a crime. The committee based its recommendation on the conviction that there is a realm of private morality that is not within the province of the law and that there is an important difference between crime and "sin." The report said that the function of the law is "to preserve public order and decency, to protect the citizen from what is offensive or injurious, and to provide sufficient safeguards against exploitation and corruption of others, particularly those who are specially vulnerable because they are young, weak in body or mind, inexperienced, or in a state of special physical, official or economic dependence."[8] They went on to say that they did *not* consider it the function of the law "to intervene in the private lives of citizens, or to seek to enforce any particular pattern of behavior further than is necessary to carry out the purposes we have outlined."

Lord Patrick Devlin, an eminent British jurist, opposed the Wolfenden Report and maintained that the law not only may but ought to enforce morals. His argument was based on his conviction that there are certain standards of

Mohandas Karamchand Gandhi

Mohandas Karamchand Gandhi (1869–1948) was born in India within the traditional caste of grocers and moneylenders (*Gandhi* means "grocer"). His mother was a devout member of Jainism, an Indian religion emphasizing nonviolence. Gandhi was married by arrangement at age thirteen and began to study law in London five years later. He was admitted to the bar in 1891 and practiced law in South Africa until 1914.

In South Africa Gandhi experienced prejudice against people of color, which he resolved to root out. In pursuit of this aim, he founded the Natal Indian Congress, which publicized the general condition of Natal Indians, including their disenfranchised state. The time he spent in South Africa was formative in that it enhanced his regard for Hinduism and made him aware of the interrelation of self-realization, the realization of God, and the service of others.

Gandhi's belief in the absolute oneness of God and humanity and the interrelation of Truth had far-reaching social and political implications. He became involved in labor organizing and in civil disobedience against British Colonialism which ultimately led in 1947 to independence from Great Britain. Gandhi's religious beliefs also determined his attitude toward the untouchables, whom he regarded as children of God; toward women, whose status in traditional Hindu society was far from enviable; toward education, where in his view equality of opportunity should prevail; and toward self-rule, which for him was grounded on Truth and the undisputed right of the people of India.

Gandhi's assassination at the hands of a Hindu fanatic ended the life of one of the most remarkable men of this century. He rejected the title of saint as being too sacred a term to be applied to a simple seeker after truth, but there can be no doubt that he was India's Mahātma, *Great Soul*.

His writings include *An Autobiography; or the Story of my Experiments with Truth* (1959), *Hindu Dharma* (1950), and *My Religion* (1955).

behavior or moral principles that society insists upon, and their violation is an offense against society as a whole as well as against the injured person.[9] Today, the controversy about whether society has the right to enforce moral standards through the law is much in evidence.[10]

Contemporary Moral Issues

Many keen observers have called attention to the loss of a sense of values that has accompanied the growth of modern technology.[11] They tell us that we have been living under

Excerpt from Gandhi:

Non-Violent Resistance (1918)

I have come to see, what I did not so clearly before, that there is non-violence in violence. This is the big change which has come about. I had not fully realized the duty of restraining a drunkard from doing evil, of killing a dog in agony or one infected with rabies. In all these instances, violence is in fact non-violence. Violence is a function of the body. . . . our offspring must be strong in physique. If they cannot completely renounce the urge to violence, we may permit them to commit violence, to use their strength to fight and thus make them non-violent.

Source: E. H. Erikson, *Gandhi's Truth* (New York: W. W. Norton, 1969).

the illusion that more automobiles, labor-saving devices, and the like will bring happiness and usher in a better life. Without a strong sense of values derived from value-giving institutions such as the family and religion, however, the human spirit tends to weaken or deteriorate. Technical devices can liberate us from drudgery and open up new possibilities for cultural development; they can also have a dehumanizing effect and be potentially dangerous if we have no self-discipline and dedication to enduring values.

John Locke

John Locke (1632–1704), an Englishman known for his charm and wisdom, had many influential friends. He lived through one of the most turbulent periods in English history—the conflict between royalty and the parliamentary forces. Locke's father, a lawyer, fought on the parliamentary side against Charles I. After graduating from Oxford, Locke lectured there for some years; then, under suspicion for treason, he took refuge in Holland and returned after the Revolution of 1688 with William of Orange and Mary. Locke had strong Puritan sympathies, stood for constitutional government, opposed tyranny, and defended tolerance of opposing political and religious convictions, freedom of the press, and the need for educational reform. His writings and philosophy had profound influence on Thomas Jefferson and the United States Declaration of Independence. It has been said that, during the American Revolution, the "party line" was John Locke. Locke's most influential political writings are *Two Treatises of Government* (1690), and *First Letter Concerning Toleration* (1689). His *Essay Concerning Human Understanding* (1690), a book more widely read than any other philosophical work in epistemology, discusses how the mind operates in learning about the world. It places emphasis on experience, distinguishes between primary and secondary qualities, and refutes the doctrine of innate or inborn ideas.

Why was it that in Germany the educated classes did so little to resist the rise of Nazism? Was it because during the nineteenth and early twentieth centuries, with the rapid development of many special fields in science and technology, the value studies were pushed aside with the result that the highly trained specialists were unconcerned about the larger problems of the community and the world? A number of scholars have told us that modern civilization is successful in transmitting to the young technical knowledge but fails to transmit the moral, cultural, and historical heritage of that civilization.

John E. Smith (see biography and excerpt, pp. 154–155), an experienced teacher and moral philosopher who has concern for contemporary society, writes:

> The most urgent problem of our time is posed by the awesome extent to which moral sensitivity and respect in the face of responsibility have

Excerpt from Locke:

The Second Treatise of Government, "Of The State of Nature" (1690)

To understand political power right and derive it from its original, we must consider what state all men are naturally in, and that is a state of perfect freedom to order their actions and dispose of their possessions and persons as they think fit, within the bounds of the law of nature, without asking leave or depending upon the will of any other man.

A state also of equality, wherein all the power and jurisdiction is reciprocal, no one having more than another; there being nothing more evident than that creatures of the same species and rank, promiscuously born to all the same advantages of nature and the use of the same faculties, should also be equal one amongst another without subordination or subjection. . . . The state of nature has a law of nature to govern it, which obliges every one; and reason, which is that law, teaches all mankind who will but consult it that, being all equal and independent, no one ought to harm another in his life, health, liberty, or possessions; for men being all the workmanship of one omnipotent and infinitely wise Maker—all the servants of one sovereign master, sent into the world by his order, and about his business—they are his property whose workmanship they are. . . . Every one, as he is bound to preserve himself and not to quit his station wilfully, so by the like reason, when his own preservation comes not in competition, ought he, as much as he can, to preserve the rest of mankind, and may not, unless it be to justice to an offender, take away or impair the life, or what tends to be the preservation of the life, the liberty, health, limb, or goods of another.

John Locke, *The Second Treatise of Government* and *A Letter Concerning Toleration,* ed. J. W. Gaugh (Oxford: Basil Blackwell, 1947).

eroded. The twin gospels of success and greed have literally dehumanized us by obscuring the one dimension of life which alone defines us as human—the ethical capacity for evaluating our conduct and for appraising our goals.[12]

The American student of the sixties and seventies often was considered to be a radical prone to disregard the traditional values of society. From today's perspective, however, these students were attempting to establish a set of values different from those of the ordinary community. For a time, the young people of the sixties and seventies turned their backs on the materialistic, competitive culture in which they were raised. They often exhibited moral sensitivity and energy.

Although contemporary young people have abandoned the extreme forms of protest often adopted by the sixties generation, they are often seriously concerned about such issues as the threat of nuclear weapons and the challenge that

John Edwin Smith

John Edwin Smith (1921–) teaches and writes about American philosophy and the philosophy of religion. He is Clark Professor of Philosophy Emeritus at Yale University, former chairman of the Yale Philosophy Department, and director of the National Humanities Institute at Yale. Professor Smith has lectured at Harvard, Fordham, Princeton, and other academic institutions. He joined the Yale faculty in 1952 and was appointed Clark Professor of Philosophy in 1972. Author of *The Spirit of American Philosophy* (1963), *Experience and God* (1968), *Reason and God* (1961), he has written a definitive study of American pragmatism: *Purpose and Thought; The Meaning of Pragmatism* (1978). In 1992 his *America's Philosophical Vision* was published.

Professor Smith was born in Brooklyn, New York, graduated from Columbia College, and subsequently received degrees from Union Theological Seminary and Columbia University. He is the husband of Marilyn Smith, one of the authors of this text.

the invention of those weapons has placed before us. Protests on behalf of minority groups and women are still held; many groups exert pressure to protect the environment; applied ethics—such as problems in medicine, human sexuality, and business—is probably the most active philosophical area today. On the whole, however, it would not seem unfair to say that ours is a period in which the moral energy of the sixties and seventies appears to have abated; it is very likely that economic needs and concerns have taken precedence over value questions.

In the modern world, institutions related to education, religion, science, the professions, recreation, business, government, and the like, have multiplied rapidly. They have a powerful influence over people and help to shape sentiments and standards of value. Although specialization

brings benefits, specialists may see life in segments or fragments and give their attention to their own world, with little or no concern about human welfare as a whole. Today moral philosophers emphasize that an individual should transcend special interests and serve the larger society to which all persons belong.

With a focus on major philosophical issues and questions, we shall now examine three areas of morality—medical ethics, sexual ethics, and business ethics.

MEDICAL ETHICS

There has been a vigorous resurgence of interest in medical ethics during the past three decades. As technology is applied to human life, value issues are raised; biological and medical re-

Exerpt from Smith:

Value Convictions and Higher Education (1958)

As we look within and discover ourselves and the nature of our own experience, we come upon what is actually the distinguishing mark of the human species—the capacity not only to think and feel but to *judge* and *evaluate*. As human beings we are not confined to being *in* the world as a part among other parts in a gigantic collection of things and powers, but we are able to respond to it in a critical way, to compare and contrast, to accept and reject. The power to exercise judgment and make the critical response not only proves our humanity, but this capacity is at the basis of all discussion concerning what has come to be called value. Without the critical response, the world before us would be just what it is and nothing more; there would be no question of better or worse, of right and wrong, of true and false, for all such distinctions imply judgment and the ability to evaluate.

J. E. Smith, *Value Convictions and Higher Education* (New Haven, Conn.: Edward W. Hazen Foundation, 1958).

searchers request guidance from moral philosophers. Several teaching hospitals have hired philosophers to help their medical staff make better decisions affecting the life and death of patients. Participation of medical ethicists in clinical settings, however, is not without controversy. Some physicians are decidedly ambivalent about these ethical contributions; on the one hand, they are eagerly searching for assistance in resolving the increasingly complex ethical dilemmas now so common in medical practice. On the other hand, they are wary and disappointed because they believe that, until now, the ethicists' contributions have been of dubious value.

Some of the more controversial and pressing ethical questions concern birth control and abortion; new methods of reproduction (including surrogate parenting); human experimentation; genetic engineering; fetal research; patients' rights; euthanasia; assisted suicide; organ transplantation; truth/confidentiality and the physician; definitions of death; care of the dying; prison psychiatry; and health care costs.

Entwined in these questions are both general philosophical problems and specific value issues: What is "life"? When does something become a "person" or acquire personal worth and status? When does one cease to be a human being? If a procedure, such as organ transplantation, has the possibility of abuse, ought it to be forbidden? Are there legitimate distinctions between killing, murder, and helping persons to die? How does the moral philosopher distinguish between "ordinary means" (e.g., intravenous feeding) and "extraordinary means" (e.g., heart-lung respirators) in regard to the artificial prolongation of certain functions? What medical and surgical procedures ought to be governed by civil law? What are the rights of the individual in contrast to the "common good" when, for example, only a limited number of dialysis machines are available. We will briefly examine the case of "Baby Jane Doe," as it was known, to illuminate the kind of issues medical ethicists consider. On October 11, 1983, Baby Jane Doe was born in Port Jefferson, Long Island. She had spina bifida (failure of the spinal cord to close properly) and hydrocephalus (excess fluid in the brain). Without surgery, physicians said, she was likely to die within two years; with it, she could survive into her twenties but would be severely retarded and bedridden. The parents, in consultation with neurosurgeons, social workers, moral philosophers, and clergy, decided to forgo surgery. The role of the medical ethicist was to weigh conflicting values: prolonging living versus prolonging dying; the quality versus the quantity of life, and the use of extraordinary as opposed to ordinary means. Is the surgery an "aggressive" treatment? The law was introduced into the case when an attorney acted as spokesperson for the infant and endorsed the surgery. Ultimately, the courts decided that the parents had the right to determine the course of treatment of their infant and therefore had the right to withhold corrective surgery. Important as is the solution to the "right" and "wrong" (the morality) of this dilemma, it was equally vital to identify, clarify, and define the conflicting issues. That is the task of the medical ethicist.

One philosopher has proposed that medicine has saved the life of ethics.[13] Interest in moral philosophy has waned since the turn of the century for a variety of reasons—the secularization of the university; the reduction of value questions to a "meaningless" status by the analytic philosophers; and the assertion that all serious questions could be solved if only we understood how to state them properly. Now it has become necessary to revive moral questioning in order to cope. New biological technologies have highlighted bioethical problems. Many of us welcomed a new consideration in the curriculum of classical and humanistic moral questions. Even more important, however, is that one look to the resurgence of bioethics for two reasons: to enrich the understanding and to develop the sense of responsibility in the individual physician and to help lay people know more about the potential effects of advances in biology and medicine so that they could share in the decisions affecting themselves and their loved ones. Whether or not these two goals have been achieved after three decades is difficult to evaluate; governmental channels have been formed—The President's Commission for the Study of Ethical Problems in Medicine and Biomedical and Behavioral Research—which provide badly needed guidelines for physicians and researchers, but guidelines should never usurp the role of the individual conscience. As we have seen,[14] our Western society is convinced that individuals should be free to do as they like unless what they do can be shown to injure someone else. Thus, we hope that these moral questions posed by biomedical technologies will follow certain broad guidelines proposed by the medical ethicist while at the same time recalling that each individual case is unique.

One example of an ethical dilemma in bioethics is *euthanasia*. There are major moral and legal questions concerning euthanasia. Is euthanasia morally permissible, or is it morally wrong? Should it be against the law, or should it be legal? It is not an easy task to define the word *euthanasia*: its basic meaning is "a good or gentle death"; however, in general usage it has acquired the meaning "mercy killing." According to one scholar, in order to justify euthanasia, five features must be present:

1. The patient would be deliberately killed.
2. The patient would die soon in any case.
3. The patient was suffering.
4. The patient asked to be killed.
5. The killing would have been an act of mercy; that is, the reason for the killing would be to prevent further needless suffering and to provide the patient with a "good death," or at least as good as it could be under the circumstances.[15]

Further terms need to be explicated in connection with the dilemma of euthanasia. There is a clear distinction between active and passive euthanasia. The phrase "active euthanasia" is used to refer to cases in which the patient is killed, for example, by being given a lethal injection. "Assisted suicide" is a variation of this approach, wherein chronically or terminally ill patients are helped to administer substances causing their own deaths. The phrase "passive euthanasia" refers to cases in which the patient is not killed but merely allowed to die, for example, by being refused surgery as in the case of Baby Jane Doe, or not being administered medication, or not being furnished with a respirator. It is important to note this distinction because many people believe that active euthanasia is immoral, but passive euthanasia is morally all right.

And so the controversy arises. We urge the reader to delve deeper into the controversial issues by consulting a text in bioethics.[16] The two main issues are: First, is it morally permissible to kill or let die, or assist to die, someone who is going to die soon anyway, at the person's own request, as an act of kindness? Should the seriously chronically ill be allowed to die similarly? And, second, should such killing, assisting to die, or letting die be against the law? As the latter question is in process of being answered in different ways by different states, let us confine ourselves to the moral arguments. The arguments which support the morality of euthanasia are two. The argument of mercy states that terminal patients sometimes suffer horrible pain; thus, the argument says, euthanasia is justified because it puts an end to *that*. The second supportive argument is known as the argument from the Golden Rule: "Do unto others as you would have them do unto you." The relevance is clear, moral rules apply impartially to everyone, therefore you cannot say that you are justified in treating someone else in a certain way unless you are willing to admit that that person would also be justified in treating you in that way if your positions were reversed.

There are two kinds of arguments opposing the morality of euthanasia and even their supporters are not in total agreement. The first is that killing is always wrong, whatever the motivation. On this view, human life is precious and ought to be protected. The second is a group of religious arguments which have often been misinterpreted and currently are losing ground with religious authorities. Briefly, the religious arguments consist in saying that (1) God forbids killing; (2) It is for God alone to decide when a person shall live and (3) suffering is a part of life. It is noteworthy that religious thinkers are reassessing the traditional ban on mercy killing.[17]

One final argument. Euthanasia may be opposed on the grounds that we cannot tell when a patient's condition is hopeless; there is always the possibility of an unexpected cure. What relevance does this have for a patient in irreversible coma such as Karen Ann Quinlan? In this famous case, in April 1975, a 21-year-old woman, allegedly because of a combination of pills and alcohol, ceased breathing for at least two fifteen-minute periods. As a result, she suffered severe brain damage and was reduced (in the words of the attending physicians) to a "chronic vegetative state." Accepting the judgment that there was no hope of recovery, her parents sought permission from the courts to disconnect the respirator that was keeping her breathing. The Quinlans are Roman Catholics and made this request only after consulting with their priest, who assured them that there would be no moral or religious objection if Karen were allowed to die.

The Supreme Court of New Jersey agreed that the respirator could be removed; Karen Ann, however, continued to breathe for ten years in the same comatose state until June 1985, when she died of pneumonia.

SEXUAL ETHICS

The basic moral standard of sexual morality for many people is the sexual expression between wife and husband united in a lifelong monogamous relationship; the intent to become parents has often been incorporated within this moral code. World history has shown that this standard is not universal and has not prevented alternative sexual views and behaviors. During the past three decades challenges to traditional norms have emerged in public discussion and in people's lives. However, the issue of sexual ethics has rarely been approached rationally. Agreements to differ or to develop laws encompassing a diverse citizenry have been subordinated to militant extremism, self-justification, and strident appeals to the moral absolutes of one's own group. (See Obstacles to Clear Thinking, pages 171–176.) In this section we shall explore four representative answers to the fundamental philosophical question about sexual conduct, "What is the primary purpose of human sexuality?"

Procreation. One response is that the primary purpose of sexual relations is to have children. Consequently, only those acts (at least potentially) leading to conception are normal, natural, and ethical. Traditional Western moral constraints limit procreative activities to monogamous marriage. (A very strict variation on this theme is that if a person is unable to have children, he or she should be celibate.) However, apart from tradition, one might wish to argue for procreative sexuality within other relationships, such as unmarried couples or communal living. In any case, masturbation, heterosexual acts without intending conception, and homosexual behaviors are not consistent with a procreative intent and are consequently abnormal, unnatural, and unethical.

Procreation and Love. Another position is that the primary purpose of sexual relations is to have children and express love. Consequently, only those acts (at least potentially) leading to conception while expressing love between the partners are normal, natural, and ethical. Familiar moral codes limit procreation and sexual love to monogamous marriage, but as with the preceding interpretation, one might wish to argue for nontraditional relationships as alternative moral contexts. Inconsistent with this view and regarded as abnormal, unnatural, and unethical are masturbation, heterosexual acts not intending conception, and homosexual behaviors.

Love. Mutual self-giving in love is the third primary purpose of human sexuality. Conception, whether planned or at random, is not necessary to sexually expressed love. Consequently, sexual acts manifesting love are natural, normal, and ethical. Additional stipulations to this position will depend on one's answers to subordinate questions, such as: "Should all love making be within marriage?" "May love making occur outside of marriage?" "If so, within what contexts (e.g., unmarried partners, communal relationships, with friends)?" "Is love making between people of the same gender morally permissible?" "Is there a particular age when sexually expressed love is ethically sanctioned?" and "What are the characteristics of love?"

Pleasure. A fourth representative primary purpose of human sexuality is pleasure. Neither reproduction nor love is the basic intent. An individual's own sense of pleasure, physical and/or emotional, is sought and is by definition natural, normal, and ethical. As with the three purposes already discussed, variations on this theme are possible as conditions are imposed. In this regard, considerations could include issues of marital status, sexual orientation, masturbation, prostitution, age, sadomasochism, and the limits of pleasure.

A Word about Homosexuality. Within the first and second primary purposes of human sexuality all homosexual, genital relations are regarded as morally wrong, regardless of the causes (genetic or otherwise) of sexual orientations. Within the third purpose only loving homosexual expressions could be included. The fourth purpose might include a variety of heterosexual and homosexual relations. There is no topic in sexual ethics that generates more emotion than homosexuality. The discipline of philosophy can help to clarify this volatile issue as a topic within sexual ethics, so that more thoughtful positions may be reached.

Conclusion. Our focus in this brief exploration of sexual ethics is to highlight a number of significant philosophical issues. A philosophical approach to sexual ethics requires patient, rational discussion and well-founded justifications of one's convictions. As a result, thoughtful laws incorporating appropriate civil rights and liberties regarding sexual behavior may be enacted.

BUSINESS ETHICS

Moral philosophers take a special interest in right and wrong, good and bad, duty and obligation. When this interest is focused primarily on economic matters, on "business" in the widest sense, the examination is called business ethics, another field of applied ethics.

Textbooks and anthologies abound in the business ethics field.[18] After a brief, general introduction to descriptive and normative ethics and metaethics, authors frequently begin by pointing to issues of preferential hiring and reverse discrimination. Because of recent federal decisions to issue new rules that relax requirements for federal contractors to recruit and promote blacks, women, and Hispanic people, this issue has become more controversial. The new rules have generated intense criticism from civil rights leaders and equally intense approbation from business organizations. It is the task of the moral philosopher to make some useful distinctions as to kinds of preferential hiring— for example, using a quota system or assigning "extra credit" to individuals from certain groups. Affirmative action presents a serious moral dilemma. Other qualifications being equal, preferential hiring is the hiring of one person rather than another on the basis of some non-job-related characteristic, such as sex, race, or religion. Is preferential hiring a form of discrimination and therefore immoral?

A second economic topic of interest to the moral philosopher is that of free expression in the marketplace and so-called whistle-blowing, in which an employee makes known, either within the corporation or publicly, business activities he or she believes are unethical. This form of free speech is prompted by an event or condition that the whistle-blower views as immoral and that would probably go unnoticed otherwise. The crucial moral issue is that an employee's views about an activity or business practice (for example, the safety of a product) can conflict with the economic well-being of the company. Can the employee's right to free expression be defended in this instance? Once again, the task of the moral philosopher is to analyze the question of the right to free expression in the workplace and to help develop policies for protecting that free expression.

Other moral issues in the business arena include an employee's autonomy in the workplace; the responsibilities and duties to an employer; ethical issues in advertising; the concept of corporate responsibility; business concerns versus environmental protection; or the responsibility the corporation has to maintain a safe, clean environment, and the possible conflict of ethics in a multinational situation in which a complete set of moral principles may differ one from the other. In recent years, both institutional and individual investors have seen that they have a responsibility to invest in fund only those institutions whose policies are in keeping with the investors' political and moral values. Investors are urged to be more socially conscious and to analyze their portfolios for political and philosophical implications.

There are, of course, no simple solutions to these issues, but philosophy can help people delineate the problems and develop general guidelines. As one distinguished corporate leader has written: "If the company, from the top executives on down, embraces a stated standard of ethical and moral conduct, it can create an environment that supports consistent ethical conduct and leads to greater cohesiveness within a corporate structure."[19]

Reflections

♦ ♦ ♦ ♦ ♦ ♦ ♦ ♦ ♦ ♦ ♦

In the first edition of this book, about a half-century ago, the author wrote:

> Mankind appears to be engaged in one of its rare moods of shifting its outlook, its basic assumptions, and its way of acting. Great decisions are being made, and more will be made in the years ahead. We may live in a much better world than any race of men and women have yet known.

That, I think, is possible; but it is also possible that we live in a much more dangerous and cruel world than we have recently known. . . .

What is the explanation of the unrest, the confusion, the bewilderment, the social and economic and political disorders, the revolutions, and the wars of our time? . . . [An] answer is that we are in the midst of a world revolution, a revolution which is intellectual and moral as well as political and economic.[20]

Dr. Titus' comments, still pertinent, were written at a time when individual and social morality was changing. During the past five decades new individual and social issues of morality have emerged with regard to civil liberties, medical care, sexual behavior, and business practices. Actually, almost every moral dimension of individual and social conduct is under review today. One might conclude that during the last half of the twentieth century a moral revolution as significant as the scientific revolution has been inaugurated!

Inevitably, at any historical period there are strains among various individuals and groups as they confront conflicting moral sensibilities. For philosophers and other thinking people it is regrettable that moral dilemmas are infrequently approached rationally in the public arena. However, tensions can be resolved creatively over time when all parties agree to place controversial issues (e.g., abortion, sexual behavior) on the public agenda *for rational discussion*. Those who prefer to retain moral solutions already in place deserve to be heard, as do others with new and different proposals. Utilizing philosophical methodology (the dialectic),[21] thoughtful persons with opposing convictions can explore any issue thoroughly and dispassionately. When views remain in dispute, legislative and judicial bodies may be necessary to resolve, at least for the time being, those issues requiring public judgments. In this chapter we have explored some of the philosophical elements in the areas of civil liberties, medical ethics, sexual ethics, and business ethics. These topics are among those that challenge us as we continue to reflect on what is right and wrong in individual and social relations.

◆ ◆

Glossary Terms

CIVIL DISOBEDIENCE   Public refusal to obey a law, expressed through deliberate but nonviolent means.

CIVIL LIBERTIES   Immunities from governmental interference (e.g., freedom from arbitrary arrest); see *civil rights*.

CIVIL RIGHTS   Rights belonging to people by virtue of their citizenship; "civil rights" sometimes encompasses and is often used interchangeably with "civil liberties."

HUMAN RIGHTS   Often understood as the universal moral rights belonging equally and absolutely to all human beings.

◆ ◆

Chapter Review

A CONTEMPORARY CHALLENGE

1. As we prepare to enter a new millennium, several issues of individual and societal living remain problematic, all requiring philosophical considerations.

CIVIL LIBERTIES

1. "Human Rights," "Civil Rights," and "Civil Liberties" need to be clarified for discussion.

2. Freedom of thought, speech, press, assembly, and religion, and the right of dissent are

among the most cherished rights frequently called civil liberties.

3. Some people believe in complete freedom; others believe there should be limitations on freedom that preserve order and security. A balance protects the rights of both the individual and the community.

4. John Stuart Mill believed that the only purpose for which power can rightfully be exercised over individuals against their will is to prevent them from doing harm to others.

5. For a considerable portion of the world population, civil liberties are limited.

6. In the United States in the late sixties and early seventies, many people were concerned about threats to civil liberties, such as political spying and limitations on the news media.

CIVIL DISOBEDIENCE

1. Protest and opposition may take the form of civil disobedience, or open refusal to obey a law that a person believes to be immoral and perhaps unconstitutional; opposition is expressed nonviolently.

2. A number of possible courses of civil disobedience are open to members of a democratic society.

THE LIMITS OF LIBERTY

1. Legal safeguards assure fairness in the administration of justice; for example, we have rules of procedure to prevent arbitrary arrest.

2. Order, one necessary element in the preservation of liberty, requires the enforcement of law by some governmental authority.

THE ENFORCEMENT OF MORALS

1. Many people believe that the law is designed to protect the moral tone of society, such as by enforcing a heterosexual standard. Others argue that society does not have the right to enforce moral standards.

CONTEMPORARY MORAL ISSUES

1. Many observers say society as a whole has been subject to the loss of a sense of values as a corollary of the growth of modern technology.

2. Applied ethics is probably the most active contemporary philosophical area. Medical ethics, sexual ethics, and business ethics are issues of applied ethics.

3. Issues of medical ethics include several philosophical problems and value issues.

4. Interpretations of sexual ethics are largely based on answers to the philosophical question, "What is the primary purpose of human sexuality?"

5. The topic of business ethics results from value and moral issues applied to business practices.

REFLECTIONS

1. During the past five decades new individual and social issues of morality have emerged; actually, almost every moral dimension of individual and social conduct is under review today.

2. Utilizing the dialectic, thoughtful persons with opposing convictions can explore any issue thoroughly and dispassionately. When views remain in dispute, legislative and judicial bodies may be necessary to resolve, at least for the time being, those issues requiring public judgments.

♦ ♦

Study Questions and Projects

1. Distinguish between right, left, and center in social and political philosophy, and indicate where you stand and why. List specific groups in society that you think can reasonably be placed under each of these headings.

2. Make a list of events—including elections, court decisions, industrial changes, and significant declarations—that indicate a trend toward: (1) individualism, (2) greater governmental control. What overall conclusions are to be drawn from this list?

3. Are there principles that limit or ought to limit the right of the community to interfere with the individual? State the principles you accept, and defend them.

4. Some years ago a majority of the citizens in one state developed a strong "personal-liberty complex" that was directed against the compulsory vaccination law. There were then very few cases of smallpox, and the law was repealed. As the number of cases of smallpox increased, in some years doubling, more and more people began to wonder if that was the kind of freedom they really wanted. Eventually a majority decided to reenact the law. Should all the people have been forced to accept vaccination? Do people have the right to reject public health measures?

5. Indicate why you agree or disagree with the following statement by Samuel Eliot Morison in *Freedom in Contemporary Society* (Boston: Little, Brown, 1956), p. 29:

    In my opinion, the growth of democracy in the United States has not contributed to the growth of political freedom. And the reasons, I think, are clear: (1) Political education has never caught up with political power. (2) The religious sanction to government has declined, with commensurate loss of public virtue; character and intelligence are losing the race to greed and selfishness. It is only by comparison with totalitarian governments, where the religious sanction is wholly wanting, and where free rein is given to cruelty and other abominable traits of human nature, that we are reconciled to the milder ills and supportable disadvantages of democracy.

6. Indicate which of the following activities you would leave to personal choice without governmental regulation, which you would prefer to see handled by some voluntary group or cooperative society, which by a state or local government, and which by the national, or federal, government. Give reasons for your choices.
   (a) traffic regulation; (b) the building of roads, highways, cross-country freeways, and bridges; (c) private sexual conduct; (d) operation of schools and colleges; (e) regulation of currency; (f) handling pure food and drug problems; (g) control of child labor; (h) wage legislation; (i) slum clearance; (j) establishing stock market standards; (k) population control; (l) determining the location of one's dwelling or home; (m) deciding the location of one's business; (n) choosing the school to which one's children are sent.

7. Explain the problem of maintaining a just balance between freedom and order, and relate it to the need for legal safeguards in the administration of justice.

8. Do you accept the distinction between "civil disobedience" in the traditional sense and "uncivil disobedience," which many wish to label "rebellion" or "revolution" since there is resort to the use of force or violence?

9. Why is "academic freedom," or freedom in the field of education, so important? Do you agree with the statement by James P. Baxter III that "freedom in education . . . underlies all the others, and anything that weakens it necessarily threatens them"?

10. What political, moral, and other issues are involved in the question of censorship?

11. Discuss the following statements, indicating the extent to which you agree or disagree with them, and why.
    (a) "Remember it is much easier to fight to keep the freedoms you have than to fight to regain the freedoms you have lost."
    (b) "This country with its institutions belongs to the people who inhabit it. Whenever they shall grow weary of the existing government, they can exercise their constitutional right of amending it, or their revolutionary right to dismember or overthrow it."
    (c) "There is no right to be wrong."
    (d) "The worst enemy of freedom is the person who obeys the community because he or she fears it."

12. A bibliography of recent and forthcoming books on men and masculinity is available on page A6 of the February 3, 1993, issue of *The Chronicle of Higher Education*. After reading one or more of the titles, write a thoughtful essay exploring relationships between traditional American masculinity and sexual ethics and/or business ethics.

13. In "Compassion on Campus" by George F. Will (*Newsweek*, May 31, 1993, p. 66), the author states:

    The right not to be offended, far from promoting civility on campus is . . . provoking acrimonious contests to see who can claim to be most, and most frequently offended, and to decide which groups' being offended matters. Special solicitude is shown to "historically oppressed classes"—basically, everyone except white heterosexual males. Being offended has become a political agenda, even a full-time vocation for some people.

Write a critique of Will's comments.

14. Discuss the following advice to Christian religious groups, quoted by Martin Marty in *Context* (June 15, 1993, p. 6):

> [We] might well pause in the rooting out and booting out of gays and lesbians among clergy, office-bearers, and members of our churches until we give more attention to the more numerous, more explicit, more definitive New Testament teachings about divorce.

15. In "The Spread of Rights Babble" (*U.S. News and World Report*, June 28, 1993, p. 17), John Leo asserts:

> We have reached the point where it's nearly impossible to discuss any problem or desire without hearing someone declare it a right. . . . Why do so many people talk this way? Well, it's a very useful language for demanding services. . . . Most groups that want something from the public have learned to put the word "rights" in their title: disability rights, animal rights, children's rights against parents, parents' rights against schools, grandparents' rights against parents. . . . Fourteen killers on death row sued for their right to reproduce through artificial insemination. . . . Their lawyer argued that rocks and streams should be treated legally like human beings who have rights but cannot speak, such as infants and other incompetents.

In an essay comment on Leo's assertions as they relate to this chapter's understanding of civil rights and liberties. Include considerations of whether rights and liberties pertain to individuals, groups, other forms of life, and/or inanimate objects.

◆ ◆

Suggested Readings

Baker, R., and Elliston, F. A. (eds.). *Philosophy and Sex.* N Rev. Ed. Buffalo, N.Y.: Prometheus, 1984.

Essays on adultery, monogamy, feminism, abortion, homosexuality, promiscuity, and perversion.

Bawer, B. *A Place At The Table: The Gay Individual In American Society.* New York: Poseidon, 1993.

The author attempts to set things right on the nature of homosexuality by stripping away the misconceptions underlying homophobia, by critically scrutinizing gay subcultures, and by defining the complex moral predicament of the gay person. Most gay people, he proposes, are as mainstream as most heterosexuals, have serious careers, want committed relationships, and hold religious beliefs.

Bedau, H. A. (ed.). *Civil Disobedience in Focus.* New York: Routledge, 1991.

A collection of a dozen essays on civil disobedience, divided into two groups. The first set include Plato's "Crito"; the well-known essays by Thoreau and Martin Luther King, Jr.; and two essays by recent critics. The second set, which begins with Rawls' position in "A Theory of Justice" includes critical essays and alternative views of six contemporary philosophers.

Bok, S. *Lying: Moral Choice in Public and Private Life.* New York: Pantheon, 1978.

A professor of ethics, the author asks, "What is a lie? Is it ever right to lie?" She looks at lying and deception in government, medicine, law, academia, journalism, the family, and friendships.

Council on Ethical and Judicial Affairs, *Codes of Medical Ethics, Current Opinions with Annotations—1994 Edition.* Chicago: American Medical Association, 1994.

This American Medical Association booklet states its principles of medical ethics and opinions on social policy issues, interprofessional relations, hospital relations, confidentiality, fees, and professional rights and responsibilities.

Cruikshank, M. *The Gay and Lesbian Liberation Movement*. New York: Routledge, 1992.

The gay and lesbian movement is examined in this book from three different perspectives: as a sexual freedom movement, as a political movement, and as a movement of ideas.

Donnelly, J. *Universal Human Rights in Theory and Practice*. Ithaca, N.Y.: Cornell University Press, 1989.

The author looks closely at the theoretical issues and practical dilemmas involved in protecting human rights internationally.

Kekes, J. *The Morality of Pluralism*. Princeton, N.J.: Princeton University Press, 1993.

Current controversies about abortion, the environment, pornography, AIDS, capital punishment, and similar issues naturally lead to the question of whether there are any values that can be ultimately justified, or whether values are simple conventional. The author's central claim is that pluralism is both reasonable and a preferable alternative to dogmatism and relativism.

Lacey, M. J., and Haakonsses, K. (eds.). *A Culture of Rights: The Bill of Rights in Philosophy, Politics and Law—1791 and 1991*. New York: Cambridge University Press, 1992.

These essays explore the cultural, moral, philosophical, legal, and political moorings of rights as they were established and have developed throughout American history.

Meyer, M. J. and Parent, W. A. (eds.). *The Constitution of Rights: Human Dignity and American Values*. Ithaca, N.Y.: Cornell University Press, 1992.

In this collection of original papers, twelve philosophers and legal thinkers focus on the relationship between our constitutional rights and human dignity.

Outka, G., and Reeder, J. P. (eds.). *Prospects For A Common Morality*. Princeton, N.J.: Princeton University Press, 1992.

This volume centers on debates about how far moral judgments bind across traditions and epochs. The contributors hope to advance the substance of the debates without prejudging the outcome.

Paul, E. F. (ed.). *Reassessing Civil Rights*. Cambridge, Mass.: Blackwell, 1991.

This exploration focuses on the attempt by democratic societies to construct laws guaranteeing that the rule of law will apply to everyone equally.

Rawls, J. *A Theory of Justice*. Cambridge, Mass.: Harvard University Press, 1971.

The author develops a theory of justice based on individual rights that, he believes, even the welfare of society as a whole should not override; he sees utilitarianism as the dominant moral view for the past two centuries and develops an alternative concept of justice.

Rion, M. *The Responsible Manager: Practical Strategies for Ethical Decision Making*. San Francisco, Calif.: Harper and Row, 1990.

An academic and corporation ethicist, the author has provided a brief text of seven chapters: (1) Six Managers and Their Questions; (2) Why Is This Bothering Me? (3) Who Else Matters? (4) Is It My Problem? (5) What Do Others Think? (6) Am I Being True To Myself? (7) Now What?

Ruse, M. *Homosexuality: A Philosophical Enquiry*. Cambridge, Mass.: Blackwell, 1988.

Writing as a philosopher, the author examines homosexuality, both historically and in the present in an attempt to understand what it is, why we have shaped certain attitudes toward it, and what intellectual challenges it presents.

Shaw, W. *Business Ethics*. Belmont, Calif.: Wadsworth, 1991.

A comprehensive survey of business ethics as an area of applied philosophy; topics include sexual harassment, business abuse of animals, drug testing, insider trading, job discrimination, whistle-blowing, affirmative action, and more.

Soble, A. (ed.). *The Philosophy of Sex: Contemporary Readings*. 2nd ed. Savage, Md.: Rowan and Littlefield, 1991.

An anthology that brings together important philosophical writings to offer an informed, critical, and imaginative investigation of the fundamental concepts surrounding human sexuality.

Sowell, T. *Preferential Policies: An International Perspective*. New York: W. Morrow, 1990.

Rights and affirmative action are examined from a conservative black viewpoint.

Veatch, R. M. (ed.). *Cross Cultural Perspectives in Medical Ethics: Readings.* Boston: Jones and Bartlett, 1989.

A collection of significant global writings that have contributed to systematic thought about medical ethics, including its basis and principles.

West, C. *Race Matters.* Boston: Beacon, 1993.

As he offers insights on issues ranging from black sexuality to the 1992 upheaval in Los Angeles, Professor West exposes flawed racial reasoning involved in the Clarence Thomas–Anita Hill affair, critiques the "ideological blinders" of the new black conservatism, and examines the roots of Malcolm X's rage.

◆ ◆

Notes

1. J. Dewey, *Freedom and Culture* (New York: Capricorn Books, 1963), p. 3.

2. J. S. Mill, *On Liberty* (London: J. M. Dent, Everyman's Library, 1910), pp. 72–73.

3. *The Right of the People,* pp. 83, 121–22, by William O. Douglas. Copyright © 1958 by William O. Douglas.

4. H. Arendt, *Crises of the Republic* (New York: Harcourt Brace Jovanovich, 1972), pp. 74–75.

5. M. L. King, Jr., *Why We Can't Wait* (New York: Harper and Row, 1963), p. 84. Copyright 1963 by Martin Luther King, Jr.

6. Arendt, *Crises of the Republic,* p. 77.

7. H. Zinn, "The Force of Nonviolence," *The Nation* (March 17, 1962).

8. *The Wolfenden Report,* entitled "Report of the Committee on Homosexual Offences and Prostitution presented to Parliament by the Secretary of State for the Home Department and the Secretary of State for Scotland by Command of Her Majesty," September 1957 (Cmmd. 247), para. 13.

9. Sir P. Devlin, *The Enforcement of Morals* (Oxford: Oxford University Press, 1965), p. 6.

10. Homosexual persons are citing instances when they are denied equal protection of their civil rights and denied equal access to vocational opportunities. See *Christianity and Crisis* 37, nos. 9 and 10 (1977).

11. H. J. Muller, *The Children of Frankenstein: A Primer on Modern Technology and Human Values* (Bloomington: Indiana University Press, 1970).

12. J. E. Smith, in "A Responsible Animal," *Yale Alumni Magazine and Journal* (November 1976), p. 2.

13. S. Toulmin, "How Medicine Saved the Life of Ethics," *Perspectives in Biological Medicine* 24 (1982): 736.

14. See the earlier discussion in this chapter on J. S. Mill, p. 142.

15. See J. Rachels, "More Impertinent Distinctions and a Defense of Active Euthanasia," in *Biomedical Ethics,* 3rd ed. ed. T. A. Mappes and J. S. Zembaty (New York: McGraw-Hill, 1991), pp. 374–81.

16. R. Munson, *Intervention and Reflection: Basic Issues in Medical Ethics,* 4th ed. Belmont, Calif.: Wadsworth, 1992.

17. See D. Maguire, *Death by Choice* (Garden City, N.Y.: Doubleday, 1973).

18. See, for example, W. H. Shaw and V. E. Barry, *Moral Issues in Business,* 5th ed. (Belmont, Calif.: Wadsworth, 1992); R. T. DeGeorge, *Business Ethics* (New York: Macmillan, 1990); and J. W. Kuhn and D. W. Shriver, Jr., *Beyond Success: Corporations and Their Critics in the 1990s* (New York: Oxford University Press, 1991).

19. D. V. Seibert, "Time To Revive a Commitment to Ethics," *New York Times,* December 25, 1983.

20. Harold H. Titus, *Living Issues in Philosophy* (New York: American Book Company, 1946), pp. 411*ff.*

21. See Chapter 1, pp. 10–11.

PART THREE

Knowledge
and Science

The Sources of Knowledge

CHAPTER OBJECTIVES

In this chapter we will address the following questions:

◆ What Are the Central Questions in Epistemology?

◆ Are Tradition and Common Sense Helpful?

◆ How Do Obstacles to Clear Thinking Impede Acquiring Knowledge?

◆ Are There Possible Sources of Knowledge?

What each man knows is, in an important sense, dependent upon his own individual experience: he knows what he has seen and heard, what he has read and what he has been told, and also what, from these data, he has been able to infer.[1]

Central Questions in the Theory of Knowledge

♦ ♦ ♦ ♦ ♦ ♦ ♦ ♦ ♦ ♦

"I *know* that for a fact!" or similar assertions occur in many ordinary conversations. Students of philosophy may hear such claims with new awareness because, as we shall discover in these three chapters on knowledge and science, the justification of statements requires more than simple assertions of certainty.

The question "What can we know?" has occupied a central place in philosophy since the time of Plato in ancient Greece. From the Renaissance on, this issue has been keenly debated in the writings of philosophers. Some knowledge of the problems involved is necessary as a background for understanding many of the major systems of philosophy that we shall consider in Part IV. It is not only one of the most important but also one of the more difficult questions in the field of philosophy. We will state the problem in nontechnical language as far as possible without sacrificing meaning and accuracy.

What is the nature of human knowledge? What is the human mind capable of knowing? Do we have any genuine knowledge on which we can depend, or must we be satisfied with mere opinions and guesses? Are we limited to the bare facts of experience, or are we able to go beyond what the senses reveal?

EPISTEMOLOGY

The technical term for the theory of knowledge is *epistemology,* which comes from the Greek word *episteme,* meaning "knowledge." There are three central questions or problems in this field: (1) What are the *sources* of knowledge? Where does genuine knowledge come from, or how do we know? This is the question of origins. (2) What is the *nature* of knowledge? Is there a real world outside the mind and, if so, can we know it? This is the question of appearance versus reality. (3) Is our knowledge *valid*? How do we distinguish truth from error? This is the question of the tests of truth, of verification. These questions are considered in this and the next chapter. In Chapter 11, we shall consider scientific methods of inquiry and the relation between science and philosophy.

Many beliefs, once considered genuine knowledge, have turned out to be false. People once firmly believed that the earth was flat, that disease demons could be driven out by loud noises, and that in dreams our souls actually visited spots distant in time and space. These beliefs, at one time so securely held, have now been almost universally discarded. May the same thing be true of much of our present-day knowledge?

Tradition and Common Sense

♦ ♦ ♦ ♦ ♦ ♦ ♦ ♦ ♦ ♦

Philosophy is a comparatively recent development in the long human struggle to understand the conditions of living. Even today, only a small percentage of the population has any real insight into the fundamental problems of human existence with which philosophers are concerned. The vast majority subscribe to commonly held opinions or beliefs based largely on tradition and custom. Let us consider briefly this less specialized fund of opinions before we examine the main sources of knowledge.

We are born into social groups that have definite ways of acting, feeling, and thinking. We become conscious of ourselves and of a world around us. We get acquainted with other persons and with things through an everwidening range of experience. Our emerging consciousness includes the sensations of touch, sight, sound, taste, and smell. As objects (or relations, qualities, and so on) and sounds are brought together through association or deliberate conditioning, we form words and learn the names of things. Words are grouped into sentences as we acquire a language. The events of our consciousness are distinctly private; no one else can be aware of our sensations. We assume, however, that the experiences of others are similar to our own.

As we grow and have further experiences, we acquire habits, feelings, thoughts, beliefs, and memories that appear to be fairly reliable. These ways of acting and thinking, engaged in without serious doubt or questioning by the members of a group, are the customs and traditions that tend to hold the individual in line. We often look to group opinion to help form our own ideas. Ways of acting and thinking are passed on from generation to generation by tradition, imitation, and instruction. These common ways of looking at things are often referred to as "common sense." **Common sense** is thus a broad term for the fund of opinion each member of the group is expected to have.

This acquired wisdom may include practical maxims and proverbs, opinions about the practices that people are expected to follow, and the unarticulated beliefs held by members of the group. That children ought to obey their parents, that animal organisms have a definite life span, that objects heavier than air fall to the ground, and that things exist independently of us and our knowledge of them—all these may be included among the countless convictions growing out of human experience.

HABITUAL AND IMITATIVE THINKING

Among the characteristics of common-sense opinion, four are worthy of note. First, common-sense opinion tends to be habitual and imitative—that is, to be inherited largely from the past. It rests on custom and tradition. What is custom and tradition for the group tends to become habit and belief for the individual. These common-sense beliefs sometimes are stated as proverbs or maxims handed down from the past, such as "Spare the rod and spoil the child." Common-sense belief places limits on the whims and the caprices of the individual, and emphasizes the tested and approved ways of the group. For this reason *common sense* often is considered to be synonymous with *good sense,* and a person of common sense is considered a person of sound judgment.

VAGUE AND AMBIGUOUS NOTIONS

Second, common-sense opinion often is vague and ambiguous. It is superficially grounded and may vary from individual to individual, from group to group, or from area to area. It is a mixture of fact and prejudice, of wisdom and emotional bias. It includes notions and opinions that have been formed without careful reflection and criticism: for example, "The good die young." Furthermore, common-sense opinion is inclusive of all areas of life in the sense that it is unspecialized belief. At times, this may be an element of strength and balance. It enables us to appeal to common sense as opposed to the one-sided and extreme claims of some specialists, who may see the world and life from a narrow point of view. Common-sense belief, however, may lead people astray. In a complex and rapidly changing world, it is frequently inadequate to meet or cope with new and unfamiliar situations.

UNTESTED BELIEF

Third, common-sense opinion is in considerable part untested belief. It is not, as some are prone to believe, a mere statement of "facts" based on first-hand sensations or other experiences. For example, "Red-headed people are quick-tempered." Like people who are not red-headed, some red-heads are quick-tempered and some are not. Positive cases seem to confirm the opinion; negative cases are seldom used to refute it. Although those who hold them may think these notions are self-evident, the ideas actually are based on assumptions that are often unexamined and need to be checked and criticized. Although some notions of common sense can be verified, the history of science and philosophy makes it clear that the "first look" is not always correct, and that things are not always what they appear to be.

SELDOM-EXPLAINED ASSUMPTIONS

Fourth, common-sense opinions seldom are accompanied by supported explanations of why things are as they are alleged to be. Explanations are missing or, if they are present, usually are so general that they overlook exceptions and limiting conditions. For example, if water is said to freeze at low temperatures, why is this? Why is it that flowing water and salt water do not freeze under the same conditions as do still and fresh water? In distinguishing science from common sense, Ernest Nagel says, "It is the desire for explanations which are at once systematic and controllable by factual evidence that generates science; and it is the organization and classification of knowledge on the basis of explanatory principles that is the distinctive goal of the sciences."[2]

We never leave common-sense belief wholly behind us, regardless of how far our education carries us or how specialized our knowledge becomes. It may be fortunate that we never completely abandon common-sense belief, because it may serve as a check against the "blind spots" some people develop through intensive specialization. But common-sense belief, if it is to serve this useful purpose, needs constant and careful reexamination.

Obstacles to Clear Thinking

Just as speech defects may prevent a person from speaking clearly, so thought impediments may prevent a person from thinking clearly. Emotion, personal interests, or outside pressures may lead our thinking astray. These obstacles to clear thinking may cause our science and our philosophy to be biased, and they are especially likely to influence and to distort our fund of common-sense opinions.

IDOLS OF THE MIND

Francis Bacon (1561–1626) (see biography and excerpt, pp. 172–173) has given us a classic statement of the errors of thinking in his famous "Idols of the Mind."[3] These are, first, the *Idols of the Tribe*. We are apt to recognize evidence and incidents favorable to our own side or group (tribe or nation). Second, there are the *Idols of the Cave*. We tend to see ourselves as the center of the world and to stress our own limited outlook. Third, the *Idols of the Marketplace* cause us to be influenced by the words and names with which we are familiar in everyday discourse. We are led astray by emotionally toned words—for example, in our society such words as *communist*

or *liberal*. Finally, the *Idols of the Theater* arise from our attachment to parties, creeds, and cults. These fads, fashions, and schools of thought are like stage plays in the sense that they lead us into imaginary worlds; ultimately, the Idols of the Theater lead us to biased conclusions.

Handicaps to clear thinking may be stated in other than these classic terms. Some that we would recognize are prejudice, susceptibility to propaganda, and authoritarianism.

PREJUDICE

Prejudices always inhibit clear thinking. The human mind frequently finds it difficult to suspend judgment until all the evidence is in.[4] Even after the evidence has been gathered, our prejudices make it difficult for us to draw accurate conclusions. A prejudice is a prejudgment, a mental bias, that leads us to ignore or to minimize some of the evidence and to overestimate other parts of it. Prejudices usually rest on emotional grounds and tend to be in line with our comfort, pride, and self-interest. When confronted with our prejudices, we are likely to try to rationalize them—that is, we try to find "reasons" or arguments for continuing to believe what we wish to believe.

PROPAGANDA

Another obstacle to clear thinking is our susceptibility to propaganda. Even when we want to face facts and think clearly, our thinking may go astray because our information is tainted or manipulated by its sources. The propagandists of special-interest groups use media such as radio, television, the press, and motion pictures to control our thinking. Propagandists attempt, first, to arouse in us a strong emotion or desire and then, through suggestion, to present a line of action that appears to be a satisfactory way of expressing the emotion or satisfying the desire. There is, however, no necessary—that is, logical—connection between the emotion to be aroused, such as one's love for one's spouse, and the proposed line of action, which may be buying anything from flowers to a grand piano.

Francis Bacon

Francis Bacon (1561–1626), English philosopher and statesman, was born in London. His father was Lord Keeper of the Great Seal under Queen Elizabeth. He studied at Cambridge University and later held important governmental posts. He was elected to Parliament in 1584 and knighted in 1603. He was one of the earliest and most influential supporters of the English empirical movement and the use of scientific methods. Previous claims to knowledge, he thought, were largely false, yet he believed that people could discover truth by the inductive method. First, however, the mind had to be cleared of various prejudices he called "idols."

Bacon's most important writings in philosophy and science are *The Advancement of Learning* (1605), which relates the progress in human knowledge to his own day, and the *Novum Organum* (1620), a discussion of the method of induction based on observation and experiment. He also wrote much in the fields of history and political affairs: *The Wisdom of the Ancients* (1609), *The New Atlantis* (1624), a discussion of the ideal state; and his *Essays,* which deal with a wide range of observations on humans and affairs. At the height of his career, when short of funds, he was convicted of taking bribes (1621) and sentenced to a short imprisonment and a large fine. He spent his last few years in retirement.

Excerpt from Bacon:

Novum Organum (1620)

There are four classes of idols which beset men's minds. To these for distinction's sake I have assigned names,—calling the first class *Idols of the Tribe;* the second *Idols of the Cave;* the third, *Idols of the Marketplace;* the fourth, *Idols of the Theater.*

The Idols of the Tribe have their foundation in human nature itself, and in the tribe or race of men. For it is a false assertion that the sense of man is the measure of things. On the contrary, all perceptions, as well of the sense as of the mind, are according to the measure of the individual and not according to the measure of the universe. And the human understanding is like a false mirror, which, receiving rays irregularly, distorts and discolors the nature of things by mingling its own nature with it.

The Idols of the Cave are the idols of the individual man. For everyone (besides the errors common to human nature in general) has a cave or den of its own, which refracts and discolors the light of nature; owing either to his own proper and peculiar nature or to his education and conversation with others; or to the reading of books, and the authority of those whom he esteems and admires; or to the differences of impressions, accordingly as they take place in a mind preoccupied and predisposed or in a mind indifferent and settled; or the like.

There are also idols formed by the intercourse and association of men with each other, which I call Idols of the Marketplace, on account of the commerce and consort of men there. For it is by discourse that men associate; and words are imposed according to the apprehension of the vulgar. And therefore the ill and unfit choice of words wonderfully obstructs the understanding. . . . But words plainly force and overrule the understanding, and throw all into confusion, and lead men away into numberless empty controversies and idle fancies.

Lastly, there are idols which have immigrated into men's minds from the various dogmas of philosophies, and also from wrong laws of demonstration. These I call Idols of the Theater; because in my judgment all the received systems are but so many stageplays, representing worlds of their own creation after an unreal and scenic fashion. Nor is it only of the systems now in vogue, or only of the ancient sects and philosophies, that I speak: for many more plays of the same kind may yet be composed and in like artificial manner set forth; seeing that errors the most widely different have nevertheless causes for the most part alike. Neither again do I mean this only of entire systems, but also of many principles and axioms in science, which by tradition, credulity, and negligence have come to be received.

Francis Bacon, *Novum Organum,* in *The English Philosophers from Bacon to Mill,* ed. E. A. Burtt (New York: Modern Library, 1939).

AUTHORITARIANISM

The uncritical or blind appeal to authority is an unphilosophical and unscientific method of gaining knowledge, whether the authority is custom, tradition, the family, the church, the state, or the mass media of communication. Uncritical acceptance of authority is called **authoritarianism.**

Authoritarianism is different from the mere acceptance of the views of a particular authority (such as a specialist) on certain occasions; it is the belief that knowledge is guaranteed or validated by the authority's words alone. When we accept authority uncritically, we cease our independent efforts to find out what is true or false. Regardless of its form, testimony that is accepted on unsupported faith, and without regard to the extent to which it does or does not harmonize with experience and reason, is a dangerous thing.

The weaknesses and dangers of authoritarianism are numerous. First, as a dominant attitude, which uses no tests for knowledge except authority, it tends to block progress and to be a substitute for thinking and further investigation. We live in a rapidly changing social order, in which the beliefs and practices of one age may be quite inadequate in a later period. Second, when authorities disagree or conflict, as they frequently do, we are left in confusion unless we have other sources to which we can turn. Third, we are likely to be led astray by the prestige of our authority and fail to realize when he or she speaks outside the range of his or her competence. People who are competent in one field are quite likely to be believed when they speak on some other subject about which they may have no special knowledge. Fourth, we may be led astray by the fact that a belief has been persistent and widespread. Such widespread acceptance may add to its prestige and appeal and make it difficult for us to discover ancient errors. Many of these beliefs may be wrong; indeed, many have been disproved.

As a classic illustration of authoritarianism we can cite the scholastic thinkers of the Middle Ages, who dared not deviate from the teachings of the Church and the writings of Aristotle. Modern counterparts exist; a political "party line" comes to mind most quickly, but you can think of others.

Many people welcome authority because they have little confidence in themselves or are intellectually lazy: to accept the word of someone else is the easy way of gaining comfort and assurance. People in general tend to be imitative, credulous, and suggestible. To hear or to read is to believe, and so they accept the idea, "follow the crowd," "toe the party line." To follow the crowd and fall in line with public opinion is the refuge, too, of confused and weary minds. Such conformist tendencies in human beings create fertile soil for modern advertising and propaganda.

FALLACIES IN THINKING

The pressure of public opinion, prejudice, propaganda, and blind acceptance of authority are not the only obstacles to thinking. We are all creatures of impulse and habit. Although habits are useful in taking care of the routine details of life, they do not help and they sometimes hinder us when we are faced with new and unfamiliar situations.

There is also a wide range of fallacies in thinking, or violations of the principles of logic and consistency. While discussing logic in the opening chapter of this text, we referred to the need to distinguish between valid and invalid arguments.[5] When an argument violates a rule of inference it is said to be fallacious. It is important not to confuse a false statement with a fallacy. We should not say, for example, "The belief that a child's sex is determined by its mother is an ancient fallacy." This belief is an ancient *error*, but it is not fallacious. Only *arguments* can be fallacious.[6] A *formal fallacy* is a fallacy of inference; formal fallacies cause us to draw invalid conclusions from our premises, such as when we make an assertion about all the members of a group when the premises permit us to speak of only some.

Informal fallacies are common errors in reasoning into which we may fall either because of carelessness and inattention to our subject matter or through being misled by some ambiguity in the language with which we formulate our argument.[7] We can divide informal fallacies into fallacies of *ambiguity* and fallacies of *relevance*.

A fallacy of ambiguity occurs in arguments the formulations of which contain ambiguous words or phrases, the meanings of which shift and change subtly in the course of that argument and thus render it fallacious. For example, if the term *law* in a discussion of natural law is changed surreptitiously to refer to a civil or moral law (in the sense of a rule of conduct), we have a shift of meaning.

Common to all arguments that commit fallacies of relevance is that their premises are *logically irrelevant* to, and therefore incapable of establishing the truth of, their conclusions. A common example of a fallacy of relevance is **begging the question,** in which we assume as a premise for our argument the conclusion we intend to prove. If the proposition to be established were formulated in exactly the same words both as premise and as conclusion, the mistake would be so glaring that it would deceive no one. Often, however, two formulations can be so different that they obscure the fallacy. For example, we may argue that Shakespeare is a greater writer than Agatha Christie because people with good taste in literature prefer Shakespeare. If asked how we tell who has good taste in literature, we reply that such persons are identified by their preferring Shakespeare to Christie. Such a *circular argument* clearly begs the question.

One of the most frequent obstacles to clear thinking is the **ad hominem** ("to the man") fallacy. This faulty reasoning shifts from an issue to a personality. We find it in news stories, editorials, political speeches, religious debates, and ordinary conversations.

"I know there is no God, because all persons believe in God for psychological reasons." Notice what has happened! The issue is the existence of God. This kind of reasoning, however, shifts from any examination of the issue to a focus on personal motivations for belief; human motivations do not prove or disprove the existence of God. Even if it could be *proved* that all religious people are out of their minds, the separate issue of God's existence has been ignored. In fact, human motivations do not affirm or deny *any* issue; they simply offer possible reasons for some people's support of or opposition to an idea.

"My opponent is a liar; he cannot be believed." Attacking a person's character is another ad hominem method. The speaker has not relied on evidence to prove or disclaim an issue; instead she has depended on name-calling. She has not called into question her opponent's stand on issues; she has attacked the opponent personally.

"Jones believes in busing. What would he know, he has no children." "Don't trust what *he* says; he's different." An ad hominem method avoids the mental effort of examining an issue. It fails to prove or disprove a statement; it substitutes "getting personal" for relevant evidence.

Additional informal fallacies with examples follow.

> *Use of threat.* "If you insist on teaching that view, you will find everyone against you, and then it will be *too late* for you to change your mind."
>
> *False cause.* "The incidence of crime in contemporary Western civilization is less than it was when the Christian Church \prevailed, therefore Christianity generates crime."
>
> *Appeal to ignorance.* "I believe in reincarnation because there's no reason not to."
>
> *Appeal to the mob.* "Of course Columbus discovered America; everyone knows that!"
>
> *Hasty conclusion.* "I saw them together late last night; they're clearly committed to each other."
>
> *Guilt by association.* "They were walking with a member of the KKK; they must be members, too."
>
> *Slippery slope.* "If you have a cocktail at the weekly social, you'll be an alcoholic in no time." (One thing will definitely lead to another.)

Straw man. "Darwinism is in error. It claims that we are all descendants from an apelike creature, from which we evolved according to natural selection. No evidence of such a creature has been found. No adequate and consistent explanation of natural selection has been given. Therefore, evolution according to Darwinism has not taken place." (Attack a proposal indirectly by setting up and destroying a substitute proposal that is more vulnerable but beside the point.)

CLOSED MINDS

An individual's commitment to particular "idols of the mind" prevents creativity in thought and action. For example, the firmly held conviction that the earth was the center of the universe prevented many people from seriously considering a different explanation, namely, that the earth is one of several planets revolving around one of billions of suns in the universe. Among many medieval scholars of Western civilization it was unacceptable to conceive of our planet as anywhere but at the center of God's creation. For those individuals a commitment to the idea of an earth-centered cosmos had prevented alternative understandings. Other inquirers with open minds led to advances in our explanations of the earth's place in the universe.

Firmly held ideas by people with closed minds can also prevent variations in human relations. For example, a televised news series contained interviews with several married couples; the women were six or more years older than their husbands. In one reported case of the six-year age difference, immediate relatives of both the man and the woman refused to speak to either of them; family members as well as friends considered the couple "unnatural." The couples were subjected to cruel remarks suggesting mental illness or financial motives for the relationships. Not fitting the customary idea that husbands should be of the same age or older than their wives, such marriages were viewed by some people as unacceptable.

Whenever people with closed minds cling to particular ideas and view other ideas on a subject as automatically unacceptable, they hinder the pursuit of new ideas.

The Possible Sources of Knowledge

In his well-known *Essay Concerning Human Understanding,* John Locke (1632–1704) points out how the problem of the sources of knowledge is fundamental.

> Were it fit to trouble thee with the history of this Essay, I should tell thee, that five or six friends meeting at my chamber, and discoursing on a subject very remote from this, found themselves quickly at a stand, by the difficulties that arose on every side. After we had a while puzzled ourselves, without coming any nearer a resolution of those doubts which perplexed us, it came into my thoughts, that we took a wrong course; and that before we set ourselves upon inquiries of that nature, it was necessary to examine our own abilities, and see what objects our understandings were, or were not, fitted to deal with. This I proposed to the company, who all readily assented; and thereupon it was agreed, that this should be our first inquiry.[8]

Immanuel Kant (1724–1804) also placed this issue first among the central questions of life. Since the time of Locke and of Kant, the problem of knowledge has occupied a prominent place in philosophical discussions.

Where did we get the beliefs we now hold? Is there some one source of knowledge, or are there many sources of knowledge? If there are many sources, are some more important than others? Four sources of knowledge usually are recognized by modern philosophers.

THE APPEAL TO AUTHORITY

How do we know that Socrates and Julius Caesar ever lived? Are they perhaps fictitious characters, like many others about whom we read in ancient mythology and in modern novels? We know that Socrates and Julius Caesar lived because of the testimony of their contemporaries and of the historians. In fact, the most common way of gaining knowledge about the past is to rely on the testimony of others—that is, on authority. Much of the knowledge we use in everyday living also has been gained in that way. Thus, we have gained this knowledge neither by intuition, nor by thinking it out for ourselves, nor by personal experience, but through the thoughts of others and the facts discovered in the special fields of the various sciences.

Authority as a source of knowledge has its values as well as its dangers. Testimony or authority that is open to free and honest inquiry as to its validity is a legitimate source of knowledge. We need to accept such testimony in areas that we cannot investigate adequately for ourselves. We should make reasonably certain, however, that those we accept as authorities are people of integrity who have had more opportunity than we to gain the information desired. We need to know that these people have used the best methods available at the time. We must leave the solution of some questions to experts in whose knowledge and skill we have reasonable confidence. The testimony of others may be valuable in bringing us a summary of the conclusions to which they have been led by their experience. Such testimony may suggest to us where and how to look for evidence and so direct our attention to what we might otherwise overlook. In discussing "the grounds of belief," Max Black says, "Among the most useful tests of qualification applied to alleged authorities are *recognition by other authorities* (especially as evidenced by such official signs of respectability as titles, diplomas, and degrees), *agreement with other authorities,* and *special competence* ('being in a position to know')."[9]

Testimony or authority is a secondary source, not a primary one. When we ask, "From what source did our authority gain his or her knowledge?" we should not be satisfied with merely additional authorities. We want to know whether our authority gained information by experience, or reason, or some other way, and whether we can examine the steps by which the conclusions were reached.

Appeal to authority has both values and dangers. Authority as a source of knowledge is dangerous only when we surrender our independent judgment and make no effort to discover what is true or false. In the previous section, we considered some of the main dangers of the blind acceptance of tradition and authority.

THE SENSES AS A SOURCE: EMPIRICISM

How do we know that water will freeze or that it will revive a drooping plant? We may say that we know by means of our sensory organs from our own past experience.

What we see, hear, touch, smell, and taste—that is, our concrete experience—constitutes the realm of knowledge, according to the *empiricists.* Empiricism stresses our power of perception, or observation, or what the senses receive from the environment. Knowledge is obtained by forming ideas in accordance with observed facts. Stated briefly, empiricism maintains that we know what we have found out from our senses.

Empiricism may take a number of forms. As a narrow sensationalism (that is, referring to the senses), it asserts that knowledge is essentially sensation and that there is no other knowledge. In the eighteenth century, John Locke regarded the mind as analogous to a piece of wax: as wax shows the form of what is pressed against it, so the mind registers impressions as they come from the world outside.

More recent empiricism has abandoned this theory of knowledge. Pragmatism views the mind as active in selecting and molding its experiences in accordance with the interests and purposes of the organism. It emphasizes the changing world of experience. (Pragmatism is considered separately as a philosophical perspective in Part IV.)

Modern science, which is especially interested in particular facts and relations, is empirical. Scientists are interested in controlled observations and experiments, not merely in general sense perceptions and experiences, and they strive to keep irrelevant factors from disturbing their examination of some special problem or event. Items can be changed or manipulated, and the effects can be recorded. Furthermore, if the conditions are controlled, the experiment can be repeated by other observers; thus more accurate and objective information can be obtained. Special instruments can be used to aid observation, help eliminate errors, and measure results. The conclusions, however, are always tentative and are set forth in the form of hypotheses, theories, or possibly laws, which, after further observation and research, may need to be modified or changed. The process of building the great body of scientific knowledge is a slow one, involving the labor of thousands of scientists in many parts of the world. This knowledge enables us to exercise considerable control over our world, and it is of constant service in our daily lives.

DIFFICULTIES WITH SENSATIONALISM

When philosophers and others reflect on the sources of knowledge, they find that it is much more complicated and baffling than most people realize; they find, as we have seen, that the beliefs of sensationalism are frequently unexamined. Let us look at some of the problems that arise in sense perception, a source of knowledge, using some of the simpler examples that occur frequently in the literature on the subject.

The Sense of Sight. As we look at objects, they appear to have some color. Where or what is color? If I put on blue-colored glasses, the world looks blue. If I put on red glasses, the world looks red. If we ingest an overdose of santonin or put it in our eyes, everything looks yellow. Color appears to be either wholly or in part affected by the condition of our visual organs. In the cases mentioned, nothing has been done to the "outer" world. A person with "normal" vision may see an object and call it red, whereas a color-blind person sees it as green. But if two people with supposedly normal eyes look at the same object and call it red, have we any assurance that

they both see the same shade of red? Even if they do see exactly the same thing, does that mean anything more than that they both have the same type and quality of visual apparatus?

If our eyes were constructed more like microscopes, would we appear to live in the world that we now inhabit? On the other hand, if they were gauged more like telescopes, would we seem to live in a still different world? Some animals, we are told, can see by ultraviolet light, which gives us no color sensation. Light from some of the stars I saw last evening took thousands of years to come to the earth. What I see is not the star but a little bit of light. It is possible that the star disappeared years ago.

There is a coin on my desk. People say it is circular, but from most points of view it looks elliptical. There are only two points from which it appears circular: that directly over it and that directly under it. Many observers could have many different "coinlike" sense data. Apparently, the sense data and the coin (whatever it is) are not identical. When I say that I "see" a book on my desk, what I see ordinarily is a part of the cover or jacket and one end or one side of the book. The book is in part perceived, but it is in part a mental construct. This is characteristic of most of the objects we are said to experience. When I apply pressure to my eyeball at precisely the right place, I see double; for example, I can see two pencils on my desk, not just one. If all of us had grown up with a bone pressing at that point, would we all see two things where we now see just one?

The Sense of Sound. In hearing we are presented with problems similar to those in vision. If I am standing by the railway tracks and a whistling locomotive rushes past me, the pitch of the whistle changes definitely as the engine approaches me, is opposite me, and recedes. The engineer or the fireman will insist that the pitch was the same throughout. Here are two different sense data apparently from one object.

At a track meet, the starting pistol must sound before any of the runners leave the starting line. If you are at the far end of some tracks, you can see the runners start before you hear the pistol report—that is, the order of your sense data reverses what other observers insist are the "facts" of the situation. In dreams and hallucinations, we may have a vivid impression of voices or other sounds when there are no corresponding external factors.

The Sense of Touch.   As the philosopher George Berkeley pointed out years ago, water may feel warm to one hand and cool to the other if, when we plunge both hands into the same water, one of our hands is cool and the other is warm.

If I stand near the fire, I experience the sensation of heat. In common practice, we speak of the heat as a quality of the fire. But is it? As I move nearer the fire or into it, I experience the sensation of pain from the greater degree of heat. Yet the pain is my pain and not in the fire. Is the heat, also, a sensation of mine rather than a property of the fire? Raise the temperature of our bodies only a few degrees and the world feels and looks different. C. E. M. Joad, who points out some of these facts, suggests that there is no particular reason that the sensations possessed by an adult with a body temperature of 98.6° F should be privileged to be considered "real."[10]

If parts of our nervous system are appropriately stimulated, we can get various sensations of touch. A person who loses a limb may still experience a sense of touch, or of twitching, or of pain in the missing limb, as if it were still there.

The Senses of Smell and Taste.   The sense organs of smell and taste are especially fickle, as many people can testify. They are sometimes influenced by what we have just been eating or smelling, and a head cold may greatly diminish their range and consistency. Here again our experiences seem to be affected by the nature and the condition of the sense organs, as well as by what may be "out there."

Memory, Dreams, and Hallucinations.   We can remember past objects, people, and events. Sometimes our memory is clear and vivid. We can imagine all sorts of things with equal vividness. In dreams and hallucinations, we seem to see, hear, touch, smell, and taste things that have no present position in the spatiotemporal order, as we and others may judge the situation at a later time. There is a dualism here that leads us to ask whether in ordinary perceptions we may be creating our sense data wholly or in part. How reliable are these as sources of knowledge?

Although we depend on empirical knowledge for our acquaintance with the particular facts and relations of our everyday world, we need to exercise caution and realize that we can be led astray even in the area of sense data. Prejudices and emotions may distort our view so that we select our "facts" to support our expectations. We tend to see what we expect to see or are trained to see. Our knowledge is influenced by a personal and subjective coloration. The fact that philosophers and scientists can easily invalidate our mental and physical concepts of the world should make us more cautious in our judgments. The extent to which the world as we know it is appearance or reality is considered in the next chapter.

THINKING AS A SOURCE: RATIONALISM

How do we know that two contradictory statements cannot be true at the same time? How do we know that if two things each are identical to a third thing, they are identical to each other? We say that such things are self-evident or that they appeal to our reason.

The thinkers who stress reasoning or thought as the central factor in knowledge are known as *rationalists*. Rationalism is the view that we know what we have thought out, that the mind has the ability to discover truth by itself, or that knowledge is obtained by comparing ideas with ideas. The rationalist, in emphasizing the human power of thought and what the mind contributes to knowledge, is likely to assert that the senses, by themselves, cannot give us coherent and universally valid judgments. The highest kind of knowledge consists in universally valid judgments that are consistent with one another. The sensations and experiences that we gain through the senses—sight, sound, touch, taste, and smell—are just the raw material of knowledge. These sensations must be organized by the mind into a meaningful system before they become knowledge. For the rationalist, knowledge is found in concepts, principles, and laws, not just in physical sensations.

In its less extreme form, rationalism makes the claim that we have the power to know, with certainty, various truths about the universe that the senses alone cannot give us. For example, if A is larger than B and B is larger than C, then A is larger than C. We know that this is true quite independently of any actual instances. We know that it applies generally to boxes, to cities, or to people, even when we have not experienced it or tried it out. Among other "necessary truths"—truths that do not depend on observation for either their discovery or their verification—are: five plus five equals ten; the three interior angles of a triangle are equal to two right angles; a square has four sides of equal length.

In its more extreme form, rationalism makes the claim that we are capable of arriving at irrefutable knowledge independently of sense experience. From this point of view, the rationalist claims to be able to provide us with genuine knowledge, truths (laws) about the world and not merely laws of thought. Furthermore, the thoroughgoing rationalist is likely to interpret these laws, discovered by thought, as basic principles of nature in general.

CONTROVERSIAL ISSUES ABOUT RATIONALISM

A priori knowledge refers to knowledge that is self-evident or to principles recognized to be true apart from observation or experience. By way of contrast, **a posteriori** knowledge is knowledge based on actual observation, empirical evidence.

The question of whether there is any a priori knowledge is exceedingly controversial. The examples most frequently cited are from the formal disciplines of logic and mathematics, in which the principles used appear to have a high degree of certainty and universality. Logic and mathematics are products, not of the senses, but of reason; yet they give us reliable knowledge. For example, consider the statements "If equals are added to equals, the sums are equal," and "A thing cannot both exist and not exist at the same time." We can see by *thinking* about them that these principles and relations must be true, although we have not tested them in all possible situations. Concrete experience does not increase or diminish our assurance of them. To think clearly, we are obliged to accept the validity of certain laws of thought, such as: the Principle of Identity, "If p is true, then p is true" (All A is A); the Principle of Noncontradiction, "Not both p is true and p is false" (Not both A and not-A); and the Principle of Excluded Middle, "p is either true or false" (Either A or not-A).[11] The mind, it is said, has certain preformed principles, or certain innate ways of operating. The empiricist (the person who emphasizes sense perception or experiences) regards these principles as the laws of thinking—directives without which meaningful discourse cannot occur—and not genuine knowledge.

Many philosophers admit that we do possess some knowledge not directly derived from sense experience. However, we need not extend the claims for the power of reason too far, as some of the more extreme rationalists do. One criticism of the rationalist's position is that it is probable that some sense experience is necessary to draw out or to make clear these general principles. We need to deal with particular things before we get a sense of numbers, and to experience lines, angles, and triangles before we can build geometrical systems. This criticism, however, misses the point because it confuses psychological and temporal priority with the real question, which is logical priority. The issue, for example, is not whether we have sense experience before we can know certain mathematical truth, but whether the justification of such truth consists in an appeal to sense experience. The rationalist insists that the question is one of logical priority and what is required for verification. Another criticism is that it appears to be clear that such a priori knowledge as we have in fields like logic and mathematics is purely formal or abstract, and that it does not inform us of what actually exists in the world. Such knowledge deals not with the existing external world but with our world of relations and meanings. All this knowledge is of the "if . . . then . . ." variety. To say that "five plus five equals ten" is not to say that any particular thing exists; it is to say that if you have five items (of anything) and receive five other items, then you have ten items. So far as the external world is concerned, we learn about its rich variety by means of the senses and not by means of any a priori knowledge.

The danger of the extreme forms of rationalism is that we may substitute deductive reasoning for empirical observation. In so doing, we may come to accept some system that has logical consistency but little relevance to the world in which we live. The medieval scholars, as well as Descartes, Spinoza, Kant, and other thinkers, have set forth systems of thought that have a high degree of logical consistency. Quite obviously they cannot all be true. The medieval scholars, assuming that perfect motions were circular and that planetary motions were perfect, reasoned that planetary motions must be circular motions; this conclusion is now rejected as false.

THE APPEAL TO INTUITION

How do we know, as we occasionally seem to know when we meet someone for the first time, that here is a person who can be trusted? Some people do feel that they know such things. Similarly, some people fall in love almost at first sight. Do we have some sense or intuition that sometimes gives us immediate insight into situations?

A possible source of knowledge is intuition, or the direct apprehension of knowledge that is not the result of conscious reasoning or of immediate sense perception. In the literature dealing with intuition, one comes across such expressions as "immediate feeling of certainty," "imagination touched with conviction," a "total response" to some "total situation," and a "direct insight into truth." We may note the following positions regarding intuition.

1. *There is an element of intuition present in all knowledge.* George Santayana uses *intuition* to mean our awareness of the immediate data of consciousness. W. E. Hocking (see biography and excerpt, pp. 182–183) speaks of self-knowledge as the "best case for intuition;" knowledge of oneself appears to be present as an element in all knowledge of other objects.[12] When I hear a whistle, in addition to hearing it, I am aware of my hearing and aware of myself as the one who does the hearing. Intuition is present in the knowledge of oneself and one's own life, in the axioms of mathematics, and in what we "take for granted." It is present in our understanding of the connection among the propositions that constitute the various steps of an argument. Reasoning itself depends on some connection that we grasp or fail to grasp.[13] An intuitive element is the foundation of our recognition of the beautiful, of the moral standards that we accept, and of our religious values.

2. *Intuition is merely the result of the accumulation of one's past experience and thinking.* Valid intuitions are shortcuts to the knowledge that the senses and reflective thinking would reveal. They are the outcome of subconscious induction or deduction. Those who have had considerable experience in thinking and working in a field are more likely than others to have good intuitions in that area. "The following are among the most frequently accepted uses of the term 'intuition' in contemporary scientific literature: quick perception, imagination, abbreviated reason, and sound judgment."[14] Scientific insight comes to those who have labored persistently over scientific problems; poetic inspirations come to those who are practiced in writing poetry; musical inspirations come to those who know and practice music; philosophical and religious intuitions come to those who devote time and attention to these fields.

3. *Intuition is a higher kind of knowledge, different in nature from that disclosed by the senses or by the intellect.* The outstanding representative of this point of view is Henri Bergson (1859–1941) (see biography and excerpt, pp. 184–185), the French philosopher. For Bergson, intuition and intelligence are pointed in opposite directions.

William Ernest Hocking

William Ernest Hocking (1873–1966), philosopher and metaphysician, was born in Ohio. His early years were spent in the Middle West while studying civil engineering at Iowa State University. As a result of private reading which stimulated his interest in philosophy, Hocking went to Harvard University; there he completed undergraduate and graduate studies, greatly influenced by William James and Josiah Royce. After posts at the University of California and Yale, he served on Harvard's faculty for most of his long teaching career until his retirement in 1943.

Hocking defended "objective idealism." He claimed that an integral relation exists between ideas (intellect) and feeling (intuition) expressed in a "principle of alternation" through which we arrive at truth. Mind is the creative principle and the primary certitude of experience. Other Mind, or God, as ultimate reality is known directly and intuitively. His philosophical system embodies aspects of both pragmatism and realism.

Among his writings are *The Meaning of God in Human Experience* (1912), *Human Nature and Its Remaking* (1918), and *Science and the Idea of God* (1944).

Intelligence, or intellect, is the tool science uses to deal with matter. It deals with things and with quantitative relations. It solidifies whatever it touches and is incapable of dealing with the nature of life or with duration. Intuition, which is instinct become self-conscious, can lead us to the very inwardness of life. If intuition can extend itself, it will give us the clue to vital operations. We discover the *élan vital,* the vital impulse of the world, by intuition, which is inward and immediate, rather than by intellect, which is external and describes the living in static terms.

4. *Intuition as found in mystical expressions may enable us to gain an immediate knowledge that transcends knowledge gained through reason and the senses.* Mysticism or mystical knowledge has been defined as "the condition of being overwhelmingly aware of the presence of the ultimately real."[15] Mystical intuition may be manifested as union of the self with spiritual reality, communion between the self and personal deity, or as cosmic consciousness (a sense of merging into the totality of the universe). This form of intuitive knowledge will be discussed further in Chapter 17.

Wherever we have feeling, we have an awareness of some object or situation. Fear, anger, and jealousy arise because of our awareness of some unpleasant situation. Love, sympathy, and laughter involve knowledge. Feeling ap-

267. Our business hitherto has been to understand the fundamental types of philosophy rather than to pass judgment upon them. I have made critical comments on various of these types in passing, not as offering a final assessment, but as indicating the motives which lead me in each case to go farther in my own search for truth. It is now our business to consider, each for himself, where he stands; certainly not in the vain hope of finishing one's world-view, but by way of demanding of ourselves what result is left by the working of these types upon our minds, whether any coherent view or direction.

Your philosophy will be made of the sum of the truths you see. The review of these types must have aided this seeing, by bringing into clearer expression many an idea which you had vaguely apprehended before. It may be that you have recognized some one of these types as your own. On the other hand, it is not likely that any great strand of human thought, such as these types are, is wholly alien to you. It is conceivable that you may find yourself belonging to all types, and to none. Mental hospitality is in danger of finding itself encumbered with an ill-fitting assortment of beliefs, composed of fragments from various types: there is "something in" all of them! This state of mind is intelligent and liberal; but also deficient in strength and decisiveness—a success, which is a relative failure. No one wants to live with a patchwork philosophy.

W. E. Hocking, *Types of Philosophy* (New York: Scribner's, 1939).

pears to contain essential elements of truth needed to meet various life situations and bring about our adjustment to them. Animals have a "feeling knowledge" in connection with food gathering, nest building, and migration that gives them a true sense of situations and sustains their life. Hocking, in pointing out such facts, suggests the possibility of this feeling sense becoming in humans a "valuable organ of knowledge." The intuitionists believe that a "total response to the total situation" may supplement the particular senses and the efforts of the intellect. The student of this problem should watch experiments that deal with possible causative factors in the behavior of animals, such as the migration of birds, and also the experiments in human extrasensory perception.

Intuition may function more adequately in connection with elemental, or basic, life interests as distinct from those judgments that are complex, or composite. William Pepperell Montague says:

> We might take as an example of an elemental interest romantic love and the judgment of faith on which it is based. It would surely be a vain and preposterous undertaking to discover one's true sweetheart by accepting the authority of others, by using deductive reasoning and calculation, by cold-blooded empirical analysis of her perceivable qualities, or by considering the

Henri Bergson

Henri Bergson (1859–1941), a French philosopher born in Paris of Anglo-Polish parentage, taught at the College of France from 1900 to 1921, when he retired because of ill health. Born the same year in which Darwin's *Origin of Species* was published, Bergson became the leader of a new life philosophy that gave attention to the concepts of evolution, creative life impulses, time and duration, intuition, and freedom. He opposed the positivism, materialism, and mechanism of his age in a number of books including *Time and Free Will* (1889); *Matter and Memory* (1896); and *Creative Evolution* (1907), his masterpiece and best-known work. Bergson became famous as a teacher, lecturer, and writer and received many honors, including election to the French Academy and the Nobel Prize for literature.

extent to which she might be a practical utility. All of these nonmystical methods would doubtless be appropriate in the selection of a business partner, a housekeeper, or even in making a marriage of convenience. But no one either could or would fall in love for any other reason than that the beloved appealed in a direct and unanalyzable manner to his heart or his feelings. In other words, the lover as such is and must always remain a mystic. And even in forming the belief on which one bases his choice of a friend, intuition is almost as indispensable as in choosing a sweetheart. True friendship is certainly not based upon either calculation or utility, but upon the direct appeal to our sympathies and affections. The same might be said of objects of art, the primary enjoyment of which is not based upon considerations that are rationally analyzable.[16]

The weakness or danger of intuition is that it does not seem to be a safe method of obtaining knowledge when used alone. It goes astray easily and may lead to absurd claims unless it is controlled or checked by reason and the senses. "No intuition or experience is so secure that it can elude rational criticism."[17] Intuition must turn to the percepts of the sense organs and the concepts of reason when it attempts to communicate and explain itself or to defend itself against false interpretations or attacks. Intuition seems to presuppose and to be affected by our previous experience and thought. An intuited "truth," supported by evidence, may be acceptable where intuition alone or reason alone would be insufficient.

A comparison of the definitions of metaphysics and the various conceptions of the absolute leads to the discovery that philosophers, in spite of their apparent divergencies, agree in distinguishing two profoundly different ways of knowing a thing. The first implies that we move round the object; the second that we enter into it. The first depends on the point of view at which we are placed and on the symbols by which we express ourselves. The second neither depends on a point of view nor relies on any symbol. The first kind of knowledge may be said to stop at the *relative;* the second, in those cases where it is possible, to attain the *absolute.*

Consider, for example, the movement of an object in space. My perception of the motion will vary with the point of view, moving or stationary, from which I observe it. My expression of it will vary with the system of axes, or the points of reference, to which I relate it; that is, with the symbols by which I translate it. For this double reason I call such motion *relative:* in the one case, as in the other, I am placed outside the object itself. But when I speak of an *absolute* movement, I am attributing to the moving object an interior and, so to speak, states of mind; I also imply that I am in sympathy with those states, and that I insert myself in them by an effort of the imagination.

H. Bergson, *An Introduction to Metaphysics,* trans. T. E. Hulme (New York: G. P. Putnam's, 1912).

Whether we think of intuition as present to some extent in all awareness and knowledge, as the accumulation of our experiences, as immediate insight into the totality of some situation, or as supersensible revelation, there appears to be an element of intuition in knowledge. Intuition, however, must abandon any claim to certainty or infallibility. Intuition, intellect, and sense experience must be utilized together in our quest for knowledge.

Reflections
♦ ♦ ♦ ♦ ♦ ♦ ♦ ♦ ♦ ♦ ♦

The various sources of knowledge, in our view, are complementary and not antagonistic in attempts to discover truth. The senses, reason, and intuition, as well as the secondary sources of the testimony of others, are genuine sources of knowledge. Each has value and something to contribute, and each may be superior to the others in certain areas.

A number of philosophers, writing from various points of view, have stressed the complementary nature of these sources of knowledge. For example, John Dewey has pointed out that a new conception of experience and of the relation between sense perception and reason is needed to conform to the newer developments in biology and psychology.[18] Wherever there is life there is activity or behavior. There is a continuous interaction between the organism and the environment; each tends to mold or to modify the other. The higher the form of life, the greater the control exercised over the environment. An organism explores and interacts constantly with its environment, and gains knowledge in the process. Knowledge is experience that is organized by the self or mind.

Knowledge thus is not something that comes in neat packages that can be easily traced to separate sources. It is rather the result of growth, of constant contact and interaction with a changing environment. An organism becomes aware of various specific things, relations, events, and persons; acquaintance, language, meaning, and thinking emerge. Nonetheless, we do not yet know which sources of knowledge most accurately reflect different kinds of situations. We also have not determined how to assess, for example, which forms of rationalism are appropriate for what kinds of knowledge.

◆ ◆

Glossary Terms

AD HOMINEM FALLACY   Faulty reasoning that shifts from an issue to a personality; from the Latin "to the man."

A POSTERIORI   *A posteriori* knowledge is based upon actual observation; from the Latin "from what comes after."

A PRIORI   *A priori* refers to knowledge that is self-evident or refers to principles recognized to be true apart from observation or experience; from the Latin "from what comes before."

AUTHORITARIANISM   The belief that knowledge is guaranteed or validated by some source; an uncritical acceptance of testimony as opposed to an independent effort to discover what is true or false.

BEGGING THE QUESTION   When one assumes as a premise for the argument the conclusion one intends to prove.

COMMON SENSE   A broad term used by philosophers to mean a way of looking at things independently of specialized knowledge or training; "common sense" is often uninformed opinion; the fund of opinion each member of a group is expected to have.

◆ ◆

Chapter Review

CENTRAL QUESTIONS IN THE THEORY OF KNOWLEDGE

1. The technical term for "theory of knowledge" is *epistemology*.
2. The central questions are
   a. What are the sources of knowledge?
   b. What is the nature of knowledge?
   c. Is our knowledge valid? What are the tests of knowledge?

TRADITION AND COMMON SENSE

1. We have been dependent on tradition and common sense as sources of knowledge; common-sense opinion has four characteristics: It is habitual and imitative, often vague and ambiguous, in part untested, and seldom accompanied by explanation.

OBSTACLES TO CLEAR THINKING

1. Francis Bacon formulated "Idols of the Mind," which include four distinct obstacles to clear

thinking: Idols of the Tribe, Cave, Marketplace, and Theater.

2. Prejudice has an emotional basis; judgments are made prior to research and logical considerations.

3. Propaganda is an attempt to manipulate perceptions. Emotions are aroused and solutions are suggested that probably have no correlation.

4. Authoritarianism is the position that knowledge is guaranteed or validated by the authority's words alone. Independent thought therefore ceases.

5. Formal and informal fallacies are logical inconsistencies or errors of reasoning in arguments. The frequently used *ad hominem* fallacy occurs when the emphasis changes from the issue to the individual.

6. "Idols of the Mind" prevent creativity and varied experiences.

THE POSSIBLE SOURCES OF KNOWLEDGE

1. The most common way of gaining knowledge about the past and about new data is to rely on the testimony of others. Grounds for qualification include: recognition by other authorities, agreement with other authorities, and special competence. Testimony is a secondary, not primary, source.

2. Empiricism is the position that we know what we have found out from our senses. Modern science is empirical. We can be led astray even in the area of sense data.

3. Sensationalism involves difficulties with relying uncritically on our senses.

4. Rationalism stresses reasoning or thought as the central factor in knowledge. Knowledge is found in concepts, principles, and laws, not just physical sensations.

5. There are controversial issues about rationalism.

6. Intuition is the direct apprehension that is not a result of conscious reasoning. It may be considered "immediate knowledge" and has its weaknesses.

REFLECTIONS

1. The various sources of knowledge may be seen as complementary, and not antagonistic, attempts to discover truth.

2. Nonetheless, we do not yet know which sources of knowledge most accurately reflect different kinds of situations.

• •

Study Questions and Projects

1. Which of the fallacies and obstacles to clear thinking described in this chapter do you find most often in the people around you? Which obstacles do you find in yourself? How do you account for the fact that people may continue to experience these obstacles even when they are aware of them and want to be able to think more clearly?

2. What personal experiences, if any, have you had with intuition as a source of knowledge? Are there areas in which you believe that intuition can be a valid source of knowledge?

3. How far or to what extent can you accept authority: (a) in the physical sciences; (b) for the facts of history, including causal explanations; (c) as a source of moral standards; (d) in politics, social philosophy, and religion?

4. Are some of the natural sciences more empirical and some more rational? Some students of the sciences speak of sciences like botany as more simply descriptive and less highly developed than sciences like physics, which involve a high degree of mathematical insight, logical analysis, and the formulation of abstract principles.

5. Are there any inborn or innate ideas? Until the late seventeenth century many men thought there were. In his *Essay Concerning Human Understanding,* John Locke made such a strong case against innate ideas that few men since then have been able to accept the notion. What are

Locke's arguments? His essay or any good history of philosophy will enable you to restate his position.

6. We sometimes hear it said that on the whole, women are more intuitive and men more rational in their general reactions. Can you find any evidence to support such a statement?

7. Some conservative religious people use the term *rational* in a derogatory sense and imply that reason is a danger in the realm of religion. What explains this fear of reason? Is reason an obstacle to religious belief, or may it be used in defense of religion? Most philosophers and many religious leaders would agree with John Wesley who said, "It is a fundamental principle with us that to renounce reason is to renounce religion, that reason and religion go hand in hand, and that all irrational religion is false religion."

8. Should faith and revelation be included as possible sources of knowledge? Faith may be a prerequisite for discovery and achievements in all areas of action, including science. Revelation and discovery may be different aspects of one dynamic process. (In a later chapter we consider questions of religious knowledge.)

9. Explain in your own words the central questions or problems of epistemology, or the theory of knowledge.

10. Describe some of the steps by which we acquire our earliest beliefs and ways of acting, feeling, and thinking, and indicate how these are related to the customs and traditions of our social groups.

11. What is common sense? Indicate its main characteristics, its advantages, and its disadvantages or dangers.

12. Describe authoritarianism, indicating (a) why some people easily welcome authority, (b) when the appeal to authority is justified and when not, and (c) the main weaknesses or dangers of authoritarianism in the advance of knowledge.

13. Discuss *empiricism*, indicating the forms it may take, its strong points, and the dangers of excluding other sources of knowledge.

14. Are all people who think *rationalists*? State the position known as rationalism, and indicate the forms it may take. In what fields does reason appear to be predominant? What is meant by a priori knowledge and by the "laws of thought"?

15. Analyze a moral or political spokesperson's *method* of persuasion for the presence of "obstacles to clear thinking."

◆ ◆

Suggested Readings

See also the Suggested Readings for Chapter 10.

Aaron, R. I. *Knowing and the Function of Reason.* Oxford: Clarendon Press, 1971.

This analysis of the elements of cognition—knowing, thought, and reason—makes room for intuition, which has had a prominent place in the history of thought.

Audi, R. *Belief, Justification, and Knowledge.* Belmont, Calif.: Wadsworth, 1988.

Audi starts with the origins of justification and knowledge, covers their development and structure, and goes on to questions about what they are and how far they extend.

Bunge, M. *Intuition and Science.* Englewood Cliffs, N.J.: Prentice-Hall, 1962.

Bunge provides a critical evaluation of intuition and intuitionism in the fields of philosophy, mathematics, and science.

Lehrer, K. *Theory of Knowledge.* Boulder, Colo.: Westview, 1990.

A textbook introducing students to the major traditional and contemporary accounts of knowing.

Morton, A. *A Guide Through the Theory of Knowledge.* Encino, Calif.: Dickenson, 1977.

Morton presents a useful introduction to epistemology.

Moser, P. K., and Vandernat, A. (eds.). *Human Knowledge*. New York: Oxford University Press, 1987.

An extensive set of classical and contemporary readings on the underlying foundations and issues in epistemology.

Pears, D. *What is Knowledge?* New York: Harper and Row (Harper Torchbook), 1971.

This small paperback is an introduction to epistemology. A distinction is made between factual knowledge, knowing how, and knowledge by acquaintance, as in "I know Mary."

Pollock, J. L. *Contemporary Theories of Knowledge*. Totowa, N.J.: Rowman and Littlefield, 1986.

A rigorous treatment of leading current theories in epistemology.

◆ ◆

Notes

1. B. Russell, *Human Knowledge; Its Scope and Limits* (New York: Simon and Schuster, 1948), pp. xi–xii.

2. E. Nagel, *The Structure of Science* (New York: Harcourt, Brace and World, 1961), p. 4.

3. M. T. McClure, ed., *Bacon Selections* (New York: Scribner's, Modern Student's Library, 1928), pp. 288–90.

4. There are situations, as William James and others have made clear, in which it is undesirable or impossible to suspend judgment. In cases where immediate action is demanded, we have to act on the basis of the evidence we have at the time.

5. See pp. 6, 7.

6. M. C. Beardsley, *Practical Logic* (Englewood Cliffs, N.J.: Prentice-Hall, 1956), p. 17.

7. I. M. Copi, *Introduction to Logic,* 9th ed. (New York: Macmillan, 1993), pp. 52–88.

8. From S. P. Lamprecht, ed., *Locke Selections* (New York: Scribner's, 1928), pp. 84–85.

9. M. Black, *Critical Thinking* (New York: Prentice-Hall, 1952), p. 256.

10. C. E. M. Joad, *Guide to Philosophy* (New York: Random House, 1936), p. 30.

11. J. Hospers, *An Introduction to Philosophical Analysis* (Englewood Cliffs, N.J.: Prentice-Hall, 1953), p. 123.

12. W. E. Hocking, *Types of Philosophy,* 3rd ed. (New York: Scribner's, 1959), p. 123.

13. A. C. Ewing, *Reason and Intuition* (New York: Oxford University Press, 1942).

14. M. Bunge, *Intuition and Science* (Englewood Cliffs N.J.,: Prentice-Hall, 1962), p. 68. (Spectrum Book.)

15. D. V. Steere, "Mysticism," in *A Handbook of Christian Theology* (Nashville, Tenn.: Abingdon, 1958), p. 236.

16. From W. P. Montague, *The Ways of Knowing* (New York: Macmillan, 1925), p. 226.

17. Bunge, *Intuition and Science,* p. 25.

18. See especially J. Dewey, *Reconstruction in Philosophy,* enl. ed. (Boston: Beacon, 1948). [Beacon Paperback, 1957, Chapter 4]

The Nature and Tests of Knowledge

CHAPTER OBJECTIVES

In this chapter we will address the following questions:

- ◆ What Are the Basic Issues Related to the Nature Of Knowledge?

- ◆ Is All or Some Knowledge a Matter of Subjective Opinion?

- ◆ Is Any Knowledge Objective?

- ◆ How Is Knowledge Tested for Truthfulness?

- ◆ Does Pluralism Deny the Existence of Truth?

From the naïve viewpoint of a little child anything and everything that appears is believed to be real; but as the child grows older, he learns to make a distinction between appearance and reality. He finds, for example, that what appears on the other side of the looking glass is really not in front of him at all but behind him, and . . . the happenings of his dreams, which seem real enough at the time, cannot be fitted into the world of his waking experience. . . . Thus does the child quickly gain the view that things are not always what they seem.[1]

Basic Issues in the Nature of Knowledge

◆ ◆ ◆ ◆ ◆ ◆ ◆ ◆ ◆ ◆ ◆

In the previous chapter we explored the *sources* of knowledge, one of the three basic areas in epistemology. We shall now study another basic issue, the *nature* of knowledge.

The nature-of-knowledge issue poses the following questions: Do we have any genuine knowledge on which we can depend, or must we be satisfied with mere opinions and guesses? Are we limited to the bare facts of empirical knowledge, or are we able to go beyond what the senses reveal? Do knowledge statements/ideas exist only in human minds (subjectivism)? Are knowledge statements and conclusions reached from reliable experiences of an independently real world (objectivism)? So-called "common sense" answers to these questions, as mentioned in the previous chapter, are intellectually inadequate.

We shall proceed by distinguishing "sensations" from "sense data"; next, *subjectivism* and *objectivism* will be explored. Finally, we shall examine three historical tests of truth.

SENSATIONS AND SENSE DATA

A **sensation** is a state of consciousness, an awareness, or a mental condition resulting from stimulation of a sense organ; sensations include thirst, cold, pressure, itches, and pain. A **sense datum**, on the other hand, is the immediately given content of sense experience, such as a color, sound, or the like. It is occasionally said that "we *sense* sense data," whereas "we *have* sensations." It is conceivable that two or more of us might sense the same sense datum; sensation, however, is private, personal, and peculiarly our own.

Subjectivism

◆ ◆ ◆ ◆ ◆ ◆ ◆ ◆ ◆ ◆

Subjectivism is the view that objects and the qualities we perceive through our senses do not exist independently of a consciousness of them. Reality consists of consciousness and its states, though not necessarily *my* consciousness and *my* states of mind. For some subjectivists, statements of knowledge are ideas existing only in human minds.

DREAMS, HALLUCINATIONS, AND ILLUSIONS

Ask yourself the following questions and take time to reflect on their meaning and possible answers. Where are the things in dreams located—in the world outside us or in our subjective or inner personal experiences? Just what is the nature of dreams? Some of these experiences seem clear and genuine. They may be so vivid that we can relate the details a long time afterward. They may stir us to a high pitch of emotional excitement. They may be pleasant or terrifying. Primitive people were so impressed by these experiences that they thought their selves had wandered off and had these experiences. In addition to dreams, we all have illusions at times and perhaps occasionally hallucinations. Drugs or fever may induce hallucinations. In illusions we mistake the identity of some person or object and give what we call a false interpretation; the hallucination is something we have created, in the sense that it has no external basis or counterpart. We put the objects of these experiences in the mind or within ourselves and not in the outer world. That is, we call them **subjective.** If you are willing to accept the subjectivity of such experiences as dreams, hallucinations, illusions, you have taken the first step toward subjectivism.

"MY" SENSE DATA

What is the nature of my images or sense data? The image in the dream, we say, was subjective or uniquely mine. We can have many images of one object, such as a mountain. Evidently there is a distinction between what is "out there" and my sense data. These sense data seem to vary from time to time and to be peculiarly mine. If two things can vary independently, they are not identical. As between the various sense data of the mountain and what we call the real mountain, what is mere appearance and what is "out there" in the "real" world? If you accept the subjectivity of these images, and of sense data in general, then you have taken a further step toward subjectivism.

PRIMARY AND SECONDARY QUALITIES

What is the nature of qualities such as color, sound, taste, smell, and tactual qualities? Here we are talking not just about the images we get of them, but of the qualities themselves, which are called **secondary qualities.** John Locke (1632–1704), who believed in the reality of material substance and ideas, separated the qualities of material substance into two groups. There were the **primary qualities,** such as form, extension, solidity, motion, number, and so on, which belong to the external world. Then there were the secondary qualities, such as color, sound, taste, odor, and so on, which do not belong to bodies in the external world. Colors and sounds are merely the effect of light and sound waves of certain lengths on human sensory organs. Philosophers like Locke, and various modern scientists as well, have attributed only quantitative relations to the outer world, and have attributed the nonquantitative qualities to conscious states. These secondary qualities vary from person to person, and may vary within the experience of one person as he or she views the world under different circumstances. These qualities are said to be in the mind, in states of consciousness, or to be subjective. The way we experience secondary qualities depends on the nature of our sensory equipment.

If you can accept or at least understand the subjectivity of secondary qualities, are you now ready to take another step and accept the subjectivity of the primary qualities, which include extension, figure, motion, mass, size, and shape? Experience indicates that the primary qualities, like the secondary qualities, seem to vary or change and to be affected by the condition of the sensory organs. Historically, this position is

most ably defended by the philosopher George Berkeley (1685–1753). (See biography and excerpt, pp. 194–195.) His famous expression is "To be is to be perceived." Berkeley accepted Locke's arguments for the subjectivity of the secondary qualities and then went on to show that the same arguments can be applied to the primary qualities. If all the qualities, both secondary and primary, are mental constructs, the concept of material substance as the place where primary qualities reside is no longer needed. There are only spiritual substances and ideas, or conscious beings and their sensations and ideas. If both the primary and the secondary qualities are in the mind, what is left to the object itself? All that the term *matter* can mean is a certain group of qualities, impressions, or ideas; Berkeley thus denies the existence of matter and overcame Locke's problems with the notion of "material substance." Berkeley also rejected "external bodies." It was difficult to see what purpose these external bodies could serve because, as Locke himself insisted, we could not be aware of them; in fact, they afforded the sole pretext for skepticism, which Berkeley abhorred. If external bodies are rejected, then the houses and trees, tables and stars that we perceive in the world can be *identified* with the ideas that we have, not *contrasted* with our ideas, as Locke proposed. Because it is beyond dispute that we do have ideas, Berkeley could argue "that houses, trees, tables and stars do really exist and are just as they appear to us to be."[2]

SUBJECTIVISM PROPER

If this step is taken, we have arrived at the stage of subjectivism proper, or the belief that there is no reality outside of individual experience. There is now a single realm consisting of conscious beings and their ideas. How, then, do we account for the distinctions that have been made between primary and secondary qualities? The primary qualities seem to be fixed and measurable—that is why they have been called "physical qualities" or "states," to distinguish them from the qualities that are variable or purely private experiences, which we call "mental" or "psychical."

Berkeley. Berkeley said that these common or measurable experiences, the primary qualities of our world, are caused by something beyond ourselves, and are different from the secondary qualities, which arise out of our own mental activity. The agency, however, is still a conscious being infinitely wiser and more powerful than we are. The order of nature arose, according to Berkeley, from the objective ideas in the mind of God.

Kant. Are you able to interpret space and time and the order and laws of nature as forms of the mind? We cannot perceive except in spatial and temporal terms. Does this mean that these are mind-dependent functions of a universal mind, or essentially subjective? The work of Berkeley did not reach to the laws or relations that unite our various experiences, but Immanuel Kant (1724–1804) gave attention to this problem. The mind, he said, imposes its own forms of organization or synthesis on the unorganized sensations it receives from an unknown source. The mind functions through the three faculties of sensibility, understanding, and reason. The first set of forms consists of space and time. The second set is called the "categories," the higher classes or divisions within which things are organized. These include such forms of relationship as quality, quantity, cause, effect, unity, and plurality. The third set is the "ideas." When, as scientists, we marvel over the mathematical relations and harmonies of the world, we are merely projecting onto the outer world the relations and the harmonies of our own minds.

Kant's arguments are difficult and complicated and cannot be presented here in detail. We will, however, give a brief statement regarding his arguments for the subjectivity of space and time. We can imagine the nonexistence of any particular object in space and time—say, the building we occupy—but we cannot imagine the nonexistence of space and time themselves. Try to think of a limit to space. What is beyond your limit? Is there "a time when time was not"? That time and space adhere to the mind is a proof of their subjectivity. They exist, therefore, in Kant's view, logically prior to the bodies that occupy them. Space and time exist *within* consciousness. Our thinking about the properties of space and time appears to possess a certainty and a necessity that are not present when we think about the various objects of our world. This can be explained most adequately by the assumption that they are forms of the mind itself. If space and time were objective, we would have to think of them as either finite or infinite; yet we are unable to do so. If we think of them as finite, we can easily pass in thought beyond their limit. To think of them as infinite seems, according to Kant, to imply their completion. To call a completed or actually existent series "infinite" would be self-contradictory; it would imply the completion of something that, according to his definition, was incomplete.

Solipsism. Have you ever wondered whether you alone exist and the world were your idea? A final possible stage in the line of thought we have been developing is **solipsism,** the view that the individual self alone exists, or the view of "the subjectivity of the absolute subject." This position has not been held by any school of philosophers or by any outstanding thinker. The term *solipsism* comes from the Latin *solus,* meaning "alone," and *ipse,* meaning "*self.*" It is the *reductio ad absurdum* of subjectivism.

THE EGOCENTRIC PREDICAMENT: SUBJECTIVISM AND THE NATURE OF KNOWLEDGE

The problem before us in this section on subjectivism is what Ralph Barton Perry called the *egocentric predicament.* No matter what we do or how hard we try, we cannot get outside of or beyond our own experience; a person can never know anything which is not a content of his private experience. All our knowledge of objects is of the subject–object variety. What the object would be apart from this relationship, there is no

George Berkeley

George Berkeley (1685–1753) was an Irish philosopher and Anglican bishop who became disillusioned by conditions in the society of the Old World in which he lived. After being promised a government grant of £20,000, he set out for America intending to found an ideal state and to set up a college in Bermuda for the conversion to Christianity of Native Americans, blacks, and some settlers. After two years in Newport, Rhode Island, during which the grant did not materialize, he returned to London and was appointed Bishop of Cloyne, Ireland. A deeply religious man, Berkeley wanted to reconcile the emerging science of his day with the doctrines of Christianity. He is called an "idealist" and an "immaterialist" because he held that things are mind-dependent: the world exists as it is thought in the mind of God. Berkeley was a strong opponent of skepticism.

Berkeley began to publish at the age of 24 years. His best-known works are *An Essay Towards a New Theory of Vision* (1709), *A Treatise Concerning the Principles of Human Knowledge* (1710), and *Three Dialogues Between Hylas and Philonous* (1713). In an age when materialism was popular, he sought to show that the world is composed of ideas.

way of knowing. When you think of an object, you must think of it as having various sensorially perceived qualities. The object is red or smooth or sour. We have already seen that mental factors and the condition of the sense organs enter into the perception of objects. Possibly there are no independent objects; the world may be a mental construct. To say that you can think of objects and can experience them as existing independently does not alter the situation: you are still dealing with your own perceptions or sense data. Therefore, we are caught up in a predicament, namely, that *statements we intend as knowledge may be no more than ideas existing in the perceiver's mind.*

Objectivism

OBJECTIVISM AND THE NATURE OF KNOWLEDGE

For **objectivists**, statements intended as knowledge are reliable descriptions or explanations of an independently real world; we are able to have genuine knowledge on which we can depend. Objectivists reject the view of Berkeley that to exist is to be a mind or an idea in some mind. They insist that there is an independent reality apart from minds. During the eighteenth century, the "copy theory" of John Locke was widely accepted: primary qualities were in the outer world, and the secondary qualities were in the mind. The mind knows the copies (images)

Excerpt from Berkeley:

A Treatise Concerning the Principles of Human Knowledge
(1710)

Philosophy, being nothing else but the study of wisdom and truth, it may with reason be expected that those who have spent most time and pains in it should enjoy a greater calm and serenity of mind, a greater clearness and evidence of knowledge, and be less disturbed with doubts and difficulties than other men. Yet so it is, we see the illiterate bulk of mankind, that walk the highroad of plain common sense, and are governed by the dictates of nature, for the most part easy and undisturbed. To them nothing that is familiar appears unaccountable or difficult to comprehend. They complain not of any want of evidence in their sense, and are all out of danger of becoming Sceptics. But no sooner do we depart from Sense and Instinct to follow the light of a superior Principle—to reason, meditate, and reflect on the nature of things, but a thousand scruples spring up in our minds concerning those things which before we seemed fully to comprehend. Prejudices and errors of sense do from all parts discover themselves to our view; and endeavouring to correct these by reason, we are insensibly drawn into uncouth paradoxes, difficulties, and inconsistencies, which multiply and grow upon us as we advance in speculation, till at length, having wandered through many intricate mazes, we find ourselves just where we were, or, which is worse, sit down in a forlorn Scepticism.

G. Berkeley, *A Treatise Concerning the Principles of Human Knowledge,* ed. C. Turbayne (New York: Liberal Arts Press, 1957).

of the external things. The *critical realists* of the twentieth century claim that what we perceive are sense data, not objects.

WHERE ARE THE SENSE DATA?

Before considering the case for objectivism, let us ask: *Where* are the sense data? Where are these elements of our experience that we think are immediately in consciousness? This is one of the most baffling issues in philosophy. Let us state some possibilities, without elaborating the answers.

First, the qualities that produce sense data may be out in the physical world, where they seem to be. If they are in the external world, then they may exist independently of their being sensed, or they may be created in the external world by the knower at the time of perception. These views seem difficult to hold in the light of the facts presented earlier in the chapter, but a few realists have held the belief that sense qualities exist independently of perception, or in the physical objects about us.

Second, the sense data may exist within the person who is the knower or perceiver. In that case, they may be the result of stimulation of the nervous system, or they may be explained as mental events, implying a dualism of mind and matter.

Third, what produces sense data may not be located anywhere in particular. We cannot locate them exclusively in the outer world or within the person. Signals in the form of a wave pattern produce, it is said, a pattern of "brain events," which correspond to the events from which the signals come. The sense data, then, would be imaginative projections that arise as a result of organic events stimulated by, say, light waves.

ARGUMENTS FOR OBJECTIVISM

Let us turn to some of the simpler arguments for objectivism. Some of these arguments are negative in that they attempt to show the weakness of the subjectivist's position; others are positive.

1. Objectivists accuse the subjective idealists of the fallacy of **non sequitur,** or of drawing a false conclusion from a true proposition.

> The true proposition is, "It is impossible to discover anything that is not known," since it becomes known by the mere process of being discovered. From this proposition it follows that it is impossible to discover with certainty what characteristics things possess when they are not known. The idealist then proceeds falsely to conclude, "Things have no characteristics when they are not known; therefore, the characteristic of being known is that which constitutes their existence: therefore, things only exist when they are known."[3]

The only valid conclusion is that "all known things are known," and this is merely a **tautology.** The fact that we cannot tell for certain what characteristics things possess when they are not known does not mean that all things are known or that being known is a prerequisite to existence. The fact that we cannot know a thing unless it has been experienced does not mean that there cannot be unexperienced things.

2. The subjectivists are accused of a misuse of the word *idea* when they use it both for "the concept held by the knower" and for "the object known." This double use of the word begs the question and assumes without proof that there is no real difference between the mind and that to-ward which the mind's experience is directed. Bertrand Russell says:

> There is a confusion engendered by the use of the word "idea." We think of an idea as essentially something *in* somebody's mind, and thus when we are told that a tree consists entirely of ideas, it is natural to suppose that, if so, the tree must be entirely in minds. But the notion of being "in" the mind is ambiguous. We speak of bearing a person in mind, not meaning that the person is in our minds, but that a thought of him is in our minds. When a man says that some business he had to arrange went clean out of his mind, he does not mean to imply that the business itself was ever in his mind, but only that a thought of the business was formerly in his mind, but afterwards ceased to be in his mind. And so when Berkeley says that the tree must be in our minds if we can know it, all that he really has a right to say is that a thought of the tree must be in our minds. To argue that the tree itself must be in our minds is like arguing that a person whom we bear in mind is himself in our minds.[4]

The object of an act of thought should be clearly distinguished from the act of thought itself.

3. Belief in the existence of a world quite independent of our experience and knowledge of it conforms to the assumptions of everyday life and is implied in all our special sciences. Such an assumption, although it cannot be proved with finality, explains the events and peculiarities of our lives better than does any alternative approach. In all our conscious acts, we are aware of something outside of or beyond ourselves. We are not only aware, but at times we are aware that we are aware. A common characteristic both of our sense perceptions and of our moments of reflection is that we are aware of something other than ourselves. This something, most believe, is unaffected by our consciousness of it.

The fact that the evidence from the different sense organs converges and builds up a unified picture of our world furnishes us with additional evidence. Elements of time and space fit into the series of events and appear to be genuine aspects of a world outside us. Astronomers, geologists, historians, and others report the details of a long process of development, which seems to be explained most adequately as an environing nature that we are gradually learning to describe.

Within our human experience, there appears to be a clear distinction between those experiences that we ourselves create, such as our imaginings, thoughts, and dreams, and the sense perceptions that are forced upon us by an external world. If objectivism is to some degree true, this distinction is easily understood. If it is false, then the distinction is baffling. Our sense perceptions ordinarily are vivid, steady, and consistent, whereas those other images are less distinct, unsteady, and often confused.

4. Causal interactions occur both within and beyond the realm of our experiences. Our perceptions or experiences must also have a cause. Events that break into our field of consciousness often are quite unrelated to our previous train of thought. Furthermore, these events seem to obey laws that are quite independent of our minds, so that we are unable to get rid of them even by great effort.

A fire is burning briskly in our fireplace. We leave it, then return an hour or two later to find that it has burned low. These and other events lead us to believe that causal sequences continue to operate in the same way whether or not they are being perceived by anyone. Both Berkeley and Kant recognized this problem and attempted to address it. Berkeley said that God was the cause of the order of the external world. Kant posited a thing-in-itself that was unknown and unknowable. The realist says that to accept the world of our experience at its face value is to hold the most reasonable position.

The Nature of Knowledge: Further Considerations

♦ ♦ ♦ ♦ ♦ ♦ ♦ ♦ ♦ ♦

The answer to the problem of the nature of knowledge depends, at least in part, on the type of philosophy—especially a metaphysical position—a person is inclined to accept. In a problem that is so complex, it is especially easy to take some part of the knowledge relationship and attempt to make that part appear to be the whole. Both the more extreme forms of subjectivism and the more extreme forms of objectivism are equally guilty of this error. A reasonable compromise is to hold that undoubtedly there are important subjective elements in our knowledge. We experience things from a particular frame of reference and by a particular set of sense organs, which might be quite different from what they are. Our perceptions are relative to the self. When I see a tree or a man, there is a specific neural or organic process that is the condition of that experience. As the conditions of our organism vary, the objects of our experience change. The world of things is in some sense relative to the conscious self that experiences those things. On the other hand, there is a "given" from outside us. That there are objects that have an existence quite independent of our experiences appears to be certain. This seems to be the most tenable assumption that enables us not only to explain and reconcile the numerous experiences we have but also to relate these experiences to those of our fellow human beings.

Although we cannot prove the existence of an external world, it appears that such facts as the sequence of events in our world, the discovery of objects that are unexpected and that "break in" on our consciousness, and the assumptions of everyday living and of scientific progress are explained more adequately by the hypothesis of the existence of an external world than by any of the more extreme forms of subjectivism.

TYPES OF KNOWLEDGE

In considering the different ways in which we come to have knowledge of things, persons, and events, philosophers have arrived at two useful distinctions for identifying types of knowledge. The first distinction is between knowing an object, a person, and event by actually being present, or being directly *acquainted* with it, and *knowing about* it by way of general concepts. The second distinction is between knowing factual information about something—called knowing "that"—and knowing what one must be capable of doing in order to achieve a certain result—called knowing "how." Let us consider the two distinctions in turn. We can read descriptions in an encyclopedia about, for example, Southern France and come to know about its farmhouses and villas, its vineyards and fields of lavender, its ancient churches, monasteries, and Roman ruins without actually visiting the region ourselves. That is knowledge about the region; when we travel there and experience at first hand the ruins, the vineyards, and so forth, we are said to be acquainted with what we formerly knew only through the descriptions of others.

The second distinction—the difference between knowing "that" and knowing "how"—has to do with the difference between having information and having the skill needed to bring about a desired result. We have information, for example, when we know "that" there are thirty-six inches in a yard and that Lincoln delivered the Gettysburg Address. Something different is involved when we know "how" to ride a horse, bake a cake, or master a sport such as tennis or golf. In all these cases we must, to be sure, know that a horse must be saddled in a certain way, that the beaten egg whites must be folded into the yolks, that a racket or a club must be swung in a particular manner in order to make a good shot. The central point is that although we need to know that this or that needs to be done, that information does not teach us "how" to carry out the task. Knowing how means skills such as coordinating hand and eye or striking a ball with the right force and from a particular angle. The gap between the instruction manual telling us what to do and knowing how to execute the instructions is often large; knowing how is always a matter of practice and repeated effort.

The Tests of Knowledge

♦ ♦ ♦ ♦ ♦ ♦ ♦ ♦ ♦ ♦ ♦

SKEPTICISM

Opinions, Beliefs, and Truth. Many beliefs once thought to be true have later been discovered to be false. What makes some beliefs true and others false? Can we ever be sure that we have discovered the truth? Is the human mind capable of discovering or finding any genuine knowledge? When or under what conditions may we have reasonable assurance that we are dealing with facts rather than opinions? Centuries ago, when Jesus stood trial before him, Pilate asked, "What is truth?" Before this, Socrates, Plato, and other Greek philosophers had thought about the question. Reflective persons are still seeking the answer.

Throughout time, opinions and beliefs have changed—not only the common everyday beliefs but also the beliefs of science and philosophy. Scientific theories that were once accepted as true have been replaced by other theories. Are these beliefs more than guesses or opinions based on the "climate of opinion" of the day? Things by themselves are neither true nor false; they just are or are not. Our judgment about things and our propositions are true or false. Truth has to do with the assertions or the claims that we make about things. Among the philosophers of the past and of the present there has been and is a great diversity of belief.

Issues of Skepticism. Before we attempt to examine the three main "tests of truth" that have survived the philosophical discussions of recent centuries, let us question the underlying assumption that there *is* such a thing as truth and that we can hope to discover it. How can we answer the skeptic who claims that there is no such thing as valid knowledge or expresses an attitude of uncertainty and doubt?

Skepticism, in its narrow sense, is the position that knowledge is impossible and that the quest for truth is in vain. Gorgias asserted that nothing exists and that, if it did, we couldn't know it, and that even if we did come to know anything, we could not impart this knowledge to our fellows. René Descartes, raised in the skeptical atmosphere of early seventeenth-century France, insisted that it was possible to overcome all doubt and to find an absolutely certain basis for knowledge. By applying the skeptical method more thoroughly than the skeptics had, Descartes claimed that the very act of doubting one's own existence makes one aware of the truth that one exists. Cartesian theory thus takes skepticism as its point of departure, and uses it to reveal a basis for certainty.

Thoroughgoing skepticism leads to an attitude so noncommittal as to make any intelligent and consistent action almost impossible; as such, it is not a satisfactory ideal for personal life or society. Few outstanding thinkers have denied the possibility of any knowledge. Skepticism is self-refuting; the denial of all knowledge is a claim that refutes itself. If nothing can be known, then how does the skeptic know that this position is a valid one? If skeptics affirm their own position as the truth, they are attempting to distinguish between the true and the false. They must have some idea of what the truth is to appeal to the principles of valid reasoning in arguing against the possibility of truth.

In its broader meaning, skepticism can be merely the attitude of questioning any assumption or conclusion until it can be subjected to rigorous examination. The skeptics in this sense tend to stress the possibilities for error inherent in the various ways of attempting to gain knowledge. They point out that all knowledge is human, that our human faculties are frail and limited, and that the senses and reason seem to be equally unreliable. They remind us that even the so-called experts in all areas have greatly diverse opinions.

A certain amount of skepticism has tended to precede and stimulate philosophical reflection. It is a reminder of the need for caution and the dangers of dogmatism. It says to us "Don't be too sure," "Don't be dogmatic," "You may be wrong," "Be tolerant and open-minded." This type of skepticism, represented by the questioning attitude of Socrates, has much in its favor, because it helps free us from superstition, prejudice, and error and clears the way for intellectual progress. The arguments advanced by skeptics from Greek times on, and the use to which these arguments have been put, have helped to shape both the problems dealt with by the major Western philosophers and the solutions these people have offered.

Three Tests of Truth

♦ ♦ ♦ ♦ ♦ ♦ ♦ ♦ ♦ ♦

In attempting to determine what beliefs are true, philosophers have relied, in the main, on three tests of truth. Individuals believed many things and acted on the basis of those beliefs before it occurred to them to ask, Why are some beliefs true and others false? Today, few informed people accept custom or tradition as a sufficient justification for declaring something to be true. Although customs and traditions often are valuable, they also may lead us astray. They sometimes contain conflicts, and they do not provide for change and progress. The appeal to "universal agreement" is equally insecure; some beliefs that have been widespread and firmly believed over long periods (for example, that the earth was flat) have later been found to be false. Other thinkers, in the past, have appealed to instinct. The instinct theory, however, has been under attack, and many things formerly explained as "instincts" are now explained more adequately as the results of "conditioning." Still other people have appealed to the strong feeling that a thing is true; yet feelings may be determined by our moods, health, or training.

We shall find that there is no complete agreement regarding the tests of truth. Each answer will call forth some severe criticisms from people with opposing points of view. Ask yourself: Is only one of these tests sound, or does each test contribute some insight? Do the tests need to be combined in some way? The three theories of the test of truth that we shall consider are the correspondence theory, the coherence theory, and the pragmatic theory.

THE CORRESPONDENCE THEORY: AGREEMENT WITH "FACT"

The test of truth called the *correspondence theory* is the one most widely accepted by the **realists.** According to this theory, truth is "fidelity to objective reality." Truth is the agreement between the statement of fact and the actual fact, or between the judgment and the situation the judgment claims to describe. Truth has to do with the assertions or the claims that we make about things.

If I state that the United States is bounded on the north by Canada, my statement is true, according to this approach, not because it happens to agree with other statements previously made or because it happens to work, but because it corresponds to the actual geographical situation. This, it is said, is what the word *truth* means in everyday usage. It is also the characteristic view of the scientist, who checks ideas with data or findings and is glad to submit conclusions to similar objective tests by others.

According to the correspondence theory, the presence or absence of belief has no direct bearing on the issue of truth or falsity, because truth and falsity depend on the conditions that have been affirmed or denied. If a judgment corresponds with the facts, it is true; if not, it is false. If I say, "There is an automobile parked in our driveway," my statement can be verified by empirical investigation.

The critics of the correspondence theory, however, do not think that the question of the verification of statements can be as clear and self-evident as the supporters of the theory affirm. The first critical question usually is this: "How can we compare our ideas with reality?" We know only our own experiences. How can we get outside our experiences so that we can compare our ideas with reality as it actually is? The correspondence theory, they say, assumes that we know not only our judgments but also the actual circumstances apart from our experiences.

The theory of correspondence seems to assume that our sense data are clear and accurate, that they disclose the nature of the world just as it is. Idealists and pragmatists, as well as scientific researchers in human perception, seriously question this assumption, pointing out that in perception the mind tends to modify our views of the world. If our powers of perception were diminished or increased or if we possessed fewer or more sense organs, the world might appear quite different. Because we cannot know an object or an event apart from our sense data, it is foolish to

talk about whether our judgments correspond with the thing itself.

Finally, we have knowledge of meanings (definitions), relations, and values, as in mathematics, logic, and ethics. Some of the ideas that we want to verify have no objects outside the area of human thought with which we can make comparisons and check for correspondence. In those areas, at least, the correspondence theory of truth does not seem to apply. Yet knowledge in these fields possesses a high degree of certainty. Supporters of the correspondence theory reply to this criticism by pointing out that in mathematics and logic no truth claims *about the world* are made and therefore they do not have to be verified—they need have only internal consistency.

THE COHERENCE THEORY: CONSISTENCY

The coherence, or consistency, theory is the test of truth quite generally accepted by **idealists**, although its acceptance is not confined to that school of thought. Because we cannot directly compare our ideas and judgments with the world as it is, the coherence theory judges validity by the consistency or harmony of all our judgments. A judgment is true if it is consistent with other judgments that are accepted as true. True judgments are those logically coherent with other relevant judgments.

Under ordinary circumstances, we often judge a statement to be true or false on the ground that it is or is not in harmony with what we have already decided is true. On this basis, we reject many ideas as absurd and denounce some experiences as illusions or false perceptions. They do not "fit in" with what has happened in the past or with what, from our past experience, we may reasonably expect to happen. This does not mean, however, that we reject new ideas or new truths without careful examination. Occasionally, new facts or ideas force themselves on us and impress us so strongly with their truth that we need to revise many of our previous conceptions, if not a whole system of thought. The Copernican world view and the biological theory of evolution are examples of new ideas that led to outstanding changes. We accepted them because they gave us a larger degree of coherence and consistency—they explained some things previously unexplained.

The simplest form of the coherence theory demands an inner or formal consistency in the particular system under consideration, quite apart from any interpretation of the universe as a whole. For example, in mathematics, assuming certain definitions and axioms, one can build the system of geometry implied by the definitions and axioms consistent with them. This system is then accepted as true. The principle of consistency or logical implication underlies our systems of mathematics and formal logic and, to a considerable extent, any science or organized body of knowledge. Conformity to certain formal laws of thought—like the law of noncontradiction, which it seems altogether impossible to deny—is the basis of such systems of truth, according to this approach.

A. C. Ewing writes of the coherence theory:

> Advocates of the coherence theory are well aware that complete coherence must be regarded as an unattainable ideal, but views may still be judged according to their greater or less distance from it. The nearest approach to it is to be found in mathematics. Here the different propositions are so connected that each follows necessarily from others and that you could not deny any one without contradicting a vast number of others. If we assumed that 2 + 2 = 5, we could, I think, without making any further mistake draw conclusions which contradicted every arithmetical truth there is about any number.[5]

Adherents of the coherence theory claim that any adequate theory of truth, besides satisfying other requirements, must be able to explain "the relativity of truth," or how a belief can be held to be true at one time and false at a later time. The coherence theory meets this requirement. Insofar as every judgment is merely partial when separated from the whole, it is to some extent one-sided and possesses only a degree of truth. From this viewpoint, truth grows, and it would never be complete or final until it encompassed all of reality.

Inconsistency and incoherence are disturbing and lead philosophers to seek unity, but the critics of the coherence theory point out that we can construct false as well as true coherent systems. The theory, they say, does not distinguish between consistent truth and consistent error. To say that a judgment is true if it is consistent with other judgments that are accepted as true could lead to a dangerous circularity in which we have a number of false statements, each one of which we judge to be true because it is consistent with the others. The critics point to numerous past systems that, although logically consistent, were false. Correspondence to fact is a condition even the most self-consistent system must meet. If, however, our view of coherence embraces *inclusiveness, simplicity,* and systematic *orderliness* as well as consistency, these criticisms have less validity.

Critics of the coherence theory say also that the approach is rationalistic and intellectualistic and deals mainly with the logical relations among propositions. Because of this, it fails to furnish an adequate test for the judgments of everyday experience. If the test of coherence is used, then it needs to be stated more with reference to factual consistency; that is, the agreement between a judgment and a definite environmental situation. This, of course, is really a correspondence, and not a coherence, test. Other critics of these tests of truth suggest a different approach—the test of utility.

THE PRAGMATIC THEORY: UTILITY

Pragmatism as a philosophy is considered in a later chapter. Here we give merely a brief statement of the pragmatic conception of truth and of the tests of truth.

For the pragmatists, truth cannot be understood as simple correspondence between the idea and the thing to which it refers. The reason is

Charles Sanders Peirce

Charles Sanders Peirce (1839–1914) was born in Cambridge, Massachusetts, and graduated from Harvard University, where his father was a leading mathematician. After his graduation he worked simultaneously as an astronomer at Harvard and as a physicist for the United States Coast and Geodetic Survey. He is said to have remarked that he was brought up in a laboratory. For a short period, 1879–1884, he was lecturer in logic at the Johns Hopkins University.

Within a few years, Peirce retired to Milford, Pennsylvania, where he lived in relative isolation and wrote papers in many fields of philosophy, most notably in logic, epistemology, and scientific method. He wanted to connect thought and action and to clarify terms and ideas. During his life he published little, but since his death eight volumes of his papers have been printed by Harvard University Press: *The Collected Papers of Charles Sanders Peirce*. Interest in Peirce's philosophy has grown steadily in recent decades. New enlarged and revised writings are in the process of being published.

that we must have some way of testing whether what the idea claims is to be found in the object itself. On the other hand, the coherence theory is formal and rationalistic. Pragmatism claims that we can know nothing about "substances," "essences," and "ultimate realities." It opposes all authoritarianism, intellectualism, and rationalism. For the pragmatists, the test of truth is utility, workability, or satisfactory consequences. Charles S. Peirce (see biography and excerpt, pp. 202–203), who is sometimes called the father of pragmatism, held that the best test of the truth of an idea is to ask, What would be the effect on the conduct of our lives if this idea were true? There

is no such thing as static or absolute truth. Truth is redefined to mean something that happens to a judgment or an idea. Truth is made in the process of human adjustment. According to William James, "True ideas are those that we can assimilate, validate, corroborate, and verify. False ideas are those that we can not."[6]

The pragmatic redefinition of the nature of truth leads naturally to a repudiation of the older tests of truth and to the defense of new ones. An idea or a theory or a hypothesis is true if it works out in practice, if it leads to satisfactory results. The phrase "satisfactory results" may be highly ambiguous. The supporters of this test of truth,

It appears that there are certain mummified pedants who have never waked to the truth that the act of knowing a real object alters it. They are curious specimens of humanity, and as I am one of them, it may be amusing to see how I think. It seems that our oblivion to this truth is due to our not having made the acquaintance of a new analysis that the True is simply that in cognition which is Satisfactory. As to this doctrine, if it is meant that True and Satisfactory are synonyms, it strikes me that it is not so much a doctrine of philosophy as it is a new contribution to English lexicography.

But it seems plain that the formula does express a doctrine of philosophy, although quite vaguely; so that the assertion does not concern two words of our language but, attaching some other *meaning* to the True, makes it to be *coextensive with* the Satisfactory in cognition. . . . I suppose that by the True is meant that at which inquiry aims. . . . To say that an action or the result of an action is Satisfactory is simply to say that it is congruous to the aim of that action. Consequently, the aim must be determined before it can be determined, either in thought or in fact, to be satisfactory. An action that had no other aim than to be congruous to its aim would have no aim at all, and would not be a deliberate action.

C. S. Peirce, *Collected Papers of Charles Sanders Peirce*, Vol. I, eds. C. Hartshorne and P. Weiss (Cambridge, Harvard University Press, 1934).

however, have tended to stress one or more of three approaches: (1) That is true which satisfies our desires or purposes. True beliefs must satisfy not just some whims but our whole natures, and satisfy them over a period of time. An important question here is whether a belief that satisfies us thereby demonstrates its truth or merely its comfort value. (2) That is true which can be demonstrated experimentally. This test, it is claimed, is in harmony with the spirit and practice of modern science. Whether in the laboratory or in daily life, when a question of truth and falsity arises we should "try it and see." (3) That is true which aids in the biological struggle for existence. The instrumentalism of John Dewey, discussed in a later chapter, stresses the biological function of ideas and doctrines.

The test of workability has keen critics as well as able supporters. Critics have called it a "dangerous doctrine," because it seems to justify many satisfying beliefs that ought not to be held unless they conform to the facts. Many beliefs that comfort and fortify people are plainly untrue. In our everyday life, we had better not believe that the price of common stock we hold is going up because it gives us comfort to think so when in reality it is not, or that some business venture in which we are interested is going to prosper just because it is an inspiring belief. We are more likely to use this test, the critics say, in the areas where we can more safely live in happy illusion and where we are not likely to be checked by more stringent tests.

To define truth in this way and to accept satisfactory consequences as a test of truth is to imply, at least, that there can be one truth for you and another for me. Such relativism tends to blind our judgment and make us less able to judge evidence impartially and objectively. Critics contend that we ought to learn to view things as they are and to control our hopes, wishes, cravings, and prejudices.

Innumerable theories—in religion, economic life, science, and other fields—have "worked" for a considerable time. Untrue ideas often lead to what many people call "satisfactory results." On the other hand, some judgments cannot be verified pragmatically. Although beliefs that are true tend to work in the long run, it is not necessarily the case that beliefs that work are therefore true.

Reflections

♦ ♦ ♦ ♦ ♦ ♦ ♦ ♦ ♦ ♦ ♦

Each of the separate tests of truth appears to have value under certain circumstances.[7] The test of correspondence is widely used in everyday experience, as well as in the various sciences. There are many occasions on which we seem to be able to check our "ideas" with the "facts," and to receive confirmation after other investigators have checked our results. Frequently, however, in complicated areas of human experience and thought, the correspondence theory does not seem to apply. In such cases we may have to appeal to coherence, or consistency. At still other times, we may properly defend the theory behind a concept like democracy by showing that it has worked well and has produced satisfactory results in human experience.

TRUTH

Because the theories supplement rather than directly contradict each other, they can be combined in a definition of truth: Truth is the faithful adherence of our judgments and ideas to the facts of experience or to the world as it is; but because we cannot always compare our judgments with the actual situations, we test them by their consistency with other judgments that we believe are valid and true, or we test them by their usefulness and practical consequences.

PLURALISM

Since the Enlightenment, philosophers have had sharp differences on epistemological issues. Some disagreements can be traced to one or more of the obstacles to clear thinking. Differences among experts about what claims constitute valid knowledge, however, usually are not caused by fallacious thinking. Instead, differing explanations result from differing assumptions.

Is there a method by which these differences can be resolved? Although some of us might be persuaded that one or more of our postulates[8] are inadequate to account for our experiences or those of others, some assumptions remain for which there is no agreed method of verification. For example, there is no way the empiricist can disprove a mystic's postulate that the world of time and space is only an appearance, not a fundamental reality. That assertion is, to the mystic, a self-evident truth, an axiom requiring no validation. The three tests of truth described in this chapter are irrelevant to the view that fundamental reality is beyond the empirical and rational world.

By way of contrast, your axioms may include the assertion that the world of time and space is fundamentally real, not merely an appearance. For you, this conviction is a self-evident truth, an axiom requiring no proof. Can you refute the mystic's view? With what methods?

If you try to disprove the mystic's claim, you will use assumptions and methods unacceptable to mysticism. Your methods and views will never converge, because your premises are different.

The inevitable result of beginning with different postulates is different interpretation of issues. For example, if a group of psychologists is asked to determine the reasons for certain behaviors, each responds according to the axioms of their school of thought—behaviorism, Freudian, Jungian, Gestalt, and so on. Each school has its own postulates that provide the framework for interpreting the same data.

By "philosophical pluralism" we mean the inevitable existence of different interpretations of reality, knowledge, and values. Does philosophical pluralism imply that all views are equally true? That each system or school of thought is as true as its opposite is illogical; our inability to discover the absolute truth does not mean that no truth exists nor that all positions are equally true: we do not advocate relativism. We assert, however, that there is a certain degree of tentativeness to any school of thought, any interpretation or explanation, indeed to any axiom. We propose that our capacities to discover and articulate truth infallibly are subject to human limitations.

◆ ◆

Glossary Terms

IDEALISTS (IDEALISM)   The view that asserts that reality consists of or is closely related to ideas, thought, mind, or selves rather than matter; there are many types of idealism.

NON SEQUITUR   From the Latin, "it does not follow"; an inference or a conclusion that does not follow logically from the premises; drawing a false conclusion from a true proposition.

OBJECTIVISTS (OBJECTIVISM)   (1) The view that statements we intend as knowledge reveal what really is; ideas are formed by reliable sense experiences; (2) Also, objects and qualities we perceive through our senses do exist independently of a consciousness of them.

PRIMARY QUALITIES   The qualities that are said to inhere in material substance and that do not depend on a knower. These qualities are usually thought to include form, extension, solidity, motion, and number. John Locke and others have distinguished between primary and secondary qualities.

REALISTS (REALISM)   The view that the objects of our senses exist independently of their being known or related to mind.

SECONDARY QUALITIES   The sense qualities (color, sound, taste, odor) that John Locke and others claimed were determined by the mind and not by the external world. See also *primary qualities*.

SENSATION   A state of consciousness, an awareness, or a mental condition resulting from stimulation of a sense organ.

SENSE DATUM   The image or sense impression. Sense data are the immediately given contents of sense experience, such as colored patches and shapes, which, according to some epistemologists, serve as cues to the presence and nature of perceived objects.

SOLIPSISM   The view that I alone exist, the *reductio ad absurdum* of subjectivism.

SUBJECTIVE   That which pertains to the subject, the self, or the knower; that which exists in consciousness but not apart from consciousness. The term stands in contrast with *objective*.

SUBJECTIVISM   (1) The view that reality consists of conscious beings and their mental states; (2) The position that all we can know is one's own sensory and mental states; (3) The theory that value and other statements are about feelings, and therefore have no independent status; they exist only in minds.

TAUTOLOGY   In contemporary logic, a statement that is necessarily true because of its logical form, for example, "Black dogs are black." A tautology imparts no new knowledge.

Chapter Review

BASIC ISSUES IN THE NATURE OF KNOWLEDGE

1. Basic issues in the nature of knowledge may be understood in terms of several questions, one of which is, Do we have any genuine knowledge on which we can depend, or must we be satisfied with mere opinions and guesses?

2. There is a distinction between a sensation and a sense datum.

SUBJECTIVISM

1. Subjectivism is the view that statements of knowledge are ideas existing only in human minds.

2. Objects and qualities that we perceive through our senses do not exist independently of a consciousness of them.

3. Increasing states of subjectivism include the subjectivity of dreams; sense data; primary and secondary qualities; reality; space and time and the laws of nature; and the extreme position of solipsism, the view that only the individual self exists.

4. In all cases, we are dealing with our own perceptions or sensations.

OBJECTIVISM

1. Objectivism is the view that statements we intend as knowledge reveal what really is; ideas are formed by reliable sense experiences.

2. Objects and qualities that we perceive through our senses do exist independently of a consciousness of them.

3. The location of sense data remains a problem.

4. Arguments for objectivism include rejection of the subjectivists' method of reasoning and of their use of the word *idea*.

5. More positively, objectivists argue that the assumption that there is an order of reality "out there" is a better, more adequate view than any other; it conforms to our actual experience of life and understanding of thought processes.

THE NATURE OF KNOWLEDGE: FURTHER CONSIDERATIONS

1. Concerning the nature of knowledge, it is easy to take some part of knowledge and attempt to make that part appear to be the whole. Extreme forms of objectivism and subjectivism are guilty of this error.

2. There are different ways in which we come to have knowledge of things, persons, and events; philosophers have arrived at two useful distinctions for identifying types of knowledge.

THE TESTS OF KNOWLEDGE

1. Throughout time, many beliefs that were thought to be true have been proved false. Skeptics either claim that there is no such thing as valid knowledge or express uncertainty and doubt.

2. Skepticism is an expression of doubt or disbelief, which in its stricter meaning is a denial of the possibility of any knowledge, and in its broader meaning is an attitude of suspending judgment until critical analysis is complete or all available evidence is at hand.

THREE TESTS OF TRUTH

1. All the tests of truth are concerned with verification of assertions.

2. The correspondence theory is the test of truth widely accepted by realists. It states that truth is the agreement between the statement of fact and actual fact. According to this theory, truth is "fidelity to objective reality."

3. The coherence, or consistency, theory is the test of truth generally accepted by idealists. A judgment is true if it is consistent with other judgments accepted as true.

4. The pragmatists believe that the test of truth is workability or satisfactory consequences. There

is no static or absolute truth. Truth happens to an idea or judgment. A theory is true if it works in practice.

REFLECTIONS

1. Because the theories supplement rather than directly contradict each other, they can be combined in a definition of truth: truth is the faithful adherence of our judgments and ideas to the facts of experience or to the world as it is; but because we cannot always compare our judgments with the actual situations, we test them by their consistency with other judgments that we believe are valid and true, or we test them by their usefulness and practical consequences.

2. Philosophical pluralism asserts the inevitable existence of different interpretations of reality, knowledge, and values.

3. Our capacity to discover and articulate truth infallibly is subject to human limitations.

♦ ♦

Study Questions and Projects

1. Think about the ways in which our sense data and images may vary apart from actual changes in the objects of our experience. See if you can supply examples other than those given in the chapter. Do objects appear to be independent of our perception of them?

2. Some animals can "see in the dark"; others are color-blind. Is it true that "every animal species inhabits a homemade universe" and that this world of sense perception is only a small part of the world as a whole? If we possessed other or different types of sense organs or if the range of power of our senses were keener or duller than they are now would the world vary accordingly?

3. Do our training or education and our past experiences affect our perception? Is it true that we see largely what we are trained to see or expect to see? Can you give some other examples in which training and experience tend to influence perception?

4. Even though a person may accept objectivism and a realistic approach to epistemology, does it appear that there are some subjective elements in all our knowledge? (For example, Ralph Barton Perry has spoken about the egocentric predicament, and John Dewey has said that he was never able to get beyond or outside of his own experience. Note also that there are many differing interpretations of history and many psychologies and philosophies set forth by very able thinkers.)

5. The problem of appearance versus reality, or subjectivism versus objectivism, is an old issue in philosophy. If we never penetrate beyond sense data so that we can compare sense data with what is beyond sense data, how can we make such distinctions?

6. Explain what is meant by the problem of the nature of knowledge. Why is it one of the more difficult problems in philosophy?

7. State in your own words the common-sense view of the nature of knowledge. Why is it called the "common-sense" view?

8. What difficulties arise when the common-sense view of the nature of knowledge is subjected to careful examination? Illustrate the difficulties in the areas of the senses of sight, sound, and touch.

9. What is the case for objectivism? Do the facts that this position is closer than subjectivism to the common-sense view and is implied in the various sciences carry much weight with you?

10. State as clearly as you can your own position regarding the nature of knowledge. Evaluate the concluding statements of the chapter.

11. State as clearly as you can the distinctions among reason, rationalism, and rationalization. Why do people frequently confuse these terms?

12. Give your reaction to the following statement: "Any truth is many sided, even simple truths. But the complex truth of today needs approach

by many different methods and many different types of mind before we can arrive at even an approximation of the truth." (Attributed to Lord Stamp of England.)

13. In court witnesses are asked to swear "to tell the truth, the whole truth, and nothing but the truth." What assumptions underlie this oath? Are you able to accept these assumptions?

14. Elaborate on some of the main questions connected with the problem of the tests of knowledge. Is there any knowledge that is final or infallible?

15. Define and then evaluate critically: (a) the correspondence theory, (b) the coherence theory,

(c) the pragmatic theory of truth. Indicate the strengths and weaknesses of each of the tests.

16. Distinguish between skepticism and agnosticism, and indicate the degrees or types of skepticism. What are the dangers of these negative attitudes toward knowledge, and what values can we nevertheless derive from them?

17. How would you define truth? You need not follow or accept the definition given in this chapter, but be ready to defend your position.

18. When may a philosophical theory reasonably be accepted as tentatively verified or true?

◆ ◆

Suggested Readings

Alston, W. P. *Epistemic Justification: Essays In The Theory of Knowledge*. Ithaca, N.Y.: 1990. University Press, Cornell.

Foundationalism, justification, internalist and externalist approaches to epistemology, and the epistemology of self-knowledge are the main topics of the essays. An advanced-level text.

Ayer, A. J. *The Problem of Knowledge*. London: Macmillan, 1956.

In this book Ayer takes the question of what is meant by knowledge as an example of a philosophical inquiry. He also deals with the questions of skepticism and certainty and concludes with a detailed analysis of the philosophical problems of perception, memory, and knowledge of other minds.

Carruthers, P. *Human Knowledge and Human Nature: A New Introduction To An Ancient Debate*. New York: Oxford University Press, 1992.

This advanced-level book focuses on the sources of debates in epistemology, especially on the question of inborn knowledge.

Chisholm, R. M. *Theory of Knowledge*. 3rd ed. Englewood Cliffs, N.J.: Prentice-Hall, 1989.

In the publisher's *Foundations of Philosophy* series, this exploration of the theory of knowledge is introductory and scholarly.

Dancy, J., and Sosa, E. (eds.). *A Companion to Epistemology*. London: Blackwell, 1992.

Over 250 articles ranging from summary discussions to major essays on topics of current controversy.

Dewey, J. *The Quest for Certainty*. New York: Putnam, 1929.

The subtitle for Dewey's Gifford Lectures of 1929 reads: "A study of the Relation of Knowledge and Action." In this classic, Dewey discusses the age-old struggle of philosophers to attain certainty. He sees the modern role of philosophy to be one of interpreting the conclusions of science with respect to their consequences for our beliefs about the values and purposes of life.

Ellis, B. D. *Truth and Objectivity*. London: Blackwell, 1990.

The author traces the argument from the ontology of scientific realism to an evaluative theory of truth. An advanced-level text.

Goldman, A. H. *Empirical Knowledge*. Berkeley, Calif.: University of California Press, 1988.

This advanced-level book defends common sense and scientific realism within the explanationist framework and provides a new foundational approach to justification.

Hill, C. S. *Sensations: A Defense of Type Materialism.* New York: Cambridge University Press, 1991.

Hill argues that sensory states are identical with neural states with which they are correlated. An advanced-level text.

Kirkham, R. L. *Theories of Truth: A Critical Introduction.* Cambridge, Mass.: MIT Press, 1992.

Kirkham surveys all the major philosophical theories of truth for the nonexpert.

Kurtz, P. *The New Skepticism: Inquiry and Reliable Knowledge.* Buffalo, N.Y.: Prometheus, 1992.

Professor Kurtz distinguishes among (1) nihilism; (2) mitigated skepticism; and (3) skeptical inquiry, which he regards as constructive and positive.

Lucey, K. G. (ed.). *On Knowing and the Known: Introductory Readings in Epistemology.* Buffalo, N.Y.: Prometheus, 1993.

A contemporary collection of introductory readings.

Moser, P. (ed.). *Empirical Knowledge: Readings In Contemporary Epistemology.* Lanham, Md.: Rowan and Littlefield, 1986.

An introduction to the leading approaches and current developments in epistemology.

Pojman, L. P. (ed.). *The Theory of Knowledge: Classical and Contemporary Readings.* Belmont, Calif.: Wadsworth, 1993.

An introductory textbook with bibliographies at the end of each chapter.

White, A. R. *Truth.* Garden City, N.Y.: Doubleday, Anchor Books, 1970.

This small paperback carefully examines and gives examples of the different meanings of the term *truth.* This is followed by a discussion of theories of truth.

◆ ◆

Notes

1. W. P. Montague, *The Ways of Things* (New York: Prentice-Hall, 1940), pp. 15–16.

2. G. Berkeley, *The Principles of Knowledge and Three Dialogues Between Hylas and Philonous* (New York: World, Meridian Books, 1969) pp. 20–21. (From the introduction by G. J. Warnock.)

3. Joad, *Guide to Philosophy,* pp. 65–66.

4. B. Russell, *The Problems of Philosophy,* No. 35 of the *Home University Library* series (London: Oxford University Press, 1912), pp. 62–63.

5. A. C. Ewing, *The Fundamental Questions of Philosophy* (London: Routledge and Kegan Paul, 1951), p. 62.

6. W. James, "Pragmatism's Conception of Truth," in A. Castell, ed., *Essays in Pragmatism* (New York: Hafner, 1955), p. 160.

7. For a discussion of these tests of truth by a philosopher who believes that we cannot do with only one criterion of truth, see Ewing, *The Fundamental Questions of Philosophy,* Chapter 3.

8. A discussion about postulates is included in the next chapter.

♦ ♦ ♦ ♦ ♦ ♦ ♦ ♦ ♦ ♦ ♦ ♦ ♦

Science and Philosophy

CHAPTER OBJECTIVES

In this chapter we will address the
following questions:

♦ How Has Science Developed
  Historically?

♦ What Are the Basic Issues
  in Philosophy of Science?

♦ Is There a Specific Scientific
  Method?

♦ How Are Paradigms
  and Models Justified?

♦ Do Scientific Methods Have
  Limitations?

♦ On What Points Do Philosophy
  and Science Agree and Differ?

♦ How Does Science View the
  Universe and Life Processes?

*It is becoming the thumb rule of science
that nothing is the way we thought it was,
and whatever we think we understand
today will be changed to something else
when looked at more closely tomorrow.*[1]

The Development of Science

Scholars in many fields have pointed out that there has been more scientific progress in the last 175 years than in all previous history. Certainly the pace of scientific growth has been greatly accelerated—so much so that our age is frequently called the age of science and **technology.** The development of science is predominantly the work of Western civilization in its modern period. Other civilizations have made important contributions to human progress mainly in nonscientific fields. The early Greeks made many advances in philosophy, art, and government. When they turned their attention to science, they showed interest chiefly in pure science or in theory. Nonetheless, ancient Greeks developed basic mathematics, astronomy, and medicine. During this period, philosophy and science overlapped; little or no sharp distinction was made between them. The ancient Hebrews are known for their insights in religion and morality. The Romans were administrators, lawgivers, and practical builders. Theology was one of the main interests of the medieval period. Since the Renaissance, however, and especially during the last century, progress in the West has been focused on science and its practical applications.

Science has been called "trained and organized common sense." Its distinctive characteristic is its critical and accurate observation and description of things and events. The term *science* comes from the Latin *scire,* "to know." Today, the word *science* is used in a narrower sense to designate a quantitative, testable and objective knowledge of nature.

Pure science is objective knowledge for its own sake, without consideration for any practical application. *Applied science* is scientific knowledge put to practical use or applied within science itself (e.g., the application of mathematics to physics). *Technology* often is used to mean "applied science"; an example is the application of pure science that enables industry to manufacture computers. *Technology* also refers to inventions that work even though people have no scientific understanding of why they function (such as the early steam engines); medieval technology was technology in this sense.

The development of science is one of the greatest achievements of the human mind. Without some knowledge of the growth of science, it is difficult to understand modern history. A glance at the history of scientific accomplishments in both pure science and technology will help us to appreciate the curiosity and inventiveness of the human mind.

SCIENCE AND EARLY CIVILIZATION

Early civilization, with primitive agriculture and industrial arts, appears to have originated in or near the valleys of great rivers, such as the Nile, the Euphrates, and the Yellow River. The land was fertile and water was available for people and herds. More than two thousand years before the common era began, the Babylonians and Egyptians possessed a considerable body of knowledge. They used fixed units of measurements, such as standards of length, weight, and volume; a multiplication table; tables of squares and cubes; and a decimal system based on our ten fingers. In Egypt, the periodic rise of the waters of the Nile, resulting in lost boundary marks, led to a system of land surveying that stimulated the growth of geometry. Instruments such as set squares, levels, beam balances, and plumb lines, as well as a considerable amount of mathematical knowledge, were needed to build the pyramids. Weaving and spinning were practiced, and wheeled chariots were in use.

Both the Egyptians and the Babylonians thought the world resembled a box, of which the earth was the floor. There was a rudimentary astronomy based on observations of the regularities of the "heavenly bodies." There was a calendar containing 365 days. The days of the week were named after the sun, the moon, and the five known planets, and the months and the years were determined from the movement of the moon and the apparent movement of the sun. By the sixth century B.C.E., eclipses could be predicted. In India and China, too, progress was being made. Paper and the compass were invented in China. The system of numerals we use today came from India by way of Arabia.

GRAECO-ROMAN SCIENCE

With the Greeks, human consciousness and interest in humanity and nature expanded rapidly. The Greeks wanted to know for the sake of knowing, and the scientific as well as the philosophical spirit was born. The contribution of the Greeks was so great that many of the scientific and philosophical terms we use today originated with them. Thales (c. 624–546 B.C.E.), the first Ionian nature philosopher, who lived in the Greek colonial city of Miletus in Asia Minor, is reported to have visited Egypt and to have become acquainted with the system of land surveying in use there. Later he advanced geometry and set forth his views about the watery nature of the world. Other pre-Socratic thinkers were instrumental in advancing interest and knowledge in areas that were to become important for the development of science and philosophy.

Other achievements of classical Greece included the first detailed example of what mathematical astronomy could be and the first extended attempt at a mathematical structure of matter (Plato); proposals that the earth was spherical (Pythagoras); drawings of parallels of latitude and longitude on a map of the known world and calculations of the circumference of the globe with only a 1 percent error (Eratosthenes); development of the theory that the earth rotated on its axis and moved in orbit around the sun (Aristarchus); systematizing of the theorems of plane and solid geometry (Euclid); discovery of specific gravity (Archimedes); advancements in medicine that included outlining the nervous system, and, although this was not a universally shared view, ascertaining that the brain was the center of consciousness (Hippocrates and followers); a basic atomic theory of matter (Leucippus and Democritus); the ordering of thought by means of logic, and development of classification schemes for the various branches of knowledge (Aristotle). The idea of nature as a rational, orderly whole (*kosmos*) is of Greek origin.

However, we should not conclude that the interpretations mentioned in the preceding paragraph were unerring or dominant at the time. For example, many of Aristotle's views were more prevalent than other Greek interpretations of that era (e.g., his understanding of nature's basic elements—earth, air, fire and water). Furthermore, Ptolemy had proposed the erroneous, long-lasting view of the earth as center of the universe, with the sun, moon, and stars revolving around it.

The Romans were a practical people who excelled as administrators and builders. They had little interest in pure science or knowledge for its own sake. Their amphitheaters, aqueducts, forums, and roads reflected their concern with engineering and the practical or useful arts. For a thousand years, during the Middle Ages, Europe made only slight advances in pure science. During the earlier part of the Middle Ages, the influence of Plato's philosophy was strong, and Aristotle was known mainly for his logic. During the later part, the period of cultural flowering, Aristotle's philosophy was accepted as the great authority. Thinkers of that period looked to deductive reasoning (syllogistic logic) and divine revelation as their sources of knowledge. They thought they knew the meaning and the purpose of their own lives and of the universe. The scholastic philosophers and theologians continued the Greek concept of nature as a rational, orderly whole, a concept basic to modern science.

THE MIDDLE AGES

However, the Middle Ages in Europe was one of the most inventive periods in the history of technology. Among the achievements were the stirrup, horse collar, ox yoke, iron plow with mould board, three- and four-field system of crop rotation, windmill, Gothic arch and vault, mechanical clock, optics, and systematic utilization of natural sources of power. It would be hard to characterize medieval technology as "applied science," however, because this inventiveness consisted of efforts to control nature before scientists learned to understand it.

From the ninth to the eleventh century, Greek knowledge was translated into Arabic. Islamic civilization, which included most of the Mediterranean world, produced new scientific developments written in Arabic. Mathematics, medicine, astronomy, and optics, were among the sciences advanced by the Arabic world. Eventually, the knowledge of ancient Greece and the scientific progress of this civilization were translated into European languages. Without the Arabic resource, the scientific developments of European civilization would have been seriously retarded.

Europe enjoyed the technical heritage of the Middle Ages from the sixteenth through the eighteenth centuries, the period of the Scientific Revolution.

THE SCIENTIFIC REVOLUTION

During the Renaissance and Enlightenment periods (c. 1500–1800), Aristotle's authority and medieval theology were replaced by different methods of discovering knowledge about the world and by a new view of the universe. The Copernican Revolution, named for the Polish monk Copernicus (1473–1543) (see biography and insert, pp. 214–215), was the replacement of the belief that the earth is the stationary center of the cosmos with the theory that the sun is the center of our solar system, the earth one of the planets. Copernicus reached this conclusion by mathematical and analytical reasoning.

Francis Bacon (1561–1626) relied on the inductive method, by which facts drawn from experimentation are used to formulate hypotheses and eventually to describe scientific laws and universal principles. He proposed that inquirers must first empty their minds of preconceptions or "self-evident truths," then make observations and generalize. Bacon's simple notion of induction assumed that it is possible for a scientist to be totally neutral, free from all assumptions—a condition not possible for even the most detached investigator. Also, his assertion that direct observation was essential to science would eliminate theoretical science, in which theories are built by mathematical inferences and indirect evidence; the nature of submicroscopic particles such as quarks and gluons (see p. 229) is within theoretical science. However, Bacon's conclusions regarding the inductive method and the importance of doubting all received knowledge has had immense influence in the history of modern thought.

Descartes (1598–1650) relied on deduction and used the method of mathematics to reason to the concept of a mathematically intelligible, mechanical universe. He proposed that scientists begin with self-evident axioms and then, by logical reasoning, deduce various inferences. Descartes attempted to extend the deductive method to all fields of human knowledge. Although he did not reject the value of experimentation, he relied on the attainment of knowledge through reason. A weakness in this approach is that scientists disagree about what principles are truly self-evident. Among his achievements were the development of analytic geometry, a concept of a unified, mathematically ordered universe explainable in mathematical terms, and an independent spirit of scientific investigation.

Galileo (1564–1642) combined mathematical and experimental methods. Questioning many of Aristotle's teachings, he defended Copernicus and readily used experimentation to attack accepted beliefs about physical laws. He devised an improved telescope and also established the law of falling bodies (regardless of the size or weight of falling bodies, their acceleration is constant); he made other discoveries in astronomy and physics. At several times during his life, Galileo suffered persecution by church officials who resisted his methods and conclusions which were offensive to the medieval intellectual establishment.

Johannes Kepler (1571–1630) worked out a complex geometric hypothesis to account for

Nicolaus Copernicus

Copernicus (1473–1543) was born in Torun, Poland. He studied at the University of Kracow, and was appointed a canon of the cathedral of Frauenberg, which gave him an income for life and enabled him to study law and medicine in Italy. Although he did not take courses in astronomy, he collected books in astronomy and mathematics and is often considered the father of modern astronomy. He developed the theory that the earth revolves and moves with the other planets around the sun—the heliocentric view that was to replace the Ptolemaic view. This was a major development, but equally important was the method Copernicus had employed, which included independent mathematical reasoning. The masterpiece for which he is famous is *Concerning the Revolutions of the Celestial Spheres* (1543). The printed form reached him only a few hours before his death.

distances between the elliptical planetary orbits previously thought to be circular. He also discovered that the motions of the planets are relative to their distance from the sun. His astronomical conclusions have since been called Kepler's Laws. In addition, Kepler made contributions in optics and mathematics; his *Epitome of Copernican Astronomy* (1618–1621) became the first textbook of astronomy based on Copernican principles.

Newton (1642–1727) (see biography and excerpt, pp. 216–217) united into one all-embracing law of gravitation the explanation of the motion of all bodies in the planetary system; the universe is presented as one great unity operating according to unalterable principles.

Among his important discoveries were the law of gravitation, the principles of calculus, and the compound nature of light.

The implications of Newton's research were those of the scientific revolution: opinions accepted in the past, whether philosophical, theological, or scientific, could be challenged and the issues reexamined; the universe was governed by rational, universal laws, which could be formulated as precisely as mathematical principles. The scientific revolution was not intrinsically antireligious but by implication called for a radical departure from past views of reality and from authoritarian declarations, especially on matters best researched through experimentation and observation.

Excerpt from Copernicus:

The Preface to the Books of the Revolutions to the Most Holy Lord, Pope Paul III (1543)

I may well presume, most Holy Father, that certain people, as soon as they hear that in this book *On the Revolutions of the Spheres of the Universe* I ascribe movement to the earthly globe, will cry out that, holding such views, I should at once be hissed off the stage. . . . That I allow the publication of these my studies may surprise your Holiness the less in that, having been at such travail to attain them, I had already not scrupled to commit to writing my thoughts upon the motion of the Earth. How I came to dare to conceive such motion of the Earth, contrary to the received opinion of the Mathematicians and indeed contrary to the impression of the senses, is what your Holiness will rather expect to hear. So I should like your Holiness to know that I was induced to think of a method of computing the motions of the spheres by nothing else than the knowledge that the Mathematicians are inconsistent in these investigations.

For, first, the Mathematicians are so unsure of the movements of the Sun and Moon that they cannot even explain or observe the constant length of the seasonal year. Secondly, in determining the motions of these and of the five other planets, they do not even use the same principles and hypotheses as in their proofs of seeming revolutions and motions.

Copernicus, Nicolaus, *On the Revolutions of the Heavenly Spheres*, trans. A. M. Duncan (New York: Barnes and Noble, 1976).

MODERN SCIENCE

The nineteenth century witnessed the rapid growth of science and industry. John Dalton (1766–1844) and others advanced the atomic theory, which in turn advanced all thought relative to matter and led to the particle concept for matter and energy. There was significant growth in the studies of electricity, heat, energy, light, and magnetism. Another great work of the nineteenth century was the application of scientific methods to the study of living organisms. Although the idea of evolution had been known to some Greek philosophers, it was not widely accepted before Charles Darwin (1809–1882) published the *Origin of Species* in 1859. The concept of evolution has had widespread influence on modern thought.

The twentieth century has brought unparalleled advances in many fields of science and abandonment of many interpretations that had been taken for granted during the previous centuries. The sciences of the nineteenth century, for example, took matter, space, and time as basic and fixed entities. Matter was thought to be composed of simple and indivisible atoms existing in absolute space and time. Concepts of relativity, subatomic particles, and the quantum theory have profoundly altered the older models. Explanations, subject to revision, of a cosmos in which random events occur and laws are statistically probable inferences allow scientists

Isaac Newton

Isaac Newton (1642–1727), British mathematician, physicist, and philosopher, formalized Galilean mechanics, discovered the inverse square law of universal gravitation, and made notable contributions to the theory of light. One of Newton's major works was *Optics* (1704). He was educated at the University of Cambridge, where he was a professor of mathematics from 1675 to 1707.

Philosophiae Naturalis Principia Mathematica (1687), generally known as *Principia,* is Newton's most philosophically oriented work. No one without a comprehensive knowledge of mathematics can understand it properly, which contributes to its inaccessibility. *Principia* provides an inclusive system of mechanics accounting for the motion of bodies on or near the surface of the earth and for all motion throughout the universe.

Newton claimed that his method was empirical and inductive. Furthermore, he asserted that his discovery of universal gravitation was evidence for belief in a deity.

Several seventeenth- and eighteenth-century philosophers, especially the British empiricists and Kant, were influenced by Newton. For example, much of Locke's philosophy can be seen as developing the philosophical implications of Newtonian mechanics.

to examine new information and make new interpretations.

Science is now closely tied to mathematics; scientists are more conscious of the limits of what is known and the vast areas yet to be explored. Recently, scientific inquiry has been used in the humanities and social sciences, such as psychology and economics. We will consider some modern views of the universe and life later in this chapter.

Philosophy of Science: Basic Issues

Knowledge resulting from scientific conclusions plays an important role in our understanding of the world around us. Because science to a large extent shapes our understanding of reality, philosophers are analyzing the methods and concepts of science. These studies have emerged as an area called philosophy of science.

The basic issues of philosophy of science can be grouped into two categories. The first is the analysis of the logic and the language of science. In this category philosophers have understood that the natural sciences (such as physics, chemistry, and biology) as well as the social sciences (such as psychology and sociology) offer explanations, formulate laws, and propose theories. However, concerned with the language of science, philosophers of science ask, "What constitutes a satisfactory scientific explanation, law, or theory?" They explore the criteria or standards for acceptable scientific explanations. The criteria or standards are made more explicit as

The forces of gravitation with which bodies tend to the sun and the several planets can be discovered from the celestial phenomena. . . . I wish we could derive the rest of the phenomena of nature by the same kind of reasoning from mechanical principles; for I am induced by many reasons to suspect that they all depend upon certain forces by which the particles of bodies, by causes hitherto unknown, are either mutually impelled towards each other and cohere in regular figures, or are repelled and recede from each other; which forces being unknown, philosophers have hitherto attempted the search of nature in vain.

. . . It may be that there is no body really at rest, to which the places and motions of other bodies can be referred. . . . It is indeed extremely difficult to discover and distinguish effectively the true motion of particular bodies from the apparent; because the parts of that immovable space in which these motions are performed do by no means come under the observation of our senses.

Newton, Sir Isaac, *Philosophiae Naturalis Principia Mathematica*, ed. A. Koyrè (Cambridge, Mass.: Harvard University Press, 1972).

philosophers endeavor to set forth the patterns in the process whereby scientists structure and organize their findings into theories and laws. Also, concerned with the logic of science, philosophers analyze the methods by which hypotheses are tested and theories are supported; the logical relationships between hypotheses and laws or between laws and theories are studied.

The second major category of philosophy of science is the relationship between scientific knowledge and broader concerns. For example, to what extent does science offer us a quite abstract and partial knowledge of things, accurate as it otherwise might be? Some philosophers have attempted to make use of this knowledge to answer such general questions as, "Is there anything unique about human beings, or are they just another species of animal?" Others have made use of scientific knowledge to address theological concerns about the possibility of a creator, that is, whether there is any place for a traditional God in the world portrayed by science.

As philosophers investigate science, the validity of scientific explanations and the superiority of scientific statements over intuitive, rational, and religious knowledge, become significant issues. Therefore, philosophy of science has become an important study attempting to establish greater precision about what constitutes scientific facts, scientific methodologies, and the limitations of science. Current issues in philosophy of science (related to the previous chapters on the sources, nature, and tests of knowledge) include explorations of the sources for arriving at scientific knowledge, the objectivity of such knowledge, and the tests of scientific truth.

Scientific Methods

◆ ◆ ◆ ◆ ◆ ◆ ◆ ◆ ◆ ◆

THREE POSSIBLE MEANINGS OF "SCIENCE"

Because the terms **science** and **scientific methods** are both used in a number of different ways, an examination of some of these different usages will help us understand the nature of the processes and the terms involved. The word *science* is used, first to denote any of the many sciences. These include physics, chemistry, astronomy, geology, and biology. Mathematics and logic are sometimes referred to as formal or abstract sciences, and disciplines such as botany and mineralogy often are called descriptive or empirical sciences. There are a great many sciences, and their fields overlap.

Second, the term *science* may be used for the entire body of systematic knowledge, including the hypotheses, theories, and laws that have been built up by the work of numerous scientists through the years. This knowledge is mainly theoretical, in contrast with the practical skills and the arts.

Third, a considerable number of people use the term *science* to designate the results of a method of obtaining knowledge that is objective and verifiable. In this sense, a documented biography is scientific.

SCIENTIFIC POSTULATES

Before we attempt to examine how scientific truth can be tested, it is important to examine the notion of *proof.* All proof must begin with certain assumptions. This is true in science, philosophy, or religion. Some ideas or facts must be accepted as **postulates**—that is, must be taken for granted. These include the fundamental laws of thought or logic, such as the principles of identity ("all A is A"), noncontradiction ("not both A and not-A"), and excluded middle ("either A or not-A"); these are commonly spoken of as self-evident. Ordinarily, we also accept the evidence of immediate experience. Anyone working in the sciences usually proceeds on the basis of some or all of the following basic assumptions, postulates, axioms, or conditions.

1. The principle of *causality* is the belief that every event has a cause and that, in identical situations, the same cause always produces the same effect.

2. The principle of *predictive uniformity* states that a group of events will show the same degree of interconnection or relationship in the future as they showed in the past or show in the present.

3. The principle of *objectivity* requires the investigator to be impartial with regard to the data. The facts must be such that they can be experienced in exactly the same way by all normal people. The aim is to eliminate all subjective and personal elements insofar as possible and to concentrate on the object being studied.

4. The principle of *empiricism* lets investigators assume that their sense impressions are reliable and that they can test truth by an appeal to the "experienced facts." Knowing is the result of observation, experience, and experiment, as opposed to authority, intuition, or reason alone.

5. The principle of *parsimony* is that, other things being equal, take the simplest explanation as the most valid one. A check on unnecessary intricacy, this principle cautions against complicated explanations. It is sometimes called **Occam's razor,** after William of Occam, a fourteenth-century English philosopher who said that "entities should not be multiplied beyond necessity."

6. The principle of *isolation,* or *segregation,* requires that the phenomenon under investigation be segregated so that it can be studied by itself. However, in so doing, the phenomenon is somewhat altered, thereby reducing the universality of the theory put forth; the results are true "under these circumstances."

7. The principle of *control* emphasizes that variables not under investigation must be held constant during experimentation. Otherwise, many factors may vary at the same time, and the experiment could not be repeated in the same way. If the conditions change while the experiment is being conducted, the results may be invalid. More important, it is not always possible to tell which variation caused the result.

8. The principle of *exact measurement* requires results to be such that they can be stated in quantitative or mathematical terms. This is the goal at least of the physical sciences, which seek verifiable objective measurements.

A scientist, E. G. Conklin, years ago raised the question of whether there can be such a thing as a "purely objective science." He reminds us that there can be "no observation without an observer, no experiment without an experimenter, no classification without a classifier."[2] In the physical or inorganic sciences, the postulates and conditions we have set forth can be met fairly adequately. We can isolate and control and measure with a high degree of success. When we come to a study of living creatures, especially humans and society, new and difficult conditions are encountered. Life on its higher levels cannot be isolated and controlled without altering the nature of that which is to be studied. Separate a person from society and you change the nature of his or her being.

Neither the scientist nor the philosopher has any secrets or methods of obtaining knowledge that are not open to people in general. Science differs from ordinary common sense in that it is more critical, more penetrating, and more controlled and exact in its observations and analyses.

Scientific method can be divided into two parts: the logical methods and the technical or technological methods. The logical methods are those of reasoning or drawing inferences. These logical processes are the same in all the sciences, in philosophy, and in all clear and accurate thinking. They include such principles of reasoning as the method of agreement, the method of difference, and the method of concomitant variation.

The technical methods are those of manipulating the phenomena under investigation. This is what many people think of as "science." These methods are many and varied. Here we include the constantly growing mass of apparatus and equipment that aids in observation and experimentation. These instruments immediately come to our attention as we enter a scientific laboratory. They extend our powers of observation and control. Without a knowledge of the field and the methods of reasoning, however, they are of little use.

A VARIETY OF SCIENTIFIC METHODS

There is no universal agreement, even among scientists, about what is meant by *scientific method*. Science has evolved from common sense, and the transition from one to the other has been gradual and continuous. A careful examination of the sciences—such as physics, astronomy, and botany—fails to reveal any single method in use. Sciences such as astronomy proceed by means of observation and mathematical calculations from these observations. Other sciences, such as physics and chemistry, emphasize controlled experimentation. In still other sciences, trial and error, statistics, and sampling are used. Thus there are scientific methods rather than *the* scientific method. The method used depends on the nature of the material or problem to be studied.

Observation. Some sciences, such as astronomy and botany, have been built up by careful and methodical observation. Observation is a matter of sense perception: we see, hear, touch, feel, or smell something. On the basis of our observations we draw conclusions regarding relations, causal sequences, and the meaning of the situation.

The *method of agreement,* one of the inductive methods, is sometimes called the *observational* method of agreement.[3] The principle involved is that "the sole invariable circumstance accompanying a phenomenon is causally connected with the phenomenon." Some years ago, for example, eight well-known leaders in the United States lumber industry became ill and died. Even though they lived in widely separated areas of the country, the fact that they all died within a short period led some people to think that there might be a common cause. On examination of the circumstances of the deaths and the events leading up to them, it was noted that not only had all the men died of amoebic dysentery but also all of them had attended the same conference of lumber dealers a few weeks before. All of them had stayed at the same hotel and had used water that was later found to be contaminated with microorganisms that cause dysentery; the sewage system was blocked. In the light of all the circumstances, the contaminated water at the hotel was identified as the cause of the untimely deaths, or "the sole invariable circumstance." There were, of course, a number of common conditions besides the use of the contaminated water. In such circumstances one needs to make a judgment of relevance based on general knowledge and past experience. In this case, the water supply was first assumed to be the cause; further investigation disclosed that this water was contaminated with organisms that caused the illness.

Trial and Error. The method of trial and error, sometimes called trial and success, or trial and chance, does not need lengthy discussion. Trial and error is used by animals as they try to solve their problems. It is a technique used by psychologists who study animals and human beings. A rat uses trial and error to get out of a maze or around some obstacle in its path. A chimpanzee tries various means to secure food that is out of reach. A person uses this method to find out how some gadget works. Trial and error can be used deliberately by scientists as they try different hypotheses and by philosophers as they test ideas and systems of thought for coherence and factual and logical consistency.

The trial-and-error method does involve reflection. Reflective thinking has been called "trial and error by ideas." In reflective thinking, the fumbling is done in the imagination. We may carry out in our imagination a number of proposals or hypotheses and conclude that some may work and others will not.

Experimentation. Active experimentation is the principal method of discovering and verifying causes. Experimentation involves *manipulation* and *control*. Although observation and trial and error have been widely used, they have their limitations. Great advances in scientific research were made possible when techniques of control were discovered and put to use. In an experiment, the observer controls the conditions relating to the subject of study. He or she then manipulates these conditions, changing one factor at a time so that the results can be correlated with the different conditions. The *method of difference*, sometimes called the *experimental* method of difference, is widely used in science: the rule is to vary only one factor or condition at a time, keeping all other factors unchanged or constant. The investigator makes a difference in only one variable to see whether it will make a difference in the result.

A simple illustration of the method of difference is the coin-and-feather experiment in physics. Why does a feather fall to the ground more slowly than does a coin? An experiment is designed to see whether the cause is the resistance of the air. A coin and a feather are dropped at the same time in the chamber of an air pump in which air is present. The coin drops quickly, whereas the feather's fall is retarded. With the other factors kept constant, the air is pumped from the chamber. The coin and the feather are dropped again. This time they reach the bottom of the chamber at the same time. It is reasonable to conclude that buoyancy slowed the fall of the feather.

Statistical Method. The term *statistics* refers to the mathematical science of the collection, analysis, and classification of numerical data as a basis for induction. Statistical methods arose in early times to help rulers and states gather information about population, births, deaths, wealth, taxes, and the like. These methods have been greatly refined, and today statistical methods are used in everyday affairs, in business and financial activities, in education, and in many of the sciences. Counting, measurement, averages, means, medians—all enable us to make our information more exact and to find order in a mass of detail. Although the use of statistics helps us to understand particular features of groups (for example, white male drivers in America between the ages of 19 and 25), we learn nothing definite about a certain individual of that group; what can be said of a general nature about a group based on statistical evidence cannot be said in the same sense of any individual in it. Statistics help us to determine the probability of events so that we can make predictions, to explain causes and effects, to describe types of phenomena, and to make comparisons. Data often are presented in tables, charts, and graphs, which make it easy to see the distribution of events.

Sampling. In sampling, we assume that the nature of some members of a class is an indication of the nature of all the members. When is a single instance likely to be an accurate representative of the whole and when is it not likely to be? When the material to be examined is known to be homogeneous throughout, a single sample will give accurate results. A random sample will suffice, because there are no varying conditions the distribution of which must be considered. Such samples often are valuable for comparison of the same material at different times or places.

As the heterogeneity of the material increases, the number of samples needed increases. If we know that the sand on a seashore is uniform, then a single sample may be sufficient. If we suspect that the sand is not uniform throughout, then we will take samples at many different places. These can be mixed, and we can "sample the sample."

When differences among items must be taken into account, as in public polls, the investigator must be careful to see that the sample is representative. We must consider whether age, gender, occupation, economic status, education, religion, politics, and other factors influence the results. In this case, the sample constructed needs to be a cross section of the population. The bacterial content of water in a pond may vary in different parts of the pond and be affected by inlet or outlet, running or stagnant areas, surface or depth, vegetation and wind direction. In this situation, a sample from each area must be examined.

The Nature and Role of Models and Paradigms

♦ ♦ ♦ ♦ ♦ ♦ ♦ ♦ ♦ ♦ ♦

The concept of models in science is an important one. Although models usually mean nothing more than pictorial, mechanical, or physical representations of things in the physical universe, they are successful in guiding scientific practices. It is useful to think of a model as a set of rules, or an algorithm. For example, a number of computer games are based on models that provide the logic by which decisions are made in the games even though the logic may not work in the "real" world. In science, models are often mathematical. The laws of physics and the techniques of calculus, for example, can be used to construct a model that will predict how objects behave when certain forces are applied under certain conditions. Its purpose is to enable scientists to "try out" a number of experimental conditions and to test hypotheses without actually manipulating physical objects. Often models are used to represent objects that are not actually seen by scientists, such as molecules and atoms. They allow scientists to make predictions and to hypothesize and experiment with things that are otherwise unavailable, thereby helping new discoveries to come about.

Models, however, are not the only thing which guide scientific practices. True enough, they are the tools by which scientific practices are made possible and scientific progress is advanced. But there is another sense in which science is guided. The very questions that are asked, the modes of investigation that scientists are inclined to use, the way they analyze data, and the way their findings supplement a larger body of theory are all a matter of the context in which these activities take place. For philosopher of science Thomas S. Kuhn,[4] the context or background of conditions, or set of fundamental assumptions, within which science actually takes place, is called a **paradigm**. Paradigms are not necessarily explicitly recognized by a scientific community. Nevertheless, they guide the way science is actually practiced. A paradigm guiding scientific activities is like a pipe through which water flows, directing it without necessarily being apparent to the flow itself. Paradigms are not merely the pictorial tools that are meant by models, but are the very picture itself, adhered to by the community of scientists, within which the world is interpreted. On Kuhn's view, "normal" scientific investigation proceeds within the framework of a reigning paradigm just as long as there are no new discoveries to challenge it. When that happens, as it did in the case of Einstein's theory of relativity, a crisis occurs and then the question is whether to adopt a new paradigm. Two persistent philosophical questions which may be addressed to scientists are: "Does today's science agree with reality as it *is,* or is today's science a current intellectual agreement among contemporary scientists?" and "Is all scientific knowledge limited to some degree of approximation, subject to ongoing refinement and correction?"

Adherence to a paradigm or model is at heart a matter of faith, of taking particular ideas for granted, however reasonable they seem. The fact that scientists of a given historical period, or individual scientists at any time, prefer one paradigm or model over others indicates that valuing is present in the selection process. Hence, science cannot be regarded as totally value free.

A Method of Acquiring Knowledge

♦ ♦ ♦ ♦ ♦ ♦ ♦ ♦ ♦ ♦ ♦

The methods we considered earlier in this chapter are not separate and distinct; they are interrelated and supplement one another. In fact, it is not possible to use one of them apart from all the others. In a general way, we may say that *scientific method* is a collective term designating numerous processes and steps by which the various sciences are built up. Scientific method enables scientists to test their hypotheses, to determine whether rejection or conditional acceptance and further testing should occur; it is a way that scientific knowledge is accumulated.

To avoid a false impression, we need to recognize that scientific method cannot be reduced to an absolute formula or a master plan. As noted by one physicist:

> If by scientific method we mean the sequence and rule by which scientists now and in the past have actually done their work, then two truths soon become obvious. First, as for every task, there are here not one but many methods and uncountable variants and, second, even those different methods are for the most part read into the story after it has been completed, and so exist only in a rather artificial and debatable way. The everpresent longing to discover some *one* master procedure underlying all scientific work is understandable, for such a discovery might enormously benefit all fields of scholarship; but . . . this hope had to be given up.[5]

What follows, then, are general steps present in scientific method.

1. *Recognize that a problem exists and state the problem.* Thinking ordinarily begins when there is some definite obstacle, or difficulty, or possibly when we are merely curious about something. It is crucial to state the problem clearly and correctly. Without a clear statement of the problem, an investigator cannot proceed with the development of a hypothesis and subsequent steps of the research.

At this point it is helpful to state the major assumptions or postulates directly related to the defined problem. Whatever is taken for granted as true at the outset of research influences the development of a **hypothesis** and subsequent steps of investigation. For example, if a proposed study assumes that the results of a previous research project are valid, this assumption should be stated as a postulate.

2. *The available and relevant background information is collected.* Determine what else has been done about the problem or closely related problems. This material may be readily available or require considerable research and analysis. Occasionally, this step is minimized as an investigator leaps intuitively to step 3.

3. *A hypothesis is formulated.* Science has no real rules for thinking up an hypothesis, which is a proposed solution or possible explanation

stated in general terms. Hypotheses are often the result of a leap of imagination speculating on a certain problematic issue; they may occur to the scientist during research into background information. The investigator may make educated guesses as the problem is clearly stated. The researcher selects for testing the hypothesis that appears to be most probable on the basis of available evidence. There may be no limit to the number of hypotheses that may be set forth as possible solutions to a problem, but each must undergo the same rigorous investigation.

4. *Deductions are drawn from the hypothesis.* The principles of formal logic are used to decide what results would indicate the validity of a hypothesis; that is, if a hypothesis is true, it implies that particular consequences are observable and can be tested directly. The investigator predicts a result based on the hypothesis; that is, if A and B are true, then C must be true.

5. *An appropriate research plan is developed and implemented.* Having determined in the fourth step what else will be true if the hypothesis is true, the researcher then attempts to see whether these other conditions are true or actually occur. Empirical procedures for collecting and treating data (i.e., observation and other scientific methods discussed earlier in this chapter) are planned. Once developed, the procedures should be so clear that any qualified scientist could follow them and obtain the same data.

The data resulting from implementing the research plan are collected, organized, and classified.

6. *Verification is the final stage.* An interpretation of the data (which may include conclusions, generalizations, and applications) is developed. If this explanation corresponds to the hypothesis, the investigator is able to conclude that the hypothesis is confirmed or verified. Hypotheses that stand up to further empirical testing may eventually be considered scientific laws, principles, or theories.

A hypothesis is rejected when it is used to make a prediction that is not confirmed by the observed outcome. If a hypothesis is not verified, another hypothesis may be developed and tested.

Steps similar to these six are followed in any research study that requires reflective thinking and empirical verification. Those who claim that scientific method is limited are usually thinking of the more restricted approach, in which the material is objective and the results must be stated in mathematical or quantitative terms. For example, some people working in the natural sciences object to the use of the terms *science* and *scientific method* when applied to the social sciences, such as psychology, sociology, or economics.

Limitations of Scientific Methods

In our discussion in this section we are thinking of *science* and *scientific methods* in the more restricted sense—as the terms are used by most scientists in the natural sciences, in which the methods are strictly empirical and objective and the purpose is to interpret the world quantitatively and mathematically. We are assuming that scientists are free to investigate anything with which their methods are capable of dealing. The purpose of this section is not to urge that the sciences be kept out of any particular areas of human experience; rather, it is to indicate the limitations inherent in scientific methods.

If one reads widely in the literature of the sciences, many questions arise in one's mind. For example, why are there several psychologies, each claiming to be the valid approach and to represent the truth? What are the dominant factors in human behavior and social progress? Are they geographic, hereditary, psychological, cultural, religious, or economic, to mention a few of the possible answers? The conflicting evidence and claims are bewildering.

There are principles that will help to point up some of the limitations of science. Keep these suggestions in mind when considering science and scientific methods.

1. *In scientific research, you can find only that which your methods and your instruments are*

capable of finding. You can discover only that which is discoverable with the technique you use. This seems so obvious that one wonders why it is so frequently overlooked. If you use an objective method, you find only what can be stated objectively. If you proceed on the basis of the postulates of physics and chemistry, you find only what can be stated in physical or chemical terms. If you get in touch with your friend by telephone, you hear his voice; you get what the instrument transmits, and nothing more. If you investigate an object with a pair of scales, you get its weight. There may be other interesting things about it, but you are entitled to claim as scientifically valid knowledge only what your instrument and method are capable of giving you.

A number of scientists who proceed on the basis of the postulates of the physical sciences say that they never find such things as sensations, thoughts, or acts of will. Others have told us that they cannot detect purpose or meaning in any part of the universe disclosed by powerful telescopes. But should a person expect to find thoughts, acts of will, purpose, or meaning by looking through a telescope or using any scientific method?

2. *Scientific classification gives valuable information, but no single classification includes everything in the subject being classified.* Classification is one of the fundamental bases of scientific knowledge. We do not know what a thing is until we can classify it or put it into a meaningful context. If a thing cannot be analyzed and classified, it eludes science.

The kind of classification, however, depends on our purpose in making it. Things may be classified in many different ways. Buildings may be classified according to location, type, or valuation. Ill people may be classified according to their ailments, the doctors attending them, their ages, races, economic statuses, and so on. It is especially obvious in the case of ill people that classification is a means of dealing with things by the simple device of disregarding their differences. For example, several people with many different characteristics may all be classed as having typhoid fever. Scientific classification frequently includes details of the differences by the use of subdivisions or subclasses. However, the fact remains that the original classification was based on some one common characteristic. Therefore we are justified in asserting that simple classification treats a group of people or things that have certain qualities in common as if they possessed only those qualities. Scientists are entirely justified in doing this, if they do not forget what they have done.

3. *The whole may have qualities absent in the parts.* If we analyze an object, its elements or simple units are not more real than the object or event with which we began. Scientific method is concerned with breaking objects down into their constituent elements. Some people are inclined to believe that these simple units have a reality not possessed by the complex object. This may be called the **fallacy of reduction**, or reductionism. The explanations of science add something to our knowledge; they give us new facts or point out things that we would have overlooked otherwise, but they do not take anything away from the actual world. To explain is not to explain away. To explain the colors of the sunset as electromagnetic vibrations is not to explain away the sunset, but merely to analyze it, to add to our knowledge of the nature of light and colors.

If we analyze a living organism, we may not find life in the same sense in a particular part. Yet there is life in the total organism; the whole has a quality not found in parts.

Reductionism often leads to the *nothing but* syndrome. For example, "humans are nothing but a complex of biochemical mechanisms"; a possible implication is to equate human beings with rats, which are also a complex of biochemical mechanisms. Pondering, reflection, and decision making are not characteristics of biochemical mechanisms; the function of feelings is equally irrelevant.

When we analyze things into simple units, it is a mistake to believe that these units are more "real" than the whole of which they are parts, or of the same kind of reality as the whole. The real nature of things is found as much in wholes and in qualities as in parts or elements. The world that any science gives us may be a real world, but it is neither the whole world nor the only world. No one can interpret adequately any situation without considering it as a whole, as well as knowing its parts and the relations of those parts to one another.

4. *There may be many interpretations of a thing, a person, or an event, each of which is valid in certain contexts.* Each interpretation may be illuminating from one point of view. The farmer who sees the boys stealing his apples gets extremely excited. The psychologist describes the state of the man by saying that a stimulus has called forth an emotional response. The physiologist describes the reaction as accelerated heart action. The physicist may describe it by reference to the increased velocity of the molecules in the blood. A bystander may simply remark that the man is angry. Each is describing the event properly from her or his own viewpoint.

The uncritical attempt to explain or describe everything in one language or with reference to one principle or type of interpretation is one of the more frequent misuses of the scientific methods. It may be called the **fallacy of oversimplification**. It occurs whenever all things are thought to be exhaustively treated by inclusion in one single category. Examples of hasty oversimplification include the simplistic explanations of history or of human conduct. Some explain history solely on the basis of climatic changes, others solely on the basis of economic forces, and still others on the basis of biological factors. Human conduct has been explained entirely by genetic conditions, by psychological urges, and by environmental pressures. Although all these factors are important, we may well be suspicious of attempts to explain complex events with reference to a single set of concepts. There are multiple approaches to understanding our world.

5. *When we consider anything that is in a process of development, we find the later stages as real as the earlier stages, and the latter are probably more informative about the nature of the process.* A prevalent mistake is that of regarding what is earlier in development as more real than what follows. The genetic method, which traces things back to their beginnings, is useful if it does not cause us to neglect the more advanced stages. We cannot explain later stages adequately or fully by the earlier stages. If we could see the earth as it was many millions of years ago, we would be impressed by the fact that no life was present. Later we might see life but no human beings. Of the first view, we would say that only mechanical forces were present. It would be observed still later that living organisms were present. Eventually the process produced *Homo sapiens* with self-consciousness and a degree of intelligence.

Aristotle once asked how we should study an oak tree. Where should we start? Should we start with the acorn or the young sapling, with the tree in its maturity or in its period of decay? Clearly all the processes belong to the concept "oak tree," and a mere description of its parts or a cross section of it at any one period does not describe the unity of the organism. For Aristotle, reality was a process of development from potentiality to actuality. The later stages of an evolutionary process indicated most clearly the nature of the force or forces that have been present throughout the process.

6. *The sciences are dependent on our sense organs and our views of reality.* Scientific instruments are extensions of the human senses. We can increase the range of our senses with instruments such as the telescope, microscope, and computer, but we cannot provide new ones or change the nature of our organs.

When we observe, it is always with some "interest." We have a tendency to see what we are trained to see or expect to see. After we receive the image or the sensation, we have to move on to inference or generalization. This involves the logical operation of the human mind.

Observation and theories develop hand in hand. Different observations lead to different theories, and different theories lead us to make different observations. Science depends on the human sense organs and the processes of human reason. The "standpoint of the observer", the viewer's "frame of reference," is increasingly recognized in all fields. Because science is often said to be based on observation and experimentation, we emphasize again that scientific knowledge depends also on assumptions and postulates and that these in turn rest essentially on informed faith.

7. The sciences cannot prescribe values. The biological and physical sciences seek to describe and predict the empirical events within their spectrum; the behavioral and social sciences attempt to describe and predict many areas of human (and nonhuman) interaction. The biological and physical scientist might describe methods by which new life forms are created; the social scientist might describe trends and consequences of population growth. Neither scientist as *scientist* has a method by which she or he can provide what *ought* to be done; the value or moral issues are beyond the scientist's methods.

A scientist can, of course, *describe* objectively the values idealized and practiced by individuals and groups of people, but what *ought to be* is a prescription beyond scientific method. Furthermore, a scientist can point out that an object is "valuable" as a tool, but whether the object has intrinsic value is a nonscientific judgment. When scientists prescribe values, they are no longer restricting themselves to scientific methods; they are practicing philosophy.

Many sciences, perhaps all of them, employ objective, quantitative, and mechanical methods because of the greater accuracy of these methods. When they are used, however, the sciences are not telling the whole story. Scientific methods are among our most useful intellectual tools, but, like the others, they can be misused.

Philosophy and Science: Agreements and Contrasts

♦ ♦ ♦ ♦ ♦ ♦ ♦ ♦ ♦ ♦

During the last few centuries, philosophy has developed in close association with science. Many of the outstanding philosophers have made important contributions in the sciences. For example, Leibniz shared in the discovery of the differential calculus. The contributions of Alfred North Whitehead and Bertrand Russell to mathematical theory are well known to students of mathematics and advanced philosophy. Both philosophy and science use the methods of reflective thinking in their attempt to describe the facts of the world and of life. Both exhibit a critical, open-minded attitude and an impartial concern for the truth. They are interested in organized and systematized knowledge.

Science supplies philosophy with a large amount of factual and descriptive material. Indeed, the philosophy of any period is related to the scientific outlook of that period. Science exerts a check on philosophy by helping to eliminate such ideas as are incompatible with scientific knowledge, and philosophy critically examines the foundations of science.

Philosophy takes the piecemeal knowledge of the various sciences and organizes it into a more complete and integrated world view. In this connection the progress of the sciences makes philosophy necessary, because the discovery of new facts and relationships forces us to revise our notions and interpretations not only in the sciences but in most other fields. For instance, the acceptance of the concept of evolution forced us to revise our thinking in nearly all other areas. Further contributions of philosophy to science are the criticism by philosophy of the assumptions and postulates of the sciences and the critical analysis of many of the terms used.

The contrasts between philosophy and science generally represent tendencies or points of emphasis, not absolute distinctions. Whereas particular sciences deal with restricted or limited fields, philosophy attempts to deal with the whole of experience. Philosophy thus attempts to gain a more comprehensive view of experience in general. Whereas science is more descriptive in its approach, philosophy is more synthetic, dealing with the properties and qualities of nature and life as a whole. Science attempts to analyze the whole into its constituent elements; for example, the study of a virus considers its smaller divisions as well as its interrelationship with the entire auto-immune system. Whereas science tends to eliminate the personal factor and to ignore values in its drive for objectivity, philosophy assesses personality, values, and all realms of experience.

Although there are many areas in which the scientist gives us much knowledge, there are other areas into which scientists do not venture, such as religious commitment, devotion, and worship; the values, ends, and purposes and meanings of life; beauty in the arts and literature; a life view and a world view that integrate human knowledge and insights, in which the scientist, as scientist, has no method of investigation.

Scientific Views of the Universe

♦ ♦ ♦ ♦ ♦ ♦ ♦ ♦ ♦ ♦ ♦

The purpose of considering briefly some scientific views of the universe and life is twofold. First, these views are taken seriously by those philosophers who intend to incorporate scientific information into their philosophical positions. Second, readers unfamiliar with such information may gain a sense of awe about the cosmos as well as respect for the men and women engaged in scientific pursuits. How did the universe begin? Is the universe everlasting, without beginning and end, or will it someday cease to exist? Of what is the universe made? The study of these issues is **cosmology** (*cosmos* means "universe"). Questions about the origins, destiny, and basic structure of reality have occupied many thinkers since ancient times. Religions have offered conflicting answers; philosophers have contributed various explanations, and scientists propose differing interpretations of their findings.

What is "life"? How did life begin? To what extent is life present elsewhere in the universe? The study of the origin, nature, and extent of life has no widely used name; yet biologists, chemists, physicists and other scientists study these topics with whatever methods their instruments allow.

Scientific views of the universe and life contribute significantly to contemporary metaphysics. Once a matter of speculation and belief, the study of the nature of reality relies heavily on scientific inquiry. Let us consider some representative answers to questions about the origin, nature, and extent of life.

THE ORIGIN AND DESTINY OF THE UNIVERSE

The Steady State Theory. According to the steady state theory, the universe has always existed and will continue to exist indefinitely. Although the universe is expanding at a constant rate, its density remains constant because of the creation of matter out of nothing; newly created matter fills the expanding cosmos such that the density remains stable. This theory, also called *continuous creation,* is not widely accepted by contemporary scientists.

The Big Bang Theory. According to the modern big bang theory, developed in the 1930s and 1940s, the cosmos began with a gigantic explosion. As long ago as twenty billion years, the universe burst forth from a singular state of unimaginable density and high temperatures. In the course of that event—called the big bang—space and time were created and all the matter in the universe released; today's expanding cosmos is the result of that initial explosion.

According to the essential elements of the big bang theory (which has more than one interpretation), there are two possible destinies for the universe. The first theory asserts that the cosmos is constantly expanding, although at a progressively slower rate. Such an *open* universe eventually will cool off, the stars will burn out, and space will become a giant cemetery of dead stars and other matter, with neither heat nor light.

Equally bleak is the second theory, that of a *closed* universe: the cosmos at some distant time will contract and form a fireball that resembles its origin. An 80-billion-year periodic cycle of big bangs and contractions pulsates from explosion to explosion, from evolving universe to evolving universe. This theory is frequently called the *pulsating cosmos.*

One troublesome question can be put to the proponents of the big bang theory: Why does the universe appear so uniform? Another question revolves around what happened in the first instant following the gigantic explosion. The inflationary-universe understanding of the big bang theory rests on the idea that, shortly after creation, the new universe went through a brief and extremely rapid expansion, before and after which everything expanded at a relatively slow rate. For contemporary physicists and astronomers, this inflationary theory solves some of the complex scientific problems inherent in the big bang theory.

Unanswered Questions.

We have been considering a metaphysical issue, the origin and destiny of the universe; but is it not possible that several parallel universes bubble up rather than explode with one or more initial big bangs? Might such universes be connected in some way? In a scientific view assuming cause-and-effect relations, what caused the big bang? What caused the cause of the big bang? What caused the "state of unimaginable density" to exist in the first place? Why is there something rather than nothing? How fast is the universe expanding? How did the initially smooth universe become so clumpy with various galactic structures? How old is the universe? Are there dimensions to the universe besides three of space and one of time? These questions are among those facing cosmologists today.

THE NATURE OF THE UNIVERSE

The Expanse of the Cosmos.

The immensity of the universe is beyond our imaginations. Our planet is a small part of the solar system. As far as we know, the solar system consists of one star (the sun), nine planets, thirty-two moons, about 50 thousand asteroids, millions of meteorites, 100 billion comets, dust specks, and an assortment of gas molecules and atoms. Yet 99.86 percent of the solar system's substance is contained in the sun. Our planet represents only .0014 percent of the substance of the solar system.

Our sun, which has a diameter of 864,000 miles (the earth has a diameter of just under 8,000 miles), is one of 100 billion suns or stars in our galaxy, the Milky Way. This galaxy stretches for about 920 quadrillion miles. About 100 billion galaxies of different shapes dot the universe.

The earth is traveling 67,000 miles per hour in its annual journey around the sun. The Milky Way galaxy speeds along at 1.3 million miles per hour, propelled farther into an expanding cosmos. Every four seconds the universe adds to itself a volume equivalent in size to the Milky Way!

Nature of Matter.

Equally fascinating are the matter and energy studies that investigate the minute parts of our world. We might ask, why should a stone or a tree or a human hand be analyzed into anything different from a stone or a tree or a human hand? There are several reasons. First, particular things, such as stones, trees, human bodies, oceans, and land forms undergo alterations. Processes such as growth, decay, weathering, and erosion are always taking place. Second, physical objects undergo or are affected by inner transformations of various kinds. Under certain conditions they may pass back and forth between solid state, liquid state, and gaseous state. Third, although we can have contact or have experience with particular physical objects through our various sense organs, we cannot experience matter itself. **Matter** is the substance of which any physical object is composed.

During the sixth and fifth centuries B.C.E., certain people became curious about the nature of the world. They started a new line of thinking and investigation that, by various paths, led to our modern conceptions of matter. To trace this development in any detail would carry us too far afield and would embrace a considerable portion of the history of philosophy and science. However, early in the nineteenth century, when chemists and physicists were again turning their attention to the constitution of matter, John Dalton proposed, as Democritus had in the past, but on new knowledge, a possible explanation of certain chemical and physical actions and reactions.

Two methods of studying the nature of matter have been used side by side: that of chemical and physical analysis, with instruments and apparatus, and that of mathematical or logical speculation.

Careful and elaborate research has revolutionized our views of the material universe and ushered in the nuclear age. Many able investigators have offered both mathematical and empirical evidence in support of the view that the atom is an exceedingly complicated system—one might say it is "a little world in itself."

Quarks and Gluons. In the first half of the twentieth century, a picture of the atom as a miniature solar system developed. At the atom's center is the nucleus (like the sun), consisting of a cluster of relatively massive particles called protons and neutrons. Around the nucleus spin the electrons, one for each proton in the nucleus. As research progressed, other particles, known as elementary particles, were discovered. In 1964, quarks (considered the most basic constituent of matter) were proposed as the mathematical and possibly physical bases of the relationships among subatomic particles; experiment has also indirectly suggested their existence. Some physicists are still not sure whether quarks really exist; they might be merely inferred mathematical abstractions that help explain the behavior of the particles they supposedly constitute. (A few scientists posit a prequark structure.)

The significance of quarks was first implied by the Roman philosopher Lucretius, when he proposed that the succession of things inside other things had to end. Lucretius' argument, however, was for indivisible atoms as the "end." Some physicists believe that with the discovery of quarks, the end is at hand, that the fundamental structure of all matter has been established.

Theoretically, quarks are structureless; there is no division within them. They are at the base of all material structure. There are thought to be six types of quarks. In 1979, gluons were proposed as the embodiment of the force that holds quarks together. Although quarks and gluons are not directly observable, their existence is supported by the behavior of the particles they constitute. Gluons carry the strong nuclear force, which holds the nucleus of an atom together and is one of the four forces of nature. The other three forces are the weak nuclear force (responsible for radioactive decay), the electromagnetic force, and the gravitational force. Physicists are searching for one underlying force for all four, a unified theory of the four forces of nature, which would be as fundamental a statement of the universe's laws as scientists can currently conceive.

At the fundamental level of quarks, matter may be dematerialized; the extent to which quarks can be called material is under discussion. Also being studied is the extent to which order, predictability, chaos, and chance are characteristic of subatomic reality.

The principle of indeterminacy has been widely accepted among scientists and has influenced thinking in philosophy. Realities beyond appearances at both the macrocosmic and microcosmic levels have fascinated thinkers since ancient times through today. At either level, the issues of space, time, and relativity are considerations.

SPACE–TIME AND RELATIVITY

Space and Time. Views of space and time have changed as the horizons of human knowledge have been extended. The terms *space* and *time* each are used with two different meanings. *Perceptual* space is the space in which we live and move—for example, the distance between objects and the areas through which these objects move. Perceptual *time* is the time we experience day by day as we make and keep appointments. These experiences are parts of direct awareness or sense perception.

Conceptual space and time are the idealized space and time of mathematics. They are that to which philosophers refer when they ask whether space and time are limited or unlimited, subjective or objective. Apart from a few philosophers like Immanuel Kant, who argued that space and time were categories of the human mind or ways in which the mind perceives and organizes the world, most thinkers until recently have thought that space and time were real, separate entities, albeit entities of a special kind.

The traditional view not only described space and time as fixed and definite, but as experienced in essentially the same way by all normal people. Although motion takes place in space and time, the latter were not thought to be materially affected by the motion. Space was distinguished by the property of extension in all directions, and all the elements and units of space were of the same nature. Time was characterized by duration, and each instant or division of time was similar to every other bit of time. Until early in the twentieth century, the traditional views of space and time were not seriously questioned.

As a result of the investigations of a number of scientists in the late nineteenth century and the early decades of the twentieth, great changes were taking place in human thinking about space, time, motion, and the like. With the verification in 1919 of some of Einstein's predictions, the theory of relativity came to be almost universally accepted. Soon people were talking about space–time, the curvature of space, relative motion systems, and frames of reference.

Relativity. What is meant, in simple terms, by the notion of relativity? Consider some common human experiences. A man standing on the bridge of a wide river, looking over the railing at the water below, may get the impression that the river is standing still and that he and the bridge are moving. Many persons have had the peculiar experience of sitting in a plane at an airport and receiving the impression that the plane is moving, only to find in a moment or two that it was a nearby plane that was in motion. Again, a woman leaning over the rear of a moving boat may suddenly get the sensation that she is at rest and the water is moving. Until we can see some other "fixed" object, we cannot trust our perceptions.

The theory of relativity arose from the need for a frame of reference—a standard that scientists could use in analyzing the laws of motion. The need for such a standard is apparent when we ask ourselves "Motion with respect to what?" One central precept for relativity is that there is no "correct" place from which to view the universe; there is no "God's-eye" view of things; every observer sees the same laws of nature.

Albert Einstein (1879–1955) (see biography and excerpt, pp. 232–233), through his special and general theories of relativity, showed that absolute space and absolute time do not exist. The space–time continuum consists of four dimensions, including the three space dimensions and time on an equal footing. The presence of matter in space causes space to "curve," forming gravitational fields—a property of space itself.

In 1905 Einstein proposed a special theory of relativity (called special because it refers to a special kind of motion) based on two postulates: the *special relativity principle* and the *constancy of the speed of light.*

The *special relativity principle* is limited to the description of events as they appear to observers in a state of uniform, relative motion; it assumes that absolute speed cannot be measured, only speed relative to some other object; the motion of one object can be defined only with respect to that of a second object; no absolute meaning can be given to the statement that an object is at rest. All observers moving at constant velocities with respect to each other should find the same laws of nature operating within their frames of reference. For example, experiments done within a moving laboratory (a plane or train) are completely unaffected by the laboratory's motion, provided it continues to move in a straight line at a constant speed. In fact, no experiment carried out inside a closed laboratory can reveal the speed at which the lab is moving.

The second postulate of the special theory of relativity proposes that the *speed of light* appears to be the same to every observer; the speed of light is always the same no matter how fast the observer or light source is moving. For example, if an observer is approaching a light source at 100 miles per hour or 100,000 miles per hour, the speed of light will be 186,000 miles per second in either case. Implied in this postulate is that the maximum velocity that can be attained in every frame of reference in the universe is that of light; we can accurately describe relative motion by using the speed of light as a basis.

Among the consequences of accepting the two postulates of special relativity are length contraction, mass increase, and time dilation. As the speed of an object approaches the speed of light, its length—along the direction of motion—decreases, it becomes heavier, and time measured on its clock runs more slowly than time measured on the clock of a "still" observer; events occurring simultaneously according to one observer may happen at different times according to an observer moving past the first. Experiments carried out in particle accelerators have confirmed these postulates.

In 1915 Einstein extended his special theory to a general theory of relativity applicable to all observers not in uniform relative motion; this led to an elaborated concept of gravitation; it states that all observers, regardless of their state of motion, see the same laws of physics operating in the universe. This general theory attempts to show that the structure of space is determined by matter, thus eliminating "absolute space," and that the laws of physics are the same everywhere. This general theory treats gravity not as a force that acts directly across empty space between bodies (the Newtonian view) but as an apparent force that arises because the presence of matter in space causes space to curve, forming gravitational fields; thus, gravity becomes a property of space itself. Therefore, bodies and even rays of light follow curved paths near massive bodies, and clocks run slow where gravity is strong, and light becomes redshifted (stretched in wavelengths) when moving up through a gravitational field. These effects have also been confirmed by observation and experiment.

The implications of the special and general theories of relativity show that no frame of reference for observations of nature is more privileged than any other.

The Origin and Nature of Life

♦ ♦ ♦ ♦ ♦ ♦ ♦ ♦ ♦ ♦ ♦

As we look around ourselves, we are impressed by the amazing variety of living things on and in the earth, the waters, and the air. The microscope discloses a further world of life. Living forms seem to occupy almost every conceivable place in nature. How do organisms differ from the inorganic processes that we have been considering? Where did life come from, and what are some of its characteristics?

Since early times, people have observed that living things tend to reproduce their kind. Does all life come from one source or are all the different kinds of life separate and distinct in origin? There have been several theories.

1. *All matter is alive,* and there is no need to make any rigid distinction between organic and inorganic matter. This view, held by a number of early Greek thinkers, was known as *hylozoism.* The discovery of viruses, filter passers, and the like, and the knowledge that living and nonliving matter are composed of the same elements, tends to make the separation seem less rigid.

2. The notion of *spontaneous generation* appears in the writings of Lucretius in the first century B.C.E. This concept was held by many people until about 1860, when Louis Pasteur proved fairly conclusively that it was false. He compared sterilized and unsterilized liquids and demonstrated that microorganisms are carried in the dust-laden air.

3. The idea of *panspermia,* that life originated other than on earth and arrived here by space-traveling spores, and the view that chemical building blocks for life arrived from space, have been revived recently. Panspermia transfers the problem of life's origin elsewhere but does not answer the fundamental question of how life originated.

4. Based on a literal reading of biblical material, there is the belief in *direct creation* by a special act of God, which confines the entire creative process to six days of twenty-four hours each (Genesis, Chapter 1:1–2:4a, but not Genesis 2:4b*ff.*). There also have been attempts to mediate between biblical and modern scientific accounts by the use of explanations like the geological-day interpretation theory (that "day" means a geologic era). To many people, these views fail to do justice to the biblical or to the scientific accounts of creative processes.

5. *Present living forms, including humans, originated through a gradual process of develop-*

Albert Einstein

Albert Einstein (1879–1955) was a German-born Swiss–American theoretical physicist and mathematician. He studied at Zurich's Federal Institute of Technology and received his doctorate from the University of Zurich. From 1913 to 1933, he taught at the University of Berlin. Deprived of citizenship in 1933 when Hitler came to power, he came to the United States and accepted a position at the Institute of Advanced Studies, Princeton, where he spent the rest of his life.

The most important consequence of Einstein's theory of relativity for philosophical thought has been the change in concepts of time and space. He destroyed the assumption that there is an all-embracing time in which all events in the universe have their place. Einstein proved that there is no experiment capable of determining absolute motion. Because time and space are measured separately, there always remains a degree of subjectivity that not only affects human observers but all other things. Time and space are dependent on each other, forming a relationship that can be analyzed in many different ways. Time had previously been regarded as a fixed cosmic measure. Einstein introduced the idea of local time connected with the earth's motion.

His works include *Groundwork of the General Theory of Relativity* (1919), *The Meaning of Relativity* (1921), *On the Method of Theoretical Physics* (1933), and *Out of My Later Years* (1950).

---

ment. This does not rule out the idea of creation by God, if God is interpreted as the creative agency, although the idea of a special act of creation at one time or place would be rejected. Life seems always to arise from life. If, as the story is pressed back, the distinction between animals and plants and between living and nonliving forms tends to disappear, and if living matter was, at some time, created from the nonliving, it need not seriously affect our general outlook on life. The chief effect could be to increase our appreciation of what has been called "nonliving" matter. Philosophers and scientists today, with few exceptions, believe that the living forms on earth developed through some process of evolution.

Recently it has been suggested by some scientists that life may have evolved repeatedly during the Earth's first billion years, only to be obliterated by periodic, rare impacts by asteroids.

Human Beings and Evolution

Advances in the physical sciences, especially those connected with the new power from nuclear fission and fusion, have been spectacular. But perhaps they are no more important in the long run than advances in the life sciences, which have great implications for our understanding of humans. New knowledge in the life sciences

You will hardly find one among the profounder sort of scientific minds without a peculiar religious feeling of his own. But it is different from the religion of the naive man. For the latter, God is a being from whose care one hopes to benefit and whose punishment one fears; a sublimation of a feeling similar to that of a child for its father, a being to whom one stands to some extent in a personal relation, however deeply it may be tinged with awe.

But the scientist is possessed by the sense of universal causation. The future, to him, is every whit as necessary and determined as the past. There is nothing divine about morality; it is a purely human affair. His religious feeling takes the form of a rapturous amazement at the harmony of natural law, which reveals an intelligence of such superiority that, compared with it, all the systematic thinking and acting of human beings is an utterly insignificant reflection. This feeling is the guiding principle of his life and work, insofar as he succeeds in keeping himself from the shackles of selfish desire. It is beyond question closely akin to that which has possessed the religious geniuses of all ages.

Einstein, *The World As I See It,* trans. A. Harris (New York: Philosophical Library, 1949).

gives rise to philosophical problems of primary importance, as we shall see.

ORGANIC EVOLUTION

Evolution in the biological sense, or organic evolution, is a process of growth or development of all forms of life. It means that "the present is the child of the past and the parent of the future." The theory of organic evolution posits that the plants and animals we see about us today are the descendants of ancestors that were, on the whole, somewhat simpler. These ancestors were the offspring of still simpler ancestors, reaching back for millions of years to exceedingly low forms of life or to life's beginnings. The numerous species of animals and plants have developed by natural descent, with modification, from previously existing types. In general, the theory is that life proceeds from the simple to the more complex or from the lower to higher forms. The term *higher* here means increased structural complexity and range of functions or powers. *Evolution* is the name for this process of change; a theory of evolution is an interpretation of how the process occurs. Theories of evolution attempt to identify the major factors that have produced new species. Though the fact of evolution is well established by a large body of evidence (see Evidence for Organic Evolution below), there is much debate among scientists over the theory of evolution. (We must keep in mind that a *hypothesis* is a proposal or informed guess with research yet to be completed; a *theory* is a confirmed hypothesis, an explanation of evidence gathered by means of research.)

To understand this process of change, we will examine the term **Darwinism.** In the narrow sense, Darwinism refers to a theory of organic evolution presented by Charles Darwin (1809–1882) (see biography and excerpt, pp. 236–237) and by other scientists who developed various aspects of his views. We call this narrow sense *biological Darwinism*. In the broad sense, Darwinism refers to a collection of scientific, social, theological, and philosophical thought that was historically stimulated by Darwin's theory of evolution.

Natural Selection. The most important feature of Darwin's theory, and the most important single contribution ever made to the understanding of evolution, was the idea of *natural selection.*

Darwin, extending the ideas of the Reverend Robert Malthus to all species, noted that populations increase rapidly, and if unchecked will exceed the means of support—especially food resources—available for the species. As a result of this overpopulation, a struggle for survival ensues, to be resolved by natural selection. "It may metaphorically be said that natural selection is daily and hourly scrutinizing, throughout the world, the slightest variations; rejecting those that are bad, preserving and adding up all that are good; silently and insensibly working, whenever and wherever opportunity offers, at the improvement of each organic being in relation to its organic and inorganic conditions of life."[6]

In Darwin's original theory, natural selection played both a negative and a positive role. In a species whose members were unable to adapt to changed circumstances, natural selection would lead to extinction. Where a sufficient number of members of the population were able to adapt ("survival of the fittest"), natural selection would lead to species transformation. Dar-

win argued that those individuals which possessed chance variations favored by the new and unpredicted environment would be selected and survive. They would tend, by the laws of heredity, to pass these novel characteristics to their offspring. As the result of many such combinations of chance variations and selections for changed environments, a modified population would result. Biologists considering this process of "descent with modification" would classify the later population as a species distinct from the ancestor one. In this way, the process of natural selection would lead to the origin of a new species.

Although Darwin, in *Origin of Species,* placed the greatest weight on evolution by natural selection, he cited two additional factors that, in conjunction with natural selection, affect the evolution of populations: sexual selection and the inheritance of characteristics acquired during the lifetime of the individual organism.

Sexual Selection. The second mechanism of evolution was described by Darwin as the "struggle of males for females." This is a special case of a more general phenomenon: selection in favor of a characteristic that will increase the tendency to produce young will occur even though it may not be favored by natural selection. All such cases Darwin calls *sexual selection.* It is clear that different sorts of characteristics can influence the probability of having offspring. Darwin regards sexual selection as especially significant in the evolution of human beings. The loss of body hair, for example, is attributed to systematic choice by our ancestors of mates who exhibited large regions of bare skin.

Inheritance of Acquired Characteristics. Because Darwin predated the clear formulation of the concept of mutation, the modern theory of the origin of genetic variation was not available to him. Consequently, he suggested that some variations are due to the action of the environment on the germ plasm and that others are due to the effects of use and disuse. For example, if an animal's skin is tanned by sunlight, this might result in changes in its germ plasm that would result in its offspring possessing pretanned skin; or, if a wolf developed its muscles by chasing rabbits, its pups might inherit larger muscles. These mechanisms, if they exist, would account for some variability. But they would also account for some evolutionary change even in the absence of natural or sexual selection. Darwin stressed the inheritance of acquired characters as an aid in explaining both variability and evolutionary change. Although now defunct, this theory had a strong influence on further progress in the study of evolution and contributed significantly to present understanding of the subject.

Darwinism and Genetics. Darwin's theory of natural selection as the chief (but not the sole) factor of evolution was criticized even by his contemporaries. Some, such as the co-founder of the theory, Alfred Russel Wallace (1823–1913), believed that natural selection alone sufficed, whereas others, such as Darwin's collaborator on animal instincts, George John Romanes (1848–1894), added additional factors, believing natural selection to be inadequate for the production of new species. A major weakness in Darwin's work was his theory of heredity, as he was unaware of the contemporaneous work of Gregor Mendel (1822–1884), who in 1865 discovered the basic laws of genetics.

The new science of genetics was based on the idea of "characters" that arose as a unit and could be transmitted whole from one generation to the next, and it rapidly replaced the outmoded concept of partial transmission of characters upon which Darwin had largely based his theory of heredity.

The study of genetics, the modern science of heredity, has increased our understanding of both life and the theory of evolution. The bearing of genetics on the theory of evolution has to do with the phenomenon of *mutations,* the abrupt, random changes in heredity observed by geneticists; to explain evolution on this basis alone is *mutationism.* When we look more closely at the random elements in evolution, we discover that it is impossible for evolution to occur entirely at random; there is more to it than accident and chance.

In the period from the mid-1930s to the mid-1940s, Mendelian genetics was reconciled with Darwinian natural selection in what is now termed the "modern synthesis." This theory (sometimes called neo-Darwinism) combined the stepwise process of genetics with the cumulative process of selection, and is widely, though not universally, accepted among biologists today. Some biologists, such as Stephen Jay Gould, have proposed alternative theories of evolution. According to Gould's theory of "punctuated equilibrium," many species do not change over long periods of time—the "equilibrium" which produces a new species in a relatively short geological period of time (5,000 to 50,000 years). Other biologists argue that evolution is not an entirely random process—that evolutionary change does have an orientation or direction. Once a certain sort of structural change has started in a given group, it tends to continue until the group becomes extinct or gives rise to a new species. Although all biologists accept evolution as a foundation fact for their science, they disagree—as is normal in science—concerning theories to explain that process.

Evidence for Organic Evolution. For about two hundred years, the evidence for evolution has been accumulating. The main fields from which the evidence has come include:

1. *Comparative anatomy.* This is a study of the structural correspondence (bones, muscles, bodily organs, and the like) that exists among the great divisions of animals.

2. *Study of vestigial remains.* In some lower animal forms, these vestigial remains—organs and glands—continue, but they have lost their function or use in later or higher forms.

3. *Embryology.* Embryology consists of a study of organisms in the early stages of development from the fertilized ovum. The embryos of the different species of animals tend to be similar in the early stages.

Charles R. Darwin

Charles R. Darwin (1809–1882) was a British naturalist whose theory of organic evolution through natural selection led to great changes in the biological sciences, philosophy, and religious thought. Educated at Edinburgh and Cambridge Universities, he joined a British expedition aboard the H.M.S. *Beagle* for a five-year study (1831–1836) of the plants, animals, fossils, and geological formations at widely separated points on the globe, mainly the coast of South America and islands in the Pacific Ocean. His *Origin of Species* (1859) and *Descent of Man* (1871) gave factual evidence for the view that species are related in ascending order and that humans came from the same group of animals as did the chimpanzee and other apes. However, he never asserted that we descended *from* the apes. Darwin's writings led to heated debates that still continue today.

4. *Blood and fluid tests of animals.* These tests tend to confirm relationships among the various species.

5. *Examination of fossils.* Fossil forms or other remains of extinct forms of animals, and of early stages of animals that exist today, have been preserved in the earth's crust.

6. *Study of geographical distribution.* The location and distribution of the plants and animals in the various parts of the world seem to be explained only on the basis of evolution.

7. *Domestication and experimentation.* By various methods of selective breeding, it is possible to do in a short time what the slower processes of unmanipulated nature might do over a long period of time.

8. *Classification.* Animals are arranged in an ascending order of complexity from unicellular organisms to humans.

What is sometimes said to be the *strongest argument for evolution* is the fact that the evidence from these various fields of research dovetails, or fits into a single pattern, thus forming one united theoretical whole.

Excerpt from Darwin:

Voyage of the Beagle, Chapter 5
(1839)

A very singular little bird, Tinochorus rumicivorus, is here common: in its habits and general appearance, it nearly equally partakes of the characters, different as they are, of the quail and snipe. The Tinochorus is found in the whole of southern South America wherever there are sterile plains, or open dry pasture land. It frequents in pairs or small flocks the most desolate places, where scarcely another living creature can exist. Upon being approached they squat close, and then are very difficult to be distinguished from the ground. When feeding they walk rather slowly, with their legs wide apart. They dust themselves in roads and sandy places, and frequent particular spots, where they may be found day after day: like partridges, they take wing in a flock. In all these respects, in the muscular gizzard adapted for vegetable food, in the arched beak and fleshy nostrils, short legs and form of foot, the Tinochorus has a close affinity with quails. But as soon as the bird is seen flying, its whole appearance changes; the long pointed wings, so different from those in the gallinaceous order, the irregular manner of flight, and plaintive cry uttered at the moment of rising, recall the idea of a snipe. The sportsmen of the *Beagle* unanimously called it the short-billed snipe. To this genus, or rather to the family of the Waders, its skeleton shows that it is really related.

C. Darwin, *Journal of Researches into the Natural History and Geology of the Countries Visited during the Voyage of H.M.S. Beagle* (New York: Heritage Press, 1957).

MISINTERPRETATIONS OF EVOLUTION

To understand clearly what evolution is, we must rid ourselves of some prevalent misconceptions.

1. *We are not descendents of the apes.* First, the theory of evolution does not mean or imply that all living forms are tending toward *Homo sapiens* or that any present species is changing into any other species. It does not mean that we "came from" the monkey or are a "made-over monkey." We have had a long ancestry, extending back through earlier species. Although apes and humans likely have common ancestors, the ape is not our ancestor. The other mammals that exist today have also had a long ancestry. Most students of evolution illustrate the relationships among living creatures by a tree with many long branches. Once a branch has been separated from the trunk, or main branch, it does not return; it goes off in a new and separate direction. Existing species are represented by the tips of the branches only. Many of the branches probably have reached "dead ends," so to speak. A few others have died and disappeared in the past.

There is no possibility of any present species of animal giving rise to animals that are in a different evolutionary line. To locate connections and relationships, it is necessary to delve into the distant past.

2. *The theory of evolution is not synonymous with* Darwinism. Darwinism is one explanation of how one species may have arisen from another. A few years ago, when an outstanding scientist said that he did not accept Darwinism, he was quoted, incorrectly, as stating that he did not believe in evolution. One may reject Darwin's explanation of how one species arose from another, as many do, and still accept the theory of evolution.

3. *The theory of evolution is not an explanation of the origin of life.* It is the theoretical interpretation of a process, or a description of the mechanisms by which one species was derived from another. Such interpretations may be mechanistic, vitalistic, or teleological; they may be nontheistic or theistic. Just as a knowledge of the development of the individual does not imply any single attitude toward life, so an acceptance of the theory of evolution does not in itself force on us any single philosophy of life or any one interpretation of the universe.

4. *The theory of evolution is not necessarily a denial of religion and of belief in God.* If you do not find it difficult to believe in God when you know that the individual has come to adulthood as the result of a slow process of growth, why should the knowledge that humanity has been the result of a process of development cause so much concern?

Keep in mind that the theory of evolution does not explain the origin or the nature of life and the will to live. Philosophically, natural selection leaves much unexplained. Natural selection is not the creative factor in evolution; it is a mere act of sifting or eliminating forms of life that cannot cope with the environment. Natural selection guides or selects variations, but it does not create these variations. (See earlier discussion on p. 234.)

The terms *competition,* the *struggle for existence,* and the *survival of the fittest,* used in the discussion of evolution, also need to be criticized

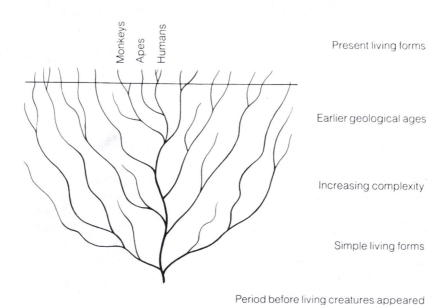

Simplified Genealogical Tree of Animals

and evaluated carefully. Both competition and cooperation are present in nature; competition and struggle by no means tell the whole story. The "survival of the fittest" may mean only that those who survive are able to survive in some particular environment, and this may depend on various chance factors. There are many degrees and types of adaptation as well as of fitness. In some environments, only low forms of life can survive.

Although the evidence for organic evolution appears to be conclusive, some people remain unconvinced. Historically, most of the opposition has come from a branch of religious conservatives, known as *fundamentalists,* who have defended a literal interpretation of the account of creation contained in Genesis. Early Roman Catholic opposition was modified in later pronouncements, especially by the *Papal Encyclical* of 1951. The mainstream of Protestants accepted evolution, whereas various fundamentalist groups took a stand against it in denominational conventions and state legislatures. The controversy came to its peak between 1920 and 1930, and especially during the Scopes trial in Dayton, Tennessee, in 1925.[7]

There has been a recent resurgence in this country of *creationism,* or *creation science.* It is important to distinguish this view from others that have preceded it, such as the nineteenth-century theory of *special creation,* which asserted that God in some way *directly* intervened in the order of nature to originate each new species. Darwin was extremely hostile to special creation in his *Origin of Species.* Contemporary creationists assert that they have an alternative scientific view to the theory of evolution based on the "biblical account of creation," by which they mean, of course, the account found in the first chapter of Genesis, in which all of creation lasts six days. They regard the description of the creation in Genesis as a genuine scientific alternative to the theory of evolution, and want it to be taught as such in the public schools of the United States. Recent court decisions in Arkansas and elsewhere, however, have rejected "creation science" as a disguised form of religious teaching,

and have concluded that as a consequence it cannot be given "equal time" with evolution in science courses.

One response to the creationists' assertion is that their views are neither biblical nor scientific. Biblical scholars in major universities point out that there are several other accounts of creation in the Bible; for example, both the Book of Job (Job 38:7) and Proverbs (Proverbs 8:22–31) contain descriptions of creation. To call one account the "literal" one, they believe, is arbitrary and whimsical. The conclusion of those who support evolutionary theory and biblical thought is that nothing in the long history presented in the Bible on the subject of creation precludes the findings of modern science.

SOME QUESTIONS ABOUT EVOLUTION

Millions of stars in the Milky Way may have habitable planets; this magnitude is a possible truth for other galaxies as well. Whether intelligent life or simple forms of life exist elsewhere in the cosmos is not known. If intelligent beings are discovered on some distant planet, the psychological effect on humanity would be substantial; a reassessment of the place and significance of human life in the universe would be on our philosophic agenda.

As scientists look for the origins of life by means of laboratory experiments and space probes, many questions remain unanswered. Although we may discover the origin of the constituent building blocks of life, that is not the same as discovering the origin of life itself. We wonder how these building blocks came together as a living entity, that is, how they were able to reproduce themselves. How was the transition made from chemical evolution to biological evolution and natural selection?

Currently, scientists believe that the earliest signs of life on our 4.5 billion-year-old earth occurred between 3.5 to 3.8 billion years ago. "Recent life," including that of mammals, is only 70 million years old; *Homo sapiens* emerged less than 250,000 years ago. But the reasons for the rates of evolutionary change of life; how the fertilized egg becomes the developed organism, and what kinds of information are built into the human nervous system are not completely known.

Reflections

♦ ♦ ♦ ♦ ♦ ♦ ♦ ♦ ♦ ♦

SCIENCE AS EXPLANATION AND TECHNOLOGY

Science is founded on informed faith in particular views of the universe. The precise expanse and nature of the universe as well as the origin of its natural laws are mysteries. It is possible that these mysteries will remain issues of faith or theoretical hypotheses, forever beyond direct observation and experimentation.

Contemporary scientists are far more modest in their claims of certainty than citizens anxious to invest all-knowing certitude in anything or anyone "scientific."

Schools of thought are found in the physical and social sciences, and surprising to many persons, in mathematics.[8] Not even Einstein's theory of general relativity is beyond revision; other interpretations offering more refined explanations may be developed. For any scientific explanation to be adequate, it must accommodate new data obtained by reliable scientific methods. More than one interpretation of data can be expected on most issues; high degrees of probability seem to be more attainable than certainty.

During the last century, applied science took us from the motor car to interplanetary probe, from the nucleus of the atom to the edge of the universe, from deciphering the genetic code to personal computers in homes. The interplay between basic and applied science has broadened the scope of both disciplines. In the area of technology, we have seen the ongoing development of sophisticated methods of communication, transportation, and entertainment. As a result of medical knowledge and technology, the average human life span has increased significantly, and the average American lives in better health and comfort than did any nineteenth-century monarch.

Critics of technology frequently blame both pure science and technology for the bomb, pollution, futile prolongation of life in terminally ill patients, exploitation of limited natural resources, and inaccurate bills generated by a computer. But technology is neither blameworthy nor praiseworthy; human beings and their decisions deserve the criticism. Human error causes computer error; humans invent lethal weapons. The bewildering array of options offered by science requires human competence and judgment to make well-informed and moral choices.

CONTEMPORARY PHILOSOPHY OF SCIENCE

In this chapter we have been introduced to the history of science, philosophy of science, and scientific views of the universe and life. Historians of science continue their research, as do pure and applied scientists. Philosophers of science continue to study the methods by which science is able to progress and make advances in human knowledge. The standard philosophical approach is that science—with its methods for hypothesizing, testing, and confirming hypotheses as theories, laws, and principles about our world—provides us with a steady progress in the accumulation of knowledge; this approach is being debated vigorously among philosophers of science. Dissatisfied with the standard view, some philosophers are studying the extent to which science and scientific knowledge are conditioned by the human community in which research is carried on. They are also challenging some of the basic assumptions that underlie scientific methods and scientific laws. Other issues under examination today include (a) whether scientific theories, when held to be true, give an exact analysis of a reality independent of those theories, or is it impossible to posit a reality independent of the human minds that are aware of it? (b) the relation of science and religion: are the two types of knowledge contradictory? complementary? independent from each other? (c) the role of mathematics in science: why are the laws of nature formulated in mathematical terms; is this necessary or merely convenient? and (d) the role of major scientists—from Aristotle to Newton to Einstein to current theorists—in particle physics, cell biology, evolutionary theory, and the neurosciences.

As such, philosophy of science is in a state of turmoil. It has become difficult for philosophers to be able to agree on the criteria by which scientific knowledge can be held as certain truth. Some philosophers still hold to the view that science is steadily progressive in the accumulation of knowledge, while others are of the opinion that there are discontinuities and "leaps" in the process brought about by changes in paradigms so that the question has been raised whether we can think of Newton and Einstein, for example, as referring to the same "world."

It is fair to say that the nature of science is no longer regarded as something clear-cut and settled, as was the case before the impact of studies in the history of science brought to light the way sciences actually develop. These studies revealed that the scientific enterprise is far more complex than previous philosophical theories would lead us to believe.

◆ ◆

Glossary Terms

COSMOLOGY   The study of the origin, nature, and development of the universe as an orderly system; theories formulated from such study.

DARWINISM   The Darwinian theory that the origin of species is derived by descent, with variation, from parent forms, through the natural selection of those best adapted in the struggle for existence.

FALLACY OF REDUCTION   The belief that an object's simpler units have a greater reality than the larger, complex object itself.

FALLACY OF OVERSIMPLIFICATION   The uncritical attempt to explain everything with one principle or type of interpretation.

HYPOTHESIS   A tentative proposal or possible explanation; often an early step in scientific method; an informed guess with research yet to be completed. (See theory.)

MATTER   The substance or substances of which any physical object consists or is composed.

OCCAM'S RAZOR   The principle that, other things being equal, one should always take the simpler explanation as the valid one.

PARADIGM   A model or an example that identifies certain scientific phenomena and guides the inquiries of scientists; the context, background of conditions, and the set of fundamental assumptions within which science takes place.

POSTULATES   A postulate is a fundamental assumption used as a basis for developing a system of proofs, but not subject itself to proof within the system. Though some logicians use *axioms* and *postulates* as synonymous, for others an axiom is a self-evident truth, whereas a postulate is a presupposition or premise of a train of reasoning and not necessarily self-evident. In this latter sense, all axioms are postulates, but not all postulates are axioms. A postulate is a basic statement "taken for granted" from which other statements may be deduced.

SCIENCE   (1) Used to denote any of the many sciences; (2) Knowledge of nature that is quantitative, objective, and testable; (3) The entire body of systematic knowledge built up through experimentation and having a valid theoretical base.

SCIENTIFIC METHOD   The processes and steps by which the sciences obtain knowledge.

TECHNOLOGY   A body of useful and practical knowledge which deals with applied science, engineering, industrial arts, and the like.

THEORY   The general conclusion after evidence is gathered and anlyzed; a confirmed hypothesis; an explanation of evidence gathered by means of research.

Chapter Review

THE DEVELOPMENT OF SCIENCE

1. The development of science is predominantly the work of Western civilization in its modern period.

2. Today the word *science* is used in a narrow sense to designate a quantitative, testable and objective knowledge of nature. Pure science is objective knowledge for its own sake, without consideration of any practical application. Applied science is scientific knowledge put to practical use as technology or applied within science itself.

3. Because of curiosity and technology, the scientific spirit was born in the Graeco-Roman period.

4. Medieval science included much inventiveness and provided the technical heritage for the period of the Scientific Revolution; Islamic Civilization was highly significant for European Civilization.

5. During the Scientific Revolution, new methods of discovering knowledge about the world and a new view of the universe replaced former interpretations.

6. During the nineteenth century, modern science advanced the atomic theory and concentrated on matter and energy. Scientific methods were applied to living organisms and Darwin's *Origin of Species* introduced the concept of evolution.

PHILOSOPHY OF SCIENCE: BASIC ISSUES

1. Philosophical examinations of science can be classified as "philosophy of science."

2. There are two major categories of philosophy of science.

SCIENTIFIC METHODS

1. The word *science* can be used to refer to any of the many sciences.

2. Scientific postulates are at the foundation of scientific inquiry.

3. The various scientific methods include observation, trial and error, experimentation, statistical analysis, and sampling.

THE NATURE AND ROLE OF MODELS AND PARADIGMS

1. Models are the pictorial, mechanical, or physical representations of things in the physical universe; paradigms are the world views or set of fundamental assumptions that identify certain scientific phenomena and within which scientific activities take place. Some philosophers view these concepts as fundamental in philosophy of science.

2. The fact that scientists of a given historical period, or individual scientists at any time, prefer one paradigm or model over others indicates that valuing is present in the selection process. Hence, science cannot be regarded as totally value free.

A METHOD OF ACQUIRING KNOWLEDGE

1. Recognize that a problem exists and state the problem.

2. Collect the available and relevant background information.

3. Formulate an hypothesis.

4. Draw deductions from the hypothesis.

5. Develop and implement an appropriate research plan.

6. Verify the hypothesis; verification is the final stage.

LIMITATIONS OF SCIENTIFIC METHODS

1. Results of scientific research are hampered by the techniques and instruments used. What we claim as factual is only as accurate as the instrument allows.

2. Classification of information is essential but no classification is all-inclusive.

3. The whole may have qualities absent in the parts. No simple unit is more real than the ob-

ject investigated. Scientific explanation is another form of interpretation; it does not give us the "pure truth."

4. There may be many interpretations of things or people illuminating equally significant points of view. Complex events need many approaches for total understanding.

5. When we consider anything in the process of development, we must consider the entire process. We cannot explain later stages adequately by earlier stages alone.

6. We tend to see what we expect to see; therefore, we are never completely "objective" in our observations.

7. Values or ethical issues are beyond scientific methods. When scientists choose to prescribe values, they have entered the realm of philosophy.

PHILOSOPHY AND SCIENCE: AGREEMENTS AND CONTRASTS

1. The contrasts between philosophy and science generally represent tendencies or points of emphasis, not absolute distinctions.

SCIENTIFIC VIEWS OF THE UNIVERSE

1. Interpretations of the origin and destiny of the universe include the steady state theory and the Big Bang theory.

2. Issues about the nature of the universe include the expanse of the cosmos and the nature of matter (including quarks and gluons).

3. Views of space, time, and relativity have undergone change in recent years.

THE ORIGIN AND NATURE OF LIFE

1. There are several theories describing the origin and nature of life.

HUMAN BEINGS AND EVOLUTION

1. Darwinism in its narrow sense refers to a theory of organic evolution presented by Charles Darwin and by other scientists who developed various aspects of his views.

2. The most important feature of Darwin's theory was the idea of natural selection.

3. The study of genetics has increased our understanding of both life and the theory of evolution.

4. There is much empirical evidence for organic evolution.

5. Misinterpretations of evolution include misconceptions about humans as descendants of the apes, Darwinism, the origin of life, and the role of evolutionary theory in religious thought.

6. The views of "creation science" can be argued to be neither Biblical nor scientific.

REFLECTIONS

1. Science is founded on informed faith in particular views of the universe.

2. Contemporary scientists are far more modest in their claims of certainty than citizens anxious to invest all-knowing certitude in anything or anyone "scientific."

3. Tentative explanations are called theories and are subject to continual study, testing, revision, and rejection.

4. Schools of thought are found in the physical and social sciences and in mathematics.

5. In the area of technology we have seen the ongoing development of sophisticated methods of communication, transportation, and entertainment.

6. Technology itself is neither blameworthy nor praiseworthy: human beings decide how technology will be employed.

7. Philosophy of science is in a state of turmoil; standard philosophical views of science are being debated vigorously.

8. It is fair to say that the nature of science is no longer regarded as something clear-cut and settled. Studies in the history of science have revealed that the scientific enterprise is far more complex than previous philosophical theories would lead us to believe.

9. As different thinkers endorse and defend different and changing philosophic conceptions of science, the controversy serves to cast light on science itself. Although there are no settled answers, there is ongoing inquiry. In this respect, philosophy of science resembles science itself.

Study Questions and Projects

1. Read the following quotations, discuss their implications, and indicate why you agree or disagree with them.
   (a) "All scientific descriptions of facts are highly selective . . . , they always depend upon theories. . . . Similarly, a scientific description will depend, largely, upon our point of view, our interests, which are as a rule connected with the theory or hypothesis we wish to test; although it will also depend upon the facts described."
   (b) Warren Weaver says, "Science is what scientists do . . . and scientists are human." Scientists, he points out, differ from people in general only in their "schooling in scientific method, their knowledge of the vast successes science has had, their proud partnership in the profession that has measured the star, split the atom, and probed the cell. This inheritance is, I am bound to tell you, magnificent but dangerous."[9]

2. Evaluate the following quotations:
   (a) "Even the most 'unprejudiced' science is imbedded in philosophy—sometimes in a philosophy that is not very sound or consistent."
   (b) "If science could tell with certainty all that it is capable of telling, it would still leave our most pressing questions unanswered."
   (c) "In Western culture science . . . is the discovery of useful facts. . . . This factualness of science makes it blind to the difference between the trivial and the significant, the odious and the exquisite, the good and the bad."
   (d) "If a scientific age is to be a good civilization, it is essential that increase in knowledge be accompanied by increase in wisdom or in a sense of human values."

3. What would be your reaction if life were successfully synthesized in a laboratory? Compare your reaction to evolutionary theory with that of an earlier generation.

4. Justify the statement that there are "a variety of scientific methods" rather than one method only. Give examples.

5. Discuss briefly the methods, problems, and possible disadvantages involved in observation, experimentation, and statistical procedure and sampling.

6. Read the cover story of *Time* for December 28, 1992, entitled "What Does Science Tell Us About God?" In what ways is the magazine report related to this chapter, "Science and Philosophy?" Note points of agreement and disagreement.

7. Comment on philosophical issues present in the twelve vital challenges facing science as reported in the December 1992 edition of *Scientific American*.

8. Evaluate the following statement, in terms of the issues presented in Chapter 11:

   "We believe that the world is knowable, that there are simple rules governing the behavior of matter and the evolution of the universe. We affirm that there are external, objective, extrahistorical, socially neutral, external and universal truths and that the assemblage of these truths is what we call physical science. Natural laws can be discovered that are universal, invariable, genderless and verifiable. They may be found by men or by women or by mixed collaborations of any obscene proportions. Any intelligent alien anywhere would have come upon the same logical system as we have to explain the structure of protons and the nature of supernovae. This statement I cannot prove, this statement I cannot justify. This is my faith." (S. Glashow, "We Believe That The World Is Knowable" in the *New York Times,* October 22, 1989, p. E24.)

9. Read a weekly science section from a Tuesday's *New York Times*. What philosophical issues exist in one or more of the reports?

10. Write an essay on "Science and Values."

11. Two articles on human evolution were published in *Nature: International Weekly Journal of Science* 368, (March 31, 1994). Read Waddle's "Matrix Correlation Tests Support a Single Origin for Modern Humans" (pp. 452–454) and Bowcock et al. "High Resolution of Human Evolutionary Trees with Polymorphic Microsatellites" (pp. 455–457). Incorporating your own comments on scientific method and the

theses of the two articles, write an essay entitled "Human Evolution: Hypothesis or Theory?"

12. Read Coppens's "East Side Story: The Origin of Humankind" in *Scientific American* 270 (May 1994): 88–95. Considering Chapter 2, "Human Nature: What Is It?" and Chapter 11, "Science and Philosophy," what philosophical issues remain unresolved in the Coppens article?

◆ ◆

Suggested Readings

Boyd, R. et al. (eds.). *The Philosophy of Science*. Cambridge, Mass.: MIT Press, 1991.

With more than forty readings, this anthology covers the most important developments in the past six decades; a thorough glossary and bibliography are included.

Brody, B. A., and Grandy, R. E. (eds.) *Readings in the Philosophy of Science*. 2nd ed. Englewood Cliffs, N.J.: Prentice Hall, 1989.

An anthology whose four parts cover theories, explanation and causality, confirmation of scientific hypotheses, and selected problems of particular sciences. The text concludes with a bibliographical essay.

Fetzer, J. H. *Philosophy of Science*. New York: Paragon, 1992.

The author provides a foundation for inquiry into the nature of science, the history of science, and the relationship between the two; he investigates the aims, methods, and explanations of empirical science.

Feyerabend, P. K. *Realism, Rationalism and Scientific Method,* Vols. I and II. Cambridge: Cambridge University Press, 1981.

By one of the most important contemporary philosophers of science, these volumes deal mainly with three ideas that the author believes have played an important role in the history of science, philosophy, and civilization: criticism, proliferation, and reality.

Hesse, M. B. *Models and Analogies in Science*. London and New York: Sheen and Ward, 1963.

A basic exploration of scientific models.

Kitcher, P. *The Advancement of Science: Science Without Legend, Objectivity Without Illusions*. New York: Oxford, 1993.

The author attempts to resurrect the notions of objectivity and progress in science by identifying both the limitations of idealized treatments of the growth of knowledge and overreactions to philosophical idealizations.

Kosso, P. *Reading the Book of Nature: An Introduction to the Philosophy of Science*. New York: Cambridge University Press, 1992.

Why should we believe what science tells us about the world? Observation data, confirmation of theories, and the explanation of phenomena are all considered at an introductory level.

Kourany, J. A., (ed.). *Scientific Knowledge: Basic Issues in the Philosophy of Science*. Belmont, Calif.: Wadsworth, 1987.

An introductory exploration of philosophy of science.

Laudan, L. *Science and Relativism*. Chicago: University of Chicago Press, 1990.

The author explores some key controversies in the philosophy of science.

Lindberg, D. C. *The Beginnings of Western Science*. Chicago: University of Chicago Press, 1992.

A full, unified account of the European scientific tradition in philosophical, religious, and institutional context from 600 B.C.E. to 1450 C.E.

Salmon, W. C. *Four Decades of Scientific Explanation*. Minneapolis, Minn.: University of Minnesota Press, 1990.

The author provides a definitive introduction to scientific explanation by recounting and analyzing the major developments during the past fifty years.

Notes

1. Lewis Thomas, "On Life In A Hell Of A Place," *Discover* (November 10, 1983): 42.

2. E. G. Conklin, *Man, Real and Ideal* (New York: Scribner's, 1943), p. 5.

3. See J. S. Mill, *A System of Logic* (London: John W. Parker, 1851), 3rd ed., Vol. I., Book 3, Chapter 8.

4. T. S. Kuhn, *The Structure of Scientific Revolutions,* 2nd ed. (Chicago: University of Chicago Press, 1970).

5. G. Holton, *Introduction to Concepts and Theories in Physical Science* (Cambridge, Mass.: Addison-Wesley, 1952), pp. 218*f*.

6. Darwin, *Origin of Species,* 6th ed. (London: J. Murray, 1872), p. 126.

7. See G. Ray, *Six Days or Forever? Tennessee vs. John Thomas Scopes* (Boston: Beacon, 1958); W. B. Gatewood, *Preachers, Pedagogues and Politicians: The Evolution Controversy in North Carolina, 1920–1927* (Chapel Hill: University of North Carolina Press, 1966). The play *Inherit the Wind,* by Jerome Lawrence and Robert E. Lee, is a popular treatment of the Scopes trial, although it does not list the dominant characters by name. More recent explorations of the issues may be found in M. Ruse, ed., *But Is It Science?: The Philosophical Question In The Creation/Evolution Controversy* (Buffalo, N.Y., Prometheus, 1988); L. B. Gilkey, *Creationism on Trial: Evolution and God at Little Rock* (San Francisco: Harper, 1985); and T. M. Berra, *Evolution and the Myth of Creationism: A Basic Guide to the Facts in the Evolution Debate* (Stanford, Calif.: Stanford University Press, 1990).

8. See "Mathematics, Philosophy of," in A. Flew, *A Dictionary of Philosophy* (New York: St. Martin's, 1979); the more advanced essay "Mathematics, Foundations of" in the *Encyclopedia of Philosophy* (New York: Macmillan, 1967); or M. Kline, *Mathematics: The Loss of Certainty* (New York: Oxford University Press, 1980).

9. "Science and the Citizen," *Bulletin of the Atomic Scientists* 13 (December 1957): 365; *Science* 126 (December 13, 1957): 1223.

PART FOUR

Philosophical Perspectives

Naturalism

CHAPTER OBJECTIVES

In this chapter we will address the following questions:

♦ What Is Naturalism?

♦ How Do Mechanistic and Dialectical Materialism Differ?

♦ What Is the Humanist World View?

I submit that it [naturalism] presents a philosophical outlook of the nature of the universe, and the place of the human species within it, and of the foundations of ethical value that still are viable today — especially when compared with alternative philosophical conceptions. In a sense, naturalism is the heir, and perhaps the climax, of what has been labeled, "The Golden Age of American Philosophy."

Naturalism Defined

Naturalism is a theory that accepts "nature" as the sum total of reality. The term *nature* has been used in philosophy with a wide variety of meanings, ranging from the physical world as observable by humans to the total system of spatio-temporal phenomena. It is the world disclosed to us by the natural sciences. The term *naturalism* stands in contrast to the term *supernaturalism,* which implies a dualistic world view with some form or idea, power or Being above or beyond nature.

Broadly conceived, naturalism uses the methods of science, evidence, and reason to understand nature, including humanity. This perspective may be defined as "the philosophical generalization of the methods and conclusions of the sciences."[2] Some of the basic tenets of naturalism are: (1) the universe (nature) is the only reality; (2) there is no supernatural or nonnatural realm beyond or within nature; (3) the universe may consist of many different types or levels of natural realities; (4) if human beings have the correct instruments and methods, all phenomena can be explained in terms of natural processes; and (5) human nature, values, and morality are best explained in terms of the inherent human position in nature.

MATERIALISM

Materialism is a narrow or more limited form of naturalism, which in general asserts that there is nothing in the world except matter, or that "nature" and the "physical world" are one and the same. The term *materialism* can be defined in various ways: as the theory that extended, self-existent atoms of matter in motion are the constituent elements of the universe, and that mind and consciousness—including all psychical processes—are mere modes of such matter and are reducible to the physical elements; and as the doctrine that the universe can be fully interpreted by the physical sciences. These two definitions have identical implications, and represent the more traditional forms of materialism. In recent times, the doctrine has been expressed as "energism," which reduces everything to some form of energy, or as a form of "positivism," which emphasizes the exact sciences and disclaims concern about such things as the "ultimate" nature of reality.

> Modern Materialism holds that the universe is an unlimited material entity; that the universe, including all matter and energy (motion or force), has always existed, and will always exist; that the world is a hard, tangible, material, objective reality that man can know. It holds that matter existed before mind; that the material world is primary and that thoughts about this world are secondary.[3]

Materialists, like members of other schools of philosophy, do not agree on all points or make all the claims found in the quotation above. In the contemporary world, materialism is likely to take one of two main forms: mechanism, or mechanistic materialism, with emphasis on the natural sciences, and dialectical materialism, the official philosophy of the former Soviet Union, the People's Republic of China, and other communist groups around the world.

Mechanistic Materialism

Is the world a mechanism to be interpreted solely according to the principles of the physical sciences? Can the structure, function, and behavior of living creatures be interpreted exclusively by physics, chemistry, and related sciences? We know that the same physical elements that are found in rocks and stars are found in organisms. Does this mean that the same mechanical laws operate universally?

Materialism, in the narrow sense, is the theory that all things can be explained in accordance with the laws that govern matter and motion. Materialism holds that all events and conditions are necessary consequences of previous events and conditions. The organic or "higher" forms in nature are merely more complex than the inorganic or lower forms; the higher forms contain no new materials or forces, and the principles of the physical sciences are sufficient to explain all that occurs and exists. All of nature's processes, whether inorganic or organic, are determined and would be predictable were all the facts about previous conditions available.

From the early Greeks we have inherited two quite different interpretations of the world. The line of thought most representative of the Greek outlook is that embodied in the works of Pythagoras, Plato, and Aristotle. According to this view, the regularity and orderliness of the world are due to the presence of mind or purpose. Other Greek philosophers believed that the universe could be interpreted merely as matter in motion. The quantitative atomism of Democritus (see biography and excerpt, pp. 252–253) was probably the first systematic presentation of mechanism. Democritus formulated a theory about the nature of things that bears a striking resemblance to some twentieth-century scientific views. Psychic activity is merely the motion of fine, highly mobile atoms. Epicurus and the Roman poet Lucretius popularized similar views for a short time before mechanism went into almost total eclipse during the medieval period.

From the fifteenth to the twentieth century, materialism gained considerable support in Western thought with the development of the mathematical sciences and of objective, experimental methods in the natural sciences. The world, some thought, consisted solely of physical quantities that could be measured mathematically. Descartes (1596–1650) applied mechanical concepts to the physical universe only—that is, unlike the materialists, he accepted the existence of nonphysical entities. Thomas Hobbes (1588–1679) went further and attempted to raise the science of his day to a philosophy by presenting a thoroughgoing mechanistic materialism. By the twentieth century, various physiologists, biologists, and psychologists were employing physical and mechanistic explanations in their interpretations of all living creatures, including humans. All movements, from those of the distant stars to the thoughts of humans (thoughts being regarded by these thinkers as movements), could be explained, it was asserted, by appealing to materialistic principles.

According to mechanistic materialism, mind and its activities are forms of behavior. Psychology is a study of behavior, and mind and consciousness are interpreted as muscular, neural, or glandular behavior. These processes may then be explained by physics and chemistry.

For the mechanistic materialist, all changes in the world, from those involving the atom to those involving people, are strictly determined. There is a complete and closed causal series. This causal series is explained by the principles of the natural sciences alone, and not with resort to such notions as "purpose." Mechanistic materialism is the doctrine that the world is governed by natural laws that can be stated in mathematical terms when the necessary data are available. It is the type of metaphysics that enlarges the concept "machine" and stresses the mechanical nature of all processes, organic as well as inorganic. The mechanistic materialist claims that all phenomena are subject to the same kinds of explanation that we use in the physical sciences—that is, the concepts of mechanism, determinism, and natural law have universal application. The only world that we know or can know is the one that reaches us through the physical sense organs.

The foundations of materialism were laid by the mathematical and physical sciences; these principles of explanation were later employed by the biological, psychological, and social sciences.

APPEAL OF MECHANISTIC MATERIALISM

Mechanistic materialism has considerable appeal because of its simplicity. In accepting this approach, we seem to get rid of many difficult problems that have perplexed us through the centuries. What is "real" in humans is their bodies, and the tests for truth or reality are touch, sight, sound—the tools of experimental verification.

Mechanistic materialism is attractive because most individuals are occupied for a large part of the time with physical things, and a philosophy that calls these things and only these things "real" appeals to some people. The problems of obtaining food, clothing, and shelter are constant. The materialist is impressed with the stability and permanence of these physical things and their necessity for life. It is easy to go on from here to believe that the material things are the only real things in life—the only genuine determinants—and that what are called "nonmaterial things" depend on these physical things. If people claim that there are "things" that are not physical, these claims are said to be the result of imagination or wishful thinking.

Mechanism as a theory and a method has produced great results in the natural sciences. Why, then, should mechanism not be the key to the explanation of all other things in life? Many people do not think that they have explained things adequately until they have interpreted them mechanistically. In this sense intelligibility, for many, appears to be synonymous with a mechanistic and a materialistic explanation.

Finally, mechanistic materialism, in its thoroughgoing forms, seems to relieve us of personal or moral responsibility. Moral standards and appeal to ideals have meaning only if we are to some degree free agents. For some, this lack of responsibility is comforting, because it causes problems of ethics and morality to drop out of the picture or to become purely subjective and relative.

IMPLICATIONS OF MECHANISTIC MATERIALISM

Some thinkers have argued that if the sciences are able to explain all things by simple mechanical causation, then there is little justification for believing in God or in a cosmic purpose. The same laws operate in humans as in the lower animals and the stars, and "consciousness" and "thinking" are the result of changes in the brain or the nervous system. The universe is governed by the physical laws of matter, even to the most refined and complex processes of the human mind. For the materialist, living is merely a physiological process with only a physiological meaning.

Mechanistic materialism interprets mind and consciousness as physiological behavior of a neural, hormonal, or muscular type. All human activity obeys physical laws. The action of stimulus and response in the nervous system is automatic and mechanistic. Consciousness must be discarded or interpreted as an **epiphenomenon** (a phenomenon accompanying some bodily processes, such as a glow or emanation from the brain), and thinking is "subvocal speech"—it is talking under one's breath or silent talking—or brain movements. We are conditioned to react to certain words as we would react to the objects for which they stand. When this happens we are said to know the meaning of the symbols or words. The law of cause and effect operates universally, and the human organism offers no exceptions.

A complete mechanism implies complete and universal determinism and rules out any real freedom of choice. One must merely accept the physical facts as they occur and as they are described by the natural sciences, except where we use material forces to alter the physical facts. These are the implications of a thoroughgoing mechanistic materialism.

CRITICAL COMMENTS ON MECHANISTIC MATERIALISM

Although mechanistic materialism has appealed to some people because it is a simple interpretation of the universe in line with science, attacks on the doctrine have been many and varied. Developments in the natural sciences have weakened, if not completely shattered, the foundations of the older mechanism and materialism. Studies in the history of science and its development have called attention to the limited view represented by the classical mechanism and materialism, which stemmed from Newtonian mechanics. Scientists are giving more attention to such varied concepts as organism, novelty, potentiality, possibility, becoming, and the point of view of the observer. These concepts, as we have seen earlier, seem to imply a greater degree of spontaneity and freedom than are present in both mechanism and materialism.

Democritus

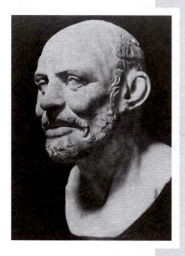

Democritus (c. 460–370 B.C.E.), an early Greek philosopher, was the first atomist, the first materialist, and a forerunner of mechanistic science. When asked what the universe was made of, or what was real, he said that it consisted of two parts—first, there were the atoms, infinitesimal bits of matter infinite in number, the same in quality, but differing greatly in size and shape. Second, there was the void or empty space in which the atoms move. The atoms, too small to be observed and indestructible, combined in many different ways to form people, animals, plants, rocks, and the like. Different things appeared when atoms came together in large numbers, collided and rebounded in different directions. These atoms and their motion in space explained all phenomena. Moreover, Democritus was a rationalist who said that reason knows things truly. Sense perception gives only relative knowledge.

Leucippus, a contemporary of Empedocles (490–430 B.C.E.), was the founder of the atomist school. It is now immensely difficult to disentangle the individual contributions Leucippus and Democritus each made to this atomist theory, inasmuch as their writings for the most part are lost. It is known that Democritus supplied much of the detailed elaboration of the atomist school. Democritus stated with clarity his abstract theory of atomism: that everything is made up of atoms moving in space.

Mechanistic materialism seems to be forced to do one of two things: either deny many things that are fundamental realities to large numbers of people or to endow "matter" with the power to become a self-conscious person interested in the promotion of truth, beauty, goodness, and love. The universe has produced people who are the discoverers of mechanisms and the builders of machines; this fact should not be overlooked. Nature has produced individuals with loves and hates, with hopes and aspirations, with consciousness and reason. They strive to attain ideals. They engage in creative activity, and they look into the past and the future.

In an age in which we are inventing even more complicated machines and elaborate computers, and in which articles are being written on "reading machines," "teaching machines," and "thinking machines," it is undoubtedly easy for some people to accept mechanistic materialism. After acknowledging "that the behavior of men can in principle be duplicated by machines," Paul Weiss says:

> What cannot be loved by one who can love, and what cannot love what can be loved, are less than human, no matter how much they look like and behave like men. Machines fail on both counts. They are not on a footing with men. They are, in short, not human, and thus cannot be said to have selves or minds, rights or responsibilities. The conclusion is not surprising, for we all know that a machine is an artifact whose parts are united so as to enable them to act together, whereas a man is a unity in which the

Excerpt from Aristotle:
Physics

Note: *As we have almost no remaining writings of Democritus, the following selections are taken from Aristotle's* Physics. *Clearly, Aristotle had access to the teachings of Democritis.*

Aristotle:
Physics. A. 5. 188 a 22.

Democritus asserts the solid and the void exist, of which the former is like Being and the latter like Non-being. Then again [there are differences] in position, shape and order. The following are their generic contraries: of position, up and down, backwards and forwards; of shape, angular, straight, and round.

Aristotle:
Physics. VIII. 252 a 32.

But in general, to think that, because something always is or always happens in a given fashion, we have sufficiently explained it, is not to understand the manner aright. By such a principle Democritus reduces the explanation of nature to the statement that, thus it happened formerly also, and there is no sense in looking for an explanation of what always happens.

Aristotle, *Physics,* ed. W. D. Ross (Oxford: Oxford University Press, 1936).

whole governs the behavior of the parts. Only such a unity has a self, with feelings, mind, will, and the rest.[4]

A considerable number of philosophers—humanists, idealists, pragmatists, and others yet to be considered—claim that mechanism does not tell the whole story. Most people acknowledge that there are systems in the world that are best interpreted mechanistically, and few question the value of using mechanistic interpretations in any field where they aid our understanding or control. But many do doubt the ability of mechanistic principles to supply a satisfactory basis for the explanation of *all* the facts of human existence. These critics claim that materialism is an example of the "reductive fallacy" that occurs when some complex situation or whole is de-

scribed as "nothing but" some simple element or part. For example, when the materialist asserts that mind is merely a form of matter, the critic claims that he or she is guilty of a crude reductionism. The reductionist reduces all phenomena to one type and thereby denies or at least blurs useful distinctions.

Dialectical Materialism

♦ ♦ ♦ ♦ ♦ ♦ ♦ ♦ ♦ ♦

Dialectical materialism grew out of the intense social struggle that arose as a result of the Industrial Revolution. It is connected with the names of Karl Marx (1818–1883) (see biography and excerpt, pp. 258–259) and Friedrich Engels (1820–1895) (see biography and excerpt, pp. 260–261). It was the official philosophy of the former Soviet Union and continues to be so for The People's Republic of China, and the doctrines of Marx and Engels have been interpreted and expanded by Lenin, Stalin, Mao Ze-dong, and others. We are dealing here, however, with dialectical materialism as a philosophical position and not with the views and practices of current governments.[5]

Dialectical materialism is not identical with mechanistic materialism, which we have just considered. Dialectical materialism, although it holds science in high esteem and claims that the sense perceptions of science provide our only real knowledge, is an approach from the point of view of politics and history rather than from that of the natural sciences. Emphasis is placed on a view of historical development in which matter in the form of the economic organization of society is regarded as basic. Thus, the terms *historical materialism* and *economic determinism* are both used.

BACKGROUND FOR THE DIALECTIC

To understand dialectical materialism, we need to go back to Georg Hegel (1770–1831) (see biography and excerpt, pp. 256–257). Hegel, an idealist whose writings influenced Marx, held that the universe is an unfolding process of thought out of which develop the processes of nature, human history, and the organizations and institutions of society. Matter, for Hegel, was less real than mind, because thought or mind is the essence of the universe. Marx rejected the idealism of Hegel. He inverted Hegel's philosophy and said that matter, not mind and ideas, is fundamental. Matter, especially as it is revealed in the economic organization of society and the modes of production, determines the social and political institutions of society. These in turn influence ethical, religious, and philosophical notions.

Although Marx and Engels rejected Hegel's idealism, they did accept his philosophical methodology almost completely. The world, according to Hegel, is in a continual process of development. All such processes of change are dialectical—that is, these changes proceed through an affirmation, or thesis, to some denial, or antithesis, to an integration, or synthesis.[6] All development, both of things and of ideas, is brought about through the overcoming of contradictions. For example, the idea of "being" leads logically to the idea of "nonbeing." Nonbeing and being, when united, logically entail the concept "becoming." In society, to give another illustration, a trend in the direction of extreme individualism tends to generate a countermovement toward its opposite, collectivism. Out of these extremes may come a society that recognizes the value of both individual freedom and collective action.

Marx and Engels accepted the dialectic. They said that although the early Greeks discovered it, Hegel was the first to explain it fully. His mistake, according to Marx and Engels, was to give it a mystic form; when stripped of its idealistic form and turned around, the proposition that historical development is dialectical is a profound truth. The dialectical process, Marx and Engels contended, is a pattern that exists in nature. It is an empirical fact, knowledge of which is derived from a study of the order of nature and supported by further knowledge of the causal interconnections brought to light by historians and scientists. Marx and Engels did not think of the dialectical process as mechanistic or completely determined. They emphasized a plurality of factors and causal interaction, in which the production of the goods necessary for life is the predominant factor. Change and development take place continually. When a synthesis has been reached, it tends in time to generate its own contradictions (or antithesis), and so the process proceeds. There is a continuous emergence of new qualities that grow out of the interpenetration and unity of opposites.

HISTORICAL MATERIALISM

Dialectical materialism, like mechanistic materialism, rejects the primacy of mind and all dualisms (such as the view that mind and body, humans and nature, are different substances) as well as all forms of supernaturalism. Material forces are the societal determinants and determine evolutionary development, as well as all other phenomena—inorganic, organic, and human. Dialectical materialism is a physical realism that is sometimes spoken of as "historical materialism" or "economic determinism." In dialectical materialism, the decisive factor in historical change and human society is the production and reproduction of life. The first need is to live and therefore to attend to life's necessities. Thus, the mode of production at any particular stage in history is of prime importance.

Marx and Engels had read widely in the fields of the physical, biological, and social sciences. The sciences, these philosophers claimed, disclose a world in constant change. Stability and rigidity can no longer be accepted as descriptive terms or desirable goals; the physical universe has a history and exhibits changes through time, just as do the organic world and human society. Darwin's theory of natural selection eliminates the need for teleological concepts in the natural sciences. There was a time when no humans existed, and there was an earlier time when there was no life. Quite clearly, Marx and Engels assert, everything has had a natural development with origins in the inorganic, or matter.

Although Marx vigorously opposed idealism as the exclusive interpretation of reality, he did not question the existence of conscious mind. He was not a "moral materialist," who stressed eating, drinking, and the acquisition of things. He wanted to free people from "wage slavery" and he thought that to do this changes in the material base of society were necessary.

According to dialectical materialism, people can influence their own lives and history to some degree. Life has its origins in the inorganic, and humans are part of nature; therefore, humans and animals differ in degree rather than in kind. Humans are able to make other parts of nature serve their ends. They alone can alter the conditions of their lives and, in a sense, help make their own history. The springs of action, however, reside neither in ideas, nor in an individual's desires, nor in her or his brains, but primarily in the processes of production and the class relations of society.

A PHILOSOPHY OF SOCIAL CHANGE

In dialectical materialism, action is primary and thought is secondary. There is no such thing as knowledge that is mere contemplation of the world of nature; knowledge is inseparably bound up with action. In the past, Marx tells us, philosophers explained the world in many different ways. The present task is to change the world, and that is the task and historic mission of the communists. In this task, the communists do not necessarily hesitate to take direct action and use violence to obtain their objectives.

Society, like all things, always is in process of change. It cannot be static, because matter itself is dynamic. Change, or the process of development, however, is not a simple, straight, or linear growth process. Small, indiscernible changes take place, apparently not altering the nature of what is changing, until finally there comes a point beyond which a thing cannot change without becoming different. Then there is an abrupt change—for example, if water is heated slowly, it gets hotter and hotter until suddenly, at a specific point, it turns to steam—and a change of state occurs. There is "a development which passes from insignificant and imperceptible quantitative changes to open, fundamental changes, to qualitative changes; a development in which the qualitative changes occur not gradually, but rapidly and abruptly, taking the form of a leap from one state to another."[7] Similarly, in the economic relations of a society and in the conflict of interests among the classes, revolutionary situations arise. Interpreted in this way, dialectical materialism provides a basis for the "class struggle" and for revolutionary action.

In 1848, Karl Marx and Friedrich Engels published *The Communist Manifesto,* a document that inspired many revolutionary movements. Later, Marx published his great work *Das Kapital,* the first volume of which appeared in 1867. Marx constructed an economic interpre-

Georg Wilhelm
Friedrich Hegel

G. W. F. Hegel (1770–1831) was a German idealistic philosopher whose adult life was spent almost entirely in academic circles. After attending a theological seminary, he was a private tutor for some years, then taught successively at the universities at Jena, Heidelberg, and Berlin. At the latter post, where he remained until his death, he exercised a wide influence. Quite apart from his view of history and type of idealism, Hegel became famous for his dialectical method of thinking or logic, which was adapted by Karl Marx even though Marx rejected his metaphysics. Hegel's writings during his lifetime include *The Phenomenology of Mind* (1807), *The Science of Logic* (1812), *The Encyclopedia of the Philosophical Sciences* (1817), and *The Philosophy of Right* (1821). After his death from cholera, his students used his lecture notes to publish four books: lectures on the history of philosophy, on the philosophy of history, on the philosophy of religion, and on the philosophy of art.

tation of history that has had its most widespread influence during the last one hundred years. For Marx, economic factors are central determinants in human historical development. History is interpreted as a record of class conflict in which the means of production, distribution, and exchange exert a determining influence on the social process. Changes in the economic structure of society cause changes in class relations, and these influence the political, social, moral, and religious customs and traditions.

Five types of productive systems can be distinguished. Four of them have appeared in succession in human society; the fifth is forecast for the immediate future or is now taking form. The first is the system of primitive communism. It is the first economic stage and is characterized by the communal ownership of property, by peace-

ful relations, and by lack of technology. The second stage is the ancient or slave system of production. It is marked by the rise of private property, which comes into existence when agriculture and cattle raising tend to displace hunting as a means of livelihood. Soon aristocratic, upper-class groups enslave other people. Conflict of interest appears as the minority groups gain control of the means of support. The third stage is characterized by military feudal groups in control of a large number of serfs. The feudal nobles appropriate the surplus products from the serfs, who eke out a bare living.

The bourgeois, or capitalist, system of production comes in with the increase of commerce and inventions and the division of labor; this is the fourth stage. The factory system creates the industrial capitalist, who owns and con-

Was there any historical evidence for this?

Dogmatism as a way of thinking, whether in ordinary knowledge or in the study of philosophy, is nothing else but the view that truth consists in a proposition, which is a fixed and final result, or again which is directly known. To questions like, "When was Caesar born?", How many feet made a furlong?" etc., a straight answer ought to be given; just as it is absolutely true that the square of the hypotenuse is equal to the sum of the squares of the other two sides of a right-angled triangle. But the nature of a so-called truth of that sort is different from the nature of philosophical truth. . . .

As regards philosophy in its proper and genuine sense, we find put forward without any hesitation, as an entirely sufficient equivalent for the long course of mental discipline—for that profound and fruitful process through which the human spirit attains to knowledge—the direct revelation of the divine and the healthy common sense of mankind, untroubled and undisciplined by any other knowledge or by proper philosophical reflection. These are held to be a good substitute for real philosophy, much in the way as chicory is lauded as a substitute for coffee.

G. W. F. Hegel, *The Phenomenology of Mind,* trans. J. B. Baillie (London, Allen and Unwin, 1910). [2d ed. 1931]

trols the instruments of production. The workers have only their labor power, and they are forced to offer themselves for hire. Just as the hand mill creates a society with a feudal structure, the steam engine creates a society with the capitalist employer.

The history of society since the breakup of the primitive communal society is a history of class struggle. During the last one hundred and fifty years industrial capitalism, with its doctrine of self-interest, has split society into two opposed groups; the bourgeois, or owning, group and the proletarian, or wage-earning, workers. Because the owning class controls the key institutions of society and will permit no thoroughgoing changes by peaceful means, the way out is "the forcible overthrow of all existing social conditions."

After the revolution, according to dialectical materialism and communist philosophy, there are two stages of society. There is, first, a transitional stage, the period of the dictatorship of the proletariat. During this interval, revolutionary social changes are made and classes are abolished through the elimination of private ownership of the means of production, distribution, and exchange. The second stage after the revolution is the fifth and final type of productive system. It is the "classless society," or pure communism. In this era, conflicts and exploitation will have ended, and all men and women will be assured of the means to achieve a good life. The state will cease to be a class instrument, and the dialectic will cease to operate in a classless society. There is supposed to be freedom, equality, peace, and abundance. Society will realize the formula:

Karl Marx

Karl Marx (1818–1883) is highly respected, even revered, in communist circles as one of the greatest thinkers of all time; his theories are regarded as dangerously revolutionary by many leaders in capitalist countries. Marx was born in Germany, studied law at the University in Bonn, philosophy and history in Berlin, and received a Ph.D. from the University of Jena, where his thesis was on the philosophers Epicurus and Democritus. After his short career in journalism, the paper he was editing (the *Rheinische Zeitung*) was suppressed and he was expelled. He went first to Paris, later to Brussels, and finally to London, where he found freedom to write and express his views. While in Paris he met and became a friend of Friedrich Engels, a British industrialist, who collaborated with Marx in writing the *Communist Manifesto* (1848) and who supported Marx financially and intellectually during Marx's later life. Marx spent most of his life (1849–1883) as an exile in London working in the library of the British Museum on *Das Kapital* (Vol. I, 1867; Vols. II–III, 1885–1894), his major writing, in which he discusses the strengths and weaknesses of the free enterprise system, its place in history, and its coming overthrow. Marx's writings have been printed in most countries and have influenced mass movements, including democratic forms of socialism and revolutionary communism.

from each according to his ability, to each according to his need.

CRITICAL COMMENTS
ON DIALECTICAL MATERIALISM

Insofar as dialectical materialism is a form of materialism, it is subject to the same criticisms. Let us here consider those points in dialectical materialism that are distinctive and open to criticism.

Although economic factors are exceedingly important, an economic or materialistic interpretation of life and society is one-sided. The course of history may not be so fixed and inevitable as the Marxists seem to believe. Marx apparently assumed that the blind forces of economic change are the determining factors in human history.

But the productive forces in society are as much a result of human intelligence as the thoughts of people are a result of the productive forces. Dialectical materialism fails to explain why people living under similar systems of production have developed quite different types of cultures, and why people who share the same economic and cultural conditions often embrace quite different systems of thought. The social and ethical attitudes of people are perhaps more important than Marx was willing to acknowledge.

The Marxian interpretation of the dialectic is open to serious question. Other historians have discovered no dialectical "necessity" in history. In addition, this concept offers no objective standard by which to judge events. Any historical event can be asserted to be the thesis, an-

Excerpt from Marx:

Das Kapital, "The Production of Absolute Surplus-Value" (1867)

Labour is, in the first place, a process in which both man and Nature participate, and in which man of his own accord starts, regulates, and controls the material reactions between himself and Nature. He opposes himself to Nature as one of her own forces, setting in motion arms and legs, head and hands, the natural forces of his body, in order to appropriate Nature's productions in a form adapted to his own wants. By thus acting on the external world and changing it, he at the same time changes his own nature. He develops his slumbering powers and compels them to act in obedience to his sway. . . . Besides the exertion of the bodily organs, the process demands that, during the whole operation, the workman's will be steadily in consonance with his purpose. This means close attention. The less he is attracted by the nature of the work, and the mode in which it is carried on, and the less, therefore, he enjoys it as something which gives play to his bodily and mental powers, the more close his attention is forced to be.

K. Marx, *Capital,* ed. F. Engels (New York: The Modern Library, 1906).

tithesis, or the synthesis in a process of change, depending on one's point of view. The theory of the dialectic assumes however, that each new stage in the process is "higher" than preceding stages; however, there seem to be processes of disintegration and decline to be reckoned with in history—there appears to be no one-way process operating throughout the course of human history. In other words, one may, with Marx, choose to describe history solely with reference to a dialectical process of thesis, antithesis, and synthesis, but such a description ignores important distinctions and reduces all historical events to those of a single kind. Such *reductionism* may be considered to be at best unenlightening and at worst misleading.

Undoubtedly, many people oppose the use of dialectical materialism as a philosophical justification for direct action, violence, and revolution. This philosophy places too great an emphasis on force, in the expectation that a revolution or some drastic change in the structure of society will solve most of humanity's problems. If a program is really good for the majority, leaders ought to be, and generally have been, able to persuade the people of that fact.

Humanistic Naturalism

♦ ♦ ♦ ♦ ♦ ♦ ♦ ♦ ♦ ♦

Humanistic naturalism is a philosophy that emphasizes humans or human interests and affairs. It has been defined as follows:

Friedrich Engels

Friedrich Engels (1820–1895) is best known as collaborator, friend, and financial backer of Karl Marx. Engels was the son of a wealthy German industrialist who adhered to Protestantism and political conservatism. As a youth, Engels planned to become a poet; he admired German romanticism, the historical past, and nature in art. A brief visit to London and service in the Prussian army altered his beliefs. He abandoned German nationalism and all plans of succeeding his father. Instead, after meeting Marx in the mid-1840s, he devoted his life to fight for the rights of the working class and to the realization of Marx's plans.

Most of Engels' work was done in collaboration with Marx, but some of his contributions are clearly identifiable, including the notion of dialectical materialism. The thesis–antithesis–synthesis pattern was presumed by Engels to work at all levels of reality. In nature, this process generates new qualities; in history, the pattern works toward the elimination of classes and the establishment of a harmonious, classless society.

In his later years, Engels blended dialectical materialism with philosophical materialism. Also, he tried to expand the meaning of Marx's terminology. His writings include *Socialism, Utopian and Scientific* (1883), *The Origin of the Family, Private Property and the State* (1884), and *Principles of Communism* (1925).

Humanism is a way of life which relies on human capacities and natural and social resources. Humanists see man as a product of this world—of evolution and human history—and acknowledge no cosmic mind or supernatural purpose or force. Humanism expresses an attitude or conviction which requires the acceptance of responsibility for human life in this world, emphasizing mutual respect and recognizing human interdependence.[8]

Humanistic naturalism, sometimes referred to as *secular humanism,* is distinguished from three other philosophical positions: mechanistic materialism, Renaissance humanism, and religious humanism. It should not be confused with mechanistic materialism, which is based on a rigid determinism and tends to make everything subservient to the laws of the physical sciences. In contrast, humanistic naturalism emphasizes the social studies and seeks to do justice to the organic and to human interests and aspirations. It acknowledges that which is unique in people, and its defenders claim that it is as sensitive as is idealism to human interests and welfare.

Humanistic naturalism is clearly distinguished from the humanism of the Renaissance, although it has been called "Renaissance humanism modernized and brought up to date." The humanists of the Renaissance admired the Greeks—especially their reasonable and balanced lives—and they studied the classics. The Renaissance movement was to a great extent a literary one, which developed a new confidence in humans and human reason. People turned to

Excerpt from Engels

Speech at the Graveside of Karl Marx (Delivered at Highgate Cemetery, London, March 17, 1883)

On the 14th of March, at a quarter to three in the afternoon, the greatest living thinker ceased to think. He had been left alone for scarcely two minutes, and when we came back we found him in an armchair, peacefully gone to sleep—but forever.

An immeasurable loss has been sustained both by the militant proletariat of Europe and America, and by the historical science, in the death of this man. The gap that has been left by the death of this mighty spirit will soon enough make itself felt.

Just as Darwin discovered the law of evolution in organic nature, so Marx discovered the law of evolution in human history; he discovered the simple fact, hitherto concealed by an overgrowth of ideology, that mankind must first of all eat and drink, have shelter and clothing, before it can pursue politics, science, religion, art, etc.; and that therefore the production of the immediate material means of subsistence and consequently the degree of economic development attained by a given people or during a given epoch, form the foundation upon which the state institutions, the legal conceptions, the art and even the religious ideas of the people concerned have been evolved, and in the light of which these things must therefore be explained, instead of *vice versa*.

K. Marx, *Selected Works,* Vol. I., trans. A. Adoralsky (New York: International Publishers, 1933).

---

classical, as opposed to ecclesiastical, studies. A modern movement, known as *literary humanism,* advocates a classical type of liberal education. This movement, resembling Renaissance humanism, should not be confused with humanistic naturalism.

Humanistic naturalism is different from religious humanism. Indeed, the term **humanism** has been used in many senses: there are scientific, religious, atheistic, and ethical humanists. All declare that they are *for humans,* that they wish to "actualize human potentialities, enhance human experience and contribute to happiness, social justice, democracy, and a peaceful world. All say that they are opposed to authoritarian or totalitarian forces that dehumanize man. All profess compassion for human suffering and commit-

ment to the unity of mankind."[9] More specifically, as John Herman Randall, Jr. writes: "Humanism is a certain religious temper, a certain set of values."[10] In fact, humanist religion is primarily an effort to free religious faith and devotion from the dogma of theistic theologies. As a result of their alienation from religious institutions, the humanists' conceptions of religious experience are usually individualistic and humanists hesitate to establish a religious organization. According to Herbert W. Schneider, humanist interpretations of religion have become increasingly radical with the growth of a genuine science of religion, on which humanists depend. Such thinkers attempt to rid religious institutions, myths, creeds, prayers, and sacraments of superstitious beliefs. Assuming that a religion is neither true nor false as a whole, humanists attempt to make a critical evaluation of religion. As Schneider writes: "Like other arts and philosophies, it runs the danger of becoming narrow, dogmatic or fashionable; and therefore religious humanists should be religiously alert to criticize each other as well as religion."[11]

METHOD OF HUMANISTIC NATURALISM

The humanistic naturalists have profound respect for modern science: they accept its assumptions, postulates, and discoveries. They are especially interested in biology, psychology, medicine, and the social studies because the attention of these disciplines is centered on people and human welfare. Science is viewed not as a transcript of reality but as a human construct to secure control over the world. Humanistic naturalists recognize that the "laws" of nature are formulated as such by people. Humanistic naturalism is a philosophy based on the empirical scientific method, and its proponents are interested in hypotheses and experimentation for the purpose of control.

Humanistic naturalists stress the principle of continuity. There are no sharp distinctions among intellectual, biological, and physical processes. There is, the humanistic naturalists assert, in accord with evolutionary theory, continuity from the less complex to the more complex. Intellectual processes "grow out of" organic or biological processes, and organic processes arise from physical processes without being identical with them. This is a methodological postulate—a directive for investigation—and in no sense an attempt to "reduce" one to the other.

The humanists contend that the richness of human experience and the great variety of natural phenomena can be neither "explained away" nor "reduced" to something else. This opposition to reductionism distinguishes this form of naturalism from the older materialism. The world is what it is or appears to be; the new naturalism accepts the reality of physical and intellectual processes, and accepts the existence of these processes as empirical facts.

THE HUMANIST WORLD VIEW

Humanistic naturalists regard the universe as self-existing, not created. They have abandoned all concepts of a supernatural Being and all forms of cosmic support. Life is dependent on a physiochemical order, and it is likely that "life is a local and episodic phenomenon in the cosmos at large."[12] The quest for an understanding of the "ultimate" origin, nature, and goal of the universe as a whole is thought to be futile. Thus, humanists support an "unreservedly naturalistic" view of the universe and of life. "For present-day naturalists 'Nature' serves rather as the all-inclusive category, corresponding to the role played by 'Being' in Greek thought, or by 'Reality' for the idealists."[13]

The categories of "matter" and "motion" have been replaced by the categories of "events," "qualities," and "relations." To experience change or process is to be aware of differences of the kind called "qualitative." The naturalists insist that they are not committed to any one interpretation of the nature of anything; they subscribe to neither the theory of levels nor the principle of reduction. Observation merely indicates that some objects and events differ sharply from one another and some differ less sharply. An explanation is acceptable to the extent to which it is supported by evidence. Scientific method is not limited to any field; it may deal with the processes of history, with values, with the fine arts, and with human purposes and goals.

Some humanists retain the word *religion* and redefine it; other humanists prefer to drop the term and substitute "the humanist way of life." In either case, the orthodox or traditional concepts of religion are abandoned. The humanist's religion is a social product; it is loyalty to the values of life and the cooperative human quest for a better life. The religious or the spiritual is not something alien to people or imposed from without; it is a quality of human life that is grounded in human activity. Our spiritual side fights for the values of life, cooperates for human welfare, projects ideals and struggles to attain them, and makes room for sympathy and love. "Any activity," says John Dewey, "that is pursued in behalf of an ideal and against obstacles and in spite of threats of personal loss because of conviction of its general and enduring value is religious in quality."[14] The essence of religion is seen as the integration of the human personality around loyalty to some high ideal. The humanist's religion is a religion without God, but the humanists claim that it meets the needs that religion has always met in that it unites individuals in devotion to human interests and values. The humanists hope to integrate scientific, social, and religious thought into one unified philosophy that aspires to the best possible life.

CRITICAL COMMENTS ON HUMANISTIC NATURALISM

Many people commend humanistic naturalists for their emphasis on people and their distinctively human traits, for their emphasis on scientific method, and for their willingness to face facts. People also admire humanists' faith in creative intelligence and their notion that the world is still in the making.

What is more difficult for many to accept is the humanists' exclusive faith in the methods of the objective sciences and in people's ability to attain a satisfactory life in a universe that is indifferent to our interests and aspirations. If nature has produced humans, as the naturalists say, then it would seem that humans give some indication of the nature of nature and that humans probably give as good an indication of the nature of the universe as do rocks and stars.

The modern naturalists want to guard against the charge of **anthropomorphism** (attributing human qualities to the nonhuman realm). They wish to avoid the danger of projection or of "reading into nature" our human hopes and aspirations. Isn't there an equal danger that we may go to the opposite extreme and, in our desire to be strictly objective and empirical, "read out of nature" some qualities

and aspects that may be present? If "wishful thinking" is a bad thing, isn't it equally undesirable to assume that the truth is contrary to what we desire?

The question of whether the universe is friendly in the sense that there is purpose and concern for humans at the center of things, or unfriendly to humans is fundamental. Is it true that a cold and suspicious attitude toward the cosmos is hard to combine with a trustful and affectionate attitude toward human beings? Although the humanists say that they do not make a separation between humans and the process that has produced humans, their critics say they do make such a separation when they see the power beyond humans as indifferent to the human venture. The creative processes of the universe have produced self-conscious beings with a degree of intelligence and a drive to search for truth, beauty, and goodness. Is it reasonable to believe that a process devoid of purpose and intelligence could produce such a being? If humans are interpreted as a part of nature and nature is simply a blind force operating without concern for the goals of human life, is life, as some of the critics assert, likely to be seen as only a struggle for existence? Are self-interest and power eventually likely to emerge as guides for action? Does humanism leave human ideals and standards without any secure foundations?

Reflections

♦ ♦ ♦ ♦ ♦ ♦ ♦ ♦ ♦ ♦

The contemporary role of philosophical naturalism is disputed. One scholar has claimed that this viewpoint had its day during late 1930s and through the 1940s.[15] Another philosopher has recently proposed its viability. (See the initial chapter quotation on page 248.) Perhaps a fair observation is that forms of naturalism remain active and productive in American philosophy, but this perspective has been overshadowed by other philosophical views and methods (e.g., analytic philosophy, phenomenology, existentialism, and process philosophy).

Glossary Terms

ANTHROPOMORPHISM   The attributing of human qualities to the nonhuman realm or to nature. The term may refer to the portrayal of God as having human form, characteristics, or limitations.

EPIPHENOMENON (EPIPHENOMENAL)   A phenomenon accompanying some brain processes.

HUMANISM   A general outlook that emphasizes distinctively human interests and ideals. The humanism of the Renaissance was based on the Greek classics; Christian humanism focuses upon human concerns within a theological context; secular humanism underscores the significance of humanity as free agents independent of any supernatural realm or forces.

MATERIALISM   In its extreme form, the view that nothing is real except matter. Mind and consciousness are merely manifestations of such matter and are reducible to the physical elements.

NATURALISM   An outlook that accepts the empirical world as the whole of reality, usually without a deity. Naturalism, as opposed to *supernaturalism*, holds that explanations of the world produced by scientific methods are the only satisfactory ones.

Chapter Review

NATURALISM DEFINED

1. Nature is the sum total of reality. Nature is the world disclosed to us by the natural sciences.

2. Materialism is a narrow form of naturalism, which asserts there is nothing but matter; nature and the physical world are one.

MECHANISTIC MATERIALISM

1. The theory that all things are explained by laws that govern matter and motion is called mechanistic materialism.

2. Mind and its activities are forms of behavior; mind and consciousness are explained by physics and chemistry.

3. Mechanistic materialism states that the world is governed by natural laws stated in mathematical terms. All phenomena are explicable in concepts used by physical sciences.

4. Mechanistic materialism is appealing because of its simplicity. Only that which is perceived by the senses is "real."

5. Humanists, idealists, pragmatists, and others criticize mechanism for its inability to explain satisfactorily many of the facts of human existence.

DIALECTICAL MATERIALISM

1. Hegel, an idealist, stressed the primacy of mind and the dialectic. Marx rejected idealism and replaced it with a materialism—hence, we get dialectical materialism.

2. In dialectical materialism, the decisive factor in historical change and human society is the production of goods necessary for life. Humans have some influence over their own lives; they can make other parts of nature serve their ends, thereby controlling processes of production.

3. Dialectical materialism asserts that action is primary and thought is secondary; there is no knowledge apart from action. The philosophical task is to change the world.

4. History, to Marx, is a record of class conflict. He distinguishes five types of productive systems.

5. Criticisms of dialectical materialism are similar to the criticisms of materialism insofar as dialectical materialism is a materialism. There are,

however, other criticisms that can be applied to the Marxist dialectic.

HUMANISTIC NATURALISM

1. Humanistic naturalism, sometimes called *secular humanism,* emphasizes the significance of humans as free agents independent of any supernatural forces.

2. Humanistic naturalism is a philosophy based on the empirical scientific method; its proponents are interested in biology, psychology, medicine, and the social studies.

3. Humanistic naturalists, in accord with evolutionary theory, stress continuity of development from the simple to the complex. Intellectual, biological, and physical processes are incorporated into a broad overview of existence.

4. Humanistic naturalists believe that life is dependent on a physiochemical order. They have abandoned all concepts of a supernatural Being.

◆ ◆

Study Questions and Projects

1. In addition to the types of humanism mentioned or discussed in this chapter, the term *humanism* has been applied to other groups and movements of thought. For example, Nicola Abbagnano, who wrote the article "Humanism" in *The Encyclopedia of Philosophy* (Vol. 4, p. 72), after discussing mainly Renaissance humanism, says that the term has been used to designate communism, pragmatism, personalism, and existentialism. Jacques Maritain says that the only true humanism is a Christian humanism. See how many uses of the term you can find. Do the different uses have anything in common?

2. Dialectical materialists (Marxists and communists in general) have claimed that their approach is strictly scientific. Others have claimed that these movements are ideologies, philosophies, or even theologies. Arnold Toynbee, the historian, says that communism is a Christian heresy, since it carries over the Judeo-Christian passion for a better world. Discuss these claims as fully as you can.

3. Critically evaluate the following statements, indicating where you agree and disagree with them:
   (a) "If there is no God, then anything goes."
   (b) "The mechanistic conception of life is a structural approach in the main, whereas the teleological view places emphasis mainly on function. These are complementary rather than antagonistic approaches."
   (c) "In materialism the emphasis was upon order, law, immutability. In the new way of thinking which is developing, the emphasis is upon spontaneity, creativeness, initiative."

4. Explain the meanings of *naturalism, materialism, mechanistic materialism, dialectical materialism, and humanistic naturalism.*

5. What are some of the things that mechanistic materialists affirm and deny? Why does this position appeal to some people?

6. Explain how dialectical materialism differs from other types of materialism. How can it be used to justify revolutionary tactics.

7. Critically evaluate dialectical materialism.

8. Indicate clearly the points of agreement and disagreement of the three types of naturalism discussed in this chapter. Be ready to compare these positions.

9. Read "Cosmogony, Cosmology" in the 1992 publication of *The Anchor Bible Dictionary* (Vol. 1; pp. 1162–71); focus on section B9, "The Hebrew Bible's Portrait of the Cosmos." Do the ancient Hebrew people experience and understand God within a form of naturalism? Is naturalism compatible with belief in a personal God, such as is found in the Bible? Justify your position.

10. Secular humanism is frequently regarded as lacking values and as an enemy of religion. Is this assessment accurate? Justify your response.

Suggested Readings

Cornman, J. W. *Materialism and Sensations*. New Haven: Yale University Press, 1971.

This work discusses "reductive materialism," which reduces sensations to physical entities; "eliminative materialism," which seems forced to deny pain, after-images and the like; and "sensing and sensa."

Feibleman, J. K. *The New Materialism*. The Hague: Martinus Nijhoff, 1970.

A new theory of matter based on modern physics calls for a new theory of materialism that has consequences for human nature and suggests a new approach to religion.

Garver, N., and Hare, P. H. (eds.). *Naturalism and Rationality*. Buffalo, N.Y.: Prometheus, 1986.

A collection of papers that struggle with the problems arising out of the ancient view of humans as half-rooted in nature and half-transcending into the world of norms and reason; contrasts between freedom and constraint are discussed as well as naturalized epistemology, belief formation, and decision making.

Hook, S. *The Quest for Being*. New York: St. Martin's, 1961.

Favoring humanism, the author rejects the claim that religious experience and metaphysical insight alone discover truths that are outside the domain of scientific inquiry.

Krikorian, Y. (ed.). *Naturalism and the Human Spirit*. New York: Columbia University Press, 1944.

A classic work of collected essays regarding naturalism as it applies to religion, democracy, ethical theory, logic, and America.

Kurtz, P. (ed). *The Humanist Alternative*. Buffalo, N.Y.: Prometheus, 1973.

The subtitle of this collection of humanists' writings directly points to the content: "Some Definitions of Humanism." Every conceivable area of thought and existence is examined from a humanistic standpoint; topics range from atheistic humanism to Zen and humanism.

Kurtz, P. *Philosophical Essays In Pragmatic Naturalism*. Buffalo, N.Y.: Prometheus, 1990.

A major advocate of "secular humanism," the author presents the philosophies of scientific naturalism and pragmatism—two dominant schools in current American philosophy.

Marx, K., and Engels, F. *The German Ideology*. Parts I and III. New York: International Publishers, 1947.

This joint work of Marx and Engels is their first and most comprehensive statement of historical materialism. It is the first systematic account of their view of the relationship among the economic, political, and intellectual activities of humans, and is thus the first full statement of dialectical materialism.

Ryder, J. (ed.). *American Philosophic Naturalism in the Twentieth Century*. Buffalo, N.Y.: Prometheus, 1994.

This comprehensive collection of essays by leading philosophers of the twentieth century is divided into five parts: (1) conceptions of nature; (2) nature, experience, and method; (3) values—ethical and social; (4) values—aesthetic and religious; and (5) naturalism and contemporary philosophy.

Shea, W. M. *The Naturalists and the Supernatural*. Macon, Ga.: Mercer University Press, 1984.

A discussion of American naturalism and its understanding of religion, and marginally about an alternative.

Woodbridge, F. J. E. *An Essay on Nature*. New York: Columbia University Press, 1940.

A classic discourse in which the author considers nature as the domain where both knowledge and happiness are pursued.

Notes

1. P. Kurtz, *Philosophical Essays in Pragmatic Naturalism* (Buffalo, N.Y.: Prometheus, 1990), p. 7.

2. Kurtz, *Philosophical Essays,* p. 12.

3. S. Seely, *Modern Materialism: A Philosophy of Action* (New York: Philosophical Library, 1960), p. 7.

4. P. Weiss, "Love in a Machine Age," in Sidney Hook, ed., *Dimensions of Mind: A Symposium* (New York: Collier Books, New York University Institute of Philosophy, 1961), pp. 179–80.

5. We are aware of the fact that scholars differ in their interpretation of Marx. Some prefer to stress the early writings, up to 1844, which are more subjective and humanistic, rather than the later writings, which emphasize the materialistic interpretation of history. See A. Schaff, *Marxism and the Human Individual* (New York: McGraw-Hill, 1970). Of special interest is the first chapter, "Rediscovery of the Old Content of Marxism."

6. Many scholars are wary of using these terms. "The terms 'thesis,' 'antithesis' and 'synthesis,' so often used in expositions of Hegel's doctrine, are in fact not frequently used by Hegel: they are much more characteristic of Fichte." J. N. Findlay, *Hegel: A Re-Examination* (London: Allen and Unwin, 1958), pp. 69–70.

7. J. Stalin, *Dialectical and Historical Materialism* (New York: International Publishers, 1950), p. 8.

8. *The Humanist* (San Francisco: American Humanist Association, July–August 1968), inside front cover.

9. P. Kurtz, ed., *The Humanist Alternative* (Buffalo, N.Y.: Prometheus, 1973), p. 6.

10. Kurtz, *The Humanist Alternative,* p. 58.

11. H. W. Schneider, "Religious Humanism," in Kurtz, *The Humanist Alternative,* pp. 65–66. It is difficult to find a statement of the meaning of religious humanism that all practicing religious humanists would accept; we have chosen Schneider because of his influence in the field as well as the clarity and rationality of his writing.

12. E. A. Burtt, *Types of Religious Philosophy,* rev. ed. (New York: Harper, 1951), p. 341.

13. J. H. Randall, Jr., "Epilogue: The Nature of Naturalism," in Y. H. Krikorian, ed., *Naturalism and the Human Spirit* (New York: Columbia University Press, 1946), p. 357.

14. J. Dewey, *A Common Faith* (New Haven: Yale University Press, 1934), p. 27.

15. A. C. Danto, "Naturalism," in P. Edwards, ed., *The Encyclopedia of Philosophy,* Vol. 5, (New York: Macmillan & The Free Press, 1967), p. 450.

Idealism and Realism

CHAPTER OBJECTIVES

In this chapter we will address the following questions:

- What Are the Respective Outlooks of Idealism and Realism?
- Are There Various Types of Each?
- Who Are Some Historically Significant Idealists and Realists?
- Do the Two Movements Have Contrasting Implications?

At first, as a youth, we smile over its silliness; somewhat further on the way we find [idealism] interesting, clever, and forgivable. . . . With maturity we are likely to find it meaningful, to annoy ourselves and others with it, but on the whole scarcely worth disproving, and contrary to nature. It is hardly worth the trouble of further thinking because we feel that we have thought often enough about it already. But later, and with more earnest reflection and more extensive knowledge of human life and its interests, idealism acquires a strength which it is difficult to overcome.[1]

Realism as a general temper of mind is a disposition to keep ourselves and our preferences out of our judgment of things, letting the objects speak for themselves. . . .[2]

Contrasting Philosophical Movements

◆ ◆ ◆ ◆ ◆ ◆ ◆ ◆ ◆ ◆

In this chapter we consider idealism and realism as contrasting philosophical movements. To some extent, they both contain outlooks that go back to the ancient world. Even a brief sketch of the history of idealism in its many forms would involve recounting a considerable portion of the history of philosophy from Plato to the present. Idealism has held the allegiance of many prominent scholars in both Western and Eastern thought for more than two thousand years. During the latter half of the nineteenth century, idealism was the dominant Western philosophy. On the other hand, realism, with its assumption of an external world existing independently of the human mind, has been widely accepted throughout history. Realism was not seriously questioned by large numbers of Western thinkers until the seventeenth century. Most people think of themselves as existing in the midst of a world of objects that are independent of them. The mind and the external world interact, but this interaction does not affect the basic nature of the world. The world existed before mind was aware of it, the realists say, and will exist after mind ceases to be aware of it. Let us clarify the meaning of and tension between these two types of speculative philosophy.

Idealism Defined

◆ ◆ ◆ ◆ ◆ ◆ ◆ ◆ ◆ ◆

The term *idealist* as used philosophically has a meaning quite different from its meanings in ordinary language. Popularly, the word may mean (1) one who accepts and lives by lofty moral, aesthetic, and religious standards or (2) one who is able to visualize, and who advocates, some plan or program that does not yet exist. Every social reformer is an idealist in the second sense because he or she supports something that has not yet come into existence. Those who work for permanent peace or for the elimination of poverty can also be called idealists in this sense. The term may be used either as a compliment or a disparagement. The person who stands for goals that other people generally believe to be quite unattainable or who ignores the facts and practical conditions of a situation is likely to be called a "mere idealist."

The philosophical meaning of the term **idealism** is determined more by the ordinary meaning of the word *idea* than that of *ideal*. W. E. Hocking, an idealist, says that the term *idea-ism* would be more to the point. Idealism, in brief, asserts that reality consists of ideas, thoughts, minds, or selves rather than of material objects and forces. Idealism emphasizes mind as in some sense "prior to" matter. Whereas materialism says that matter is real and mind is an accompanying phenomenon, idealism contends that mind is real and matter is in a sense a byproduct. Idealism thus implies a denial that the world is basically a great machine to be interpreted as matter, mechanism, or energy alone.

Idealism is a world view or a metaphysics that holds that the basic reality consists of or is closely related to mind, ideas, thoughts, or selves. The world has a meaning apart from its surface appearance. The world is understood and interpreted by a study of the laws of thought and of consciousness, and not exclusively by the methods of the objective sciences.

Because the universe has a meaning and purpose of which the development of people is an aspect, the idealist believes that there is a kind of inner harmony between the rest of the world and humanity. What is "highest in spirit" is also "deepest in nature." The individual is "at home" in the universe and is not an alien or a creature of chance; the universe is in some sense a logical and a spiritual system that is reflected in a person's search for the good life. The self is not an isolated or unreal entity; it is a genuine part of the world process. This process at its high levels manifests itself as creativity, mind, selves, or persons.

Nature, or the objective world, is real in the sense that it exists and demands our attention and adjustment to it. Nature, however, is not sufficient in and of itself; the objective world depends to a certain degree upon mind. Idealists believe that the later and higher manifestations of nature are more significant in disclosing the characteristics of the world process than are its earlier and lower ones. Idealists are willing to let the *physical* scientists tell us what *matter* is, provided the latter do not attempt to reduce everything in the world to that category. The idealists are willing to let the *biological* scientists describe *life* and its processes, provided the latter do not attempt to reduce all other "levels" to the biological or the physiological.

Idealists stress the organic unity of the world process. Whole and parts cannot be separated except by a dangerous abstraction that centers attention on single aspects of things to the exclusion of other, equally important aspects. According to some idealists, there is an inner unity, an unfolding series of levels from matter through vegetable forms through animals to humanity, mind, and spirit. Thus, a central principle of idealism is organic wholeness. Idealists tend to emphasize the coherence or consistency theory of the test of truth—an assertion is judged to be true if it is in agreement with other assertions that are accepted as true.

Types of Idealism

◆ ◆ ◆ ◆ ◆ ◆ ◆ ◆ ◆ ◆ ◆

The history of idealism is complicated because the term *idealism* is broad enough to include a number of different, although related, theories. Some students of philosophy use the term in a broad sense to include all the philosophies that maintain that spiritual (nonmaterial) forces determine the processes of the universe. Idealistic philosophies thus oppose naturalistic philosophies that view these forces as emerging at some late stage in the development of the universe. In a narrower sense, the term *idealism* is used for those philosophies that view the universe as, in some crucial sense, dependent on mind.

In our discussion in this chapter we shall refer mainly to the idealistic tradition as reflected in the thinking of some of its outstanding representatives in Western civilization. Keep in mind, however, that there are significant idealistic systems and movements in Asia, especially in India, within the Hindu tradition. Although there are differences in outlook and emphasis between Western and Asian idealism, P. T. Raju tells us that "the idealistic systems of the West and of India seem to be complementary to each other," and that "the orthodox Indian thought and Buddhist philosophy became idealistic when they reached their highest developments."[3] (See Radhakrishnan biography and excerpt, pp. 272–273.)

There are many classifications of the types of idealism, yet no one classification seems to be entirely satisfactory as there is much overlapping. In this chapter, we shall briefly consider subjective idealism, objective idealism, and personalism; this classification is useful, relatively simple, and clear.

SUBJECTIVE IDEALISM— IMMATERIALISM

Subjective idealism is sometimes called *mentalism*, sometimes *phenomenalism*. It is the least defensible, least prevalent, and most frequently attacked form of idealism. The subjective idealist holds that minds, or spirits, and their perceptions, or ideas, are all that exist. The "objects" of experience are not material things; they are merely perceptions. Things such as buildings and trees exist, but they exist only in a mind that perceives them. The subjective idealist does not deny the existence, in some sense, of what we call the "real" world; the question at issue is not its existence but how it is to be interpreted. It does not exist independently of a knower. The sense in which the external world is said to "exist" by the subjective idealist is special—that is, the word *exist* is used differently from the way it is used ordinarily. For the subjective idealist, all that exists (in the more ordinary sense) are minds and their ideas.

Subjective idealism probably is best represented by George Berkeley (1685–1753), an Irish philosopher who preferred the term **immaterialism** to describe his philosophy. To say that an idea exists means, according to him, that it is being perceived by some mind. For ideas, *Esse est percipi:* "To be is to be perceived." Minds themselves, however, are not similarly dependent for their existence on being perceived. Minds are *perceivers.* To be is to be perceived (ideas) or to be a perceiver (mind). All that is real is a conscious mind or some perception or idea held by such a mind. How, Berkeley asks, could we speak of anything that was other than an idea or a mind?

When we assert that we can imagine objects existing when they are not seen, and that we do believe in the independent existence of an external world, Berkeley tells us that the order and consistency of the world of nature are real and are a result of active mind, the mind of God. God, the supreme mind, is the author and the governing spirit of nature, and God's will is the law of nature. God determines the succession and the order of our ideas. This explains why we cannot determine merely by willing it what we shall see when we open our eyes.

The subjectivist holds that there can be no object, as well as no perception of it, without a knower; that the subject (mind or knower) in some way creates its object (what we call matter, or things that are known); and that all that is real is a conscious mind or a perception by such a mind. To say that a thing exists is to say that it is perceived. What anything would or could be apart from its being known, no one can think or say. What we see or think is mind-dependent, and the world is a mental world.

OBJECTIVE IDEALISM

Many idealists, from Plato through Hegel to contemporary philosophers reject both extreme subjectivism, or mentalism, and the view that the external world is in any real sense created by humans. They regard the organization and form of the world, and hence knowledge, to be determined by the nature of the world itself. The mind discovers what there is in the order of the world. They are idealists in that they interpret the universe as an intelligible realm, the systematic structure of which expresses rational order and value. When they say that the ultimate nature of the universe is mental, they mean that the universe is one all-embracing order, that its basic nature is mind, and that it is an organic whole.

Although the term *idealism* has been used only in recent times to designate a school of philosophical thought, the beginnings of idealistic speculation in Western culture often are attributed to Plato (c. 427–347 B.C.E.) (see biography and excerpt, pp. 274–276). Plato called the fundamental realities *Ideas,* but this did not mean that they were dependent for their existence on a mind, human or divine. Plato believed that behind the empirical world of change—the phenomenal world that we see and feel—there is an ideal world of eternal essences, *forms,* or "Ideas." The world was divided into two realms. There was the world of sense perception, the world of sights, sounds, and individual things. This concrete, temporal, perishable world was not the real world; it was the world of appearances only. There was also the supersensible world of concepts, Ideas, universals, or eternal essences. The *form* of "humanity" has more reality than has any individual person, and any individual human being is real only to the degree that the person "shares in" the *form* of humanity. We recognize individual things through our knowledge of eternal patterns. This second realm contains the patterns, forms, or types that serve as standards for the things we perceive with our senses. Ideas are the original transcendent patterns, and perceptions and individual things are mere copies or shadows of these Ideas. Although reality is immaterial, Plato would not say that there is nothing real except mind and its experiences. The unchanging Ideas, or essences, which are real, are known to us through our reason. The soul of a person is an immaterial essence imprisoned for a time in the body. The changing world of matter, as apprehended by the senses, yields only opinion, not genuine knowledge.

Modern objective idealists typically maintain that all parts of the world are included in one all-embracing order, and they attribute this unity to the ideas and purposes of an Absolute Mind. Hegel (1770–1831) propounded one of the

Sarvepalli Radhakrishnan

Sarvepalli Radhakrishnan (1888–1975) became one of India's leading contemporary philosophers, educators, and statesmen. After being educated at various mission schools, he earned an M.A. in philosophy at Madras Christian College. He served as Indian ambassador to Russia, and then became Vice-President (1952–1962) and then President (1962–1967) of India.

Radhakrishnan preached spiritual revolution as an answer to humanity's problems. In many of his writings, he expressed the view that the materialism and skepticism generated by the scientific and technological revolution could be overcome only through a revitalized spirituality, a life of simplicity and asceticism, and a balance between contemplation and activity. He studied the major religions and concluded that they have a common bond that can be perceived through mystical insight, but not by reason alone.

Radhakrishnan's principal writings include *The Hindu Way of Life* (1927), *An Idealist View of Life* (1932), *Indian Philosophy*, 2 vols. (1923–1927), and *Religion in a Changing World* (1967).

best-known systems of absolute or monistic idealism. Thought is the essence of the universe, and nature is the whole of mind objectified. The universe is an unfolding process of thought. Nature is Absolute Reason expressing itself in outward form. Consequently, the laws of thought are also the laws of reality. History is the way the Absolute appears in time and human experience. Because the world is One and is purposive and intelligent, it must be of the nature of thought. When we think of the total world order as embracing the inorganic, the organic, and the spiritual levels of existence in one order, we speak of the Absolute, or the Absolute Spirit, or God.

Instead of the fixed or static reality and the separate and complete self of traditional philosophy, Hegel sets forth a dynamic conception of a self and its environment so interrelated that a clear-cut distinction cannot be drawn between the two. The self experiences reality at all times. The "universal" is present in all the particular experiences of the dynamic process. In such a philosophy, distinctions and differences belong to the phenomenal world and are relative to the observer; they do not affect the unity of the one purposive intelligence.

The objective idealists do not deny the existence of an external or objective reality. In fact, they believe that their position is the only one that does justice to the objective side of experience, because they find in nature the same principles of order, reason, and purpose that we find within ourselves. There is purposive intelligence at the heart of nature. This is discovered, they

Excerpt from Radhakrishnan:

Indian Philosophy (1927)

The philosophic attempt to determine the nature of reality may start either with the thinking self or the objects of thought. In India the interest of philosophy is in the self of man. Where the vision is turned outward, the rush of fleeting events engages the mind. . . . If we put the subjective interest of the Indian mind along with its tendency to arrive at a synthetic vision, we shall see how monistic idealism becomes the truth of things. To it the whole growth of Vedic thought points; on it are based the Buddhistic and the Brahmanical religions; it is the highest truth revealed to India. Even systems that announce themselves as dualistic or pluralistic seem to be permeated by a strong monistic character. If we can abstract from the variety of opinion and observe the general spirit of Indian thought, we shall find that it has a disposition to interpret life and nature in the way of monistic idealism, though this tendency is so plastic, living and manifold that it takes many forms and expresses itself in even mutually hostile teachings.

S. Radhakrishnan, *Indian Philosophy,* 2 vols. (London: Allen and Unwin, 1923–1927).

believe, and not "read into" the world. Nature existed before me, the individual self, and will exist after me; nature also existed before the present community of selves. The existence of meaning in the world, however, implies something akin to mind or thought at the core of reality. Such a significant order of reality is given humanity to comprehend and participate in. This belief in meaning and intelligence in the structure of the world is a basic insight underlying idealism.[4]

PERSONAL IDEALISM—PERSONALISM

Personalism emerged as a protest against both mechanistic materialism and monistic idealism. For the personalist, the basic reality is neither abstract thought nor a particular thought process, but a person, a self, or a thinker. Reality is of the nature of conscious personality. The self is an irreducible living unit, which can be divided only by a false abstraction. The personalists believe that recent developments in modern science, including the formulation of the theory of relativity, have added support to their position. Reality is a system of personal selves—hence, it is pluralistic. Personalists emphasize the reality and the worth of individual people, moral values, and human freedom.

Nature, for the personalists, is an objective order; however, it does not exist in and of itself. People transcend or rise above nature when they interpret it. Science transcends its material through its theories, and the world of meaning

Plato

Plato (427–347 B.C.E.) was born in Athens amid aristocratic surroundings. As a young man he planned to enter politics, but gave up that goal when Socrates, whom he admired and followed, was sentenced to death by the state. After the death of Socrates, he left Athens and traveled until 387 B.C.E., when he returned to the city and founded a school known as the Academy, of which he was leader for forty years. Like his brilliant student, Aristotle, he was one of the most influential thinkers and writers in the history of Western society.

Plato's writings have a beauty and purity of diction. They use a literary form known as the dialogue that consists of a conversation between two or more persons and centers on some important idea. The early writings probably reflect the point of view of Socrates, whereas in the later writings the character designated as Socrates is the spokesman for Plato's own philosophical position. His better-known writings include the *Apology* and *Crito*, which deal with Socrates' trial and last conversations; *Euthyphro*, which discusses piety, or reverence; and *The Republic*, Plato's great masterpiece, which is concerned with justice and the ideal state.

and of values surpasses the world of nature as final explanation. Rudolf Hermann Lotze (1817–1881), Borden P. Bowne (1847–1910), Edgar Sheffield Brightman (1884–1953) (see biography and excerpt, pp. 276–277), and Peter Bertocci (1910–1989) have emphasized this point of view.

Brightman thought of personalism as a mediating position between the absolute idealism of Josiah Royce and the pragmatism of William James, as well as between **supernaturalism** and naturalism. Reality is a society of persons that includes the uncreated Person (God) and the created persons found in human society.

According to the personalists, nature was created by God, who is the Supreme Self in a society of persons. The Supreme Spirit has expressed Himself in the material world of atoms and in conscious selves, which emerge at particular stages in the world process. There is a society of persons, or selves, related to the Supreme Personality. Ethical and spiritual values are reinforced by and gain their meaning from the Personal Creative Spirit, to whom all are related. Personalism is theistic; it furnishes both religion and ethics with metaphysical foundations. God may be thought of as finite, as a struggling hero working for lofty moral and religious ends. The goodness of God is retained, even though there is some limitation placed on his power. The proper goal of life is a perfect society of selves who have achieved perfect personalities through struggle.

The personal idealists hold that the process of life is more important than any verbal forms of expression or fixed meanings, and they stress the

Next, I said, compare the effect of education and the lack of it upon our human nature to a situation like this: imagine men to be living in an underground cave-like dwelling place, which has a way up to the light along its whole width, but the entrance is a long way up. The men have been there from childhood, with their neck and legs in fetters, so that they remain in the same place and can only see ahead of them, as their bonds prevent them from turning their heads. Light is provided by a fire burning some way above and behind them. Between the fire and the prisoners . . . there is a path across the cave and along this a low wall has been built, like the screen at a puppet show in front of the performers who show their puppets above it.

See then also men carrying along that wall all kinds of artifacts, statues of men, reproductions of other animals in stone or wood fashioned in all sorts of ways. . . .

They are like us, I said. Do you think, in the first place, that such men could see anything of themselves and each other except the shadows which the fire casts upon the wall of the cave in front of them?

Plato, *The Dialogues of Plato,* Vol. I, trans. B. Jowett (New York: Random House, 1937).

realization of the capacities and powers of the person through freedom and self-control. Personality has greater value than anything else, and thus society must be so organized as to give each person fullness of life and opportunity.

Implications of Idealism

THE UNIVERSE IS PURPOSEFUL

For the idealists, there is a purposeful universe, the real nature of which is spiritual. Although they accept the interpretations of the modern empirical sciences, they point out that these are limited by the nature of the methods used and the fields investigated. The sciences tend to eliminate all mental aspects of the world and to construct a world that is "closed to mind." The laws of the universe, according to the idealist, are in harmony with the demands of the intellectual and moral nature of human beings.

Although humans are a part of the world process and in that sense "natural," they are spiritual beings in that there is in them something not reducible to bare matter. All interpretations of human beings that make them merely animals or place them in the control of purely physiological or mechanical processes are viewed as inadequate by idealists. Human nature has only begun to realize its possibilities. Moreover, it is through the individual person and his or her aspirations that we find the best clue to the nature of God.

For the idealists, God is not apart from the world, but is the indwelling life principle. Al-

Edgar Sheffield Brightman

Edgar Brightman (1884–1953) was a leading advocate and defender of the philosophy of personalism, or personal idealism. He was also the philosopher in the United States to develop in detail the personalistic outlook and its implications for society. He taught at Nebraska Wesleyan University (1912–1915), at Wesleyan University (1915–1919), and at Boston University (1919–1953). At Boston University he studied under Borden Parker Bowne and was the Borden Parker Bowne Professor of Philosophy from 1925 until his death. He was president of the Eastern Division of the American Philosophical Association in 1936. He conceived of personalism as a mediating position between James' pragmatism and Royce's absolute or monistic idealism. He held that personalism could resolve the impasse between supernaturalism and naturalism, and that his concept of the total person retained the elements of truth in both positivism and existentialism.

His writings include *Introduction to Philosophy* (1925); *Nature and Values* (1945); *A Philosophy of Religion* (1940); and a book edited and published after his death—*Person and Reality, An Introduction to Metaphysics* (1958).

though transcending the world process, God is also immanent in it. God is found in the processes of nature, in history, in the social order, and preeminently in the human heart. Consequently, the older distinction between the natural and supernatural tends to break down. In monistic idealism, such as that presented by Radhakrishnan, God is the purpose and the creative spirit of the cosmic process. The absolute idealist thinks of God as infinite and as the ground of all existence. The personalist, who is a **pluralist** as well, may think of God as finite, a struggling hero, the Supreme Self or Person in a society of persons. In any case, God's administration is no longer external, and we do not have to look to some outside agent or event for divine revelation; it is to be found in all of life.

SOCIAL IMPLICATIONS

What are the social implications of idealism? Does it lead to an acceptance of conditions as they are or to a spirit of reform and progress? The answers depend on the type of idealism being considered. Idealists in general tend to have considerable respect for culture and tradition. They think of the values of life as grounded in a realm beyond the individual and the social groups. In absolute idealism, the universe precedes and is superior to the particular, so we may come to believe, with Hegel, that the absolute is expressed in history and through the institutions of society. In such cases, there is less tendency to recognize individual rights and values as opposed to those of society and the state.

Excerpt from Brightman:
Personality and Religion (1934)

No abstract discussion can ever plumb the depths of personality. Personality is not a psychological theory or the sum of them all, nor is it a definition. Neither is it exhausted by the experience of any one of us. Personality is Pericles and Abraham Lincoln, Alcibiades and Aaron Burr, Alexander the Great and Aristotle, Saint Francis, Saint Thomas Aquinas, Napoleon, Charlemagne, Bismarck, Hitler, Gandhi, George Fox, Nero, Euripedes, Wagner, Einstein, Spinoza, Raphael, Jesus, the unknown soldier, and the forgotten man. If a philosophy or a psychology or a religion fails to take account of all that personality has been and may be, it cannot be said to be the whole truth. In a world where so much of truth is beyond our grasp, can we afford to neglect truth which is readily available?

E. Brightman, *Personality and Religion* (New York: Abingdon Press, 1934).

Although Plato's political philosophy is at heart a blueprint for social change, his idealism with its view of Ideas or universals as transcendent essences often led to a conceptual separation of this world and the next; this view dominated medieval society and tended to fix all human relationships. This outlook supported the idea of a static society.

In contrast to Platonic and Hegelian types of idealism, many modern idealists, from Descartes and Liebniz to the contemporary personalists, have emphasized the person or the consciousness of the individual. People are viewed as free moral agents capable of discovering values. Idealism, thus, gives an objective basis for moral values and obligations as opposed to relativistic views, which stress customs and opinion. Self-realization, or the development of selfhood, is the supreme value to which all other values are subordinate.

Realism Defined

♦ ♦ ♦ ♦ ♦ ♦ ♦ ♦ ♦ ♦ ♦

We have pointed out that idealism was the dominant Western philosophy in the late nineteenth century. With the opening of the twentieth century, however, there was an upsurge of realism, especially in Great Britain and North America. Let us be clear about the meanings of the terms **real, reality,** and **realism.** The *real* is the actual, or the existing; the term refers to things or events that exist in their own right, as opposed to that which is imaginary or in our thought. *Real* refers to what is. *Reality* is the state or quality of being real or actually existent, in contrast to what is mere appearance. In a popular sense, *realism* may mean devotion to fact, to what is the case, as opposed to what is wished, hoped, or desired. In philosophy, however, the word *realism* is used in a more technical sense.

Realism, in its strictly philosophical sense, is the position that the objects of our senses are real in their own right; they exist independently of their being known to, perceived by, or related to mind. For the realist, the universe is so inexorably "out there" that the only thing we can do is to come to the best terms possible with it. The realists attempt to do this, not to interpret the world according to their special hopes or unverified beliefs. A Scottish realist, John Macmurray, says:

> We cannot get away from the primary fact that there is a distinction between things and ideas. For ordinary common sense an idea is the idea of something, a thought in our minds which *represents* the things that it is the idea of. In that case the thing is the reality while the idea is merely "how the thing appears to us." Our thought must, therefore, adapt itself to things if it is to be proper thought, that is to say, if our idea is to be true. If the idea does not correspond with the thing of which it is the idea, then the idea is false and useless. The thing will not accommodate itself to our idea of it. We have to change our ideas and keep on changing them till we get them right. Now, such a common-sense way of thinking is essentially realist, and it is realist because it makes the "thing" and not the "idea" the measure of validity, the center of significance. It makes the thing real and the idea the true or false appearance of the thing.[5]

In discussing the psychological genesis of positions other than realism, Macmurray says that, because philosophers are so concerned with ideas, they tend to emphasize the world of ideas or thought. Because thought tends to be important to them, they naturally—although mistakenly—come to think that ideas have a reality not found in things. If we regard the life of the mind, or reflective thinking, as something higher or nobler than practical activity or than our interest in things, we may falsely come to assume that the idea is more important than the thing of which it is the idea. If we confine ourselves to thought, then thought seems to be the only significant thing. According to Macmurray, the realistic view is the common-sense view and the only one that will stand up amidst the practical activities of life.

Another realist, Alfred North Whitehead, sets forth his reasons for believing that the things we experience should be distinguished clearly from our knowledge of them.[6] In defending the objectivist position of realism, which, he says, is adapted to the requirements of science as well as to the concrete experiences of humanity, Whitehead makes three affirmations. First, we are *within* a world of colors, sounds, and other sense objects. The world is neither within us nor dependent on our sense perception. Second, history discloses long ages when no living beings existed on earth and when important changes or happenings were taking place. Third, one's activity seems to transcend the self and to find and to seek ends in the known world. Things pave the way for our awareness. A common world of thought seems to imply and require a common world of sense.

Many philosophers, notably the idealists and the pragmatists, have claimed that an object known or experienced is different from the object before it entered such relationships. Because we can never know an object except as it is known or experienced by us, the object's being known or experienced forms an integral part of the object known. Thus, knowledge and experience tend to modify or constitute the object to some extent. The realist holds that such reasoning is fallacious, because it draws a false conclusion from certain accepted propositions. We cannot, of course, know a thing until we have some experience of it. It is also true that we cannot know what qualities a thing possesses when it is unknown. The only valid conclusion is that all known things are known, which is a truism, or that awareness is an element of knowledge. From this we cannot draw the conclusion either that things have no qualities when they are not known or that the experience of knowing changes them in any way or constitutes their existence. The realist insists that the widely accepted common-sense position is sound—that is, that the realm of nature, or physical objects, exists independently of us and that our experience does not change the nature of the object experienced.

Types of Realism

Realism is a term that covers many different trends in or types of philosophy that have certain basic tenets in common. At least three tendencies are evident in modern realism. There is, first, a tendency toward materialism in some of its modern forms. For example, mechanistic materialism is a realism as well as a materialism. Second, there is a tendency toward idealism. The basis of existence may be thought of as mind or spirit that is an organic whole. Third, there are many realists who claim that reality is pluralistic and consists of many types of entities of which mind and matter may be only two. In this chapter, the pluralistic type of realism receives greatest attention because it appears to be the dominant trend.

What is sometimes called Platonic, conceptual, or classical realism is nearer to modern idealism than to modern realism. Assuming that the real is the permanent or the unchanging, Plato said that the Idea, or the universal, was more real than the individual thing. During the Middle Ages, there was a controversy between the Platonic or classical realists and the **nominalists,** who insisted that class terms or universals are names only, and that reality is found in percepts or individual things.

Aristotle was more of a realist, in the modern sense, than was his teacher, Plato. Aristotle was an observer interested in the details of individual things. He believed that reality exists in concrete things or in the process of their development. The real world is the world we sense, and form (the idea or principle of organization)

and matter are inseparable. From the twelfth century on, the influence of Aristotle tended to replace that of Plato, Thomas Aquinas (c. 1224–1274) brought Aristotelian metaphysics and Christian theology into harmony and gave Medieval Scholasticism its most complete expression. His great synthesis was made within the realistic tradition.

Space does not permit a detailed account of the various groups or schools of realism that have existed during the last few hundred years. In the United States, during the early decades of the twentieth century, two realistic movements that showed considerable vigor were the new realism, or neo-realism, and critical realism. The new realism was an attack on idealism, and critical realism was a criticism of both idealism and the new realism. The discussions tended to center around highly complex and technical problems of epistemology and metaphysics. Some prominent realists not associated with these groups also were active during the first half of this century. All these realists have tended to transfer attention from the mind that interprets nature to the world that is interpreted.

The first decade of the twentieth century was a time of intellectual ferment. By 1910, six men—all teachers of philosophy in the United States—discovered that they were in considerable philosophical agreement and formed a group that published, in 1912, a cooperative book entitled *The New Realism.*[7]

The new realists reject subjectivism, monism, **absolutism** (belief in an Absolute or that which is without limitation), all mystical philosophies, and the view that nonmental things are either created or modified in any way by the knowing mind. The new realists claim that they are returning to the common-sense doctrine of a real, objective world, which is known directly by sense perception. For them, the knowledge of an object does not change the object known. Our experience and awareness are *selective,* not *constitutive*—that is, we choose to give attention to some things rather than others; we do not create or alter them merely by experiencing them. For example, that there is a chair in this room is not affected by our experiencing or not experiencing the chair. Certain thinkers have set forth fairly complete philosophies derived from the new realism.[8]

During the 1910–1920 decade, seven men set forth a philosophy with a slightly different outlook. In 1920 they published a volume entitled *Essays in Critical Realism.*[9] Although they agreed with the new realists that the existence of objects is independent of knowledge, they criticized the new realists for making the relationship between objects and observer so immediate or direct.

The *critical realists* do not think that the awareness or perception of objects is as direct and immediate as the new realists claimed. The outer object is not actually present in consciousness. Only the sense data are present in human consciousness. The sense data reflect the nature of the external object, as well as the nature of the perceiving mind. Except by inference, we cannot go beyond or get behind the sense data to the object from which they are derived. We have, then (1) the perceiving mind, the knower, or the conscious organism; (2) the object, with its primary qualities; (3) the sense data, which connect the perceiving mind and the object. The critical realist thinks that the sense data give us fairly direct contact with objects. The critical realist believes that this approach enables us to understand and explain illusions, hallucinations, and errors of various kinds, because the sense data may be distorted.

The realists distinguish clearly between the objects of thought and the act of thought itself. Realists on the whole stress the correspondence theory for the verification of statements: truth is the faithful adherence of our judgments to the facts of experience or to the world as it is.

Most realists respect science and are likely to stress the close relationship between science and philosophy. Yet, many of them are critical of one aspect of earlier science, which either implied a dualism or denied the realm of values. For example, Alfred North Whitehead, who set forth a "philosophy of organism," criticized the traditional scientific outlook that separates matter and life, body and mind, nature and spirit, substance and its qualities. Such an approach empties nature of sense qualities and tends to lead to the denial of the values of ethics, aesthetics, and religion. Newton's methodology led to success in the physical sciences, but it left nature without meaning or value; some people came to believe that values and ideals are illusory and have no objective basis. This attitude is the result of abstracting and emphasizing certain aspects of reality and ignoring other aspects. Whitehead calls this process of abstraction the "fallacy of misplaced concreteness." It occurs whenever we take one aspect of a thing and treat it as the whole. In this way, arbitrary lines are drawn between what the investigator is willing to regard as important and what he or she considers unreal.

Implications of Realism

◆ ◆ ◆ ◆ ◆ ◆ ◆ ◆ ◆ ◆ ◆

Whereas the pragmatists, as we shall see in Chapter 14, emphasize the world of *our experience*, the realists emphasize *the world* of our experience. The world is what it is, no matter what is thought about it. Whereas the idealists emphasize mind as the primary reality, the realists tend to view mind as only one of many things that make up the world. The realist is suspicious of any tendency to substitute our wishes or desires for the "facts," or to make our conscious selves the center of importance in the universe. This emphasis on an external world independent of but disclosed just as it is to the mind is congenial to the natural sciences. Attention is directed not to the mind that understands but to the reality that is understood. Realism thus reflects the objectivism that underlies and supports modern science. Realism is less likely than idealism to concern itself with problems of the whole. Realism depends on reason rather than on our sentiments and wishes; it is prepared to find that the world is quite different from what we might wish it to be.

Because realism stands in sharp contrast to idealism and is said to "dementalize" the world, a statement regarding the realist's attitude toward mind is in order. In arguing that realism does not defame mind or rob it of its riches and value, one realist says, "Realism strips mind of its pretensions but not of its values or greatness. On the contrary, in leaving to other things their rights mind comes into its own . . . if it dethrones the mind, it recognizes mind as chief in the world it knows."[10] (See Alexander biography and excerpt, pp. 282–283)

We spoke earlier about realism as a disposition to keep ourselves . . . out of our judgment of things, letting the objects speak for themselves. Is there a relation between philosophical realism and what realism means in ordinary language? Does this attitude carry over into everyday affairs and affect our outlook in education, art, literature, and religion? Many people think there is a definite relationship, whereas others have suggested caution in making such applications. Is it possible that philosophical realism might influence an individual to stress content-centered rather than pupil-centered education? In literature, has the outlook of philosophical realism led writers to stress fidelity to real life as opposed to sentimental, extravagant, or romantic, glorification of human nature and the world? Has there been a similar influence on other art forms? Realism in art avoids an abstract or ideal treatment and limits itself to a portrayal of the object as actually observed. Realists aim at correspondence with nature; they attempt to represent their subject matter in its concrete and particular details.

Although some realists deny religion any validity, there was a revival of religious realism during the first half of this century. Philosophical realism influenced thinking in the field of religion. Within Roman Catholicism, a religious realism is found in the form of **neo-Thomism,** a restatement of the religious philosophy of Thomas Aquinas that repudiates all relativistic philosophies as well as idealistic metaphysics. A group of Protestant religious leaders (often known as Christian realists) also formulated their theological beliefs within the general outlook of realistic philosophy. In general, we can say that the influence of realism has been to encourage recognition of the presence of evil in life. Realism is thus a repudiation of extreme optimism, sometimes found where the influence of idealism is prominent. This recognition does not lead to the denial of the good or of God. Real deliverance from evil is possible; salvation may be obtained if the right adjustment to the religious Object (or God) is made.

Evaluation of Idealism

◆ ◆ ◆ ◆ ◆ ◆ ◆ ◆ ◆ ◆ ◆

The fact that idealism has survived for many centuries and has been supported by many outstanding thinkers, in both the East and the West, seems to indicate that it has filled some need. The strength of idealism is that it emphasizes the significance of the person and the mental or spiritual side of life. Idealism justifies philosophically the notion that the individual self has meaning and dignity; people have abiding worth and are superior to institutions and "things."

Although they accept the modern scientific account of the world, idealism makes room for religion. Moral and religious values are present in the world of nature. Idealism is thus in harmony with many human intuitions and aspirations. Idealism, its supporters claim, gives intellectual support to the spiritual intuitions of the species. The appeal of idealism is based in part on human moral aspirations and not only on logical or epistemological grounds.

The critics of idealism, on the other hand, say that it is vague and abstract in its terminology, that it is merely of traditional interest, and that it lacks a genuinely scientific outlook. Pragmatists such as John Dewey claim that idealism tends to substitute an antiquated attitude of otherworldliness for vigorous participation in the struggle for a new society here and now. To regard institutions as expressions of a universal reason may lead us to think more about order and stability and less about change and progress.

Realists and philosophical analysts are likely to charge that idealism goes beyond all empirical

Samuel Alexander

Samuel Alexander (1859–1938) was born in Sydney, New South Wales, and was educated at Wesley College (Melbourne) and Oxford University. After completing his studies in mathematics, classics, and philosophy, he became the first Jew to be appointed as a Fellow at Oxford; his earliest work, *Moral Order and Progress,* influenced by the prevailing idealism at Oxford, was published in 1889.

Alexander gave up his Fellowship to explore an approach to philosophy more closely related to the development of the empirical sciences. From 1893 to his retirement in 1924, he occupied the chair in philosophy at the Victoria University of Manchester. As a realist, he believed that only observation can lead to objective knowledge about space, time, and *nisus* (an urge to move in an evolutionary way from simpler to more complex forms of reality).

Alexander's books include *Space, Time and Deity,* 2 vols. (1920), and *Beauty and the Other Forms of Value* (1933). Many of his essays appear in *Philosophical and Literary Pieces,* edited by J. Laird (1939).

evidence and that its "proofs" resort to metaphor and flights of the imagination based on hopes and wishes. The tough-minded person finds it difficult to accept the assumptions the idealist makes. If the universe is an expression of mind or reason, the critic asks, why is it that experience reveals so much that is irrational and apparently purposeless, if not actually malevolent?

Other opponents charge that the idealists confuse the "accidental" with the "essential" features of objects. When idealists claim that existence is dependent on some mind, the realist insists that "being perceived" is an accidental feature of an object, whereas existence is an essential feature. The fact that we can never refer to an object without holding some idea of it does not mean that the object does not exist apart from the presence of an idea or a mind or even that it is in any way changed by the act of perception. There is the danger in idealism of equating mere thought with being or of confusing the environment with the mind that thinks about the environment.

Idealism receives criticism from some theologians who say that an intellectualistic view of God or an Absolute can be no substitute for a contrite heart and an act of decision. Idealism, they say, has too optimistic a view of humanity and the world. It does not deal satisfactorily with the problem of evil. For most people, evil is real and the problems of evil are how to identify it, how to reduce its power, and how to eliminate it.

Excerpt from Alexander:

Proceedings of the British Academy, "The Basis of Realism"

*The spirit of Realism.** The temper of Realism is to deanthropomorphize: to order man and mind to their proper place among the world of finite things; on the one hand to divest physical things of the colouring which they have received from the vanity or arrogance of mind; and on the other to assign them along with minds their due measure of self-existence. But so deeply ingrained and so natural is the self-flattering habit of supposing that mind, in its distinctive character of mind, is in some special sense the superior of physical things, so that in the absence of mind there would be no physical existence at all, that Realism in questioning its prerogatives appears to some to degrade mind and rob it of its riches and values.

But this apprehensive mood is the creature of mistake. Realism strips mind of its pretensions but not of its value or greatness. On the contrary, in leaving to other things their rights mind comes into its own.

---

*When I speak in this paper of Realism I mean contemporary realism, and for the most part my own form of it.

S. Alexander, *Philosophical and Literary Pieces,* ed. J. Laird (London: Macmillan, 1939).

For idealism, there is the additional and perhaps insoluble problem of how there can be any evil or imperfection in the world. Monistic idealism, at least, appears to permit a tolerance of evil and to justify the status quo, because whatever *is* is defined as good or as a part of the World Spirit.

Evaluation of Realism

◆ ◆ ◆ ◆ ◆ ◆ ◆ ◆ ◆ ◆

Realism is a broad philosophical movement that ranges from materialism at one extreme to a position close to objective idealism at the other. Consequently, it is not easy to defend or criticize it briefly. To deal with all the various types of realism is impossible. The presentation of each type raises questions, of course, about the soundness of other positions. Our general statements about realism are made with caution and the realization that they may not apply to all realists and that most realists would not accept all these criticisms as valid.

Realism is the view that the objects of our senses are real or exist in their own right quite independent of their being known to, perceived by, or related to mind. Being known or becoming an object of experience does not affect the nature of the object or alter it in any way. Objects exist and we may be aware of them now, and later not be aware of them, without their characteristics being changed. Objects thus may be related to consciousness, but they are not in any way created or altered by the mere fact of being known.

Realists think that their position is the only one that is supported by common sense, as well as by the assumptions underlying the sciences. The "human mind," says Ralph Barton Perry, is "instinctively and habitually realistic; so that re-alism does not so much need to be proved as to be defended against criticism."[11] Referring to his own position as that of "provisional realism," Alfred North Whitehead says, "I do not understand how a common world of thought can be established in the absence of a common world of sense."[12]

◆ ◆

Glossary Terms

ABSOLUTISM   (1) Belief in an ultimate reality that is without limitation; (2) the view that truth is objectively real, that there is only one correct explanation of reality, truth, and values.

IDEALIST (IDEALISM)   The view that asserts that reality consists of or is closely related to ideas, thought, mind, or selves rather than matter; there are many types of idealism.

IMMATERIALISM   With reference to George Berkeley, a theological form of subjective idealism.

NEO-THOMISM   A restatement of the religious philosophy of Thomas Aquinas.

NOMINALISTS (NOMINALISM)   The view that "universals," or general terms, are only names and represent no objectively real existents; all that exists is particulars; reality is found in individual things.

PERSONALISM   A type of idealism that asserts that reality is a system of personal selves. The self is said to be an irreducible living unit.

PLURALIST (PLURALISM)   (1) The view that reality consists of not one or two but many substances, in contrast to monism and dualism. (2) The position that more than one informed explanation or interpretation of most issues will be possible. (This is not to imply that all such explanations are equally true.)

REAL   Being an actual thing; having objective existence.

REALISM   The doctrine that the objects of our senses exist independently of their being known or related to mind.

REALITY   The state or quality of being real or actually existent, in contrast with what is mere appearance. Encompasses everything there is.

SUBJECTIVE IDEALISM   The belief that reality consists of minds, or spirits, and their perceptions or ideas.

SUPERNATURALISM   The outlook that there is a reality above or beyond the empirical world of nature.

◆ ◆

Chapter Review

CONTRASTING PHILOSOPHICAL MOVEMENTS

1. Idealism and realism contain outlooks that go back to the ancient world.

IDEALISM DEFINED

1. The term *idealist* may mean, in popular terms, one who accepts and lives by high moral and religious standards or one who advocates some program that does not yet exist.

2. Idealism in philosophy asserts that reality consists of ideas, thoughts, and selves rather than material objects and forces. Mind is real and matter is its byproduct. Nature is not sufficient in and of itself. The organic unity of the world process is stressed. The world has a meaning and purpose.

TYPES OF IDEALISM

1. Subjective idealism is referred to as immaterialism, mentalism, and phenomenalism.

2. Objective idealism asserts that the mind discovers what is already in the order of the world.

3. The basis for personalism, or personal idealism, is individuals, their value, and their struggle toward perfection of self.

IMPLICATIONS OF IDEALISM

1. The universe is purposeful, and although humans are a part of the world process, they are spiritual beings and therefore are not reducible to mere matter.

2. Depending on the type of idealism, the emphasis is either on the development of the person or the spiritual aspirations of the species.

REALISM DEFINED

1. There are differences in the meanings of *real, reality,* and *realism.*

2. Realism asserts that objects exist independent of their perception by the mind.

TYPES OF REALISM

1. There are many different trends in realism; all share certain common characteristics. Three tendencies evident in modern realism are those of mechanistic materialism, objective idealism, and pluralism.

2. Two movements prominent in the early twentieth century were neorealism and critical realism.

Neorealism was in complete opposition to idealism and critical realism criticized both idealism and neorealism.

3. Most realists respect science and stress a close relationship between philosophy and science.

IMPLICATIONS OF REALISM

1. Realists describe the world as it is and not as they would like to see it. They emphasize an independent external world. Realists depend on reason, aiming at correspondence with nature.

2. In religion, realism has recognized the presence of evil in life. Theories of realism have been adopted by certain religious leaders such as Thomas Aquinas and by Christian realists.

EVALUATION OF IDEALISM

1. Idealism has justified the idea that humans have dignity and meaning.

2. Idealism is based in part on the moral aspirations of people. It harmonizes with religion as it gives religious views intellectual support.

3. Critics of idealism claim that it goes beyond empirical evidence and that it equates thought with being.

4. Some theologians contend that idealism is too optimistic concerning humans and the world. How can idealists deal with the problem of evil?

EVALUATION OF REALISM

1. Realism ranges from materialism to a view that is similar to objective idealism. Such a broad category creates difficulty when we try to analyze the theory.

2. Objects may be related to the awareness of them, but they are not created or changed simply by being perceived.

3. The realist is convinced this position is the only one supported by common sense and science.

Study Questions and Projects

1. What in your opinion are the main appeals of idealism and the chief objection to idealism?

2. Give your reaction to the idealism of George Berkeley. The following limerick attributed to Ronald Knox, was written about Berkeley's immaterialism:

There was a young man who said, "God
Must think it exceedingly odd
If he finds that this tree
Continues to be
When there's no one about in the Quad."

REPLY

Dear Sir:
Your astonishment's odd.
I am always about in the Quad.
And that's why the tree
Will continue to be,
Since observed by
Yours faithfully,
God.

3. Is Christian Science within the general framework of or closely related to, idealistic philosophy? If so, to which of the types is it most closely related? Mrs. Mary Baker Eddy, the founder of Christian Science, said: "I gained the scientific certainty that all causation was Mind, and every effect a mental phenomenon."[13] "God is good. Good is Mind." "God, Spirit, being all, nothing is matter."[14]

4. Theosophy has been called "the body of truths which forms the basis of all religions." Look up some facts regarding theosophy and its beliefs. Does it have any relationship to idealistic thought?

5. Give the derivation of the term *idealism* and distinguish the philosophical meaning from the common or popular uses of the term.

6. What are the common assumptions and convictions underlying the various schools or types of idealism?

7. Explain as clearly as you can the distinctive points of subjective idealism, objective idealism, and personal idealism.

8. List a few Western idealists, and indicate where idealism has flourished. Can you give any reasons for its relative decline in the West in recent decades?

9. What are the implications of idealism for our views of the universe, God, humans, and social relationships?

10. The new realists claim that they are returning to the common-sense doctrine of a real, objective world that is neither created nor modified by the knowing mind. The critics of realism claim, however, that perceptual errors refute this type of realism. Do you think the critical realists, by emphasizing the sense data and thus making the relationship between the knower and the object known less direct, have strengthened the case for realism? Give reasons for your answer.

11. What, in your view, are some of the implications of realism for political thought, literature and the other arts, and religion?

12. Define the terms *real, reality,* and *realism* as they are used in philosophy.

13. Indicate the chief characteristics of, or points of emphasis in, philosophical realism.

14. Discuss the history of realism, indicating a few of the different forms it has taken in different periods of Western thought.

15. State some of the implications of realism for political thought, literature and other arts, and religion.

Suggested Readings

Alexander, S. *Space, Time and Deity.* 2 vols. New York: Macmillan, 1920.

The author's philosophy of realism is contained in this detailed, well-known study.

Bertocci, P., et al. (eds). *Person and Reality: An Introduction to Metaphysics.* New York: Ronald, 1958.

This text provides an introduction to metaphysical problems from the standpoint of a personalist.

Brightman, E. *Person and Reality, An Introduction to Metaphysics.* P. Bertocci et al. (eds.). New York: Ronald, 1958.

An introduction to metaphysical problems from the standpoint of a personalist.

Ewing, A. C. *Idealism: A Critical Survey.* 3rd ed. New York: Humanities Press, 1961.

Ewing writes a critical discussion of the idealism that dominated philosophy during the nineteenth century.

Harris, E. E. *Nature, Mind, and Modern Science.* New York: Humanities Press, 1954.

The author is especially critical of logical empiricism and of any philosophy that rejects the immanence of mind in nature.

Reck, A. *Speculative Philosophy.* Albuquerque: University of New Mexico Press, 1972.

Professor Reck's helpful book defines what speculative philosophy is as well as ascertaining its four major types: realism, materialism, idealism, and process philosophy. He concludes with a chapter on the uses of speculative philosophy.

Reeve, C. D. C. *Philosopher-Kings: The Argument of Plato's Republic.* Princeton, N.J.: Princeton University Press, 1988.

An exploration that makes the case for the enduring relevance of Plato to contemporary issues in moral and political philosophy.

Urban, W. M. *Beyond Realism and Idealism.* New York: Humanities Press, 1949.

The author maintains that there is an irrefutable element in both idealism and realism and that these philosophies are complementary. For advanced students.

Notes

1. W. M. Urban, *Beyond Realism and Idealism* (London: Allen and Unwin, 1949), p. 38.

2. W. E. Hocking, *Types of Philosophy* (New York: Scribner's, 1939), p. 389. See also the 3rd ed., 1959, with the collaboration of R. Hocking, p. 225.

3. P. T. Raju, *Idealistic Thought of India* (London: Allen and Unwin, 1953), pp. 7, 13. Others, including S. N. Dasgupta and S. Radhakrishnan, have spoken of the dominant philosophies in India as *idealistic.*

4. Since the time of Hegel there have been many systems of objective idealism. Omitting the contemporary thinkers, there are Josiah Royce, W. M. Urban, and W. E. Hocking in the United States, and T. H. Green, Edward Caird, and F. H. Bradley in England—to mention only a few.

5. J. Macmurray, *The Philosophy of Communism* (London: Faber and Faber, 1933), pp. 21–22.

6. A. N. Whitehead, *Science and the Modern World* (New York: Macmillan, 1925), pp. 129*ff.*

7. E. B. Holt et al., eds. *The New Realism* (New York: Macmillan, 1912). The group consisted of Edwin B. Holt, Walter T. Marvin, William Pepperell Montague, Ralph Barton Perry, Walter P. Pitkin, and Edward G. Spaulding.

8. For example, S. Alexander, *Space, Time and Deity* (New York: Macmillan, 1920).

9. D. Drake et al., eds. *Essays in Critical Realism* (New York: Macmillan, 1920) [Reprint, New York: Peter Smith, 1941]. This group included Durant Drake, A. O. Lovejoy, James B. Pratt, A. K. Rogers, George Santayana, Roy W. Sellars, and C. A. Strong.

10. Alexander, "The Basis of Realism," in Roderick M. Chisholm, ed., *Realism and the Background of Phenomenology,* (Glencoe: Free Press, 1960), p. 186.

11. R. B. Perry, *Philosophy of the Recent Past* (New York: Scribner's, 1926), p. 201.

12. Whitehead, *Science and the Modern World,* p. 131.

13. *Retrospection and Introspection* (Boston: Published by the Trustees under the Will of Mary Baker G. Eddy, 1892) p. 24.

14. *Science and Health with Key to the Scriptures* (Boston: 1906), p. 113.

Pragmatism

CHAPTER OBJECTIVES

In this chapter we will address the following questions:

◆ What Is Pragmatism?

◆ Who Are the Major Pragmatists and How Do They Differ?

◆ How Is Pragmatism Related to American Philosophy?

Pragmatism grew out of American life and experience; it was not in the main an academic movement, and its chief expositors were marked by independence of judgment.[1]

Pragmatism Defined

❖❖❖❖❖❖❖❖❖

Pragmatism is essentially an American philosophical movement that has come to prominence during the last hundred years. It has been called "a new name for an old way of thinking." It strongly reflects some of the characteristics of American life. Pragmatism is connected with such names as Charles S. Peirce (1839–1914), William James (1842–1910), and John Dewey (1859–1952). Pragmatism seeks to mediate between the empirical and idealist traditions and to combine what is most significant in each of them. Pragmatism is an attitude, a method, and a philosophy that uses the practical consequences of ideas and beliefs as a standard for determining their value and truth. William James defined pragmatism as "the attitude of looking away from first things, principles, 'categories,' supposed necessities; and of looking towards last things, fruits, consequences, facts."[2]

Pragmatism places greater emphasis on method and attitude than on a systematic philosophical doctrine. It is the method of experimental inquiry extended into all realms of human experience. Pragmatism uses the modern scientific method as the basis of a philosophy. Its affinity is with the sciences, especially the biological and social sciences, and it aims to utilize the scientific spirit and scientific knowledge to deal with all human problems, including those of ethics and religion.

As a movement in philosophy, pragmatism was founded for the purpose of mediating between two opposing tendencies in nineteenth-century thought. There was empiricism and science, to which Darwin's theory of evolution had contributed the most recent description of who human beings are. This tradition looked at the world and humans as parts of a mechanical or biological process in which the mind was an observer. There was also the tradition coming from Descartes and his rationalism and moving through the critical idealism of Kant, the absolute idealism of Hegel, and later romantic thought. In this, the human mind had enormous power, so that philosophers proceeded to construct theories about the whole nature of things, ending up with a "block universe."

Between these two traditions there was a gulf. From the scientific point of view, rationalist and idealist philosophies lacked objective evidence to support their claims. From the rational and idealist points of view, the assumptions of science were a threat to the humanistic side and the moral and religious convictions of human beings. Pragmatism sought to mediate between these two traditions.

The pragmatists said that philosophy in the past had made the mistake of looking for ultimates, absolutes, eternal essences, substances, fixed principles, and metaphysical "block systems." The pragmatists emphasized empirical science and the changing world and its problems, and nature as the reality beyond which we cannot go. For John Dewey, *experience* is central. Experience is the result of the interaction of the organism with its environment. Although the idea of experience for the pragmatists was not limited to "sense experience," nonetheless they agreed with the empirical tradition that we have no conception of the whole of reality, that we know things from many perspectives, and that we must settle for a pluralistic approach to knowledge.

Charles S. Peirce

❖❖❖❖❖❖❖❖❖❖

Charles S. Peirce (pronounced *purse*), sometimes called the founder of pragmatism, was influenced by Kant and Hegel. Peirce considered that problems, including those of metaphysics, could be solved if one gave careful attention to the practical consequences of adherence to various ideas. Pragmatism is sometimes said to have originated in 1878, when Peirce published the article "How To Make Our Ideas Clear."[3] *Popular Science Mo.*

The philosophical writings of Peirce consist of essays and manuscripts, many of which are fragmentary or incomplete. Although he never wrote a book in philosophy or organized his thoughts into systematic or final form, his literary activity covered many years. With the publication of his papers in recent decades, interest in Peirce's philosophy is increasing, and he is coming to be recognized as an intellectual genius of outstanding originality. He was the rare combination of a natural scientist with a "laboratory habit of mind," a careful student of philosophy, and a man with strong moral convictions. He is sometimes referred to as a philosopher's philosopher, rather than a public or popular philosopher, such as James.

Peirce was primarily a logician concerned with the more technical problems of logic and epistemology, and the methods of the laboratory sciences. He was interested in deductive systems, methodology in the empirical sciences, and the philosophy behind the various methods and techniques. His logic included a theory of signs and symbols, a field in which he did pioneer work. He viewed logic as a means of communication and a cooperative or public venture. His approach was to invite critical examination and seek aid from others in a continuous quest for the clarification of ideas. Peirce wished to establish philosophy on a scientific basis and to treat theories as working hypotheses. He called his approach **pragmaticism.**

One of Peirce's main contributions to philosophy is his theory of meaning. He coined the word *pragmatism* from the Greek word *pragma* ("act" or "deed") to emphasize the fact that words derive their meanings from actions. He set forth one of the first modern theories of meaning by proposing a technique for the clarification of ideas. The meaning of many ideas, Peirce said, is best discovered by putting them to an experimental test and observing the results. His criterion of meaningfulness was to appeal to the way an object *would* behave if it had a certain character or were of a certain kind. If an object were "hard" it would scratch other objects; if it were "volatile," it would evaporate rapidly, and the like. Peirce argued that thinking always occurs in a context, not in isolation. Meanings are derived not by intuition but by experience or experiment. For these reasons, meanings are not individual or private but are social and public. If there is no way of testing an idea by its effects or public consequences, it is meaningless. To be able to distinguish between meaningful and meaningless is particularly important, Peirce thought, when you are considering opposing systems of thought.

Peirce's empiricism is intellectualistic rather than voluntaristic; that is, emphasis is on the intellect and understanding rather than on will and activity. The irritation of doubt leads to the struggle to attain belief. The end of this inquiry, which aims to dispel doubt, is knowledge. Thus he does not stress sensation or volition as much as do later forms of popular pragmatism. Peirce is critical of positivism and mechanistic determinism, on the one hand, and intuitionism and a priori principles, on the other hand. Although he shares some of the positivists' views, he does not share with them the idea that empiricism requires a denial of the possibility of metaphysics. In the field of metaphysics as well as in all other areas of discourse, we must avoid the belief that we have attained finality. Peirce supports "fallibilism"; even the most intelligent people are apt to be mistaken. Progressive inquiry leads to constant modification. There is chance (tychism) because, Peirce maintained, although nature behaves in a lawlike way, that regularity is never exact. Chance, as well as habit, plays a real part in the occurrence of events in the world. Fallibilism and an open future replace skepticism and absolutism, and pragmatism replaces fixed systems of belief in philosophy and in science. Although Peirce gave his major attention to logic and methodology, his writings make clear that he left a place for an evolutionary idealism that stresses the need for a principle of love opposed to any narrow individualism in human affairs.

William James

◆ ◆ ◆ ◆ ◆ ◆ ◆ ◆ ◆ ◆

A complete discussion of the people who influenced William James (see biography and excerpt, pp. 292–293) would take us back to Lange, Mach, Pearson, and Renouvier, as well as to Peirce; we will have to be content with a mere mention of these names. The rapid development of pragmatism was due

William James

William James (1842–1910) was born in New York City in a home where there was spirited and wide-ranging discussion that stimulated free intellectual growth. James became an original thinker; he read widely in the literature of experimental psychology and studied the works of John Stuart Mill, Kant, and Hegel. From 1855 to 1860, he studied in England, France, Switzerland, and Germany. His interests shifted from painting to natural science and medicine, to psychology, and then to philosophy. From 1872 until his death, he taught at Harvard University, first in physiology, then psychology, and finally philosophy. He wrestled with questions such as: What does it mean to be a human being? To what extent are humans free? How do ideas affect our lives? We need, James thought, to exercise a "will to believe."

James was a highly social person whose friends, including Oliver Wendell Holmes and Ralph Waldo Emerson, formed an influential intellectual community. He gave public lectures, became a leader in the movement known as *pragmatism*, and wrote a number of books that are classics in American philosophy. His writings include *The Principles of Psychology* (1890); *The Will to Believe* (1897); *The Varieties of Religious Experience* (1902); *Pragmatism* (1907); *The Meaning of Truth* and *A Pluralistic Universe* (1909); and, published after his death, *Some Problems in Philosophy* (1911); and *Essays in Radical Empiricism* (1912).

largely to the fertile soil it found in America and to the brilliant exposition made by William James. In his book *Pragmatism,* James contrasts the tender-minded rationalist, who usually has an idealistic and optimistic outlook, with the tough-minded empiricist, the lover of facts, who is often a materialist and a pessimist. To both of these James says, "I offer the oddly-named thing pragmatism as a philosophy that can satisfy both kinds of demands. It can remain religious like the rationalisms, but at the same time, like the empiricisms, it can preserve the richest intimacy with facts."[4]

RADICAL EMPIRICISM

James defines the term *radical empiricism* this way: "I say 'empiricism' because it is contented to regard its most assured conclusions concerning matters of fact as hypotheses liable to modification in the course of future experience."[5] He says, "To be radical, an empiricism must neither admit into its constructions any element that is not directly experienced, nor exclude from them any element that is directly experienced."[6] James includes relations, such as *greater than*, among the latter (directly experienced) elements.

[Determinism] professes that those parts of the universe already laid down absolutely appoint and decree what the other parts will be. The future has no ambiguous possibilities hidden in its womb: the part we call the present is compatible with only one totality. Any other future complement than the one fixed from eternity is impossible. The whole is in each and every part, and welds it with the rest into an absolute unity, an iron block, in which there can be no equivocation or shadow of turning.

> With earth's first clay they did the last man knead,
> And there of the last harvest sowed the seed.
> And the first morning of creation wrote
> What the last dawn of reckoning shall read.

Indeterminism, on the contrary, says that the parts have a certain amount of loose play on one another, so that the laying down of one of them does not necessarily determine what the others shall be. It admits that possibilities may be in excess of actualities, and that things not yet revealed to our knowledge may really in themselves be ambiguous. Of two alternative futures which we conceive, both may now be really possible; and the one becomes impossible only at the very moment when the other excludes it by becoming real itself. Indeterminism thus denies the world to be one unbending unit of fact. It says there is a certain ultimate pluralism in it; and, so saying, it corroborates our ordinary unsophisticated view of things.

W. James, *The Will to Believe and Other Essays and Popular Philosophy* (New York: Longmans, Green, 1904).

Pragmatism, as we have seen, is the practice of looking toward results and facts instead of toward first principles and categories. It accepts the experiences and facts of everyday life as fundamental. Reality is just what it is experienced as being—flux or change. Because experience is fragmentary, pragmatists find things partly joined and partly disjoined, and accept them as they are. Consequently, they insist that reality is pluralistic rather than monistic or dualistic. There is *the given*—the data of the senses—which is brought in as stimuli from the region beyond us. Added to this is the *interpretative element,* which the conscious being supplies. The creative whole of experience, which includes both the given and the interpretative element, is the one reality we know. Knowledge is thus based directly on sense perception, or experience, which constitutes the continuous, flowing stream of consciousness.

JAMES' THEORY OF TRUTH

William James said, "Truth happens to an idea." What was so startling about this statement was that the more traditional theories of truth took virtually the opposite view—namely, that truth was a fixed or static relation. When James examined the traditional theories of truth, he demanded to know what "truth" means in operation. Truth must be the cash value of an idea. What other motive could there be for saying that something is true or not than to provide guides for practical behavior? James would ask, "What concrete difference will it make in life?" "A difference that makes no difference *is* no difference," but only a matter of words. An idea becomes true or is made true by events. An idea is true if it works or if it has satisfactory consequences. Truth is relative; it also grows. The true is "the expedient in the way of our thinking," just as the right is "the expedient in the way of our behaving." Ideas, doctrines, and theories become instruments to help us meet life situations; doctrines are not answers to riddles. A theory is created to suit some human purpose, and the only satisfactory criterion of the truth of a theory is that it leads to beneficial results. *Workability, satisfactions, consequences,* and *results* are the key words in the pragmatic conception of truth.

PRAGMATIC VIEW OF MORALITY

Within James's view, morality, like truth, is not fixed but grows out of present life situations. The source and authority for beliefs and conduct are found in human experience. The good is that which makes for a more satisfactory life; the evil is that which tends to destroy life. James was a strong defender of moral freedom and indeterminism; he believed that determinism is an intellectualistic falsification of experience. He supported the doctrine of **meliorism,** which holds that the world is neither completely evil nor completely good but is capable of being improved. Human effort to improve the world is worthwhile and fruitful, and the trend of biological and social evolution is toward such improvement.

THE WILL TO BELIEVE

James devoted considerable attention to religion. The doctrines of pluralism and meliorism, as well as the doctrine of the will to believe, all contributed to his views of religion and of God. He acknowledged later that "the will to believe" might have been called "the right to believe."

Let us consider first James's doctrine of the will to believe. We have pointed out that radical empiricism ceases to look beyond experience for supposed necessities and metaphysical entities and stresses the present stream of consciousness. Consciousness displays interest, desire, and attention; it is volitional as well as sensory, and the will rather than the intellect is determinative. The will determines how and what we experience; thus thinking is empirically secondary to willing. What is selected and emphasized is thereby made vital and real; thus, the world we experience is largely of our own making.

As with our sensory perceptions, so with our ideas. Those ideas that interest us and engage our attention tend to exclude others and to dominate the scene; and these ideas tend to find expression in our actions. In life, individuals have to make numerous decisions. How are they to make these decisions and formulate their beliefs? In some situations the evidence is reasonably certain and clear, and in these circumstances they need to act in accordance with the evidence. In other situations, in which a choice between the proposed lines of action either is not forced or is trivial, they can postpone their decisions or even refrain from choosing at all. There are still other situations, however, in which individuals facing some crucial issue must choose and act, because failure to decide will commit them to one of the alternatives. If such issues are *living, forced,* and *momentous,* people need to act even though they do not have all the evidence on the basis of which they would like to make their decisions. James' doctrine of the will to believe applies to this third type of situation, where some decision is demanded by the structure of the situation. For example, shall I marry this woman (or man) or shall I wait until I know for certain how the marriage will turn out? I cannot know for certain that the marriage will be harmonious and successful. All the facts are not known and I cannot wait until all the evidence is in, yet the issue is living, forced, and momentous. To fail to act is in itself a decision—not to marry this person at this time. When the will to believe leads to decision and action, it leads to discovery and conviction, or to truth and value simply through the fact that the will exists. Life's values are empirical and are found and tested in the process of living.

According to James, in many of life's experiences, we have contact with a "More." We feel that which is sympathetic and gives us "support." We rely on it in worship and in prayer. This sense of the "More" brings comfort, happiness, and peace; furthermore, it is an almost universal experience. In the religious sense, God is the name of this ideal tendency or encompassing support in human experience.

James, as we have seen, was impressed by the novelty, freedom, individuality, and diversity inherent in our world. Consequently, he insisted that God is finite. There are real possibilities for evil as well as for good in our world; no good, all-powerful God could have created the world as we know it. God is, however, moral and friendly, and we can cooperate with God in creating a better world. *Tie in w/ Hegel's A.S.*

John Dewey

♦ ♦ ♦ ♦ ♦ ♦ ♦ ♦ ♦ ♦ ♦

The continued growth and strength of pragmatism can be attributed to John Dewey's (see biography and excerpt, pp. 296–297) prolific writings and his application of the principles of the movement to all phases of life and thought. Dewey achieved prominence in logic, epistemology, ethics, aesthetics, and political, economic, and educational philosophies. For Dewey and his many followers, the term **instrumentalism** is preferred to the term *pragmatism,* but both are used.

Dewey was a keen and a constant critic of the classical or traditional types of philosophies, with their search for ultimate reality and their attempt to find the immutable. Such philosophies, Dewey claimed, attempt to minimize or transcend human experience. In *The Quest for Certainty,* Dewey says that we have used two methods to escape dangers and gain security. One is to appease or conciliate the powers around us by ceremonial rites, sacrifices, supplication, and so on. The second is to invent tools to control the forces of nature to our advantage. This is the way of science, industry, and the arts, and it is the way Dewey approves. The aim of philosophy is the better organization of human life and activity here and now. Interest thus shifts from traditional metaphysical problems to the methods, attitudes, and techniques for scientific and social progress. The method is that of experimental inquiry as guided by empirical research in the area of values.

EXPERIENCE AND THE CHANGING WORLD

Experience is one of the key words in Dewey's pragmatic theory. Dewey's philosophy is *of* and *for* daily experience. In his essay "The Need for a Recovery of Philosophy," Dewey sets down his criticisms of the traditional or inherited view of experience as found in empiricism and offers a substitute interpretation. The orthodox empirical view regards experience primarily as a knowledge affair (see Chapter 9). Dewey prefers to see experience as "an affair of the intercourse of a living being with its social and physical environment."[7] Experience for Dewey is primarily experimental and is not tied to what has been or what is "given"; experience involves an effort to change the given by reaching forward into the unknown. Dewey refuses to attempt to transcend human experience or to believe that anyone else has ever succeeded in doing so. In the past, philosophers attempted to discover some "theoretical superexperience" on the basis of which they might build a secure and meaningful life. Dewey insists that "experience is not a veil that shuts man off from nature"; it is the only means we have of penetrating further into the secrets of nature.

This present world of men and women, of fields and factories, of plants and animals, of bustling cities and struggling nations, is the world of our experience. We should try to understand it and then attempt to construct a

John Dewey

John Dewey (1859–1952) was born in Burlington, Vermont, and grew from a shy youth to a man whose influence spread throughout the world. After his graduation from the University of Vermont, he taught classics, science, and algebra for a short time in high school and later received his Ph.D. degree from The Johns Hopkins University. He taught for ten years at the University of Michigan, for a short period at the University of Minnesota, and for ten years at the University of Chicago. In 1904, he went to Columbia University and remained on the staff there until his retirement in 1930.

John Dewey was a defender of the democratic process and an outspoken champion of social reform. He wanted to make philosophy relevant to the practical problems and affairs of humanity. He lectured in the United States and in a number of other countries. He was in Beijing, the capital of China, for two years lecturing and aiding in the reorganization of the educational system. He spent shorter periods in Japan, Turkey, Mexico, and Russia. After his retirement, Dewey remained active and continued to write many articles and books not only on philosophy and logic but also on art, education, science, and social and political reform. He was a leader in various humanitarian causes. A bibliography of his writings runs to more than 150 pages. Among his books are *Democracy and Education* (1916); *Reconstruction in Philosophy* (1920); *Experience and Nature* (1925; 2nd ed., 1929); *Art as Experience* (1934); and *Freedom and Culture* (1939).

society in which all can grow in freedom and intelligence.

Dewey takes evolution, relativity, and the time process seriously. The world is in the making; it is constantly moving forward. This view of the world stands in marked contrast to that of a fixed and permanent reality, which dominated Greek and medieval thinking and has characterized many areas of modern science.

Dewey was born in 1859, the year Darwin published *Origin of Species*. Not since Aristotle has any philosopher built his or her thought so completely on biological foundations. The vision of human beings as always changing and developing in the midst of an environment that fosters and at the same time threatens their lives was decisive for Dewey. Organism and environment, development and struggle, precariousness and stability—these are the basic elements that humans face. Dewey put these elements together in the unifying idea of *experience*.

According to Dewey, we live in an unfinished world. Dewey's attitude can best be understood by an examination of three aspects of what we call his instrumentalism. First, the notion of temporalism means that there is real movement and progress in time. We can no longer hold a spectator view of reality. Our

Plato's Allegory of the Cave

A criticism of current philosophizing from the standpoint of the traditional quality of its problems must begin somewhere, and the choice of a beginning is arbitrary. It has appeared to me that the notion of experience implied in the questions most actively discussed gives a natural point of departure. For, if I mistake not, it is just the inherited view of experience common to the empirical school and its opponents which keeps alive many discussions even of matters that on their face are quite remote from it, while it is also this view which is most untenable in the light of existing science and social practice. . . .

Suppose we take seriously the contribution made to our idea of experience by biology,—not that recent biological science discovered the facts, but that it has so emphasized them that there is no longer an excuse for ignoring them or treating them as negligible. Any account of experience must now fit into the consideration that experiencing means living; and that living goes on in and because of an environing medium, not in a vacuum. Growth and decay, health and disease, are alike continuous with activities of the natural surroundings. The difference lies in the bearing of what happens upon future life-activity. From the standpoint of this future reference environmental incidents fall into groups: those favorable to life-activities, and those hostile.

J. Dewey, *Creative Intelligence: Essays in the Pragmatic Attitude* (New York: Henry Holt, 1917).

knowledge does not merely mirror the world; it reshapes and changes it. Second, the notion of futurism bids us to look mainly to the future and not to the past. The future, which is growing out of the past, will not be a repetition but will be in some sense novel. Third, meliorism is the view that the world can be made better by our efforts, a view also held by William James.

THE METHOD OF INTELLIGENCE

Basic to Dewey's philosophy is the instrumental theory of ideas, the use of intelligence as a method. Thinking is biological; it is concerned with the adjustment between an organism and its environment. All thinking and all concepts, doctrines, logics, and philosophies are, in Dewey's words, part of the "protective equipment of the race in its struggle for existence."

Reflective thinking occurs when we face a problem or when our habits are blocked in particular crises. Intelligence is an instrument for the individual or society to gain some goal. There is no separate "mind stuff" gifted with a faculty for thinking. Mind is manifested in our capacity to respond to what is *doubtful* or *problematic* in experience. Knowing and acting are continuous. Knowing occurs within nature, and sensory and rational factors cease to be competitors and are both parts of a unifying process. Ideas are plans of action. Scientific theories, like other tools and instruments, are created by us in pursuit of particular interests and goals. The aim of thinking is to remake experienced reality through the use of experimental techniques.

FREEDOM AND CULTURE

According to Dewey's pragmatic outlook, humans and nature always are interdependent. We are not part body and part mind; we are naturalized within nature, and nature is so interpreted as to take account of us. Nature in humans is nature grown intelligent. Nature is neither rational nor irrational; it is intelligible and understandable. Nature is not something merely to be accepted and enjoyed; it is something to be modified and experimentally controlled.

Dewey and the modern instrumentalists have been staunch defenders of freedom and democracy. Dewey was a defender of moral freedom—or freedom of choice—of intellectual freedom, and of the political and civil liberties, including freedom of speech, of press, and of assembly. He advocated an extension of the democratic principles in the political and social realms to all races and classes. *Intellectual and political freedom contributes to adaptability.*

EDUCATIONAL PHILOSOPHY

Nothing is more important than education in remolding a society. If we are creatures of habit, education should provide the conditions for developing our most useful and creative habits. Instead of some catastrophic upheaval, such as a revolution, changing the habits of a culture, education can provide a more controlled approach to change. Instead of revolution, Dewey believed that those habits may be altered by education, but education of the sort that is available to every man in every walk of life. Thus he believed in universal education, which should extend over the entire culture and penetrate to its foundations. The demand that education be universal is

bound up with Dewey's conviction that there is a need to find a way to reorient society as a whole.

The spirit of education should be experimental. The mind is basically a problem-solving instrument and needs to try alternative means for solving problems. However, Dewey never said that education ought simply to cater to the needs and whims of the child. In one of his earliest writings on education, *The Child and the Curriculum,* he criticizes the child-oriented theory of education by noting that it contains an empty concept of development. Children are expected to "work things out for themselves" without receiving proper guidance. According to Dewey, advocating complete freedom for the child "reflects a sentimental idealization of the child's naive caprices and performances" and inevitably results in "indulgence and spoiling."[8] When unlimited free expression is allowed, children "gradually tend to become listless and finally bored." Dewey argues instead for the necessity of deliberate guidance, direction, and order. Education is, or ought to be, systematic and ordered, and thus the intelligent guidance of the teacher is necessary.

Dewey insisted that there be clear objectives in promoting the art of critical thinking. "Though there is widespread belief that American education has suffered from Dewey's influence, it would be more accurate to say that insofar as it has failed to develop the tough-minded habits of intelligence, it has failed to be influenced by what is most basic for Dewey."[9]

A COMMON FAITH

Dewey and many of his supporters reject all supernaturalism and ground both ethical and religious values solely in the natural relations of humans. The values of life are capable of verification by the methods through which other facts are established.

> There exist concretely and experimentally goods—the values of art in all its forms, of knowledge, of effort and of rest after striving,

of education and fellowship, of friendship and love, of growth in mind and body. These goods are there and yet they are relatively embryonic. Many persons are shut out from generous participation in them; there are forces at work that threaten and sap existent goods as well as prevent their expansion. A clear and intense conception of a union of ideal ends with actual conditions is capable of arousing steady emotion.[10]

Dewey was critical of the traditional institutional church, with its stress on fixed ritual and authoritarian dogma. He uses the adjective *religious* to describe those values through which one's personality is integrated and enriched. Thus any activity pursued on behalf of an ideal, because of an abiding conviction of its genuine value, is religious. The term *God* may be used if it refers to the unity of all ideal ends in their tendency to arouse us to desire and action.

Reflections

◆ ◆ ◆ ◆ ◆ ◆ ◆ ◆ ◆ ◆ ◆

Pragmatism has grown out of certain aspects of living, especially of contemporary American life. It is an expression of the mood of America, of the emphasis of modern technological society on getting things done and on satisfactory consequences. Pragmatism attempts to bring philosophy "down to earth" and to deal with the living issues of the day. According to Dewey, the aim of philosophy should be the improvement of human life and its environment, or the organization of life and its activities to meet human needs. We need, he says, a philosophy that makes life better here and now; the world is in the making, and our efforts will in part shape the future. If we accept the melioristic attitude and believe that life can be made better, we are more likely to create a better world. We need to face the facts of experience and to discover and live by those principles that stand the test of time and of daily living.

According to pragmatism, our knowledge does not merely mirror or reflect the world; thinking is a creative process that reshapes the world. Ideas and doctrines are instrumental and serve the process of adjustment between the organism and its environment. Beliefs are developed and tested by experimental methods and experience.

Pragmatism has generated a liberal habit of mind and a beneficial enthusiasm for social progress. Most pragmatists have been keen supporters of democracy and human freedom.

However, pragmatism has had various criticisms directed against it. Some people assert that pragmatism has an inadequate metaphysics. Pragmatists are likely to claim that speculations regarding the ultimate nature of reality misdirect our energies away from concrete problems. Pragmatists use scientific methods of inquiry and distrust traditional metaphysics, which rests on the spectator attitude toward the world. If the pragmatists stress experience and assert that reality is as it is experienced and that nature is to some extent created by people, they move in the direction of the subjective forms of idealism. However, if they stress the objective independent world, they move in the direction of realism.

Another criticism is that pragmatism has an inadequate view of mind. Mind is undoubtedly a biological aid to survival, as the pragmatists claim. However, some people believe that mind is much more than an instrument for satisfying the practical needs of food, clothing, and shelter. People are problem solvers but they also function in the realm of aesthetic contemplation and of ideas and ideals. We ask about the "why" and not only about the "how" of things. Some critics think that the instrumentalist view of mind as merely a description of certain kinds of behavior is unsatisfactory.

Critics also attack the pragmatic view that the discovery of truth is conditioned by human inquiry and that truth has no independent existence. Pragmatists may commit a fallacy when they say that "true propositions work in the long run" means that "all propositions that work are true." As truth is ordinarily understood, we do not think of ourselves as creating it by living correctly; on the contrary, we live correctly by grasping and following the truth.

Finally, critics ask whether pragmatism can be used to justify any social attitude that an individual or a group wishes to call progress. If the good is that which can be lived, is everything belonging to the evolutionary process good? Possibly pragmatism places too much emphasis on the goals we do seek—and not enough on the goals we *should* seek.

◆ ◆

Glossary Terms

INSTRUMENTALIST (INSTRUMENTALISM)   (1) Another term for the pragmatism of John Dewey and others. (2) Instrumentalism stresses experience and interprets thinking, ideas, and beliefs as means for the adjustment of an organism to its environment.

MELIORISM   The view that the world is neither entirely good nor entirely evil but can be made better through our efforts.

PRAGMATICISM   At one point of time, the name given by Peirce to his own thinking. (See pragmatism.)

PRAGMATISM   A philosophical outlook generated by C.S. Peirce and William James and further developed by John Dewey that emphasizes experience, experimental inquiry, and truth as that which has satisfactory consequences.

◆ ◆

Chapter Review

PRAGMATISM DEFINED

1. Pragmatism is an attitude, a method, and a philosophy that uses the practical consequences of ideas and beliefs as a standard for determining their value and truth.

2. Essentially an American philosophical movement, pragmatism has come to prominence in the last one hundred years.

3. Pragmatism is essentially empirical in method. However, experience for the pragmatists is not limited to "sense experience." We have no conception of the whole of reality; we know things from many perspectives and we must settle for a pluralistic approach to knowledge.

CHARLES S. PEIRCE

1. Peirce is often credited with founding pragmatism in 1878, when he published an early essay.

2. Concerned with logic, epistemology, and the methods of the laboratory sciences, he contributed an early modern theory of meaning to philosophy.

3. He proposed that by putting ideas to an experimental test and observing the results, we can discover their meaning.

4. Peirce supported "fallibilism" and "tychism."

WILLIAM JAMES

1. James' "radical empiricism" broadened the base of empiricism from the laboratory to human experiences and facts of daily life.

2. James' theory of truth stressed the criteria of satisfactory consequences, the difference an idea makes in life, the idea's workability.

3. He applied pragmatism to interpretations of morality; the doctrine of meliorism is important to his understanding of the world.

4. James was convinced that the will determines how and what we experience, and that therefore thinking is empirically secondary to willing. Thus, the world we experience is largely of our own selecting, our own choices.

5. His sense of the "More" is central to his views on religion. James interprets "God" as this "More."

JOHN DEWEY

1. Experience is one of the key concepts in Dewey's pragmatic outlook.

2. A critic of traditional philosophies that sought ultimate truths. Dewey was concerned with the better organization of human life and activity here and now. His method was experimental inquiry and guided by empirical research in the areas of values.

3. An understanding of daily experience and the construction of a better society are goals of Dewey's thought. The present world and society are evolving, and our efforts to shape its values are central human tasks.

4. Intelligence is an instrument for gaining goals. Mind is not a separate entity; the aim of thinking is to remake experienced reality through the use of experimental techniques.

5. Dewey was a defender of freedom of choice for all persons in all areas of life.

6. The spirit of education should be experimental, because the mind is basically a problem-solving instrument and therefore needs to try out alternatives. Deliberate guidance, direction, and order are necessary in education; clear objectives in promoting the art of critical thinking are central to Dewey's educational philosophy.

REFLECTIONS

1. American philosophy has been dominated by pragmatism. However, its critics have raised important issues for further consideration.

◆ ◆

Study Questions and Projects

1. Are you able to accept William James' doctrine of the will to believe? What are its values and its dangers? Are there safeguards you would like to add?

2. Give an account of the life of John Dewey, emphasizing his intellectual development and the factors that influenced his thinking.

3. Wherein does pragmatism agree with and differ from (a) idealism, (b) realism?

4. Do you think there is any justification for the charge sometimes made that pragmatism could be used to support many widely different systems of metaphysics or social philosophy? It is conceivable that several hypotheses about the same thing might "work" equally well?

5. Are there beliefs that cannot be verified on pragmatic grounds? Consider beliefs about the meaning of life, the worth of man, democracy, and life after death in the light of the above question.

6. What are the distinguishing features or emphases of pragmatism?

7. Indicate the part played by Charles S. Peirce in the development of pragmatism.

8. Give an exposition of the philosophy of William James, indicating his views of empiricism, truth, meliorism, and the will to believe.

9. How does the pragmatic view of truth differ from traditional interpretations?

10. Discuss the instrumentalism of John Dewey, indicating the distinctive points of emphasis in his philosophy.

11. What are the implications of accepting pragmatism, or instrumentalism, for logic, psychology, education, social philosophy, and religion?

12. What do you consider to be the strengths and weaknesses of pragmatism as a general philosophy of life?

13. The index of *The Encyclopedia of Philosophy,* under "Pragmatism," lists references to figures frequently classified as pragmatists (for example, C. I. Lewis, G. H. Mead, Ernest Nagel). Choose one person, not discussed in this chapter, and write a short report that brings out some of the distinctive ideas stressed by him or her.

• •

Suggested Readings

Boydston, J. A. (ed). *Guide to the Works of John Dewey.* Carbondale: Southern Illinois University Press, 1970.

A group of scholars have collaborated to produce this valuable guide to the writings and thinking of John Dewey in a dozen different fields.

Boydston, J. A. (ed). *John Dewey: The Collected Works.* Carbondale, Ill.: Southern Illinois University Press, 1975–1991.

Dewey's writings have been collected in thirty-seven volumes: *Early Works 1882–1898* (5 vols.); *Middle Works 1899–1924* (15 vols.); and *Later Works 1925–1953* (17 vols.), with an index published in 1992.

James, W. *Pragmatism.* New York: Longmans, Green, 1907. (Also Meridian paperback, 1965).

The beginner should start with these "popular essays" before reading *The Meaning of Truth; A Pluralistic Universe;* and *The Will to Believe* by the same author.

Morris, C. *The Pragmatic Movement in American Philosophy.* New York: Braziller, 1970.

Pragmatism is seen as a unified movement of ideas in which four leading exponents—Peirce, James, Dewey, and Mead—have unique but not conflicting points of emphasis.

Murphy, J. P. *Pragmatism: From Peirce to Davidson.* Boulder, Colo.: Westview, 1990.

A comprehensive discussion of American pragmatism which traces the development of pragmatism from Peirce through post-Quinean pragmatism.

Rorty, R. *Consequences of Pragmatism: Essays 1972–1980.* Minneapolis, Minn.: University of Minnesota Press, 1982.

The author interprets the story of philosophy from Plato to the contemporary period and suggests a new role for philosophy in contemporary culture.

Smith, J. E. *America's Philosophical Vision.* Chicago: University of Chicago Press, 1992.

The author proposes that American philosophers like Peirce, James, Royce, and Dewey have forged a unique philosophical tradition—one that is rich and complex enough to represent a genuine alternative to the analytic, phenomenological, and hermeneutical traditions that have originated in Britain or Europe.

———. *Purpose and Thought: The Meaning of Pragmatism.* London and New Haven: Hutchinson and Yale University Press, 1978.

In this book, the author sets out to rescue the philosophical ideas of pragmatism from obscurity and misunderstanding. He discusses the pragmatic theory of meaning, the relationship between the nature of action and thought, and contrasts the meaning of experience to the pragmatists with the meaning of experience in empiricism.

———. *The Spirit of American Philosophy.* New York: Oxford University Press, 1963.

Using Peirce, James, Royce, Dewey, and Whitehead as examples, the author says that American philosophy has its own original spirit. This spirit is found in three basic beliefs: that thinking is an activity, that ideas must make a difference, and that progress is guaranteed by the application of knowledge.

Notes

1. J. E. Smith, *The Spirit of American Philosophy* (New York: Oxford University Press, 1963), p. 198.

2. W. James, *Pragmatism* (New York: Longmans, Green, 1907), pp. 54–55.

3. It was to this paper that James referred in his address of 1898 "Philosophical Conceptions and Practical Results," in which he established Peirce as the founder of Pragmatism. The paper is reprinted in J. J. McDermott, ed., *The Writings of William James* (New York: Random House, 1967), pp. 345–62.

4. James, *Pragmatism,* p. 33.

5. W. James, *The Will to Believe and Other Essays* (New York: Longmans, Green, 1896), p. vii.

6. W. James, *Essays in Radical Empiricism* (New York: Longmans, Green, 1922), p. 42.

7. J. Dewey, *Creative Intelligence* (New York: Octagon Books, 1970), p. 7.

8. J. Dewey, *The Child and the Curriculum* (Chicago: University of Chicago Phoenix Books, 1902) with *The School and Society* (Chicago: University of Chicago Phoenix Books, 1900), p. 15.

9. R. J. Bernstein, ed., *On Experience, Nature, and Freedom: Representative Selections from John Dewey* (New York: Bobbs-Merrill, 1960), p. xii.

10. J. Dewey, *A Common Faith* (New Haven: Yale University Press, 1934), p. 51.

Analytic Philosophy

The traditional disputes of philosophers are, for the most part, as unwarranted as they are unfruitful. The surest way to end them is to establish beyond question what should be the purpose and method of a philosophical enquiry. And this is by no means so difficult a task as the history of philosophy would lead one to suppose. For if there are any questions which science leaves it to philosophy to answer, a straightforward process of elimination must lead to their discovery.[1]

Language and Philosophy

• • • • • • • • • • •

Language is the chief tool of philosophers and the medium through which they find expression. Consequently, they are sensitive to its ambiguities and defects, and sympathetic to efforts to clarify and improve it. The twentieth century has witnessed a growing interest in the problems of language and communication and the function of signs and symbols. This has led to the development of **semantics,** or the study of the meaning and the function of words and the relations between words and things, schools of linguistic or philosophical analysis, and symbolic logic. It has also led to a renewed attention to details of grammar and syntax. Most people take language pretty much for granted, like the air we breathe. At present, however, many specialists, including philosophers who use a "logical–analytic method," see the study of meaning and the principles and rules of language as the central problem of philosophy. The philosophers of the ancient world and the Middle Ages were concerned mainly with a reality that transcended that of the temporal world. Their search was for "being." The philosophers from the Renaissance to the nineteenth century looked inward; they were interested mainly in the self, ideas in the mind, and the problem of knowledge. These earlier interests have not disappeared from philosophy; some contemporary philosophers, however, restrict their attention to linguistic analysis and the details and theory of discourse. Words, definitions, propositions, hypotheses, axioms, principles of verification, and the like have come increasingly to be regarded as central topics of philosophical investigation. This field is complex and highly technical. We shall limit our discussion to a few of the issues raised.

Naming is an early step in acquiring knowledge. Ordinarily we are said not to know what a thing is unless we can name it, classify it, and locate it in some meaningful context. If we wish to say something about a thing we need a name (or symbol) for it, so that we can distinguish it from other things. The **name** is the symbol that stands for the thing named, which is called the **refer-**ent. By this device we take a word or symbol (spoken or written) and use it to refer to something (object, quality, relation) or to connect other words that stand for things, and so on. Different names *could* have been chosen, but once a particular one is selected in a given language, there must be an element of permanency about its use if confusion is to be avoided. Words are combined into sentences, which also have meaning, and we have a language as an instrument of discourse.

The ability to use language is one of our distinctive traits. Animals are restricted to natural cries, which are few in number and which seem to express feelings of pleasure or pain. Such sounds or expressions may accompany the presence of food, mates, or danger. With the development of consciousness, intelligence, and a social group, and with the invention and use of verbal symbols, humans acquired a potentiality for freedom and knowledge that no other animal possesses.

A spoken language, which appeals to the ear, has a great advantage over pictorial signs and gestures, which appeal to the eyes. Hearing has advantages over sight in that using the voice leaves the hands free, and sound radiates in many directions and can be heard even in the dark—the speaker does not need to be seen. All groups of people the world over have a spoken language. However, a spoken language has no independent objective permanence and may soon be lost from memory, and whatever knowledge the group may have acquired may also be lost.

The development of a written language is one of the important steps in the growth of a civilization. Without a written language there would be little progress. Speech is broken into its fundamental elements, and symbols are used for these as in the alphabet; a relatively permanent medium of expression and communication is created. A written language can be a storehouse of past knowledge, and it has the power to transcend some of the more obvious limitations of time and space and to resist the changes that take place in oral transmission. New methods of recording sounds, of course, may give speech (spoken language) a greater degree of permanency.

Language has many functions. Language has a **cognitive** function: it expresses propositions that we can test for accuracy and accept or reject. This is the knowledge sought in the various sciences, as well as in philosophy. Much of our language is *emotive:* it may be *expressive* of our feelings and moods or **evocative** and call forth an emotional response from others. Language may be *imperative:* it may command or direct in an attempt to control the actions of others. It may be *ceremonial,* as in many of our greetings and some of our conversations and rituals. Different disciplines may have their own terminology, so that we may have the language of science, literary and aesthetic pursuits, poetry, love, morals, and piety. Is it possible to confuse these different kinds and functions of languages and to assume that a statement is cognitive when it is emotive or imperative? Can an expression of a wish be accepted on occasion as verified knowledge?

We need to distinguish clearly between statements that point out or describe actual things in the world and the way these things are related and statements that have no referent in the external world. That is, we may use language to talk about objects or to talk about language or words. When we talk about objects like pencils, desks, animals, and the like, we are said to be using an "object-language," but when we talk about this object-language itself we are using a **meta-language.** We could even take a further step and talk about the language in which we talk about the object-language, but let's not complicate this problem any more than necessary! That I said something may be true; what I said may be false. A statement may be true in one language and be false or meaningless in the other language.

Language is more intimately connected with human experience than is often recognized. Some think of language merely as a fairly accurate recording of the items of experience that seem important to the individual and to society. People think of language as reflecting or portraying the world much as it is. However, language itself not only reflects our experiences

and the environmental conditions under which it has developed, but it also has a powerful influence on these experiences. Language imposes certain perceptual and conceptual viewpoints and in this way has an influence on our thoughts and actions. Language and thought may also at times take wings, so to speak, and create their own world.

Language may influence experience and thinking in innumerable and subtle ways because of our projection of the way it structures the world. Language may help mold the thoughts of those who use it, because there is an interaction between the culture and the linguistic forms that are in use. Concealed in the structure of different languages are a wide range of unconscious assumptions about life and the world of nature. After asserting that there are "as many different worlds upon the earth as there are languages," Clyde Kluckhohn says, "The lack of true equivalences between any two languages is merely the outward expression of inward differences between two peoples in premises, in basic categories, in the training of fundamental sensitivities, and in general view of the world."[2] These linguistic forms, like other cultural elements, usually have a long history and carry traditional meanings whose origins are obscure. Although there are often difficulties in translating accurately from one European language into another, the difficulties mount as one compares the languages of groups more widely separated in historical backgrounds and cultures. For example, the English language and European languages in general tend to center attention on objects and their characteristics. These languages are traditionally regarded as subject–predicate languages. The language of the Navaho Indians in America, on the other hand, is verb-centered—the main attention is paid to actions rather than to objects. Navaho language is more specific than English in some areas and less so in other areas. The world appears somewhat different to people using different symbols, vocabularies, and languages.

Is it possible that some of the baffling problems we face are the result of confusions in our linguistic forms and usages, and that clarification of the language might solve or at least eliminate these problems? This is the claim of a considerable number of philosophers.

Locke, Hume, and the Traditional Outlook

Before we consider some of the newer linguistic positions, we shall summarize the outlook to which they are a reaction. In the past two thousand years, Western philosophy, reinforced by Christianity, has attempted to furnish a world view, a life view, and a scale of values by which to live. One philosopher, C. E. M. Joad, sums up this traditional outlook as follows:

> The traditional Philosophy of Western Europe holds that, transcending the familiar world of things known to us by our senses and explored by science, there is another order of reality which contains values. Of these, Goodness, Beauty and Truth are preeminent, and constitute the grounds of ethics, aesthetics and logic respectively. In other words, it is because the universe is—or contains—a moral order that some things are right and some are wrong; because it contains an aesthetic order that some things are beautiful and some ugly, and because there is such a thing as truth that some judgments are true and some false. Many philosophers would add that the universe also includes deity and that deity is the source of the values, Goodness, Truth and Beauty, being, as religion puts it, the modes of God's revelation of Himself to man. Metaphysics—the study of the reality which transcends and underlies the familiar world—is, therefore, in part, the study of the values and of God.[3]

Alongside what is sometimes called the "Great Tradition" there developed, especially in England during the last few centuries, an empirical movement that has gained strength and has succeeded in confining the idea of experience to "sense experience." Including such thinkers as John Locke and David Hume, this movement was critical of metaphysics and what they considered to be merely speculative thinking and held that knowledge comes through our senses. John Locke (1632–1714) held that at birth the mind is like a blank tablet or photographic plate on which are registered impressions from the outside. Knowledge is derived only from the senses. Through reflection aided by memory, sensations are organized into the various disciplines or bodies of knowledge. Locke denied the existence of inborn, or innate, ideas and said that universals (or Platonic Ideas) are not transcendental but rather are "the inventions and creatures of the understanding, made by it for its own use." David Hume (1711–1776) carried the empirical tradition even further. Simple ideas, he said, are copies of simple sensations, and complex ideas are formed from the combination of simple ideas or from complex impressions. The general effect of Hume's position was to deny the validity of the notion that there are abstract and general ideas. Hume attacked the traditional concepts of substance and causality and carried the skeptical implications of his position over into the fields of ethics and religion. This empiricism received further support in the nineteenth and twentieth centuries from the influence of the sciences.

The Empirical Tradition

The groups that carried on and supported the empirical tradition were the French positivists of the nineteenth century, the **logical positivists** and the Vienna Circle, and the English schools of philosophical analysis. These groups support and reinforce one another although they have not combined. They constitute, along with such philosophers as John Locke and David Hume, a school of thought that we refer to as the empirical tradition.

AUGUSTE COMTE

The tendency to base knowledge on sense perceptions and the investigations of objective science and to discard metaphysical world views led to a position known in France as positivism.

Positivism limits knowledge to statements of observable facts and their interrelations. The French philosopher Auguste Comte (1798–1857) (see biography and excerpt, pp. 310–311), a pioneer in sociology and an advocate of a "religion of humanity," was the founder and leading exponent of positivism. Comte chiefly directed his efforts toward political philosophy and the reform of society. He divided the history of humanity into three periods, each of which is characterized by a certain way of thinking. The first period is the theological, in which imagination has free play, events are explained by the control and intervention of spirits and gods, and the world is defined in animistic or supernatural terms. The second period is the metaphysical, in which events are explained by such abstractions as causes, inner principles, and substances. These abstractions replace supernatural agencies. The third, or "positive," is the final and highest period. This is the period of scientific description, which does not attempt to go beyond observable and measurable facts. People give up their earlier efforts to discover the causes, the destiny, and the ultimate nature of things. What, if anything, is "beyond" this world of experience is of no concern, and we should confine our attention to this world. Positivism is the final stage of human thought, and the task of science at this stage is to make the present world safe for humanity.

According to this school of thought, knowledge is valuable only because it helps people modify conditions in the material world and society. For this purpose, we need to know only phenomena and the laws under which things operate. Comte replaces supernatural religion and metaphysical unity with humanity and social progress.

LOGICAL POSITIVISM AND THE VIENNA CIRCLE

Largely because of Ernst Mach and Moritz Schlick, who succeeded Mach in 1922 as professor of the philosophy of the inductive sciences at the University of Vienna, a group of positivists influenced philosophical thought not only in Austria and Germany but also eventually throughout the West. The members of this group, especially active during the 1920s and 1930s, were scientists, mathematicians, or people who had done their main professional work in symbolic logic and scientific methodology. Whereas the earlier positivism was founded on nineteenth-century science, the new developments were based on more recent logical and scientific concepts. The movement has been variously designated "logical positivism," the "Vienna Circle,"[4] **logical empiricism,** and "scientific empiricism." It is said of this school of thought that:

> The forerunners of logical empiricism are, in the opinion of the members of the movement themselves, all those philosophers and scientists who show a clear antimetaphysical or antispeculative, realistic or materialistic, critical or skeptical tendency—as well as everyone who has contributed essentially to the development of their most important methodological instrument: symbolic logic.[5]

The members of the Vienna Circle were especially interested in working out a secure intellectual foundation for all science. They thought that the sciences, although not now highly unified, belong logically to one coherent system. The problem was to find an inclusive terminological and conceptual system common to all the sciences and not limited to one or only a few of them. This led to a study of the language of particular sciences and an analysis of language in general in the hope of finding a universal language of science. The members of this philosophical group believe the proper task of philosophy to be the analysis of language, especially the language of science.

The approach represents a definite shift from the methods and tactics of traditional philosophy. Instead of attacking the arguments of the traditional philosophers per se, the members of this school turned to an analysis of language in an attempt to show that some of the older issues are meaningless as presented. Logical positivists tend to claim that their method or approach is independent of a metaphysics. Their critics, however, challenge this claim.

In the 1930s, the threat and reality of totalitarianism overcame Central Europe and forced the members of the Vienna Circle to flee to England and the United States, where they continued their investigations. Thus their influence reached the English-speaking world.

ENGLISH SCHOOLS OF PHILOSOPHICAL ANALYSIS

Early in the twentieth century, certain philosophers, including G. E. Moore, Bertrand Russell, C. D. Broad, and Ludwig Wittgenstein, became interested in linguistic study and the logical analysis of terms, concepts, and propositions. The new direction was in part a reaction to certain idealists, namely F. H. Bradley, who held a position somewhat similar to that of Hegel, considered in Chapter 13.

Some late-nineteenth-century rationalists who were absolute idealists had viewed the world as a single, indivisible whole in which the only self-contained entity was reality itself—the Absolute or God. One reaction to such a rigid monism was an extreme pluralism, which described the world as consisting of an indefinitely large number of separate elements. Partly because of the desire to avoid the metaphysical implications of the concept "pluralism," and partly because of revised analytic methods, the philosophical analysts shifted their outlook and the terms *logical empiricism* and *analytic philosophy* came to be used. Although they claimed that linguistic analysis is the only legitimate activity of philosophers, the analysts were not in agreement regarding many philosophical questions, such as determinism, behaviorism, or even some religious beliefs and metaphysical questions. With some exceptions, however, the later analysts either avoid making metaphysical statements or reject metaphysical questions as meaningless.

The fact that Russell and Wittgenstein had come to philosophy by way of symbolic logic and mathematics was also partly responsible for the rise of philosophical analysis. The philosophical analysts and the members of the Vienna Circle also influenced one another. Could the disagreement among philosophers, they asked, be rooted in the ambiguities of ordinary language rather than in the complicated nature of the world? A belief that this might be so led some philosophers to be concerned with the language in which ideas are expressed and with an analysis of the structure of that language.

Looking back over the history of philosophy, the linguistic analysts thought they saw evidence that analysis of language had in fact always been stressed, although superficially it appeared that nonlinguistic points were at issue. They called attention to Plato's analysis of concepts like "justice," to Socrates' effort to clarify the meaning of terms like *courage, goodness,* and *piety,* and to Hume's rigorous examination of statements about causality.

Hume held that statements about matters of fact are contingent and that, although their contradictories are false, they are not self-contradictory. Certain statements about relations between ideas, on the other hand, such as "a plane triangle has three sides and three angles," are necessary and are certified as true solely in accordance with the principle of contradiction. Thus, to say, "a plane triangle has two sides" not only is false but is self-contradictory. Hume separated the empirical and the rational; what is empirical (contingent) is not necessary and what is necessary is not empirical.

Kant reformulated the issue by introducing two distinctions: the first between *analytic* and *synthetic;* the second between *a priori* and *a posteriori.* The former involves the relation between the subject and predicate of a judgment, and the latter involves the status of a judgment as a whole. In an analytic judgment, the predicate is part of what is thought in the subject ("all triangles have three angles"); it is governed by the principle of contradiction and is said to be *necessary.* In synthetic judgment, the predicate is not part of what is thought in the subject ("the building is tall") and the connection between the two, although subject to the principle of

Auguste Comte

Auguste Comte (1798–1857) was born in Montpellier, France, and became a leader of French Positivism, which emphasized the objective examination of all phenomena. While in his teens he rejected many of the traditions of his family, including their devout Catholicism and support of royalty. He studied in a polytechnic school in Paris and was a brilliant student in mathematics and science, but he was expelled in 1816 for participating in a student rebellion. He remained in Paris and continued his research in science, economics, history, and philosophy. He developed a new science of humanity, which he called Sociology. He sought to discover the laws that governed the development of the mind and explained social phenomena. In a six-volume work, *Course of Positive Philosophy* (1830–1842), he described the three ways by which people try to understand their world (see accompanying text). Despite mental illness during his later years, he was able to produce this major work.

Kant was right; only they're not judgments, they're forms of life.

contradiction, is not wholly determined by it and depends on experience. By *a priori*, Kant meant a judgment that is universal and necessary and stems from the faculties of understanding and reason. An *a posteriori* judgment is based on experience and is contingent. The singular trait of Kant's theory of knowledge is his claim that there are some fundamental judgments in science and philosophy that are *both* synthetic and *a priori* ("every event has a cause"). If these judgments create difficulties in metaphysics (as Hume insisted), they create the same ones in mathematics and physics. Kant believed, therefore, that if synthetic *a priori* judgments could be explained or justified in mathematics and physics, they would also be justified in metaphysics. This was Kant's challenge to empiricism:

there are judgments that are universal and necessary but not analytic and hence not certifiable by the principle of contradiction.

The crucial transformation of Kant's view at the hands of the logical empiricists was the collapsing of a priori into analytic; not only was Kant's problem eliminated, but it became impossible to *state* the problem because one would have to speak of "analytic synthetic" judgments, which is absurd. The result was that the logical empiricists returned to the position of Hume: what is necessary cannot be empirical (or synthetic) and what is empirical cannot be necessary.

Analysis was not a new device but a well-established philosophical method stressed especially by the empiricists. What was new, the linguistic analysts said, was the extra rigor and

They reduced judgments to statements, mental acts to linguistic acts; they changed the rules of the language game Kant was playing and then declared victory.

Studying the total development of the human intelligence in its various spheres of activity, from its first trial flights up to our own day, I believe I have discovered a fundamental law to which it is subjected from an invariable necessity, and which seems to me to be solidly established, either by rational proof drawn from a knowledge of our nature, or by the historical test, an attentive examination of the past. This law is that each of our principal conceptions, each branch of our knowledge, passes successively through three different theoretical states: the theological or fictitious, the metaphysical or abstract, and the scientific or positive. In other words, the human mind, by its nature, employs in all its investigations three methods of philosophising, of an essentially different and even opposed nature: first the theological, then the metaphysical, and finally the positive. Hence there are three mutually exclusive kinds of philosophy, or conception systems regarding the totality of phenomena: the first is the necessary starting-point of human intelligence; the third its fixed and final state; the second is only a means of transition.

A. Comte, *Introduction to Positive Philosophy*, ed. F. Ferré (Indianapolis, Ind.: Bobbs-Merrill, 1970). This book represents the first two chapters of the first volume of *Course in Positive Philosophy*.

precision, the increased subtlety and exactness of the symbolic methods, and the explicit claim that what is being done is linguistic analysis. Sometimes, the aim is to make every statement correspond, insofar as is possible, to the data or experience to which it refers. At other times, the aim is to clarify just what is at issue—a linguistic point, an empirical matter—and eliminate confusion. For example, a philosopher may be stipulating a definition when he or she appears to be giving a new insight about the world.

Contemporary analysts generally are empiricists, and most of them accept as meaningful only statements that are capable of empirical verification or that are about how we use terms. Statements that are not based on experiences or that cannot be verified are regarded as nonsensical or as having some noncognitive function. All the genuine data of experience, they say, are the province of some special science. Philosophy properly deals with language—in other words, once the philosopher has decided that a statement is meaningful and makes some claim about the world and not merely about the way we use words, it is up to the scientist to verify the statement. What is new is that attention is directed toward analysis and criticism, with synthesis and the synoptic outlook pushed into the background; metaphysics and speculative philosophy are repudiated. Critical philosophy, in the form of logic, semantics, philosophy of language, philosophy of science, and epistemology, has become the chief interest in many college and university philosophy departments.[6]

Analytic Philosophy and Questions of Knowledge

◆ ◆ ◆ ◆ ◆ ◆ ◆ ◆ ◆ ◆ ◆

Certain questions particularly concern the analytic philosopher: What judgments can we make? How much can we infer from our sense data, or the data of experience? What is meant by *meaning* and *verification*? How can we proceed through analysis to clarify language? What are the implications of the answers to these questions?

Many brilliant men and women have participated in the debates of the last six or seven decades. Apart from some general discussion, we shall limit our presentation to two men, Ludwig Wittgenstein and A. J. Ayer. We selected these two men because of their outstanding influence, because they have set forth fairly systematic accounts of their philosophies, and because they illustrate the shifts in points of view that have taken place in recent years.

LUDWIG WITTGENSTEIN

Few philosophers in the twentieth century have had greater influence on philosophy or have been more concerned with linguistic problems than Ludwig Wittgenstein (1889–1951) (see biography and excerpt, pp. 314–315). Born in Vienna, educated in Austria and at Cambridge University in England, he came under the influence of Bertrand Russell and G. E. Moore. In 1930 he succeeded Moore and taught philosophy at Cambridge, from where he influenced many thinkers in England and the United States. He has the rare distinction of producing two different, highly original systems of thought: one in the *Tractatus,* a short work published in 1922, and a longer work, *Philosophical Investigations,* published posthumously in 1953. The latter work is a criticism and rejection of many of the central ideas of his earlier book.

The *Tractatus* is an account of the conditions under which language has meaning and can make a claim to truth. Meaningful sentences are pictures of a state of affairs. A proposition is a "picture of reality," but in any picture there must be a one-to-one correspondence between the picture and the state of affairs it purports to represent. The *picture theory* of propositions is central at this early stage of his thought. To understand a sentence, we must know the referent or state of affairs to which it directs our attention. Statements that are capable of meaningful application to the world must meet certain rigid conditions, otherwise they make no sense. Wittgenstein brands as nonsensical many utterances of traditional metaphysicians and theologians as well as mystical utterances. His early thought influenced and was developed by the logical positivists of the Vienna Circle. Philosophy, from this point of view, does not aim at intellectual discovery. It is a method of bringing into light the linguistic confusions that give rise to pseudo-problems of many different kinds.

If philosophy is primarily a study of language, how should we proceed in making such a study? The early Wittgenstein, along with Russell, Carnap (see biography and excerpt, pp. 316–317), and their followers, distrusted ordinary language as a vehicle of philosophical expression and favored the construction of an ideal, artificial language, such as that of symbolic logic, with more precise signs and symbols than those in ordinary use. An artificial language, a logical system with semantic rules to function in special areas (quantum theory, learning theory, and so on) was thought to have advantage in precision and clarity; the natural languages, such as English, French, and German seemed ambiguous, vague, and imprecise in meaning.

With the appearance of Wittgenstein's *Philosophical Investigations,* analytic philosophy adjusted to a new point of view. It was still concerned with language, but Wittgenstein saw the nature of language in a different light. He repudiated a large portion of the *Tractatus* on the grounds that he had assumed that language has only one function, namely, to state facts. What struck Wittgenstein now was that language has many functions, and attention should be shifted from a preoccupation with logic and the construction of a "perfect" language to the study of the ordinary usages of language. The later

Wittgenstein moved away from what Russell and Carnap were doing and turned in the direction of G. E. Moore's emphasis on "common sense": the meaning of any expression is its use. Language has many uses and we need to examine the way key words and expressions function in ordinary language. By means of language we play various games as we shift from one type of discourse to another. In the "language games," words can be used to describe, to order, and to direct persons and things, or to express some play of the imagination. An artificial language does not solve the problems that arise in usage and may even lead to serious distortions and one-sided views. Ordinary language can be subjected to a rigorous, extended program of analysis.

By recognizing the diversity of the functions of language, Wittgenstein altered the task of philosophy. Unlike the positivists, he would not reject the statements of metaphysics outright. We bring words back from their metaphysical to their everyday usage. "In philosophy we do not draw conclusions. . . . Philosophy only states what everyone admits."[7] Thus it is that philosophy does not provide us with new or more information, but adds clarity by a careful description of language.

ALFRED JULES AYER

After graduating from Eton and Oxford, Alfred Jules Ayer (1910–1989) (see biography and excerpt, pp. 318–319) spent some time at the University of Vienna studying logical positivism. Soon after returning to Oxford as a lecturer in philosophy, he published *Language, Truth and Logic* (1936), a highly influential book that acknowledges its debt to Russell, Wittgenstein, and the Vienna Circle, as well as to the earlier empiricism of Berkeley and Hume. The second edition of this book (1946) modifies some but does not retract the main contentions of the first edition. Ayer's later books cover topics such as logic, meaning, mental states, and the idea of a person.

As a background for some of Ayer's views, we need to see his relation to Immanuel Kant.

According to Kant, who had a powerful influence on modern thought, there are *analytic propositions*—propositions in which the predicate is "contained in" the subject. For example: white swans are white; all bachelors are male. The predicate merely states something that is contained in the ordinary meaning of the subject; the predicate is a defining characteristic of the subject. In contrast with analytic statements, there are synthetic propositions, which cannot be verified by analyzing the statement. For example: this watch is gold; there is a chair in my office. Synthetic judgments being two ideas together in a new relationship; propositions that tell us something about the world (and not about how we use words) and must be verified empirically are called *synthetic propositions*. While Kant believed that most synthetic propositions could be verified sensorially, he held that there are some synthetic propositions that are *a priori*—that is, known to be true prior to experience and not dependent on experience for verification. An example of a *synthetic a priori* proposition, according to Kant, would be: every event has a cause. Synthetic *a priori* propositions are necessarily true, yet they give information about the world.

According to A. J. Ayer, who in his earlier writings combines British philosophical analysis and logical positivism, there are no synthetic *a priori* judgments, as Kant had held. There are, as Hume had earlier claimed, only two kinds of statements that convey knowledge and that can be judged true or false. There are analytic statements or propositions, the truth of which depends solely on the definitions of the terms or symbols involved. Especially good examples are found in the fields of mathematics and logic; for instance, "two plus two equals four." Kant said that this kind of statement was synthetic a priori, since it seemed to be necessarily true and seemed to give information about the world. Ayer and his followers insisted that the statements of mathematics were necessarily true only insofar as they were analytic and depended on the meaning of mathematical terms. When, however, these statements had empirical referents, they were no

Ludwig Wittgenstein

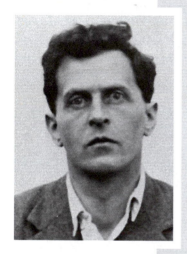

Ludwig Wittgenstein (1889–1951) was born in Vienna, and educated at home until he was fourteen years old. He became interested in mathematics and the physical sciences, and spent two years studying mechanical engineering in Berlin. He moved to England and was engaged in aeronautical research for three years. Influenced by Bertrand Russell's *Principles of Mathematics,* he went to Cambridge to study logic with Russell. When World War I broke out, he joined the Austrian army as a volunteer and was taken prisoner in 1918 by the Italians. After his release, he taught school, but in 1929 he returned to Cambridge to devote himself to philosophy. In 1939, he succeeded G. E. Moore to the chair of philosophy at Cambridge University in England. His work was a major factor in the rise of various schools of logical positivism, linguistic analysis, and semantics. Wittgenstein was a man of rare scientific, literary, and artistic ability who brought about a revolution in modern philosophy. His thought underwent great change so that it is sometimes said that he worked out two systems of thought: the first in the *Tractatus* (1922), in which he takes his stand with logical positivism; the second in *Philosophical Investigations* (1953), in which he puts the emphasis on language use and linguistic problems. Two other volumes are important: *The Blue and Brown Books* (1958) and *On Certainty* (1969).

Excerpt from Wittgenstein:

Philosophical Remarks (1964)

Note: Wittgenstein's writings, on the whole, are written in the form of short reflections, just as seen here.

57 One misleading representational technique in our language is the use of the word "I", particularly when it is used in representing immediate experience. How would it be if such experience were represented without using the personal pronoun?

58 Like this, say: If I, L. W., have toothache, that is expressed as "There is toothache." In other cases: "A is behaving as L. W. does when there is toothache." Language can have anyone as its centre. That it has me as its centre lies in the application. This privileged status cannot be expressed. Whether I say that what is represented is *not* one thing among others; or that I cannot express the advantages of *my* language—both approaches lead to the same result.

59 It isn't possible to believe something for which you cannot find some kind of verification. In a case where I believe someone is sad I can do this. But I cannot *believe* that I am sad.

60 Does it make *sense* to say two people have the same body?

61 What distinguishes *his* toothache from *mine*?

62 "When I say he has toothache, I mean he now has what I once had." But is this a relation toothache once had to me and now has to him?

63 I could speak of toothache (datum of feeling) in someone else's tooth in the sense that it would be possible to feel pain in a tooth in someone else's mouth.

64 If I say "A has toothache," I use the image of feeling pain in the same way as, say, the concept of flowing when I talk of an electric current flowing.—The hypotheses that (1) other people have toothache and that (2) they behave as I do but don't have toothache—possibly have identical senses.

L. Wittgenstein, *Philosophical Remarks*, ed. R. Rhees, trans. Raymond Hargreaves and Roger White (Oxford: Blackwell, 1975).

Rudolph Carnap

Rudolph Carnap (1891–1970), philosopher and teacher, was born at Ronsdorf, near Bremen, Germany. After attending The Gymnasium at Bremen, he studied at the universities of Freiburg and Jena from 1910 to 1914, specializing in physics, mathematics, and philosophy. After service in World War I, Carnap resumed his studies and in 1921 obtained his doctorate in philosophy at Jena. In 1926, at the invitation of Moritz Schlick, Carnap went to the University of Vienna and became a member of the Vienna Circle. After emigrating to the United States, he served on the faculty of the University of Chicago from 1935 to 1952, and subsequently taught at the University of California at Los Angeles until his retirement in 1961.

Carnap firmly believed that progress in philosophy requires an exact analysis of concepts, especially those of logic and science. The development of a formal language is the first essential step in philosophical analysis. His own contributions to semantics are important, especially to the development of modal systems.

Carnap was a formalist and applied symbolic logic to the problems he considered. His first philosophical attempt was to make a logical construction of the world. He held that the world can be built up starting with "primitive ideas," or the immediate data of experience, and one basic relation, that of similarity; following this, the formal constitution of quality classes, sense classes, sensory fields, and things is developed. Carnap finally abandoned this project because of the difficulty of reaching the public world from the starting point of private experience.

Carnap published several works, including *The Logical Construction of the World* (1928), *The Unity of Science* (1932), *Introduction to Semantics* (1942), and *Meaning and Necessity* (1947).

longer necessarily true, but depended on observation for their verification. The notion of the synthetic a priori is thus rejected.

There are affirmations or denials of questions of fact, synthetic statements, that can be verified empirically. All synthetic propositions—statements of fact about the world—are grounded in sense perception or are relevant to some actual or possible experience. According to this analysis, a statement is meaningful if and only if it is either analytic or empirically verifiable. That is, Ayer established what is referred to as the *verificationist meaning criterion*: nonanalytic statements are meaningful only if they are empirically verifiable.

In *Language, Truth and Logic*, Ayer makes a distinction between the "strong" and the "weak" sense of verification:

> It will be seen that I distinguish between a "strong" and a "weak" sense of the term "veri-

Excerpt from Carnap

Introduction to Semantics (1942)

A *language,* as it is usually understood, is a system of sounds, or rather of the habits of producing them by the speaking organs, for the purpose of communicating with other persons, i.e. of influencing their actions, decisions, thoughts, etc. Instead of speech sounds other movements or things are sometimes produced for the same purpose, e.g. gestures, written marks, signals by drums, flags, trumpets, rockets, etc. It seems convenient to take the term "language" in such a wide sense as to cover all these kinds of systems of means of communication, no matter what material they use. Thus we will distinguish between speech language (or spoken language), language of writing (or written language), gesture language, etc. Of course, speech language is the most important practically, and is, moreover, in most cases the basis of any other language, in the sense that this other language is learned with the help of the speech language. But this fact is accidental; any of the other kinds of language could be learned and used in a way independent of the speech language.

R. Carnap, *Introduction to Semantics* (Cambridge, Mass.: Harvard University Press, 1948).

fiable," and that I explain this distinction by saying that "a proposition is said to be verifiable in the strong sense of the term, if and only if its truth could be conclusively established in experience," but that "it is verifiable, in the weak sense, if it is possible for experience to render it probable."[8]

The weak sense of the principle leaves room for the extremely indirect method of testing some explanatory hypotheses in science. The logical empiricist would say that these hypotheses start from and eventually return to the area of empirical data and observations.

In speaking of the function of philosophy, Ayer says that the philosopher "must not attempt to formulate speculative truths, or to look for first principles, or to make *a priori* judgments about the validity of our empirical beliefs. He must, in fact, confine himself to works of clarification and analysis. . . ." He also says

Alfred Jules Ayer

A. J. Ayer (1910–1989), an English analytic philosopher, received his education at Eton, where he was a "Kings Scholar," and at Christ Church College at Oxford University. After graduation in 1932, he studied logical positivism at the University of Vienna, then returned to Oxford as a lecturer in philosophy and later as a research fellow. During World War II, he was commissioned into the Welsh Guards and was attaché at the British Embassy in Paris for a short time. Following his public service he returned to Oxford and became Dean of Wadham College and a year later Grote Professor of the Philosophy of Mind and Logic at University College, London. He returned to Oxford in 1959 as Wykeham Professor of Logic.

Ayer's thinking reflects the influence of Hume, Russell, Wittgenstein, and the Vienna Circle of logical positivism. He thinks that metaphysical and theological statements are without meaning. His writings include *Language, Truth and Logic* (1936, revised in 1946), a book that has been widely discussed and both praised and criticized. Other books are *The Foundations of Empirical Knowledge* (1940); *Thinking and Meaning* (1947); *Philosophical Essays* (1954); *The Problem of Knowledge* (1956); *The Concept of a Person* (1963), and *Philosophy in the Twentieth Century* (1982).

that "the propositions of philosophy are not factual, but linguistic in character—that is, they do not describe the behavior of physical, or even mental objects; they express definitions, or the formal consequences of definitions. Accordingly, we may say that philosophy is a department of logic."[9]

Logical analysts who limit knowledge to statements of *observable* fact make rather sweeping denials. Apart from analytical statements, they will not accept anything as meaningful that cannot be verified by empirical observation. The metaphysical thesis that there is "knowledge of a

reality transcending the world of science and common sense" is brushed aside as nonsense: what could it possibly mean? Much of traditional philosophy is repudiated, and concepts like "being," "reality," "God," and the "purpose of human existence" are disregarded or said to be meaningless. Similarly, normative ethics is eliminated. Ayer says:

> [I]n saying that a certain type of action is right or wrong, I am not making any factual statement, not even a statement about my own state of mind. I am merely expressing certain moral sentiments. And the man who is ostensibly con-

Excerpt from Ayer:

Language, Truth and Logic, "The Elimination of Metaphysics" (1946)

One way of attacking a metaphysician who claimed to have knowledge of a reality which transcended the phenomenal world would be to enquire from what premises his propositions were deduced. Must he not begin, as other men do, with the evidence of his senses? And if so, what valid process of reasoning can possibly lead him to the conception of a transcendent reality? Surely from empirical premises nothing whatsoever concerning the properties, or even the existence, of anything super-empirical can legitimately be inferred. But this objection would be met by a denial on the part of a metaphysician that his assertions were ultimately based on the evidence of his senses. He would say that he was endowed with a faculty of intellectual intuition which enabled him to know facts that could not be known through sense-experience. . . . One cannot overthrow a system of transcendent metaphysics merely by criticizing the way in which it comes into being. What is required is rather a criticism of the nature of the actual statements which comprise it. And this is the line of argument which we shall, in fact, pursue. For we shall maintain that no statement which refers to a "reality" transcending the limits of all possible sense-experience can possibly have any literal significance; from which it must follow that the labours of those who have striven to describe such a reality have all been devoted to the production of nonsense.

A. J. Ayer, *Language, Truth and Logic* (London: Victor Gollancz, 1947).

---

tradicting me is merely expressing his moral sentiments. So that there is plainly no sense in asking which of us is in the right. For neither of us is asserting a genuine proposition. . . .

We can now see why it is impossible to find a criterion for determining the validity of ethical judgments . . . because they have no objective validity whatsoever. If a sentence makes no statement at all, there is obviously no sense in asking whether what it says is true or false. . . . They are pure expression of feeling . . . unverifiable for the same reason as a cry of pain or a word of command is unverifiable—because they do not express genuine propositions.[10]

Metaphysical, theological, and ethical propositions are regarded as meaningless; they are merely emotive, are untestable, and give no knowledge. *Are human feelings — esp. feelings of respect and disrespect — untestable?*

Reflections

◆ ◆ ◆ ◆ ◆ ◆ ◆ ◆ ◆ ◆

Since the task of adding to our knowledge necessarily falls to one or another of the various sciences, just what is the task of philosophy according to this approach? Logical empiricists are likely to reply that philosophy's task is the logical analysis of language, especially the language of science. Attention is given to symbolic logic and the theory of signs or symbols.

Although no one doubts that the various sciences have achieved much and that we can look forward to even greater advances in the future, some philosophers will question attempts to limit knowledge to scientific statements. The members of the groups we have been considering in this chapter do not say that all the statements of science are true or even meaningful, but many of them do say that for a statement to be true it must be empirically verifiable. The more extreme analysts seem to combine a thoroughgoing skepticism with respect to the beliefs of religion and speculative philosophy with an almost dogmatic acceptance of the findings of the sciences. There are limitations to the methods used by the sciences, and it follows that there may be meaningful propositions that are not verifiable by these methods.

A central question is: How much can we infer from what we believe to be directly experienced? Nearly all people admit that we do make inferences both in science and philosophy. But what kinds of inferences are justified? Philosophers of different backgrounds and intellectual outlooks have claimed that their philosophies have started from what is directly known, and yet they have concluded with different kinds of systems. Rationalists such as Descartes have been willing to cast aside everything that can be doubted and to start from what is clearly and distinctly perceived. Empiricists such as Locke and Hume likewise built their philosophies on the basis of what they took to be given in experience. Can we start from that which is given directly in experience and move on to infer the existence of other entities or realities thought to be implied or required by these experiences? How far can we go in this direction? Can we infer the existence of such things as substances, a self, universals, and God? Many philosophers have thought that some such inferences were necessary; others have attacked such inferences and have insisted that we stop with that which is immediately given in sense perception or at least with that which is open to some experimental or empirical check.

If the latter view is accepted, a wide range of topics and problems that in the past have been considered to be important are rejected as meaningless.

A too-exclusive attention to language may lead us to lose sight of what language is supposed to represent. Philosophers in the past have insisted on their right and need to discuss questions of science, art, morality, religion, politics, and education, as well as symbols and language. To say that philosophy can talk only about language is to transform one method of clarification into the essence of philosophy; it is an example of reductive analysis and "losing the object."

After paying tribute to the clarity and vigor of much of the work of the analytic philosophers, one critic says:

> I cannot help but feel that there is something seriously wrong with a philosophy, in the mid-twentieth century, that takes no notice of war, revolution, nationalism, nuclear energy, the exploration of space, or anything else distinctive of the life of our time save the magnificent sweep of the intellect in the achievements of pure science and mathematics.[11]

Critics of analytic philosophy contend that its meaning criterion and its principle of verification are too exclusive and arbitrary. The principle of verification itself is neither logicomathematical nor empirical and by this accepted definition of meaning is itself undermined. If no metaphysical statements are permitted, the assumptions and statements on which logical empiricism rests are also meaningless. Is it true that what we know consists exclusively of propositions that are empirically verifiable or deduced from such propositions? Various metaphysical assumptions are hidden behind statements of this kind.

Analytic philosophy, insofar as it insists that every descriptive or factual term must be in the language of science, and that propositions must be verifiable by sensory observation, is asserting a metaphysical doctrine. This is in fact a clear-cut materialism, which was fairly prevalent in scientific circles during the nineteenth century. Insofar as logical empiricism is materialistic, the position is open to the criticisms directed against materialism.

The linguistic analysts have made it clear that philosophers have sometimes confused the various functions and meanings of language and have failed on occasion to distinguish clearly among them; such confusion has clouded philosophical issues themselves. Today, it appears that there is emerging among the analysts a more liberal attitude, which includes a recognition of not just one or two but of many modes of meaning as legitimate. This may presage a return to accepting as legitimate such issues as those of ethics, aesthetics, and metaphysics.

◆ ◆

Glossary Terms

COGNITIVE (COGNITION)   The attainment of knowledge of something; the mental process by which we become aware of objects of perception; thought.

EVOCATIVE   From *evoke,* "to call up or to produce" (memories, feelings, and so on).

LOGICAL EMPIRICISM (LOGICAL POSITIVISM)   A school of thought that would limit meaningful propositions either to those that are empirically verifiable or to those that are analyses of definitions and relations among terms. Empirically verifiable propositions are the concern of the sciences, and analysis of definitions and relations between terms is seen as the specific task of philosophy.

LOGICAL POSITIVISTS (LOGICAL POSITIVISM)   Those who would limit meaningful propositions either to those that are empirically verifiable or to those that are analyses of definitions and relations among terms. Empirically verifiable propositions are the concern of the sciences, and analysis of definitions and relations between terms is seen as the specific task of philosophy.

METALANGUAGE   The language that we use to talk about language itself, in contrast with an *object language* that we use to talk about the world.

NAME   The symbol that stands for the thing named.

REFERENT   That which is meant.

SEMANTICS   A study of the meaning of words and linguistic forms, their function as symbols, and the part they play in relation to other words.

◆ ◆

Chapter Review

LANGUAGE AND PHILOSOPHY

1. Many contemporary philosophers see the study of meaning and the principles and rules of language as the central problem of philosophy.

2. The ability to use language apparently distinguishes humans from animals. Language serves as a vehicle for knowledge and freedom.

3. Civilization progresses through use of a written language, which provides a means of transporting knowledge from past to future.

4. Language has many functions: cognitive, expressive, evocative, imperative, and ceremonial.

5. Although most people think of language as reflecting our world, language also influences our experiences. It imposes specific viewpoints and structures reality.

6. Many philosophers claim that some of humanity's problems are caused by difficulty in communication attributed to ambiguity in linguistic forms and usages.

LOCKE, HUME, AND THE TRADITIONAL OUTLOOK

1. The traditional Western world view has consistently asserted that the universe has an intrinsic moral order. Some things are right and others are wrong, unconditionally.

2. Locke and Hume were critical of metaphysics. They denied the validity of abstract and general ideas. As empiricists they maintained that knowledge was derived solely from the senses.

THE EMPIRICAL TRADITION

1. Positivism, founded by Auguste Comte, limited knowledge to statements of observable facts and their interrelations. It is concerned only with scientific description, which does not go beyond observable and reasonable facts.

2. Logical positivism, which began in Austria and Germany, spread to the rest of the West and was based on more recent logical and scientific concepts.

3. English schools of philosophical analysis all agree that analysis is the only task of philosophy, but they differ as to conclusions about certain philosophical questions.

ANALYTIC PHILOSOPHY AND QUESTIONS OF KNOWLEDGE

1. Ludwig Wittgenstein, an analytic philosopher, in his early years distrusted ordinary language and at one point proposed the construction of an ideal, artificial language such as symbolic logic. He believed an artificial language would offer more precision and clarity.

2. A. J. Ayer combined British philosophical analysis and logical positivism. For Ayer, a statement is meaningful only if it is analytic or empirically verifiable. Philosophy must confine itself to clarification and analysis; it expresses definitions. Metaphysical, theological, and ethical statements are meaningless; they give no knowledge.

3. Analytical philosophers consider the task of philosophy to be the logical analysis of language, especially the language of science.

REFLECTIONS

1. The task of philosophy according to the approach of analytic philosophy is the logical analysis of language.

2. The current status of analytic thought is moving toward the recognition of many modes of meaning as legitimate.

◆ ◆

Study Questions and Projects

1. Empiricism is the view that knowledge comes through experience or through the senses. How do you explain the fact that empiricists have moved in so many directions and have included idealists, pragmatists, logical positivists, and others?

2. Many metaphysical and theological assertions are such that, if they are held with conviction, they make a difference in human decisions and actions. What, in your opinion, will be the effects on ethics, politics, religion, and theology of the spread of the more extreme empirical views?

3. What are the different functions of language, and how may a confusion of these different functions lead to errors in thinking?

4. State the views of Ludwig Wittgenstein and point out some differences between his earlier and later philosophical approaches.

5. Distinguish between analytic and synthetic propositions and discuss the "synthetic a priori" controversy.

6. Explain what is meant by the "principle of verification." What is the difference between the "strong" and the "weak" application of the principle?

7. State the position of A. J. Ayer and point out what this position implies about what questions are meaningful, and which are meaningless.

8. What is the main task of philosophy as seen by the linguistic analysts?

9. Evaluate analytic philosophy, indicating what you believe to be the strengths and weaknesses of these related movements.

10. The statements below say or imply that logical empiricists and positivists sacrifice certain questions and problems to a method. Indicate the extent to which you agree or disagree with the quotations.

    (a) In *The Self as Agent* (New York: Harper, 1953), p. 28, John Macmurray says: "Philosophy, like any branch of serious reflective inquiry, is created and defined by its problems; and its problems are not accidental, but necessary; grounded in the nature of experience. If I find that my method of attempting to answer them is unsuccessful, if it fails even to discover a meaning in them, then I must conclude that there is something wrong with the method, and seek a better one. To discard the problems in order to retain the method; to seek for problems which the method *could* solve, would be neither serious nor reasonable."

    (b) In Carl Michalson, ed., *Christianity and the Existentialists* (New York: Scribner's, 1956), pp. 81–82, J. V. Langmead Casserley says: "Positivist philosophers in particular behave rather like an investigation and censorship committee determined upon the suppression of inconvenient questions by calling in question and libelling the philosophical integrity of those who insist on asking them. But to censor and suppress human questioning must in the long run erode and destroy human intellectualism."

    (c) In *A Critique of Logical Positivism* (Chicago: University of Chicago Press, 1950), p. 148, C. E. M. Joad asks: "Can a man really continue to feel indignant at cruelty, if he is convinced that the statement 'cruelty is wrong' is meaningless? Again he says: "If Logical Positivism is correct, you can say, 'one atom bomb can destroy 50,000 people' (statement of fact), but not 'it is a bad thing to destroy 50,000 people' (statement of evaluation), or, rather, you can say it, but the word 'bad' adds nothing to the factual content of the statement."

◆ ◆

Suggested Readings

Ammerman, R. R. (ed.). *Classics of Analytic Philosophy*. Indianapolis, Ind.: Hackett, 1990.

A comprehensive anthology.

Andreski, S. (ed.). *The Essential Comte*. London: Croom Helm, 1974.

This volume contains a relatively recent selection from Comte's *Course in Positive Philosophy* with an excellent introduction by Andreski that delineates Comte's place in the history of sociology. Important for understanding all varieties of analytic philosophy.

Ayer, A. J. *The Central Questions of Philosophy*. New York: Holt, Rinehart and Winston, 1973.

This is the series of Gifford Lectures delivered by Ayer in 1972–1973. The book contains discussions of what philosophy is; what the special character of metaphysical arguments is taken to be; various theories of meaning; and the problems covered by philosophical analysis. Ayer concludes with a chapter on "The Claims of Theology," which is mainly concerned with showing that we have no good reason to believe that there is a God.

Bell, D., and Cooper, N. (eds.). *The Analytic Tradition: Meaning, Thought and Knowledge*. Oxford: Blackwell, 1990.

A collection of nine original papers on the nature and history of the analytic tradition in contemporary philosophy.

Chomsky, N. *Cartesian Linguistics*. New York: Harper and Row, 1966.

Chomsky concentrates on the development of the leading ideas of Cartesian linguistics and points to the ways in which they have reemerged in current linguistic thought.

Martinich, A. P. (ed.). *The Philosophy of Language.* 2nd ed. New York: Oxford University Press, 1990.

A general anthology.

Pears, D. *Ludwig Wittgenstein.* New York: Viking Press, 1970.

This paperback is a good introduction to the thought of Wittgenstein. Pears' discussion is a helpful guide to the general character of Wittgenstein's philosophy.

Rorty, R. (ed.). *The Linguistic Turn: Recent Essays in Philosophical Method.* Chicago: University of Chicago Press, 1967.

This is an introduction and selections that show the development of linguistic philosophy during the last few decades.

————. *Philosophy and the Mirror of Nature.* Princeton, N.J.: Princeton, 2nd printing with corrections, 1980.

A controversial discussion of the whole problem of truth and its complications.

Weitz, M. (ed.). *Twentieth Century Philosophy: The Analytic Tradition.* New York: Free Press, 1966.

A collection of essays about twentieth-century analytic philosophy, focusing on realism, logical analysis, logical positivism, and conceptual elucidation.

◆ ◆

Notes

1. A. J. Ayer, *Language, Truth and Logic,* 2nd rev. ed. (New York: Dover, 1946), p. 33. The first edition was published in 1936.

2. C. Kluckhohn, *Mirror for Man* (New York: Whittlesey, 1949), pp. 160, 166–67.

3. C. E. M. Joad, *A Critique of Logical Positivism* (Chicago: University of Chicago Press, 1950), p. 27.

4. For the work of the Vienna Circle and the activity of some of its members, see J. Jorgensen, *The Development of Logical Empiricism* (Chicago: University of Chicago Press, 1951); see also V. Kraft, *The Vienna Circle: The Origin of Neo-Positivism,* trans. A. Pap (New York: Philosophical Library, 1953).

5. Jorgensen, *Logical Empiricism,* p. 6.

6. Mortimer Adler, in his book *The Conditions of Philosophy* (New York: Atheneum, 1965), makes a helpful distinction between "first-order" philosophical questions—questions about that which is and happens in the world—and "second-order" questions—questions about the content of our thinking when we try to answer first-order questions, or questions about the way in which we express such thought in language. Analytic philosophy concerns itself exclusively with second-order questions.

7. L. Wittgenstein, *Philosophical Investigations,* trans. G. E. M. Anscombe (Oxford: Blackwell, 1953), p. 156e.

8. Ayer, *Language, Truth and Logic,* p. 9.

9. Ayer, *Language, Truth and Logic,* pp. 51, 57.

10. Ayer, *Language, Truth and Logic,* pp. 107, 108–109.

11. A. Kaplan, *The New World of Philosophy* (New York: Random House, 1961), p. 90. (Copyright by Abraham Kaplan.)

◆ ◆ ◆ ◆ ◆ ◆ ◆ ◆ ◆ ◆

Existentialism, Phenomenology, and Process Philosophy

CHAPTER OBJECTIVES

In this chapter we will address the following questions:

◆ What Are Some Major Characteristics of Each Movement?

◆ Who Are Some of the Major Proponents of Each Outlook?

◆ What Features Do All Three Movements Share?

Almost everybody who is at all familiar with traditional philosophy has been struck by its variety. Even in the Middle Ages, when practically all thinkers adhered to Christian doctrine, several philosophical schools with vastly different outlooks emerged. In the twentieth century, however, philosophy is marked by a diversity without parallel in the historical tradition.[1]

In addition to the traditional philosophical views known as materialism, naturalism, idealism, and realism, we have discussed the more recent outlooks of pragmatism and analytic philosophy. There are at least three other perspectives currently on the philosophical scene: the philosophy of existence (**existentialism**); **phenomenology**, and **process philosophy.** Our intention is to examine first the characteristics of the philosophy under question and second to mention some philosophers who subscribe to the particular view.

Some Characteristics of Existentialism

♦ ♦ ♦ ♦ ♦ ♦ ♦ ♦ ♦ ♦ ♦

A MOVEMENT OF PROTEST

The term *existentialism* does not connote any one particular philosophical system. There are considerable differences among the various philosophies that usually are classed as existentialist, but nonetheless there are common themes that characterize the existentialist movement. Primarily, existentialism is a revolt against some features of traditional philosophy and modern society. It is in part a protest against the rationalism of the Greek, or classical, tradition in philosophy, especially the speculative world views of thinkers such as Plato and Hegel. In such "systems," the individual self or the thinker is lost in abstract universals or in a universal ego. Existentialism is a protest in the name of individuality against the concepts of "reason" and "nature" that were so strongly emphasized during the eighteenth-century Enlightenment. "The refusal to belong to any school of thought, the repudiation of the adequacy of any body of beliefs whatever, and especially of systems, and a marked dissatisfaction with traditional philosophy as superficial, academic, and remote from life—that is the heart of existentialism."[2]

Existentialism also is a revolt against the impersonal nature of the modern industrial or technological age and against the mass movements of our time. Industrial society tends, as the existentialists see it, to subordinate the individual to the machine: humans are in danger of becoming tools, computers, objects. Scientism recognizes only the external behavior of people and interprets them as merely a part of a physical process. Existentialism also is a protest against totalitarian movements, whether fascist, communist, or whatever, which tend to crush or submerge the individual in the collective or the mass.

A DIAGNOSIS OF THE HUMAN PREDICAMENT

Existentialism is concerned with describing and diagnosing the human predicament. In this respect, it is a reemphasis of some older ways of thinking. Some of its supporters claim that it is not just ancient and modern, but actually timeless. "Existentialism as a universal element in all thinking is the attempt of man to describe his existence and its conflicts, the origin of these conflicts, and the anticipation of overcoming them. . . . Wherever man's predicament is described either theologically or philosophically, either poetically or artistically, there we have existentialist elements."[3]

Insofar as existentialism emphasizes the human situation and our prospects in the world, it is found in Judaism, Christianity, and in the attempts at self-analysis and self-understanding of philosophers such as Socrates. In this sense, it is indeed ancient as well as modern. As a modern movement, existentialism gained prominence only in the twentieth century. During the nineteenth century, however, certain "lonely prophets"—Kierkegaard, Nietzsche, Dostoevsky—were voicing their protests and registering their concern about the human condition. During the twentieth century, the expression of concern over our sense of estrangement and meaninglessness has grown into a strong chorus. People, it is asserted, do not feel at home in the world in which they must make their home.

A BELIEF IN THE PRIMACY OF EXISTENCE

Existentialism emphasizes the uniqueness and primacy of existence—the inner, immediate experience of self-awareness. The fundamental drive or urge is to exist and to be recognized as an individual. If we are so recognized, we may gain a sense of meaning and significance in life. The most meaningful point of reference for any person is his or her own immediate consciousness, which cannot be contained in systems or abstractions. Abstract thinking tends to be impersonal and to lead away from the concrete human being and the human situation. Reality or being is existence that is found in the "I" rather than the "it." Thus the center of thought and meaning is the existing *individual* thinker. For the Danish philosopher, Søren Kierkegaard, for example, people who pretend that their view of life is determined by sheer reason are both tiresome and unperceptive; they fail to grasp the elementary fact that they are not pure thinkers, but *existing individuals.*[4]

Existentialists make a clear-cut distinction between **existence** and **essence.** Existence means the state of being actual, or occurring within space and time, or it refers to "something given here and now." It is used in the sense in which selves or human individuals are recognized to exist, or to live. For the existentialists, however, the verb *to exist* has a richer and more positive content than the verb *to live.* People sometimes say of those who live a drab and meaningless life, "They do not live, they merely exist." The existentialists would turn the sentence around and say, "They do not exist, they merely live." Existence for them means a full, vital, self-conscious, responsible, and growing life.

The term *essence,* in contrast with *existence,* refers to that which distinguishes a thing from other types of objects. It is that which makes a thing what it is, or that which all things called by the same name have in common. The essence is common to the many individuals, and we may speak meaningfully of an essence even though no instances of the thing actually exist at any given time. "We distinguish between *what* a thing is and *that* it is. What a thing is we call its essence; that it is, its existence. The thing I hold in my hand is by essence a pencil. And this pencil, as I believe on the evidence of my senses, exists."[5] Once we have grasped the idea or concept of the essence of a thing, we can think of it quite apart from its existence. For Plato and many classical thinkers, the concept of, say, "man" had more reality than the individual human being John Doe; they thought that the participation in the idea, or form, or essence, called "man-ness" is what makes a man, any man, what he is. Existentialists reject this Platonic view and assert that there is something that cannot be conceptualized—the personal act of existing. They insist on the primacy of the state of existence.

Jean-Paul Sartre, the French author and philosopher, would say that the expression "*Existence comes before essence,*"[6] is what existentialists have in common, but other existentialists would not put it this way. What does it mean to say that existence precedes essence? Sartre tells us that when we consider, for example, a paper knife, we know that it has been made by someone who had in his or her mind a conception of it; thus, even before it is made, the paper knife is already conceived as having a definite purpose and as being the product of a definite process. The paper knife's essence can be said to come before its existence. In the case of humans, however, humans as such exist and only later make their essential selves.

AN EMPHASIS ON SUBJECTIVE EXPERIENCE

Existentialism places a new emphasis on our inner life and experience and thus on our immediate, subjective awareness. There is no knowledge, the existentialists say, apart from a knowing subject. A person's inner life, with its moods, anxieties, and decisions, becomes the center of attention. Existentialism opposes all forms of objectivity and impersonality insofar as they pertain to the life of human beings. Objectivity, as expressed in modern science and Western industrial society and by their philosophical and psychological representatives, has tended to make the person of secondary importance to things. Life in general and humans in particular often have been interpreted objectively and impersonally, so that life becomes hollow and meaningless. Existentialism, in contrast, stresses the importance of our inner life and is not afraid of introspection. It raises anew the problems surrounding that which is unique—individuality and personality. Existentialism stresses the necessity of rebelling against all attempts to ignore or suppress the uniqueness of subjective experience.

Truth, existentialists say, is revealed in the subjective experience of living. We experience the truth within us. The truth about the nature of humans and their destiny is not grasped and stated adequately in abstract concepts or in propositions. A purely rational approach is likely to deal with universal principles that absorb the person into some all-embracing unity or system. Because the existentialists stress the intimate, concrete aspects of experience, or that which is unique and personal, they are likely to turn to literary and other artistic forms of expression, through which feelings and moods can be portrayed more vividly.

A RECOGNITION OF FREEDOM
AND RESPONSIBILITY

The emphasis on personal existence and subjectivity has led in turn to a new emphasis on freedom and personal responsibility. The various determinisms, whether biological or environmental, do not tell the whole story. In existentialism, interest is directed not so much to humanity in general, or to human institutions and achievements, or to the impersonal world of nature, but to the individual person and his or her choices and decisions. Existentialism is an assertion of the significance of personal existence and decisions even in the face of interpretations of the world that appear to eliminate meaning and significance.

Freedom is not something to be proved or argued about; it is a reality to be experienced. We have considerable freedom within reach if we will but grasp it. Freedom is working out the demands of one's inner nature and expressing one's genuine or authentic self; it is facing choices, making decisions, and accepting responsibility for them. Above all, humans must accept responsibility for the decisions that have contributed to making them who they are.

Some Existentialist Thinkers

♦ ♦ ♦ ♦ ♦ ♦ ♦ ♦ ♦ ♦ ♦

SØREN KIERKEGAARD

Søren Kierkegaard (1813–1855) (see biography and excerpt, pp. 330–331) usually is considered to be the founder of modern existentialism. The writings of this Danish thinker furnished the stimulus for later members of the movement. Kierkegaard is difficult to interpret. He never intended to be a systematic thinker, and he gloried in paradoxes. His writings are made more difficult by his use of indirect communication, of irony, and of pseudonyms. As for almost all the existential thinkers, Kierkegaard's biography acts as an important clue to understanding his philosophy. We cannot here give the details of Kierkegaard's personal life, but his melancholy, the Lutheran orthodoxy under which he was reared, and his broken engagement undoubtedly were responsible to a great extent for his existential emphasis.

For Kierkegaard, the central issue in life is what it means to be a Christian. He is concerned not with "being" in general, but with individual existence. He wants us to come to an understanding of authentic Christianity. There are, Kierkegaard believes, two great enemies of Christianity. One is the Hegelian philosophy so prevalent in his day. Abstract speculation, he believes, whether in the Cartesian or the Hegelian form, depersonalizes humans and leads to the impoverishment of life. Kierkegaard attacks Hegel for writing about "pure thought"; pure thought is comical, says Kierkegaard, for it is thought without a thinker. Kierkegaard is especially scornful of all attempts to make Christianity "reasonable" or any defense of Christianity that employs objective arguments.

The second enemy of Christianity is convention, especially the conventional churchgoer. Unreflective or perfunctory church members may be good functionaries, but they do not live their faith. Instead, they have a depersonalized religion, and probably do not know what it means to *become* or *be* a Christian. Kierkegaard is highly critical of much in "Christendom," especially the established church, its clergy, and rituals. Kierkegaard is opposed to any mediating factor—minister, sacrament, church—that comes between the individual of faith and God, the absolute sovereign.

According to Kierkegaard, there is an "unbridgeable gulf" between God and the world, the Creator and the creature. God stands above all social and ethical standards. How are humans to overcome this gap? To be suspended in doubt is to experience existential anguish. "Every man who has not tasted the bitterness of despair has missed the significance of life, however beautiful and joyous his life might be."[7] When people are in anguish they must abandon reason and embrace faith. In the agonized "leap of faith," we embrace the absurd and the paradoxical. "Christianity takes a prodigious giantstride . . . a stride into the absurd—there Christianity begins . . . how extraordinarily stupid it is to defend Christianity."[8] To Kierkegaard, faith is everything. There must be either wholehearted obedience to God or open rebellion. One is either for or against Christ, for or against Truth; Christianity is absolutely true or absolutely false. Kierkegaard says, "What our age lacks, however, is not reflection but passion." Factual knowledge simply cannot overcome a defect of motive and will.

FRIEDRICH NIETZSCHE

Whether Nietzsche (1844–1900) (see biography and excerpt, pp. 332–333) is an existentialist is an open question, but in any event he has exerted a strong influence on the movement.

"In the story of existentialism, Nietzsche occupies a central place: Jaspers, Heidegger, and Sartre are unthinkable without him. . . . Existentialism without Nietzsche would be almost like Thomism without Aristotle; but to call Nietzsche an existentialist is a little like calling Aristotle a Thomist."[9]

Nietzsche and Kierkegaard agree and disagree on many points. Both men lived unhappy and lonely lives, and their experiences undoubtedly colored their views of humanity and the world. Both opposed the rationalistic thought of the nineteenth century and concerned themselves passionately with the human predicament. They saw in each person an existential being whose life cannot be described in the conventional ways. They found much that was wrong with human nature, and they opposed what they considered the shallowness of middle-class morality. On the other hand, the points of sharp contrast stand out clearly. Whereas Kierkegaard's main problem was how to become a Christian, Nietzsche attacked Christianity and said, "God is dead." Nietzsche opposed Christianity as the enemy of reason, as a life-denying force, and his problem was how to live without God. His emphasis was on life, instinct, and power, which, he believed were being perverted by a culture that catered to the masses. He recognized the "Will to Power" as the basic human motive. He wanted to make way for the "higher man," who would embody higher values, not the virtues of mediocrity that Nietzsche found exhibited in Christianity, democracy, and nineteenth-century bourgeois morality.

What would Nietzsche have us put in place of the traditional morality, which he believed to be dying? He is not as clear in his positive advice as he is in his criticisms and attacks. There must occur, he says, a "transvaluation of all values." By **transvaluation,** however, he does not intend the creation of a new table of moral values. He means mainly to declare war on the presently accepted values in the name of honesty and accuracy. The will to dominate is a fundamental drive in human beings, and ultimately that drive will produce a master morality and a rare number of

Søren Kierkegaard

Søren Kierkegaard (1813–1855), a Danish religious thinker, is considered by many persons to be the founder of existentialism. He was brought up in a home where he acquired a deeply emotional faith. At the University of Copenhagen, he studied Hegelian philosophy and reacted strongly against it. Abstract speculation, he believed, depersonalizes human beings in that it emphasizes thought and reason, and tends to disregard the thinker as well as personal faith and convictions. He reacted against the Danish Lutheran Church of his day as well as against efforts to make Christianity reasonable. His writings are often autobiographical and make use of irony and paradox; he stresses the gulf between God and humans and God and the world. True faith, he thought, involved accepting what is "absurd." His writings include *Either-Or* (1843), *The Sickness Unto Death* (1849), and *Fear and Trembling* (1843). He has had considerable influence on philosophy and literature, as well as on religious thought, in the twentieth century.

exceptional people, whom Nietzsche has called "supermen," or "overmen." The superman will be the truly free individual for whom nothing is forbidden—the passionate, vibrant person whose passions are checked by superior intellect.

Nietzsche's main contribution was to confront humanity with the implications of existence in a world in which there were no secure values and goals. This **nihilistic** outlook has been reflected in much literature and art that express the sense of hopelessness and meaninglessness of today's world. Nietzsche is one of many who see dangers in a technical and industrial age that they believe has discarded the guidance of human values and wisdom. Yet his own views introduce other dangers equally great.

KARL JASPERS

One of the most perceptive studies of Nietzsche has been written by Karl Jaspers (1883–1969).[10] Jaspers is interested in the good life and in the

Excerpt from Kierkegaard:

Attack upon "Christendom"
(1855)

The Christianity of the New Testament simply does not exist. Here there is nothing to reform; what has to be done is to throw light upon a criminal offense against Christianity, prolonged through centuries, perpetrated by millions (more or less guiltily), whereby they have cunningly, under the guise of perfecting Christianity, sought little by little to cheat God out of Christianity, and have succeeded in making Christianity exactly the opposite of what it is in the New Testament.

In order that the common Christianity here in our country, the official Christianity, may be said truly to be even so much as related to the Christianity of the New Testament, we must make it known, as honestly, as openly, as solemnly as possible, how remote it is from the Christianity of the New Testament, and how little it can truly be called an endeavor in the direction of coming nearer to the Christianity of the New Testament.

So long as this is not done, so long as we either make as if nothing were the matter, as if everything were all right, and what we call "Christianity" is the Christianity of the New Testament, or we perform artful tricks to conceal the difference, tricks to support the appearance that it is the Christianity of the New Testament—so long as this Christian criminal offense continues, there can be no question of reforming, but only of throwing light upon this Christian criminal offense.

And to say a word about myself: I am not what the age perhaps demands, a reformer—that by no means, nor a profound speculative spirit, a seer, a prophet; no (pardon me for saying it), I am in a rare degree an accomplished detective talent.

Søren Kierkegaard, *Attack upon Christendom,* trans. W. Lowrie (Princeton, N.J.: Princeton University Press, 1944).

---

self that makes decisions. For him, philosophy is a guide to reasonable living; it is a perpetual quest in which living, feeling, deciding, acting, and risking cannot be ignored. Jaspers' chief concern is the age-old question of Being, which must now (in a post-Kierkegaardian age) be studied from the vantage point of *existence philosophy.*

People are always more than what they think they know. In striving for meaning or orientation in the world, we can go to one extreme by stressing only the objective sciences; we can take the opposite approach by emphasizing subject or spirit and accept some form of idealism. Jaspers thinks that matter, life, self, and mind are qualitatively different from each other and that they cannot be reduced to any common term or terms. In addition to the way of objective science and the way of metaphysics, there is the approach through an examination of personal existence. Here there are at least three areas to consider: an individual's immediate consciousness of

Friedrich Nietzsche

Friedrich Nietzsche (1844–1900) was born in Prussia, Germany, and educated at the universities of Bonn and Leipzig. He is variously described as a philologist, classical scholar, philosopher, and poet. Nietzsche was the grandson of two Lutheran ministers and the son of another. His father died early, and he was brought up by his mother, sister, grandmother, and two maiden aunts.

Nietzsche attacked Christianity, democracy, feminism, and socialism. He stressed strength, virility, and power. Asserting that "God is dead," he looked for leaders in the *übermensch* (overmen), those who would exhibit a higher morality. After teaching classics at the University of Basel in Switzerland for ten years, he retired because of ill health and spent his time writing. In 1889 he had a mental breakdown from which he never recovered.

His writings include *The Birth of Tragedy* (1872), *The Four Meditations* (1873–1876), *Thus Spake Zarathustra* (1883–84, 1891), *Beyond Good and Evil* (1886), *Toward a Genealogy of Morals* (1887), and after his death, *The Will to Power* (1901; rev. 1910–1911).

---

selfhood, the communication of humans with their fellows in society, and the various historical structures of community life—morals, law, the family, the state, and the like. Jaspers was greatly influenced by Kierkegaard's writings and speaks of how we must express a *philosophic faith* that will enable us to have an almost mystical union with the depths of life.

In the individual, Jaspers says, we find a historically conditioned empirical self. This self is conditioned by the physical and physiological background and cultural environment. This is the self studied by sciences such as psychology; but there is a gap between the findings of objective psychology and the intimate human experience of love and hate, joy and tragedy, aspiration

Excerpt from Nietzsche:

Beyond Good and Evil (1886)

Gradually it has become clear to me what every great philosophy so far has been: namely, the personal confession of its author and a kind of involuntary and unconscious memoir; also that the moral (or immoral) intentions in every philosophy constituted the real germ of life from which the whole plant had grown.

Indeed, if one would explain how the abstrusest metaphysical claims of a philosopher really came about, it is always well (and wise) to ask first: at what morality does all this (does he) aim? Accordingly, I do not believe that a "drive to knowledge" is the father of philosophy; but rather that another drive has, here as elsewhere, employed understanding (and misunderstanding) as a mere instrument. . . . For every drive wants to be master—and it attempts to philosophize *in that spirit*.

To be sure: among scholars who are really scientific men, things may be different—"better," if you like—there you may really find something like a drive for knowledge, some small, independent clockwork that, once well wound, works on vigorously *without* any essential participation from all the other drives of the scholar. The real "interests" of the scholar therefore lie usually somewhere else—say, in his family, or in making money, or in politics. Indeed, it is almost a matter of total indifference whether his little machine is placed at this or that spot in science, and whether the "promising" young worker turns himself into a good philologist or an expert on fungi or a chemist: it does not *characterize* him that he becomes this or that. In the philosopher, conversely, there is nothing whatsoever that is impersonal; and above all, his morality bears decided and decisive witness to *who he is*—that is, in what order of rank the innermost drives of his nature stand in relation to each other.

Friedrich Nietzsche, *Beyond Good and Evil,* trans. W. Kaufman (New York: Random House, Vintage Books, 1966).

and anxiety. There is also an authentic self that the sciences cannot discover. This authentic self gives life its meaning. As persons, we have a temporal existence—we live in time—yet we are not merely temporal, we touch "existential eternity." This breaking through of the authentic self into the historical and empirical process makes choice and freedom possible.

Subjectivity and objectivity are both genuine aspects of reality. Subjectivity is not a passing phase or a byproduct of objectivity. There is in us the breath of the transcendent, and we must strive, despite all difficulties, to maintain our deeper insights and our freedom. Yet only through life in society and through communication can individual existence be developed and fulfilled. We cannot say just what the nature of the world is or understand Being with any completeness. But with the aid of intelligence we can keep up the quest for understanding and endure the struggle patiently.

GABRIEL MARCEL

Gabriel Marcel (1889–1973), a French Roman Catholic existentialist, centers his philosophy, as does Jaspers, on the question of Being. The proper theme of philosophy, according to Marcel, is the human predicament. He is concerned with the answers to two questions: "Who am I?" and "What is Being?" Although he shows his distrust of metaphysical *systems,* which seem to imply that thinking has arrived at some stopping place, he does not avoid metaphysical questions. His ideas often are presented in informal and unsystematic ways—in his diaries, journals, and plays. Marcel sees philosophy as a search moved by "an unusual sense of inner urgent need," and a "deep sense of inner disquiet." Philosophy does not attempt to view things in a purely detached objective manner, because philosophers must be in continuous living contact with the reality in the midst of which they live.

Marcel says, "The dynamic element in my philosophy, taken as a whole, can be seen as an obstinate and untiring battle against the spirit of abstraction."[11] Thus Marcel opposes a rationalism that elevates reason above life and experience, and an empiricism that goes to the opposite extreme and interprets humans too exclusively as creatures of sense perceptions. Marcel speaks of our world as "a broken world" that has lost its real unity and is at war with itself. He is critical of many things that go with a mass society and tend to depersonalize people and discredit privacy, brotherhood, and creativity. "The more techniques advance, the more reflection is thrust into the background."

Three distinctions made by Marcel can help us to understand the trend of his thinking. The first is between "first reflection" and "second reflection." The former is the reflection of the "person in the street," as well as of technical and scientific people. It separates subject and object and views things from the outside, as objects of scientific study. It is the spectator view of the world. The other type of reflection transcends science, technology, and objective knowledge. It is the effort of human thought to reach beyond itself into the realm of Being. This is philosophical reflection, which has become more completely aware, so that it is able to bear witness to the presence of Being. We are capable of nonsensuous intuition or understanding. Knowledge can be gained through philosophical reflection, including metaphysics, as well as through the objective methods of many special sciences.

A second distinction is that between "having" and "being." Having implies a relationship between me and some object outside or independent of me. It may indicate mere possession or refer to some other internal or external relationship, as when we say, "I have a body." Being, on the other hand, involves that which I *am* and not just that which I *have.* It reaches into the depths of my nature and involves participation and some degree of transcendence of the merely physical level of existence. A living person, however, cannot abolish all "having" from his or her life, and this would not be desirable in any event. Danger arises when we unduly emphasize the "having" area of our experience. To make the change of emphasis from "having" to "being," we need to experience love—love in the sense of "the subordination of the self to a superior reality, a reality at my deepest level more truly me than I am myself"[12] is the core of being.

The Gifford Lectures that Marcel delivered in 1949 and 1950, published in a two-volume work entitled *The Mystery of Being,* generally are regarded as Marcel's most systematic statement. A third distinction central to Marcel's philosophy is that between a problem and a mystery; this distinction is indicative of the nature of the existentialist approach. Marcel writes:

> A problem is something which I meet, which I find complete before me, but which I can therefore lay siege to and reduce. But a mystery is something in which I myself am involved, and it can therefore only be thought of as *a sphere*

where the distinction between what is in me and what is before me loses its meaning and its initial validity. A genuine problem is subject to an appropriate technique by the exercise of which it is defined; whereas a mystery, by definition, transcends every conceivable technique. It is, no doubt, always possible (logically and psychologically) to degrade a mystery so as to turn it into a problem. But this is a fundamentally vicious proceeding, whose springs might perhaps be discovered in a kind of corruption of the intelligence.[13]

Central concepts in Marcel's philosophy are those of participation, transcendence, and being. The reflective person seeks to overcome the broken world and rise from the insignificant to the level of the significant. We need to start from the realization that we are in a concrete situation, "tied to a body," immersed in matter and in the historical process. My body, he says, is not external to me; I am not independent of it; yet I am more than a mere body. Through this body I function in the world and am in continuous sensuous (feeling) contact with the universe around me. Marcel uses the term *incarnation* to symbolize our relation to the world. I am incarnate or embodied in my body, and the world of nature is thus expressed in me. We are a part of objective nature, but we are more than "things"; a person is "the only being who may make promises," a phrase of Nietzsche's that aptly expresses the nonobjective side of our nature that Marcel wants to stress.

Marcel wishes to avoid many of the traditional dualisms. The classical distinction between subject and object is too arid and stale. Reality is both transsubjective and transobjective. A person as participant stands in contrast to a person as spectator. The latter remains largely passive and is not "open to the situation." Participants allow themselves to be drawn into that which they encounter, so that the oppositions are overcome. Both feeling and contemplation are modes of participation. At one extreme, we are in contact and interaction with the objective world of things; at the other extreme objectivity has been transcended and we participate through prayer, meditation, or contempla-

tion as we encounter an authentic and transcendent reality. A finite and concrete self can be in contact with a living, personal God. To refuse God is to refuse to be.

JEAN-PAUL SARTRE

Existentialism emerged in its contemporary form in Paris immediately following World War II. At first it appeared to be a philosophical fad; Sartre (1905–1980) (see biography and excerpt, pp. 336–337) notes: "For since it [existentialism] has become fashionable, people cheerfully declare that this musician or this painter is 'existentialist.'"[14] However, due mainly to the essays, plays, and novels of Sartre, Simone de Beauvoir, and Albert Camus, existentialism has achieved more than a fashionable acceptance.[15]

Sartre started as a free-lance writer, taught philosophy for five years, and took part in World War II and the French Resistance. Although he is most widely known for his plays, short stories, and essays, his main philosophical work, *Being and Nothingness,* brought him recognition as a philosopher.[16] In a short, popular work, *Existentialism and Humanism,* Sartre says that "existentialism, in our sense of the word, is a doctrine that does render human life possible; a doctrine, also, which affirms that every truth and every action imply both an environment and a human subjectivity."[17]

Sartre follows Nietzsche in denying the existence of God and elaborating on the implications of this view, which include seeing humans as lacking a formed or given nature.[18] We have to make ourselves and to choose the conditions under which we are to live. Sartre denies us any external support; we must rely on our own resources and be held totally responsible for our free choices.

For Sartre, we have freedom to create ourselves as we will and act. Our situation may seem meaningless, absurd, and tragic, but we can still live by the rules of integrity, nobility, and valor, and we can create a human community. Because our destiny is within ourselves, our hope is choosing and acting so that we can live.

Jean-Paul Sartre

Revol

Jean-Paul Sartre (1905–1980), educated in Paris at the Ecole Normale Supérieure, exhibited at an early age his gift for literary expression. He is known mainly to us through his novels, plays, short stories, and psychological studies. His chief philosophical text is *Being and Nothingness*, a large volume that deals with the nature and forms of being, but his best-known work is his lecture, *Existentialism and Humanism* (1946), which has become famous despite Sartre's later attempts to state the definition of existentialism in different terms.

During World War II, Sartre was in the French army, was a German prisoner of war, and was active in the Resistance movement. He was a supporter of liberal causes and a defender of human freedom. Because of his political and philosophical convictions, he refused the Nobel Prize for literature in 1964. Of philosophical interest are his novel *Nausea* (1938), his plays *No Exit* (1947) and *The Flies* (1947), and his short story "The Wall" (1939), which contains his psychology of death.

At some points, Sartre dwells on the tragic nature of life. In our aloneness, we experience dread and anguish, and we fear the nothingness and death that face us. The "other" is either the uncaring stranger or the enemy who wishes to possess and dominate. In Sartre's play *No Exit,* one of the characters describes hell: "You remember all we were told about the torture-chambers, the fire and brimstone, the 'burning marl.' Old wives' tales! There's no need for red-hot pokers. Hell is—other people!"[19] The majority of people are in "bad faith" with themselves. They attempt to shift responsibility for who they are to the determining factors of heredity and environment, to the will of a superior power, or to the mass or collective in which a sense of personal responsibility is lost.

Sartre illustrates one type of "bad faith" by his story (which, incidentally, also has been used by the French existentialist, Simone de Beauvoir) of a girl who is taken to a restaurant by a man, and who, to put off the moment when she must face making a definite decision and say either "yes" or "no" to him, pretends to herself

Excerpt from Sartre:

Existentialism and Humanism
(1946)

Atheistic existentialism, of which I am a representative, declares with greater consistency that if God does not exist there is at least one being whose existence comes before its essence, a being which exists before it can be defined by any conception of it. That being is man. . . . What do we mean by saying that existence precedes essence? We mean that man first of all exists, encounters himself, surges up in the world—and defines himself afterwards. If man as the existentialist sees him is not definable, it is because to begin with he is nothing. He will not be anything until later, and then he will be what he makes of himself. Thus, there is no human nature, because there is no God to have a conception of it. Man simply is. Not that he is simply what he conceives himself to be, but he is what he wills, and as he conceives himself after already existing—as he wills to be after that leap towards existence. Man is nothing else but that which he makes of himself. That is the first principle of existentialism. . . . But what do we mean to say by this, but that man is of a greater dignity than a stone or a table? For we mean to say that man primarily exists—that man is, before all else, something which propels itself towards a future and is aware that it is doing so. Man is, indeed, a project which possesses a subjective life, instead of being a kind of moss, or a fungus or a cauliflower. Before that projection of the self nothing exists; not even in the heaven of intelligence: man will only attain existence when he is what he purposes to be.

J.-P. Sartre, *Existentialism and Humanism,* trans. Philip Mairet (London: Methuen, 1948).

that she does not notice his intentions toward her. Finally there comes a moment when he takes her hand; she must make a decision. Instead, she becomes totally absorbed in intellectual conversation, and leaves her hand to be taken by him, without noticing it, as if he has just picked up some *thing,* any thing, off the table. She has dissociated herself from her hand, for the time being, and is *pretending to herself* that it is nothing whatever to do with her. Her hand just rests in his hand, inert and thinglike. If she had removed it, or deliberately left it where it was,

she would apparently have come to some decision. But by simply not taking responsibility for her hand, she avoided the need to decide; this is "bad faith."[20]

Although people experience themselves as fragmentary and discordant, they are free and therefore are responsible for their lives and decisions. This freedom, Sartre believes, gives us dignity and saves us from being mere objects:

The essential consequence of our earlier remarks is that man being condemned to be free carries the weight of the whole world on his shoulders;

he is responsible for the world and for himself as a way of being. . . . Furthermore this absolute responsibility is not resignation; it is simply the logical requirement of the consequences of our freedom. . . . Thus there are no accidents in a life; a community event which suddenly bursts forth and involves me in it does not come from the outside. If I am mobilized in a war, this war is my war; it is my image and I deserve it. I deserve it first because I could always get out of it by suicide or by desertion; these ultimate possibilities are those which must always be present for us when there is a question of envisaging a situation. For lack of getting out of it, I have chosen it.[21]

The goal of human striving is a heightened consciousness and awareness that may come to those who are free and responsible. For Sartre, the individual stands as a tragic and lonely specimen of humanity. We must look to ourselves, because there is no God and no purpose or meaning in the universe:

> Sartre's view of atheism is so stark and bleak that it seems to turn many people toward religion. This is exactly as it should be. The choice must be hard either way; for man, a problematic being to his depths, cannot lay hold of his ultimate commitments with a smug and easy security. It may be that, as the modern world moves on, the Sartrean kind of freedom will be more and more the only kind man can experience. As society becomes more totalitarian, the islands of freedom get smaller and more cut off from the mainland and from each other—which is to say from any spontaneous interchange with nature or the community of other human beings.[22]

Some Characteristics of Phenomenology

♦ ♦ ♦ ♦ ♦ ♦ ♦ ♦ ♦ ♦

In whatever context the term *phenomenology* is used, it refers to the distinction introduced by Kant between the **phenomenon,** or appearance of reality in consciousness, and the **noumenon,** or being of reality in itself. The problem of reconciling reality and thought about reality is as old as philosophy itself. It is complicated by the fact that we cannot know reality independently of consciousness, and we cannot know consciousness independently of reality. Philosophers are committed to penetrating the mystery; phenomenologists attempt to solve this apparent dualism. They begin by asserting that, if there is a solution at all, it is that only phenomena are presented and that therefore is where we must first look. As Maurice Merleau-Ponty has written, "Phenomenology is an inventory of consciousness as milieu of the universe."[23] If we are to know what anything is, and this is the commitment of the phenomenologist, we must examine the consciousness we have of it; if this does not give us an answer, nothing will.

Phenomenology, as a philosophical movement, came to prominence in Germany in the first quarter of the twentieth century and has since spread mainly to France and the United States. The founding father of phenomenology is Edmund Husserl (1859–1938), who was 54 years old before he brought out of his preliminary explorations the first developed description of phenomenology as a rigorous *method* for analyzing consciousness. He was followed by Max Scheler (1874–1928), whose conviction was that philosophy is above all concerned with humanity's historical situation. Scheler was eclipsed by both Martin Heidegger (1899–1976) and Maurice Merleau-Ponty (1908–1961). Heidegger's outlook often is discussed under "existentialism," but although he has exerted considerable influence on it, he expressly indicated that he did not want to be identified with the philosophy represented by Sartre.

The principal characteristics of phenomenology can be broadly indicated, remembering that there is the strict sense in which it is to be regarded only as a method. For the phenomenologist, philosophy should begin with a concerted effort to *describe* the content of consciousness. *An express effort* is necessary for description; by "description" is meant a careful look at the essential structures of the things exactly as they appear. The phenomenologist is concerned with concrete things, not so much as they are in everyday affairs, but rather with the

Since there is no escape from consciousness, the only way to solve the problem is more phenomena and, perhaps, better phenomena.

essential structures of those things as they are objectively present in our consciousness, which is the matrix of experience.

Some Phenomenological Thinkers

♦ ♦ ♦ ♦ ♦ ♦ ♦ ♦ ♦ ♦

EDMUND HUSSERL

If we are to understand what phenomenology means as a contemporary philosophical attitude, we must first understand what it meant in the mind of its founder, Edmund Husserl (1859–1938) (see biography and excerpt, pp. 340–341). As we pointed out, phenomenology is both a method and a philosophy. As a method it outlines the steps that must be taken to arrive at the pure phenomenon: we must start with the human subject and her or his consciousness and endeavor to get back to a "pure consciousness." To attain the sphere of pure consciousness, one must strip away one's everyday experiences and images; when this is done, there remain certain essential features or an "intuition of essences." For example, the color "red" is no less a thing than is a horse; each has an "essence" that is entirely independent of any concrete, contingent existence it may have. It is sufficient that the experience of red can be as clearly distinguished from the experience of green as can the experience of horse from that of man.[24]

Further, the phenomenologists aim to present philosophy as an autonomous and basic method—a "root-science"—that can serve all knowledge. In contrast to the methods of objective science, formal logic, and the dialectic method of overcoming oppositions, the phenomenological method begins with the *experiencing knower*—the one who perceives.

As a philosophy, phenomenology, according to Husserl, gives necessary, essential knowledge of that which is. In the course of its investigations, therefore, it discovers those objects (infinite in number) that make up the experienced world. These objects can be described in terms of the consciousness wherein they are found. Phenomenology is thus often conceived as a return to "things," as opposed to illusions or mental constructs, precisely because a "thing" *is* the direct object of consciousness in its pure form.

MARTIN HEIDEGGER

In 1916, Husserl accepted the chair of philosophy at the German University of Freiburg. One of his students was Martin Heidegger (1889–1976) (see biography and excerpt, pp. 342–343), who had been convinced to study philosophy by Husserl's book *Logical Investigations.* Husserl's method of instruction took the form of leading the students in phenomenological "seeing"; he discouraged the introduction of untested ideas from the philosophical tradition; he rejected appeals to authority or to the great figures in the history of philosophy. Heidegger found in this method the best approach to his own philosophical problems. Heidegger poses three central questions: Who is a human? What is concrete being? and, most serious, What is Being (ultimate reality)?

Heidegger asks: "What does it mean to say 'I am'?" We are creatures "thrown" into the world without our consent. We need to acknowledge our finiteness. We came out by the abyss, and before us lies the abyss of death. Confronted with nothingness, we are anxious, but this anxiety enables us to become aware of our existence. As we study ourselves, questions of temporality, fear and dread, conscience and guilt, nothingness and death, come to the fore.

Heidegger is especially critical of people who live superficially and who emphasize things, quantity, and personal power. Modern people are rootless and empty because they have lost their sense of relationship to Being in its fullness. Concrete being must be transcended so that we are open to the totality of Being as such. Only through the discovery of the dynamic nature of existence can we be saved from the chaos and frustration that threaten us.

Heidegger's discussion of Being is found in his famous, albeit difficult, book *Being and Time.* There he attempts to redirect the path of Western philosophy. "The history of Western

The primary content of consciousness is physical objects, not sense data, therefore there is no need to reconstruct them.

Edmund Husserl

Edmund Husserl (1859–1938), a German philosopher, is the central figure in the phenomenological movement. He began his career in mathematics but moved to philosophy and taught at Halle, Göttingen, and Freiburg. He came to see a career in philosophy as a calling or sacred moral duty as he worked out a new philosophical approach, the phenomenological method. Husserl distinguished between the world as known to science and the world in which we live. The latter includes awareness and the intentionality of consciousness. Although we can "think away" any object, we cannot think away our consciousness. The existence of consciousness is the one thing that cannot be thought away. The study of the lived world and our direct experience of it is the central task of phenomenology. Husserl's views about intentionality and intuition have exercised a strong influence on philosophy, especially in Germany, France, and America. His books include *The Idea of Phenomenology* (1906–1907), *Cartesian Meditations* (1931), and *Ideas: General Introduction to Phenomenology* (1913 and 1952).

philosophy begins with the Greeks posing the question of the Being of the things-that-are; it ends with Nietzsche answering that question in a way that renders impossible any further inquiry, at least on traditional grounds. Heidegger proposes to create a climate in which the questioning of Being might reopen."[25] He does this by establishing a new basis for ontology; Being, for Heidegger, does not lie in a world beyond our world. Instead, Heidegger's existential phe-

Excerpt from Husserl:

Ideas: General Introduction to Phenomenology "The World of the Natural Standpoint: I and My World About Me—" (1913)

Our first outlook upon life is that of natural human beings, imagining, judging, feeling, willing, "*from the natural standpoint.*" Let us make clear to ourselves what this means in the form of simple meditations which we can best carry on in the first person.

I am aware of a world, spread out in space endlessly, and in time becoming and become, without end. I am aware of it, that means, first of all, I discover it immediately, intuitively, I experience it. Through sight, touch, hearing, etc., in the different ways of sensory perception, corporeal things somehow spatially distributed are *for me simply there,* in verbal or figurative sense "present," whether or not I pay them special attention by busying myself with them, considering, thinking, feeling, willing. Animal beings also, perhaps men, are immediately there for me; I look up, I see them, I hear them coming towards me, I grasp them by the hand; speaking with them, I understand immediately what they are sensing and thinking, the feelings that stir them, what they wish or will. They too are present as realities in my field of intuition, even when I pay them no attention. But it is not necessary that they and other objects likewise should be present precisely in my *field of perception.* For me real objects are there, definite, more or less familiar, agreeing with what is actually perceived without themselves being perceived or even intuitively present. I can let my attention wander from the writing-table I have just seen and observed, through the unseen portions of the room behind my back to the verandah, into the garden, to the children in the summer-house, and so forth, to all the objects concerning which I precisely "know" that they are there and yonder in my immediate co-perceived surroundings—a knowledge which has nothing of conceptual thinking in it, and first changes into clear intuiting with the bestowing of attention, and even then only partially and for the most part very imperfectly.

Edmund Husserl, *Ideas: General Introduction to Phenomenology,* trans. W. R. Boyce Gibson (New York: Collier Books, 1962).

nomenology must show that human existence is the key to interpreting the history of philosophy and that by exposing the essence of that existence we arrive at a true understanding of Being itself.

People may (and most do) live an unauthentic existence as members of a collective absorbed only in the things and details of everyday affairs. But we can, if we so choose, live an authentic human existence; we fix our gaze on the truth as

Martin Heidegger

Martin Heidegger (1889–1976) was born in Baden, Germany, and exercised considerable influence on many philosophers of Continental Europe and South America. He received a doctoral degree in philosophy from the University of Freiburg, where he studied under and then assisted Edmund Husserl, the founder of phenomenology. For a time he was professor of philosophy at the University of Marburg, but returned to Freiburg to succeed Husserl.

With the rise of the Nazi movement, he disavowed his allegiance to Husserl (who was a Jew), and in 1933 became the first National Socialist rector of the University of Freiburg, where he delivered a public lecture on the "Role of the University in the New Reich," stressing the emergence of a new and glorious Germany—there was a nationalistic strain in Heidegger's thinking. In 1934, when he became disillusioned with the Nazi regime he resigned as rector, but he continued to teach until he retired in 1957. Most of his writings deal with such questions as "What is Being?" "Why is there something rather than nothing at all?" and with human existence, anxiety, alienation, and death.

His most influential works are *Being and Time* (1927) and *Introduction to Metaphysics* (1953).

we are able to discover it, live our lives in the light of death, and thereby view our lives in a new perspective.

MAURICE MERLEAU-PONTY

Until recently, perhaps the least known of the phenomenologists was Maurice Merleau-Ponty (1908–1961). Merleau-Ponty's main work was done in the field of philosophical psychology, in which he used the phenomenological method as a philosophical tool. He had a vast acquaintance with the findings and experiments of modern psychology—particularly of Gestalt psychology—which encouraged him to turn his attention away from the behavioristic character

of psychology to the "essential" aspects of experience.

> Like Husserl, he is convinced that the genuine philosopher must begin by painstakingly examining his own experiences of reality, thus avoiding the two extremes of merely examining and re-examining *what has been said* about reality and that of considering only the outward manifestations of experience with no reference to reality at all.[26]

Merleau-Ponty agreed with Husserl that there can be no knowledge of things-in-themselves but only of things as they are accessible to human consciousness. He insisted, however, that all perceptual experience carries with it

Excerpt from Heidegger:

What Is Philosophy?

When we ask, "What is philosophy?" then we are speaking *about* philosophy. By asking in this way we are obviously taking a stand above and, therefore, outside of philosophy. But the aim of our question is to enter *into* philosophy, to tarry in it, to conduct ourselves in its manner, that is, "to philosophize." The path of our discussion must, therefore, not only have a clear direction, but this direction must at the same time give us the guarantee that we are moving within philosophy and not outside of it and around it.

The path of our discussion must, therefore, be of such a kind and direction that that of which philosophy treats concerns us personally, affects us and, indeed, touches us in our very nature.

But does not philosophy thereby become a matter of affection, emotions, and sentiments?

"With fine sentiments bad literature is made." These words . . . apply not only to literature but even more to philosophy. Sentiments, even the finest, have no place in philosophy. Sentiments, it is said, are something irrational. Philosophy, on the other hand, is not only something rational but is the actual guardian of reason.

Martin Heidegger, *What Is Philosophy?* trans. Jean T. Wilde and William Kluback (New Haven, Conn.: College and University Press, 1956).

an essential reference to a world that transcends consciousness. Therefore, phenomenological description, as Merleau-Ponty conceived it, does not deal with sense data or essences alone; instead we have a perceptual encounter with the world. Merleau-Ponty announced the "primacy of perception" as a mode of access to the real.[27]

The importance of Merleau-Ponty for phenomenology lies in the introduction of the notion of dialectic into phenomenology. He has been called a "philosopher of ambiguity," which is not to say that his thought is ambiguous but rather that Merleau-Ponty sees dialectic as essential to philosophy—in much the same way that Sartre regards "absurdity."[28] In his book *Les aventures de la dialectique*, Merleau-Ponty believes that if the subject–object dialectic is to have any validity at all, it must remain ambiguous or it will destroy itself.[29] Because of this view of the dialectic, Merleau-Ponty sees phenomenological description as unable to be completed; phenomenological description is concerned with a world in process, and the process cannot be predicted; only that is given that can be described. The world in its history does not follow a preconceived model; rather it takes on sense through its history, which is truly a history only through a subject–object dialectic. Our understanding of the world depends on our ability to enlarge reason such that it will include both the nonrational and the irrational. "Philosophy's attention to the contingent, the vague, the dark underside of things is for Merleau-Ponty only a way to be more faithful to the task of reason itself, the task of unrestricted reflection."[30]

Some Characteristics of Process Philosophy

"The term 'process philosophy' is one way of pointing to a profound change which has come over speculative philosophy or metaphysics in the modern period in Europe and America."[31] Perhaps the most widely accepted type of speculative philosophy in America today is process philosophy. This is fundamentally a metaphysical position concerned with the categories and principles necessary for interpreting process and development; **becoming** is its watchword. Its basic doctrine is that the universe is essentially a creative advance and that everything in the universe is in the process of moving toward self-realization and fulfillment. Process is marked by creativity; things are constantly trying to create new experiences for themselves. Each new phase of a thing as it completes the process of self-realization adds novelty to the pluralistic universe, contributing to other parts of the universe as they also struggle toward self-realization. Natural scientists, social scientists, humanists, and theologians recognize the reality of change and development. They measure their efforts and achievements in terms of adaptation to and control of change.

CREATIVITY

Creativity, as the term implies, aims at novelty; each new self-realization is also a new way of perceiving the world. Perhaps the most difficult part of understanding Whitehead's thought is what is meant by the fundamental units of existence, which are not static, material entities, but events or what he calls "actual occasions." They are realized in experience by what he calls "actual entities."

HISTORICAL DEVELOPMENT

Charles Hartshorne, a contemporary process philosopher, has shown that process philosophy stemmed from a neoclassical tradition that coexisted with the classical approach in both Western and Asian philosophy. He writes: "Greek philosophy tended to depreciate becoming and exalt mere being,"[32] and as a result the reality of process was underestimated. In the Western world a neoclassical theology remained, until recently, overshadowed by the classical systems of Aristotle and Aquinas. Moreover, in the modern scientific period—the second half of the nineteenth century and the early decades of the twentieth century—the major assumption of science was that nature consisted of fixed, material objects located in time and space. Matter was regarded as the irreducible stuff of the universe. Accordingly, the model for thinking about the contents and behavior of nature was that of a machine—all the particular things of nature were thought to be rigidly determined parts of a large mechanism. Things were related to each other in a sequence of cause and effect that allowed no room for novelty. Human nature also was viewed in similar material and mechanical terms.

CHALLENGE MADE BY PROCESS PHILOSOPHY

Those thinkers committed to the ideas of change, creativity, organism, and evolution (such as Bergson and Whitehead) questioned these basic assumptions of modern science and of philosophies based on it. They attacked the principles of substance and determinism, substituting the concept of events and the principles of process and creativity. How can there be any genuine novelty in nature, they asked, if the basic reality is material and mechanistic and movements merely repeat themselves? Is there any room for human freedom in such a universe? If not, we need to modify the mechanistic view. This is not to say that process philosophy denies the insights of science; it moves away from an outdated mechanistic physics to a new dynamic physics and especially to a metaphysics in which the novel results of becoming and the values that attach to self-realization are taken into account. Process philosophy discovered the reality of time, not as the medium of perishing but as the means whereby new values are added to existence. If the physical universe is "running down," they say, a spiritual order is ascending.

Two Process Philosophers

◆ ◆ ◆ ◆ ◆ ◆ ◆ ◆ ◆ ◆ ◆

HENRI BERGSON

The influence of Henri Bergson (1859–1941) as a forerunner of contemporary process philosophy cannot be overestimated. Born in 1859—the year John Dewey was born and Charles Darwin's *Origin of Species* was published—Bergson prepared the way for a metaphysics of creative process, freedom, and novelty. Four major ideas serve as indicators of his commitment to the tenets of process philosophy: *intuition* as a way of knowing reality; the *self* as exemplifying the most concrete reality; and the ideas of *duration* and *élan vital*.

Analysis and Intuition.
Bergson was convinced that there are two different ways of knowing a thing: the first is to "move around" the object and the second is to "enter into" it. To move around an object is accomplished through analysis and abstraction. This kind of knowledge depends on the vantage point of the observer and therefore is different for each observer and thus is *relative*. By contrast, the second kind of knowledge, *intuition*, is absolute. Intuition overcomes the limitations of varying perspectives and allows us to grasp the object as it really is. In *Introduction to Metaphysics*, Bergson emphasizes the nonconceptual character of intuition; he sees it as a kind of *intellectual sympathy* by which one places oneself within an object to coincide with what is unique within it. Unlike the intellect (or the process of analysis)—which remains outside what it knows, requires symbols, and produces knowledge that is always abstract and relative to some viewpoint—intuition enters into what it knows, dispenses with symbols, and produces knowledge that is concrete and absolute. For example, in the case of the self we cannot perceive what constitutes a person's essence from without, because by definition someone's essence is internal. With the self, intuition is an immersion in the indivisible flow of consciousness, a grasping of pure becoming—a continuous process. Most important for the future conception of metaphysics and process philosophy was Bergson's conviction that intuition discovers about reality the truth that it is continuous and cannot be reduced to parts.

The Self.
Closely allied to the capacity of intuition that we all possess is Bergson's view of the self. We have seen that the intellect, proceeding analytically, is never capable of discovering the true self. Psychology, which uses an analytic method to examine the self, dissects the self into separate "states" such as sensations, feelings, and ideas, which it studies separately. To study the self by studying separately the various psychical states is, says Bergson, like trying to *know* Paris by studying sketches of various sections, all of which are labeled "Paris."[33] Analysis stops life and movement; moreover, it separates into several independent and static parts what is a free-flowing and enduring movement of consciousness.

Like Descartes, Bergson founded his philosophy on the immediate knowledge of the self. The inner life of the self is compared by Bergson to a continual increase, like the snowball increasing in size as it rolls down a hill. The self is known only by intuition, is immediate, and endures:

> What is really important for philosophy is to know exactly what unity, what multiplicity, and what reality superior both to abstract unity and multiplicity the multiple unity of the self actually is. Now the philosophy will know this only when it recovers possession of the simple intuition of the self by the self. Then, according to the direction it chooses for its descent from this summit, it will arrive at unity or multiplicity, or

at any one of the concepts by which we try to define the moving life of the self. But no mingling of these concepts would give anything which at all resembles the self that endures.[34]

Duration.

The key to Bergson's philosophy is the concept of real time, or duration; he centers his attention on the process in all things, which he called "duration." Duration, or becoming, Bergson maintains, was overlooked by classical Western philosophy. What does Bergson mean by "duration"? We said earlier that for Bergson the intellect is capable of comprehending only static parts and is therefore unable to understand becoming, movement, or change. Only intuition can grasp duration. Reality *is* duration; reality consists not of things but of things in the making—changing states and tendencies. A melody illustrates pure duration: "Each (moment) permeating the other and organizing themselves like the notes of a tune, so as to form what we shall call a continuous or qualitative multiplicity with no resemblance to number."[35] Duration also is process, change, becoming. Here Bergson's thought emerges as process philosophy *par excellence*.[36] He often speaks of reality as equated with real time or duration, and duration is equated with change. Duration is continuous in that the past survives in the present, and the present survives in the future. It is also creative: the flow of time changes an event such that even an act that is repeated or an event that is remembered differs from the original because it now has new neighbors in the flow of time. Finally, duration means authentic existence: "We find that, for a conscious being, to exist is to change, to change is to mature, to mature is to go on creating oneself endlessly."[37]

Elan Vital.

One of the most profound influences on Bergson's thought was the theory of evolution, which allowed science to understand duration and becoming. Bergson's vision of duration rescued the principle of evolution from a mechanistic interpretation and prepared the way for a metaphysics of creative process, freedom, and novelty. Bergson found the existing theories of evolution inadequate and thus offered a new theory of evolution, which he presented, appropriately, in *Creative Evolution*.

To obtain a true understanding of the evolutionary process, the findings of biology must be supplemented, Bergson thought, by the findings of metaphysics. The chief clue is what intuition reveals of our own inner nature as living beings. When we focus on what intuition discloses of ourselves, we find not only continuous becoming and real duration, but also a consciousness of an *élan vital* (vital impulse), of our own evolution in time. We are thus led to the idea of "an original impetus of life" that pervades the whole evolutionary process.

The *élan vital* is regarded by Bergson as a "current of consciousness" that has penetrated matter, given rise to living bodies, and determined the course of their evolution. This current passes from one generation to the next by way of reproduction and is the cause of variations that accumulate and produce new species. In this view, all organisms tend toward more complicated and higher forms, and this is accomplished through the *élan vital*, the creative aspect of evolution. Creative evolution is a cosmic process that can be grasped adequately not by the intellect but by intuition; only by intuition do we comprehend the duration, movement, and novelty stemming from the *élan vital*.

ALFRED NORTH WHITEHEAD

Alfred North Whitehead (1861–1947) (see biography and excerpt, pp. 348–349) is the philosopher most commonly associated with process philosophy. He made an outstanding attempt to construct a new and comprehensive metaphysical system in which the traditional concept of substance, with its connotation of "fixed" or "unchanging," was replaced by the idea of events that flow into and out of each other in a continual process of change. The final realities are passing and take time; they are events. Influenced mainly by Bergson, F. H. Bradley, and William James, Whitehead's Gifford Lectures of 1927–1928, *Process and Real-*

ity, defined speculative philosophy (metaphysics): "Speculative philosophy is the endeavor to frame a coherent, logical, necessary system of general ideas in terms of which every element of our experience can be interpreted."[38]

Three Periods of Thought. Whitehead's work generally is described as falling into three periods: the early years at Cambridge University up to 1910, when he was collaborating with Bertrand Russell on the logical foundations of mathematics; the middle years in London up to 1924, when he was writing on the philosophy of science; and the last years at Harvard University in America, when he constructed his metaphysics. The philosophical interests expressed in his later work can be found implicit in his earlier writing; the general assumption of Whitehead's logical and mathematical work influenced his later philosophy.

Whitehead has further reflections on the nature of metaphysics:

> Metaphysics is a description. Its discussion so as to elucidate its accuracy is necessary but is foreign to the description. The tests of accuracy are logical coherence, adequacy and exemplification. A metaphysical description takes its origin from one select field of interest. It receives its confirmation by establishing itself as adequate and as exemplified in other fields of interest.[39]

Whitehead's speculative philosophy is a form of process philosophy. Among others, his basic categories include: "actual entities," prehension; society, or *nexus;* and creativity. Whitehead's thought, particularly as expressed in *Process and Reality,* is complex and interconnected—after all, he believed that "connectedness is the essence of all things." As a result, it is difficult to present Whitehead's categories in a condensed and hence abstract way. We suggest you read Whitehead's own work to gain a full understanding of these categories.

Misplaced Concreteness. Whitehead expressed his concern to overcome the limitations of abstractions as "misplaced concreteness." He was convinced that Newtonian physics was based on the fallacy of misplaced concreteness. He also believed that there is no element whatsoever that possesses the character of simple location. The concept of an isolated atom, he says, is the result of intellectual *abstraction*. But these abstractions lift a thing out of its concrete environment. We must not mistake the abstraction for the concrete. Things such as instants of time, points in space, or independent particles of matter are helpful concepts for scientific thought, but when they are taken as descriptions of concrete reality they lead to distortion. Whitehead, when discussing Nature, distinguishes between Nature alive or fully concrete, and Nature as lifeless or as represented only by the mechanical universe of the physical sciences. For Whitehead, Nature means "the world as interpreted by reliance on clear and distinct sensory experiences, visual, auditory and tactile."[40]

Actual Entities. Whitehead views concrete reality (Nature) as atomistic—but in a novel fashion. Whitehead discards the term *atom* because it is just one more expression of abstracted lifeless Nature; he substitutes the term *actual entities* or *actual occasions.* These are "drops of experience, complex and interdependent."[41] Nothing is more real than actual entities; they are "completed facts." They are novel ways of feeling the many parts of reality in a single moment of experience. Most important, actual entities are not separate, independent entities; they are related and interdependent, which harks back to the connectedness of all things. They never exist in isolation but are "chunks in the life of nature." Whitehead's actual entities permit us to view nature as a living *organism.*

Prehension. The notion of *prehension,* another basic category of existence, comes into play when the actual entity is analyzed. Whitehead uses "prehension" to describe how the elements of actual entities are grasped and integrated into a unified whole in the process constituting an actual occasion. Nothing in the world is unrelated; prehension is "concrete facts of relatedness" in-

Alfred North Whitehead

Alfred North Whitehead (1861–1947) was born at Ramsgate, England, the son of an Anglican clergyman and schoolmaster. He entered Trinity College, Cambridge University, where he concentrated his studies in the field of mathematics. Later Whitehead and Bertrand Russell, a distinguished logician, wrote *Principia Mathematica* (1910–1913), one of the great works on the foundation of mathematics. In 1910, Whitehead moved to the University of London and in 1914 became Professor of Applied Mathematics at the Imperial College of Science and Technology. Here he became interested in the aims and problems of mass education.

In 1924, at the age of 63, Whitehead surprised those who knew him by accepting a professorship of philosophy at Harvard University. He proceeded to develop a system of metaphysics recorded in *Process and Reality* (1929), his masterpiece in speculative philosophy, and in *Science and the Modern World* (1925), *Religion in the Making* (1926), and *Adventures of Ideas* (1933). He has said that "From twenty on [he] was interested in philosophy, religion, logic, and history." In an age of analysis and specialization, he developed an intellectual drive toward synthesis and a comprehensive view of things.

volving that entity in a complex of relations to other things.[42] In stressing the role of prehension in the makeup of the actual entity (that it is related to other entities), Whitehead understands it as a kind of feeling which the developing occasion has for previous occasions, for example, attraction or rejection. Thus, for him, feeling is the primordial characteristic of concrete experience.

Nexus. We do not ever experience a single isolated actual entity but only a collection of these entities. Whitehead calls these groups either a *society* or a *nexus*. Because actual entities are microscopic, whether identified as electrically charged particles in physics or as drops of experience in psychology, they are part of the objects that common sense experiences; in fact, they are the most concrete elements in our experience. These objects are societies of occasions or a collection of interrelated drops of experience.

Creativity. Whitehead saw reality as a continual process in which actual entities are constantly becoming, a process in which *what* an actual entity becomes depends on *how* it becomes. He emphasizes the principle of creativity as the fundamental characteristic of the processes of nature. Creativity is "the category of the ultimate. . . . Creativity is the principle of *novelty.*"[43] An actual occasion is a novel entity different from any other entity in the "many" with which it unites. Thus creativity is the ultimate principle by which we arrive at complex unities. We must

Excerpt from Whitehead:

Modes of Thought—Epilogue:
"The Aim of Philosophy" (1938)

What is the special function of philosophy?

In order to answer this question, we must first decide what constitutes the philosophic character of any particular doctrine. What makes a doctrine philosophical? No one truth, thoroughly understood in all the infinitude of its bearings, is more or less philosophical than any other truth.

Philosophy is an attitude of mind towards doctrines ignorantly entertained. By the phrase "ignorantly entertained" I mean that the full meaning of the doctrine in respect to the infinitude of circumstances to which it is relevant, is not understood. The philosophic attitude is a resolute attempt to enlarge the understanding of the scope of application of every notion which enters into our current thought. The philosophic attempt takes every word, and every phrase, in the verbal expression of thought, and asks, What does it mean? It refuses to be satisfied by the conventional presupposition that every sensible person knows the answer. As soon as you rest satisfied with primitive ideas, and with primitive propositions, you have ceased to be a philosopher.

A. N. Whitehead, *Modes of Thought* (New York: Macmillan, 1938).

---

not take each actual entity separately—this is to abstract once again; rather, we have the product of a "novel togetherness." By applying the ultimate category of creativity in the interpretation of the cosmos, Whitehead, like Bergson with his view of *élan vital,* viewed the world as a process aiming at the realization of values rather than as constituted by lifeless matter.

Reflections

Although there are differing viewpoints, moods, and attitudes within both existentialism and phenomenology, all of the philosophers of these two schools are concerned with the human predicament. They all deal with the feelings of estrangement and alienation, and the separation of humans from their deeper selves, from their fellows, and from nature and the world—a separation many people experience in modern life. In one way or another these philosophers call attention to the questions: What is a person? What is the meaning of our human existence? What is our final destiny? They want all individuals to think about what is involved in being a person. For simplicity, from this point on in our discussion, we will speak of existentialists, keeping in mind that most of what we say will apply to the phenomenologists.

The existentialists protest against the methods and outlooks of many philosophers in the past. They believe that most philosophers, in dealing with speculative questions and in the formulation of "systems," have overlooked the vital problems of human existence. Consequently, philosophical thought has been divorced from concrete events. The existentialists are equally dissatisfied with the linguistic analysis and logical positivism of more recent years. They think that these movements, in their effort to avoid what they regard as pseudoproblems, have themselves become enmeshed in pseudoproblems of their own making.

Some people commend the existentialists for bringing certain contemporary problems of human experience and existence forcefully to our attention and for being sensitive to the discrepancy between thought and action. They think that the intellectuals of our time all too frequently have been satisfied to watch and describe what they should have shaped and guided. The existentialists ask the intellectuals to take a stand when life and death issues are in the balance. They recognize the need for decision and action, as well as for contemplation and analysis.

As we have pointed out, existentialism is a movement of protest and rebellion. It is a reaction against the philosophical solutions proposed by Hegel, Marx, and Engels, and modern scientists. The existentialists believe that these proposed solutions are ineffective in meeting the problems of modern humans. They think that the positivistic and linguistic emphases and the masses of descriptive knowledge of the sciences often leave our lives empty. They say that people's feeling of estrangement has increased during the last hundred years. The Industrial Revolution, the technology that has produced great cities, the collectivist trends and mass movements, the fragmentation and specialization of knowledge and life, all have tended to depersonalize human beings. "Because the very existence of man on this earth is menaced, because the annihilation of man, his dehumanization and the destruction of his humanity and of all moral values is a real danger, therefore the meaning of human existence becomes our problem."[44]

In rejecting a false and extreme objectivity that tends to deny the distinctive qualities of the human, existentialism seems to have gone to the opposite extreme and rejected all objectivity. Thus existentialists have minimized the importance of science, nature, the external world, reason, and the many valid insights of other kinds of philosophy. As a reaction to those who ignore the subject, existentialists tend to ignore the object. Furthermore, their critics claim that the existentialists are giving an inadequate description of even the human experience that is their prime concern. In addition to studying experience itself, we need to ask what it is that we experience, and hence to study the outside world. Phenomenology has made an attempt to correct this oversight.

The critics also ask how—if human reason is devalued or discredited and there are no objective standards of truth and goodness to which we can appeal—can we settle disputes except by force? They ask whether existentialism is a retreat from reason into the fascinating world of metaphor, where objective standards do not apply. In this sense, existentialism is unrelated to the historical mainstream of recent technical philosophy. This may be one reason why it has gained more support from artists, writers, and theologians than from philosophers and scientists.

Is existentialism in part the product of a particular historical epoch and of conditions that have led a disillusioned intellectual elite to center its attention on the meaningless and absurd elements in modern life? Existentialism may be the result of the swing of the pendulum away from the extremely optimistic rationalism that was the product of a different set of conditions at the beginning of this century. To emphasize any one mood or set of feelings as the clue to the understanding of life and the world in their entirety is dangerous. To stress anxiety and dread, which are not directed toward specific objects, is likely to lead to a sense of absurdity and nothingness. Nevertheless, existentialism has called our attention to serious frustrations and disorders in modern life and to the theory that not only modern civilization but also human existence itself is in a precarious condition.

The process philosophers share certain features with the phenomenologists and existentialists. Just as the existentialists attacked the idealist philosophy of the nineteenth century for failing to do justice to individual life and freedom, so both Bergson and Whitehead challenged the abstractness and materialist bias of modern science. Is reality, they asked, no more than what science says it is? Does nature consist of material objects located in space? Is matter the final "stuff" out of which all things are made? Process philosophy attacks these assumptions as well as the basic thesis that, because all the particular things in nature are but parts of a large machine, we need only describe the laws of the system with mathematical precision to determine how every individual item behaves.

These assumptions of modern science raised serious philosophical problems for both Bergson and Whitehead. Does Nature really consist of material objects located in space? Can the intellect discover such an arrangement of things? We have seen how Bergson, with his notion of duration, and Whitehead, with his view of actual entities, challenge the static scientific outlook. Both also reject the abstract approach to the analysis of matter: Bergson stresses intuition as a way of knowing and Whitehead is concerned with the "connectedness of all things."

Bergson's version of process philosophy was the dominant mode of philosophical thought in the early twentieth century. However, its distrust of reason and its reliance on intuition of the immediate experience of duration contributed to its decline, even during Bergson's life.[45] Speculative philosophy or metaphysics needs systematic formulation and requires language, whereas intuition tends to be unsystematic and ultimately is reduced to silence.

Whitehead, it appears to us, avoids the pitfall of immediacy that Bergson faced. For Whitehead, process is not the sole theme of metaphysics. To formulate "the complete problem of metaphysics" in *Process and Reality,* Whitehead cited two lines of a famous hymn:

> Abide with me!
> Fast falls the eventide . . .

He comments:

> Here the first line expresses the permanences, "abide," "me" and the "Being" addressed; and the second line sets these permanences amid the inescapable flux. . . . Those philosophers who start with the first line have given us the metaphysics of "substance"; and those who start with the second line have developed the metaphysics of "flux." But, in truth, the two lines cannot be torn apart in this way.[46]

Whitehead insists that process is equally important as permanence. The major difficulty of Whitehead's metaphysics lies elsewhere. Even the most careful effort to determine what Whitehead meant leaves us with questions about the internal consistency and coherence of his speculative system and its adequacy and relevance as an interpretation of pre- and post-philosophical experience.[47] Whitehead, moreover, chose to solve the problem of how to express a new viewpoint in traditional language by devising a novel and formidable vocabulary that only specialists are able to comprehend. Despite these problems, however, the main drift of Whitehead's philosophy of organism has had a significant effect on philosophy in this century.

◆ ◆

Glossary Terms

BECOMING   To be in the process of coming into being.

CREATIVITY   The state of producing something novel or original that will lead to further self-realization (Whitehead).

ESSENCE   The substance or intrinsic nature which makes a thing what it is. Ordinarily *essence* is considered distinct from *existence*.

EXISTENCE   (1) For Thomists, *existence* is the act of being as ordinarily contrasted with essence; it is the state of occurring within space and time. (2) Existentialists use *existence* in a limited sense, so that *to exist* applies to personal experience and calls for creative commitment. (3) The term is often used as the opposite of *essence*.

EXISTENTIALISM   An attitude and outlook in philosophy, theology, and the arts that stresses the human predicament or people's feeling of anxiety, and emphasizes human existence and the qualities distinctive of individuals rather than "humankind" in the abstract or nature and the world in general.

NIHILISM (NIHILISTIC)   (1) An extreme form of skepticism; the denial of an objective basis for truth and meaning. (2) The doctrine that nothing exists; therefore, nothing can be known or have value. (3) The term is often used to refer to social doctrine that conditions are so evil that the present order ought to be swept aside or destroyed to make room for something better.

NOUMENON   According to Kant, the reality as it is in itself, beyond the phenomenal world we can experience and have knowledge about.

PHENOMENOLOGY   A school of philosophy of which Edmund Husserl (1859–1938) was a leader. It starts with the human subject and his or her consciousness, the experiencing knower; the knowledge we have is only of things as they are accessible to human consciousness.

PHENOMENON   According to Kant, the appearance of reality in consciousness.

PROCESS PHILOSOPHY   A school of thought in philosophy and theology which stresses process or becoming, relations, and relativity as new views of viewing reality.

TRANSVALUATION   A reappraisal or a reestimate of the accepted standards of a given society.

◆ ◆

Chapter Review

In addition to the philosophical movements discussed in previous chapters, there are at least three other contemporary perspectives: existentialism (the philosophy of existence), phenomenology, and process philosophy.

SOME CHARACTERISTICS OF EXISTENTIALISM

1. Existentialism is primarily a protest movement against traditional Western philosophy and modern society.

2. Existentialists refuse to belong to any school of thought. They resent the impersonal nature of technology and of totalitarianism.

3. Existentialism is concerned with the human predicament. Human estrangement has been a focal point during the twentieth century.

4. Existentialism stresses the awareness of being, of existing. The value of living occurs through recognition of the individual, the "I" rather than the "It."

5. Existentialists believe there is no knowledge apart from a knowing subject. The truth is experienced within us. That truth cannot be grasped abstractly; therefore, the existentialists use literary or artistic forms to express feelings and moods.

6. Existentialism emphasizes the individual and his or her freedom and responsibility.

7. Sartre, like Nietzsche, denies the existence of God. People are not driven; they create their own lives and therefore are totally responsible for their choices.

SOME CHARACTERISTICS OF PHENOMENOLOGY

1. Kant introduced the distinction between phenomenon—the appearance of reality in con-

sciousness—and noumenon—being of reality in itself. Phenomenology examines the consciousness of reality.

2. Husserl, considered the founder of phenomenology, started with the experience of human consciousness in an attempt to arrive at "pure consciousness."

3. Heidegger, a student of Husserl's, asked three questions: What is a person? What is concrete being? What is being?

4. Merleau-Ponty contributed to the field of philosophical psychology. He used the phenomenological method as a philosophical tool.

SOME CHARACTERISTICS OF PROCESS PHILOSOPHY

1. Process philosophy is fundamentally a metaphysical position concerned with the categories and principles necessary for interpreting process and development; "becoming" is its watchword.

2. Its basic doctrine is that the universe is essentially a creative advance and that everything in the universe is in the process of moving toward self-realization and fulfillment.

TWO PROCESS PHILOSOPHERS

1. Bergson was an influential forerunner of contemporary process philosophy, and Whitehead is most commonly associated with this perspective.

REFLECTIONS

1. Existentialism, like phenomenology, is a protest against traditional philosophies. Both movements are concerned with humans as individuals and with their estrangement from themselves, their fellows, and modern society.

2. Existentialists emphasize decision and action; contemplation and analysis are not sufficient.

3. Existentialists revolt against the depersonalization of humans as a result of a mass technological society, which they believed poses a threat to humanity and morality.

4. Critics contend that by stressing subjectivity, existentialists have rejected all objectivity. They have minimized the importance of science, nature, reason, and the external world.

5. Other critics assert that existentialism is a retreat from reason and is unrelated to the historical mainstream of recent technical philosophy.

6. Some critics conclude that an exaggerated emphasis on meaninglessness will become a self-fulfilling prophecy.

7. Nevertheless, the existentialists can be commended for promoting an awareness of some of the problems present in modern society.

8. The philosophers of process challenged the abstractness and materialist bias of modern science.

9. Open questions about the internal consistency and coherence of Whitehead's speculative system and its adequacy and relevance remain, as do reservations about Bergson's notion of intuition.

* *

Study Questions and Projects

1. Write an essay on "Alienation in Modern Society" indicating wherein you agree or disagree with existential interpretations. Use your library guides to periodical literature in locating up-to-date articles on such topics as alienation, anxiety, and the like.

2. Which existentialist thinker is the most sound in your judgment? Why?

3. Evaluate Kierkegaard's philosophy in the light of the following questions: What are the roles of reason, emotion, and authority in life? Should one exercise his critical faculties regarding the nature and direction of faith and decision? Are Kierkegaard's dualisms valid or distorting? Are his views on religion adequate?

4. In what respects are the following people existentialists? (a) Nicholas Berdyaev, (b) Martin Buber, (c) Fyodor Dostoevsky, (d) José Ortega y Gasset, and (e) Miguel de Unamuno. Your library can probably furnish you with reading material about each of these men.

5. Compare existentialism with logical empiricism as revolts against traditional philosophy.

6. How has existentialism been expressed in art? See Paul Tillich, "Existential Aspects of Modern Art," in Carl Michalson, ed., *Christianity and the Existentialists* (New York: Scribner's, 1956).

7. In 1958 Albert Camus, a French author, received the Nobel Prize for his literary achievements. His main philosophical work is *The Myth of Sisyphus* (New York: Knopf, 1955). Report on Camus' philosophy of life.

8. What is the relation between Christianity and existentialism? Judaism and existentialism? Some writers see a close relationship; others have said that, while there is no "Christian existentialism," some Christians are also existentialists.

9. What are central points of emphasis in phenomenology? What justification is there for grouping existentialists and phenomenologists together even though there are differences in approach and outlook?

10. To what extent and in what ways do you personally experience your life as totally and radically free as Sartre indicates? To what experience or learning in your life do you attribute this?

11. What is existentialism?

12. What are the things against which nearly all of the existentialists have been protesting?

13. Discuss the meaning of "the human predicament," "the primacy of existence," and "the leap of faith."

14. Explain and give examples that clarify the distinction between existence and essence as used in existentialism.

15. What is distinctive about the existentialist view of man? Indicate some major differences among existentialists concerning human nature.

16. Discuss process philosophy and theories of evolution with regard to human nature.

◆ ◆

Suggested Readings

Barrett, W. *The Illusion of Technique.* Garden City, N.Y.: Anchor Press, Doubleday, 1978.

Barrett, among the first to introduce existentialism to America, here attacks the question of freedom. Technology and technique threaten freedom; furthermore, they cannot deal with the deeper human problems. Barrett selects three representative thinkers—Wittgenstein, Heidegger, and James—to show the limits of logic as a technique and to consider how an individual, as a member of a technical society, must struggle to find meaning for his or her existence.

Browning, D. (ed). *Philosophers of Process.* New York: Random House, 1965.

This is a collection of the writings of those philosophers identified with process philosophy: Bergson, Peirce, James, Alexander, C. Lloyd Morgan, Dewey, Mead, and Whitehead. Contains an invaluable introduction by Charles Hartshorne on "The Development of Process Philosophy."

Grossman, R. *Phenomenology and Existentialism: An Introduction.* New York: Routledge, 1984.

An introductory text in which the author contends that no matter how revolutionary a philosophical movement may appear to be, a closer look ultimately reveals the traditional underlying issues of philosophy; he then focuses on the problems of knowledge, existence, and freedom.

Hammond, M., Horwath, J., and Keat, R. *Understanding Phenomenology.* Cambridge, Mass.: Blackwell, 1991.

An introduction to phenomenology in which the authors explain what is distinctive about the perspective, how its major proponents agree and disagree, and where to look for lines of fruitful and positive criticism.

Kaelin, E. F., and Schrag, C. O. *American Phenomenology: Origins and Development*. Hingham, Mass.: Kluwer, 1988.

A picture of the many influences that phenomenology has had on North American thought.

Lauer, Q. *Phenomenology: Its Genesis and Prospects*. New York: Harper and Row, 1958.

This Harper Torchbook reveals a genuine understanding of Husserl and phenomenology. There is an especially fine opening chapter, "What is Phenomenology?"

Raymond, D. B. *Existentialism and the Philosophical Tradition*. Englewood Cliffs, N.J.: Prentice-Hall, 1990.

This text can be used as the basis for an historical introduction to existentialism or for a thematic approach; it includes classical and contemporary readings.

Reck, A. J. *Speculative Philosophy*. Albuquerque: University of New Mexico Press, 1972.

Reck has written a comprehensive study of the nature and types of speculative philosophy. He analyzes the representatives of realism, materialism, idealism and process philosophy. He concludes with a chapter on the uses of speculative philosophy.

Solomon, R. C. (ed.). *Phenomenology and Existentialism*. Lanham, Md.: Rowman and Littlefield, 1991.

An anthology of a wide range of scholars.

———. *Introducing The Existentialists: Imaginary Interviews with Sartre, Heidegger, and Camus*. Indianapolis, Ind.: Hackett, 1981.

Imaginary conversations with Sartre, Heidegger, and Camus in which central ideas and themes of each are brought to light.

Spiegelberg, H. *The Phenomenological Movement: Historical Introduction*. 2 vols., 2nd ed. New York: Heinman, 1965.

In this scholarly work, Volume 1 presents the background and German phase of phenomenology; Volume 2 treats the French phase and gives an appraisal of the movement.

◆ ◆

Notes

1. R. G. Olson, *A Short Introduction to Philosophy* (New York: Harcourt Brace and World, 1967), p. 111.

2. W. Kaufmann, ed., *Existentialism from Dostoevsky to Sartre* (New York: World Publishing, 1956), p. 12.

3. P. Tillich, "Existentialist Aspects of Modern Art," in Carl Michaelson, ed., *Christianity and the Existentialists*, (New York: Scribner's, 1956), pp. 129, 130.

4. R. Bretall, ed., *A Kierkegaard Anthology* (Princeton: Princeton University Press, 1947).

5. H. Kuhn, *Encounter with Nothingness* (Chicago: Regnery, 1949), p. 1.

6. J.-P. Sartre, *Existentialism and Humanism*, trans. P. Mairet (London: Methuen, 1948), p. 26.

7. S. Kierkegaard, *Either-Or*, Vol. II, trans. D. F. Swenson and L. M. Swenson (Princeton: Princeton University Press, 1946), p. 175.

8. S. Kierkegaard, *The Sickness Unto Death*, trans. Walter Lowrie (New York: Doubleday Anchor Books, 1954), pp. 217, 218.

9. W. Kaufmann, *Existentialism from Dostoevsky to Sartre*, pp. 21–22.

10. K. Jaspers, *Nietzsche*, trans. C. Wallraff and F. Schmitz (Chicago: Regnery, 1965).

11. G. Marcel, *Man Against Mass Society*, trans. G. S. Fraser (New York: Regnery, 1952), p. 1.

12. G. Marcel, *Being and Having,* trans. K. Farrer (Westminster: Dacre Press, 1949), p. 167.

13. Marcel, *Being and Having,* p. 117.

14. Sartre, *Existentialism and Humanism,* p. 25.

15. For a clear picture of the relation of existentialism to academic philosophy, consult W. Barrett, *The Irrational Man* (Garden City N.Y.: Anchor Books, 1962), "The Advent of Existentialism," pp. 3–23. Barrett also has a fine chapter, "The Testimony of Modern Art," which underscores the existential tendencies in contemporary painting, sculpture, literature, and music.

16. J.-P. Sartre, *Being and Nothingness* (New York: Philosophical Library), 1956.

17. In Sartre, *Existentialism and Humanism,* p. 24.

18. See Chapter 2.

19. J.-P. Sartre, *No Exit and Three Other Plays* (New York: Vintage Books, 1955), p. 47.

20. This illustration is cited in M. Warnock, *Existentialism* (New York: Oxford University Press, 1970), p. 102.

21. Sartre, *Being and Nothingness,* pp. 489, 553, 554.

22. Barrett, *Irrational Man,* p. 263.

23. M. Merleau-Ponty, *The Structure of Behaviour* (London: Methuen, 1965), p. 199.

24. We are greatly indebted to Quentin Lauer's discussion of Husserl in his fine book *Phenomenology: Its Genesis and Prospects* (New York: Harper and Row, 1958).

25. T. Langan, *The Meaning of Heidegger* (New York: Columbia University Press, 1959), p. 11.

26. Q. Lauer, *Phenomenology: Its Genesis and Prospects,* p. 179.

27. The two principal works in which Merleau-Ponty developed these views are *Phenomenology of Perception,* trans. C. Smith (London: Routledge and Kegan Paul, 1962) and *The Primacy of Perception,* ed., James Edie (Chicago: Northwestern University Press, 1964).

28. A. de Waehlens, *Une Philosophie de l'Ambiguité* (Louvain: Publications Universitaires de Louvain, 1951).

29. M. Merleau-Ponty, *Les aventures de la dialectique* (Paris: Gallimard, 1955).

30. A. L. Fisher, ed., "Introduction," *The Essential Writings of Merleau-Ponty* (New York: Harcourt, Brace and World, 1969), p. 8.

31. C. Hartshorne, "Introduction: The Development of Process Philosophy," in D. Browning, ed., *Philosophers of Process* (New York: Random House, 1965), p. v.

32. Ibid.

33. H. Bergson, *Introduction to Metaphysics,* trans. T. E. Hulme (New York: G. Putnam's Sons, 1912) pp. 27–28.

34. Bergson, *Introduction to Metaphysics,* pp. 38–39.

35. H. Bergson, *Time and Free Will: An Essay on the Immediate Data of Consciousness,* trans. F. L. Pogson (London: Macmillan, 1913), p. 105.

36. A. J. Reck, *Speculative Philosophy* (Albuquerque: University of New Mexico Press, 1972), p. 202.

37. H. Bergson, *Creative Evolution,* trans. A. Mitchell (New York: Modern Library, 1944), p. 10.

38. A. N. Whitehead, *Process and Reality* (New York: Macmillan, 1930), p. 4.

39. A. N. Whitehead, *Religion in the Making* (Cleveland: Meridian Books, World Publishing, 1960), pp. 86–87.

40. A. N. Whitehead, *Modes of Thought* (New York: Macmillan, 1938), p. 174.

41. Whitehead, *Process and Reality,* p. 28.

42. Whitehead, *Process and Reality,* p. 32.

43. Whitehead, *Process and Reality,* p. 32.

44. F. H. Heinemann, *Existentialism and the Modern Predicament* (London: Adam and Charles Black, 1953), p. 178.

45. Reck, *Speculative Philosophy,* p. 207.

46. Whitehead, *Process and Reality,* p. 318.

47. G. Kline, ed., *Alfred North Whitehead: Essays on His Philosophy* (Englewood Cliffs, N.J.: Prentice-Hall, 1963), p. 4. These essays provide further interpretation and criticism of Whitehead's philosophy.

Religion: East and West

The Nature of Religion

The nature of religion is a vast and complex subject that can be approached from a bewildering variety of viewpoints. . . . As a result there are a great variety of anthropological, sociological, psychological, naturalistic, and religious theories of the nature of religion. There is, consequently, no universally accepted definition of religion, and quite possibly there never will be.[1]

What Is Religion?

◆ ◆ ◆ ◆ ◆ ◆ ◆ ◆ ◆ ◆

Along with art, philosophy, and science, religion has been one of the dominant interests of humanity. "Religion" is not easy to define or describe because it takes many different forms among the peoples and nations of the world. Although there is no universally accepted definition of religion, throughout history humanity has exhibited a sense of the **sacred** and religion has to do with the sacred.

Sacred is a somewhat poetic word referring to whatever or whoever is regarded as holy, spiritually distinct from human initiatives, worthy of reverence, wondrous, respectful, and awesome. For example, in Judaism, Christianity, and Islam the God of Abraham, Jesus, and Mohammed is sacred in an ultimate sense; no one or thing is more holy than God, the "Sacred Ultimate." *Sacred* scriptures are the revered writings of religions, and *sacred* places or objects are worthy of reverence; but neither scriptures nor places or objects are sacred in the ultimate sense reserved for deity alone. Religious individuals feel that they have an unconditional commitment to whatever they regard as the Sacred Ultimate; that is, the source and basis of existence, the supreme foundation of all truth, reality, and goodness.

THE NATURE OF FAITH

We may read or hear of "The Hindu Faith," an individual's faith in God, faith in one's country, faith in one's physician, and faith in a body of teachings. Underlying all these usages is an attitude of trust. "The Hindu Faith" refers to the religious teachings and practices trusted by millions of people of India for nearly four thousand years. Moses' faith in God refers to his personal trust in God. Patriotic faith means the allegiance or loyalty to one's country. Faith in a physician denotes confidence in the doctor's professional judgments. Faith in teachings (also called *doctrines*) signifies agreement with particular beliefs. Faith can be primarily a matter of the heart (such as trust in someone), a matter of the mind (such as trust in particular beliefs), or a blend of emotional and rational trust in someone or something.

Naive faith is an attitude of trust without justification; faith is present without sufficient experience or explanation. Examples of naive or uninformed faith are (a) trust in mere acquaintances, such that they are unquestioningly loaned your car and (b) trust placed in unexamined teachings. *Informed faith* is an attitude of trust justified by adequate experience and explanation. Examples of informed faith are (a) trust in some friends you know well, such that they are loaned your car confidently and (b) trust in teachings supported by a suitable rationale. Not surprisingly, philosophers prefer informed faith.

RELIGION AS DOCTRINE

Is religion primarily a set of teachings, doctrines, rituals, feelings, or beliefs? As we examine the history of religion, it is evident that some individuals have been put to death for not believing the doctrines others thought they ought to believe. Religion has been interpreted as assent to correct teachings by some. Intellect and explanation are essential, they say, to any respectable religion; otherwise, it will lose its scholarly foundations as well as its appeal to thinking men and women.

RELIGION AS FEELING

Is religion largely a matter of feeling? What part does feeling play in religion? Probably the most thoroughgoing case for the interpretation of religion as feeling was set forth by Schleiermacher, a German theologian of the nineteenth century. For him, pure religion was pure feeling, a feeling of absolute dependence on God. Another "feeling" aspect of religion is the exhilaration resulting from rituals intensely praising God. We know from history and from contemporary life that the emotional element has been evident in religion; yet some people say emotions are not enough. Emotions can lead us astray unless they are accompanied and guided by intellect.

RELIGION AS ORGANIZATION

The mere mention of religion sparks hostility in many people; they think of problems connected with "organized religion," that is, a specific denomination (such as the Methodist Church) or a congregation (such as a local temple). Often their grievances are directed against inadequate or condescending replies received in answer to questions directed to clergy and religious educators. They cite a lack of effective pastoral care. Oftentimes, parents have forced religious instruction on their children. They have observed hypocrisy among professed believers. There frequently is an apparent preoccupation with fundraising among religious institutions. Rigid moral rules sometimes have discouraged natural human pleasures. Some people perceive a focus on this world as merely preparatory for the next. Others experience impersonal and boring worship, are subjected to brainwashing methods, and are offered simplistic outlooks on life's issues.

Such grievances are frequently focused on specific leaders and believers rather than on religion in general or a particular religion. However, the angry feelings often blur the distinctions among religions in general, the official beliefs of a religion, the organizational structure of a particular religion, and poorly taught or practiced religion. Some individuals feel so betrayed that they abandon their religions and claim disenchantment with all religion. The same people might not consider abandoning all government or surrendering their citizenship because political leaders fail to embody or articulate adequately their nation's ideals. To abandon a human institution because it imperfectly embodies its ideals is to demand unattainable perfection. Although legitimate grievances exist against the conduct of any human community, an angry, hasty exit often reflects a lack of consideration of the official beliefs, ideals, and principles of a given religion as well as the possibility of gradually correcting the inadequacies. If individuals are offended, they might ask themselves: Am I angry with the very notion of religion? Am I disenchanted with the official beliefs of a particular religion? Am I alienated by all forms of organized religion? Am I feeling betrayed by poorly taught and practiced religion? Do I demand perfection from religious people and organizations?

A common response by disenchanted men and women reflects varying degrees of anger against all organized religions: "I don't need a structure in order to pray or be a good person." Most persons responding this way have not raised for themselves questions such as those in the preceding paragraph. They may not have considered that organization is essential, not for the sake of structure, but for enhancing relationships among believers, for the development of leadership, for education, and for continuity. Whenever people assemble to commit themselves to anything or anyone, some degree of organization, however minimal, is needed for the promotion of human relationships, the selection and training of leaders, the education of members, and the continuance of the group beyond its present membership. When it seems to exist for its own preservation with little effective attention to its tasks, organization is often challenged. To be rid of religious organization entirely is to reduce or eliminate its community and educational dimensions, leadership, and continuity.

RELIGION AS LIFE

When it is the reaction of a person's whole being to a highest loyalty, religion is not segregated from the rest of life. Religion is felt and thought; it is lived and translated into action. In this view, religion is not a segment of life; it is not limited to any one time or place. It is not just ceremonies, doctrines, or organization, even though these may all be aids in stimulating and expressing religious thought.

RELIGION AS RITUAL

Participation in formal religious observances can nurture beliefs, feelings, organization, and daily living. This is true for governmental, civic, educational, and military observances as well. The practices and ceremonies of these observances are called *rituals*. However, people attending a Memorial Day ceremony can overlook the meaning of the speeches and simply watch the parade. Similarly, people observing a religious ritual can fail to grasp its meaning and merely watch the ceremony. Without some preparatory explanation, a ritual may appear to use unintelligible language and peculiar actions. Unfortunately, some individuals equate religion with the ritual as seen and heard. A philosopher of religion generally stresses the symbolic character of ritual.

A ritual (such as confirmation) which is comprehended and appropriated by the participants dramatizes their beliefs, feelings, organization, and daily living; it is not an isolated hour separated from the other moments of one's existence. If religion were only ritual, religion would be confined to ritual observances; such a limitation seems too restrictive for a definition of religion.

But, what *is* "religion?" How is it studied? What has religion to do with philosophy? These are our next topics.

The Nature of Religion

♦ ♦ ♦ ♦ ♦ ♦ ♦ ♦ ♦ ♦

Our discussion thus far suggests the following tentative definition of religion: a **faith** in (that is, beliefs about and commitment to) a Sacred Ultimate; a faith often organized around community, leadership, and continuity, integrated with daily living, frequently expressed in and nurtured by ritual. We stress that this definition is tentative; other responsible definitions are available.

SCHOLARLY APPROACHES TO RELIGION

The study of religion can be undertaken by anyone: by atheists, agnostics, and persons with particular faiths, just as they would study psychology, physics, or literature. One's personal outlooks need not hinder the study of any topic.

Obstacles to Religious Studies. Unresolved grievances related to any subject can be an obstacle to scholarship; if a person hates all psychologists, his or her emotions may be so strong that he or she cannot study psychology until the hostile feelings are resolved. Anger toward religion or some aspect of religion can similarly prevent effective study of religion.

An unquestioning adherence, which includes the assertion that one's own religion is the only true one and all others are demonic, also handicaps a student of religion. Unexamined fervor for any ideal—religious, political, or others—is an obstacle to clear thinking.

Although it is humanly impossible to turn off all feelings and personal convictions when studying any subject, scholars attempt to investigate topics as open-mindedly and dispassionately as possible.

Areas of Study. Religion can be studied in many ways. A list of areas of religious studies, with occasional parenthetical clarifications, follows:

1. The nature of religion and methods of studying religion
2. Scriptures (texts in original languages, analytical tools such as literary criticism and historical context, interpretations)
3. Historical studies (a particular religion, a period of a particular religion's history, religions in a geographical area, religions in a historical period)
4. Religious thought (a particular religion's beliefs and ethics, concepts such as "human nature")
5. Ritual (of a particular religion, comparative rituals)
6. Social-scientific study of religion (psychology of religion; sociology of religion)
7. Comparative examination of traditional religions
8. Religion as exhibited in art and literature

This list is not exhaustive but is designed to introduce you to the diverse studies about religion. Various disciplines have many areas of study, and religion is no exception.

PHILOSOPHY AND RELIGION

Individual religions offer, when approached as an attempt to gain a view of perennial problems, contributions to some philosophic issues. Most religions address the metaphysical questions concerning the origin and nature of the cosmos, the meaning of human nature and ultimate reality, and the presence of purpose in the universe. Theories about the sources, nature, and validity of religious knowledge are germane to epistemological enquiries. Norms for morality offered by religions can be studied by people interested in value theory.

Religion can contribute to a comprehensive philosophy as, for example, physics can. Whether a religious, physical, or any other explanation can be integrated within a comprehensive philosophy depends on whether it fits logically; for example, many naturalistic philosophies would not accommodate "spiritual enlightenment." Philosophy of religion is philosophical thinking about religion, just as philosophy of art is philosophical thinking about art. The study of the philosophy of religion need not be undertaken from a religious standpoint. The atheist and the agnostic, as well as the person with religious convictions, can and do study philosophy of religion. Scholars examine several topics, including the various concepts of the Sacred Ultimate or God, the origin and growth of religion, religious experience, religious knowledge and language, explanations of evil, and survival after death.

The Origin and Growth of Religion

♦ ♦ ♦ ♦ ♦ ♦ ♦ ♦ ♦ ♦

ORIGIN

What has fostered our sense of the sacred? Numerous explanations have been given—fear, awe, an instinct, a faculty of some kind; two merit attention here.

1. *Religion grew out of human social and psychological needs.* It is part of the struggle for a fuller life and a more adequate adjustment to the world. Religion is part of the ever-present quest for life that expresses itself in the search for food, shelter, and safety, and in the search for social, intellectual, and spiritual values.

2. *Religion grew out of humanity's awareness or recognition of a "More" that gives meaning and significance to life.* Religion is the response to the presence and appeal of an unseen world that evokes awe, reverence, and confidence. Stated theologically, religion grew out of our response to God. The search may be a complementary one, in which we are searching for God and God is seeking our voluntary commitment.

GROWTH

Primitive people, in contact with a little-known and sometimes frightening world of nature, found themselves in circumstances beyond their control. Students of early societies speak of belief in a widely diffused power or in an influence operative wherever anything striking or unusual occurs. It is present at the birth of a child, in the medicine man, and in the great warrior, or whenever anything mysterious takes place, as well as at death. Human reaction is one of awe, caution, or reverence. This early or primitive reaction is sometimes called the **mana reaction**. The mana reaction may be manifested in many different ways, and it is found at all stages of human history. It is found in concepts and practices such as taboo, magic, totemism, and fetishism.

The term **animism** means that nature is regarded as filled with innumerable spirits. In animistic cultures, people attribute a kind of soul to all the phenomena of nature. The trees, brooks, mountains, stars, and other objects are held to be the dwellings of spirits. All things are thought of as possessing a life somewhat like our own; the spirits of things can be influenced by rites of various kinds.

When the spirits are thought of as "free" and able to move about, the term *spiritism* is used. The spirits may be of many different kinds—the spirits of natural objects, great Nature Spirits (Sun, Moon, Stars), or the spirits of departed ancestors.

When the spirits are given names and personalities, we have **polytheism,** or belief in many gods. The spirits are elevated to the status of gods and dwell above or beyond the human world. The gods usually come to be invested with human faculties and passions. Stories arise about the gods and their actions; stories account for the beginnings and endings of humanity and the world.

Monotheism, or the belief in one god, can take a number of forms. One god may be elevated over the others in a heavenly hierarchy; for example, Zeus became supreme among the Greek gods, and Jupiter among the Roman gods. In the course of time, the worshiper devotes attention to one deity, although he or she recognizes that other gods exist. This outlook is seen among the early Hebrews, who recognized Yahweh as their god and Baal as the god of the Philistines.

During the prophetic period, as found in the Hebrew Bible, the prophets assured the people that there was only one God and, moreover, that He loved righteousness and justice and hated iniquity and injustice. The idea of God became increasingly ethical: God's will included love, justice, mercy, and truth.

The history of religion includes the history of the development of the religious acts or rites through which humanity has sought to come into a harmonious relationship with God. Forms of prayer have tended to progress from simple appeals for help to more elaborate prayers with the emphasis on praise, fellowship, communion, and meditation. Institutions or organizations have developed to provide fellowship for the worshipers and to carry out a program of ritual, education, pastoral care, and social service. Scriptures or sacred literatures and creeds have arisen in connection with most religious groups.

Even within the modern world religions, we find people at all stages of development; thus, the various forms of religious development mentioned may be present concurrently. The history of religion is not a record of unbroken growth; we find arrested development and, at times, decadence. There are no particular stages through which all religions have passed or must pass. The point reached in religious development, however, is related to the culture of the society in which it is functioning.

CULTS AND SECTS

"Cult" (from the Latin *cultus,* "worship") means a system of religious beliefs and observances or the group of persons who accept a system of religious beliefs. In this sense, each major religion and every local congregation is a cult.

In recent years "cult" has been used pejoratively about new or unfamiliar groups exhibiting certain characteristics (including the introduction of novel or esoteric theories having little or no relation to the beliefs of "traditional" or "mainline" religions); these gatherings quickly and superficially satisfy many human needs for values, fulfillment, and authority. In terms of values, each cult provides a simplistic purpose for life and unambiguous moral rules. To gratify needs for emotional, intellectual, and spiritual fulfilment, cults offer a sense of belonging, conformity, enthusiasm, resolution of personal dilemmas, protection, credal certainties, intense rituals, and thorough indoctrination. The need for authority is met by an absolute ruler who is usually the cult's immediate focus and on whom members are entirely dependent. Devotees typically regard nonmembers with suspicion, even as the enemy.

Characteristics such as these, however, are not necessarily limited to new and unfamiliar groups. Some movements or congregations within a mainstream religion might exhibit the same traits.

Sect (from the Latin verb *sequi,* "to follow") has come to refer to any religious group formed out of a more dominant body, sometimes by a persuasive leader or by some principle of greater strictness or dedication. In this sense, Christianity was at the outset a Jewish sect; today the Amish and the Christian Science Church may be regarded as Christian sects.

Myth in Sacred Literature

♦ ♦ ♦ ♦ ♦ ♦ ♦ ♦ ♦ ♦

We tend to use "myth" or "mythical" as a negative value judgment about a belief or report. However, it can be used in a purely descriptive manner without negative connotations. Myth can refer to (1) fables, (2) literary forms that describe spiritual matters in everyday terms, and (3) a method of thinking about ultimate truths.[2] The first form is often an allegorical tale with animal characters; its purpose is to convey a moral or principle of behavior and not to report the details of a historical event.

The second form of myth may include, but reaches beyond, a moral intent. By referring to heaven as "above," one does not necessarily mean literally "above" in the sky somewhere. The specific meaning would depend on its religious context; the majority of religious philosophers and theologians of the world's traditions do not teach that *every* word in their respective scriptures is to be understood literally (Islam is a notable exception). The existence of the poetic element in myth does not denigrate sacred literature; on the contrary, it enlivens expression and points to profound beliefs.

The third use of myth is as a form of thinking and expressing ultimate truths, and of awakening and nurturing in people a sense of wonder and participation in the mystery of the universe. Human language is thought to be an inadequate way to express all *ultimate* truths. Words are limited in their capacity to capture the essential meaning of "God," "love," "purpose," or whatever else a particular religion views as being ultimate. Myths often are intended as expressions of ultimate "beginnings" and ultimate "endings" of the universe, of life, and of human existence. Scholars continue to wrestle with the sacred literatures of the world to understand the functions of myth in the various religions; myth has different roles and purposes among the traditions.

Simultaneously, scholars are attempting to understand better those sacred writings that claim to be historical and literal. During the current century, such inquiry into sacred writings has been undertaken extensively. These analyses enrich our understanding of the world's religions.

Religious Experience

♦ ♦ ♦ ♦ ♦ ♦ ♦ ♦ ♦ ♦

As we have indicated, the word *religion* is used in a variety of ways; the expression *religious experience* is also difficult to define. There are varieties of experiences that persons call religious, and they differ in interpretation and content. We will consider three contrasting types.

MYSTICAL EXPERIENCE

Mystical experience has been defined as "the condition of being overwhelmingly aware of the presence of the ultimately real."[3] It would be convenient if all interpretations of **mysticism** were identical, but they are not.

Union. A form of mystical experience found among some Hindus and others is the shedding of one's ego and self-awareness so that the true spiritual self is united with the sacred, nonpersonal Ultimate Unity. Through contemplation and self-surrender, a person's true self, the impersonal soul, is absorbed in a Void. Like a nonconscious "dreamless sleep," the experience is inaccessible to reason and beyond words or thoughts.[4] Indirect communication such as poetry, paradoxes, or riddles are often used by this type of mystic in an attempt to "describe" or point to the ineffable (that which cannot be spoken or written). However, mystical experiences of this type logically should conclude in silence. Mystics are said to be enlightened by their world-denying moments, which unite them with the "wholly other." They also believe that in what is called "death" their souls will eventually fuse with the Sacred Ultimate, somewhat the way a drop of water merges with the sea.

Communion. Another form of mystical experience found among some Jews, Christians, and

Muslims, is characterized by a sense of the immediate, loving presence of God. God is self-disclosing or revelatory to the individual, and the individual is self-disclosing and receptive to God. Primarily an encounter of divine love between God and a mortal, in which the distinction between Creator and creature is retained, the experience enhances one's conscious awareness of the Divine.

These mystics are said to be nurtured or empowered by their communal moments with God. Although some mystics of the West have been world-denying, others have been world-affirming, emphasizing strengthened human activity. Their silence or inability to express their experiences may be an indication of the poverty of any language to describe true love.

Those who believe in mystical union and mystical communion share the conviction that the experiencer is in touch with ultimate reality, but their interpretations of the relationship with the sacred, of enlightenment, of loving self-disclosure between Creator and creature, and of the consequences for daily living are quite different.[5]

Tranquility. The inner quiet and tranquility resulting from systematic relaxation, or from an experience such as sitting in solitude by the seashore, are regarded as religious, or mystical, by some people. The exhiliration produced by beautiful music and its quieting after-effects can also be viewed in this manner. Gazing into a clear sky at night may produce a feeling of being at one with the Universe. Such oceanic feelings (a phrase often used by Freud) need not be regarded as religious or mystical. Feelings of conscious at-oneness with the cosmos are different from the experiences of mystical union and communion. However, many persons identify these emotions as religious experiences.

Human Love. For some individuals, love among human beings is the Sacred Ultimate. For these people, there is no "wholly other" of mystical union, no personal God of mystical communion, and no ultimate sacredness ascribed to the cosmos. If the term "god" is used at all, it refers to human affections; in this sense, each person has within her- or himself love, the only Sacred Ultimate.

In a form of religious humanism (see Chapter 12, p. 260), the experiences of love can be understood as a religion. Beliefs, feelings, organization, life, and ritual are frequent components of this outlook. Such religious humanists gather periodically to provide resources of love among themselves and to reflect on ethical issues; they may also include inspirational readings at these meetings. Some religious humanists are found within traditional religions and interpret creeds and rituals as poetry designed to promote human love.

PRAYER

Another form of religious experience is prayer to a personal God. A theologian views prayer in this manner:

> Prayer is the intentional opening of human lives to, the alignment of human wills with, and the direction of human desiring toward, the cosmic Love that is deepest and highest in the world. . . . Public prayer or church worship is the way in which we unite with others in expressing dependence on this Love, opening ourselves to it, and willing cooperation with it as "fellow-workers with God." Private prayer is the way we do this in our own particular ways.[6]

This form of religious experience includes a "communion," a sense of the immediate presence of the Divine; it is marked by a personal I–Thou relationship between God and persons, privately and in groups.

A COMMON CHARACTERISTIC

Although there is diversity among religious experiences, there appears to be one common element. Each person interprets the experience as a feeling or conviction of a momentous disclosure;

a disclosure that true reality, the Sacred Ultimate, has been revealed as it "really" is.

Three Universal Religions: Judaism, Christianity, Islam

A "universal" religion is one in which beliefs are offered to all humanity. Each universal religion views itself as possessing the full truth about reality, knowledge, and values; therefore its adherents have a sense of mission to all humanity. The three universal religions originating in the Middle East are **Judaism, Christianity,** and **Islam.** (Asian religions are discussed in Chapter 19).

JUDAISM

Judaism is one of the oldest of the world's living religions. Its scriptures are regarded as holy by Christianity and Islam as well as by Judaism. The most cherished writings of the Jews are the Hebrew Bible (including the Law, Prophets, and Writings) and the *Talmud* (from the Hebrew word for "learning"), the primary written source of Jewish oral law and tradition. The *Talmud* itself consists of the *Mishnah* (a collection of oral law regarding regulations and beliefs basic to rabbinic Judaism) and the *Gemara* (commentaries on the *Mishnah*).

Torah sometimes refers to the *Pentateuch* (the first five books of the Bible), to the entire Hebrew Bible, or to the entire content of Judaism.

The following five beliefs are central in Judaism: (1) The Creator of the Universe, of all that is seen and unseen, is the personal "One, Only, and Holy God." Sometimes called *ethical monotheism,* this central teaching, often viewed as Judaism's gift to the world, is called to mind by the *Shema,* "Hear, O Israel, the Lord our God, the Lord is One." (2) The created universe is basically real; it is not an illusion. Furthermore, it is fundamentally good; the universe is neither morally neutral nor evil. (3) As was discussed in Chapter 2, human nature also is understood as basically good; made "in the image of God," all human beings have the capacity to choose other gods (idolatry) and therefore sin. (4) The one true God has chosen Israel to be His servant to bring all persons to a true knowledge of God. The Jewish community accepts this election and covenants to fulfill the obligations imposed. God's will is revealed through the Prophets of Israel and through the events of history; the primary role of the Prophets was not to predict future happenings but to discern God's will as revealed in the pattern of historical events. (5) Within such a covenant community, God's will affects all of life. There was no special word in the Jewish scriptures for "religion." The whole person responded to God's call in every aspect of life. Loving obedience to God's will marks the ethical comprehensiveness of Judaism. Living in the community of faith, a continuing witness to the Exodus event, binds Jews together no matter where they reside geographically.

There are three major divisions within modern Judaism. Orthodox Judaism is rigorous about ritual observances, the dietary laws, and the keeping of the Sabbath. It stresses the absolute authority of the revealed Law and looks for the coming of the Messiah. Conservative Judaism, although continuing rabbinical Judaism, claims the right to adapt traditions to the conditions of the modern world. There is a less rigid formulation of the requirements than among the orthodox groups. Reform Judaism stresses the ethical teachings of the prophets and the growth of a messianic age of justice, truth, and peace; Judaism is regarded as an evolving religious experience that is subject to change.

CHRISTIANITY

The New Testament continues the five beliefs of Judaism concerning (1) God, (2) the universe, (3) human nature, (4) revelation, and (5) ethical consequences for daily life. However, the writers of the New Testament amplified some of these beliefs. Jesus of Nazareth was believed to be the resurrected Messiah, who embodied and revealed God's ultimate purposes for humanity. There was considerable reluctance to accept Jesus as the Messiah, because those awaiting God's "Anointed One" (the meaning of *Messiah* and its Greek equivalent *Christ*) believed that political peace would be established for the Jews when the true Messiah came. Jesus' followers, however, believed the inner peace preached by their leader was primary and had precedence over political liberation. The witness to Jesus' presence after his resurrection became central to Christianity. The heart of Jesus' teaching is that the love of God, neighbor, and self should be elevated above all ritual observances and customs; his own life is reported in the New Testament as having exemplified fully that ideal—an ideal for which he was eventually executed and resurrected. His teaching of love is augmented by his insistence that the Kingdom of God is at hand. By "Kingdom of God," Jesus meant that God, not humanity, is sovereign. The present reality of the Kingdom is seen in Jesus' person and ministry; the messianic age has begun. The complete fulfillment or consummation of the Kingdom, however, is yet to come. The Kingdom as a present reality begun in himself and a future reality for humanity are the two emphases in Jesus' teachings.

The convictions of Christians have been expressed in three major traditions: Eastern Orthodoxy, Roman Catholicism, and Protestantism.

Eastern Orthodoxy.

Eastern Orthodoxy is the form of Christianity practiced in the ancient Byzantine Patriarchates (religious provinces) of Constantinople, Alexandria, Antioch, Jerusalem, and the national churches of Russia, Greece, Yugoslavia, Bulgaria, Rumania, Georgia, and so on. The Patriarch of Constantinople is the honorary head of Eastern Orthodoxy, but each church is governed by its own bishops, priests, and deacons; final authority is vested in the bishops.

The norm of belief (called "Sacred Tradition") for Eastern Orthodox Christians includes three essential elements: (1) the dogmatic tradition (the historic teachings), including scripture and the "spiritual reading" of scripture, doctrines formed by the Seven Ecumenical Councils, testimonies of the ancient church fathers, the canons that describe and defend the church's life, and teachings expressed in worship; (2) the liturgical tradition (the church at worship and in life); and (3) the spiritual tradition (the classical texts on spirituality).

The Eastern Orthodox Church has never had a crisis similar to the Reformation; it resists "definitions" and stresses the *whole* life of the believer and the church within "Sacred Tradition."[7]

Today, members of the Eastern Orthodox Churches are exploring ways by which their historic faith can transcend ethnic expressions. For example, in the United States, Orthodox churches with Greek customs have introduced the English language into worship and religious education; while continuing to celebrate their ethnicity, the churches accommodate American cultural diversity without compromising Sacred Tradition. Contemporary moral dilemmas are addressed within the established faith; ecumenical dialogues search for understanding and possibilities of Christian unity; and, cooperation with others in humanitarian efforts is offered where possible and consistent with Orthodox belief.

Roman Catholicism.

Roman Catholicism includes those Christians throughout the world who acknowledge the Bishop of Rome—the Pope—as the earthly representative of Jesus Christ and head of the whole Christian Church. They believe there is an unbroken line of authority vested in all bishops of Rome beginning with and derived from Saint Peter. When the Pope speaks **ex cathedra** on matters of faith and morals, his teachings are infallible; however, other pastoral counsels from the Pope such as encyclicals are not pronounced *ex cathedra* and hence are not regarded as infallible. There is much discussion today among Roman Catholic theologians about the issue of infallibility and distinctions between *ex cathedra* pronouncements and other teachings of the Pope.

Today, the Roman Catholic Church is exploring questions concerning the roles of the clergy and laity, the limits of theological freedom and dissent, varied forms of worship, the Church's relationship with other Christian churches and other religions, many contemporary moral dilemmas, and the nature of the papacy itself. Once seen as a rigid, monolithic structure relying on the doctrinal and philosophic work of Thomas Aquinas, the Roman Catholic Church today, while remaining faithful to the Bible, ancient creeds, and councils, is in a lively but cautious period of self-examination, inquiry, and outreach. At the heart of Roman Catholicism is the *Mass,* the central act of worship required for all believers, in which Jesus' command to "Do this in remembrance of me" is celebrated.

Protestantism. "Protestantism" in popular usage embraces those Christian churches that differ from the Eastern Orthodox and Roman Catholic Churches.[8] The original meaning of the term *Protestant* was "one who makes a solemn declaration or affirmation to profess a conviction." As a movement in Western Christianity, Protestantism stresses the Bible as the source and standard of belief; authority is vested only in scripture. Although reform movements have been characteristic of Christianity throughout its history, most Protestants date the movement's beginning in the sixteenth century to Martin Luther's challenge to papal authority as superior to the authority of the Bible.

Differing interpretations of the Bible have produced hundreds of Protestant churches. Attitudes toward the Bible range from **fundamentalism** to **liberalism**. Fundamentalists advocate the literal interpretation of the Scriptures as revealing without error God's truths—which yields a fixed set of beliefs for all time. Liberals interpret the Bible in the context of its own history, literary structures, and forms of thought, and as subject to human error in its composition. They then apply relevant biblical insights to contemporary issues. Between the two extremes, many moderates share with liberals the same methods of interpreting the Bible but are more apt to speak of the "Word of God" rather than "insights."

Also important to all Protestants is belief in "justification by faith alone." Persons do not become acceptable (justified) to God either by partaking of miraculous sacramental powers or by credit gained by doing good works. God accepts persons by his grace alone. A person's faithful response to this act of grace is central, and from it alone flow forms of worship and good works. Often mistakenly represented as individualistic, Protestantism instead views personal faith in God as being rooted within a community of faith, united in a common spirit of loyalty to the God of the Bible, but diverse in both the understanding and expressions of that spirit.

Modern Movements. Although Eastern Orthodoxy has remained firmly committed to its historical beliefs and customs, Roman Catholic and Protestant Christians have become diverse in their convictions. Although each church or denomination has its boundaries, the exact limits of those borders are being redefined. Among Roman Catholics and Protestants alike one can find fundamentalists, "born-again" believers, "charismatics," liberals, neoorthodox (see Tillich and Niebuhr biographies and excerpts, pp. 370–373) followers, and others.

"Born-again" Christians, not necessarily fundamentalists, stress that to be a Christian is to be more than a citizen of a particular country, or to abide by some version of the Golden Rule, or to be a church-goer. To be a Christian means to respond to God's empowering activity (the "Holy Spirit") in life, to commit oneself basically to a covenant relationship with God through Jesus. The experience of making a decision, a conscious choice of this commitment is what is meant by being "born again." Such a decision can be a quiet and gradual process of realization, or it might be a decisive, emotional moment of acceptance. Born-again Christians argue that by definition every real Christian is born again (John 3:1–17); they imply that habitual church-goers and persons living a humanitarian life who have not been born again have missed the meaning of Christianity.

Charismatic Christians are those that emphasize *charismata*, the Greek word for "gifts," from God. Such gifts may be seen as natural talents and abilities raised to new effectiveness by God and new capacities (such as healing) given by the Creator. In the New Testament, the *charismata* "vary in character from the strongly emotional outpourings of the ecstatic to the normal everyday practice of God's will; from talents and activities contributing to worship to those equally necessary for meeting the needs of the Christian community. All such powers and activities are given by God and their worth is to be judged by the measure in which they promote the well-being of the church."[9] Every Christian is believed to possess some of these, the greatest being love. Not all who identify themselves as Charismatics are fundamentalists.

In the third and fourth decades of this century there developed a theological movement known as neoorthodoxy.[10] Critical of both fundamentalism and liberalism, it emphasized the transcendence of God and human dependence. Salvation must come from God, not through human strivings. Neoorthodox theologians propose that the church is the bearer in history of God's revelation. Other emphases include a demand for moral and intellectual humility, recognition of inconsistencies as part of the human predicament, a biblical view of humanity, concern for social issues, and respect for scientific, scholarly, and artistic achievements. A revival of interest in theology developed, but doctrinal diversity remained. The influences of neoorthodoxy remain to the present day. One observer notes, "Most important, perhaps, it built bridges that opened communications not only with modernists who had all but decided that Christianity was obsolete, but also with conservatives who had all but decided that true Christians must repudiate modern modes of thought and action."[11]

Liberation theologies, black theologies, the theology of hope, process thought, television Christianity, and the "New Right" are other movements in contemporary Christianity. Apparently, this is a time of growth and diversity for many Christian groups.[12]

ISLAM

Jews and Christians view Islam as the latest of the world religions; they often call this heritage *Mohammadanism.* From a Muslim standpoint, this view is a distortion. Adherents of Islam understand their religion as the "final religion" and the "primal religion."[13] As "final," Islam is God's final revelation of prophetic religion, in fulfillment of all that had preceded. Moses was given the Law; David was given the Psalms; Jesus was given the Gospel. Judaism offers God's message of justice, and Christianity proclaims the love of God. To Mohammed (570–632 C.E.) God revealed the **Qur'an.**

As the "Seal of the Prophets," the apostle of Allah (which means "the God" in Arabic), Mohammed is not the focal point of Islam; hence, the religion should not be called by his name. For Muslims, Islam—which means "submission to God"—is the middle way between Judaism and Christianity; it restores the unity of the children of Abraham and overcomes the exclusiveness of Judaism and Christianity. Jesus, the prophet to "the lost sheep of Israel," limits Christianity; Judaism is similarly limited. Islam proclaims a practical synthesis of Judaism and Christianity for all humanity. Overcoming the incompleteness of the justice of Judaism and the idealistic love of Christianity, Islam brings to fulfillment all that Judaism and Christianity anticipated. For the Muslim believer, Islam is perfected Judaism and perfected Christianity.

As "primal," Islam is the real religion of Adam, of Abraham, of human nature. Islam is not younger than Judaism and Christianity; it preceded both. Not only is it the religion of the "Spoken Book" (the Qur'an), it is as well the religion of the "Created Book," the fabric of the universe itself. According to the Muslim faith, every person is born a Muslim, and distortions of

Paul Johannes Tillich

Paul Tillich (1886–1965) was born in Germany, son of a Lutheran minister. He studied at the Universities of Berlin, Tübingen, Halle, and Breslau, and became a Lutheran minister and an army chaplain during World War I. He rejected traditional otherworldliness and, while also rejecting Marxism, joined in the social struggle for justice in society. During the 1920s and 1930s he taught at various German universities. An outspoken critic of Hitler and the Nazi movement, he fled to the United States in 1933 and taught first at Union Theological Seminary in New York, later at Harvard University and the University of Chicago.

The articles and books written by Tillich are numerous. They include works on theology, philosophy of religion, depth psychology, books of sermons, and articles. Among his better-known works are *The Religious Situation* (1932), (written before he left Germany); *Systematic Theology* (1951–1963) (three volumes); *The Courage to Be* (1952); *The New Being* (1955); *Love, Power, and Justice* (1954); *Shaking of the Foundations* (sermons) (1948); and *Dynamics of Faith* (1957).

Tillich became an American citizen in 1940. Until the end of World War II he was politically active, working for a democratic Germany and giving aid to emigrés and refugees. A man of broad humanistic interests, he communicated an appreciation of religion as humanity's universal ultimate concern and of philosophy as humanity's search for being.

---

his or her environment lead a person astray to become a Christian, a Jew, or an unbeliever. To be human means to be Muslim.

Beliefs. The doctrines underlying the outlook of Islam, and those accepted by orthodox Muslims, usually are stated as follows: (1) *Belief in one absolute and transcendent God.* Allah is the omnipotent ruler of the universe and his will is supreme. He has decreed the processes of nature and he judges, punishes, and rewards all. Because all stand constantly in the presence of Allah, there is no need of mediators in the form of priests, sacraments, and churches. (2) *Belief in angels.* There are good angels, who may intercede for humanity, and there is an evil angel. (3) *Belief in the Qur'an,* which is inspired and verbally infallible. According to the account, the angel Gabriel appeared and revealed to Mohammed the contents of this sacred book.[14] (4) *Belief in the Prophets of Allah, of whom Mohammed is the last and the greatest* and the one commissioned to deliver Allah's message to humanity. Abraham, Moses, and Jesus of Nazareth also are recognized prophets. (5) *Belief in a time of judgment* when all people will be judged for their

Excerpt from Tillich:

The Protestant Era (1948)

"The End of the Protestant Era?"

Protestantism now faces the most difficult struggle of all the occidental religions and denominations in the present world situation. It arose with that era which today is either coming to an end or else undergoing fundamental structural changes. Therefore, the question as to whether Protestantism can face the present situation in a manner enabling it to survive the present historical period is unavoidable. It is true, of course, that all religions are threatened today by secularism and paganism. But this threat, at least as far as pure secularism is concerned, has perhaps reached its culminating point. The insecurity which is increasingly felt by nations and individuals, the expectation of catastrophes in all civilized countries, the vanishing belief in progress— all have aroused a new searching for a transcendent security and perfection. . . . The conflict between the natural sciences and religion has been overcome in all important philosophies. But the question as to whether Protestantism in particular has become stronger must be answered in the negative, although sometimes it seems, if one considers the general growth of religious interest and neglects the peculiar situation of Protestantism, that the opposite has been the case.

Paul Tillich, *The Protestant Era* (Chicago: University of Chicago Press, Phoenix Books, 1948).

deeds. There is a heaven and a hell, but eventually all Muslims will be saved.

Islam also teaches that peace should be established in the human societies of this world. To participate with Allah in the establishment of peace, Muslims are called upon to be engaged in *jihad,* meaning in Arabic "striving" or "struggle." The basic *jihad* is the struggle of the self, to bring it in obedience to God, to make sure that one is living a holy and righteous life. A lesser struggle is *jihad* as "holy war," fought only when the faith is being attacked or when Muslims are not allowed to practice their faith.

The *ummah,* or Islamic community or state, is the dynamic vehicle for the realization of God's Will and should serve as an example to the rest of the world. (See Avicenna biography and excerpt, pp. 374–375.)

Shi'ites and Sunnis. After Mohammed died, the leadership role was assumed by four of his closest companions, the last of whom was Ali. At this point, a division arose within Islam over the succession. One group, the Sunnis—now constituting about 90 percent of all Muslims—consider themselves the orthodox branch of Islam.

Reinhold Niebuhr

Reinhold Niebuhr (1892–1970), after receiving his B.D. and M.A. degrees from Yale Divinity School, served as pastor in Detroit for thirteen years. He said this experience "determined my development more than any books which I may have read." In 1928, he joined the faculty of Union Theological Seminary in New York as Professor of Christian Ethics, and remained there until his retirement in 1960.

His first major work, *Moral Man and Immoral Society* (1932), was his statement of the thesis that the Liberal movement, both religious and secular, seemed not to be conscious of the basic differences between the morality of individuals and the morality of groups. He argued that the morality of groups inevitably fell short of personal moral standards, because groups exercise coercive power over others in order to serve the group's self-interest. Individuals are capable of higher, but not perfect, moral living. However, the morality of groups should not be entirely rejected just because their standards cannot meet individual moral ideals.

In 1939, Professor Niebuhr became the fifth American invited to deliver the Gifford Lectures at the University of Edinburgh. These appeared as *The Nature and Destiny of Man* (1941–1943), in which he compares biblical with classical and modern conceptions of the nature of humanity. Later he incorporated studies undertaken for the Lyman Beecher Lectures at Yale, and a lectureship at the University of Uppsala in Sweden, in a volume *Faith and History* (1949). Both these volumes are dedicated to Niebuhr's main thesis that the Biblical view of humanity is superior to both classical and modern views. Collections of his inspiring and influential sermons are *The Children of Light and the Children of Darkness* (1944) and *Discerning the Signs of the Times* (1946).

In addition to his immense power as a preacher, Reinhold Niebuhr served as an adviser to presidents and statesmen; in 1946 he received the Presidential Freedom Award for Distinguished Service. He wrote many works on the relation between religion and political realities.

The other group, the Shi'ites, who primarily live in Iran, also consider themselves as authentic Muslims. Sunnis and Shi'ites differ on the issue of succession and in some of their interpretations

of the Shari'ah, a comprehensive code of morality and religious duties.

Characteristics of Shi'ite Islam are (1) infallibility of the "hidden" Imam, true successor of

Excerpt from Niebuhr:

"The Wheat and the Tares" (1960)

Which brings us now again to the strategy of life as we have it in the faith of the Bible. We look at the brevity of life. We admit that we are creatures. We know that we are unique creatures, that God has made us in his image, that we have a freedom to do something that nature does not know, that we can project goals beyond the limitations, ambitions, desires, and lusts of nature. We are the creatures who, gloriously, tragically, and pathetically, make history. As we make it, we have to make distinctions between good and evil. We know that selfishness is dangerous. We must be unselfish. The more we rise above our immediate situation and see the situation of the other person, the more creative we are. Therefore, our life story is concerned with making rigorous distinctions between right and wrong, between good and evil. Part of the Christian faith corresponds to this interpretation. . . .

But now we come to . . . the puzzling lesson of the parable of the wheat and the tares. The man sowed a field of wheat and the enemy sowed tares among the wheat. And the servants, following the impulse of each one of us, asked if they should root out the tares so that the wheat could grow. This is a parable taken from agriculture to illustrate a point of morals, and it violates every principle of agriculture or of morals. After all every farmer and every gardener makes ceaseless war against the tares. How else could the flowers and the wheat grow? And we have to make ceaseless war against evil within ourselves and in our fellowmen, or how could there be any kind of decency in the world? Against all moral impulse, we have this eschatological parable.

Reinhold Niebuhr, *Justice and Mercy,* ed. Ursula M. Niebuhr (New York: Harper and Row, 1974).

Mohammed; the hidden Imam is expected to return someday; (2) leadership by ayatollahs, who are believed to be representatives of the Imam; (3) tradition of honorable martyrdom memorializing the murder of Ali's son Hussein in the seventh century; and (4) in times of crisis the need to employ strong action, including holy war. According to Shi'ite beliefs, the govern-

Avicenna

Avicenna (980–1037), an Islamic philosopher and physician born in Persia, was known in the Arab world as "the third Aristotle." A brilliant student, he became a physician at age 16; his interests included logic, metaphysics, mathematics, and physics. By the age of 17, he had mastered most of the available knowledge of his time.

Avicenna achieved medical fame when he wrote *The Canons of Medicine,* a treatise that dominated European universities from the twelfth to the seventeenth centuries.

He studied Aristotelian and neo-Platonic philosophy with his contemporary Al-Farabi; he wrote several volumes on Aristotle. The translation of his philosophical writings into Latin initiated the great Aristotelian revival in the twelfth and thirteenth centuries.

Avicenna's metaphysics made concessions to the demands of his religion. The goal of philosophy, he stated, is to know God and to be like God, as far as this is possible. The goal can be reached by instruction as well as divine illumination.

His logic held that universals do not exist as separate entities prior to things, except in the mind of God. In our own minds they exist after things, as abstractions from the particulars, and they exist also in things, but not unmixed with their accidents.

Avicenna was a prolific writer, and authored over 100 treatises. They include *The Healing, The Deliverance, The Directives and Remarks,* and *The Divisions of the Intellectual Sciences.*

---

ment of a nation is a **theocracy**—a government ruled by God acting through the Imam.

Current Religious Issues

In all areas of religious studies and among the religions explored in this chapter, much vitality can be observed. We cannot possibly catalog all of the current issues and movements; only a sampling of philosophical and religious issues follows.

ISSUES IN PHILOSOPHY OF RELIGION

Are there any norms for accuracy in deciding religious claims? This question arises because there is a multitude of such claims. A shallow relativism proposing the truth of all religious claims (that is, one is as true as another) leads to self-contradiction: if X is true, then not-X cannot also be true, whether in religion, psychology, or physics. Or, are religious claims so unique that they are exempt from rules of logic? How can we distinguish between claims that purport to be

Excerpt from Avicenna:

On Prophecy

Now it is well known that man differs from all other animals in that he cannot enjoy a good life in isolation and alone, managing all his affairs without any partner to assist him in the fulfillment of his needs. A man must perforce attain satisfaction by means of another of his species, whose needs in turn are satisfied by him and his like: thus, one man will act as conveyor, another as baker, another as tailor, another as sewer [sic]; when all unite together, the needs of all are satisfied. . . . This being so, it is necessary for men both to associate with each other, and to behave like citizens. This is obvious; it also follows that it is necessary to the life and survival of mankind that there should be co-operation between them, which can only be realized through a common transaction of business; in addition to all the other means which secure the same purpose. This transaction requires a code of law and just regulation, which in their turn call for a lawgiver and regulator. Such a man must be in a position to speak to men, and to constrain them to accept the code; he must therefore be a man.

It follows therefore that there should exist a prophet, and that he should be a man; it also follows that he should have some distinguishing feature which does not belong to other men, so that his fellows may recognize him as possessing something which is not theirs, and so that he may stand out apart from them. This distinguishing feature is the power to work miracles.

Avicenna, *Avicenna on Theology,* trans. A. J. Atberry (London: Murray, 1951).

---

about objective reality and those that express only subjective feelings?

Are there standards by which one group can be designated as a fraudulent "cult" and another as a legitimate religion? Can we distinguish a false from a genuine prophet? The Unification Church, an association of political idealists, a society of religious humanists, a corporation of a television evangelist, or the traditional organizations of Jewish, Christian, and Muslim believers may each qualify as a religious community within the definition we proposed in this chapter. Is there another quality that could help us to distinguish genuine religions from tax evaders claiming to be religions?

On what bases does one approve or disapprove of prayer in U.S. public schools, the teaching of the Genesis account of creation as an alternative to the theory of evolution in a science class, the hiring of military chaplains, and the contents of library books and textbooks? On what bases does atheism in its many forms deserve a constitutionally protected place among the philosophies and religions in the United States?

What is the relation of Judaism, Christianity, and Islam to Asian religions, such as Hinduism and Buddhism? Is the real God known by one ethnic group, nation, or church or is God revealed in some degree to all people? One extreme view is to say that all religions, except my own, are false and that I alone have the truth. The other extreme is to say that all religions are alike and there are no differences in their validity. Is there an abiding experience that has been shared, interpreted, and expressed in many different symbols and ways by different peoples? Does all sincere and genuine religion rest on the fundamentally identical experience of the presence of the sacred? Is rivalry among religions and denominations of a religion inevitable?

ISSUES IN JUDAISM, CHRISTIANITY, AND ISLAM

Jewish Issues. Two issues presently being debated within Judaism are: What does it mean to be a Jew? and Can an atheist be a Jew? Several years ago Rabbi Sherwin Wine founded "Humanistic Judaism,"[15] which now has small congregations in Canada, England, the United States, and Israel. Humanistic Jews believe in human self-reliance for decisions and salvation; they celebrate the Jewish holidays, but they are atheists. By what method and with what criteria is a person entitled to be designated "Jewish"?

Another issue is whether the current nation Israel can be linked politically, geographically, and religiously to the Israel of biblical times. With what justification is Orthodox Judaism, representing a minority of Israel's population, the only "official" Judaism of the nation?

Whether Jewish identity follows the maternal or the paternal line in a mixed marriage is of concern to Jews, especially in the United States. Concern is frequently expressed that the children of such marriages may well be estranged from the religious and cultural aspects of Judaism. Furthermore, the anticipated loss of numbers because of mixed marriages is viewed as a serious threat to the Jewish community. Many American Jews marry outside their faith.

Christian Issues. The development of Christian beliefs in the early centuries C.E. included some changes from biblical views. Some of these changes were consequences of reflections by church members as they tried to better understand their own beliefs and to communicate them to the world. Others were the outgrowth of the church's incorporation of certain philosophical outlooks from other cultures.

For example, the doctrine of the Trinity as an interpretation of God and Christ emerged by the early fourth century. In the same general period, humans were viewed as emerging from the womb with innate shackled freedom and a natural tendency for idolatry; only undeserved help (grace) from God could save individuals from inherent corruption. This view of human nature in one or more versions has been fostered primarily by Christian thinkers with few exceptions throughout the ages. It is still a matter of scholarly debate whether these developments and many others represent authentic Christianity or are intrusions representing beliefs alien to Biblical foundations.[16]

To what extent do Christian beliefs need a major overhauling? Should the doctrine of the Trinity be discarded or restated? Is a different view of human nature and morality needed? One of the most lively contemporary discussions among theologians is about who Jesus was.

Current Christian thinking is responding to a multitude of influences: process philosophy, existentialism, and the experiences of sexual and ethnic minorities. The social sciences are having a profound effect on religion and morality; Christian belief continues to respond to scientific discoveries, and there is a renewed interest in spirituality. The church is examining its relationship to culture; is secular citizenship synonymous with church membership? Is the church a *public* utility for rites of passage from birth to death? For Christianity, the consequences of incorporating such diverse influences and of examining such questions remain to be seen.

Islamic Issues. Issues facing Muslims on a global basis are of a practical nature and have to do with Muslim society. Philosophical–theological concerns continue to be of secondary importance, for the faith has already been delivered in final form. However, the effect of Western colonial domination during the nineteenth and early twentieth centuries on many regions of the Muslim world has led to conflict between traditionalists and modernists.

Traditionalists are committed to the original beliefs and practices of Islam, including faithfulness to a literal understanding of Qur'anic law and its applications to contemporary life. Modernists believe that the principles, goals, and fundamental purposes of religious law are unchanging, but the specific forms in which the eternal truths are expressed must change constantly in the face of changing human circumstances. The traditionalists' vision of life's possibilities has been so rooted in the past that they have not developed a Muslim framework for many modern technological developments; in contrast, modernists attempt to accommodate recent developments within a Muslim spirit, also faithful to the Qur'an's unchanging truths.

Muslim leaders are divided over national loyalties. As a result of colonialism, the Muslim world has broken into many nation states. Some leaders applaud this development, but others fear that the unifying spirit of Islam is betrayed by political nationalism. Although it has had no centralized authority for centuries, Islam has retained a remarkable spirit of unity; with the emerging variety of political structures in the Muslim world, however, some believers—probably a minority—would prefer a more centralized leadership for religious unity. Others believe that God alone should rule without any earthly mediating authority.

Other questions for the Muslim world include: Is the ancient traditional way of life the only authentic Islamic life? To what extent, if any, can tradition accommodate the modern world? Should the Qur'an be restudied according to principles of modern historical and literary research, or would that call into question basic divine revelation as understood for centuries?

Reflections

♦ ♦ ♦ ♦ ♦ ♦ ♦ ♦ ♦ ♦ ♦

For the most part, men and women are raised with a particular religious outlook. Sometimes the religion of one's family or community is presented as the one, true, and only faith; often it is well understood as informed faith. Moreover, an individual's convictions and practices might be an ignorant, even a bizarre, rendering of a religion; or, the beliefs and practices of an individual might be well informed and exemplify the official, sophisticated stance of a religion. However, some people now choose to practice religions other than those of their families and communities, and others consciously exclude religion from their lives. The freedom to examine religious ideas, as well as to embrace or reject religion, is integral to most institutions of higher education in the United States; indeed, this freedom is inherent to being a citizen of the United States.

♦ ♦

Glossary Terms

ANIMISM   The primitive belief that nature is filled with innumerable spirits. All things are thought of as possessing a life somewhat akin to human life.

CHRISTIANITY   The religion of those who confess Jesus as Lord and Messiah, including the Roman Catholic, Anglican, Protestant, and Eastern Orthodox churches.

EX CATHEDRA   From the Latin "from the chair or seat"; used most frequently to designate the Pope's infallible teachings on matters of faith and morals that are binding upon Roman Catholics; such pronouncements are different from "non-infallible" addresses, sermons, and so on.

FAITH   An attitude of trust or confidence in a person, doctrine, system of beliefs and practices, or thing; faith may be informed or uninformed (naive).

FUNDAMENTALISM   In religions, conservative views that include literal interpretations of scriptures as revealing God's truths and so yielding a fixed set of beliefs for all time.

ISLAM   The world-wide religion of Muslims, followers of Mohammed; literally means "submission to God."

JUDAISM   The religion of Jews living all over the world.

LIBERALISM   As a modern Christian movement, a social and political philosophy favoring freedom of the individual and the rational consent of human beings, as opposed to an authoritarian ideal. As an approach to the Bible, the critical and analytical study of biblical literature with the purpose of distinguishing among myths, legends, history and other literary forms (as opposed to fundamentalism).

MANA REACTION   A primitive reaction exhibiting belief in a widely diffused power or in an influence operative wherever anything striking or unusual occurs.

MONOTHEISM   The belief that there is only one (usually personal) God.

MYSTICISM   The belief that an immediate consciousness of God or a unity within the Divine is attainable; there are many interpretations of mysticism.

POLYTHEISM   Belief in many personalized gods.

PRAYER   A form of private or group religious experience intending to establish a personal relationship with God.

RITUAL   Practices and ceremonies that nurture beliefs, feelings, organization, and daily living.

QUR'AN   The most holy writings of Islam; sometimes "Koran."

SACRED   Whatever or whoever is regarded as holy, spiritually distinct from human initiatives, worthy of reverence, wondrous, respectful, and awesome.

THEOCRACY   A government believed to be ruled by God acting through God's human agents.

◆ ◆

Chapter Review

WHAT IS RELIGION?

1. There are a variety of viewpoints concerning the nature of religion; there is no universally accepted definition of religion.

2. Throughout history, humanity has exhibited a sense of the sacred; religious individuals feel that they have an unconditional commitment to whatever they regard as the Sacred Ultimate—that is, the source and basis of existence, the supreme foundation of all truth, reality, and goodness beyond the human senses.

3. *Sacred* is an imprecise, somewhat poetic word referring to whatever or whomever is regarded as holy, spiritually distinct from human initiatives, worthy of reverence, wondrous, respectful, and awesome.

4. The element of faith has been prominent in the history of religion. Distinctions may be made between "naive" and "informed" faith.

5. The intellectual, doctrinal component of religion is significant.

6. The emotional or feeling element has been evident in religion.

7. To one degree or another organization is a recurring aspect of religion.

8. Religion has been described as involving the whole of life; it is the reaction of a person's whole being to a highest loyalty.

9. Participation in formal religious rituals can express and nurture beliefs, feelings, organization, and daily living.

THE NATURE OF RELIGION

1. Our tentative definition of *religion* is "a faith in a Sacred Ultimate; a faith often organized around community, leadership, and continuity, integrated with daily living, frequently expressed in and nurtured by ritual."

2. Scholarly approaches to religion seek to bypass obstacles to religious studies and can focus on many areas of inquiry.

3. Individual religions can offer contributions to certain philosophic issues.

4. Philosophy of religion is philosophical thinking about religion.

THE ORIGIN AND GROWTH OF RELIGION

1. One theory of origin proposes that religion grew out of human social and psychological needs. It is part of the struggle for a fuller life.

2. A second theory of origin proposes that religion grew out of humanity's awareness of a "More" that gives meaning and significance to life.

3. Growth in religion includes the primitive mana reaction, animism, polytheism, and monotheism.

4. Cults and sects are categories of some religious groups.

MYTH IN SACRED LITERATURE

1. The use of myth in sacred literature can refer to (1) fables, (2) literary forms that describe spiritual matters in everyday terms, and (3) a method of thinking about and expressing ultimate truths.

RELIGIOUS EXPERIENCE

1. One form of religious experience is mysticism; there are three contrasting types.

2. One common element among religious experiences appears to be a conviction of a momentous disclosure, a disclosure that true reality, the Sacred Ultimate, has been revealed as it "really" is.

THREE UNIVERSAL RELIGIONS: JUDAISM, CHRISTIANITY, ISLAM

1. Judaism is one of the oldest of the world's living religions; five beliefs are central to Judaism.

2. Three major divisions within modern Judaism are Orthodox, Conservative, and Reform.

3. Christianity continues the five beliefs of Judaism, amplified by specific belief in the New Testament.

4. Three major traditions in Christianity include Eastern Orthodoxy, Roman Catholicism, and Protestantism. Several modern movements contribute to diversity among Christians.

5. Adherents of Islam view their religion as the "final religion" and the "primal religion."

6. Doctrines upheld by Muslims include belief in one absolute and transcendent God, angels, the Qur'an, the Prophets of Allah (Mohammed is the last and the greatest), and a time of judgment.

7. Peace, *jihad,* and *ummah* are significant Islamic concepts.

8. Two branches of Islam are the Sunnis and Shi'ites. Shi'ites live primarily in Iran and Iraq.

CURRENT RELIGIOUS ISSUES

1. Many issues in the philosophy of religion are being explored by contemporary scholars.

2. Jews, Christians, and Muslims are debating several issues important to their adherents.

REFLECTIONS

1. The freedom to examine religious ideas, as well as to embrace or reject religion, is integral to most institutions of higher education in the United States; indeed, this freedom is inherent in being a citizen of the United States.

Study Questions and Projects

1. Read Professor Alston's essay "Religion" in the *Encyclopedia of Philosophy*, and discuss the adequacy of at least five of the quoted definitions of religion on page 140 (Vol. 7). State clearly your standards for adequacy.

2. With regard to this chapter's interpretation of "informed faith" (page 359), develop criteria for "a suitable rationale."

3. Consider the statement, "All proof must begin with certain assumptions. This is true in science, philosophy, or religion" (page 218 in Chapter 11). Discuss your understanding of "faith" as related to religion and to science.

4. "The origin of all religions can be traced entirely to various human needs and the human imagination." "My religion originated in God's self-disclosure to humanity." Can these statements be reconciled? Is there a method by which one assertion can be proven superior to the other?

5. Write a paper describing similarities and differences among Judaism, Christianity, and Islam with respect to their basic beliefs about God and/or morality.

6. Discuss the relationship between religion and philosophy, indicating the extent to which you think that religion needs support from philosophy and whether or not religion has anything to fear from philosophical investigation and discussion of religious questions.

7. What parts do the following play in religion: the organized group, the scriptures, ceremony, prayer, worship? Describe these parts in theory and practice.

8. How does religion differ from (a) philosophy, (b) science, and (c) art? You will need to keep in mind the discussions in previous chapters.

Suggested Readings

See also the Suggested Readings in Chapter 18.

Carmody, D. L. *Women and World Religions,* 2nd ed. Englewood Cliffs, N.J.: Prentice-Hall, 1988.

> A survey of female images and roles in major religious traditions past and present.

Carter, S. L. *The Culture of Disbelief: How American Law and Politics Trivialize Religious Devotion.* New York: Basic Books, 1993.

> The Yale law professor-author argues that in our zeal to keep religion out of politics, we force the religiously devout to act as if their faith doesn't really matter.

Driver, T. *The Magic of Ritual.* San Francisco: Harper, 1992.

> The author explores the vital role that ritual plays in the life of every culture.

Esposito, J. L. *Islam: The Straight Path,* expanded ed. New York: Oxford University Press, 1990 [Paperback edition, 1992].

> An introductory study written in a clear and lively style.

Forman, R. K. C. (ed.). *Religions of the World,* 3rd ed. New York: St. Martin's, 1993.

> Written by scholars in their respective areas of specialization, this text provides a detailed overview of significant faiths of the past and the major religions of the world today.

Freedman, D. N. (ed.). *The Anchor Bible Dictionary.* New York: Doubleday, 1992.

> A six-volume, multicultural reference resource written by major international scholars with essays such as "Christianity"; "Israel, History of";

"Judaism"; "Myth and Mythology"; "Philosophy"; "Platonism"; "Roman Religion"; "Sex and Sexuality"; and "Women."

Hick, J. (ed.). *Classical and Contemporary Readings in the Philosophy of Religion*, 3rd ed. Englewood Cliffs, N.J.: Prentice-Hall, 1990.

An anthology of readings, with introductory notes on major issues in the philosophy of religion.

———. *Philosophy of Religion*, 4th ed. Englewood Cliffs, N.J.: Prentice-Hall, 1990.

Professor Hick examines the central ideas in the philosophy of religion.

Marty, M., and Appleby, R. S. (eds.). *Fundamentalisms Observed*. Chicago: University of Chicago Press, 1991.

The inaugural volume in the series "The Fundamentalism Project," examining characteristics and consequences of fundamentalist movements around the world. Also in the series: *Islamic Fundamentalisms and the Gulf Crisis* (1991), *Fundamentalisms and the State* (1993), and *Fundamentalisms and Society* (1992).

Melton, J. G. *Encyclopedic Handbook of Cults in America*. Rev. ed. Hamden, Conn.: Garland, 1992.

Developments and controversies within 500 "cults," including the Unification Church, Church of Scientology, and Hare Krishnas.

Neusner, J. *An Introduction to Judaism*. Louisville, Ky.: Westminster/John Knox, 1992.

Written expressly as an exploration for a one-semester course.

———. (ed.). *World Religions in America: An Introduction*. Louisville, Ky.: Westminster/John Knox, 1994.

Native American Religions, Buddhism, Christianity, and most other world religions as practiced in American life are presented by specialists including Martin Marty, Andrew Greeley, and Jaroslav Pelikan. "Religion and Women in America," "Islam in the World and in America," "The Religious World of African Americans," and "The Religious World of Hispanic Americans" are among the fourteen chapters.

Porter, B. F. (ed.). *Religion and Reason*. New York: St. Martin's, 1993.

An anthology addressing the central questions of religion and philosophy via contemporary and historic writings.

Smith, H. *The World's Religions*. San Francisco: HarperSanFrancisco, 1991.

A clear, objective, and basic description of major world religions in this revision of Smith's classic *The Religions of Man*.

Sullivan, L. E. *Native American Religions*. New York: Macmillan, 1987.

A paperbound selection from Eliade's *Encyclopedia of Religion*, introducing readers to the religious life and expressions of Native North America.

Swidler, A. (ed.). *Homosexuality and World Religions*. Valley Forge, Penn.: Trinity Press International, 1993.

The contributors illuminate the ambiguous status of homosexuality in traditional native American, African, and Asian religions as well as in Judaism, Christianity, and Islam.

Wilson, A. (ed.). *World Scripture: A Comparative Anthology of Sacred Texts*. New York: Paragon, 1991.

A topical journey through the sacred writings of major world religions.

♦ ♦

Notes

1. J. H. Hick, *Philosophy of Religion*, 2d ed. (Englewood Cliffs, N.J.: Prentice-Hall, 1973), p. 3.

2. This threefold distinction is made by Erich Dinkler in his essay "Myth (Demythologizing)," in

M. Halverson and A. Cohen, eds., *A Handbook of Christian Theology* (Nashville, Tenn.: Abingdon, 1958), pp. 238–43. See also Mary Gerhart, "Myth," in D. W. Musser and J. L. Price, eds., *A New Handbook of Christian Theology*, (Nashville, Tenn.: Abingdon, 1992), pp. 321–23.

3. D. V. Steere, "Mysticism," in Halverson and Cohen, *A Handbook of Christian Theology*, pp. 236–38; see also J. R. Price, "Mysticism," in Musser and Price, *A New Handbook of Christian Theology*, pp. 318–20.

4. H. Zimmer, *Philosophies of India* (Princeton: Princeton University Press, 1951), pp. 328–32.

5. G. Parrinder, *Mysticism in the World's Religions* (New York: Oxford University Press, 1976), p. 161.

6. W. N. Pittenger, *Praying Today* (Grand Rapids, Mich.: Eerdmans, 1974), p. 27.

7. A. Schmemann, "Eastern Christianity," in Halverson and Cohen, *A Handbook of Christian Theology*, pp. 85*ff.*; See also T. A. Idinopulos, "Eastern Orthodox Christianity," in Musser and Price, *A New Handbook of Christian Theology*, pp. 130*ff.*

8. Several churches (such as the Anglican Church, the Old Catholic Churches, and the Philippine Independent Church) are generally viewed as Protestant; however, they prefer to emphasize their faithfulness to historic Catholicism without recognition of Roman authority.

9. E. Andrews, "Spiritual Gifts," *The Interpreter's Dictionary of the Bible* (New York: Abingdon, 1962), Vols. R–Z, pp. 435*ff.*

10. Among the leaders of the neoorthodox movement in Europe were Karl Barth and Emil Brunner and, in the United States, Reinhold Niebuhr, Richard Niebuhr, and Paul Tillich. In the 1950s, neoorthodoxy was the dominant movement in Protestant theology. By the 1960s, it was showing signs of diversity as the trend toward a "secular religion" developed. In the 1970s, the movement was toward an experiential basis for religion. See J. E. Smith, *Experience and God* (New York: Oxford University Press, 1968).

11. S. E. Ahlstrom, *A Religious History of the American People* (New Haven and London: Yale University Press, 1972), p. 948.

12. See Musser and Price, *A New Handbook of Christian Theology*, for brief essays on modern Christian (and other) movements.

13. This interpretation, empathetic to Islam, was developed in 1963 by Dr. Willem A. Bijlefeld, Director *Emeritus* of the Duncan Black Macdonald Center of The Hartford Seminary in Connecticut.

14. In addition to the Qur'an, the Sunna (Customs of the Prophets), the Hadith (traditions), and the Ijma (agreement) aid followers in gaining the right interpretation of doctrine, and they cover points not dealt with in the Qur'an. On the basis of the Qur'an and Hadith, the Islamic way of life is expressed in the Shari'ah—Islamic law.

15. S. Wine, *Humanistic Judaism* (Buffalo, N.Y.: Prometheus, 1978).

16. See T. Boman, *Hebrew Thought Compared With Greek* (Philadelphia: Westminster, 1960); E. Hatch, *The Influence of Greek Ideas on Christianity* (New York: Harper, 1957); W. H. V. Reade, *The Christian Challenge to Philosophy* (London: S.P.C.K., 1951); G. E. Wright, *The Old Testament and Theology* (New York: Harper and Row, 1969).

Belief in God

CHAPTER OBJECTIVES

In this chapter we will address the
following questions:

- Are There Different Notions
  of God?

- Can God's Existence Be Proved?

- Can God's Existence
  Be Disproved?

- Is There Life after Death?

*Religious thinking, believing, feeling are
among the most deceptive activities of the
human spirit. We often assume it is God
we believe in, but in reality it may be a
symbol of personal interests we dwell upon.
We may assume that we feel drawn to
God, but in reality it may be a power
within the world that is the object of our
adoration. We may assume it is God we
care for, but it may be our own ego we
are concerned with.*[1]

The Nature of God

"Do you believe in God?" has become a common question. A simple "yes," "no," or "I'm not sure" might appear to be adequate, but further probing could indicate that these are less-than-satisfactory responses. Unless explained, the meaning of the word "God" for the questioner might be different from that for the respondent; the person asking the question could mean "an energy force," the individual responding could mean "a spiritual essence within." Without some explanation, communication of ideas does not take place.

Belief in God, in one of its many forms, has occupied a central position in religious faith and practice. Humans throughout the ages have felt a sense of dependence on someone or something beyond their own resources. This sense of dependence may manifest itself in many ways, depending on the intellectual and cultural development of the individual or group. The non-literate tribe smears a stone with grease to appease their deity; Plato expresses reverence for the Idea of the Good; Muslims kneel and pray to Allah at various times of each day; worshippers participate in praise of God in synagogues and cathedrals; mystics reach that "dreamless sleep" of the soul's liberation—in all these there is a similar goal, a relationship with ultimate reality, or the "Sacred Ultimate."

THREE ISSUES

There are three basic issues associated with belief in God: God and the Idea of God, worship preceding ideas, and the incompleteness and insufficiency of ideas.

God and the Idea of God. There is a difference between God and any idea of God. To say that God *is* means that there is an objectively real God independent of human needs and ideas. By definition, God is ultimate reality and exists whether or not humanity exists.

However, *ideas* about God are human attempts to explain or interpret God. Convinced of the objective existence of God, theologians and some philosophers attempt to "put God into concepts" for the purpose of clarification. Their explanations or ideas are symbols about God; but because symbols change from culture to culture, ideas about God or ultimate reality vary. It is possible that some or all views about God bear little, if any, resemblance to objective ultimate reality. (See *Theology* in Glossary.)

Worship Preceding Ideas. Humanity worshipped a God or gods long before doctrines and philosophical problems concerning God arose. When people discovered other groups with different ideas of God, they were led to ask which ideas, if any, correctly represented God. With the growth of knowledge, some of the older conceptions came to seem inadequate. Thinking people were forced to defend the older views, modify them, or give them up.

The Incompleteness and Insufficiency of Ideas. No individual's view of God is either final or complete. Our knowledge is growing and incomplete. In addition, we find it difficult to express satisfactorily some of our deepest convictions. The religious person is likely to say that what he or she discovers is not propositions but a relationship with the Sacred.

TERMS ASSOCIATED WITH GOD

Let us clarify some of the terms used in discussions about the nature and existence of God. **Theism** is the belief in a personal God who is creator of the world and a participant (immanent) in its processes, and with whom human beings can enter "I–Thou" relationships. **Monotheism** is a form of theism that proposes *one* such personal god; **polytheism** says there is more than one God.

Deism, a form of theistic belief popular among eighteenth-century and contemporary people, emphasizes the remoteness (transcendence) of God from the world. Several of the founding fathers of the United States were deists, including Benjamin Franklin, Thomas

Jefferson, George Washington, and Thomas Paine.[2] God is the creator and lawgiver, who permits his creation to administer itself through natural laws. This view has been called the "watchmaker view" of the universe: God creates an instrument, the natural universe; he permits it to operate without his interference or participation. A rigorous deist does not view any writings, including the Bible, as revelations from God or participate in private or group prayer to the "absent God." However, many less rigorous deists pray or seek inspiration from group participation on sentimental occasions or in times of crisis.[3]

Pantheism is the belief that God is all, and all is God. "God" is the name we give to all things taken in their totality. The pantheism of the European Middle Ages held that because "God alone truly *is*, all that *is* must in some sense be God, or at least a manifestation of God."[4] This form of pantheism remains personal; in some sense God is believed to be "someone." A different view of pantheism understands God as the *non-personal*, universal spirit that is total reality; here, too, all existence is in God. Both the personal and nonpersonal forms of pantheism understand total existence as an all-inclusive divine reality.

God-As-Goodness is the notion of God as a metaphor for some kind of all-encompassing goodness. This view is accepted by many contemporary intellectuals who reject all forms of theism and mysticism. This concept of God is concerned with how we ought to live; among intellectuals living in Western civilizations, an emphasis on community and social responsibility is central to notions of God-As-Goodness.

Agnosticism means "not knowing." It continues to be used most frequently in a religious sense. "We do not know whether there is a God"—such is the agnostic's suspension of judgment about God's existence. It is possible neither to affirm nor to deny God's existence. The term **atheism** (without God—*a theos*—or Godless) has a different meaning; the atheist asserts there is no personal God. Far from being a suspension of belief, atheism is the firm conviction that God does not exist.

The views represented here are fundamental ideas about the nature and existence of God. Each has several schools of thought, and most can be found in some form in all the major religions of the world. Philosophers and theologians have for centuries debated the merits of each view and whether one best captures the nature of God in a given heritage. Let us now turn our attention to the concepts of God representative of three traditions: the Hebraic, Greek, and Asian.

THE HEBRAIC VIEW OF GOD

Throughout their history the Hebrew people perceived different relationships with God; love, mercy, justice, and awe characterized God's relationship with Israel. That God is the someone who creates what comes into existence is a continuing conviction of Judaism, Christianity, and Islam.[5] The God of Israel is not a crude projection of a human being; rather he is perceived as the creative intelligence who fashions reality and reveals his purpose for humanity through chosen agents and events. The "personhood" and other human characteristics of the Hebraic God as portrayed in the Bible and Qur'an are not intended to reduce deity to mortal dimensions and limitations; rather, they portray vividly a God who is some*one*, not some*thing*. An extension of this view is represented in the following passage:

> The categories which come to the fore in this interpretation of God's nature are person and the various qualities essential to personality, . . . God is literally related to his creation, affecting and being affected by it, is literally involved in space and time, literally suffers and literally intervenes in the historical order to bring about the accomplishment of his purposes so far as he can. God is a free, personal being with various super powers. . . . God has all the essentials which constitute personality.[6]

As symbols of God reflecting their cultures, words such as "Father" and "He" were used in holy writings and in prayers by Jews, Christians, and Muslims. Male symbols conveyed a personal God in language acceptable to those peoples. "It" or "She" would have failed to communicate their experiences of God. The intention was never to equate God with a mortal male or a "man in the sky." In fact, the writers of the Bible and Qur'an were not speculating about the essence of God; they interpreted his nature only in terms of his activity. Their accent was on his sovereign will, not on his being.

The systematic, intellectual presentation of Judaism, Christianity, and Islam accompanied reflections apart from their holy writings. Theologians sought to proclaim God's revelation to their own communities of faith and to the world; philosophers attempted to arrive at truth independently of revelation. The theologians worked from their scriptures and the experiences of their religious communities; philosophers, aided by reason, reached for God as well. The two tasks were occasionally blended in one person's efforts, such as in the writings of Thomas Aquinas.

Because the categories and methods of formal, scholarly philosophy were unknown to the Hebrew mind, the modes of thought developed by the great Greek philosophers entered the Jewish, Christian, and Muslim intellectual efforts at various stages of their respective histories. Concerns with essence, substance, and attributes became an aspect of the three religions. A focus on God's *being* accompanied emphasis on his *activity*. The God of Moses who delivered the Hebrew people from Egyptian captivity was also understood in terms of Aristotle's "pure form" and "uncaused cause." Some of the characteristics of God have been stated within this Greek philosophical mode as follows:

*God is **immanent**.* God is said to be operative within the structure of the universe, taking a vital part in its processes and in human life. This view is distinguished from the older supernaturalism, which viewed God as operating only from outside the natural order; it is distinguished as well from pantheism, in which God and the universe are one. According to the doctrine of im-

manence, God is conceived as the principle of intelligence, purpose, and causation operating within the creative processes of the world.[7]

God works in lawful and orderly ways. As they study the world, observers find a general orderliness that is universal and dependable. Views of God usually are in harmony with the processes discovered in the cosmos. *PSR*

*God is **transcendent**.* Many people also believe that God transcends the world process. Immanence and transcendence are not contradictory terms. God is said to exist prior to the world and to be superior to it. Thus "nature" and the "supernatural" can be thought of as separate, and God can be conceived of as operating from above or apart from the world as well as within it.

God is intelligent and his ways are purposeful. The world lends itself to intelligent analysis and comprehension. Consequently, we can assume that mind plays a prominent part in its processes. Whatever "more" God may be, God must be at least personal and intelligent, and God is a Being who acts with purpose.

God is good and beneficent. Belief in God represents the human conviction that there is an "eternal goodness." Whenever people have been confronted with what appeared to be a choice between defining God as good or as all-powerful, they have been willing to admit limits to his power rather than to his goodness. God is then viewed as struggling with and for humanity.

THE GREEK VIEW OF GOD

The nature of God in the ancient Greek tradition includes two components: the religious and the philosophical. It was the religious view that was held by the people; the philosophical had little to do with them. The first notions of deity were expressed in the *Iliad* and *Odyssey* of Homer. In these epics, a hierarchy of gods governed the universe; the most important of the gods was Zeus, the embodiment of order. He was omnipotent as long as he conformed to what was fated; if he acted differently, cosmic chaos would result. The father of gods and mortals, Zeus was not the creator of the universe. He was quite capricious in his dealings with humans—as was the style of the other gods. The gods of Greece, and later of Rome, were of primary political importance; they "represented the divine guardians of social order and prosperity, and all citizens were expected to participate in their public worship as evidence of their integrity and loyalty."[8] Such gods left much to be desired for the more thoughtful Greeks. Some attempted to understand the source of existence through the use of reason. Others turned to various mystery religions.

In the fifth and fourth centuries B.C.E., the first great comprehensive system of philosophy was developed by the Greek philosopher Plato; his system is the culmination of the stage set by his predecessors combined with his own reasoning. In his search for the unchanging and eternal, Plato proposed that only that which is beyond the universe, space, and time, could be ultimate reality. God for Plato was the essence or Idea of the Good. This Transcendence, of which the universe is a participating reflection, is perfect **Being.**

Aristotle viewed the Eternal as the "Prime Mover" and "Uncaused Cause." Affirming with his teacher Plato that the world of the senses is a derivative world dependent on a reality other than itself, Aristotle differed from Plato on many details, including those that were theological. However, Aristotle provided a rational method for proving God's existence, and his concept of God as Unmoved Mover was incorporated centuries later in the writings of Thomas Aquinas. The dualism proposed by these Greek philosophers established the contrasts between spirit and matter, nonphysical and physical, eternal and temporal, and changeless and changing. From this perspective we inherit the negative terms applied to that which is beyond: **infinite** (*not* finite), *in*corporeal (*not* material), and *im*mutable (*not* changing). Other designations of the Transcendent include: "wholly other" (totally beyond human existence) and Being (fundamental reality).

In the second century C.E. in Alexandria, a group of "Christian Platonists" sought to blend the conclusions of Plato with those of the biblical tradition. The philosophies of Greeks other than Plato, especially of Aristotle and Plotinus, were later to enter the mainstream of Western theological development. To this day, some scholars view this synthesis as enrichment; for others it is a corruption of the Hebraic world view.[9]

ONE ASIAN VIEW OF GOD

Like the Greek view, a classical Asian view of God includes a "popular" (held by ordinary people) and a philosophic understanding. As early as 3000 B.C.E., the Hindu peoples worshiped gods personifying natural phenomena. Storm gods, fire gods, and eventually creator and destroyer gods typified the unceasing process of life and death, a cyclic process with no ultimate purpose beyond the process itself. Among the major gods are Brahma (the creator), Vishnu (the preserver), and Shiva (the destroyer). Stories about these gods are intentionally unhistorical tales, though at the popular level they are often taken quite literally. In Buddhism, many of the gods of Hinduism have found a place, but the focus is on the "Enlightened One," Buddha himself. Although Buddha was originally the man who showed the way, idealized images of him are found in temples; they are treated as holy and are a focus of worship. In Chinese religion, the veneration of Confucius, ancestor worship, and other lesser forms of deity and spirits form a pantheon.

In an introduction to *The Song of God: Bhagavad-Gita*, a portion of Hindu holy writings, Aldous Huxley proposed a model by which he suggested most world philosophies and religions to be understood. In this introductory essay, the "Perennial Philosophy" is clearly meant to grasp the major motifs of Hindu thought. Huxley's four characteristics of this way of perceiving reality in all Hindu thought about God convey themes appearing year after year (hence, "perennial").[10]

A summary of Huxley's themes relevant to most world philosophies and religions follows:

1. The universe we perceive is dependent on a nonpersonal Divine Ground, which alone is ultimately real.

2. Human beings can "know" the Divine Ground by direct unitive experience that transcends rationality.

3. Persons consist of the perishable ego and body plus an eternal self, which is of the same nature as the Divine Ground.

4. The purpose of life is the uniting of one's true, eternal self with the Divine Ground.

Huxley's view that most religions and philosophies are versions of the "Perennial Philosophy" is criticized as an oversimplification by many scholars.

Grounds for Belief in God

Belief in God is a conviction and a faith held by many people, some of whom are concerned to know if such a belief is intellectually respectable in the light of modern knowledge. We need at this point to keep clearly in mind that there is a close relation between definitions of *God*, the nature of God, and the types of proof for God's existence. Definitions and conceptions of the nature of God that think of him as absolute and eternal (all-powerful, all-knowing, and everywhere) start from certain premises and proceed inferentially.[11] For example, because we explain events by cause and effect in our everyday lives, we assume that there is a cause of the process as a whole; because we strive for completion and a greater degree of perfection, we assume that there is that which is complete and perfect. We shall see this type of reasoning when we present the traditional "proofs" of God's existence. On the other hand, we can appeal directly to human experience and interpret God with respect to certain elements or aspects of experience, or to certain "good things" that reveal a more-than-surface depth to human experience. If we define *God* as "beneficent purpose," then to prove that God exists we must prove that love

and purpose are dominant realities and require a nonhuman cause.

We shall present first certain philosophical arguments for belief in the reality of God. These traditional "theistic proofs" are of philosophical interest and have received widespread attention from both secular and religious writers.

THE ONTOLOGICAL ARGUMENT

The ontological argument for the existence of God was first developed by Saint Anselm (1033–1109)[12] (see biography and excerpt, pp. 390–391). The argument attempts to prove the existence of God by moving from a human mental concept of God to a knowledge of his actual existence; this rationalistic proof seeks to establish that we already know the independent *reality* of God from the *idea* of God. Anselm proposed that God is "that than which nothing greater can be conceived," the human idea of perfection. However, a God who only exists as a human idea is inferior to one who exists both in the mind *and* in reality. Thus God must exist as an idea and as an independent reality.

Saint Anselm was convinced that it is *necessary* for God to exist. Given his definition of God, it is impossible to conceive of God not existing; nonexistence is an imperfection. To deny the existence of God would be to deny the existence of what logically must be.

Criticisms of the Argument.

The ontological argument has had many critics.[13] Gaunilon, a French monk, claimed that Anselm's reasoning led to absurd conclusions; Gaunilon then produced a parallel ontological argument for the most perfect island. Given the idea of such an island, we can argue that unless it exists in reality it cannot be the most perfect conceivable island. We cannot deduce the existence of a being from the idea of that being.

Descartes and Kant both centered their criticism on the same point, as do most of the modern discussions of the ontological argument: the assumption that existence is a predicate. Kant contends that existence is not a property or a predicate. The discussion was continued by Bertrand Russell in his analysis of the word *exists*.[14]

Some theologians, most notably Karl Barth, see Saint Anselm's argument not as an attempted proof of God's existence but as an unfolding of God's revelation. In this view, the argument does not seek to convert the atheist but rather to lead an already formed religious believer into a deeper understanding of God.

THE COSMOLOGICAL ARGUMENT

The next important attempt to demonstrate the existence of God was that of Thomas Aquinas (c. 1224–1274) (see biography and excerpt, pp. 392–393), who (drawing on Aristotle and on Muslim philosophy) (see Maimonides biography and excerpt, pp. 394–395) offers five ways of proving divine existence. The proofs are all based on the same premise; often the cosmological argument is referred to as *the first-cause argument*. It is a deductive argument that states that everything that happens has a cause, and this cause in turn has a cause, and so on in a series that must either be infinite or have its starting point in a first cause. Aquinas excludes the possibility of an infinite regress of causes and so concludes that there must be a first cause, which we call God.

In the Thomistic (thinkers who follow Thomas Aquinas) tradition, as represented by many Roman Catholic theologians, the cosmological argument for the existence of God has been given considerable emphasis. We must, it is affirmed, differentiate between the accidental and the essential features of reality, or between the temporary objects of experience and objects that are permanent. Every event or change presupposes a cause, and logically we must go back to an uncaused, self-existent cause or to a self-existent Being. This Being is the principle of explanation for the universe taken as a whole and the condition of its orderly development, as well as its permanent source or ground.

Criticisms of the Argument. David Hume and others criticized this argument. They ask, "What was the cause of the First Cause?" and they suggest that the series of causes may have had no beginning. If every event must have a cause, why, it is asked, do we stop with God? If there can be uncaused events, then is a concept of God necessary? To these criticisms, some have replied that this argument is not just a temporal argument from effect to cause but an argument in the "order of being," in that God is said to be the "highest order of being" and, as such, he is the "uncaused cause" of whatever exists, including, for example, an endless series of events.

THE TELEOLOGICAL ARGUMENT

The teleological argument, or the argument from design or purpose in the world, is among the most popular of the theistic arguments. The order and the progress in the universe disclose an immanent intelligence and purpose. Take, for example, the long process of development leading to the human brain and mind. The process has produced minds that begin to understand the world, and it has produced thought and understanding. How could this occur unless the course of evolution were directed by an infinite mind?

The teleological argument was elaborated by William Paley (1743–1805). He argued, for example, that the human eye must represent an intelligent creator's design; it would be absurd to attribute the biological development of the eye to "chance." Paley's analogy of the watch conveys the argument well: I may explain the existence of a rock lying on the ground by references to natural forces such as volcanic action, wind, and rain. However, if I see a watch lying on the ground, I cannot explain its existence in the same way; the complex arrangement of the watch's wheels, springs, and other parts, all operating together accurately, requires the postulate of an intelligent mind responsible for its being. Paley argued for the existence of God based on the complex and orderly functioning of the

Saint Anselm

Anselm (1033–1109), one of the greatest thinkers of the Middle Ages, was born in Aosta in the Italian Alps. After a period of study in France, he entered the monastic life at Bec, where his abilities were soon recognized and he was appointed prior and head of the monastic school. In 1093, he was called to be Archbishop of Canterbury, but when King William refused to recognize the freedom of the church from royal control, he went into exile in Italy in protest. King Henry I later summoned him back to England.

As a theologian and philosopher, Anselm is famous for his proofs of the existence of God by the use of reason. He said that we should accept faith first, then use reason to gain a deeper understanding. His writings include the *Monologion* (c. 1077), a treatise that examines the existence of God; the *Proslogion* (c. 1077), which develops the ontological argument for the existence of God; and *Cur Deus Homo?* (c. 1099) which deals with the doctrines of the Incarnation and Atonement.

---

world; there must be a Creator just as there must be a watchmaker.

Criticisms of the Argument. The teleological argument has had many able supporters who argue from the presence of order and design in the world to the source of that order in a purposeful God. Kant pointed out that at most the argument from design points to a designer who is not necessarily an omnipotent creator of the world. Other critics have thought that the Darwinian doctrine of natural selection has weakened the force of the teleological argument.

Another more severe criticism is that the argument assumes an order and design. The position can be offered that there is disorder, chance, or even chaos; human perceptions of reality are generally unaware of fundamental disorder in the universe. However, even if it could be proven that order exists, a problem of inferring a Transcendent God as its creator would remain.

Excerpt from Saint Anselm:
Proslogion; Preface (c. 1077)

After I had published, at the pressing entreaties of several of my brethren, a certain short tract (the *Monologion*) as an example of meditation on the meaning of faith from the point of view of one seeking, through silent reasoning within himself, things he knows not—reflecting that this was made up of a connected chain of many arguments, I began to wonder if perhaps it might be possible to find one single argument that for its proof required no other save itself, and that by itself would suffice to prove that God really exists, that He is the supreme good needing no other and is He whom all things have need of for their being and well-being, and also to prove whatever we believe about the Divine Being. But as often and as diligently as I turned my thoughts to this, sometimes it seemed to me that I had almost reached what I was seeking, sometimes it eluded my acutest thinking completely, so that finally, in desperation, I was about to give up what I was looking for as something impossible to find. However, when I had decided to put aside this idea altogether, lest by uselessly occupying my mind it might prevent other ideas with which I could make some progress, then, in spite of my unwillingness and my resistance to it, it began to force itself upon me more and more pressingly. So it was that one day when I was quite worn out with resisting its importunacy, there came to me, in the very conflict of my thoughts, what I had despaired of finding, so that I eagerly grasped the notion which in my distraction I had been rejecting.

St. Anselm, *Proslogion; Monologium; An Appendix in Behalf of the Fool by Gaunclon;* and *Cur Deus Homo,* trans. S. N. Deane (LaSalle, Ill.: Open Court, 1939).

THE MORAL ARGUMENT

The moral argument for belief in God is grounded in human beings' moral nature. The argument has been stated from a number of points of view, but there are basically two forms in which it is found.

One form is as a logical inference: from objective moral laws one infers a divine Law Giver, or from the fact of our conscience, sense of obligation, or sense of duty one infers a moral God. "If, as is the case, we feel responsibility, are ashamed, are frightened, at transgressing the voice of conscience, this implies that there is One to whom we are responsible, before whom we are ashamed . . . If the cause of these emotions does not belong in this visible world, the Object . . . must be Supernatural and Divine."[15]

A second form of the moral argument is based on the presence of moral values; strictly speaking, it is not an argument at all. It claims that anyone who is seriously committed to re-

Saint Thomas Aquinas

Thomas Aquinas (c. 1224–1274), Catholic theologian and philosopher, was born in Italy and educated under Benedictine and Dominican monks and at the universities of Naples, Paris, and Cologne. He received a doctorate in theology at the University of Paris and taught there until 1259. He then spent ten years lecturing at Dominican monasteries in the area of Rome, after which he returned to Paris to teach and write. He studied the major works of Aristotle extensively and engaged in various intellectual controversies.

The writings of Aquinas, all in Latin, include a number of large theological treatises, disputations on theological and philosophical problems, and commentaries on certain books of the Bible and on twelve treatises of Aristotle. His greatest works are *Summa Contra Gentiles* (1259–1264), to aid in the conversion of the Moors in Spain, and *Summa Theologica* (1265–1273), a systematic synthesis of Christian theology and Aristotelian philosophy.

Thomas Aquinas stands in a position of special respect in the field of Roman Catholic scholarship. In 1323, Pope John XXII canonized him as a saint, and he is called the *Angelic Doctor*. The ecclesiastical law of the Catholic Church, revised in 1918 (Canon 589.1), states that students for the priesthood are to study at least two years of philosophy and four of theology, "following the teaching of St. Thomas." The epithet "Thomist" has been applied to the followers of St. Thomas Aquinas.

Excerpt from Aquinas:

Summa Theologica: Question II, Third Article (1265)

I answer that, The existence of God can be proved in five ways. The first and more manifest way is the argument from motion. It is certain, and evident to our senses, that in the world some things are in motion. Now whatever is in motion is put in motion by another, for nothing can be in motion except it is in potentiality to that towards which it is in motion; . . . Therefore, whatever is in motion must be put in motion by another. . . . But this cannot go on to infinity, because then there would be no first mover; seeing that subsequent movers move only inasmuch as they are put in motion by the first mover; . . . Therefore it is necessary to arrive at a first mover, put in motion by no other; and this everyone understands to be God.

The second way is from the nature of the efficient cause. . . . There is no case known in which a thing is found to be the efficient cause of itself; for so it would be prior to itself, which is impossible. Now in efficient cause it is not possible to go on to infinity. . . . Therefore it is necessary to admit a first efficient cause, to which everyone gives the name of God.

The third way is taken from possibility and necessity, and runs thus. We find in nature things that are possible to be and not to be, since they are found to be generated, and to corrupt, and consequently they are possible to be and not to be. . . . Therefore, if everything is possible not to be, then at one time there could have been nothing in existence. . . . If at one time nothing was in existence, it would have been impossible for anything to have begun to exist; and thus even now nothing would be in existence—which is absurd. Therefore we cannot but postulate the existence of some being having of itself its own necessity, and not receiving it from another, but rather causing others their necessity. This all men speak of as God.

The fourth way is taken from the gradation to be found in things. . . . Therefore there must also be something which is to all beings the cause of their being, goodness, and every other perfection; and this we call God.

The fifth way is taken from the governance of the world. . . . Therefore some intelligent being exists by whom all natural things are directed to their end; and this being we call God.

Saint Thomas Aquinas, The "Summa Theologica" of *St. Thomas Aquinas,* Part I, trans. Fathers of the English Dominican Province (London: Burns Oates and Washbourne, 1920).

[Handwritten margin notes:]

1. Every single thing in nature is contingent (might not have existed).
2. Therefore, nature itself is contingent (might not have existed).

False: category mistake: the class of all accidental events is not necessarily an accidental event or even an event.

Moses Ben Maimonides

Moses Ben Maimonides (1135–1204) is one of the most highly regarded figures in Jewish history; the spiritual development of Judaism would have been impossible without his contributions as codifier, judge, and commentator on the Bible and the Talmud. His *Copy of the Law* (1178), was the first systematic exposition of Jewish religion. The "Articles of Faith" contained therein are quoted or poetically paraphrased in modern Jewish prayer books.

Maimonides' best known work is the *Guide for the Perplexed* (c. 1190), one of the great works of medieval philosophy. In it Maimonides attempted to harmonize the teachings of Judaism with Aristotle. Written for those with a philosophical background, the *Guide's* style and arrangement of material often are deliberately obscure. Maimonides asserted that metaphysics is the highest form of human activity, but is not open to all people. He believed that only philosophy can lead to a true understanding of the nature of God and the world, despite Aristotle's contention of world eternity, which ruled out a creator. Maimonides proved the existence of God purely on the basis of Aristotelian principles. He also demonstrated that the eternity of the world cannot be established by rational arguments, therefore implying that there can be no objection to the scriptural account of the creation.

His other writings include *Commentary on the Mishnah* (1168) and *Treatise on Resurrection* (1191).

---

specting moral values must believe in the reality of a transhuman source for those values, which religion calls God. "Is it too paradoxical in the modern world to say that faith in God is a very part of our moral consciousness, without which the latter becomes meaningless? . . . Either our moral values tell us something about the nature and purpose of reality (i.e. give us the germ of religious belief) or they are subjective and therefore meaningless."[16]

Criticisms of the Argument. Kant, who criticized the previous arguments for belief in God, argued that both immortality and the existence of God are "postulates" of the moral life; that is, God must exist if the moral order is to be intelligible. The critics of this argument say that even if moral values are acknowledged, they could be explained by human needs and desires or by the structure of human nature and society. In other words, the

The object of this treatise is to enlighten a religious man who has been trained to believe in the truth of our holy Law, who conscientiously fulfils his moral and religious duties, and at the same time has been successful in his philosophical studies. Human reason has attracted him to abide within its sphere; and he finds it difficult to accept as correct the teaching based on the literal interpretation of the Law, and especially that which he himself or others derived from those homonymous, metaphorical, or hybrid expressions. Hence he is lost in perplexity and anxiety. If he be guided solely by reason, and renounce his previous views which are based on those expressions, he would consider that he had rejected the fundamental principles of the Law; and even if he retains the opinions which were derived from those expressions, and if, instead of following his reason, he abandon its guidance altogether, it would still appear that his religious convictions had suffered loss and injury. For he would then be left with those errors which give rise to fear and anxiety, constant grief and great perplexity.

This work has also a second object in view. It seeks to explain certain obscure figures which occur in the Prophets, and are not distinctly characterized as being figures. Ignorant and superficial readers take them in a literal, not in a figurative sense. Even well informed persons are bewildered if they understand these passages in their literal signification, but they are entirely relieved of their perplexity when we explain the figure, or merely suggest that the terms are figurative. For this reason I have called this book *Guide for the Perplexed.*

Maimonides, *Guide for the Perplexed,* trans. M. Friedlander (New York: Hebrew Publishing, 1881).

norms need not be located outside the natural order; they need not point to a transcendent Sacred Ultimate.

THE ARGUMENT FROM SPECIAL EVENTS AND EXPERIENCES

People have been convinced throughout the ages that they have had a personal experience or witnessed a special event proving the existence of God. The "dreamless sleep" of the Eastern mystic, feelings of cosmic unity with the universe, healings, answers to prayers, visions, and testimonies of reliable persons are different from the purely rational and inferential arguments just discussed. The participants base their claims on varying degrees of empirical evidence ranging from a "sensed" Otherness to an immediate consciousness of the Transcendent.

Criticisms of the Argument. Personal experiences and witnessed events might move the agnostic toward a belief in God; the believer's faith might be further confirmed. But, would the atheist be convinced?

A pivotal question is often overlooked in this discussion. "Prove to me that there is a God," demands the challenger. One might appropriately respond, "What kind of proof will you accept?" If one of the classical arguments (ontological, etc.) will not fill the order, perhaps an event will, something observable. But what? Even the sudden appearance of a Being who performs all sorts of feats need not be convincing; observing and photographing an executed man emerging from a tomb would not be proof of the existence of a God. *Interpretations of any event can and do vary, according to the outlook of the perceiver.* The mystical experience of the Hindu holy man in his private event; even if the atheist achieved the identical states, he or she could interpret it atheistically. In similar fashion, the atheist witnessing a resurrection of an executed man could interpret the event in ways that do not require a belief in the existence of God. Unusual events and unique experiences of startling magnitude have occurred throughout history; in and of themselves they compel neither belief nor disbelief. They are interpreted by the observer's criteria.

Not only religious matters are subject to such interpretation. Economists, psychologists, physicists, and other investigators *interpret* data. Those who believe that the universe is not fundamentally real can logically dismiss all empirical data as a source of knowledge. What is the nature of evidence that will convince us of something? Are there different kinds of evidence for different kinds of experiences? Issues such as the existence of God, like every other problem of human knowledge, confront us with several possible answers.

REFLECTIONS ON "PROOF"

In the course of human history no universally accepted proof of God's existence has been developed. The classical proofs of reason were proposed by philosophers such as Aristotle and by those already committed to a belief in a Judeo–Christian–Islamic God. Atheists remain unconvinced by them; many theists from different traditions view them as incomplete.

It is interesting that in the biblical literature the deity never compels belief. Insisting on preserving human freedom to choose faith, the biblical writers portray God's encounters with human beings in manners that permit doubt. To do otherwise, to compel belief, would violate the sacredness of human freedom, a major motif in biblical thought.

In those forms of mysticism that view Ultimate Reality or God as beyond all thought and sense experiences, "proof" is even more elusive. Neither reasoned arguments nor appeals to observable events are capable of providing evidence for a deity or reality wholly other than time, space, and thought. Mystical experiences cannot be described or verified. Whether or not a person experiences a spiritual reality is a matter of belief, based on that person's interpretations of a profound, individualistic, inner experience. Although such experiences may be perceived as evidence of God's existence, some people explain them in terms of human psychology or physiology.

We need to recall here Blaise Pascal's (1623–1662) "Wager," which treats the existence of God as a mysterious puzzle; we can take a position on the basis of calculated risks. If we wager that God exists and we're correct, we might well gain salvation; we would lose little if we're mistaken. If we bet there is no God, we stand to gain little if we are right, and we may lose salvation if we are wrong. Pascal proposed that we wager that God exists.

It is likely that there can be no conclusive "proof" of the existence of God that all individuals will accept. John Baillie quotes with approval the statement of William Temple to the effect that "all occurrences are in some degree revelations of God," and the statement of Paul Tillich that "there is no reality, thing, or event which cannot become the bearer" of revelation.[17]

Grounds for Disbelief in God

◆ ◆ ◆ ◆ ◆ ◆ ◆ ◆ ◆ ◆

The responsible skeptic, whether agnostic or atheist, is not concerned with denying that religious people have had certain experiences that have led them to believe in the reality of God. The skeptic believes, however, that these experiences can be accounted for adequately without postulating a God. Furthermore, she or he points to certain grounds for disbelief in God.

EVIL

The presence of evil and pain in our world has been a great obstacle to religious faith. As a challenge to theism, the problem of evil has traditionally been put in the form of a dilemma: If God is perfectly loving, God must wish to abolish evil; and if God is all-powerful, God must be able to abolish evil; but evil exists; therefore God cannot be both omnipotent and perfectly loving.

Pain, suffering, and evil are not imaginary. They also do not seem to be a hidden form of good. They are real and serious, and the classic Christian teaching has regarded them as such. Augustine repudiated the theory that evil is an ultimate constituent of the universe, coordinate with good. Augustine holds firmly to the Judaeo–Christian conviction that the universe is *good*—that it is the creation of a good God for a good purpose. Evil—whether it be an evil will, an instance of pain, or some disorder in nature—has not been set there by God but represents the distortion of something inherently good.[18]

Theodicy means the justification of God's goodness in the face of evil. It does not claim to explain, or explain away, every instance of evil in human experience, but only to point to certain considerations that prevent evil from becoming an insuperable obstacle to rational belief in God.

Interpretations of Evil. As humanity has attempted to resolve the problem of the nature of evil, many interpretations have evolved. Some of the major views follow.

1. All evil is illusory; imperfections of every kind are rooted in matter, which has no final reality. When we recognize that only the spiritual is real, anything seen initially as evil can be set aside. This view locates the origin of evil in human perceptions, not in God.

2. Evil is the direct result of sin. The human will is responsible for bringing certain kinds of evil into the world. Evil is the natural consequence of sinfulness, or it is a punishment meted out by God as a consequence of sin. Evil happenings are expressions of the mysterious will of God inflicting punitive measures on deserving sinners. This view is an obstacle to belief in God for many persons. It is of particular difficulty when an apparently good person suffers.

3. Evil is the result of conflict between two opposing forces, God and Satan. Evil is a sign of Satan's victory. Like the preceding view, this evokes disbelief in God in many people. Why would a good God permit the existence of a rival who inflicts harm on good individuals?

4. The word *evil* is a label for natural occurrences that are perceived as harmful; earthquakes and diseases result from the natural evolutionary development of the universe, including humans. Creation is unfinished and in process. Suffering occurs at this stage of creation because of the incompleteness of the universe; it is a "given," of the present time.

For example, an incurable disease may occur in a person because the individual or the whole human race has not yet acquired immunity. This view reasons that the evolutionary creative process of the whole universe still continues; imperfections exist that will eventually become extinct. When a person or a group becomes involved in any natural catastrophe, it is often labeled "evil"; however, in reality the "disaster" is a natural process. On this view, *evil* suggests a human evaluation of an event; the disease and the earthquake are evil from a human viewpoint, but are not necessarily evil from the perspective of a developing universe. For persons who interpret the universe, including humanity, as completed or perfected, this view is unsatisfactory; a theist who interprets the Genesis accounts of creation literally would reject this position. For other people, it can be an obstacle to belief in God; why would a God design the process of creation such that the innocent suffer? Although the process may not be intended as punishment, it can be readily perceived as such.

5. "Evil" is a term used for immoral decisions and their consequences. Intentional and unintentional acts that inflict harm on the innocent and the guilty are moral evils. The human capacity to make good and bad choices allows for the possibility of harmful results. This view is an obstacle to belief in God for those who believe God should intervene in human affairs to keep individuals from suffering the consequences of their bad choices or the choices of others.

The Central Issue. Each interpretation of evil leaves a central question unanswered: Would God permit the conditions for evil? More specifically, would God punish both the innocent and the guilty? Would God allow a rival to inflict harm on humanity? Would God create the world in such a way that people suffer? Would God permit immoral human decisions to result in the suffering of the innocent.[19]

Theists do not ignore the central issue and allied questions. In various ways, they comprehend evil so that it is not an obstacle to belief for them.

HUMAN NEEDS

A second major ground for disbelief in God is the view that belief in God is only the result of wishful thinking and social convention. Some psychologists propose that an individual's need for a father figure, for dealing with the unknown, for overcoming fears and suffering, and for coping with other immaturities contribute to humanity's creation of all gods. Some sociologists propose that people grouping together have similar corporate needs and therefore create their gods as social fictions.

From a philosophical viewpoint, these "explanations" are inadequate. Even if all persons and all societies have been, are, and will be in need of a god or gods, the actual existence of God is thereby neither proved nor disproved. *Ad hominem* considerations must be set aside when the *issue* of God's existence is debated. Whether or not God or gods exist is a philosophical problem independent of the alleged motives and needs of humans.

LANGUAGE ABOUT GOD

Another obstacle to belief in God is that the word *God* has so frequently been expressed in language, symbols, and assumptions that have lost their meaning and appeal to modern people. "God-language" that reflects the outlook and culture of another age and is not relevant to contemporary experience tends to lose its meaning and appeal. The problem of the truth or falsity of religious language has been brought to the fore in recent decades by a group of philosophical or logical analysts who claim that there are only two kinds of statements that convey knowledge and that may be judged true or false. There are analytic statements such as are found in logic and mathematics, which are true by definition, and empirical statements of fact, which can be objectively tested or verified. Because metaphysical and theological statements are not of this nature, the metaphysical theses and the religious convictions about a reality beyond the realm of the empirical world are brushed aside as meaningless.

Influenced by the methods of linguistic analysis that seemed to deny the meaningfulness of statements that cannot be objectively verified, and by tragic events of the twentieth century such as wars, violence, and death camps, a number of Protestant leaders of the 1960s asserted that "God is Dead."[20] This outlook reflects the influence of Friedrich Nietzsche as well as of certain existential thinkers who have stressed anguish and despair and who seem drawn to concepts of negation and nothingness. Whereas Nietzsche hated Christianity with its emphasis on love and compassion for the weak, some of these "Death of God" theologians called themselves Christians, because they were devoted to the ethics of Jesus of Nazareth.

As an alternative to the alleged emptiness of language about God, the use of *analogy* has been proposed. Analogies are statements or words that capture a "likeness" of one thing to another; a resemblance is drawn. To say that "God is Father" is to convey the caring nature of deity; God is like a parent. It is not to be taken literally in the sense that God is a male progenitor. One recent discussion qualifies analogies about God by noting that "the meaning of any term or experience must be *at least* as rich as the meaning which the term or experience has for human beings."[21] In this sense, to say that God is the Void or Someone Who Acts is to make a meaningful statement. In either case, the words do not exhaust the fullness of the idea of deity; they resemble a human experience of what someone believes to be the Sacred Ultimate.

For some inquirers, the use of analogy would be another ground for disbelief. A study of the use of analogy in the language of science might modify their position.[22]

REFLECTIONS ON DISBELIEF

The arguments offered as grounds for disbelief in God are not conclusive. It is probably as difficult, if not as impossible, to establish indisputable proofs for disbelief as it is for belief. As with virtually all the basic questions of existence, more than one claim or conviction will be available. We have the usual options: (1) to make the judgment to suspend judgment; (2) to be convinced affirmatively; and (3) to be convinced negatively.[23] Each of these options is held with varying degrees of devotion; *each can be a position of informed faith.*

Personal Survival after Death

◆ ◆ ◆ ◆ ◆ ◆ ◆ ◆ ◆ ◆ ◆

Since the time of Job, people have asked whether there is a life after death. Belief in immortality, resurrection, or some form of future life was widespread in primitive times and is present in most theistic religions today. The belief is closely related to the belief in God, although the two are not inseparable. If we accept the existence of God, it is comparatively easy to believe in some future life. If we do not believe in God or some other nonmaterial "ground of existence," the belief in an afterlife is harder to support.

Personal survival after death cannot be definitely proved one way or the other. Science presents no indisputable data. Most clergy believe in some kind of afterlife. But a few people say that the belief in survival after death is a delusion and the result of wishful thinking. The difficulties arise as a result of certain scientific interpretations of the universe that describe the world as material and universally lawful. Some biological, physiological, and psychological interpretations leave little or no place for mind or consciousness; when the body dies, the person, it is said, simply ceases to exist.

Scientists have begun to gather data from persons resuscitated after being "near death" or being pronounced dead because their hearts had stopped beating. One study by a philosopher–psychiatrist discusses some of the methodological difficulties of his work, but cautions against trivializing the frontiers of controversial inquiry.[24]

Personal survival after death may mean quite different things to those who believe in it. There is biological survival, or the continuance of the germ plasm generation after generation. In this sense, there is no question about "survival" in an afterlife. There is instead social survival, or the inheritance of influence or of some social contribution; this too is generally unquestioned. Although few people become famous in history, almost everyone's influence or contribution does continue even after he or she is forgotten.

There is also impersonal immortality, which means that the person or the self is merged with its origin, a "world soul," or with an Absolute. In some Asian religions, the self may enter lower forms than that of humans, as determined by the law of *karma*. It may, however, finally escape the wheel of rebirths and gain unity with a nonpersonal Sacred Ultimate. Doctrines of *karma,* reincarnation, and the transmigration of souls are found in various forms of religions originating in India—notably, Hinduism, Buddhism, and Jainism. These views, however, are not what most people in the West mean by life after death. They believe in the persistence of personal identity in some sphere or plane other than the present earthly one. Does a person persist as a conscious self after what we call death?

The beliefs about life after death in Judaism, Christianity, and Islam are understandably entwined with their beliefs about human nature. In the earliest biblical and Qur'anic passages, a person is conceived as a "living soul," flesh-animated-by-soul, a psychophysical unity. A person is not perceived as having an immaterial soul encased in a separable body. A noted scholar of Islam has pointed out, "the Qur'anic doctrine of the soul is that man's soul is a corporeal, material substance, thin and tenuous as air, fine and light as vapor, permeating the body as sap in trees."[25]

Beliefs about life after death as it relates to human nature are found in two forms in the Hebraic traditions. First, the ancient Hebrew view stressed survival of the Hebrew people as a community rather than as achieving an individual, personal life beyond the grave. Because there is no detachable soul, death brings about the individual's demise. The ongoing people of God, including a person's legacy of children and deeds, continues. In a rather undeveloped form, some Hebrew people held to a vague notion that the dead lingered on in a region outside or under the earth, not in God's presence. Not particularly attractive terms designate this spot: "Ditch," "Pit," "Realm of Death," and "Sheol." Preventing a future of total extinction and giving sharp focus to *this* life, such a secondary religious tenet does suggest the continuance of a component, however minor, of human nature. The precise nature of this element was simply not of concern. Just before the New Testament period, Hebrew civilization pictured a different life after death, which included a restored communion with God. As was the case in earlier times, philosophical speculations about the nature of existence in the life hereafter were secondary.

Second, central to Christian and Muslim theologies is the view that by acts of God persons may be resurrected for everlasting life. Forms of continued self-awareness also found their ways into Jewish thinking. Although convictions about the features of the next life vary, the mode of understanding of the three Hebraic traditions is quite different from an automatic **immortality** of an eternal soul. Grounded in the psychosomatic unity position, the Hebraic traditions affirm a special divine act of re-creation of an embodied, recognizable human personality. Our main point here is that Western religious thought in its most ancient forms stresses human nature as an organic unity; a transfiguration of some sort is necessary (rather than the soul's automatic discarding of the body) for everlasting life. Notions of "immortality of the soul" enter the Hebraic traditions not in their scriptural roots but in later medieval thought. But at no point have they proposed an "immortal" soul that continues beyond this life unchanged.

Reflections

◆ ◆ ◆ ◆ ◆ ◆ ◆ ◆ ◆ ◆ ◆

In our criticisms of the argument from special events and experiences, we proposed that interpretations of any event can and do vary, according to the outlook of the perceiver. We also noted that most likely there can be no conclusive proof of the existence of God. We might conclude that beliefs in God and other religious matters are unique because of their requirements for faith. However, in the chapter on science and philosophy, we observed that "All proof must begin with certain assumptions. This is true in science, philosophy, or religion. Some ideas or facts must be accepted as *postulates*—that is, must be taken for granted." Therefore, whether matters of religion are unique in other ways, the presence of intellectual faith is not a hallmark of these issues. Faith in God in the sense of trust in someone is admittedly different from trust in postulates; faith in convictions *about* God is not unlike other informed, intellectual faiths.

It is possible to say that the atheist, the agnostic, and the theist are all persons of faith. The atheist believes that no God or gods exist, the agnostic believes in suspending judgment, and the theist believes in the existence of God. Each type of faith is believable if one scrutinizes the tenets of that faith. Each also can be maintained thoughtlessly; we often call this "blind, uninformed, or naive faith." A person with examined faith knows its boundaries and can agree to differ; unexamined faith can be simplistic, arrogant, and intolerant.

A central question for the current scientific age is this: can faith in God be credible enough so that a rational individual can maintain integrity as a person of faith? The answer to this query will determine the seriousness with which many other theological issues will be considered as well as the future of much religious belief and practice.

◆ ◆

Glossary Terms

AGNOSTICISM   A profession of ignorance, especially the claim that it is impossible to demonstrate conclusively either the existence or nonexistence of God.

ANTHROPOMORPHISM   The attributing of human qualities to the nonhuman realm or to nature. The term may refer to the portrayal of God as having human form, characteristics, or limitations.

ATHEISM   Denial of the existence of a personal God.

BEING   That which exists; sometimes used for the infinite, God, or ultimate reality.

DEISM   A belief that affirms the existence of a God who has created the universe, but who remains apart and permits His creation to administer itself through natural laws—a view fairly prevalent in the seventeenth and eighteenth centuries; may be understood as a version of theism.

IMMANENT   Indwelling, or operating within the process. An immanent God is within the structure of the universe and/or takes a vital part in its processes. The term is used in contrast with *transcendent*. Religions view their concepts of God as immanent, as transcendent, or as both.

IMMORTALITY   The doctrine that the soul survives death.

KARMA   In Hinduism, the cosmic law of sowing and reaping, of cause and effect in human life. The law determines the form that will be taken in each new existence or rebirth. Action is seen as bringing upon oneself inevitable results, good or bad.

MONOTHEISM   The belief that there is only one (usually personal) God.

PANTHEISM   The view that everything is coextensive with God; God is in all, and all is in God.

POLYTHEISM   Belief in many personalized gods.

THEISM   The belief in a personal God, the creator of the world and immanent in the world's processes, with whom we may come into intimate contact.

THEODICY   Justification of God's goodness in the face of evil.

THEOLOGY   Literally, the theory or study of God. In practice, the term is used for the system of doctrines of some particular religious group or individual thinker. Natural theology stresses reason and empirical evidence; revealed theology emphasizes revelation as the basis for our knowledge of God.

TRANSCENDENT (TRANSCENDENCE)   That which is beyond what is given in experience. In theology the term means that God is outside of or beyond nature.

Chapter Review

THE NATURE OF GOD

1. Belief in God has occupied a central position in religious faith and practice. Humans generally have felt dependent on someone or something beyond their own resources.

2. There are three issues concerning belief in God: the difference between the *existence* of God and the *idea* of God, worship preceding ideas, and the incompleteness and insufficiency of ideas.

3. Theism is the belief in a personal God who is creator of the world. God is a participant in its processes with whom human beings can interact. Monotheism refers to one personal God, polytheism refers to more than one god.

4. Deism, popular in the eighteenth century, emphasizes the remoteness (transcendence) of God. God creates an instrument, the natural universe, then permits it to operate without divine interference or participation.

5. Pantheism is the belief that God is in all, and all is in God. Pantheism may be personal or non-personal.

6. God-as-Goodness is the notion of God as a metaphor for some all-encompassing goodness.

7. Agnosticism means "not knowing." An agnostic suspends judgment concerning God's existence.

8. Atheism is the firm denial of a personal God's existence.

9. The Hebraic view of God emphasizes complementary understandings of ultimate reality. Love, mercy, justice, awe, and mystery characterized God's relationship with Israel. The God of Israel is the creative intelligence who fashions reality and reveals his purpose for humanity through chosen agents and events.

10. Theologians seek to proclaim God's revelation to their own communities of faith. They work from their scriptures and the experiences of their religious communities as well as from reason.

11. Philosophers attempt to arrive at truth independently of revelation. Their search for God is aided by reason alone.

12. Judaism, Christianity, and Islam were influenced by the Greek philosophers' questions concerning essence, substance, and attributes. Issues of God's *being* accompanied reflections on his activity.

13. The ancient Greek view of God included two components: the religious and the philosophical. The religious view was held by the people.

14. An Asian view of God includes a religious (popular) view as well as a philosophic understanding.

GROUNDS FOR BELIEF IN GOD

1. The ontological argument proposed by Saint Anselm attempts to prove the existence of God from the idea of a perfect being. God exists because he is defined in such a way that it is impossible to conceive of his not existing.

2. The cosmological argument is often called the "first-cause argument." This is a deductive argument that states that everything has a cause, and so a series must be infinite or have a first cause, which we call God. Thomas Aquinas proposed this theory.

3. The teleological argument, or the argument from design or purpose in the world, is the most popular of the theistic arguments. It claims that the order and design in the universe disclose a purposeful God.

4. The moral argument for belief in God may be presented as a logical inference from human conscience to a moral God to whom we are held responsible. Or the supporter of the moral argument may claim that moral values indicate a transhuman source for those values, which religion calls God.

5. Many people ground their belief in God on the basis of personal experiences and special events.

6. Throughout the course of history, no universally accepted proof of God's existence has been developed. Experiences and data are interpreted in various ways.

GROUNDS FOR DISBELIEF IN GOD

1. The presence of evil in our world has been a great obstacle to religious faith. Many interpretations of the nature of evil have attempted to resolve this problem.

2. A second ground for disbelief is the conviction that belief is only the result of wishful thinking and social convention.

3. Another obstacle to belief in God is that the word "God" has frequently been expressed in language, symbols, and assumptions that have lost their meaning and appeal to modern people.

4. The grounds for disbelief are not conclusive. Persons have several options: (1) to make the judgment to suspend judgment, (2) to be convinced affirmatively, and (3) to be convinced negatively.

PERSONAL SURVIVAL AFTER DEATH

1. People who believe in personal survival after death may mean quite different things: biological, social, impersonal, or personal survival.

2. Religious views as exemplified in Judaism, Christianity, and Islam support personal survival after death.

REFLECTIONS

1. The presence of intellectual faith is not unique to religion; such faith is also present in science and philosophy.

2. The atheist, the agnostic, and the theist are all persons of faith. Each position can be maintained after thoughtful, careful scrutiny of the arguments and evidence. Each can also be maintained uncritically.

3. A central question for the current age of science is: can faith in God be credible enough, so that a rational individual can maintain integrity as a person of faith?

◆ ◆ ◆ ◆ ◆ ◆ ◆ ◆ ◆ ◆ ◆ ◆ ◆ ◆ ◆ ◆ ◆ ◆ ◆ ◆

Study Questions and Projects

1. Do you agree or disagree with the assertion that the question of the existence of God and of religious truth or falsity is one of the most momentous issues we face because it determines whether the things we care for most are at the mercy of the things we care for least? Discuss.

2. Is it possible for people to think of God as both transcendent and immanent and be consistent in their views? Explain why you think this is or is not possible.

3. Comment on the following statements, and tell to what extent you think they can be accepted.
   (a) "The individual who refuses to face facts doesn't believe in God."
   (b) "A little philosophy inclineth man's mind to atheism, but depth in philosophy bringeth man's mind about to religion." —Francis Bacon
   (c) "Originally God made man in his image, and man has ever since returned the compliment."—Voltaire
   (d) "The God of any group of people is the object of their highest loyalty, adoration, allegiance, awe, reverence, devotion." —Durant Drake

4. What are the historic or classic arguments for belief in God? Do some of these arguments appear to have more weight than others?

5. Explain what is meant by the "argument from personal experience" as a basis for belief in God. Give some examples of the different forms such experience may take, and evaluate them.

6. Indicate some issues that need to be kept clearly in mind when one considers the problem of belief in God. Do you agree that our knowledge in this, as in other fields, is never adequate or final?

7. Why are pain and evil often obstacles to a belief in God? Does the presence of evil justify an indictment of nature or of God?

8. Discuss the assertion that belief in God is unscientific and the result of wishful thinking.

9. What in your judgment is the relation between faith and revelation, on the one hand, and reason and experience, on the other? Discuss the different meanings of the terms *faith* and *revelation* and indicate which of the various meanings appear most adequate to you and why.

10. What have been the main sources of influence of the idea of God prevalent in Western society? Indicate the ways in which these various sources differ in emphasis and outlook.

11. Are the interpretations of God in the Hebraic and Asian traditions the same? Evaluate the statement "It doesn't make any difference which religion you belong to; all religions believe in the same God."

12. Compare "immortality of the soul" with "resurrection of the body." (See "Immortality" and "Resurrection in the NT" in *The Interpreter's Dictionary of the Bible,* Supplementary Volume, 1976.)

13. What are the major differences between humanism, Deism, and the Hebraic religions? In terms of moral outlooks, what if anything do they have in common?

◆ ◆

Suggested Readings

Adams, M. and Adams, R. (eds.). *The Problem of Evil.* New York: Oxford University Press, 1991.

An up-to-date anthology of recent scholarship on the problem of evil.

Braaten, C. (ed.). *Our Naming of God: Problems and Prospects of God-Talk.* Minneapolis, Minn.: Fortress, 1989.

An interdisciplinary sourcebook that probes for new insights in philosophy of religion, feminist philosophy, Hebrew Scriptures, New Testament, trinitarian theology, mission, and worship.

Brummer, V. *Speaking of a Personal God.* New York: Cambridge University Press, 1992.

A philosophical analysis of the Christian concept of having a personal relationship with God.

Edwards, P. (ed.). *Immortality.* New York: Macmillan, 1992.

Believers and skeptics are represented in thirty-four current and contemporary selections covering the mind–body problem, personal identity, as well as Eastern and Western views on immortality.

Kirkpatrick, F. *Together Bound: God, History, and the Religious Community.* New York: Oxford University Press, 1993.

The author defends as philosophically credible the conviction that God is a personal Agent who also acts in particular historical moments to further the divine intention of fostering universal community.

Küng, H. *Eternal Life?* New York: Crossroad, 1984.

A discussion of the problems that arise from a consideration of the ancient question of eternal life; a modern analysis of life after death as a medical, philosophical, and theological problem.

MacGregor, G. *Images of Afterlife.* New York: Paragon, 1992.

A history of global beliefs in the afterlife from prehistoric times to the present.

Mackie, J. L. *The Miracle of Theism: Arguments For and Against the Existence of God.* New York: Oxford University Press, 1983.

The approaches of many historic and modern thinkers to the existence of God and the problem of evil are discussed.

Margeneau, H., and Varghese, R. (eds.). *Cosmos, Bios, Theos: Scientists Reflect on Science, Religion, and the Origins of the Universe, Life and Homo Sapiens* Peru, Ill.: Open Court, 1992.

A compilation of the views of sixty leading scientists on God, the origin of the universe, and the relationship between science and religion.

McFague, S. *Models of God*. Minneapolis, Minn.: Fortress, 1987.

Subtitled *Theology for an Ecological, Nuclear Age,* this book is a winner of the 1988 American Academy of Religion Award for Excellence.

Morris, T. *Our Idea of God*. Notre Dame, Ind.: University of Notre Dame Press, 1991.

In this book, accessible to nonphilosophers, Professor Morris challenges readers to think more deeply about matters of religious conviction; a basic introduction to philosophical theology.

Polkinghorne, J. *Science and Creation*. Boston: New Science Library, 1989.

A Cambridge University physicist–Anglican Priest addresses some fundamental questions about the relationship of scientific and theological world views.

Swinburne, R. *The Existence of God*. Rev. ed. New York: Oxford University Press, 1991.

An updated, recent defense of theism; a companion to the author's *The Coherence of Theism,* which was published in a revised edition in 1993.

* *

Notes

1. A. J. Heschel, *God In Search of Man* (New York: Farrar, Straus, and Cudahy, 1955), p. 9.

2. Studies that offer historically accurate religious views of the founding fathers are: S. Ahlstrom, *A Religious History of the American People* (New Haven, Conn.: Yale University Press, 1972); C. L. Albanese, *America: Religions and Religion,* 2nd ed. (Belmont, Calif.: Wadsworth, 1992); D. L. Carmody and J. T. Carmody, *The Republic of Many Mansions: Foundations of American Religious Thought* (New York: Paragon, 1990); W. S. Hudson, *Religion in America,* 5th ed. (New York: Macmillan, 1992); K. S. Walters, *The American Deists* (Lawrence: University Press of Kansas, 1992); and, P. W. Williams, *America's Religions* (New York: Macmillan, 1990).

3. An honest confession of "less rigorous" Deism in one form has been written by Warren Weaver, a scientist. See his essay "The Religion of a Scientist," in L. Rosten, ed., *Religions of America* (New York: Simon and Schuster, 1975), pp. 296–305.

4. A. MacIntyre, "Pantheism," *The Encyclopedia of Philosophy,* Vol. VI, p. 32.

5. In Exodus 3:13–14 God identifies himself as "Yahweh" (or "Jehovah"). Often translated as "I Am Who I Am," the name has received attention from modern scholars and is represented better by "It Is He Who Creates What Comes Into Existence." See W. F. Albright, *Yahweh and the Gods of Canaan* (New York: Doubleday, 1968), p. 148.

6. F. B. Dilley, "Is Myth Indispensable?" *The Monist* 50 (1966): 589. See also "The Attributes of God within the Witness of Scripture" in B. S. Childs, *Biblical Theology of the Old and New Testaments* (Minneapolis, Minn.: Fortress, 1992), pp. 371*ff.*

7. For a contemporary approach, see O. C. Thomas, ed., *God's Activity in the World* (Decatur, Ga.: Scholars Press, 1983).

8. S. G. F. Brandon, "Idea of God From Prehistory to the Middle Ages," *Dictionary of the History of Ideas* (New York: Scribner's, 1973), p. 341.

9. See W. H. V. Reade, *The Christian Challenge to Philosophy* (London: S.P.C.K., 1951); and C.

Tresmontant, *A Study of Hebrew Thought* (New York: Desclee, 1960).

10. A. Huxley, "Introduction" in *The Song of God: Bhagavad-Gita* (New York: Mentor Books, 1954); other sources are: A. Huxley, *The Perennial Philosophy* (New York: Harper Colophon Books, 1970); L. E. Loemker, "Perennial Philosophy," *Dictionary of the History of Ideas,* Vol. III (New York: Scribner's, 1973) pp. 457–62 (contains a good bibliography); N. Smart, "Perennial Philosophy" in *The Westminster Dictionary of Christian Theology,* ed. A. Richardson, and J. Bowden (Philadelphia: Westminster, 1983), pp. 439*ff.*

11. C. Hartshorne, *Omnipotence and Other Theological Mistakes* (Albany: State of New York University Press, 1984).

12. The ontological argument is found in Chapters 2–4 of Anselm's *Proslogion,* in *The Religion of Science Library,* No. 54, trans. S. N. Dean (La Salle, Ill.: Open Court, 1939).

13. For an excellent list, see J. Hick, *Philosophy of Religion,* 4th ed. (Englewood Cliffs, N.J.: Prentice-Hall, 1990), p. 20.

14. See R. Descartes, "Meditations," in *The Religion of Science Library,* Vol. 5, No. 51, trans. J. Veitch (La Salle, Ill.: Open Court, 1941) pp. 75–83; I. Kant, *Critique of Pure Reason,* trans. N. K. Smith (London: Macmillan, 1933), "Transcendental Dialectic," Book II, Chapter 3, Section 4; B. Russell, *History of Western Philosophy* (London: Allen and Unwin, 1946), pp. 859–60.

15. J. H. C. Newman, *A Grammar of Assent,* ed. C. F. Harrold (New York: David McKay, 1947), pp. 83–84.

16. D. M. Baillie, *Faith in God and its Christian Consummation* (Edinburgh: T. and T. Clark, 1927), pp. 172–73.

17. In J. Baillie, *The Idea of Revelation in Recent Thought* (New York: Columbia University Press, 1956), pp. 70, 74.

18. See Augustine's *Confessions,* Book VII, Chapter 12; *City of God,* Book XII, Chapter 3.

19. See the June 10, 1991, issue of *Time* for a popularized cover report entitled "Evil: Does It Exist—Or Do Bad Things Just Happen?"

20. T. J. J. Altizer and W. Hamilton, *Radical Theology and the Death of God* (New York: Bobbs-Merrill, 1966); D. E. Jenkins, *Guide to the Debate about God* (Philadelphia: Westminster, 1966).

21. J. E. Smith, *The Analogy of Experience* (New York: Harper and Row, 1973), p. 55.

22. Smith, *The Analogy of Experience,* pp. 48*ff.*

23. See G. Stein, *The Encyclopedia of Unbelief* (Buffalo, N.Y.: Prometheus, 1985) for a two-volume, scholarly resource of arguments for disbelief.

24. R. A. Moody, Jr., *Reflections on Life after Life* (New York: Bantam, 1977), pp. 123*ff.* See also, K. Ring, *Life at Death: A Scientific Investigation of the Near-Death Experience* (New York: Coward, McCann and Geoghegan, 1980).

25. E. E. Calverley, *Islam: An Introduction* (Cairo: The American University at Cairo, 1958), p. 92.

Asian Thought

CHAPTER OBJECTIVES

In this chapter we will address the following questions:

◆ What Do Hindus Believe?

◆ What Are the Basic Beliefs of Buddhists?

◆ Are the Beliefs of Confucians and Daoists the Same as Those of Hindus and Buddhists?

◆ Where Are Zen Buddhism and Shinto Practiced, and What Are Their Teachings?

◆ Are There Significant Differences among World Religions?

The wisdom and mysticism of the East have, indeed, very much to give us even though they speak their own language which is impossible to imitate. They should remind us of that which is familiar in our own culture and which we have already forgotten, and we should direct our attention to that which we have pushed aside as insignificant, namely the fate of our own inner man.[1]

The Nature of Asian Religion

We live in an increasingly international world, where relations between Asian countries and those of Europe and the Americas have become more crucial than ever before. Modern science and technology have created for the first time in recorded history a universal pattern of civilization, a world society which desperately needs some understanding of diversity.

There is great diversity among world religions. For hundreds of millions of Asians, their religion—no matter what form it takes—is a vital concern of their daily lives, not a mere one-day-a-week observance. The peoples of non-Western cultures see religion as integrally related to and inseparable from all the other areas of life and experience. They generally look upon their religion as the basis of their culture, which gives form and meaning to the rest of existence. Our attempt here is to understand certain beliefs about the transcendent, humanity, and the universe that have been the basis of well-established cultures and beautiful art in the Asian world. Asian philosophy is a way of life.

The Hindu Tradition

"Hinduism, literally 'the belief of the people of India,' is the predominant faith of India and of no other nation."[2] Taken as a whole, Hinduism is one of the oldest religious traditions in the world. But it is difficult to study, for it is also one of the most diversified religious traditions. There are divisions and subdivisions into which we cannot go, and you should be aware that we are necessarily oversimplifying in this discussion. The problem is further complicated by the fact that there are no exact equivalents in English for certain Indian terms and concepts.

Philosophy (*darshana*) in the Hindu tradition means "seeing the truth" and applying this truth to the problems of everyday life. Thus, for Indian thinkers, the purpose of studying philosophy is not merely to gain knowledge for its own sake or to satisfy one's curiosity, but to discover and live the highest kind of life, the life that will bring permanent self-realization or bliss. People must recover truths themselves, not just accept them on blind faith or from the testimony of others. Unless people have convictions and live in accordance with them, they are not philosophers.

Hinduism arose on Indian soil and is largely confined to Indian people. India, however, has known other traditions, including Buddhism, Christianity, and Islam. What is called Hinduism today has influenced many other parts of Asia and is steadily growing in parts of Europe and the United States.

HINDU SCRIPTURE

One indication of the difficulty of setting forth the central points in Hindu thought is that there are many texts that, collectively, can be called Hindu Scripture. First, there are the Vedas (literally "knowledge"—that is, sacred knowledge). These are texts written some fifteen hundred years before the common era. The earliest texts are the *Rig Veda*, a collection of over one thousand hymns addressed to the gods—hymns to Indra, the god of civilization, war, and storm; to Varuna, the guardian of morality; and to many others, most of them now forgotten. Included in the Vedas are the *Brahmanas*, lengthy treatises concerned with the details of the sacrificial ritual administered by the Brahmin class. Finally, in the eighth to fifth centuries B.C.E., there were added to these the most famous of the early Indian writings, the **Upanishads,** which attempted to explain the inner meaning of the reality behind the religious quest in a philosophical manner. All these writings form the essential canon of sacred scriptures in the orthodox Hindu tradition.

In the period following the *Upanishads,* there was, within Hinduism, a great development of devotional religion. This was expressed strikingly in the most famous of Indian scriptures, the **Bhagavadgita,** or "Song of the Lord." There is some doubt as to when the *Gita* was compiled, but it was probably some time during the period 200 B.C.E to 200 C.E. No other scripture is more widely read in India today. To read the *Gita* is to be introduced to some of the main themes of Hindu thought as well as to some of the main practices of Hindu life. It also introduces one to splendid Hindu poetry and to the god Krishna.

It is convenient to name four major periods of Hindu thought: first, the early period of Vedic polytheism; second, the period of the Vedanta (literally, "the end of the Veda"), with its descriptions of Absolute **Brahman;** third, a period beginning about 200 B.C.E., with an emphasis on *bhakti* (devotional worship of a theistic god); and last, the modern period, with its response to Western influence.[3] "During the classical period—those centuries between 450 B.C. and A.D. 600—occurred the emergence of a Hindu culture that absorbed into itself many different strands of mythology, ritual, and doctrine. This luxuriance of religious standpoints may sometimes baffle the outsider, but it testifies to an important and enduring characteristic of Indian culture—its desire to express and to nurture as many different approaches to the Truth as possible, and to conserve within itself the multiplicity of cultural influences that have affected the Indian subcontinent."[4]

BRAHMAN AND THE SELF

Central to much of Hindu philosophy is the emphasis on the one unchanging reality that transcends space, time, causality, and all particular things. This Absolute cannot be comprehended by human thought or adequately expressed in words and concepts. According to the nondualistic view (which emphasizes the oneness of existence) only Brahman is real, and the individual souls and the universe are illusory veils obscuring Brahman. Other views hold that the self and the physical world may be real, although they are finite and imperfect. There are also differences among philosophical thinkers about whether the ultimate reality is nonpersonal, superpersonal, or personal. But all agree on the possibility of every soul's attaining liberation (*moksha*) from the bondage of the physical world.

Closely allied to the concept of Brahman is the concept of the self, or soul, or **atman.** The true self of each person is identical with Brahman. From the transcendental standpoint, the self is immortal, free, and identical with Brahman. The divine nature of the self is veiled, but not destroyed, by false images and ignorance, for it is ultimately without traits and beyond language. The true destiny of the self is the realization of this identity with Brahman. From the phenomenal standpoint, there are many individual selves, enmeshed in the world of affairs and seeking deliverance from the round of births and deaths. Thus we need to distinguish between the real and the empirical self.

What are the relations among Brahman, the self, and the universe that we perceive? A Hindu scholar says: "Brahman is the sole reality, and it appears both as the objective universe and as the individual subject. The former is an illusory manifestation of Brahman, while the latter is Brahman itself appearing under the limitations which form part of that illusory universe."[5] The objects of the empirical world, although of a certain order of worldly reality, are appearances in that they belong to the world of cause and effect, to which Brahman does not belong. The individual self, however, is not illusory in this sense. The self is Brahman appearing under limiting conditions. It is not a phenomenon of ignorance the way physical objects are. Through an intuitive, non-logical experience one realizes the identity of the eternal self and Brahman.

CENTRAL VALUES IN HINDUISM

All Hindu systems of thought seem to agree that there are four main values to be completed and brought to perfection in the course of rebirth. In ascending order of importance they are: (1) *Artha* (wealth) and (2) *Kama* (sensuality). These are the worldly or secular values. They are legitimate if they are kept in their places and do not stifle other values. Material prosperity, good health, and long life are desired by most Indians. However, both the life of activity and renunciation are recognized. (3) *Dharma* (social and individual duties) includes all caste roles and obligations of occupation, gender, kin, generation, and temperament, as well as other ethical responsibilities. (4) *Moksha* (release from finitude and imperfection) is the intrinsic or eternal value, and the supreme spiritual ideal. It gives liberation from the wheel of existence, and cannot be achieved without complete experience and resolution of the other three. Discipline is essential if we are to achieve illumination, and the overcoming of selfishness is essential if we are to realize our genuine self and attain release. Unless a person achieves release in this life, which is rare indeed, she or he is destined to repeat the round of more existences.

According to Hinduism, no soul is eternally damned. The law of **karma**, the law of sowing and reaping, determines the form that will be taken in each new existence. This is the law of cause and effect in human life. Through our conduct we determine our own destiny in that good *karma* is acquired by living up to our *dharmic* duties and bad *karma* by ignoring or violating our given *dharma*. An unethical life may lead to rebirth below the station of the present life, and a life of goodness may lead to a more favored existence or to ultimate liberation from the round of rebirths. Thus, the doctrines of *karma* and rebirth are said to be grounded in the moral structures of the universe. They permit freedom and ethical advance in that they are under our control and are not determined by cosmic or environmental forces completely beyond our influence.

Because of its intricate dependence on the structure of *dharma*, the theory of *karma* and rebirth determines a person's position in the traditional caste system, in which there are four main castes and many subcastes or divisions within these. The caste system has been under attack in recent decades, having been outlawed in the Indian Constitution of 1949, and various outstanding leaders of Hinduism have called attention to the continued abuses of caste and have worked hard to bring about its practical elimination. Nevertheless, the caste system is highly resistant to change, not only because of the belief that a person's present social status is regulated by the law of *karma* but also because of ingrained social hierarchies based on notions of purity and contamination.

The concept of the four *ashramas*, or stages in the life of the individual, relates the goal of liberation to the needs and tasks of daily life in society. A man's duties are set by the stage of life at which he has arrived. The four stages are (1) the life of a celibate student under the mentorship of a teacher; (2) a long period of householdership, beginning with marriage, when a person assumes the responsibilities of parenthood and other social obligations and when one provides for those dedicated to the spiritual quest; (3) a period of increased religiosity, when householder duties can be passed on to the next generation, during which one retires to the forest with his wife to practice rituals and for meditation and reflection; and (4) by complete renunciation of family and caste and by practicing austerities and rigid self-control, a person seeks union with Brahman. If the person is successful in the fourth stage, struggle and strife cease and he gains peace and freedom through union with the all-embracing World Soul. The inner spirit of humanity is the focus of attention, and its development, illumination, and release are the highest values. These stations were primarily for men. At the time of traditional Hinduism, women were excluded from the more rigorous structures of the *ashramas* and received their spiritual merit from working to uphold the *dharmic* obligations of their husbands.

YOGA

We have already mentioned that, for the Hindu, discipline is essential if one is to achieve illumination: discipline of both body and mind. *Yoga* is a technique of physical and spiritual training by which the bodily and psychic energies are controlled, unified, and directed in order to attain liberation from the world. Yoga is the liberating union of the self (*atman*) with the Self (*Brahman*).

In classical yoga, after the yogi has undergone a long initiatory period of training under a master—the guru—no one else need exist in his or her world. The yogi sheds not only material distractions but also psychic hindrances such as memories, desires, fears, yearnings, and the residue of dreams and impressions; all with the goal of liberation. The importance of classical yoga is that it teaches the complete independence and freedom of the self based on the confidence that the individual mind is able through its own powers to transcend the suffering caused by matter, illusions, and supernatural agencies. Only knowledge can bring liberation. Without this goal, everything—study, work, meditation—is valueless.

RELIGIOUS EXPRESSIONS

Traditional worship of a god in Hinduism is known as *puja*. It can be practiced by anyone regardless of gender, age, or station in life, from the most erudite philosopher to the simplist street sweeper. Because Hinduism is not normally a congregational religion that is practiced in a house of worship by people as a group, the performance of *puja* is left to the individual. Usually there is a *puja* room or niche within the Hindu home, where an image of the god or goddess is enshrined in a painting, a sculpture, or other symbolic referent with flowers, incense, and food. The divinity is invoked with symbolic sounds, prayers, and songs, and often worship includes the use of fire or water. The choice of god or gods, whether it be Krishna, Rama, Shiva, Kali, Shri, or any one of a great variety from the Hindu pantheon, is often a matter of family affiliation or the needs of a given worship. Hindu temples, cared for and presided over by priests, are usually dedicated to a specific divinity and provide an especially quiet place for individual devotion. Seasonal festivities commemorating local myths and figures are expressive and celebratory affairs, often lasting many days and including people from all social backgrounds. Finally, Hindu worship can take the form of pilgrimage to area shrines or to the holy city of

Kashi (modern Banaras) and its sacred river Ganges. Possessing great adaptability and tolerance, Hinduism includes, rather than excludes, unique forms of religious expression. There are a number of reform movements in India today, and some outstanding thinkers have been remolding the Indian consciousness and outlook.[6]

In "The Spirit of Indian Philosophy," Sir Sarvepalli Radhakrishnan,[7] after pointing out the diversity of views held by Indian thinkers, indicates seven attitudes that are characteristic of the Indian philosophical mind. (1) Concentration on the spiritual. Philosophy and religion are closely related. Humans are spiritual in nature and are primarily interested in their spiritual destiny and not in material welfare. (2) Belief in the intimate relationship of philosophy and life. (3) The introspective attitude and concern for the inner life. The inner spirit of a person, the subject rather than the object, is the focus of attention and gives the best clue to the nature of the universe. (4) The affinity with idealism. Because reality is "ultimately one and ultimately spiritual," the tendency is toward nondualistic idealism. (5) The acceptance of direct perception as the only method through which reality can be known. When the mind becomes free from the impurities of attachment and aversion through the practice of yoga or spiritual disciplines, it perceives truth directly, as one perceives a fruit lying on the palm of one's hand. Reason is useful but insufficient; it leads the seeker as far as it can and then bows out. To know reality is to experience it or to become one with it. (6) A consciousness of tradition and an acceptance of the insights of seers who have lived in the past. This has not, however, made Indian philosophy dogmatic or creedal. (7) An "overall synthetic tradition." The systems of thought are seen as complementing each other. This stress on the synthetic vision had made possible an intellectual and religious tolerance toward differences within Hinduism and toward other faiths and systems of thought. Hinduism is thus not a fixed and uniform doctrinal system; it is broad, inclusive, and tolerant of different points of view.

The Buddhist Quest for Enlightenment

◆ ◆ ◆ ◆ ◆ ◆ ◆ ◆ ◆ ◆

THE BUDDHA

Buddhist philosophy has much in common with Hindu philosophy, but it also departs radically from it at certain points and hence was known among adherents of Hinduism as the "Great Heresy." Siddhartha Gautama, the founder of Buddhism (see biography and excerpt, pp. 414–415), lived in Northern India in the fifth century B.C.E. Gautama, although reared in luxury and under sheltered conditions, became greatly concerned about the widespread misery under which people lived. He left his home and family and wandered into the forest in search of the truth about the meaning of existence. Finally, after six years, and lengthy experimentation with asceticism, he returned to the Middle Way (see excerpt, pp. 415). One night shortly thereafter, under the Bo Tree, the truth, it is said, flashed into his mind and he became the "Enlightened One"—the Buddha. Contrary to the spirit of his teaching, Gautama was later idolized and deified, and temples, ceremonies, and a priesthood arose. As a result of Buddha's teaching and influence, Buddhist thought flourished in India for more than a thousand years. Today it is found mainly in Sri Lanka (Ceylon), Myanmar (Burma), Thailand, Tibet, China, Korea, and Japan. In the course of its expansion it has changed considerably.

Buddhism makes a fundamental break with Hinduism in its rejection not only of the Vedic scriptures but also of the concepts of Brahman and *atman*—the metaphysical absolute and the changeless self. Experience, it is said, gives no clear indication of such an all-inclusive World Soul. Gautama rejected the authority ascribed to the ancient gods and urged believers to rely mainly on the resources within themselves. He also rejected the caste system; wisdom and not birth or caste is of importance. He was impressed by ceaseless change, which he observed as pervading everything, and by finiteness and suffering. Gautama was not only a man of great human sympathy and goodwill; he was a thinker of great philosophic power who decided to spend his life in teaching others to gain understanding.

THE THREE MARKS OF EXISTENCE AND THE FOUR NOBLE TRUTHS

The central core of Buddhist philosophy is found in the Three Marks of Existence. By carefully observing our everyday experience, unimpeded by normal belief systems and opinions, we notice that the world of our senses is marked by transitoriness or impermanence. We then notice *anatta*, an inability to determine through experiential channels of knowledge whether or not there is a Self; this "no doctrine of a Self" quickly became in early Buddhism the "doctrine of no Self," whereby we can find no independent essence in existing things. Finally, we discover *dukkha*, suffering, that is experienced because of our attachment to things which change.

The doctrine of the Four Noble Truths then focuses on the relationship between suffering and attachment or desire. There is, first, the fact of the existence of suffering. Unhappiness or pain accompanies the experiences of birth, illness, failure to satisfy desires, separation from friends and loved ones, old age, and death. The problem of suffering is the universal problem of life in a world that is finite and changing. Even the more fortunate are unable to ward off old age and death.

The second noble truth discloses the cause of suffering. Suffering is caused by desires, or *tanha*, which in its original and literal meaning is "thirst." These desires or cravings are many, and they tend to grow or increase as we attempt to satisfy them. The greatest attachment, however, is to existence itself, for what we want most is to continue indefinitely, to have life as we now know it. The world, however, is marked by change and it is our attachment to these changing things (and especially to our own selves) that causes us the greatest suffering.

The third noble truth is that release is possible. Because we cannot alter the transitory nature of the experiential world, we have to focus our attention on something else: our attachment to this world. By getting rid of our attachment and desire we automatically get rid of our suffering. By eradicating our desire, we also reduce our ignorance and see for the first time the true nature of the self as a conditioned entity interdependent with all other things in a "chain of causation." Real happiness comes with this freedom from attachment and if we can gain such enlightenment, the wheel of existence can be ended and *nirvana* experienced.

The fourth noble truth is that there is a way out through the *Noble Eightfold Path*. Right knowledge about the nature of one's self is a means of removing attachment and suffering.

THE NOBLE EIGHTFOLD PATH AND NIRVANA

The Noble Eightfold Path consists of the following steps: (1) Right understanding. We need to realize that the cessation of suffering comes through the elimination of ignorance and of craving, desire, and thirst for a world and a self marked by transitoriness. Without understanding, we do not know the direction from which release is to come. (2) Right aspiration or purpose. Without the goal of enlightenment we are not likely to make a start or to put forth vigorous effort. (3) Right speech. We should be truthful, kind, and humble, and never gossip, slander, or boast. (4) Right conduct. We must not harm other living creatures and must avoid killing, stealing, eating meat, intoxication, and other evils. (5) Right mode of livelihood. Our mode of living and our vocation should be in harmony with the goals toward which we aspire and should be especially consistent with the ethics of nonviolence. (6) Right striving or effort. Discipline is necessary in the attainment of knowledge. (7) Right mindfulness. Our thoughts are important, and must not be permitted to wander or dwell on desires that need to be suppressed. (8) Right concentration. When we are able through meditation and concentration to identify ourselves with truth, the goal of mystic illumination is reached. At this

point we are no longer subject to rebirth, and we may achieve the experience of **nirvana.**

What is *nirvana?* Literally, the term means "blowing out, extinction, ceasing to be." Does this mean that Buddhist thinkers have set forth a religion or philosophy of escape? Such, however, would be a superficial interpretation, which in no way explains the sense of joyous fulfillment and the appeal of Buddhism to large numbers of people. What is extinguished is attachment to any belief in an eternal, permanent self and to all notions of individuality. The elimination of the bonds of rebirth, of suffering, of ignorance, of desire, is the liberation that is *nirvana.* Cessation of striving, being bound by rebirth, is said to bring a sense of liberation or freedom, peace and contentment, joy, insight, and love or compassion for all living beings.

In order to achieve this freedom, compassion, and wisdom, certain ethical behaviors must be followed. In the earliest Buddhist dialogues five prohibitions are given:

1. Avoid taking life (animal or human).
2. Avoid stealing (taking what is not offered).
3. Avoid illicit sexual relations.
4. Avoid lying.
5. Avoid intoxicants.[8]

The law of *karma* and the doctrine of rebirth were retained by Buddhists when they rejected Hinduism. The law of *karma* is a strong incentive to choose the good and avoid its opposite. If we realize that we are our own saviors, our sense of responsibility is likely to be keen. One should give aid to others, however, whenever this is possible, physically through almsgiving and the like, and spiritually through knowledge and enlightenment.

DIVISIONS WITHIN BUDDHISM

Although Buddhism arose in India and flourished there for more than one thousand years, it is found today mainly in other countries of Asia.[9] In the course of its development, Buddhism moved from early Buddhism and split into two

The Buddha

Siddhartha Gautama (fifth century B.C.E.) was the founder of the Buddhist religion. His father was a chieftain or king in Northern India. Siddhartha was "the man who had everything": he was handsome and wealthy and had a model wife and a baby son. It is said that at the time of his birth a prophetic sage predicted that if he became attached to the world and its ways, he would unify India and become a great conqueror; if he saw the true nature of the human condition and forsook the world, he would become a world redeemer.

His father wanted to keep him attached to the world, but Siddhartha eventually turned from material things. On one occasion when he was horseback riding, he saw in turn a decrepit old man, a man racked with pain and disease, and a corpse. Thus he discovered the facts regarding old age, disease, and death; he became troubled over the sorrows of human life and felt a deep desire to help. He also saw a wandering holy man with simple garb and a shaved head. At age 29, he left the palace and his family, and went off alone to seek release from the misery of the world, to discover the cause of human suffering, and to find its spiritual cure. This was the "Great Renunciation."

After some years of searching, during which he tried asceticism, extreme self-mortification, and more moderate programs of meditation, insight and enlightenment came while he was sitting under a sacred Bo tree. He became the Buddha, the Enlightened One. Buddha then spent his long life teaching and preaching. He established an order of monks and later an order of nuns. His teachings are founded in the "Three Marks of Existence," the "Four Noble Truths," and the "Noble Eightfold Path."

Excerpt from:

The Buddha's First Sermon, known as *The Foundation of the Kingdom of Righteousness* or *The Setting in Motion of the Wheel of the Dhamma*, taken from the *Mahavagga*

Note: To read Buddhist literature, you should understand that these are not historical documents in the sense of precise, objective recordings of events. Happenings in the life of the Buddha, reports of dialogues between various individuals, parables and stories—all these were set down long after the time of the Buddha and were shaped to teach his ideas as later generations came to understand them.

This, monks, is the Middle Path, the knowledge of which the Tathagata has gained, which leads to insight, which leads to wisdom, which conduces to calm, to knowledge, to perfect enlightenment, to Nirvana.

This, monks, is the Noble Truth of Suffering: birth is suffering; decay is suffering; illness is suffering; death is suffering; presence of objects we hate is suffering; separation from objects we love is suffering; not to obtain what we desire is suffering.

In brief, the five aggregates which spring from grasping, they are painful.

This, monks, is the Noble Truth concerning the Origin of Suffering: verily it originates in that craving which causes the renewal of becomings, is accompanied by sensual delight, and seeks satisfaction now here, now there; that is to say, craving for pleasures, craving for becoming, craving for not becoming.

This, monks, is the Noble Truth concerning the Cessation of Suffering: verily, it is passionless, cessation without remainder of this very craving; the laying aside of, the giving up, the being free from, the harboring no longer of, this craving.

This monks, is the Noble Truth concerning the Path which leads to the cessation of Suffering: verily, it is this noble Eightfold Path, that is to say, right views, right intent, right speech, right conduct, right means of livelihood, right endeavor, right mindfulness, and right meditation.

This is the Noble Truth concerning suffering. Thus, monks, in things which formerly had not been heard of have I obtained insight, knowledge, understanding, wisdom, intuition. This Noble Truth concerning Suffering must be understood. Thus, monks, in things which formerly had not been heard of have I obtained insight, knowledge, understanding, wisdom, and intuition.

Clarence H. Hamilton, ed., *Buddhism: A Religion of Infinite Compassion* (New York: Liberal Arts Press, 1952), p. 29.

main branches with various subdivisions within each of these branches. The first branch, Theravada ("Doctrine of the Elders"), or Hinayana ("Small Vehicle"), or Pali Buddhism, prevails mainly in Sri Lanka (Ceylon), Myanmar (Burma), and Thailand. It was a more conservative and individualistic philosophy of escape from suffering. Buddha is represented as a great teacher and master who taught the true way; he is not seen as an incarnation of a cosmic principle or power. Theravada Buddhism, a movement in which monks were central, is now becoming a laypersons' movement and showing considerable vitality. The second branch, Mahayana ("Great Vehicle") Buddhism, is found mainly in China, Mongolia, Nepal, Tibet, Korea, and Japan. It is a more broad-minded philosophy with a universal outlook, and it stresses the virtues of wisdom and love. Without minimizing individual enlightenment and freedom from illusion, there is greater stress on compassion for all living beings. For example, a **Bodhisattva** is one who, like Buddha, having attained enlightenment, refuses to enter the fully enlightened state so as to be able to continue to serve his or her fellows. Whereas Theravada Buddhism conceives the Buddha as a human and stresses individual enlightenment, in the Mahayana branch of Buddhism the Buddha is more likely to be conceived as the transcendental eternal principle or Absolute, which may bring release to all people.

Confucius and Lao-zi*

♦ ♦ ♦ ♦ ♦ ♦ ♦ ♦ ♦ ♦ ♦

Chinese civilization was old when Western civilization was in the process of formation. About the sixth century B.C.E., Confucius and Lao-zi attempted to organize the wisdom of the time into a more orderly system. Both men lived in a period of unrest and confusion, and they sought to restore peace and harmony among people and between them and the order of na-

---

*The Pinyin System of romanization (spelling) of Chinese characters is used in the text of this chapter.

ture. Lao-zi taught that behind all existence is the impersonal *Dao* (Way). *Dao* is the way the universe works; it is the reality that is immanent in nature and humanity. Confucius revised and systematized the earlier classics. He was an able teacher and administrator, with a practical turn of mind, more interested in helping his people live well than in considering speculative questions. The teachings of Confucius were reaffirmed by Mencius (Meng-zi), a Chinese philosopher who lived one century later. For twenty-five centuries, Chinese ethical ideals, in the form known as "Confucianism," were influential in the development of Chinese culture. With the establishment of the People's Republic in 1949 by Mao Ze-dong, the habits and customs of Chinese society were radically transformed. Many of these customs are returning.

Philosophy among the Chinese has tended, on the whole, to be practical and this-worldly. The interest is in achieving a harmonious adjustment to other people, to society in general, and to the demands of nature. There is less emphasis on questions of logic, epistemology, and metaphysics than on moral problems and social philosophy. Chinese writers, furthermore, tend to set forth their convictions in the form of aphorisms, illustrations, and stories that convey general meaning but omit analytical precision, systematic reasoning, and argument. For example, in the *Confucian Analects* the paragraphs consist of only a few words or perhaps a few sentences.

THE ORDER IN NATURE

Traditional Chinese philosophy is predominantly a system of ethical realism. Operating through human life and the universe is "one all-pervading principle, rational and ethical in nature."[10] For the Chinese, says Francis C. M. Wei, "orderliness and regularity are the fundamental characteristics of the universe."[11] The concepts of Heaven (*Tian*) and the *Dao*, or Way, are prominent. Heaven, for the Confucians, is the dependable order of the Universe and the ground and guardian of the moral law. Heaven not only governs human affairs in accordance with the moral order of things but gives us a disposition toward harmony and the right. *Dao,* for the Daoists, as we have seen, is the way the universe works and the reality that is immanent in nature and humanity. The *Dao* of Heaven transcends the ordinary experience of nature and humanity, gives meaning to the universe, and helps us do things in the right way. When Heaven is described in personal terms, it may be thought of as Transcendence or Providence. When Heaven is described in impersonal terms, it may be regarded as the "law of nature" or as fate, which determines natural and human events.

In Chinese philosophy, the stress is on the dynamic and changing nature of the process in the midst of which we live. This resembles some Western "process" philosophies. From early Chinese thinking, the concepts "Yang" and "Yin" have been inherited. *Yang* is the active force that is the initiating, creative factor in existence; *Yin* is the more passive and receptive factor. Through the interaction of these two forces, natural processes go on.

HUMANITY AND THE GOOD SOCIETY

In Confucianism, humans occupy a high place in the general scheme of things; we alone can understand the order of things and live according to a moral ideal. Normal persons ought to aspire to be superior people. They should strive for their own development, renounce worldly lusts, and become courteous and gentle. Such persons exhibit integrity of mind in that they are honest with themselves and with others. They are sincere in speech and action and moderate in all things. They avoid avarice, quarrelsomeness, and covetousness, and delight in aiding others. Such superior persons do not go to excess in any direction. They exercise moderation and strive for the "golden mean" or the "just medium," which enables virtue and happiness to continue and increase through history.

Until the Maoist revolution, the concepts of the community and of social propriety were central in Chinese culture. The basic institution was the family, which usually contained as a household not only the parents and unmarried children but all the sons with their wives and children and other dependent relatives. Reverence for ancestors and elders was extremely strong in traditional Chinese society. Different attitudes were called for depending on whether a person was dealing with parents, spouse, an official or landowner, a child, or whomever. Different persons had different duties and "places" according to their abilities and their stations in life.

Before the introduction of Buddhism in China, Chinese religious and ethical ideals were dominated by Confucianism and, to a lesser extent, by Daoism. Confucianism was concerned mainly with personal and social relations, whereas Daoism cultivated a sense of the individual's oneness or unity with the order of the universe, while putting less emphasis on conventions and rules. When Buddhism was introduced into China, many educated Chinese adopted it because of its comprehensive and systematic character. For a number of centuries, many of the ablest Chinese thinkers were Buddhists or were profoundly influenced by Buddhist ideas.

Mao Ze-dong

Marxism[12] has taken firm root in China today and perhaps may be regarded as a fourth religion in Chinese history. Mao Ze-dong (1893–1976), political leader, statesman, poet, and philosopher, took as his goal the radical transformation of Chinese society. He was guided in this enterprise by ideas of Western origin, first, nineteenth-century liberalism, and, then Leninist collectivism. But at the same time he was determined that this "people's China" should place a high value on its own culture.

A basic aspect of revolutionary change in twentieth-century China has been the effort of young intellectuals to break away from the dependent traditions of the old society. Dissatisfaction with the restrictions of traditional family life led many educated young Chinese at the turn of the century to seek new ways of modernizing their society. Mao Ze-dong was one of numerous

Confucius

Kong fu-zi (6th–5th cent. B.C.E.), whom the modern Western world calls Confucius, was a teacher and administrator whose down-to-earth philosophy has shaped the history of China to the twentieth century. He has been called the most influential and most revered person in Chinese history. The youngest of eleven children whose father died at an early age, he grew up in ordinary circumstances and became a self-educated man by hard work. He held various governmental positions, including minister of justice. His main contribution came through his teaching. He made no claim to originality and said that he was a transmitter of the wisdom of the ancient sages. He stressed literature, principles of conduct, and statecraft. The task of education, he said, was to produce the superior person. The ideal is the harmony of the individual and the well-ordered society based on the mutual respect and moral obligation between ruler and minister, father and son, elder brother and younger brother, husband and wife, and friend and friend. Among the many virtues he stressed are filial piety and benevolent love. His teachings, found mainly in the *Analects* (4th cent. B.C.E.), a collection of his aphorisms, became part of the Chinese classics.

Excerpt from Confucius:

The Analects*

Note: The Analects *is a collection of sayings by Confucius and his pupils pertaining to his teachings and deeds. It was probably put together by some of his pupils and their pupils.*

1:1. Confucius said, "Is it not a pleasure to learn and to repeat or practice from time to time what has been learned? Is it not delightful to have friends coming from afar? Is one not a superior man if he does not feel hurt even though he is not recognized?"

1:2. Yu-Tzu said, "Few of those who are filial sons and respectful brothers will show disrespect to superiors, and there never has been a man who is not disrespectful to superiors and yet creates disorder. A superior man is devoted to the fundamentals (the root). When the root is firmly established, the moral law (Tao) will grow. Filial piety and brotherly respect are the root of humanity.

1:3. Confucius said, "A man with clever words and an ingratiating appearance is seldom a man of humanity."

1:4. Tseng-Tzu said, "Every day I examine myself on three points: whether in counseling others I have not been loyal; whether in intercourse with my friends I have not been faithful; and whether I have not repeated again and again and practiced the instructions of my teacher."

1:6. Young men should be filial when at home and respectful to their elders when away from home. They should be earnest and faithful. They should love all extensively and be intimate with men of humanity. When they have any energy to spare after the performance of moral duties, they should use it to study literature and the arts.

1:8. Confucius said, "If the superior man is not grave, he will not inspire awe, and his learning will not be on a firm foundation. . . . When you have made mistakes, don't be afraid to correct them.

The Wade-Giles system of **transliteration** has been kept in this quoted material, as in others in this chapter.

Wing-Tsit Chan, ed. and trans., *A Source Book in Chinese Philosophy*, (Princeton: Princeton University Press, 1963).

Lao-zi

The age of a hundred philosophers in China (6th–5th cent. B.C.E.) gave rise to myriad new forms of thought, but none has so beguiled us spiritually as that of Lao-zi. Thought to be a contemporary of Confucius, Lao-zi was an archivist at the court palace of Loyang. Legend tells us that when he was about 60, Lao-zi grew weary of a world of chaos and social fragmentation and set off wandering to the west. The western gatekeeper asked him to deposit his wisdom before passing, and the result was the *Lao-zi,* also titled the *Dao De Jing.* These aphoristic and enigmatic passages express a view of life that is quietistic, yielding, receptive, and ultimately affirming of the world just as it is found. Humans are but a small part of the larger ebb and flow of natural change and the best chance for survival comes from perfect and invisible attunement to one's surroundings. No one knows if Lao-zi (which means "old man") really lived or not, but in the end it may not matter, for as is said in traditional China, Daoism is but a state of mind.

students alienated from old ways of life, but unlike many of his contemporaries Mao was sensitive to the social roots of China's political order. Early in his life, Mao realized the depth of popular discontent in China with the existing order of things. The problem was how to sustain and direct such mass anger in support of a social revolution. Mao's rural upbringing made him aware of the tendency of the peasants to avoid political involvement; they were inclined to eat the bitterness of life's hardships and injustices. But he also knew of China's long tradition of peasant rebellions. His solution to this problem of how to involve a basically conservative rural population in a revolution that would completely reshape peasant life developed only after years of effort to organize support for the communist movement in the Chinese countryside.

On May 4, 1919, the students of Beijing protested the compromising of Chinese interests at the Versailles Peace Conference. They staged anti-Western political demonstrations and sought to reshape their country's political tradition from elitism to mass participation. The "May Fourth" generation, as they became known, was deeply influenced by the success of the Bolshevik revolution of 1917 in neighboring Russia. Mao Ze-dong found in Marxism–Leninism concepts that could be used to revolutionize China, and he also saw that China's revolutionary intellectuals continued to use their new ideology in traditional ways.

Excerpt from Lao-zi:

The *Dao De Jing*

Empty your mind of all thoughts.
Let your heart be at peace.
Watch the turmoil of beings,
but contemplate their return.

Each separate being in the universe
returns to the common source.
Returning to the source is serenity.

If you don't realize the source,
you stumble in confusion and sorrow.
When you realize where you come from,
you naturally become tolerant,
disinterested, amused,
kindhearted as a grandmother,
dignified as a king.
Immersed in the wonder of the Dao,
you can deal with whatever life brings you,
and when death comes, you are ready.

As we have seen, the conflicts and contradictions in life did find expression in some of China's philosophical traditions, most explicitly the Daoist concepts of *yin* and *yang*. Daoism emphasized the ironies and tensions inherent in social institutions; in contrast, however, Confucianism, the philosophy that dominated China's political tradition, sought rule through elite consensus designed to produce the harmonious life. Under Mao and Communist Party influence, a philosophy of conflict has influenced Chinese culture. The Marxist–Leninist concepts of dialectical materialism and class struggle have held for many Chinese a greater sense of reality than Confucian harmony, although there is a definite resurgence of Neo-Confucianism in Taiwan,

Hong Kong, and to a degree in China itself. Mao Ze-dong was only the most influential member of a generation that rejected the Confucian tradition in favor of a doctrine of struggle and change. Inspired by the Marxist dialectic, Mao developed a philosophy of social change. He wrote:

Changes in society are due chiefly to the development of the internal contradictions in society, that is the contradiction between the productive forces and the relations of production, the contradiction between classes and the contradiction between the old and the new; it is the development of these contradictions that pushes society forward and gives the impetus for the suppression of the old by the new. . . . This dialectical world outlook teaches us primarily how to observe and analyze the movement of opposites in different things and . . . to indicate methods for resolving contradictions.[13]

The Chinese commitment to the ongoing dialectic has brought many upheavals in the political, social, and cultural traditions of China. "Once Mao Tse-tung's thought is grasped by the broad masses, it becomes an inexhaustible source of strength and a spiritual atom bomb of infinite power."[14] Mao himself remarked that he wished to be remembered by future generations only as a great teacher.[15] In the Chinese Confucian tradition, however, a teacher has long been considered a model to be emulated by students, a source of authority, rather than just an independent intellect who stimulates students to their own achievements. Thus Mao, even as a teacher of revolution, is likely to remain a powerful model figure who will long be held up for emulation by China's millions, a symbol of the transformation of China.[16]

The Value System of the Japanese

◆ ◆ ◆ ◆ ◆ ◆ ◆ ◆ ◆ ◆

Japanese culture has been strongly influenced by Confucianism and Chinese culture and also by Buddhism and Indian culture. Yet in Japan these acquisitions have been remolded into something distinctive and uniquely Japanese. Because of a common ancestry and language and because of living on a chain of islands separated from the mainland of Asia, Japanese peoples have been able to develop distinctive traits in comparative isolation.

SHINTOISM

The Japanese value system goes back to an early tribal society in which life was centered around the family, the villages, and small neighborhoods. Religious values and moral standards were scarcely distinguished from each other or from the problem of keeping order and making a living. The veneration of the sun; worship of the *kami* (the nature spirits); reverence for the

spirits of ancestors; and respect for and loyalty to parents, older people, and all those in positions of authority were part of one's duties. **Shinto** is the name used to cover many of these activities and beliefs. At an early date it was the tribal folk religion centering around the family and local shrines (Shrine Shinto), but eventually it became a patriotic state cult connected with the chieftain and court (State Shinto).

Shintoism is the traditional Japanese religion. *Shinto* means literally "the way of the gods," but the term was not applied until the sixth century C.E., when it was necessary to distinguish the ancient faith from the encroaching Buddhism. Originally, Shintoism was pantheistic and had no written records or written literature, no codified laws, no traditions of philosophical inquiry, and only a rough experience in the arts and sciences. The early belief was that all perceptible objects were in some way alive, inhabited by good or evil spirits. The first tales to be composed speak of waterways, vegetation, and stones that could talk; however, this was more than a simple animism.[17] The much-celebrated Japanese appreciation of nature—a twisted tree, snow falling gently in the distance—can certainly be traced back to early Shintoism. Later, however, the original nature deities were developed into a complex, institutional religion, with a priesthood, shrines, and monasteries all embodying the *cult of the Emperor,* as the son of the great Sun Goddess. From this conviction grew the idea of the Emperor as divine and of Shinto as the state religion.

ZEN BUDDHISM

During the early centuries of the common era, Chinese culture, especially Confucianism, and Indian cultures by way of Buddhism, had an influence in Japan. The Confucian emphasis on loyalty was carried over into the evolving ethical code of the warrior class. Buddhism was introduced and changed on Japanese soil. Zen became the most influential sect of Buddhism in Japan. As Buddhism moved slowly across Asia, it began to receive influences from the different countries through which it passed. Buddhism reached China as early as the first century C.E. and in due course passed on from China to Korea and Japan. During these travels and transitions, Buddhism developed several divergent forms of teaching, among them one in particular that, under its Japanese name of Zen, was destined to have a strong influence on Western societies in the second half of the twentieth century.

Zen became the most influential sect of Buddhism in Japan. *Zen*, from the Chinese *Chan* has as one of its chief features *zazen*, sitting meditation. Zen Buddhism came to serve not only people seeking salvation and wisdom, but also soldiers; it strengthened the soldiers' self-discipline and gave them poise and courage even in the face of death.

Although Zen has its basis in Mahayana Buddhism, it returns to some of the earliest values emphasized in the Theravada tradition. Like Theravada, Zen focuses on the simplicity of the moment. Reality is not transcendent but can be captured in the fullness of the fleeting here and now. Complete awareness of the experience of each moment as it comes and goes is the goal of Zen meditation.

> According to Zen there is no struggle in the fact itself such as between the finite and the infinite, between flesh and the spirit. These are idle distinctions fictitiously designed by the intellect for its own interest. Those who take them too seriously or those who try to read them into the very fact of life are those who take the finger for the moon. When we are hungry we eat; when we are sleepy we lay ourselves down; and where does the infinite come in here? Are not we complete in ourselves and each in himself? Life as it is lived suffices.[18]

The discovery of this "reality" is the Zen goal.

When questioned about life's "meaning," about "the reality of the Self," about the "origins of the Universe," or "the nature of nirvana," the Buddha maintained a "noble silence." This is also Zen's way. Such questions are considered essentially irrelevant in the attaining of spiritual freedom. The Zen philosopher Dogen talks about the "without-thinking" mode that "neither affirms nor denies, accepts nor rejects, believes nor disbelieves." Like the exhausted person leaning on the lawnmower whose eyes gaze downward, the ideal Zen mind thinks and feels nothing specific whatsoever: "He simply is as he is, with no intentional attitude at all."[19] Final "answers" cannot be reached by way of argument or any so-called facts. Thus Zen attempts to force the mind beyond the pattern of ordinary thought processes through the use of the *koan*, a nonsensical statement or question for which there is no logical response. In the use of the *koan*, the intention is to force attention on the truth that explanations in words or phrases explaining "meaning" belong to thought and language and not to actuality. By breaking down familiar distinctions and differences, Zen followers believe they can bring about a grasp of the empty transitory reality, which is a condition that transcends all opposites. In this fashion, the disciple of Zen is pushed toward a personal *experience*, toward an illuminating *realization* of the unity of life.

To be prepared for this experience, everything in Zen—its art, poetry, philosophy, rituals, and techniques—is presented as a tool for the destruction of our illusion that we are selves. Only with the obliteration of that self, that "temporary individuality," will persons be put in touch with "the Is-ness of the Is"—the present, ordinary moment of experience.

INDIVIDUAL VIRTUES
AND CULTURAL VALUES

The period from about 1100 to 1600 C.E. saw the development of the code, the *Bushido*, of the samurai or warrior class, the *bushi*. This was a time when many of the Japanese values that have persisted were codified. The code stressed an almost spartan life. The *samurai* was taught to live simply; to seek only the necessities in food, clothing, and shelter; not to desire great possessions; to rise early and avoid idle talk; and to avoid frivolities.

The code of the *samurai* does not differ greatly from that of the merchant and the peasant, or worker on the land, for the warrior code came to be accepted by all classes. Merchants and peasants, like others in society, are expected to be honest, to work hard, and to place public interest above private gain. Although some character traits are generally or universally desirable in that they apply to all people, many duties depend on the status of the person and on his or her social role or particular circumstances. One has different obligations to one's father, older brother, younger brother, neighbor, mere acquaintance, or a stranger. Rigid adherence to a detailed set of social conventions is expected. Formalized behavior tends to prevent conflicts and make possible a smoothly functioning society in which political values are primary and loyalty is the outstanding value.

Japanese standards and values are based mainly on a respect for external authority. The authority of the emperor, the elders, or tradition is always present. In the past, the Japanese as a people were more willing than Westerners to make their personal desires and wills subordinate to social standards and to accept authority.

The Japanese value system and rules of conduct contain contradictory elements, as do the systems of other societies. Conformism and the desire for self-expression, the suppression of emotion at times and emotional outbursts on occasion, military ruthlessness and a basic compassion and normally peaceful ways of living—these are a few of the contradictory aspects.

The end of World War II wrought many changes in the Japanese way of life. The atomic bombing of Hiroshima and Nagasaki in August 1945 brought defeat and surrender with startling suddenness. Defeat seemed to deny the validity of the foundation of Japanese national life and to undermine the national morality. Japanese moral standards, traditions, and expectations seemed to be thrown into reverse. The Japanese soon discovered, however, that the occupation forces were not going to exact severe terms but were anxious to help them discover better ways of living. Furthermore, the occupation leaders assumed the superiority of democratic ways. They praised freedom as the basis for ma-

ture and responsible moral decisions. What was to become of the Japanese emphasis on conformity and authority? What was to be the basis for moral action after the Emperor, publicly before the Diet (legislature) and the nation, disclaimed his divine origin, the racial superiority of the Japanese people, and the divine destiny of the nation? The entire value system seemed to be shattered.

Defeat, surrender, occupation, and inflation are only outstanding events in a long series of rapid changes that Japan has been undergoing for nearly a century. Industrialization, urbanization, secularization as a result of a weakening of the traditional religions, the introduction of foreign ideas and ways of doing things, and modernization along many lines also have occurred. While undergoing rapid social and economic change, Japan has moved away from a closed, tradition-bound, authoritarian society toward an open, affluent, capitalistic society patterned after the models of Western Europe and North America.

Reflections

◆ ◆ ◆ ◆ ◆ ◆ ◆ ◆ ◆ ◆

There are a few broad differences in outlook between East and West. The East and the West tend to view the objective or natural world of the senses from different perspectives. The West has tended in recent times to emphasize the empirical world, as seen in scientific progress. The Hindu thinker is more likely to emphasize the inner nature of the self and a reality beyond the world of the senses, which is regarded as fleeting and illusory. The Buddhist thinker, however, like the Westerner, takes account of the empirical world but focuses instead on its transitory quality and the need for nonattachment to it.

Partly as a result of differences in theories of knowledge and views of reality, the East and West have contrasting attitudes toward human desires and their fulfillment. In the West, there is a tendency to emphasize desires and the need to satisfy them. The effort to satisfy desires has led to an interest in things and the comforts and pleasures of this world. It has led to competition, to the acquisitive society, and sometimes to unrest and even war. In the East, on the other hand, there is greater emphasis on discipline, self-control, moderation, detachment, and even renunciation. Buddhism, with its claim that suffering and misery come from desire and striving and its stress on release from desire and the suffering it brings, did have a strong influence in China, Japan, and other Asian countries. It needs to be pointed out, however, that both China—with the People's Revolution—and Japan—through adopting capitalistic goals— have reworked much of their religious heritage.

Thinkers in the West put more emphasis than do most Eastern thinkers on the reality and the value of time. In the West, we find process philosophies and concepts of creative evolution and progress attractive. (Only recently have Asian scholars become interested in process philosophy.) Thus time has a role in Western notions of salvation. For the Hindu or the Buddhist, on the other hand, the good is not in this present world of things, and it is not to be gained by manipulating nature, altering society, or seeking pleasure for ourselves. The good is found through the quest for the One within or beyond, or in attaining liberating knowledge.

People in the West tend to view nature (in the sense of the external world) as something to be exploited. It is used for recreation and fun, and is predominantly exploited for financial gain. Western imagery is expressed in terms of "harnessing nature," "taming the wilderness," or "conquering space." Think of the problem the West has with air and water pollution, strip mining, and the defacing of nature for purposes of advertising. In the Asian world a pervasive concept is "harmony with nature." The Asians feel that nature is life-sustaining and gives them their food, shelter, and the material for their arts and sciences. There is something ineffable, a sense of oneness, and a nature mysticism that cannot be described adequately by the terms and concepts of scientific and philosophical treatises. It is perhaps best expressed in the gardens, flower arrangements, and the nature art of the Japanese.

Apart from these differences regarding the value of certain kinds of knowledge, the role of desires, the nature of the time process, and the attitude toward nature, there is considerable agreement about morals and values. That is, the things approved and called good and the things disapproved and called evil differ only in minor details. Love and compassion, freedom, and responsibility are emphasized in both Eastern and Western systems.

● ●

Glossary Terms

ATMAN The Hindu concept of the soul or self after enlightenment. The true self of each individual is identical with Brahman. The true destiny of the self is the realization of union with Brahman.

BHAGAVADGITA A particular Hindu scripture that has the form of a dialogue between the hero Arjuna and Krishna, an incarnation of the God Vishnu. The most well-known of the Hindu Scriptures; called the *Gita* and the *Song of the Lord*. (Sometimes written *Bhagavad-Gita*.)

BODHISATTVA A term used in Buddhism for a person aspiring to enlightenment, one who is a Buddha-to-be; a Buddhist wise and holy person.

BRAHMAN The central concept in Hindu philosophy of the impersonal supreme being or ultimate reality. The primal source and ultimate goal of all beings, with which Atman, when enlightened, knows itself to be identical.

KARMA In Hinduism, the cosmic law of sowing and reaping, of cause and effect in human life. The law determines the form that will be taken in each new existence or rebirth. Action is seen as bringing upon oneself inevitable results, good or bad.

NIRVANA   The extinction of the finite, changing, desiring self. A cessation of striving that liberates and enlightens one. The elimination of ignorance, lust, and selfishness, which are at the root of suffering.

SHINTO   The name given to the many activities and beliefs of the traditional Japanese religion.

TRANSLITERATION   The spelling of words translated from a different foreign script. For example, Arabic script, dissimilar to the script of English words, can yield *Qur'an* or *Koran, Muslim* or *Moslem,* and various English spellings of "Mohammed."

UPANISHADS   A group of philosophical treatises, usually in dialogue form, composed between the eighth and sixth centuries B.C.E. They comprise part of the Hindu Scripture and represent an advance beyond the Vedas, having as their principal message the unity of Brahman and Atman.

◆ ◆

Chapter Review

THE NATURE OF ASIAN RELIGION

1. We live in a world society that desperately needs some understanding of its diversity, especially the great diversity among world religions.

2. The peoples of Asian cultures view religion as integrally related to and inseparable from all other areas of life and experience.

THE HINDU TRADITION

1. Hinduism has been practiced for some 5,000 years, making it one of the oldest religious traditions in the world.

2. The purpose of Hindu philosophy is to see the truth and to apply the truth to problems of everyday life.

3. Hindu Scripture is extensive and when collected includes the Vedas and the widely read *Bhagavadgita.*

4. Four major periods of Hindu thought include Vedic polytheism; the Vedanta and the presentation of Absolute Brahman; Bhakti, or the literature of devotional theism, including the *Bhagavadgita;* and the modern period.

5. Central to Hindu philosophy is Brahman, the one unchanging reality that transcends space, time, causality, and all particular things.

6. The concept of the self, *atman,* is closely allied with Brahman.

7. Four main values of Hinduism are: *artha* (wealth), *kama* sensuality, *dharma* (duty or righteousness), and *moksha* (enlightenment or release from finitude).

8. *Karma,* the law of cause and effect in human life, determines the *dharmic* form that *atman* will take in each new existence.

9. The four *ashramas,* or stages of life, are student, householder, forest dweller, and renunciant.

10. *Yoga* is a technique of physical and spiritual training by which the bodily and psychic energies are controlled, unified, and directed in order to attain liberation from the world.

THE BUDDHIST QUEST
FOR ENLIGHTENMENT

1. Siddhartha Gautama was the founder of Buddhism, which flourished in India for more than a thousand years. He became known as the Buddha or "Enlightened One."

2. The central core of Buddhist philosophy is found in "The Four Noble Truths."

3. The Noble Eightfold Path can lead to *nirvana,* the experience of cessation of suffering, the liberation from human striving.

4. Two main branches with various subdivisions arose in Buddhism, the main divisions being Theravada and Mahayana.

CONFUCIUS AND LAO-ZI

1. Confucius and Lao-Zi attempted to organize the wisdom of the time into a more orderly system. Philosophy among the Chinese has been practical and this-worldly. They emphasized moral problems and social philosophy.

2. Traditional Chinese philosophy proposes a system of ethical realism in which man occupies a high place in nature.

3. Confucianism was concerned mainly with personal and social relations, whereas Daoism cultivated a sense of oneness with the order of the universe.

MAO ZE-DONG

1. Marxism may be regarded as the religion of China today with Mao Ze-dong as its founder.

THE VALUE SYSTEM OF THE JAPANESE

1. The Japanese value system began in an early tribal society. Standards and values were based mainly on respect for external authority, ensuring a smoothly functioning society. In Japan, since the end of World War II, there has been considerable movement toward a capitalistic society similar to that of Western Europe and America.

2. Shinto, literally "the way of the Gods," is the name used to cover many activities and beliefs of the Japanese.

3. Zen Buddhism, the most influential sect of Buddhism in Japan, stresses the universe as one indissoluble substance, one total whole, of which man is only a part. Zen focuses on everyday, ordinary experience, on living the experience of each moment.

4. Individual virtues and cultural values are reflected in the Bushido code and respect for external authority; however, contradictory elements can be found, as in systems of other societies.

REFLECTIONS

1. There are basic sources of misunderstanding between East and West: economic and technological differences; contrasting ideals; differences in outlook on reality and satisfying desires; respective differences concerning time, and attitudes toward nature.

2. The things approved and disapproved differ in minor details; there is considerable agreement about morals and values.

◆ ◆

Study Questions and Projects

1. Judaism and Christianity are Middle Eastern in origin. To what extent do their value systems agree with and differ from the Asian philosophies considered in this chapter?

2. Discuss briefly the differences between East and West in their attitude toward sense perception, human desires, the time process, and the world of nature.

3. What are some conclusions to be drawn from a study of the value systems of the Occident and Asia? What are some contributions Asia can make to the Occident, and vice versa?

4. Why is it important to study Asian philosophies? What problems are involved in making such studies?

5. Discuss the following in the Hindu tradition: the aim of studying philosophy; the relations among Brahman, the self, and the universe; the goal of life and the steps to achieve it.

6. What are the four main values in the Hindu outlook on life?

7. Give the distinctive characteristics of Indian philosophy.

8. Discuss the following in Buddhism: what it accepts and rejects in Hinduism; the Three Marks of Existence; the Four Noble Truths; the Eightfold Path; and Nirvana.

9. What are some virtues or character traits that are stressed by Buddhists?

10. Discuss the place of philosophy and the general value system found in traditional Chinese civilization, especially under Confucianism.

11. What is the relation between nature, the individual, and the good society in traditional Chinese thought?

12. Discuss the elements, native and foreign, that contributed to the Japanese value system.

13. Explain the crisis in the area of values faced by Japan in this century, and the way the crisis is being met.

14. Write a term paper on "The Functions of Myth in Hebraic and Asian scriptures."

15. Write an essay, "The Religion of Mao Ze-dong."

◆ ◆

Suggested Readings

Davis, W. *Japanese Religion and Society: Paradigms of Structure and Change*. Albany, N.Y.: State University of New York Press, 1992.

The author provides an important and timely study of the interrelationships between Japanese religion and society.

Dumoulin, H. *Zen Enlightenment, Origins and Meaning*. New York: Weatherhill, 1979.

An historical and philosophical introduction to Zen Buddhism that uses primary texts to focus on Zen experience.

Forman, R. K. C. (ed.). *Religions of the World*. 3rd ed. New York: St. Martin's, 1993.

Written by scholars in their respective areas of specialization, this text provides a detailed overview of significant faiths of the past and of the major religions of the world today.

Hardacre, H. *Shinto and the State: 1868–1988*. Princeton, N.J.: Princeton University Press, 1989.

Important Japanese religion–state issues during the nineteenth and twentieth centuries are discussed.

Hiriyana, M. *Essentials of Indian Philosophy*. Flushing, N.Y.: Asia Book Corporation 1978.

A classic treatment of six major philosophical traditions of India.

Kalupahana, D. J. *Buddhist Philosophy: A Historical Analysis*. Honolulu: University Press of Hawaii, 1976.

This introduction to Buddhism examines its basic philosophical teachings and historical development. The author's orientation is primarily philosophical.

Kasulis, T. *Zen Action/Zen Person*. Honolulu: University of Hawaii Press, 1985.

This book on Zen Buddhism is unmatched for its clarity and precision.

Kitagawa, J., and Cummings, M. (eds.). *Buddhism in Asian History*. New York: Macmillan, 1989.

A collection of essays appropriate for students interested in further information on various features of Buddhism.

Klostermaier, K. K. *A Survey of Hinduism*. Albany, N.Y.: State University of New York Press, 1989.

A recent scholarly exploration.

Munro, D. J. *The Concept of Man in Early China*. Stanford, Calif.: Stanford University Press, 1969.

An excellent discussion of Confucianism and Daoism, focusing on issues of the human mind, equality, and the nature of society. In 1977 *The Concept of Man in Contemporary China* followed from the University of Michigan Press.

Nishida, K. *An Inquiry into the Good*. New Haven, Conn.: Yale University Press, 1990.

An important work for understanding modern Japanese thought as written by a preeminent Japanese philosopher.

Pas, J. F. (ed.). *The Turning of the Tide: Religion in China Today*. New York: Oxford University Press, 1990.

A critical examination of various aspects of the present state of religion in China.

Raju, P. T. *Introduction to Comparative Philosophy*. Carbondale, Ill.: Southern Illinois University Press, 1970.

This paperback, written by an outstanding Indian philosopher, examines both Asian and Western world views.

Rice, E. *Eastern Definitions*. Garden City, N.Y.: Doubleday, 1978.

This short encyclopedia of Asian religions defines terms from Hinduism, Sufism, Buddhism, Islam, Zen, Daoism, the Sikhs, and Zoroastrianism.

◆ ◆

Notes

1. Carl J. Jung, from N. W. Ross, *Three Ways of Asian Wisdom* (New York: Simon and Schuster, 1966), p. 9.

2. R. K. C. Forman, (ed.)., *Religions of the World*, 3rd ed. (New York: St. Martin's, 1993), p. 83.

3. For a more detailed look at these periods, see Klaus K. Klostermaier, *A Survey of Hinduism* (Albany: State University of New York Press, 1989).

4. N. Smart, *The Religious Experience of Mankind*, 3rd ed. (New York: Scribner's, 1985), p. 126. We advise any student of religion to refer to this book.

5. M. Hiriyanna, *The Essentials of Indian Philosophy* (London: Allen and Unwin, 1949), p. 158.

6. See V. S. Naravane, *Modern Indian Thought: A Philosophical Survey* (London: Asia Publishing House, 1964).

7. S. Radhakrishnan, and C. A. Moore, eds., *A Source Book in Indian Philosophy* (Princeton: Princeton University Press, 1957), pp. xx–xxvi.

8. See David Little and Sumner B. Twiss, "Religion and Morality in Theravada Buddhism," in Charles S. Prebish, ed., *Buddhist Ethics: A Cross-Cultural Approach* (Dubuque, Iowa: Kendall/Hunt Publishing Company, 1992), p. 60.

9. We discuss Zen Buddhism, one of the most important divisions of Buddhism, later in this chapter under The Value System of the Japanese, pp. 422–24.

10. Quoted in C. A. Moore, ed., *Essays in East-West Philosophy* (Honolulu: University of Hawaii Press, 1951), p. 301. (East–West Philosophers' Conference.)

11. F. C. M. Wei, *The Spirit of Chinese Culture* (New York: Scribner's, 1947), p. 91.

12. See Chapter 12 for an introduction to the dialectical materialism of Marx.

13. Mao Tse-tung, "On Contradiction" (1937), in *Selected Works of Mao Tse-tung*, Vol. I (Peking: Foreign Language Press, 1961–1965), pp. 314–15.

14. Lin Piao, "Foreword to the Second Edition," *Quotations from Chairman Mao Tse-tung* (Peking: The East Is Red Publishing House, 1967), pp. vii, ix.

15. E. Snow, *The Long Revolution* (New York: Random House, 1972), p. 169.

16. For much of this discussion we are indebted to a fine, arresting introduction to Mao's China: R. H. Solomon, *A Revolution Is Not a Dinner Party* (Garden City, N.Y.: Anchor Press, Doubleday, 1975).

17. See Chapter 17, p. 362.

18. Daisetz Teitaro Suzuki, *Essays in Zen Buddhism* (First Series) (New York: Grove Press, 1961), p. 19.

19. T. P. Kasulis, *Zen Action/Zen Person* (Honolulu: University of Hawaii Press, 1985), p. 75.

◆ ◆ ◆ ◆ ◆ ◆ ◆ ◆ ◆ ◆ ◆

Concluding Reflection

Philosophy recovers itself when it ceases to be a device for dealing with the problems of philosophers, and becomes a method, cultivated by philosophers, for dealing with the problems of men.[1]

"Beauty is in the eye of the beholder."

"Everyone should do their own thing, so long as nobody else is hurt."

"Truth depends upon your point of view."

Each of us is to some degree a philosopher. The three short statements above express a conception of life and the world—a philosophy. Individuals conduct their lives, whether consciously or not, in line with their conceptions of life and the world, and their scheme of values. Even small children bring to our attention the fact that we all live—cannot avoid living—without a philosophy of some kind. For example, they sometimes ask metaphysical questions: What's time? What are things? What is death? Our answers or our avoidance of the questions clearly reveal a philosophical perspective.

Today, however, we are less likely to be able to answer such questions with any philosophical satisfaction. Men and women alike are caught in a daily existence that does not allow for much speculation and reflection. Ours is a practical age that moves toward specialization; we seldom perceive ourselves as whole persons but rather as job-seeker, mother, party-goer, student, or shopper. We live a compartmentalized and fragmented existence. What philosophy needs to do, and has done in the past, is to provide a life view or a world view that is based on a broad range of human experience. "Specialization within philosophy is virtually a contradiction in terms. . . . If philosophical specialities were pursued without regard to one another, a supraphilosophy would be needed to unite them, interpreting them in ways which would allow for general perspectives."[2]

Naturally, we begin to practice philosophy from our own perspective. The questions that we choose to ask and the tentative answers we give are, of course, initially dependent on what we think is most significant and meaningful. We have not only individual perspectives but also certain common assumptions that are derived from the society or civilization in which we happen to live. For example, in the modern period our search for answers—our search for truth—tends to be a search for "proof." Our education has been mainly directed toward providing *information,* which we accept unquestioningly as authoritative and complete. The child may ask, "Why is there that rainbow on the surface of the puddle?" You may reply, "Because there is a film of oil on the water." Your answer apparently satisfies the youngster but it is by no means a complete or "satisfactory" answer. As children, we would want to know what oil has to do with rainbows; as our education proceeds, however, we become increasingly satisfied with partial answers, partial explanations, and partial philosophies. The result is that we have an incomplete, inarticulated philosophy based on a number of unconscious presuppositions.

Every civilization rests on a number of presuppositions about many questions: about humanity, human nature, the nature of the world, and about those things that are valuable. These presuppositions are generally unstated; they are unconscious assumptions—unexamined opinions or prejudices—held by most people. They are considered part of the nature of things and are seldom made explicit. These assumptions and unreflected convictions, accepted as facts, determine the way in which we view things. They determine the standards and institutions of a society. They are like windows through which we view the world; we do not see them, but we see other things through them. For example, presuppositions about humanity and the world change radically as we move from the Middle Ages to the eighteenth century to the contemporary world. During the Middle Ages, life in this world was thought to be a period of preparation for a future life, and faith was a higher form of understanding than reason. By the eighteenth century, philosophy was mainly concerned with who people are and with our unique powers of understanding and reason. In the contemporary world, because of the influence of science and technology, the outlook is secular and empirical. People in the modern period tend to think in terms of personal achievement—they are "success oriented" and inclined to have a purely subjective perspective. Thus there are certain beliefs that, for a certain age, are regarded not only as beliefs but as statements of fact.

The beliefs of philosophers also rest on certain basic assumptions. One can point to the different frames of reference of philosophical positions. For example, the materialists interpret all existence according to their basic assumption that all is matter. They are necessarily impressed with material things and the physical reality of the universe. On the other hand, the behaviorists, who are engaged in the social sciences and psychology, have as their assumption that people be defined in terms of behavior. Like the materialists, they insist that the scientific method is the only path to valid knowledge, but they differ in that they confine their attention to the activities of "organisms" and talk about the environment rather than the world of matter. Their frame of reference is limited to examining humanity through external behavioristic signs.

The idealists have a different assumption. They are impressed with the mind, the self, and an apparent orderly relation of things. Idealists perceive humanity as having an intentionality—a meaning—that enables understanding, reason, and thought to comprehend the nature of all there is. In contrast, the realists (who hold the common-sense view) stress the world "out there," insisting that this world exists independently of our perceptions of it and that this universe is all there is.

Basic philosophical assumptions can make an immense difference in how one views the world. Pragmatists, for example, stress human, practical *experience,* experience that goes beyond sense experience and includes all experiences in daily life. John Dewey points to three classical assumptions that modern philosophy necessarily had to overcome: "The first, that certainty, security, can be found only in the fixed and unchanging; the second, that knowledge is the only road to that which is intrinsically stable and certain; the third, that practical activity is an inferior sort of thing, necessary simply because of man's animal nature and the necessity for winning subsistence from the environment."[3] With pragmatism, interest shifts from traditional metaphysical questions that do not seem to make a difference in our lives, to the problems of everyday affairs: designing a better school curriculum, developing a more equitable judiciary, or providing increased individual freedom. In contrast, analytic philosophers have as their basic assumption that clarity is enough. Again, interest shifts from the traditional metaphysical questions to other problems—not problems of daily living, but of meaning and verification. Logic, semantics, the philosophy of science, and epistemology become central; large areas of historical philosophical interest are forgotten as meaningless. Questions such as: "What constitutes the good life?" "Why is there anything at all?" and "What makes a sunset beautiful?" are neglected entirely.

These are only a few samples of how philosophical assumptions can alter one's comprehension and perception of life. What needs to be stressed, however, is how we can arrive at a life view that will encompass all areas of human experience.

In a previous chapter we pointed out that beliefs make a difference in life. Our beliefs express themselves in action. Consequently, they affect the quality of our personal lives and they influence the society in which we live. Many people, however, find it difficult, if not impossible, to look beyond their small segment of life and achieve a comprehensive view. This is the major philosophical task; in our age of increasing specialization, we need the larger view to give us a guide by which to choose to be persons. Building a philosophy is a needed and life-giving activity. Today, it is clear that there are many human difficulties of an urgent, deep-seated kind that are crying out for attention and clarification from trained reflection. Unfortunately, these problems are often difficult, challenging, and even frustrating; philosophers take a risk when undertaking a dialectic with truly philosophical issues—they may find not truth, but error. Philosophers, nonetheless, need to make choices and decisions, need to opt for a truth even though it may be unpopular and unconventional. By choosing to question simplistic and narrow answers, the philosopher chooses to be alive.

Moreover, if philosophy should abandon the task of attempting to see life as a whole, and become simply another specialty, then others will respond to the demand and take over the traditional task of the philosopher. Philosophy will not decline, but it may be carried on by scientists, theologians, cultural historians, and writers. One philosopher states this issue clearly:

> Every man [and woman] has a philosophy, in short; and if it is not provided—formulated, criticized, improved—by those identified as philosophers in the prevailing division of labor, others will inevitably perform that function. At various periods of history various groups have performed it—priests, poets, scientists, statesmen, and occasionally even professors of philosophy. In our time, journalists, psychiatrists, literary critics, and nuclear physicists seem to be carrying the burden. . . . In the arts and sciences, in law, medicine, politics, or religion, questions continually arise which, because they are so speculative, so broad in scope, or so inextricably involved with values are habitually dismissed as being too philosophical in character to be considered there. I have no quarrel with those who hold that such questions belong in philosophy; but what is to be done if philosophers also refuse to consider them? I am saying only that the division of labor in society must not be allowed to go so far as to leave no place at all for those great questions which cannot be divided, and for which every man presupposes some answer or other in going about his business or just in living his life.[4]

Contemporary philosophers should continually remind themselves to attend to human difficulties, to the problems of themselves, to the living issues of philosophy.

◆ ◆

Notes

1. J. Dewey, "The Need for a Recovery of Philosophy," in W. G. Muelder, L. Sears and A. V. Schlabach, eds., *The Development of American Philosophy,* 2nd ed. (Cambridge, Mass.: Houghton Mifflin, 1960), p. 416.

2. A. Kaplan, *In Pursuit of Wisdom* (Beverly Hills: Glencoe Press, 1977), p. 22.

3. J. Dewey, *The Quest for Certainty* (London: Allen and Unwin, 1930), pp. 51–52.

4. A. Kaplan, *The New World of Philosophy* (New York: Random House, 1961), pp. 4*ff.*

ABSOLUTE   (1) That which is entirely independent, such as ultimate reality; (2) a demonstrated or self-evident, true principle or presupposition, such as a moral absolute.

ABSOLUTISM   (1) Belief in an ultimate reality that is without limitation; (2) the view that truth is objectively real, that there is only one correct explanation of reality, truth, and values.

A.D.   From the Latin *anno Domini* "in the year of Our Lord," a Christian reckoning of the calendar years following Jesus' birth. "C.E." meaning "common era" is being used for the same period of time, but without reference to Christian theology. (See B.C.)

AD HOMINEM FALLACY   Faulty reasoning that shifts from an issue to a personality; from the Latin "to the man."

AESTHETICS   That branch of philosophy concerned with art and the nature and work of art.

AFFECTIVE   Relating to emotion or feeling.

AGNOSTICISM   A profession of ignorance, especially the claim that it is impossible to demonstrate conclusively either the existence or nonexistence of God.

ANALYTIC STATEMENTS   Statements that simply express the meaning of one of their terms. (See TAUTOLOGY.)

ANIMISM   The primitive belief that nature is filled with innumerable spirits. All things are thought of as possessing a life somewhat akin to human life.

ANTHROPOMORPHISM   The attributing of human qualities to the nonhuman realm or to nature. The term may refer to the portrayal of God as having human form, characteristics, or limitations.

A POSTERIORI   A posteriori knowledge is based upon actual observation; from the Latin "from what comes after."

A PRIORI   *A priori* refers to knowledge that is self-evident or refers to principles recognized to be true apart from observation or experience; from the Latin "from what comes before."

ATHEISM   Denial of the existence of a personal God.

ATMAN   The Hindu concept of the soul or self after enlightenment. The true self of each individual is identical with Brahman. The true destiny of the self is the realization of union with Brahman.

AUTHORITARIANISM   The belief that knowledge, or some knowledge, is guaranteed or validated by some source; an uncritical acceptance of testimony as opposed to an independent effort to discover what is true or false.

AXIOLOGY   The branch of philosophy that deals with values.

B.C.   "Before Christ"—a Christian reckoning of the calendar years before Jesus' birth. B.C.E., meaning "before the common era" is being used for the same period of time, but without reference to Christian theology.

B.C.E.   Before the common era. (See B.C. and A.D.)

BECOMING   To be in the process of coming into being.

BEGGING THE QUESTION   When one assumes as a premise for the argument the conclusion one intends to prove.

BEHAVIORISM   A theory of psychology which asserts that the proper subject matter of human psychology is the observed behavior of the human being.

BEING   That which exists; sometimes used for the infinite, God, or ultimate reality.

BHAGAVADGITA   A particular Hindu scripture that has the form of a dialogue between the hero Arjuna and Krishna, an incarnation of the God Vishnu. The most well known of the Hindu Scriptures; called the *Gita* and the *Song of the Lord*. (Sometimes written *Bhagavad-Gita*.)

BODHISATTVA   A term used in Buddhism for a person aspiring to enlightenment, one who is a Buddha-to-be; a Buddhist wise and holy individual.

BRAHMAN   The central concept in Hindu philosophy of the impersonal, supreme being or ultimate reality. The primal source and ultimate goal of all beings with which ATMAN, when enlightened, knows itself to be identical. (See BRAHMIN.)

BRAHMIN   The highest caste in Hinduism, sometimes transliterated as *Brahman*. (See Transliteration.)

C.E.   The common era. (See A.D.)

CHRISTIANITY   The religion of those who confess Jesus as Lord and Messiah, including the Roman Catholic, Anglican, Protestant, and Eastern Orthodox churches.

CIVIL DISOBEDIENCE   Public refusal to obey a law, expressed through deliberate but nonviolent means.

CIVIL LIBERTIES   Immunities from governmental interference (e.g., freedom from arbitrary arrest) (See Civil rights.)

CIVIL RIGHTS   Rights belonging to people by virtue of their citizenship; "civil rights" sometimes encompasses and is often used interchangeably with "civil liberties."

COGNITION (COGNITIVE)   The attainment of knowledge of something; the mental process by which we become aware of objects of perception; thought.

COMMON SENSE   A broad term used by philosophers to mean a way of looking at things independently of specialized knowledge or training; "common sense" is often uninformed opinion; the fund of opinion each member of a group is expected to have.

CONATION (CONATIVE)   The part of mental life having to do with striving, including desiring and willing.

CONCEPT   A general idea, as distinct from a percept. I may have a concept of "man" or "humanity," but I have a percept when I see a particular man, John Doe. We have percepts of particular, experienced objects; we have concepts of universals, classes, and unexperienced objects.

CONCLUSION   A proposition inferred from the premises of an argument.

CONSCIOUSNESS   Awareness of one's own existence.

CONSEQUENCES   The effects or results of something occurring earlier.

COSMOLOGY   The study or theories of the origin, nature, and development of the universe as an orderly system.

CREATIVITY   The state of producing something novel or original that will lead to further self-realization (Whitehead).

CULT   A system of religious beliefs and observances or the group of persons who accept a system of religious beliefs; on the popular level, often used pejoratively.

DARWINISM   The Darwinian theory that the origin of species is derived by descent, with variation, from parent forms, through the natural selection of those best adapted in the struggle for existence.

DECONSTRUCTION   A philosophical and critical movement, starting in the 1960s, that questions all traditional assumptions about the ability of language to represent reality.

DEDUCTION   An inference in which the conclusion follows necessarily from one or more premises. When the conclusion does so follow, the deduction is said to be valid.

DEISM   A belief that affirms the existence of a God who has created the universe but who remains apart and permits His creation to administer itself through natural laws—a view fairly prevalent in the seventeenth and eighteenth centuries; may be understood as a version of theism.

DEONTOLOGICAL   Refers to theories which hold that right and wrong is determined by true and binding formal rules of conduct, independently of any consideration of consequences.

DESCRIPTIVE ETHICS   The study of the ingredients of a moral situation, of the actual conduct of individuals, groups, and peoples.

DETERMINISM   The view that human choice is entirely controlled by previous conditions or governed by causal laws. The realm of nature, including human beings, is an unbroken chain of cause and effect. (Sometimes called HARD DETERMINISM.)

DIALECTIC   As most frequently used by philosophers, the critical analysis of ideas or conceptions to determine their meaning, implications, and presuppositions; the development of thought through an interplay of ideas. Also, a method of reasoning used by Socrates, Hegel, and others in which opposites are reconciled.

DIALOGIC   Pertaining to or participating in dialogue.

DUALISM   (1) The view that reality is composed of two different substances or realms, so that neither one can be reduced to the other (such as, spirit and matter). (2) In religion, DUALISM stresses the absolute difference between God and the rest of reality.

DUTY   Doing what one ought to do.

EMPIRICISM (EMPIRICAL)   The view that knowledge comes from experience or through the senses, in opposition to RATIONALISM.

ENLIGHTENMENT   A philosophical period of the seventeenth and eighteenth centuries, characterized by belief in the power of human reason.

ENTITY   Whatever has real existence or being; thing.

EPICUREANISM   The doctrine that pleasure (as understood by Epicurus) or freedom from pain is the highest good in life.

EPIPHENOMENON (EPIPHENOMENAL)   A phenomenon accompanying some brain processes.

EPISTEMOLOGY   Theory of knowledge; the branch of philosophy that studies the sources, nature, and validity of knowledge.

ESSENCE   The substance or intrinsic nature that makes a thing what it is. Ordinarily *essence* is considered distinct from *existence*.

ETHICAL MONOTHEISM   The belief in one God who has revealed moral standards all must follow.

ETHICAL RELATIVISM   The view that there are no fixed, universal moral values; also called *moral relativism*.

ETHICAL STANDARDS   Principles or norms by which moral actions are judged right or wrong.

ETHICS   The study of moral conduct. The term may also be applied to the system or code followed (such as "Buddhist ethics.")

EVOCATIVE   From *evoke;* to call up or produce (memories, feelings, etc.).

EVOLUTION   The theory of evolution is an interpretation of how the development of living forms has taken place. (See THEORY and HYPOTHESIS.)

EX CATHEDRA   From the Latin "from the chair or seat"; used most frequently to designate the Pope's infallible teachings on matters of faith and morals that are binding upon Roman Catholics; such pronouncements are different from "noninfallible" addresses, sermons, and so on.

EXISTENCE   (1) For Thomists, *existence* is the act of being as ordinarily contrasted with essence; it is the state of occurring within space and time. (2) Existentialists use "existence" in a limited sense, so that *to exist* applies to personal experience and calls for creative commitment. (3) The term is often used as the opposite of ESSENCE.

EXISTENTIALISM   An attitude and outlook in philosophy, theology, and the arts that stresses the human predicament or human feelings of anxiety, and emphasizes human existence and the qualities distinctive of individuals rather than humanity in the abstract or nature and the world in general.

EXTRINSIC VALUE   A value or good that leads to another good; valued for something other than itself (such as a common pencil whose chief value is what it *does,* not what it *is.*)

FAITH   An attitude of trust or confidence in a person, doctrine, system of beliefs and practices, or thing; faith may be informed or uninformed (naive).

FALLACY OF OVERSIMPLIFICATION   The uncritical attempt to explain everything with one principle or type of interpretation.

FALLACY OF REDUCTION   The belief that an object's simpler units have a greater reality than the larger, complex object itself.

FATALISM   The belief that events are irrevocably fixed so that human effort cannot alter them, though sometimes things appear otherwise. "What will be, will be."

FORMALISM   Adherence to prescribed forms. In ethics *formalism* means that certain types of acts follow fixed moral principles, apart from consideration of any particular situation or probable consequences.

FREE WILL   The position that human beings have some genuine power of alternate choice; the power of self-determination.

FUNDAMENTALISM   In religions, conservative views that include literal interpretations of scriptures as revealing God's truths—and so yielding a fixed set of beliefs for all time.

HEBRAIC   Refers to beliefs rooted in or compatible with basic convictions of classical, pre-Christian Hebrew civilization. Judaism, Christianity, and Islam are sometimes referred to as Hebraic religions.

HEDONISM   The term for various views that the chief good in life is pleasure.

HUMANISM   A general outlook that emphasizes distinctively human interests and ideals. The humanism of the Renaissance was based on the Greek classics; Christian humanism focuses on human concerns within a theological context; secular humanism underscores the significance of humanity as free agents independent of any supernatural realm or forces.

HUMAN RIGHTS   Often understood as the universal moral rights belonging equally and absolutely to all human beings.

HYPOTHESIS   A tentative proposal or possible explanation; often an early step in scientific method; an informed guess with research yet to be completed. (See THEORY.)

IDEALISTS (IDEALISM)   The view that asserts that reality consists of or is closely related to ideas, thought, mind, or selves rather than matter; there are many types of idealism.

IDEAS   (See WORLD OF ETERNAL FORMS.)

IMMANENT   Indwelling, or operating within the process. An immanent God is within the structure of the universe and/or takes a vital part in its processes. The term is used in contrast with TRANSCENDENT. Religions view their concepts of God as immanent, as transcendent, or as both.

IMMATERIALISM   With reference to George Berkeley, a theological form of SUBJECTIVE IDEALISM.

IMMORTALITY   The doctrine that the soul survives death.

INDETERMINISM   The belief that personal choices are independent of antecedent events. William James, for example, held that genuine possibilities exist in the future and that the universe holds a considerable amount of novelty, chance, and spontaneity.

INDUCTION   Reasoning that attempts to reach a conclusion concerning all the members of a class after inspection of only some of them. Inductive knowledge is empirical. The conclusion of an inductive argument, unlike that of a deductive one, is not logically necessary.

INFERENCE   A conclusion derived either from general premises (deduction) or from factual evidence (induction). Not to be confused with *implication;* one proposition is said to *imply* another when their relation is such that if the first is true, the second *must* also be true.

INFINITE   Unbounded or unlimited, not finite.

INSTRUMENTALIST (INSTRUMENTALISM)   (1) Another term for the pragmatism of John Dewey and others. (2) Instrumentalism stresses experience and interprets thinking, ideas, and beliefs as means for the adjustment of an organism to its environment.

INTRINSIC VALUE   A value or good that is good in itself.

INTROSPECTION   A person's awareness of his or her own thoughts and feelings; a psychological method of study that is in contrast to the study of objective behavior, though the two methods may be used together.

ISLAM   The worldwide religion of Muslims, followers of Mohammed; literally means "submission to God."

JUDAISM   The religion of Jews living all over the world.

KARMA   In Hinduism, the cosmic law of sowing and reaping, of cause and effect in human life. The law determines the form that will be taken in each new existence or rebirth. Action is seen as bringing upon oneself inevitable results, good or bad.

KORAN   See QUR'AN.

LIBERALISM   As a modern Christian movement, a social and political outlook favoring freedom of the individual and the rational consent of human beings, as opposed to an authoritarian ideal. As an approach to the Bible, the critical and analytical study of biblical literature with the purpose of distinguishing among myths, legends, history, and other literary forms (as opposed to FUNDAMENTALISM).

LOGIC   The branch of philosophy that deals with the nature and problems of clear and accurate thinking and argument.

LOGICAL EMPIRICISM (LOGICAL POSITIVISM)   A school of thought that would limit meaningful propositions either to those that are empirically verifiable or to those that are analyses of definitions and relations among terms. Empirically verifiable propositions are the concern of the sciences, and analysis of definitions and relations between terms is seen as the specific task of philosophy.

LOGICAL POSITIVISTS (LOGICAL POSITIVISM)   See LOGICAL EMPIRICISM.

MANA REACTION   A primitive reaction exhibiting belief in a widely diffused power or in an influence operative wherever anything striking or unusual occurs.

MATERIALISM (MATERIALISTS)   In its extreme form, the view that nothing is real except matter. Mind and consciousness are merely manifestations of such matter and are reducible to the physical elements.

MATTER   The substance or substances of which any physical object consists or is composed.

MEANS   An agency, instrument, or method used to attain a goal.

MECHANISM   The view that everything is to be explained by mechanical principles or by the laws that govern matter and motion.

MELIORISM   The belief that the world is neither entirely good nor entirely evil but can be made better through human efforts.

MENTAL   Of or pertaining to the mind.

METAETHICS   The study of the meaning of terms and language used in ethical discourse and the kind of reasoning used to justify ethical statements. (See NORMATIVE ETHICS.)

METALANGUAGE   The language we use to talk about language itself, in contrast with an *object language* that we use to talk about the world.

METAPHYSICS   A critical study of the nature of reality. Metaphysics is often divided into ontology and cosmology.

MOKSA or *MOKSHA*   In Hinduism, liberation or release from the bondage of the physical world.

MONISM   The position that there is one fundamental reality, which may be mind, matter, God, or some other substance.

MONOTHEISM   The belief that there is only one (usually personal) God.

MORAL AGENT   The individual participating in a moral situation.

MORAL OUGHT   Used to express duty or moral obligation.

MOTIVE   Whatever it is that prompts a person to act in a certain way or that determines volition (willing).

MYSTICISM   The belief that an immediate consciousness of God or a unity within the Divine is attainable; there are many interpretations of mysticism.

NAME   The symbol that stands for the thing named.

NATURALISM   An outlook that accepts the empirical world as the whole of reality, usually without a deity. Naturalism, as opposed to SUPERNATURALISM, holds that explanations of the world produced by scientific methods are the only satisfactory ones.

NATURAL THEOLOGY   The systems of doctrines (including the study or theory of God) that stress reason and empirical evidence. (See THEOLOGY and REVEALED THEOLOGY.)

NEO-THOMISM   A restatement of the religious philosophy of Thomas Aquinas.

NIHILISM (NIHILISTIC) (1) An extreme form of skepticism; the denial of an objective basis for truth and meaning. (2) The doctrine that nothing exists; therefore, nothing can be known or have value. (3) The term is often used to refer to social doctrine that conditions are so evil that the present order ought to be swept aside or destroyed to make room for something better.

NIRVANA The extinction of the finite, changing, desiring self. A cessation of striving which liberates and enlightens one. The elimination of ignorance, lust, and selfishness, which are at the root of suffering.

NOMINALISTS (NOMINALISM) The view that "universals," or general terms, are only names and represent no objectively real existents; all that exists is particulars; reality is found in individual things.

NON SEQUITUR From the Latin, "it does not follow"; an inference or a conclusion that does not follow logically from the premises; drawing a false conclusion from a true proposition.

NORMATIVE ETHICS The area of ethics concerned with principles by which human beings *ought* to live.

NOUMENON According to Kant, the reality as it is in itself, beyond the phenomenal world we can experience and have knowledge about.

OBJECTIVISTS (OBJECTIVISM) (1) The view that statements we intend as knowledge reveal what really is; ideas are formed by reliable sense experiences; (2) Also, objects and qualities we perceive through our senses do exist independently of a consciousness of them.

OCCAM'S RAZOR The principle that, other things being equal, one should always take the simpler explanation as the valid one.

ONTOLOGY (1) Used synonymously with "metaphysics." (2) An area of metaphysics which has to do with the nature of ultimate reality or being.

PANTHEISM The view that everything is coextensive with God; God is in all, and all is in God.

PARADIGM A model or an example that identifies certain scientific phenomena and guides the inquiries of scientists; the context, background of conditions, and the set of fundamental assumptions within which science takes place.

PERCEPTS OR PERCEPTION The organization of sensory impulses into units or wholes; apprehending by means of the senses; that which is immediately given in perception.

PERSONALISM A type of idealism that asserts reality is a system of personal selves. The self is said to be an irreducible living unit.

PHENOMENOLOGY A school of thought of which Edmund Husserl (1859–1938) was a leader. It starts with the human subject and his or her consciousness, the experiencing knower; the knowledge we have is limited to things as they are accessible to human consciousness.

PHENOMENON According to Kant, the appearance of reality in consciousness.

PHYSICAL Of or pertaining to empirical realities, including the human body.

PLURALIST (PLURALISM) (1) The view that reality consists of not one or two but many substances, in contrast to monism and dualism. (2) The position that more than one informed explanation or interpretation of most issues will be possible. (This is not to imply that all such explanations are equally true.)

POLYTHEISM Belief in many personalized gods.

POSTULATES A postulate is a fundamental assumption used as a basis for developing a system of proofs, but not subject itself to proof within the system. Though some logicians use *axioms* and *postulates* as synonymous, for others an axiom is a self-evident truth, whereas a postulate is a presupposition or premise of a train of reasoning and not necessarily self-evident. In this latter sense, all axioms are postulates, but not all postulates are axioms. A postulate is a basic statement "taken for granted" from which other statements may be deduced.

PRAGMATICISM At one point of time, the name given by Peirce to his own thinking. (See PRAGMATISM.)

PRAGMATISM A philosophical outlook generated by C. S. Peirce and William James and further developed by John Dewey that emphasizes experience, experimental inquiry, and truth as that which has satisfactory consequences.

PRAYER   A form of private or group religious experience intending to establish a personal relationship with God.

PREDESTINATION   The doctrine, stated with varying emphases, that all events in human life have been decreed or determined from the beginning of time by the sovereign will of God.

PREMISE   A proposition supporting or helping to support a conclusion.

PRESUPPOSITION   Anything that must be true for something else to be true.

PRIMARY QUALITIES   The qualities that are said to inhere in material substance and that do not depend on a knower. These qualities are usually thought to include form, extension, solidity, motion, and number. John Locke and others have distinguished between primary and secondary qualities.

PROCESS PHILOSOPHY   A school of thought in philosophy and theology which stresses process or becoming, relations, and relativity as new views of viewing reality.

PROPOSITION   A statement that is either true or false.

PSYCHICAL   Of or pertaining to the human soul or mind.

QUR'AN   The most holy writings of Islam; sometimes "Koran."

RATIONALISM   The view that the mind has the power to know some truths that are logically prior to experience and yet not analytic.

REAL   Being an actual thing; having objective existence.

REALISTS (REALISM)   The view that the objects of our senses exist independently of their being known or related to mind.

REALITY   The state or quality of being real or actually existent, in contrast with what is mere appearance; encompasses everything there is.

REFERENT   That which is meant.

REVEALED THEOLOGY   Theology that emphasizes revelation as the basis for our knowledge of God.

RITUAL   Practices and ceremonies that nurture and express beliefs, feelings, organization, and daily living.

SACRED   Whatever or whoever is regarded as holy, spiritually distinct from human initiatives, worthy of reverence, wondrous, respectful, and awesome.

SCIENCE   (1) Used to denote any of the many sciences. (2) Knowledge of nature that is quantitative, objective, and testable. (3) The entire body of systematic knowledge built up through experimentation and having a valid theoretical base.

SCIENTIFIC METHOD   The processes and steps by which the sciences obtain knowledge.

SECONDARY QUALITIES   The sense qualities (color, sound, taste, odor) that John Locke and others claimed were determined by the mind and not by the external world. (See PRIMARY QUALITIES.)

SECT   Any religious group formed out of a more dominant body.

SELF-CONSCIOUSNESS   To be aware of one's existence, sensations, thoughts, and the like is to be conscious; to be self-conscious is to be fully aware of the contents and activity of one's own mind or self. When self-conscious, individuals regard themselves as subjects.

SELF-DETERMINATION   The position that links determinism and freedom by stressing the causal effectiveness of human participation in events. The self acts as the causal agent. (Sometimes called soft determinism.)

SEMANTICS   A study of the meaning of words and linguistic forms, their function as symbols, and the part they play in relation to other words.

SENSATION   A state of consciousness, an awareness, a mental condition resulting from stimulation of a sense organ.

SENSE DATUM   The image or sense impression. Sense data are the immediately given contents of sense experience, such as colored patches and shapes, which, according to some epistemologists, serve as cues to the presence and nature of perceived objects.

SHINTO   The name given to the many activities and beliefs of traditional Japanese religion.

SITUATION ETHICS   According to Joseph Fletcher, the doctrine contending that truly moral actions produce the greatest amount of love possible in each situation; love is the only moral absolute. A version of teleological ethics.

SOCIAL CONTRACT   The voluntary agreement among individuals by which, according to any of various theories—as of Hobbes, Locke, or Rousseau—organized society is brought into being and secures mutual protection and well-being for its members.

SOLIPSISM   The view that I alone exist, the *reductio ad absurdum* of SUBJECTIVISM.

SUBJECTIVE   That which pertains to the subject, the self, or the knower; that which exists in consciousness but not apart from consciousness. The term stands in contrast with OBJECTIVE.

SUBJECTIVE IDEALISM   The belief that reality consists of minds, or spirits, and their perceptions or ideas.

SUBJECTIVISM   (1) The view that reality consists of conscious beings and their mental states. (2) The position that all we can know is one's own sensory and mental states. (3) The theory that value and other statements are about feelings and therefore have no independent status; they exist only in minds.

SUBSTANCE   That which exists in and of itself; that in which attributes, properties, and qualities reside.

SUPERNATURALISM   The outlook that there is a reality above or beyond the empirical world of nature.

TAUTOLOGY   In contemporary logic, a statement that is necessarily true because of its logical form, for example, "Black dogs are black." A tautology imparts no new knowledge.

TECHNOLOGY   A body of useful and practical scientific knowledge; applied science, including engineering, industrial arts, and the like.

TELEOLOGICAL ETHICS   The view that the consequences of a moral act determine its rightness or wrongness.

THEISM   Belief in a personal God.

THEOCRACY   A government believed to be ruled by God acting through God's human agents.

THEODICY   Justification of God's goodness in the face of evil.

THEOLOGY   Literally, the study or theory of God. In practice, the term is used for the system of doctrines of some particular religious group or individual thinker. (See NATURAL THEOLOGY and REVEALED THEOLOGY.)

THEORY   The general conclusion after evidence is gathered and analyzed; a confirmed hypothesis; an explanation of evidence gathered by means of research.

TRANSCENDENT (TRANSCENDENCE)   That which is beyond what is given in experience. In theology the term means that God is outside of or beyond nature.

TRANSLITERATION   The spelling of words translated from a different foreign script. For example, Arabic script, dissimilar to the script of English words, can yield *Qur'an* or *Koran, Muslim* or *Moslem,* and various English spellings of "Mohammed."

TRANSVALUATION   A reappraisal or a reestimate of the accepted standards of a given society.

ULTIMATE REALITY   That which is ultimately real; often refers to God.

UNCONSCIOUS   Without awareness, sensation, or cognition.

UNIVERSALS   General terms or characteristics, as distinguished from individual cases; abstract ideas, such as blueness or justice.

UPANISHADS   A group of philosophical treatises, usually in dialogue form, composed between the eighth and six centuries B.C.E. They comprise part of the Hindu Scriptures and attempt to explain the inner meaning of the Reality beyond the religious quest, having as their principle message the unity of BRAHMAN and ATMAN.

UTILITARIANISM   An ethical theory claiming that utility, in the sense that whatever increases pleasure and decreases pain, should be the aim of acts and the criterion by which we judge them.

VALUE   A guiding principle; a quality; a goal; the worth of something.

VICES   Immoral or evil habits or practices.

VIRTUES   Particular moral excellences; righteousness; goodness.

VOLUNTARY   Done, made, or brought about by one's own accord or by free choice.

WORLD OF ETERNAL FORMS OR IDEAS   Plato's supersensible world, which contains the universal definitions of ideas, known as forms.

Page numbers are in parentheses.

The Bettman Archive: Socrates (10), Aristotle (8), Hobbes (34), Rousseau (36), Arendt (38), Buber (48), Hume (52), Freud (64), Descartes (68), Leibniz (74), Skinner (86), Edwards (90), Santayana (106), Epicurus (122), Bentham (124), Kant (126), Mill (144), King (146), Gandhi (150), Locke (152), Bacon (172), Bergson (184), Berkeley (194), Peirce (204), Copernicus (214), Newton (216), Einstein (232), Democritus (252), Hegel (256), Marx (258), Engels (260), Radhakrishnan (272), Plato (274), James (292), Dewey (296), Comte (310), Kierkegaard (330), Nietzsche (332), Sartre (336), Husserl (340), Heidegger (342), Whitehead (348), Niebuhr (372), Avicenna (374), Saint Anselm (390), Saint Aquinas (392), Maimonides (394), The Buddha (414), Confucius (418), Lao-zi (420).

Boston University: Brightman (276).
Cambridge University/Master and Fellows of Trinity College: Wittgenstein (314).
Museum of Modern Art: (109).
National Gallery of Art: Saint Augustine (88).
National Library of Medicine: Darwin (236).
University of Manchester: Alexander (282).
Wide World Photos: Hocking (182), Carnap (316), Ayer (318), Tillich (370).
Yale University: Blanshard (54), Smith (154).

Philosophers Mentioned in Text
(continued from front endpapers)

The Nineteenth and Twentieth Centuries

Utilitarianism

Bentham (1748–1832)
J. S. Mill (1806–1873)

Philosophies of Evolution

Darwin (1809–1882)
Spencer (1820–1903)
Alexander (1859–1938)
Bergson (1859–1941)

Dialectic Materialism

Marx (1818–1883)
Engels (1820–1895)
Lenin (1870–1924)
Stalin (1879–1953)
Mao Tse-tung (1893–1976)

In the Idealistic Tradition

Fichte (1762–1814)
Hegel (1770–1831)
Schelling (1775–1854)
Schopenhauer (1788–1860)
Royce (1855–1916)
Bradley (1846–1924)
Hocking (1873–1966)
Blanshard (1892–1988)

Personalism {
Lotze (1817–1881)
Bowne (1847–1910)
Brightman (1884–1953)
Bertocci (1910–1989)